An INTEGRATED LANGUAGE PERSPECTIVE in the ELEMENTARY SCHOOL

Theory into Action

CHRISTINE C. PAPPAS
University of Illinois at Chicago

BARBARA Z. KIEFER
University of Oregon

LINDA S. LEVSTIK
University of Kentucky

Longman

An Integrated Language Perspective in the Elementary School

Longman, 95 Church Street, White Plains, N.Y. 10601

Associated companies:
Longman Group Ltd., London
Longman Cheshire Pty., Melbourne
Longman Paul Pty., Auckland
Copp Clark Pitman, Toronto

Senior editor: Naomi Silverman
Production editor: Helen B. Ambrosio
Text design adaptation: Lorraine Mullaney
Cover design: Betty L. Sokol
Text art: Fine Line, Inc.

Library of Congress Cataloging in Publication Data
Pappas, Christine.
An integrated language perspective in the elementary school : theory into action / Christine C. Pappas, Barbara Z. Kiefer, Linda S. Levstik.
p. cm.
Includes bibliographical references.
ISBN 0-8013-0175-0
1. English language—Study and teaching (Elementary) 2. Language arts (Elementary)—Curricula. I. Kiefer, Barbara Zulandt, 1944– . II. Levstik, Linda S. III. Title.
LB1576.P257 1990
372.6′044—dc20 89-12992
CIP

BCDEFGHIJ-HC-99 98 97 96 95 94 93 92 91 90

To our children, with love
Christina and Sara, Jon, Jennifer and Jeremy

Credits

Dialogs on pp. 10 and 12 from Gordon Wells, *Learning Through Interaction: The Study of Language Development.* New York: Cambridge University Press, 1981. Reprinted by permission.

Figure 1.2 (p. 19) from Brian Wildsmith, *The Owl and the Woodpecker.* Oxford, England: Oxford University Press, 1971. Reprinted by permission.

Figure 1.3 (p. 20) text copyright © 1984 by Gail Gibbons. All rights reserved. Reprinted from TUNNELS by permission of Holiday House, Inc.

Table 1.1 (p. 22) from Donald Holdaway, *Foundations of Literacy.* Sydney: Ashton Scholastic, 1979. Reprinted by permission.

Poem on p. 67 by Mary A. Hoberman, *House Is a House Is For Me.* New York: Viking, 1978.

Excerpt on p. 169 from *Mouse,* text copyright © 1985 by Sara Bonnett Stein, illustration copyright © 1985 by Manuel Garcia, reprinted by permission of Harcourt Brace Jovanovich.

Excerpt on p. 169 from Susan Bonners, *Panda.* New York: Delacorte, 1978.

Specified text on pp. 170 and 171 from MOJAVE by Diane Siebert. Illustrated by Wendell Minor (Crowell). Text copyright © 1988 by Diane Siebert. Illustrations copyright © 1988 by Wendell Minor. All selections reprinted by permission of Harper & Row, Publishers, Inc.

Excerpts on p. 172 from THE SEE-THROUGH ZOO: HOW GLASS ANIMALS ARE MADE, by Suzanne Haldane. Text and photographs copyright © 1984 by Suzanne Haldane. Reprinted by permission of Pantheon Books, a division of Random House, Inc.

Table 5.4 (p. 177) from Susan L. Lytle and Morton Botel, *PCRP II: Reading, Writing and Talking Across the Curriculum.* Harrisburg, PA: Pennsylvania Department of Education, 1988. To be published as *Framework for Literacy* by Heinemann-Boynton/Cook in 1990. Reprinted by permission of the authors.

Tables 5.5, 5.6, 5.7, 5.8 (pp. 181–182) adapted from Andrea Butler and Jan Turbill, *Towards a Reading-Writing Classroom.* Portsmouth, NH: Heinemann, 1984.

Figure 6.19 (p. 221) adapted from Kathy Sylva, Carolyn Roy and Marjorie Painter, *Childwatching at Playgroup and Nursery School.* Ypsilanti, MI: High/Scope Press, 1980. Reprinted by permission.

Excerpted text on p. 265 from Arthur Ellis, *Teaching and Learning Elementary Social Studies.* Boston: Allyn & Bacon, 1986.

Figure 8.19 (p. 306) adapted from *Children's Literature in the Elementary School,* 4th Edition by Charlotte Huck, Susan Hepler, and Janet Hickman, copyright © 1987 by Charlotte Huck, reprinted by permission of Holt, Rinehart and Winston.

Contents

Preface

This book is a *fully co-written* book that outlines an integrated language perspective on teaching in the elementary school. It provides the theory on which the perspective is based and provides many examples of how it may be translated into practice. Teachers in training and teachers in the field frequently believe in the principles of an integrated language perspective but cannot conceive of how to put it in action in a real classroom. Although we believe that a how-to integrated language textbook is in some ways a contradiction in terms—integrated language cannot really be found between the covers of a textbook—we think that the integrated language ideas and examples described in the book will benefit and support those persons wanting to implement changes in language learning in our elementary classrooms.

We do not mean to suggest that integrated language teachers do not now exist. Actually, we believe that teachers who foster children's using their own language (listening, speaking, reading, and writing) for authentic purposes across the curriculum (in social studies, science, math, art, and music) have always existed, but perhaps their approaches were labeled something else (and may not have been based on *current* research, which we will try to provide here). Also, there are current views that share the integrated language principles that are addressed in this book, but they may be called something else. For example, the whole-language perspective depicts language and learning in ways that are very similar to ours. Thus, although we have used the term *integrated language* to name our perspective, we want to deemphasize the label and, instead, stress the importance of the *principles* of the approach. Too frequently, important educational reforms have not lasted because people have taken on only the label without understanding the substance—the principles—that the new approach may have represented. We are inviting you to adopt the principles that the integrated language perspective provides and implies, and then we will leave you with the choice as to what you want to call your perspective and yourself as a teacher.

Although the emphasis in this book is on a language arts curriculum, we cover other curricular areas because an integrated language perspective requires that teachers promote children's use of language across the curriculum. A major contribution of the book is showing how planning a thematic unit enables a teacher to integrate listening, speaking, reading, and writing with art, music, social studies, science, and mathematics in elementary classrooms. This thematic unit approach is based on current theory and research in cognitive development and also provides an organizational framework within which children can make choices, use language for authentic purposes, and collaborate with other children and the teacher in learning.

Eight thematic units—which we call *prototypes*—are illustrated and explained at various elementary grade levels in the book. Each prototype is like the melody line in jazz improvisation in the sense that the melody line is the basic structure on which individual modifications can be created (by you as teacher and by children). These prototypes are planning guides that are based on recent ideas about how children learn in general and how they learn language specifically. However, our approach counters many prevalent educational practices and back-to-the-basics programs that view the teacher merely as a technician who employs someone else's programs and methods. Instead, our approach gives professional status to teachers as the developers and implementers of their own programs. Thus, the integrated language perspective fosters "ownership" for teachers and also for children as they learn to express their meanings in language for real social and cultural purposes.

ACKNOWLEDGMENTS

We want to acknowledge some important people for their help and support during the process of writing this book, which—we want to emphasize—was written while all three of us were juggling full-time teaching loads at our respective institutions. During that time, also, two of us moved to other institutions.

First, we want to thank one another. This is a fully co-written book that required immense collaboration. We learned a lot from one another, and even when desperately trying to meet deadlines, we have really enjoyed writing this book. We are good friends and important co-critics. Each of us has contributed our own areas of expertise to this book, but we have similar views of language, learning, and teaching derived from the educational experiences we had during our doctoral programs at The Ohio State University. Therefore, we thank our former professors who created a learning community—a characteristically OSU "way with words"—in which our individual interests and constructions of knowledge were nurtured.

We also want to acknowledge the critical feedback of the reviewers of our manuscript and especially Kay Moss, Illinois State University, who argued with and yet rooted for every word we wrote, from the prospectus to the final drafts of the book. Certain colleagues and students also helped in various ways by providing important references and useful criticism. Really important in this project is our editor, Naomi Silverman, who "nudged" us to write the book in the first place and then continued to encourage and support us to write the kind of book we wanted to write.

In addition, we are grateful to our respective families for putting up with us at various times during the writing. We appreciate the efforts of one family member in particular, Irene Zulandt, who typed and edited parts of various versions of the manuscript.

Last, but not least, we thank the teachers of integrated language whom we have seen in action in the classroom. We hope we have caught their spirit, expertise, and delight in teaching children of elementary age.

Introduction

Teachers from an integrated language perspective "own"—with their students—their language arts program. Teachers plan and develop long-range units of study so that their students have ample opportunities to use language for many meaningful purposes. In these classrooms, speaking, listening, reading, and writing are not separate subjects, ends in and of themselves. Instead, they are used together as tools, as means for learning other things. In the process, students learn both the other things *and* the language. Activities and projects span the curriculum so that there is enough time for children to engage in systematic and reflective inquiry on a range of topics. As children use language to learn, teachers collaborate, respond, facilitate, and support their efforts. Such teachers orchestrate their curriculum through thematic units. To visualize what is going on, what it's like, let's eavesdrop in three elementary classrooms where this approach is used.

VIGNETTES OF THREE INTEGRATED LANGUAGE CLASSROOMS

EXPLORATIONS in Ruby Antoncic's First Grade Classroom

Ruby's first grade classroom

EXPLORATIONS thematic unit

The children in Ruby's first grade classroom have been busy for weeks working on the thematic unit EXPLORATIONS. There are many subthemes to pursue—"Exploring Big and Little," "Exploring the Natural World," "Imaginary Explorations," "Exploring New Places," and so forth (see the WEB for Prototype 4 in Chapter 4 for the way these subthemes are organized). Today is the day for children who have been focusing on the subtheme, "Exploring the Immediate Environment," to present their projects to the whole class. These children have read books such as *Up Goes the Skyscraper!, Big City Port,* and *Flying.* As extensions of these and other books, the students have made surveys of the people-made things in their community and have charted how these things are used, where they are found, and so on. Individual children have picked one category of people-made things in the environment—for example, planes, boats, trucks, and buildings—for more intensive study.

Gibbons (1986)
Maestro & DelVecchio (1983)
Gibbons (1986)

Other children in this small group that is exploring the immediate environment have concentrated on everyday items, such as air, milk, or germs. Using books such as *Milk, Air,* and *Germs Make Me Sick!,* they have been considering how air, germs, and so forth affect us.

Carrick (1985)
Lloyd (1982)
Berger (1985)

Individual presentations to the whole class

Joey's skyscraper

We "enter" the classroom as Ruby and the children gather around to listen to the children's presentations. Joey and Maria have elected to go first. Joey carefully places on a small table his model of a huge skyscraper that he has made out of papier mâché. Then he begins to read the chart that he has written to describe the major features of skyscrapers and how they are made. Joey also has written a small booklet that he has entitled "Tips for Making a Skyscraper." All the children are aware that Joey's first skyscraper was a disaster. He worked for days on it only to have it crumble on him. With Ruby's help, he figured out a way to make a strong frame so that the skyscraper could stand straight and tall. Ruby had also suggested the booklet. Joey agreed with Ruby that other children would probably benefit from such a how-to booklet because they might encounter similar difficulties in their projects during the year. After reading the booklet, Joey passes it around, and children ask questions about skyscrapers and make comments on Joey's illustrations in his booklet. Ruby asks him if he is going to build another skyscraper. Everyone laughs when Joey answers, "Not this year!"

Maria's tunnels

Gibbons (1986)

Now it's Maria's turn. Joey removes his model so that she has room for the two tunnel models she has constructed. Relying a lot on Gail Gibbons' *Tunnels,* she has made two tunnels with different shapes—a vertical sidewall tunnel and a basket-handle tunnel. Unlike Joey, Maria has not written a chart, but she has made small cards to label her two tunnels and to designate the parts of a tunnel. These cards showing the tunnel parts—sidewalls, invert, crown, and face—are taped on big pins and stuck into the tunnels. Maria talks briefly about the kinds of tunnels that exist and why she chose to make the two she did. Apparently, she decided to do these two because she has seen these two shapes frequently. She points out to the children that the tunnel their bus goes through every day to school is a vertical sidewall tunnel and that the train tunnel near the McDonald's is of the basket-handle type. Then Maria explains how she made her tunnels. She, too, had trouble making a frame. She relates how her father helped her by twisting two wire hangers to make the ends of each tunnel, and then how they attached chicken wire to these ends to make the tunnel frames. Like Joey, she used papier mâché to mold the frame into the tunnels. She painted one tunnel brown and the other black. After her talk, Ruby asks the children if they have any comments or questions for Maria. Many children say that they can't wait to look again at the real tunnels she mentioned. John states that he hasn't paid too much attention to tunnels before, and he's going to look at them better in the future. Christina suggests that Maria should make a how-to booklet like Joey's. Because many of the children seem to nod in agreement, Maria says that she will.

Pedro's *Germs Attack*

Pedro and Susan report on germs and milk, respectively. Pedro listened to Berger's *Germs Make Me Sick!* many times to get his ideas for his project. (Ruby had made a tape of the book and put it at the listening post for Pedro because initially he could not read the book on his own.) Pedro is considered by the children to be *the* artist in the classroom, so he has written a book named "Germs Attack" that includes many illustrations. As he reads each page to the class, he turns the pages of the book toward the group so they can see his pictures. His book covers the ways germs cause colds, cavities, earaches, boils, and the like and depicts someone in agony from each ailment. As each page is read, the children roar with laughter because although Pedro's text reflects the straightforward tone of the report genre, his pictures are hilarious. When Pedro finishes reading his book, children ask him if they may read it later. Morgan and Dwayne want to know if the *Germs Make Me Sick!* tape is still around so they can listen to it. Ruby says it should be there at the listening post.

Susan's *Milk Makes Susie Sick*

After Pedro joins the class on the floor, Susan sits in the author's chair to share her story entitled "Milk Makes Susie Sick." Susan decided to study the topic of milk because she is allergic to it, as the children in the class know. Parents, who sometimes provide snacks for the class, always have to provide a different one without milk in it for her. Susan gets mad when she hears on TV or in books she has read for the project how wonderful milk is. "Well," she says as she introduces her story, "it isn't wonderful for everybody!" She explains to the class that although there is a "Susie" in her title, the story is a make-believe one. She says, however, that she did get a lot of her ideas by talking to her mother and aunt, who are also allergic to dairy products. They told her about all the times they got sick when they were kids by sneaking an ice cream cone or by eating milk or cheese accidentally. Then Susan reads her story of Susie, who becomes sicker and sicker until the doctor discovers that she is allergic to milk. Finally, Susie gets better. The story ends with a friend coming to visit her. Gerry (all children laugh when Susan reads her name, because they all know that Geraldine is her best friend), not knowing that milk makes Susie sick, brings her ice cream as a get-well present. The last page of the book has a great picture of Gerry with a large stomach because she herself ate all the ice cream that she had brought for Susie. Geraldine blushes as she and the rest of the children laugh at Susan's illustration. The group then breaks up as Ruby reminds the children that it's almost lunch time. Several children go up to Susan to take another look at her book.

LET'S EAT in Carol Hagihara's Second Grade Classroom

Carol's second grade classroom

Carol Hagihara and her second grade children have been involved with the thematic unit LET'S EAT for a while when we drop in to visit. Some of the subthemes they have explored are "Helping the Hungry," "Food Geography," "Who Eats What," and "Food Changes" (see the WEB for Prototype 5 in Chapter 4). As we enter the room, children are busy on various activities and projects at centers arranged around the room. This is one of the three integrated work times that Carol schedules every day.

LET'S EAT thematic unit

We focus on the center where several children are doing "cooking math." In the past two days, these children have been calculating measurements for recipes. They have figured out the difference between a teaspoon and a tablespoon, and they know how to put all the spoons in proper order—the 1/4 teaspoon is the smallest, then comes the 1/2 teaspoon, then finally the teaspoon and the tablespoon. They have done the same with various measuring cups and have noted that although there is a one-third measuring cup, there isn't any comparable one-third teaspoon.

Small group collaboration on math calculations

Next week the class is having thirty guests, so today the children are trying to figure out how much they need for the recipe they are going to use to feed them. Jeremy is reading the recipe while the other members of the group, Jill, Dana, and Sam, take notes on the particulars. Sam poses the important question they must deal with, "The recipe says that it makes enough for six people, so how much do we need of each ingredient for thirty people?" There is an interlude of quiet as each child thinks. Then Dana has an idea and starts adding one "six" at a time. Everyone in the group, as well as Carol, who has come to the group to see how they're doing, listens as Dana talks aloud while she adds: "Six plus six is twelve; add another six and you get eighteen; plus another six, and you get twenty-three . . . no, twenty-four; add another six and you get thirty!" Carol asks, "So, how many sixes do you have there, Dana?" Everyone watches as Dana counts each six that she added. "Five," Dana reports. "So, how many times are you going to add each ingredient of the recipe so we have enough for thirty people?" Carol asks. Dana, Jeremy, and Sam all chime in with the answer "five." Then Carol suggests that they first start with the flour ingredient; the recipe says that one cup is needed. "How many cups of flour do you need for thirty?" Carol poses. The children do some quick calculations, and all come up with the number five, which they write next to "flour" on their ingredient list. They tell Carol that was an easy one.Jill reasons, "We really didn't have to add the ones, did we? We could have just "thought it in our head, right?" Carol nods with a smile on her face. Carol leaves as they try to figure out the other ingredients on their list. "I'll be back to see if there are any problems—some of these might be tricky," she tells them as she moves to another group.

Caitlin's sixth grade classroom

DIGGING UP THE PAST in Caitlin's Sixth Grade Classroom

Pryor (1988)

As we eavesdrop in Caitlin Cooper's sixth grade class, Caitlin has just finished reading *Seth of the Lion People* by Bonnie Pryor to her students, and the whole class begins to discuss the book. This piece of historical fiction is a prehistorical saga. Seth, the main character, is different from others in his clan. Not only is he crippled, but he has ideas that threaten the brutal leader of the People of the Lion. Seth, with his friend, Esu, embarks on a perilous journey that leads to many discoveries that would make his clan's life easier and safer. The question is: Is it safe for him and his friend to return to share these discoveries?

DIGGING UP THE PAST thematic unit

Steele & Steele (1975)
Schlein (1979)
Carter (1987)

Teacher-led discussion

Over the course of the DIGGING UP THE PAST thematic unit, Caitlin has read several other pieces of historical fiction—another book on prehistory, Steele's *The Eye of the Forest,* and two books on Egyptian history, *I, Tut: The Boy Who Became Pharoah* and *His Majesty, Queen Hatsepshut.* During Caitlin's reading of this historical fiction to her students, she has been having children consider various questions: How have various authors visualized the past? What evidence do they use? What is their point of view? She begins the discussion of *Seth of the Lion People* by reviewing these questions with the children. Several of the children comment on the relative strength of ideas versus crude physical brutality in this book and others. Alan wonders if the authors consider this to be a critical issue in the course of history in general.

Hunter (1974)

Then Bill, who is a member of a small group reading and studying a range of other pieces of historical fiction (see the WEB for Prototype 8 in Chapter 4), speaks up to point out some similarities between Seth and the character in *The Stronghold* by Mollie Hunter. Bill argues, "The boy in this story doesn't 'fit in' with his people either." "Furthermore," Bill continues, "he also wants to help them by building a stronghold to protect his people from the raiders." Penny and Heather, who are also in Bill's group, then react to Bill's remarks by examining what "help" is in these two books and the other books the class has read. Right before it's time to break, Paola suggests that they ought to look at that help theme in all the historical fiction that Caitlin has shared with them. He then turns to Penny, Heather, and Bill and says, "Our group ought to at least compare this 'help' idea in *Dawn Wind, I, Tut,* and *Queen Hatsepshut* because they are all stories about ancient times. You know *Dawn Wind* has to do with ancient Britain stuff, and the *Tut* and the *Queen* books are on ancient Egypt." They all nod in agreement. Penny notes the question in her learning log so they don't forget it when they meet later in their group.

Sutcliff (1962)
Schlein (1979)
Carter (1987)

SUMMARY

The teachers in the foregoing vignettes, as well as all the other teachers you will meet in this book, represent characteristics and attributes that we have seen in real teachers in real classrooms who use an integrated language approach to teaching.

A range of interactions is possible in integrated language classrooms.

The vignettes reflect important features of integrated language classrooms, but they can provide only a flavor of what is yet to come. Teachers provide a range of interactions. In Ruby's class, we saw individual children share their projects with the whole class. These were the outcomes of their study of topics related to a subtheme of the EXPLORATIONS unit. In Carol's class, which was working on LET'S EAT, we viewed the interactions of a small group working together on a math project. Then, in Caitlin's class that was exploring the DIGGING UP THE PAST thematic unit, we noted a teacher-led group discussion on a book Caitlin had read to her students.

A broad spectrum of activities is available for children to choose from.

Another feature to note is that these teachers provided a broad spectrum of choices of activities for children to engage in. As Ruby's class indicated, various types of responses to the studies children took on were also encouraged. The making of papier mâché models and the writing of fictional and nonfictional texts were selected by individual children to present the findings of their projects. The opportunities for choices for children is probably one of the most important characteristics of the integrated language perspective. The use of a thematic unit—a broadly based topic of study—is a critical component in the approach, for such units enable teachers to provide these choices.

Authentic, integrated language is promoted.

Thematic units allow for and promote authentic language use in the classroom. Speaking, listening, reading, and writing are not separate activities but are employed by children in an integrated way. Moreover, this integrated language is used across the curriculum. "Authentic language use" here means that language is not used to learn language but for something else that *requires* language, that *requires* speaking, listening, reading, and writing. Thematic units offer this possibility in the classroom. Concepts and relationships that span curricular areas are investigated in a coherent way, yet at the same time a range of topics, or domains, can be studied in depth by children. Remember Susan's study of milk and Pedro's work on germs in Ruby's class, the intense concentration of Dana, Sam, and others in their group as they attempted to solve their recipe problem in math, and the focused, yet related, work in history and literature that the students engaged in in Caitlin's sixth grade classroom. All these children had purposes for their learning and use of language. They also demonstrated autonomy in their thinking and knowing: They were responsible for their own learning.

Many topics or domains are explored by children.

Teachers use a collaborative style of teaching.

The vignettes also showed the various roles of the teachers. Perhaps the most critical characteristic of the teachers you met is the way they collaborated with children in the classroom. This collaborative style of teaching spreads through to every facet of their interactions with their students. In the vignettes, teachers posed questions for children to entertain, supported children's hypotheses about possible solutions for their own problems, facilitated children's own intentions and choices, and so forth. Knowledge is not facts or absolute truths to be dispensed by teachers into the empty vessels of children's minds. Instead, these teachers realize that children construct their own knowledge, their own theories of the world. Moreover, the teachers are aware that knowledge is also constructed out of what other people know, and as knowing persons, they recognize that they have an important role in sharing their knowledge with children. Other classmates—other knowers in the classroom—possess knowledge to be tapped, too. The knowledge in these classrooms is constructed as part of a social process; it is negotiated by all the participants, children and teacher alike.

There is no magic formula for teaching, but we believe that for it to be successful and meaningful in the learning and the lives of children, teachers must be ready to collaborate with the children in their classrooms. The purpose of this book is to try to help you be that kind of teacher.

AN OVERVIEW OF THE BOOK

Descriptions of the various chapters

As its title suggests, this book deals with both theory *and* practice. The plan of the book is first to provide you with the big picture in the first several chapters, and then in subsequent chapters to "go in close" by filling in with more detailed, specific information. Chapter 1 provides the general principles of the integrated language perspective. Chapter 2 describes the characteristics of the participants in the integrated language classroom, both children and teachers. Chapter 3 shows how to plan thematic units. Chapter 4 then demonstrates how to implement the units in the classroom. Eight prototypes in action at various grade levels and in various school settings are provided. Chapter 5 returns to the theory of the perspective that was introduced in Chapter 1, emphasizing important aspects of literacy. It provides a model of written genres and explains more about the reading and writing processes. Chapter 6 covers a range of "kid watching" procedures and techniques. Chapter 7 goes into more detail about how to integrate language across various curricular areas—social studies, science, math, and art and music. Chapter 8 discusses in much greater detail many of the activities and routines mentioned in Chapters 3 and 4 (as well as in other chapters). Chapter 9 deals with evaluation and accountability. Finally, Chapter 10 provides suggestions for changing present programs in elementary schools along the integrated language per-

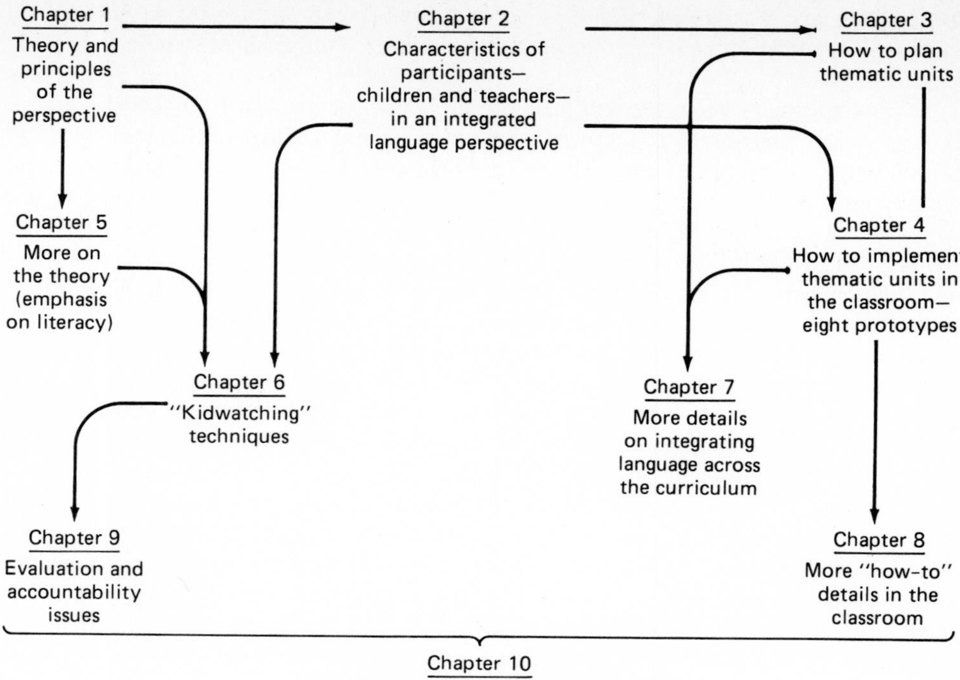

Figure I.1 Interrelated Threads of This Book

spective. Thus, these chapters are "integrated" in certain ways—Figure I.1 depicts how the major threads of ideas and themes in the various chapters are interrelated in the book.

Explanations of certain features of the book

In addition, three certain features have been incorporated into this book to help you use it more easily and effectively.

First, as you have already noted in reading this "Introduction," we have included marginal notations. Four types of notations are used throughout the book to do four jobs: (1) to cite the persons whose work and ideas we have drawn on in writing the book; (2) to refer to sources for possible further exploration of a topic, idea, or concept; (3) to highlight a specific concept, idea, or topic covered in the text; (4) to provide a shorter definition or explanation of an important concept, idea, or topic that is discussed in the text.

The second feature—certain group activities—is found in Chapters 1 and 5. These two chapters are heavy-duty theory chapters, and these activities are suggested to help you get a better understanding of the critical ideas about oral and written language that are discussed in these chapters.

The third feature has to do with how and where we have provided full bibliographic information for references we have cited. References are provided at the end of each chapter in two lists (when applicable): one that provides the scholarly works we have cited, listed alphabetically by author; the other gives the children's literature books we have mentioned, listed alphabetically by title.

CHILDREN'S LITERATURE

AIR by D. Lloyd. Illustrated by P. Visscher. Dial Press, 1982.

BIG CITY PORT by B. Maestro & E. DelVecchio. Illustrated by G. Maestro. Scholastic, 1983.

DAWN WIND by R. Sutcliff. Walck, 1962.

THE EYE OF THE FOREST by W. Steele & M. Q. Steele. Dutton, 1975.

FLYING by G. Gibbons. Holiday House, 1986.
GERMS MAKE ME SICK! by M. Berger. Illustrated by M. Hafner. Harper & Row, 1985.
HIS MAJESTY, QUEEN HATSEPSHUT by D. S. Carter. Lippincott, 1987.
I, TUT: THE BOY WHO BECAME PHAROAH by M. Schlein. Four Winds Press, 1979.
MILK by D. Carrick. Greenwillow Books, 1985.
SETH OF THE LION PEOPLE by B. Pryor. Morrow, 1988.
THE STRONGHOLD by M. Hunter. Harper & Row, 1974.
TUNNELS by G. Gibbons. Holiday House, 1984.
UP GOES THE SKYSCRAPER! by G. Gibbons. Macmillan, 1986.

1

The Theory of the Integrated Language Perspective

The integrated language perspective is based on three major interrelated principles:

Children are active, constructive learners.

Children are constructive learners. They are active meaning-makers. They are continuously making sense of their world based on what they have already learned, on what they have already constructed.

Language is used for many social purposes that are expressed by many language patterns.

Language is the major system by which meanings are communicated and expressed in our social world. Because language is used for various purposes, our meanings are expressed in various ways, by various language patterns. Thus, language cannot be understood, interpreted, or evaluated unless it is related to the social contexts in which it is being used. Moreover, language is learned through actual use; that is, various patterns of language are learned as language is used for various purposes in various social contexts.

Knowledge is organized and constructed by individual learners through social interaction.

Knowledge is in the minds of individuals. It is organized and constructed through social interaction. It is constantly changing over our lives; it is built-up mental representations that are based on our individual experiences. Thus, knowledge is always being modified; it is tentative and provisional. Knowledge is *not* a static, absolute "out-there" object. Because we are social beings, our knowledge is always affected by our culture, existing social circumstances, the historical moment, and so forth.

In this chapter we go over these principles in more detail, and then further extend and elaborate on them throughout the book. We begin by considering how children learn to use oral, or spoken, language.

HOW DO CHILDREN LEARN SPOKEN LANGUAGE?

Spoken language is learned within a natural environment of language use.

Regardless of race, class, or family background, children learn their native language during infancy and the preschool years with ease and success. Without special tutoring or formal instruction, they not only learn the structure of language but also how to use it for numerous communicative purposes. They learn language within a natural environment of language use. An integrated language perspective applies to the classroom principles operating in early language acquisition. The first question we must address, then, is: What are the characteristics of a natural environment of language use? Infants, who initially do not know what a language is or what it is for, discover both by *interacting* with their immediate family and other members of their community. The medium of these interactions is *conversation*. Our first step, thus, is to examine what goes on in our everyday face-to-face conversations.

General organization of conversations

What is the general nature of conversations? How are they organized? Try to envision what a normal conversation between two adults (a male and a female for this example) is like. Consider the pattern of a typical conversation: First, one participant, the speaker, expresses or translates the meaning of his experience, intentions, and ideas through a conventionally agreed-on communication system so that these experiences, intentions, and ideas can be shared with the second participant, the listener, who is also an active meaning-maker. The listener uses this coded message offered by the speaker and other cues provided in the situation to construct the meaning that she believes the speaker to have intended. She then signals in some way—by gesture or by what she says next—that the meaning of the speaker has been understood. This exchange between a speaker and listener (who keep taking turns being speaker and listener in the conversation) is what linguists and psychologists call *intersubjectivity*. It means: I (the speaker) know that you (the listener) know what I mean, and you (the listener) know that I (the speaker) know that you (the listener) know. For any conversation to have any success at all, speakers and listeners have to be sure that they are talking about the same thing, sharing the same meanings.

Intersubjectivity is understanding another's perspective so that meanings can be shared.

Actually, the foregoing account of a typical conversation is too simplistic. It sounds as if the speaker's meanings are totally unknown to the listener until that speaker has completed his linguistic utterances during his turn in the conversation (and vice versa, for the listener's turn as speaker). In fact, at the very point of utterance, at the very beginning of a conversation, meanings are created for both participants. That is because, based on the situation or circumstances of the conversation (which are discussed in more detail later in this chapter), the listener usually already has a good idea of what the speaker is going to say, and the speaker can also predict what the listener will say next, and so forth. Most of these predictions are subconscious, operating below the level of awareness, and they account for most of what is understood in conversations.

The example also seems to characterize intersubjectivity in conversations as an all-or-nothing affair. That is not the case at all. Rather, the intersubjectivity achieved by participants in conversations is always a matter of degree. We can all recall an extreme case, a conversation in which we felt that we and our conversational partner were not talking about the same thing at all! Nevertheless, most conversations are successful because most of the time intersubjectivity has been established.

Conversations require collaboration and negotiation.

Thus, an important aspect of typical conversations is that it is a *collaborative* activity between participants who take turns to offer, modify, extend, and sustain a meaning that is constructed by their joint efforts. In any conversation, participants *negotiate* the meanings that are expressed. They have to negotiate—and again it's done subconsciously—because each person has different ideas and experiences, and each person has different purposes and expectations about what the conversation is to achieve. Again, as with intersubjectivity, these processes of collaboration and negotiation are a matter of degree. In most typical conversation interactions, however, each participant subconsciously makes constant adjustments to take account of the perspective of the other.

Wells (1981)

Now, how do these ideas of intersubjectivity, collaboration, and negotiation function in *learning* spoken language? Following is a conversation between Mark (23 months) and his mother (taken from Gordon Wells's longitudinal study of language development). This conversation occurred in the kitchen after breakfast while Mark's mother was involved in domestic tasks. Helen, Mark's nine-month-old sister, was also there, seated in her high chair. The conversation begins with Mark's discovery that when he looks into a mirror, he can see both himself and his mother.

	Mark	Mother	
1	Mark: Mummy(v)		[Mark is looking in a mirror and sees reflections of himself and his mother]
2	Mummy		
3		Mother: What?	
4	Mark: There, there Mark		
5		Mother: Is that Mark?	
6	Mark: Mummy		
7		Mother: Mm	
8	Mark: Mummy		
9		Mother: Yes that's Mummy	
10	Mark: *		
11	Mummy		
12	Mummy(v)		
13		Mother: Mm	
14	Mark: There Mummy		
15	Mummy(v)		
16	There, Mark there		
17		Mother: Look at Helen	
18		She's going to sleep (long pause)	
19	Mark: [ɛɔæ](=look at that)		[Mark can see birds in the garden]
20	Birds Mummy(v)		
21		Mother: Mm	
22	Mark: Jubs (=birds)		
23		Mother: What are they doing?	
24	Mark: Jubs bread		
25		Mother: Oh look	
26		They're eating the berries aren't they?	
27	Mark: Yeh		
28		Mother: That's their food	
29		They have berries for dinner	
30	Mark: Oh		

Source: Wells (1981), p. 102.

Even very young children actively participate in conversations.

Even though Mark has limited linguistic resources—he uses one or two word utterances, and there is much repetition—it is clear that he is an active participant in a coherent conversation. His remarks are full of meaning and his mother is able to pick up that meaning and respond to it. They negotiate and collaborate to construct this meaning. Intersubjectivity occurs through his mother's responses in units 5 and 9. It is lost later when she introduces a new topic (that Helen has fallen asleep) in units 17 and 18, but by unit 23, intersubjectivity has been achieved again. Now Mark can add information to his topic (*Jubs bread*), and his mother can take the meaning and reply with more information about the topic he has initiated.

Thus, this conversation between Mark and his mother is like an ordinary conversation. Turn-taking is well established, topics are sustained over turns, and both participants seem to understand each other's contributions. This successful interaction did not happen overnight. Its roots can be found in the time when Mark was a tiny baby.

Early Communication Developments

See Bates (1976) and Trevarthan (1979, 1980) for more information on early infant communication.

The past twenty years of research have indicated that intersubjectivity can been seen very early in infancy. Children have an innate ability to know another human being. Researchers have carefully studied the behavior of two-month-old babies and their mothers on videotapes. They have been able to analyze how the babies move their whole bodies—how they move their mouths and faces, their hands and legs, and so forth—along with those of the mothers' movements, and they have demonstrated that there are strong reciprocal, highly synchronized interactional patterns existing between participants. The mother (or father or other important caregiver) may talk to or smile at the young baby, who in turn may gurgle and move both mouth and face (and other body parts) in such a way that researchers have termed the interaction a primitive, or proto-conversation. Thus, at the very beginning of life the infant's reciprocal behavior shows an ability to take account of another's perspective. These early interpersonal relations constitute a *primary intersubjectivity* and provide the initial communication framework by which children learn their language and how to make meaning in their culture.

Learning language and learning one's culture evolve out of early interpersonal communication.
Stern (1985)
Bower (1974, 1978); Kagan (1972); Trevarthan (1979, 1980); Trevarthan & Hubley (1978)

The past couple of decades of research have shown that young babies also appear to know much more about the properties of objects than was earlier thought. Very young babies are endowed with an ability to hypothesize about how objects "work" in their world. When infants are around six months old, they begin to interact with objects in a different way. As a result, a new kind of intersubjectivity is ushered in that influences language development in important ways. Before six months, a baby interacts with objects *or* with humans but not with objects and people *simultaneously*. At this new stage, objects begin to be incorporated into the earlier purely interpersonal intersubjectivity to form a new type of intersubjectivity called *secondary intersubjectivity*. As parent and baby interact with objects in everyday activities, the baby gains important understandings about action schemes involving objects. For example, the parent as an actor acts on an object such as a ball or cup, and the baby serves as recipient of this action. Then, the roles of participants get reversed as the baby becomes the agent of the action on the ball (giving the ball back, for example), so that now the parent is the beneficiary of the action.

Trevarthan (1979a, 1979b, 1980); Trevarthan & Hubley (1978)

Secondary intersubjectivity

Another important aspect of language has its roots in this secondary intersubjectivity stage. Babies develop an understanding with their caregiver that they can share a focus on an object or person—a topic—that can then be commented on. That is, baby or mommy or ball can serve as a topic about which something can be said—it can go or be up or pretty. So, in the middle of the first year the young infant is already discovering two important universal features of language: that these basic relationships among agents (persons), actions, and objects can be encoded or expressed in language, and that an object in the world can serve as a *joint* topic, a focus that the baby can share *with* another person, that can subsequently be commented on. Much of what young children learn about the properties of objects is mediated by conversations about various everyday physical activities. That is, their knowledge about the world of objects is largely constructed in social interaction.

Bruner (1975a, 1975b, 1983)

Babies learn important universal properties of language through social interaction.

The example of Mark's conversation shows how his present turn-taking, conversational exchanges with his mother have been supported by earlier reciprocity in routines of activity and vocalizations with another person. That is, Mark's language system has built on and extended these earlier understandings.

Mark also has clearly moved beyond what is called the *proto-language* stage of language development that has been described by the linguist Michael Halliday. Proto-language typically begins at the end of a child's first year or the beginning of the second year before conventional words, or vocabulary, and grammar develop. Proto-language emerges when the child pairs certain sounds with certain meanings or functions in a regularized, systematic way. Mark's utterance in unit 19 is a remnant of his proto-language. That is, a particular set of sounds is used by Mark to mean "look at that." Babies can do things with language with such a system, although usually only immediate family members and caregivers can understand and interpret their communication efforts. One-year-olds, for example, can use their own sound-meaning constructions to give commands, get something, ask or query about something, express a "we-ness" with another, and so forth.

Halliday (1975)

Proto-language is a baby's system of regularized sound-meaning constructions.

Before adult-like grammar and vocabulary emerge, proto-language provides a set of functions through which to communicate.

Back to Mark

Mark's language has developed from a proto-language sound-meaning system to a rudimentary level of organization that relates meaning and sounds in a different and more complex way. Here are the beginnings of a *grammar*, a structural language system that

Grammar: Language both classifies experience into categories and expresses that experience to others.

allows him to mean two things at once. For example, Mark's *Jubs bread* (unit 24) enables him to express the meaning relationship of an agent, *Jubs* (his word for "birds"), and an object, *bread,* and at the same time express the pragmatic meaning of indicating this aspect of his experience (the birds and bread) to his mother.

Wells (1981)

This primitive grammar will be gradually expanded and developed as Mark has more and more conversations about his everyday experiences. The next conversation between Mark and his mother occurred two months later and gives us an idea of how children increase their mastery of the language system. Here Mark (now 25 months old) is looking out of the window. Earlier he had been watching a neighbor working in his garden, and now the man has disappeared.

	Mark	Mother	
1	Mark: Where man gone?		[Mark has seen a man working in his garden]
2	Where man gone?		
3		Mother: I don't know	
4		I expect he's gone inside because it's snowing	
5	Mark: Where man gone?		
6		Mother: In the house	
7	Mark: Uh?		
8		Mother: Into his house	
9	Mark: No		
10	No		
11	Gone to shop Mummy(v)		[The local shop is close to Mark's house]
12		Mother: Gone where?	
13	Mark: Gone shop		
14		Mother: To the shop?	
15	Mark: Yeh		
16		Mother: What's he going to buy?	
17	Mark: Er—biscuits		
18		Mother: Biscuits mm	
19	Mark: Uh?		
20		Mother: Mm	
21		What else?	
22	Mark: Er—meat		
23		Mother: Mm	
24	Mark: Meat		
25	Er—sweeties		
26	Buy a big bag sweets		
27		Mother: Buy sweets?	
28	Mark: Yeh		
29	M—er—man—buy the man buy sweets		
30		Mother: Will he?	
31	Mark: Yeh		
32	Daddy buy sweets		
33	Daddy buy sweets		
34		Mother: Why?	
35	Mark: Oh er—[ɔ] shop		
36	Mark: Mark do buy some—sweet—sweeties		
37	Mark buy some—um—		
38	Mark buy some—um—		
39	I did		

Source: Wells (1981), p. 107.

Look how Mark has progressed in only two months! His utterances are longer and more complex (see units 11, 26, and 36 especially). He is a better respondent when his mother asks for information (see units 17 and 22). Moreover, most of his talk deals with persons and events that are not present in the here and now but, instead, are either recalled or imagined. Here is evidence of Mark's developing understanding of a certain *script* in his culture, knowledge of what typically happens at shops. A script, sometimes also called a *schema,* represents what Mark has generalized about the events that he has observed at the local shop and perhaps at other shops like it that he has visited. Mark's mother's behavior is critical in supporting this "story" about the shop. She provides a reasonable explanation for his question about where the man had gone. In units 9 and 10 Mark rejects it and provides an alternative—*gone to shop.* She checks this meaning in units 12 to 14 and then joins his game.

Nelson (1986)

Scripts or schemas are generalized event knowledge.

Scripts specify obligatory and optional actors, actions, and props or objects relevant to particular goals and circumstances. Mark's mother helps him by suggesting the action of buying (unit 16) and then urges him to come up with different props. Mark tries out three actors as customers for the services obtained at the shop (the goal and circumstances of the script). First, the man (the disappearing neighbor), then his daddy, and finally Mark himself buys certain props. Mark tries out several props for the man to buy, but only Daddy and Mark buy sweets, obviously a favorite of Mark's.

The two conversations between Mark and his mother illustrate how children's participation in everyday conversations enables them to learn language *and* learn through language. In fact, these two types of learning are almost indistinguishable in the natural environment of language use. Notice how skillful the mother is in supporting this learning. She is "teaching," but she isn't directing language lessons on sounds, words, or sentences, or lessons on birds or shops. She tracks and pays attention to what Mark is trying to express about what he already knows and what he is attempting to know. She addresses his meanings about the world and in doing so helps Mark acquire a system of language structure to express or realize these meanings.

Learning language *and* learning through language are both fostered in conversations.

Halliday (1975, 1982)

Bruner (1983); Wells (1981, 1988)

SPOKEN COMMUNICATION

People express meanings in both oral and written language through text. We do not speak or write isolated words or sentences. Instead, we speak and write through connected discourse or text. Individual words and sentences in a text can be understood only when they are related to other words, sentences, or the text as a whole. However, oral and written texts are different because they serve different purposes in our culture. This section examines the nature of oral language texts so that they can be contrasted with written language texts and the reading and writing processes in a later section.

All language is communicated through texts.

What Is a Text?

A text—spoken or written—is a social exchange of meanings, a semantic unit. *A text is both a product and a process.* It is a product in the sense that it is an output of a particular social interaction that can be recorded and studied. The two conversations between Mark and his mother that we examined in the preceding section were texts in this sense. In fact, every language example we include in this textbook is such a product (although no oral language texts could ever be duplicated exactly in print, of course).

Text is a social exchange of meaning. *Halliday & Hasan (1985)*

It is the second sense of text that we want to emphasize, however. A text is also a process in the sense that it represents a *continuous process of semantic choice* based on factors that are operating in a particular *context of situation.* For any context of situation, we can ask three general questions: (1) *What's happening?* What is the setting? What are the topics being discussed? (2) *Who are taking part?* What is the personal relationship of the participants? (3) *What role is the language playing?* What do the participants expect their language to do for them in the situation? What is the purpose of the language being used?

A text represents a process of semantic choices.

A text always relates to a context of situation.

Context of situation: (1) What's happening? (2) Who are taking part? (3) What role is language playing?

On the basis of these three contextual factors, participants select certain wordings or expressions to relate their meanings. Consequently, Mark's and his mother's linguistic contributions were choices, choices made because of particular factors operating in each conversational setting. And we couldn't have evaluated or even understood their wordings unless we also considered this situational information.

Language is a resource used to express meanings to others.

Language is a meaning potential or resource, and drawing on this resource, speakers make certain linguistic choices on the basis of what's going on in a situation. Different situations result in different linguistic choices, different wording patterns. For example, a college student's discussion of homework with a roommate in a dormitory would be different from this same student's conversation with a blind date while en route to a movie, which, in turn, would be different from the student's talk when meeting with the College Dean over some academic issue, and so forth. That is, our language varies depending on the context in which it is used. Language variation that exists in varying contexts is called *register*.

Register is language variation.

Typical Oral Language Registers

Short excerpts from several texts follow. The participants are all overheard at a place that is well known in our culture. Each text excerpt is separated with a dotted line. Read through each numbered excerpt, as though it were a clue, and see if you can guess where the language occurred:

....

1. **A:** How far do you want to go?
   B: [Shrugs shoulders]

....

2. **A:** I want to sit in the first one.
   B: Okay.

....

3. **A:** Right here.
   B: Go ahead.

....

4. **A:** Ah, it's nice and cold in here.
   B: Brrr! I'll say.

....

5. **A:** Did you forget your glasses?
   B: Nah. [Pats glasses in shirt pocket]

....

6. **A:** Why are you sitting here?
   B: Cause Joe is already sitting here.

....

7. **A:** Do I have a choice?
   B: Sure.

....

8. **A:** Here's a seat.
   B: Get in front.
   C: Not too far.

....

Well, did you figure out where the texts were produced? Some people are puzzled until they read Text 8. Many others continue to be perplexed, but then they all nod with understanding once the answer is given. The place is a movie theater. All these excerpts, as you have probably already concluded, were gathered before the movie began while people were finding their seats. We can imagine the kind of language that would have been used in the lobby while people bought their tickets and refreshments. After the movie, the language would probably have been centered on the content of the movie. This language would be more difficult for us to predict because it would be so directly related to the specific movie being seen, but we could imagine what would most likely be discussed. For example, people would probably use evaluative language; they would report whether they liked the movie. Perhaps they would also include in their conversations information about other movies of the same type or other movies done by the same actors, directors, producers, and so forth.

Spoken language usually accompanies action.
Halliday (1977); Hasan (1984a)

We want to make two important points about the language in the foregoing excerpts. First, the language is typical oral language that accompanies action—in our case, finding a seat at a movie during the summer (where there is air-conditioning in the theatre, hence the remarks in Text 4). Attention is focused only partially on what is said. Nonverbal gestures and other perceptual cues (specific objects present, the emphasis or tone of a participant's voice, and so forth) in the actual situational setting contribute and support the meanings expressed. In conversations such as those in the excerpts, words fit the world. Short responses like *okay, sure, go ahead,* as well as nonverbal gestures like shrugging one's shoulders are typical in such contexts. Terms such as *the first one* and *here,* referring to a row, a seat, or the theater itself, that may have seemed ambiguous as you initially read through the excerpts, are easily interpreted by participants in the conversations.

In typical oral language, words fit the world.
Donaldson (1978); Wells (1986)

The second point is that once you found out about the social situation, the language appeared to be familiar. This is because you already have a script, a schema, a mental representation about the events that typically occur when going to see a movie at a theater. Along with this event knowledge, you also know about the kind of language (the type of linguistic register) that is likely to be used to express the meanings at a particular instance of this script. You can even predict or consider variations of this script. For example, if you have been to an opera or symphony concert, you know that open seating is unlikely. Tickets for particular seats must be purchased ahead of time, and an usher probably helps you to find your seat. In contrast, seeing a rented movie on VCR equipment in your own home presents a related but very different variation of the going to the movies script.

Language is predictable.

During the preschool years, children acquire considerable event knowledge, or scripts, about a variety of familiar experiences (getting dressed scripts, baking cookies scripts, birthday party scripts, going to restaurants scripts, and so forth) and a range of oral language registers to express meanings in these contexts. Children learn to adjust their linguistic choices to meet the features of particular social contexts in their culture—the setting, the participants, and the specific task at hand. By the time children begin kindergarten they have remarkable oral *communicative competence;* they know how to use language appropriately in many social contexts. They have acquired a considerable vocabulary and have internalized the fundamental aspects of grammar.

Nelson (1986)

Communicative competence is knowing how to use language appropriately on the basis of context.

Unfortunately, we do not always appreciate children's already developed control of language. If a child says very little (one- or two-word utterances) to our questions in the classroom, we frequently believe that the child has impoverished language skills. Teachers do not always consider that the child's short answers may actually be appropriate in the social setting operating at that time.

What are questions and answers like in everyday social contexts? Two examples follow. Example A illustrates a typical exchange between a parent and a teenager.

EXAMPLE A

1. **Q:** Have you finished your homework?
   A: Yes.
2. **Q:** Even your math?
   A: Well, no.
3. **Q:** Cleaned up the kitchen?
   A: No.
4. **Q:** When are you going to?
   A: Soon.
5. **Q:** Promise?
   A: Yes.

EXAMPLE B

1. **Q:** Have you finished your homework?
   A: Yes. I have finished my homework.
2. **Q:** Have you even finished your math?
   A: Well, no. I haven't finished my math.
3. **Q:** Have you cleaned up the kitchen?
   A: No. I haven't cleaned up the kitchen.
4. **Q:** When are you going to finish your homework and clean up the kitchen?
   A: I am going to finish my homework and clean up the kitchen soon.
5. **Q:** Do you promise to finish your homework and clean up the kitchen soon?
   A: I promise to finish my homework and clean up the kitchen soon.

Except for question 1, all the questions in Example A are abbreviated, and all the answers are also short. Yet, you were able to understand the exchanges. These abbreviations are grammatically appropriate as well. They are what linguists call *elliptical constructions*—that is, they presuppose or rely on other information already given. For example, in answer 1, it is understood that the *yes* is an affirmative response to the question about whether the teenager had finished the homework. The one-word response does not indicate the teenager's linguistic incompetence; instead, *yes* demonstrates that the teenager understood both the *content* and *form* of the question. In this context, *yes* is enough of an answer. The parent's questions 2 and 3 are also enough. *You* (the teenager) and the act of *finished* in question 1 are meanings presumed in these questions; they do need not to be expressed again. The rest of the questions and answers are adequate for similar reasons.

Questions and answers in the real world are frequently short.

Now read through Example B, where all the presupposed understandings are included. Yet, Example B sounds unnatural, doesn't it? It sounds funny because it is not typical in everyday conversations. This example, however, represents the kind of questions and answers that are promoted in many language textbooks and programs. For example, following the routines in these programs, teachers may ask children questions like "How are you feeling?" Or, pointing to a picture of a cat in a tree, they ask, "Where is the cat?" Answers such as "fine," or "in the tree" are not acceptable responses according to these programs. Instead, children are required to answer, "I am feeling fine," or "the cat is in the tree." They are admonished to say it in a whole sentence, presumably because talking this way will teach them language skills. If they talked like this anywhere out in the world, however, their talk would be considered odd or peculiar.

Questions and answers in the real world are authentic.

Another feature of the questioning in Example A is that they are genuine and authentic. The parent actually wants to know if, in fact, the teenager has finished the homework and cleaned up the kitchen. Or perhaps, depending on the history between the parent and teenager about homework and household duties, the parent is also attempting to remind the teenager about these responsibilities. At any rate, very few questions in traditional classrooms are like those in Example A. Relying on questions from basal readers, social studies and science textbooks, and so forth, teachers tend to look for answers that they themselves already know. These materials frequently actually list questions the teachers should ask, as well as the "right answers" to these questions. For example, in a story about a boy whose dog has run away, the teacher's manual of a basal reader may tell teachers to ask questions such as: "What ran away?" "How did the boy feel?" "What was the color of the dog?" Next to these questions, the answers, "the dog," "sad," and "black" may be found. Because teachers always ask the questions and because they already have the answers, children are always in a respondent position, always being asked to provide answers to indicate the possession of certain information and vocabulary. In reading lessons and in the other lessons in other school subjects, children are given few opportunities to take an initiating role in asking their own questions. They are rarely asked about their own plans, thoughts, or feelings concerning their activities.

Teachers obviously know about the nature of spoken language because they use language appropriately in a range of communicative contexts. However, their knowledge may be subconscious or tacit. Unless this tacit understanding becomes more of an explicit awareness on the part of the teachers, several things will happen. First, if they are not sensitive to various typical oral language registers, teachers will be confused about the "correctness" of children's spoken language. They will mistake appropriate children's language behavior as deficits. Second, without an understanding of how spoken texts are created and used, teachers will not be able to provide opportunities for children to employ a range of oral language registers in the classroom. Finally, unless they recognize how spoken language differs from written language, teachers cannot support children in learning to use written language effectively. (Suggested Activity 1 at the end of the chapter can help you to explore more about spoken language registers.)

See Suggested Activity 1.

WRITTEN COMMUNICATION

As discussed in the previous section, we also communicate in written language through texts. Written texts are structured differently from typical spoken texts because we use them in our culture to serve different communicative functions. One of the most obvious differences between a spoken text and a written one is that a typical spoken text is constructed collaboratively by the participants in a conversation. In contrast, a reader's or writer's use of a written text is more of a solo enterprise. Readers and writers, usually unknown to each other, communicate across space and time. Consequently, written texts have to have a *disembedded* quality. Wordings must be organized in a different way, that is, different language registers must be employed to accomplish this type of communication.

Written texts are different from spoken texts.
Smith (1982a, 1982b); Tannen (1985); Wells (1981, 1985, 1986)
Written texts serve various communicative functions.

Halliday (1985)

Written texts are expressed by various language registers.

As will be noted in more detail later, even if a written text is usually used alone in a physical sense, a reader and writer, in a sense, can still "collaborate" with each other regarding it because each reader and writer has internalized the conventions of these language registers. Each has an idea of the kinds of interpretations that are likely, based on the ways the language patterns of the written text are expressed.

Typical Written Language Registers

What are typical written language registers? How are they different from spoken texts? It is not the channel of communication alone—oral or written—that distinguishes written from spoken texts. Written phone messages can look like oral texts; oral presentations or lectures can be like written registers. Instead, it is the entire situation, or context, in which the language is used, all factors (the setting, the location, the participants, the purpose, and so forth) operating in that context, that determines how particular language patterns are organized. Important differences between oral and written texts exist, but these differences do not represent a dichotomy based solely on the channel (oral *or* written) distinction.

To clarify some of these differences, let's start by considering the following text. Can you interpret it?

> *You* got a big *one* today.
> *It*'s got *lots. It*'s got
> *more* than *the other one.*
> Can *I do it?*

The reason you are having trouble figuring out this text is that it is the beginning of a typical conversation. Although it was completely appropriate and understood in the context in which it was uttered, only information about the actual setting will enable you to decipher it.

> **Context**
>
> A six-year-old child is getting ready to dictate an original story, and a visiting teacher is preparing to take down the child's dictation. The story will be tape recorded as it is being dictated, and this is a familiar routine for both participants. A new tape recorder has been brought to school today and is the focus of shared attention. The child is touching the buttons on the new recorder as she speaks the words above.

Now it is easy to figure out what the italicized words mean. *You* and *I* refer to the teacher and the child, the two participants in the conversation. The words *one* and *it* relate to the new tape recorder, and *the other one* refers to the old tape recorder that had been used in the past. The *lots* and *more* both are easily understood as "lots of buttons" and "more buttons" (than the old tape recorder had). Finally, *do it* means "push the buttons."

The foregoing italicized words are implicit linguistic devices. They are called *im-*

Implicit wordings

Halliday & Hasan (1976, 1985)
Two interpretative sources: situational environment or *context* and linguistic environment or *co-text*

plicit because their interpretation has to be found by reference to some other source. The question is: Where is that interpretative source? We have argued that a strong relationship exists between context and text structure, or the ways words are organized or patterned in texts. Thus, for any linguistic unit on which we want to focus, there are two environments: (1) the extra-linguistic environment or actual situation (i.e., the context) related to the total text, and (2) the linguistic environment (i.e., the co-text), the actual language accompanying or surrounding that linguistic unit. Consequently, implicit devices could either be co-textual or purely contextual (or situational). In the foregoing conversation about the tape recorder, the source of interpretation for these implicit devices is contextual. The implicit devices are called *exophoric* because the source of their interpretation lies outside the co-text; they can be understood only through an examination of the immediate context of situation. Figure 1.1 depicts aspects of the situation that provide the interpretative sources for the exophoric implicit devices used in the conversation about the tape recorder. (Suggested Activity 2 will help you to explore more about exophoric implicit wordings.)

Exophoric implicit devices *point out* to the immediate situational context.

See Suggested Activity 2.

The use of exophoric implicit wordings is typical in spoken language. Although the oral text example we have included is perhaps an extreme case with respect to its density of exophoric implicit wordings, it is a useful illustration to demonstrate what is meant when it is said that in conversations, words fit in the world. In written language, however, words create a world in that implicit and other types of wordings are chosen so that the text stands on its own. The typical written text creates its own context of situation, and the source of interpretation of implicit devices lies within the co-text, not the immediate surroundings in which a text is being used.

Wells (1986)

Words create a world in written language use.

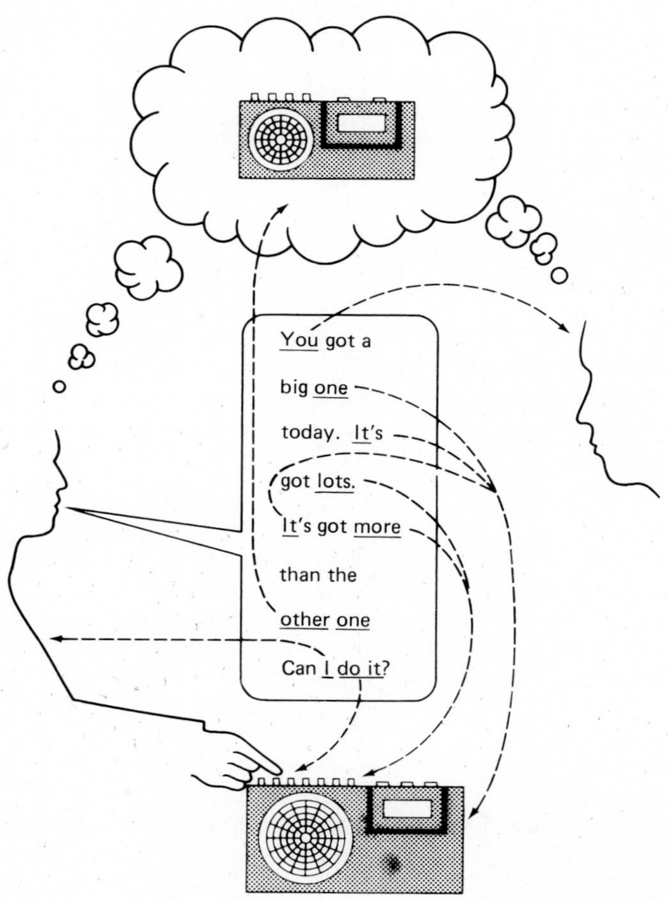

Figure 1.1

We will discuss excerpts from two written texts to better understand these differences of language variation that characterize linguistic registers of written communication.

Two Examples of Written Texts

Figure 1.2 contains the first six sentences of *The Owl and the Woodpecker,* a story written by Brian Wildsmith. Let's first look at how the author used implicit devices. In the first sentence *a Woodpecker* is introduced. This *woodpecker* then becomes the source with which to interpret subsequent implicit devices. The definite article *the* plus *woodpecker* are used (in sentences 2, 4, and 6) to refer back to the woodpecker. Other pronouns, *he, his, you, my,* and *I,* are also used to refer to the woodpecker and are thereby easily understood. The same kind of use of implicit devices is employed by Wildsmith with respect to the other main character in the story and to the woodpecker's tree. *An Owl* is presented in the third sentence and serves as the interpretative source to understand *the Owl* (sentences 4 and 5) and *I* (in 5), and *there* (in sentence 5) and *it* (in 6) through earlier mention of *tree* (in 2 and 6).

Wildsmith (1971)

You can see that the implicit devices that have been used here in this example of written language are very different from those we have seen in conversations. Rather than being exophoric, referring to items outside the text, these implicit devices in typical written language are *endophoric.* They refer to items inside the text for their interpretation. This doesn't mean that exophoric implicit wordings can be found only in spoken language and that endophoric implicit ones exist only in written language. Oral language also contains a lot of endophoric implicit wordings—for example, the elliptical constructions illustrated in the conversation about the homework (page 15) were endophoric. Moreover, certain exophoric implicit wordings may also occur in written language. It is a matter of degree: Exophoric implicit wordings are typically found in spoken language because spoken language accompanies action; endophoric implicit wordings are usually present in written language because written language is used for more "disembedded" communication.

Halliday & Hasan (1976, 1985)

Endophoric implicit devices *point into* the text.

In written texts, the use of endophoric implicit wordings creates three "threads" or "chains" of meaning. These threads or chains, illustrated for the woodpecker, owl, and the woodpecker's tree in Figure 1.2, go throughout the text. The chains help the text "hang together"; they contribute to that text's coherence. Because written texts, like stories, can be read at any time or at any place, they have to be more explicit than

Endophoric implicit wordings form threads or chains within the text.

Hasan (1984b)

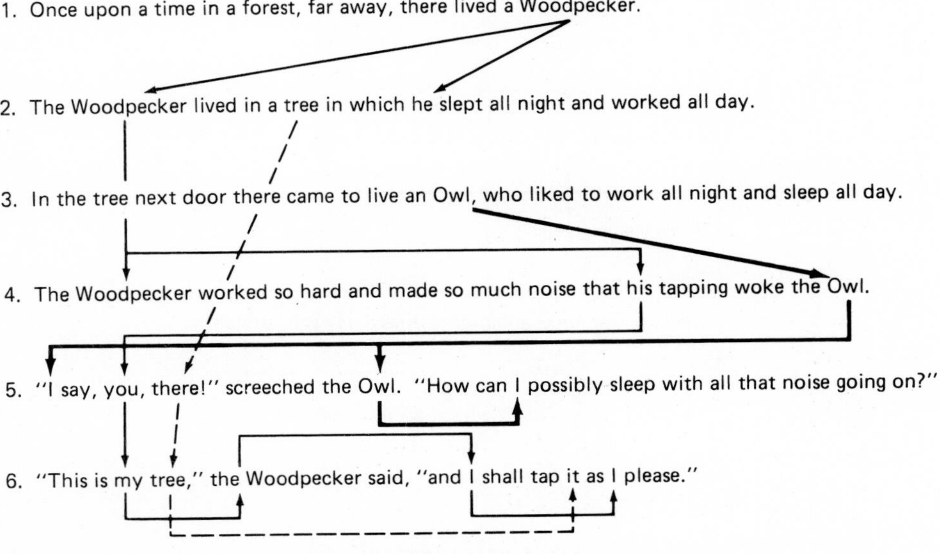

1. Once upon a time in a forest, far away, there lived a Woodpecker.
2. The Woodpecker lived in a tree in which he slept all night and worked all day.
3. In the tree next door there came to live an Owl, who liked to work all night and sleep all day.
4. The Woodpecker worked so hard and made so much noise that his tapping woke the Owl.
5. "I say, you, there!" screeched the Owl. "How can I possibly sleep with all that noise going on?"
6. "This is my tree," the Woodpecker said, "and I shall tap it as I please."

Figure 1.2 The Owl and the Woodpecker
Source: Wildsmith (1971).

spoken text. Because written texts sustain continuous messages that do not rely *directly* on particular sets of circumstances for understanding them, implicit devices are usually used endophorically, and lexical, or content, wordings—nouns, verbs, adjectives, and adverbs—are employed to a much larger extent. In addition, lexical items, or vocabulary, are frequently more formal, less colloquial. (Chapter 5 discusses these aspects of written language in more detail.)

Chafe (1985); Halliday (1985)

Written texts are also related to social contexts in our culture.

Halliday (1985); Halliday & Hasan (1985)

Gibbons (1984)

The fact that typical written texts possess a disembedded quality and cannot be seen as having a direct relation between their message and the immediate surroundings in which they are being used does not mean they are not related to some context. It is just that they are related to a context of our social system in a more complicated, indirect way. Written texts serve various purposes in our culture. Stories such as *The Owl and the Woodpecker* create imaginative worlds and are used to entertain young children in our culture. Other written texts—for example, the information book, *Tunnels,* written by Gail Gibbons—play a different role in our culture. They attempt to explain and describe animals, objects, and happenings in the world to young children. Variation in purpose and context in our culture means variation of language. Consequently, different registers, different linguistic patterns from stories are found in information books. Let's look at the first few sentences of *Tunnels* in Figure 1.3 to get an idea about some of these differences.

Information texts are expressed by different registers from stories.

Consider the implicit devices first. *They* is used twice: The first *they* (in sentence 3) refers to *ants and worms* (in 2), and the second *they* (in sentence 5) relates to *moles, chipmunks, and prairie dogs* (in 4). The possessive pronoun, *their,* in sentence 5 also refers to these three animals. Finally, *them* (in sentence 3) refers to *tunnels* (made by ants and worms in sentence 2) for its understanding. Thus, as in *The Owl and the Woodpecker,* the implicit devices used in *Tunnels* are the endophoric type. They refer to aspects of the co-text for their interpretation.

Identity chains versus classification chains
Martin (1985); Martin & Peters (1985); Pappas (1988, 1989)

However, if you take another look at the *Tunnels* excerpt, you will note that the threads or chains created are different in a subtle but important way. In *The Owl and the Woodpecker* the threads involved the same individual or animal (woodpecker and owl) or object (tree). In contrast, in *Tunnels* the threads depict the same *class* of objects (tunnels) or animals (ants and worms, moles, chipmunks, and prairie dogs). If you trace the *tunnels* chain (illustrated with a single line) in Figure 1.3, for example, you will discover that it does not refer to the same individual tunnels but to the same entire class of objects, that is, tunnels, in general.

Most information books are similar. They don't identify particular persons as characters, for example, and then follow their conflicts, motives, reactions, and exploits as stories do. Instead, information books make general statements about animals, objects,

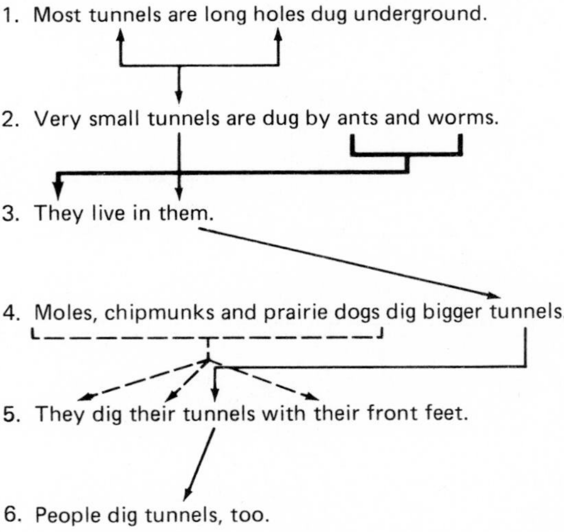

1. Most tunnels are long holes dug underground.
2. Very small tunnels are dug by ants and worms.
3. They live in them.
4. Moles, chipmunks and prairie dogs dig bigger tunnels.
5. They dig their tunnels with their front feet.
6. People dig tunnels, too.

Figure 1.3 Tunnels
Source: Gibbon (1984).

places, people, and so forth. Other linguistic features contribute to the general nature of information books that can be illustrated in *Tunnels*. Information books use the present tense—for example, *are, are dug, live, dig*. (Stories are usually in the past tense, except in quoted dialogue.) Information books contain a lot of descriptive constructions (e.g., *tunnels are long holes*). (Of course, stories also contain descriptions, but not nearly as many as information books do.)

These are only some examples of the wording patterns to be found in information books. Again, just as teachers have a subconscious awareness of various types of spoken language registers, they also have a tacit understanding of various written language registers. They subconsciously know that meanings are expressed in imaginative, fictional narrative through wording patterns different from those expressed in nonfictional expository texts. However, unless these tacit understandings become more explicit, teachers will not be able to expose children to representative examples of the written genres used in our culture or to support children's efforts to read and write these genres on their own. (Suggested Activities 3 and 4 can help you to explore more about differences between oral and written registers and about the differences between typical stories and information books.)

See Suggested Activities 3 and 4.

Emergent Literacy

How do children learn how to use written texts? The research of the 1970s and 1980s on early literacy has indicated that our previous belief that learning to read and write begins only when children are instructed in the elementary school has to be questioned. Like talking and listening, reading and writing have roots that reach back into infancy. Early literacy begins when children encounter books and other written texts in their own social, cultural environments. Beginning understandings of written language are also learned within a natural environment of language use. Children learn that written texts, too, can be used to get things done. They learn what books and other written texts are, in what circumstances they are employed, and what is in reading and writing for them. This early awareness of the purpose of written language in the environment of their homes and communities is called *emergent literacy*.

Early literacy understandings are also learned within a natural environment of language use.

Goodman & Goodman (1979); Harste, Woodward, & Burke (1984); Holdaway (1979); Teale & Sulzby (1986)

Emergent literacy

Schickedanz (1986)

Two major traditional assumptions are questioned in this new view of literacy. First, the mastery of oral language is no longer a prerequisite to the development of written language. Oral and written language develop simultaneously, each facilitating and supporting a child's understanding of the other. Second, literacy learning need not be tutored in specific ways. Instead of direct instruction, children learn written language by interacting with adults (or older children) in reading and writing situations, by exploring print on their own, and by observing significant adults, especially their parents, actually using written language for their communicative ends.

Written language develops *along with* oral language development.

Literacy learning doesn't require special tutoring.

The term *emergent literacy* is used to emphasize the continuities in becoming literate, how young children develop early concepts and skills basic to learning to read and write. All children have acquired some of these understandings because our culture is a literate one. Individual children's knowledge about literacy, however, differs as a result of the manner and extent to which written language has been shared with them.

A major element contributing to young children's understanding of typical written registers and the ways they differ from typical spoken ones is adults' practice of reading storybooks and other types of written texts to children during the preschool years. Extensive and repetitive experiences with a range of favorite books enable young children to learn about these written registers. They develop a *literacy set* as a result of these rich book-sharing experiences. Don Holdaway (1979) describes literacy set in terms of four factors—*motivational, linguistic, operational,* and *orthographic*. Table 1.1 describes these factors of Holdaway's literacy set.

Reading to children is a crucial factor in fostering understandings of written language registers.

Cambourne (1981); Smith (1982a)

Literacy set

Holdaway (1979)

An integrated language perspective fosters and further builds on this initial literate behavior. Learning to read and write is seen as children's extending the potential, or resource, of language. Reading and writing are not considered as ends in and of themselves but as tools to learn, as further means by which to communicate for many various

Halliday (1978)

Literacy is an extension of the potential of language to express meanings.

TABLE 1.1 Literacy Set

A. MOTIVATIONAL FACTORS (High expectations of print)
Enjoys books and stories—appreciates the special rewards of print.
Has had extensive, repetitive experience of a wide range of favourite books.
Seeks book experiences—asks for stories, goes to books independently.
Is curious about all aspects of print, e.g. signs, labels, advertisements.
Experiments with producing written language.

B. LINGUISTIC FACTORS (Familiarity with written dialect in oral form)
Has built extensive models for the special features of written dialect.
Syntax—grammatical structures learned through meaningful use, e.g. full forms of contractions such as 'I'm' or 'What's', structures which imply consequence 'If . . . then . . .'
Vocabulary—words not normally used in conversation, e.g. 'however', 'dine', 'ogre'
Intonation Patterns—appropriate intonations for literary or non-conversational English, e.g. 'Fat, indeed! The very idea of it!'
Idioms—special usage contrary to normal grammatical or semantic rules, e.g. same example as for intonation—illustrates that idiom often works with special intonation.

C. OPERATIONAL FACTORS (Essential strategies for handling written language)
Self-monitoring operations: Self-correction and confirmation.
Predictive operations: Ability to 'use the context' to fill particular language slots.
Structural operations: Ability to follow plot, temporal and causal sequences, logical arrangements, etc.
Non-situational operations: Ability to understand language without the help of immediate sensory context.
Imaginative operations: Ability to create images which have not been experienced or represented in sensory reality, and apply metaphorical meanings.

D. ORTHOGRAPHIC FACTORS (Knowledge of the conventions of print)
Note: Few pre-schoolers would have grasped more than a few of the orthographic principles.
Story comes from print, not from pictures.
Directional conventions—a complex progression:
- Front of book has spine on left
- Story begins where print begins
- Left hand page comes before right hand
- Move from top to bottom of page
- Begin left along line to right
- Return to next line on left margin

Print components—clear concept of 'words', 'spaces', 'letters'
Letter-form generalizations—same letter may be written in upper and lower case, and in different print styles
Punctuation conventions
Phonetic principle—letters have some relationship to speech sounds
Consistency principle—same word always has same spelling

Source: Holdaway (1979), p. 62.

purposes. Let's examine this type of communication more. How do readers and writers, the participants in the use of written texts, manage this kind of social interaction?

Reader-Writer Contract

Written texts have a disembedded quality.

Wells (1985, 1986)

Both reading and writing consist of the construction of texts.

Smith (1982b); Tierney & Pearson (1984)

A reader-writer contract exists when written texts are used.

We have noted how written texts have a disembedded quality because in written communication readers and writers are frequently unknown to each other and because they are rarely communicating in the same place in time and space. However, that does not mean that readers and writers are not related, not involved, with each other. A writer must always keep the readers in view in composing or constructing a text; otherwise those readers would never be able to interpret the writer's message. And readers must constantly construct in reading what they believe to be the writer's message. Both readers and writers construct written texts. With any use of a written text, there is a reader-writer relationship, a reader-writer contract, so to speak. The reader-writer contract is the means by which particular readers and writers achieve intersubjectivity in written communication.

Schemas are our organized mental representations of our knowledge of the world.

As do speakers and listeners, writers (during the composing process) and readers (during the comprehension process) rely on their mental representation of the world to communicate. Researchers call these mental representations by different terms—*scripts, cognitive structures,* or *schemas.* In this book, although we may at times use any one of these terms, most of the time, we use *schemas* to designate individual mental representations. The next section covers schemas in detail, but some general remarks about them are necessary now to clarify these reader-writer relationships.

Schemas are our individual organizations of what we know. They consist of what we know of persons and personal relationships in our world, what we know of the properties and features of objects in the world, and what we know of how language works to express understandings about the world. Our knowledge of conventions of written language—another way to talk about written language registers—is crucial in the reader-writer transaction. Figure 1.4 depicts the reader-writer contract.

Schemas include our people world, our object world, and our language world.

Karmiloff-Smith (1979)

From a writer's side of the contract, a particular written text is the result of a writer's intentions to communicate meanings. Those meanings, drawn from the writer's schemas, are expressed through the conventions of written language. The text represents a blueprint or a set of cues that a reader uses to evoke the particular schemas needed to comprehend the writer's message. From the reader's view, expectations about what the conventions express or stand for enable the reader to predict, according to the reader's perceptions, what the writer has communicated. Using the cues provided by the writer to spark the appropriate schemas, the reader constructs the perceived textual world the writer has envisioned. Both readers and writers bring meaning (based on their schemas) to texts.

Writer's intentions

Rabinowitz (1987); Rosenblatt (1978)

Reader's expectations

SCHEMAS: OUR MENTAL REPRESENTATIONS OF OUR KNOWLEDGE

We are learning all the time. What we learn at any time is always based on what we already know. This knowledge is not a mere accumulation of "out-there" facts about the world picked up by osmosis, by passive absorption like a sponge. Instead, knowledge is actively *constructed* by individual minds. It is a "theory of the world in the head" developed over a lifetime of experiences.

Knowledge is constructed by individual learners.

Smith (1982a, 1982b)

Piaget was an influential proponent of this constructive view of learning and knowledge. He described learning as a process of change, a continuous modification of our schemas or cognitive structures in our brain. Through two simultaneous processes, assimilation and accommodation, children add new information about the world to their schemas to adapt to their environment. *Assimilation* is the process by which knowledge is restructured by being integrated into existing schemas. In contrast, *accommodation* is the process by which knowledge is restructured by making modifications in existing schemas. In Piaget's theory, development is explained in terms of global knowledge restructuring. Children go through four broad, qualitatively different stages of development corresponding to certain ages: sensorimotor stage (birth to two years), preoperational stage (two to seven years), concrete-operational stage (seven to eleven years),

Piaget (1926, 1969a, 1969b, 1975)

Piaget's theory of development is one of *global* knowledge restructuring.

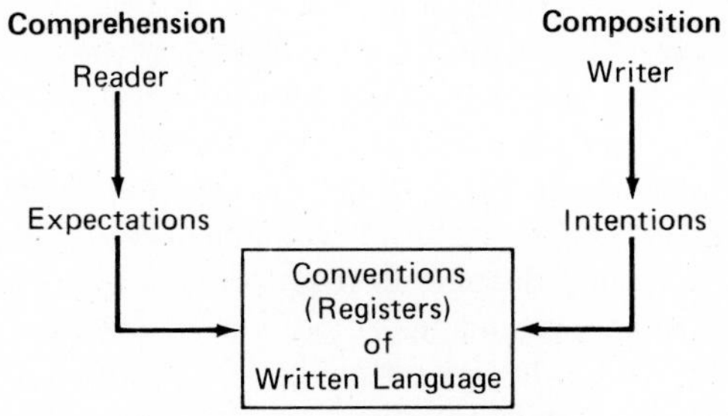

Figure 1.4 Reader-Writer Contract

and formal-operational stage (beyond the eleventh year). Children's thinking processes are constrained and determined by what stage they are in. Children's logical processes are different from adults' in Piaget's view.

More recent research in cognitive psychology and developmental psychology has extended many Piagetian ideas about development, learning, and knowledge. Some aspects of his theory have been modified and reinterpreted. Piaget, for the most part, studied how children's schemas developed as they interacted with objects in the physical world. More recent views emphasize how this knowledge is mediated and influenced through social interaction. Children act on objects and play with toys on their own, but most of their activities with objects are immersed in a sea of conversation with others, as has been already discussed and illustrated in earlier sections. Individual schemas constructed by individual learners are not developed in a void; schemas are influenced by social and cultural interactions and practices.

Bruner (1986); Donaldson (1978); Dunn (1988); Vygotsky (1962, 1978); Wells (1988)

Another feature of Piaget's theory having to do with children's early thinking and speech has also been challenged. Piaget characterized preschoolers' thought as being *egocentric.* That is, young children are not able to take the point of view of another. However, this cannot be true, as we have already noted when we discussed *intersubjectivity.* Through their reciprocal interactions with their parents, even two-month-olds demonstrate that they are sensitive to the behavior of another person. These babies are affected by the smile or other facial gestures and verbalizations of the adult *and* their facial expressions, gurgles, and body movements affect the adult's movements, articulations, and so forth. These babies are already taking account of another person, adapting their behavior to respond to another human being. In fact, children could never learn language at all if they were as egocentric as Piaget suggested. Recall Mark and how hard he worked to achieve intersubjectivity with his mother—how he made sure that his mother understood what he was trying to tell her.

Finally, questions about Piaget's theory of how knowledge is reconstructed have been raised. In his view, restructuring of knowledge is global. Children in a particular stage of development apply the same kind of thinking processes no matter what the area or topic is. The procedures or routines that children employ in each stage are independent of the content of the knowledge they operate on because it is assumed that their schemas vary little across domains. Consequently, the process of learning is affected only slightly, or not at all, by the concepts contained in a learner's schemas in each of the domains. The procedures and routines used by children change only when they enter a new stage in which these general or global structures are modified.

Carey (1985, 1988); Gelman & Baillargeon (1983); Keil (1984); Mandler (1983); Vosniadou & Brewer (1987)

Newer developmental theories emphasize knowledge restructuring in specific domains.

In the more recent views of development, the area, topic, or conceptual domain that the learner is involved with or trying to figure out does matter, is significant. Properties or concepts in particular domains affect the thinking processes, routines, strategies, and procedures that children apply in their experiences. In this view, then, children's thinking and learning processes are similar to those of adults. Moreover, young children can learn things in particular domains much earlier in development than was previously thought *and* learning in those domains also takes a much longer time during development than was previously realized. In this *domain-specific knowledge restructuring view,* inferences made by a learner at any time are based more on what and how concepts are structured and organized in particular domains—specific content—than they are on the age of the learner. For example, if children have many experiences with clay, perhaps because their parents are potters, or because they live in a place where the ground is clay-like and play with it a lot, or because they regularly play with the leftover dough when their parents make pies, then they may come to understand that a particular ball of clay is the same amount even if it is rolled into a long "snake." That is, in Piagetian terms, these children can conserve mass; they realize that the quantity of the clay is the same despite its transformation in shape. The reason these children can acquire these understandings at age four or five (instead of seven or eight, according to Piaget's theory) is because they have a schema in the particular domain of clay and its properties and transformations. In this view, children can be "experts" in a particular area in which adults may function as novices. How many five-year-old dinosaur experts do you know? How about eight-year-old Star Wars or space whizzes? Teenage computer hackers? These are all cases of children who have knowledge in a specific topic or domain, a domain that many adults may know little about.

In this book, certain important Piagetian notions are emphasized. Children are seen as active, constructive learners as they continuously generate and test hypotheses about aspects of their environment. Like Piaget, we stress the importance of cognitive conflict in children's development, that children learn when their theories are questioned. Conflict inducement leads to modification of their schemas.

Children are constructive learners.

Children generate and test hypotheses.

Foreman & Kushner (1983)

Cognitive conflict leads to changes in children's schemas.

However, we expand on these Piagetian views in two major ways. First, we emphasize the role of social interaction with others as an important source of cognitive conflict. Having to collaborate and cooperate with others about an area of interest promotes the restructuring of children's knowledge. With the assistance of others, children can go beyond their own limits to solve their own problems through interaction. Second, we emphasize the importance of content or concepts in specific domains in development and learning. Traditional elementary schools frequently concentrate on basic skills, especially at the early grades, so that children can deal with content parceled out in later grades. An integrated language perspective, in contrast, insists that skills go hand and hand with content. Children comprehend and learn how to do things on the basis of their knowledge structures of specific content, particular topics, fields, or domains. Let's look further at how this domain-specific knowledge is organized and how it is developed.

The importance of social interaction on knowledge restructuring

Bruner (1986); Lindfors (1987); Vygotsky (1978); Wells (1988)

The importance of knowledge restructuring in specific domains

The Organization of Schemas

Schemas are not random bits of information stored in any haphazard way. Instead, schemas are organized; they are coherent category systems. Schemas consist of three major components: (1) categories or concepts of knowledge; (2) features, attributes, characteristics, or rules for determining what constitutes a category or concept—that is, rules of category membership; and, (3) a network of connections and interrelationships among and between categories or concepts. Thus, our schemas can be conceived of as dynamic, always changing, structured mental representations of what we know. Each experience we have is interpreted in terms of the knowledge we have acquired, stored, and organized, and this knowledge is modified, reorganized (restructured) as a result of each experience.

Schemas are organized.

Rumelhart (1980); Smith (1982a, 1982b)

Our knowledge is restructured as a result of our experience.

Schemas As Semantic Maps of Domains

A good way to visualize schemas is to see them as *semantic maps*—that is, maps of concepts or meanings. Semantic maps are diagrams of what researchers think schemas in our brains are like. Although schemas or maps are related to each other in ways we do not quite understand, they are coherent units, or wholes, in different areas, or domains. Domains themselves are best seen as a continuum from general, broad fields or areas of knowledge to more specific, narrow topics or concepts. For example, curricular areas or academic disciplines, such as biology or history, can be seen as illustrations of broad, general domains, whereas cats, dogs, and dinosaurs exemplify concepts at the specific end of the continuum. Similarly, mathematics, art, music, and language can be thought of as general symbolic domains. Then, within each of these general domains, more narrow domains can be considered—for example, geometry and algebra in mathematics, drawing and sculpture in art, symphonies and rock songs in music, stories and information books in written language, and so forth. Domain-specific knowledge restructuring can be conceived of as occurring at various levels of generality in development. However, it is distinguished from global knowledge restructuring in that schemas are not overarching structures developed in the same way over all domains. Children may be able to conserve a substance like clay but not be able to conserve number. For example, they may not realize that there is the same number of beads in two rows when the beads in the shorter row are placed next to each other and the beads in the

Semantic Maps are diagrams depicting our concepts in domains.

Johnson & Pearson (1984); Pearson & Johnson (1978)

Domains are areas of knowledge.

Schemas are developed in specific domains.

longer row are placed with spaces between them. Children who have played marbles with their parents and siblings may be able to conserve number but not conserve substance. Some children may be already competent at reading stories when they begin school because their family has always read lots of stories to them; other children may enter school understanding many number concepts because their family has played a lot of board and card games requiring counting. In sum, knowledge structures are developed with more or less elaboration and differentiation in different, particular domains.

The Development of Schemas

How do people develop these domain-specific schemas? Children and adults alike learn by inventing new categories or concepts and by constructing and making new and different connections and relationships among these concepts. Although people have many similar experiences and therefore possess common knowledge, each individual has unique experiences and therefore develops unique schemas (unique categories, rules, and interrelationships).

Schemas are unique and individualized.

The construction of a schema in the domain of spiders

To better understand how this development of a schema may occur, let's follow Sara as she learns about or constructs a schema in the domain of spiders. We begin our story when Sara is around six or seven months old. Perhaps her first construction is the result of her observations of her parents' enactment of the cleaning the house script or schema. Sitting in her high chair, she notices how a spider, which has crawled out from a chair mommy or daddy has moved, is vacuumed up with all the other dirt that had been accumulated since the last time the room was cleaned. Figure 1.5 is a semantic map depicting Sara's initial, rudimentary spider schema.

Semantic Map of Sara's initial spider map

Because Sara has noted that the spider actively moves across the floor, she categorizes the creature as a type of animal. Also, both the action of "cleans up" and the

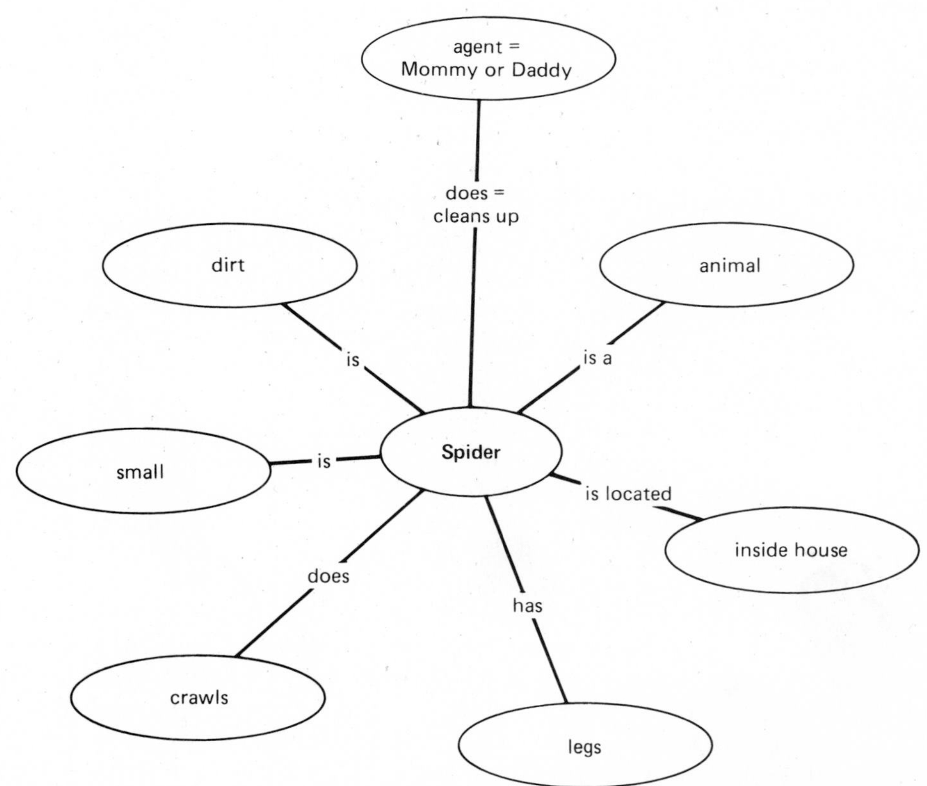

Figure 1.5

agent (mommy or daddy) of that action are somehow part of her conception of spider. She develops certain characteristics of spider—that a spider has legs, crawls, and is small. She may also include a feature of "dirt" for the spider because the spider has been so much a part of the dirt that is usually cleaned up. Similarly, she develops the idea that the concept of spider can be found at a certain location, namely, "inside the house," because this is where the events of cleaning up the spider have occurred.

Second Semantic Map for Sara's spider schema

About two months later, Sara's parents begin to play the "itsy, bitsy spider went up the water spout" game with her. Therefore, modifications in her spider schema evolve. Figure 1.6 is a semantic map showing this restructuring. She develops new connections to her spider concept. As a result of repeated instances of the itsy, bitsy spider game, her schema includes Sara and her parents, as agents, pretending to be a spider. In the game, fingers are like spider legs, so that idea is incorporated. Some idea that spiders may also possess fingers may be constructed in her schema as well. Another place that spiders can be found—in a water spout—is added, although what a water spout is Sara does not really understand. Similarly, she develops some preliminary notion that rain washes out spiders. Notice how a two-way mapping process that relates concepts and language is being evolved. Schemas provide clues to word meanings that people use, and others' word meanings help modify one's own old schemas. This is a consistent pattern that continues throughout development.

Over the years, Sara's spider schema becomes more and more elaborated, modified, reorganized, restructured. Figures 1.7, 1.8, and 1.9 attempt to depict some of these changes. There isn't enough space to show all possible changes, so only the more salient ones are included.

Figure 1.6

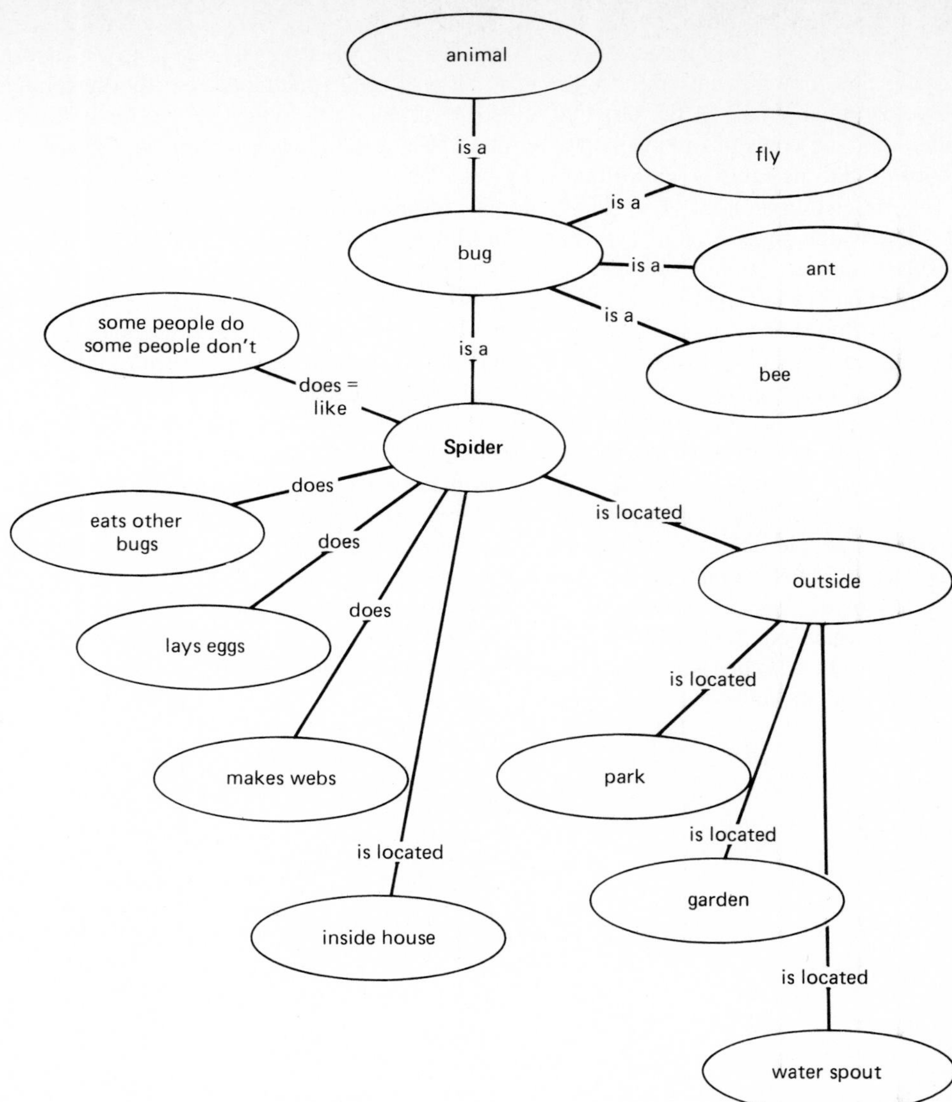

Figure 1.7

Third Semantic Map for Sara's spider schema

As the semantic map in Figure 1.7 indicates, spider, along with "fly," "ant," and "bee," has become part of a class of "bugs" in Sara's schema. The earlier dirt and fingers relationships have been dropped and new characteristics of spiders have been added—that they eat other bugs, lay eggs, and make webs. A new location connection—"outside"—has been incorporated and differentiated. Sara now understands that spiders can also be found outside in parks and gardens. She has also noted that people have varying degrees of liking for spiders.

Fourth Semantic Map for Sara's spider schema

White (1952)

As the result of hearing *Charlotte's Web* by White read aloud, and later reading on her own, Sara's schema on spiders (Figure 1.8) again shows modification. Although *Charlotte's Web* is a fantasy, it provides useful information about spiders that induces Sara to elaborate on her "lays eggs" and "outside" connections. Of course, "make-believe" connections (marked by asterisks) are also added—Charlotte, the spider in this delightful book, talks and spells words, thereby saving Wilbur, the pig, from slaughter.

Fifth Semantic Map for Sara's spider schema

Subsequently, Sara's spider becomes even more restructured (see Figure 1.9). As a result of a school project on spiders, the earlier "bugs" classification drops alto-

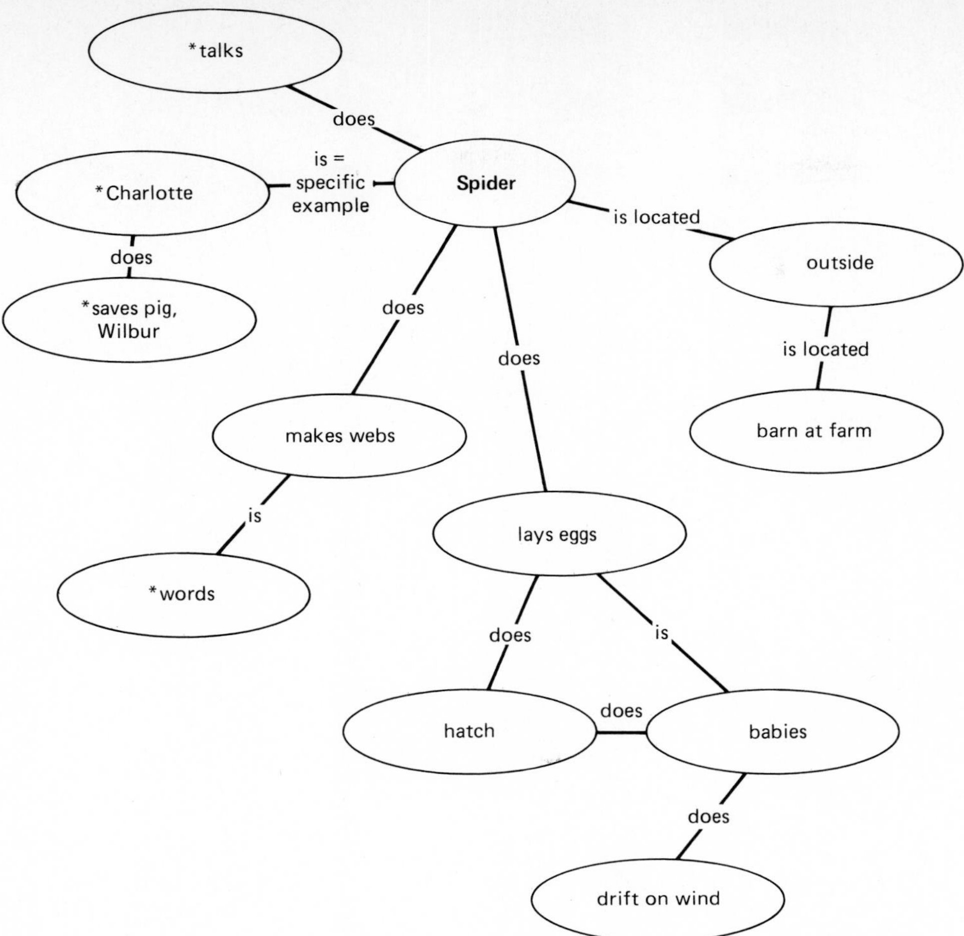

Figure 1.8

gether, and Sara begins to differentiate between the class of "insects" and the class of "arachnids," of which spiders are members. She learns that insects and arachnids have certain features that distinguish them. For example, insects have six legs and three body parts, whereas arachnids have eight legs and two body parts. In addition, as Sara incorporates this class distinction into her schema, she includes members of the insect class. She also notes that there are members of the arachnid class other than spiders and that there are many kinds of spiders—tarantulas, which are the largest ones, black widow spiders, which are poisonous, and so forth.

Of course, our account of Sara's development of the spider schema is much too simplistic of how children actually construct and reconstruct their schemas. Schemas are much more complex than we are able to illustrate here—networks of particular schemas overlap with, and link to, many other schemas. These schemas are always unique; for example, the spider schemas for an avid gardener, a biologist, and an entomologist are most likely to be very different from yours. As children learn, existing categories and connections are enlarged and restructured, and new categories are created and modified in many particular domains. These schemas develop on the basis of individual experiences and interests.

Another schema example is shown in Figure 1.10, which illustrates a seven-year-old child's schema of "living things," a more general domain than that of Sara's spider domain. The child was given a new large tablet by his mother and was told that he could write whatever he wanted in it. One of his earliest efforts was this list he constructed of

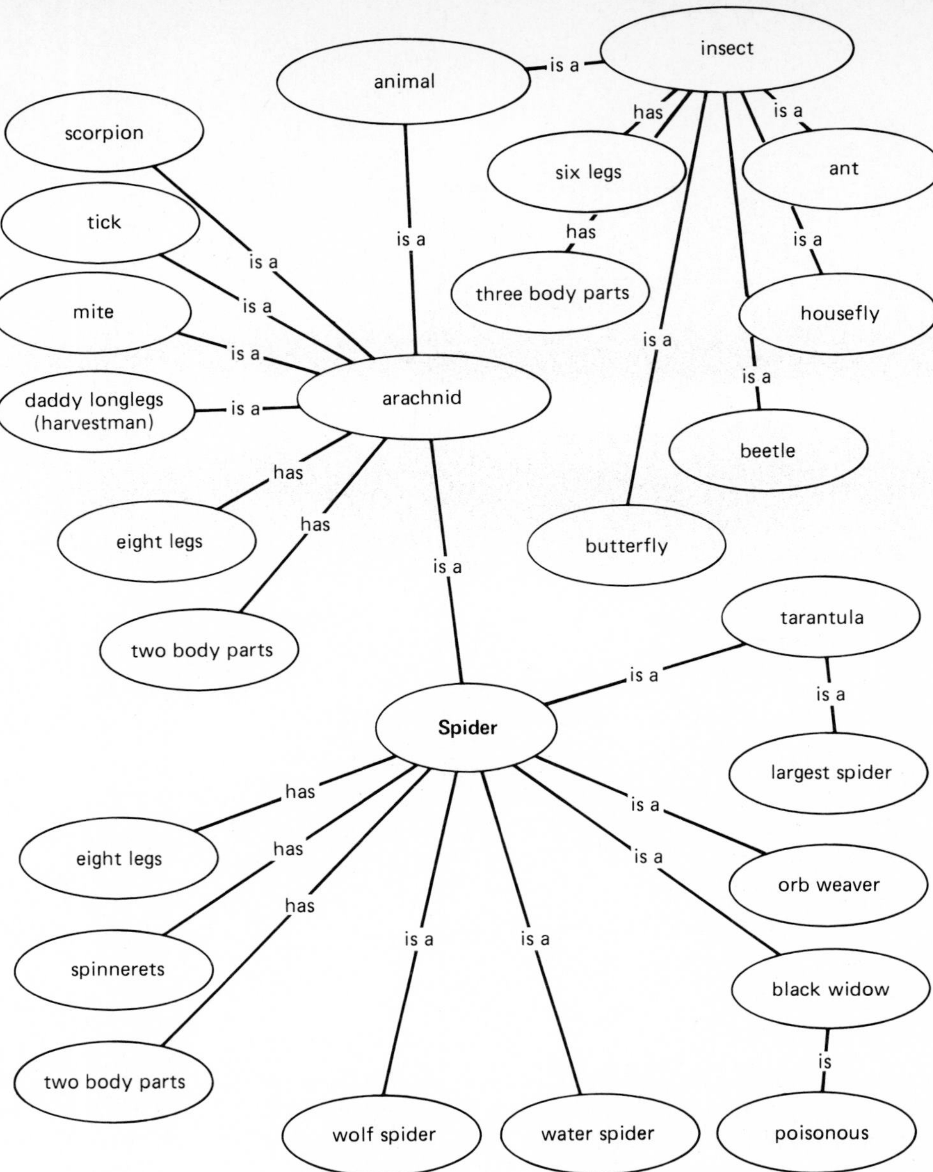

Figure 1.9

living things. Although his list is a linear display, it is easy to imagine off-shoots of subdomains, and perhaps even to infer connections and relationships of distinguishing properties for these more specific subdomains. Many of his entries are amusing, but they are organized. His list reflects both some of the concepts he has already learned in this domain and his ability to express these concepts in language.

SUMMARY

A two-mapping process that relates concepts and language occurs in development.

This chapter started by addressing the way language develops in conversation and what conversation is. Then it moved into considering differences between oral and written language. Following that, it went into schemas and their development. In development, a dynamic, two-way mapping process occurs relating concepts and language. Children's existing conceptual schemas provide them with clues to the meanings of the wordings

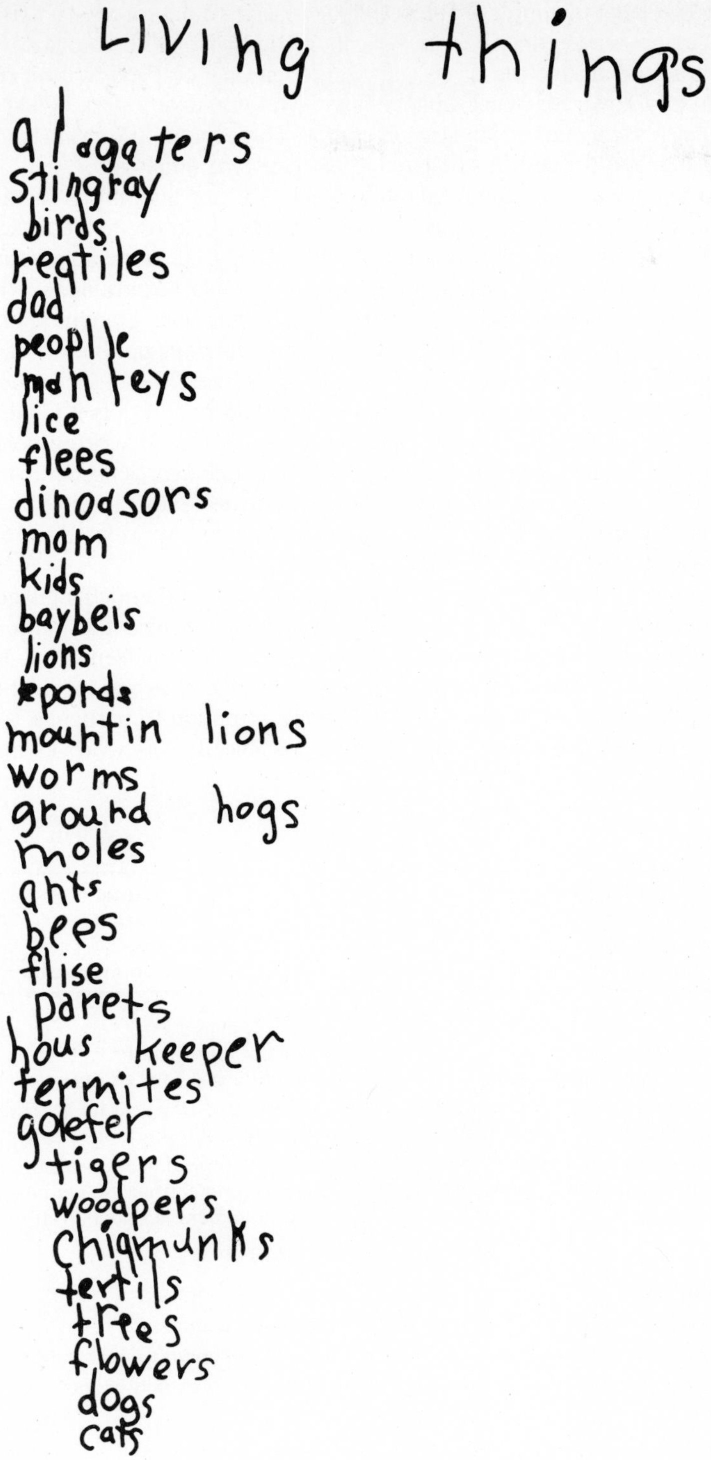

Living things

algaters
stingray
birds
reqtiles
dad
peoplle
mahkeys
lice
flees
dinodsors
mom
kids
baybeis
lions
pords
mountin lions
worms
ground hogs
moles
ants
bees
flise
parets
hous keeper
termites
golefer
tigers
woodpers
chigmunks
tertils
trees
flowers
dogs
cats

Figure 1.10

used by others in various contexts, and the language that children experience in a range of contexts leads to modification and restructuring of their schemas.

Lindfors (1987); Wells (1981)

Children do not sit on the sidelines during this process. They are active participants in the process, constantly charging into the fray. They continually learn how they can use the potential of language to communicate their meanings to others in their culture.

These developing language abilities reflect children's evolving understandings of

Contexts for oral and written communication

how language relates to context. Table 1.2 summarizes some of the factors, characteristics, and circumstances that exist in typical oral and written communicative contexts. They are organized around the three questions regarding oral and written contexts that we have already covered: What's happening? Who are taking part? What role is language playing? Varying factors and circumstances correspond to varying language registers—how language is used, how language patterns are employed.

The circumstances or factors given in Table 1.2 are only broad distinctions, and in many ways, they are too simplistic. For example, a letter to your grandmother, although it is written communication, may be very like a spoken conversation in lots of ways. Because you and your grandmother share many past experiences, you may refer to persons, objects, places, and so on exophorically, and your grandmother will understand what you mean. Retelling a story to someone who does not know it is an example of oral communication. Because such a listener is "naive," the story monologue must be linguistically complete for the listener to understand it, and thus it is very similar to a typical written text. Typical oral communication and typical written communication are best seen as the two ends of a continuum or language use. Moreover, frequently—especially in the classroom—conversations and written texts can interact in complex ways; that is, the use of a written text can be surrounded by, related to, or discussed through conversation.

An integrated language perspective stands for authentic language use in the classroom.

Edelsky (1986); Lindfors (1987)

An integrated language perspective stands for real, authentic language use in the classroom because that is how children learn language before they enter school. It requires that the classroom provide many opportunities for children to use language for a range of purposes. Children participate in a broad range of experiences of their choice to help them develop the sustained and deliberate attention to particular topics across the curriculum that makes systematic learning possible. In this view, listening, speak-

TABLE 1.2

Situational Context for Oral Communication	Textual Context for Written Communication
WHAT'S HAPPENING?	
the topic of conversation frequently spontaneous purpose	the topic of composition frequently preplanned purpose
the objects/persons/actions in the situation are frequently referred to exophorically	the objects/persons/actions in the text are mostly referred to endophorically
the actual time and place in which the communication occurs are usually pertinent and relevant	the textual communication occurs across space and time so that the actual space/time in which it occurs is usually not relevant
WHO ARE TAKING PART?	
the people present their role, status, etc. frequently known to each other need at least a speaker and listener (who take turns)	reader-writer contract their role, status, etc. usually unknown to each other reader/writer usually alone
relates to what was just said dialogue, turn-taking collaborative construction of meaning	relates to what was just 'said' monologue, continuous text solo construction of meaning (but with reader or writer in mind)
WHAT ROLE IS LANGUAGE PLAYING?	
the task or purpose that the communication is to accomplish usually accompanies overt physical action	the task or purpose that the communication is to accomplish usually the act of reading/writing is the only action

ing, reading, and writing are the tools and means to support such learning, not ends in and of themselves. Speaking, listening, reading, and writing are integrated because they are integrated in real language in use.

Speaking, listening, reading, and writing are tools for learning.

SUGGESTED ACTIVITIES

1. To enhance and help make explicit your understanding of spoken registers, collect some samples of typical conversations. With the help of other students in your class, try to tape people talking in different contexts of situation—buying donuts at a bakery, conversing over lunch, playing on the playground, and so forth. You may want to gather some examples in the classroom, too. For each sample, be sure you can answer all three questions about the context of situation: What's happening? Who's participating? What part is language playing? Transcribe as much as you can of your samples so that you can share them with others. Now, analyze and compare yours and your classmates' samples of how people used language, their linguistic patterns. How are these patterns the same? How are they different? How is the language being used related to the factors or features of the context of situation?
2. To better understand exophoric implicit wordings, go over the spoken language samples you have already collected (or obtain some new ones). Can you identify exophoric devices, whose source is not the co-text but which are understood because of some factor operating in the actual situation in which the conversation took place?

   Typical implicit devices that can be exophoric are the following:
   1. Pronouns—*I, you, me, he, she, him, her, his, it, they, them,* and so on, including the use of *the, this, that, those, here, there,* and the like.
   2. Words called *substitutions* that refer to a class of objects (e.g., *one, ones, the same*) or to actions in a general way (e.g., *do, be, have, do it/that*).
   3. Elliptical constructions in which only part of a phrase or sentence can be completed unless some aspect in the situation is considered (*lots* and *more* in the conversation about the new tape recorder are examples of ellipsis because we need a feature of the tape recorder—namely, "buttons"—to complete our understanding) (see Figure 1.1).

   Did participants seem to understand these exophoric wordings in the samples? If not, what did they do to better understand each other?

   See Halliday & Hasan (1976) for a more detailed discussion of implicit devices.
3. To better understand endophoric implicit wordings, review a range of different types of written texts. Can you identify endophoric implicit devices, wordings whose interpretative source is part of the co-text? Refer to the list of implicit devices in Suggested Activity 2; they can be endophoric implicit wordings, too. Can you find threads or chains of meanings throughout the texts? Be careful to select children's literature and other books, magazines, newspapers, and so on—texts found in stores and libraries—for your review. (Avoid basals or textbooks because many of these do not contain typical or good examples of written language.)
4. To better enhance and help make more explicit your understandings of different registers of written language, look at a sample of stories and information books. Are there different language patterns? Are there some examples that seem to be "fuzzy"? That is, are there some information books that have some story-like features? Are there some stories that have incorporated information-like properties? More will be said about this in Chapter 5.

REFERENCES

Bates, E. (1976). *Language and context: The acquisition of pragmatics.* New York: Academic Press.

Bower, T. G. R. (1974). *Development in infancy.* San Francisco: Freeman.

Bower, T. G. R. (1978). Perceptual development: Object and space. In E. C. Carterette & M. P. Friedman (Eds.), *Handbook of perception,* Vol. 8 (pp. 83–102). New York: Academic Press.

Bruner, J. S. (1975a). The ontogenesis of speech acts. *Journal of Child Language, 2,* 1–19.

Bruner, J. S. (1975b). From communication to language: A psychological perspective. *Cognition, 3,* 255–287.

Bruner, J. S. (1983). *Child's talk: Learning to use language.* New York: Norton.

Bruner, J. S. (1986). *Actual minds, possible worlds.* Cambridge, MA: Harvard University Press.

Cambourne, B. (1981). Oral and written relationships: A reading perspective. In B. M. Kroll & R. J. Vann (Eds.), *Exploring speaking-writing relationships: Connections and contrasts* (pp. 82–98). Urbana, IL: National Council of Teachers of English.

Carey, S. (1985). *Conceptual change in childhood.* Cambridge, MA: MIT Press.

Carey, S. (1988). Reorganization of knowledge in the course of acquisition. In S. Strauss (Ed.), *Ontogeny, phylogeny, and historical development: Human development,* Vol. 2 (pp. 1–27). Norwood, NJ: Ablex.

Chafe, W. L. (1985). Linguistic differences produced by differences between speaking and writing. In D. R. Olson, N. Torrence, & A. Hildyard (Eds.), *Literacy, language, and learning: The nature and consequences of reading and writing* (pp. 105–123). Cambridge: Cambridge University Press.

Donaldson, M. (1978). *Children's minds.* Glasgow: William Collins Sons.

Dunn, J. (1988). *The beginnings of social understandings.* Cambridge, MA: Harvard University Press.

Edelsky, C. (1986). *Writing in a bilingual program: Habia una vez.* Norwood, NJ: Ablex.

Foreman, G. E., & Kushner, D. S. (1983). *The construction of knowledge: Piaget for teaching children.* Washington, DC: National Association for the Education of Young Children.

Gelman, R., & Baillargeon, R. (1983). A review of some Piagetian concepts. In J. H. Flavell & E. M. Markman (Eds.), *Cognitive development,* Vol. 3 (pp. 167–230) of P. H. Mussen (Gen. Ed.), *Handbook of child psychology.* New York: Wiley.

Goodman, K. S., & Goodman, Y. M. (1979). Learning to read is natural. In L. B. Resnick & P. A. Weaver (Eds.), *Theory and practice of early reading,* Vol. 1 (pp. 137–154). Hillsdale, NJ: Erlbaum.

Halliday, M. A. K. (1975). *Learning how to mean: Explorations in the development of language.* London: Edward Arnold.

Halliday, M. A. K. (1977). Text as semantic choice in social contexts. In T. van Dijk & J. S. Petofi (Eds.), *Grammars and descriptions* (pp. 176–225). Berlin: de Gruyter.

Halliday, M. A. K. (1978). *Language as a social semiotic: The social interpretation of language and meaning.* London: Longman.

Halliday, M. A. K. (1982). Three aspects of children's language development: Learning language, learning through language, and learning about language. In Y. Goodman, M. Haussler, & D. Strickland (Eds.), *Oral and written language development research: Impact on the schools* (pp. 7–19). Urbana, IL: National Council of Teachers of English.

Halliday, M. A. K. (1985). *Spoken and written language.* Victoria, Australia: Deakin University Press.

Halliday, M. A. K., & Hasan, R. (1976). *Cohesion in English.* White Plains, NY: Longman.

Halliday, M. A. K., & Hasan, R. (1985). *Language, context, and text: Aspects of language in a social-semiotic perspective.* Victoria, Australia: Deakin University Press.

Harste, J. C., Woodward, V. A., & Burke, C. L. (1984). *Language stories and literacy lessons.* Portsmouth, NH: Heinemann.

Hasan, R. (1984a). The nursery tale as a genre. *Nottingham Linguistic Circular, 13,* 71–102.

Hasan, R. (1984b). Coherence and cohesive harmony. In J. Flood (Ed.), *Understanding reading comprehension: Cognition, language, and the structure of prose* (pp. 181–219). Newark, DE: International Reading Association.

Holdaway, D. (1979). *Foundations of literacy.* Sydney, Australia: Ashton Scholastic.

Johnson, D. D., & Pearson, P. D. (1984). *Teaching reading vocabulary.* New York: Holt, Rinehart and Winston.

Kagan, J. (1972). Do infants think? *Scientific American, 226,* 74–82.

Karmiloff-Smith, A. (1979). *A functional approach to child language: A study of determiners and reference.* Cambridge: Cambridge University Press.

Keil, F. C. (1984). Mechanisms of cognitive development and the structure of knowledge. In R. J. Sternberg (Ed.), *Mechanisms of cognitive change* (pp. 81–99). New York: Freeman.

Lindfors, J. W. (1987). *Children's language and learning.* Englewood Cliffs, NJ: Prentice-Hall.

Mandler, J. M. (1983). Representation. In J. H. Flavell & E. M. Markman (Eds.), *Cognitive development,* Vol. 3 (pp. 420–494) of P. H. Mussen (Gen. Ed.), *Handbook of child psychology.* New York: Wiley.

Martin, J. R. (1985). *Factual writing: Exploring and challenging social reality.* Victoria, Australia: Deakin University Press.

Martin, J. R., & Peters, P. (1985). On the analysis of exposition. In R. Hasan (Ed.), *Discourse on discourse* (pp. 61–92). Wollongong, Australia: Applied Linguistics Association of Australia.

Nelson, K. (1986). *Event knowledge: Structure and function in development.* Hillsdale, NJ: Erlbaum.

Pappas, C. C. (1988, November). *Exploring the ontogenesis of the registers of written language: Young children tackling the "book language" of information books.* Paper presented at the annual meeting of the National Reading Conference, Tucson, AZ.

Pappas, C. C. (1989, April). *Exploring young children's understandings of the "book language" of information books.* Paper presented at the biennial meeting of the Society for Research in Child Development, Kansas City, MO.

Pearson, P. D., & Johnson, D. D. (1978). *Teaching reading comprehension.* New York: Holt, Rinehart and Winston.

Piaget, J. (1926). *The language and thought of the child.* London: Routledge & Kegan Paul.

Piaget, J. (1969a). *The child's conception of the world.* Patterson, NJ: Littlefield, Adams.

Piaget, J. (1969b). *The psychology of intelligence.* Patterson, NJ: Littlefield, Adams.

Piaget, J. (1975). *The development of thought: Equilibration of cognitive structures.* New York: Viking.

Rabinowitz, P. J. (1987). *Before reading: Narrative conventions and the politics of interpretation.* Ithaca, NY: Cornell University Press.

Rosenblatt, L. M. (1978). *The reader, the text, the poem: The transactional theory of the literary work.* Carbondale, IL: Southern Illinois University Press.

Rumelhart, D. E. (1980). Schemata: The building blocks of cognition. In R. J. Spiro, B. C. Bruce, & W. F. Brewer (Eds.), *Theoretical issues in reading comprehension: Perspectives from cognitive psychology, linguistics, artificial intelligence, and education* (pp. 33–58). Hillsdale, NJ: Erlbaum.

Schickedanz, J. A. (1986). *More than the ABCs: The early stages of reading and writing.* Washington, DC: National Association for the Education of Young Children.

Smith, F. (1982a). *Understanding reading.* 3rd ed. New York: Holt, Rinehart and Winston.

Smith, F. (1982b). *Writing and the writer.* New York: Holt, Rinehart and Winston.

Stern, D. N. (1985). *The interpersonal world of the child.* New York: Basic Books.

Tannen, D. (1985). Relative focus on involvement in oral and written discourse. In D. R. Olson, N. Torrence, & A. Hildyard (Eds.), *Literacy, language, and learning: The nature and consequences of reading and writing* (pp. 124–147). Cambridge: Cambridge University Press.

Teale, W. H., & Sulzby, E. (1986). *Emergent literacy: Writing and reading.* Norwood, NJ: Ablex.

Tierney, R. J., & Pearson, P. D. (1984). Toward a composing model of reading. In J. M. Jensen (Ed.), *Composing and comprehending* (pp. 33–45). Urbana, IL: National Conference on Research in English.

Trevarthan, C. (1979a). Descriptive analyses of infant communication behaviour. In H. R. Schaffer (Ed.), *Studies in mother-infant interaction* (pp. 227–270). London: Academic Press.

Trevarthan, C. (1979b). Instincts for human understanding and for cultural cooperation: Their development in infancy. In M. vanCranach, K. Foppa, W. Lepenies, & D. Ploog (Eds.), *Human ethology: Claims and limits of a new discipline* (pp. 530–571). Cambridge: Cambridge University Press.

Trevarthan, C. (1980). The foundations of intersubjectivity: Development of interpersonal and cooperative understanding in infants. In D. R. Olson (Ed.), *The social foundations of language and thought: Essays in honor of Jerome S. Bruner* (pp. 316–342). New York: Norton.

Trevarthan, C., & Hubley, P. (1978). Secondary intersubjectivity: Confidence, confiding and acts of meaning in the first year. In A. Lock (Ed.), *Action, gesture and symbol: The emergence of language* (pp. 183–229). London: Academic Press.

Vosniadou, S., & Brewer, W. F. (1987). Theories of knowledge restructuring in development. *Review of Educational Research, 57,* 51–67.

Vygotsky, L. S. (1962). *Thought and language.* Cambridge, MA: MIT Press.

Vygotsky, L. S. (1978). *Mind in society: The development of higher psychological processes.* Cambridge, MA: Harvard University Press.

Wells, G. (1981). *Learning through interaction: The study of language development.* Cambridge: Cambridge University Press.

Wells, G. (1985). Preschool literacy-related activities and success in school. In D. R. Olson, N. Torrence, & A. Hildyard (Eds.), *Literacy, language, and learning: The nature and consequences of reading and writing* (pp. 229–255). Cambridge: Cambridge University Press.

Wells, G. (1986). *The meaning makers: Children learning language and using language to learn.* Portsmouth, NH: Heinemann.

Wells, G. (1988, April). *Developing literate minds.* Paper presented at the annual meeting of the American Educational Research Association, New Orleans, LA.

CHILDREN'S LITERATURE

CHARLOTTE'S WEB by E. B. White. Illustrated by G. Williams. Harper, 1952.

THE OWL AND THE WOODPECKER by B. Wildsmith. Oxford University Press, 1971.

TUNNELS by G. Gibbons. Holiday House, 1984.

2

Children and Teachers in an Integrated Language Classroom

In an integrated language perspective, the classroom represents a natural environment of language use; it is a culture in which language is used to learn. What are the participants—children and teachers—like in such a classroom culture? In this chapter, we further refine and extend the ideas about learners, language, and knowledge covered in Chapter 1 by summarizing and highlighting characteristic attributes and activities of these participants in the classroom. Chapters 3 and 4 then show how to plan and implement thematic units so that the activities of classroom participants can be realized. An integrated language perspective is child-centered. Thus, first we cover what children are like, and then, because of these characteristics of children, we consider the roles of teachers.

CHILDREN

Although we discuss individually the characteristics of children in the context of an integrated language perspective, these characteristics are not isolated, or separate, categories. Instead, they are fundamentally connected and interrelated because children learn language and learn through language in the integrated language classroom.

Children Generate and Test Hypotheses

Meaning-makers learn by generating and testing hypotheses about the world.

Children are meaning-makers, always trying to make sense of their world. Because they are active, constructive learners, they are constantly solving problems and generating and testing hypotheses. Because their hypotheses may be confirmed or disconfirmed at any time, risk-taking is inherent in the process of learning. Moreover, their hypotheses are about specific content, a specific domain of knowledge, a specific problem-space. Hypotheses are not content-free. What children already know—their schemas on a particular topic—is the basis on which their questions arise. Learning is always the result of "the having of wonderful ideas" to try out in an activity or project. Remember how Sara's earlier knowledge of spiders (in Chapter 1) became extended and differentiated as a result of the opportunity to study spiders in depth at school. The more ideas children already have on a topic—the more there is something to think about—the more ideas are generated, and the more complicated and developed their schemas become.

Smith (1982); Wells (1986)

Duckworth (1987)

Children Are Responsible for Their Own Learning

Children are responsible for what and how they learn.

Donaldson (1978)

Dunn (1988); Lindfors (1987); Wells (1986, 1988)

The fact that children create and construct their knowledge means that they are responsible for their own learning. Babies are born with a fundamental human urge to make sense of their world and to bring it under their control—to be effective and be competent, to act with skill. From the beginning of life, children want to know and do, and this intellectual autonomy of theirs is nurtured, encouraged, and supported by informed others.

Children's system of knowledge is self-governed and self-regulated; it is based on their own questions. Children mediate between their own schemas in their minds and the information available in their environment. Because children construct unique schemas and ask different questions, they follow different routes in learning for which they themselves are responsible. For example, the questions that Sara might ask about spiders (again refer to Chapter 1) would likely be very different from those asked by one of her classmates who hadn't engaged in a systematic study of the topic. That is, this child, a novice about spiders, would not initially ask questions about arachnids, for instance, because the child might be still classifying spiders as "bugs."

Children's Language and Learning Reflect Approximations

Approximations are inherent in the learning process.

Cambourne (1984); Holdaway (1979); Wells (1986)

Lindfors (1987)

Wells (1981, 1986)

Children are always modifying the ideas and concepts in their schemas. Their present theories are tentative and approximate adult (or expert) views regarding a topic. Their language also includes approximations that reflect their current understanding of the conventions of language to express their ideas. Approximations are the natural consequences of learning. They are intrinsic to the ways by which children construct their knowledge. Approximations are creative constructions. They reflect the linguistic and cultural diversity that children bring to their communication and approaches to learning. Consequently, in this book we do not refer to children's hypotheses about the world or language with negative terms such as *errors* or *mistakes*.

Parents accept and actually reward spoken language approximations all during the preschool years. They accept their baby's proto-language, their idiosyncratic constructions—remember Mark's *jubs,* an approximation of the conventional word *birds*—their child's designation of "doggie" for all four-legged, furry animals, their preschooler's attempts to regularize all plurals and past tenses with "mouses" and "goed," and so forth. Thus, although approximations, especially in reading and writing, may not be tolerated in most traditional classrooms, they are welcomed and encouraged in an integrated language classroom because they are considered to be great indicators of a child's thinking and understanding at a particular time on a particular topic in a particular context. Meaning-makers always produce approximations!

Children Use Authentic Language for Meaningful Purposes

Language is learned through authentic use.

Genishi (1985); Halliday (1975)

Cambourne (1984); Holdaway (1979); Jaggar (1985); Newman (1985a)

From the beginning of life, children are immersed in authentic, meaningful spoken language. Even as babies, they are invited to be participants in communication. They do not learn about oral language first, and then learn how to use it. They learn oral language and how to use it simultaneously—they learn spoken language for real, functional purposes.

Research in emergent literacy has indicated that those young children who have come to school already reading and writing also learned this literate behavior in this authentic, meaningful way. Parents of these children shared and discussed books with them and encouraged them to write their own messages and notes. When the conditions are right, children can learn to read and write as easily as they learn to talk and listen. Thus, in integrated language classrooms, children use authentic language for meaningful purposes—to write a report on their study of chicks that they have seen hatch, to converse with their group members about the play they are planning to give, to read books for a project they are working on, and so forth.

Authentic language is holistic. Thus, isolated drills or practice on only one part or subsystem of language (e.g., practicing phonics rules on certain letter-sound relationships, copying over and over the spelling words of the week, underlining nouns in sentences on a ditto from the language arts textbook) are not used. Instead, children learn letter-sound relations (or graphophonemic cues) by reading real books and writing their own stories or information books; they learn how to spell through exposure to words in their reading and by trying out their invented spellings to express their own ideas in writing; they understand how nouns work by encountering those employed by authors and by using those they need in their own writing.

Edelsky (1986); Newman (1985b)

It is through this kind of genuine language use that children also learn about language. At the same time that they are learning language (i.e., constructing the language system, or figuring out how symbols represent meanings in oral and written form) and learning through language (i.e., discovering how the world works in conversations with others), they are also learning about language itself (i.e., becoming aware of language as an object that has elements, forms, and functions). Although they are largely tacit or subconscious, these three aspects of language development simultaneously interact and facilitate one another. All three are social processes, learned in authentic, meaningful communication with others.

Halliday (1982); Jaggar (1985)

Children Integrate Speaking, Listening, Reading, and Writing in Their Activities/Projects

In an integrated language classroom, there are no separate listening, speaking, reading, and writing activities. The fact that children use authentic language in the classroom means that their use of language is integrated. Their activities and projects are surrounded by conversation. These projects require reading; writing is needed to share the outcomes or findings of their projects. For example, a small group of children may study slugs. As they observe the slugs, they chat among themselves about what they see, what they have read about slugs, and so forth. They take notes on their observations and about the information they have gleaned in their reading. They individually present their findings—one writing a story about slugs (entitled "Sluggo"), another a more informational piece on slugs, another a pictorial depiction (with captions) of the behavior of slugs, and so on. Much is learned through use of integrated language. Children learn about reading and writing by listening to books read to them. They also learn about reading and writing by listening and talking to their peers and teachers when they have discussions about the books they have read, or when they share the writing they have composed. They gain insights about writing from reading—they learn to write like a reader; they acquire knowledge about reading by writing—they learn to read like a writer.

Language is integrated.

Harste & Short (1988); King (1985); Lytle & Botel (1988); Wells (1986)

Children Have Choices and Ownership in What They Do

During the preschool years, children choose activities that interest them. Their purposes sustain their attention in projects and guide their motivation to understand. By having ownership in what they do, by following their own questions about topics, they are able to create new concepts and make new connections in their schemas. Children in an integrated language classroom are also provided with opportunities to initiate their own activities. They select and take on projects; they make them their own, thereby making their knowledge their own. It is this *ownership* that fosters the intellectual autonomy that we discussed earlier. "Owning" an activity or project leads to knowing how, why, and what to do. As a result, children behave responsibly.

To have choices fosters ownership and autonomy.

Graves (1983); Calkins (1986); Wells (1986)

Children Collaborate and Interact with Peers and Teacher about Learning Activities/Projects

Children learn through collaboration with others.

King (1985); Newman (1985b); Wells (1986, 1988)

Just as children use others as resources in learning about the world and language during the preschool years, children in an integrated language classroom are supported through their interactions with their peers and teacher. Rather than hours of individual "seat-work" where talk is forbidden, purposeful conversation among children is encouraged. For example, several children in a small group may collaborate with their group members in an activity. Perhaps they are going to do a survey regarding litter in the community. Some children will be responsible for drawing up a rough draft of the questions they will ask; others may be busy brainstorming to decide whom they should ask, and so forth. Decisions about their individual contributions to the project require negotiation. They have to decide among themselves who will be doing what task. Or perhaps a problem or issue may be posed by the teacher, and it is then examined by children in the classroom. Perhaps the teacher asks them to consider if they think they have enough categories of people or enough questions to make the results of their survey representative. Children bring their own knowledge to bear on the problem to come up with an answer that is constructed by a group or the class as a whole.

Heath (1983); Lindfors (1987)

To understand and be understood is the basis of communication and of learning in general. Individual children have had varying experiences and therefore may possess very different knowledge schemas on a particular topic. In addition, children have unique personal characteristics and come from a variety of cultural backgrounds. Such cultural and linguistic diversity means that children also bring their own complex customs or styles of interaction to their activities or projects. Children from different cultural backgrounds have different rules for communication. Because their "ways with words" may not be like those of the other children or of the teacher, collaboration is crucial. Negotiation is the only means by which classroom participants—children and teacher alike—can deal with their own various ways of participating or interacting. This is how intersubjectivity is achieved and how understanding is accomplished.

Children Use Feedback from Peers and Teacher to Self-Regulate Their Use of Language and Modify Their Theories

Feedback from others develops children's schemas.

Calkins (1986); Cambourne (1984); Wells (1986)

When children collaborate and negotiate with other classroom participants, they are provided with countless opportunities to reconsider and reevaluate how and what they mean. They present their ideas (orally and in writing) on the basis of their schemas, and they take note of their peers' or teacher's responses or ideas: "That's a great idea! How about . . .?" "I don't understand that." "What do you mean?" "Why do you think so?" This feedback extends their ideas, urges them on, requires them to clarify and justify their views. Listening to a fellow student's report or presentation on a particular topic or a partner's ideas about how to explore and report on their project sparks new questions and ideas. This self-regulation, fostered through social interaction, leads to knowledge restructuring and modification of their schemas.

Self-regulation also promotes children's *metacognitive awareness*—that is, an awareness of their own thinking. They begin to reflect on the thinking processes of communication, what they do when they talk, read, write, how their interpretations may affect others, and how others' interpretations may influence their own.

Children Use and Learn Language across the Curriculum

Language is used across the curriculum.

Harste, Woodward, & Burke (1984); King (1985); Lytle & Botel (1988); Wells (1986, 1988)

Understandings about language are increased and intensified when children use integrated language across the curriculum. They speak, listen, read, and write as they conduct a science experiment, as they consider problems and discover patterns in math, as they engage in an inquiry in social studies, as they reflect on some art project, and on and on. Because the content of these disciplines or curricular domains is different, children discover that different registers of language (both oral and written) must be employed in their projects. Communicative competence is fostered in complex, sophisticated ways. Metalinguistic and metacognitive awarenesses—abilities to learn about language, to consider language as an object of study in and of itself, to ponder about their own thinking processes, to examine their own strategies in solving or approaching certain problems in science, or math, or social studies—are facilitated when children recognize in a more explicit way how linguistic choices are expressed by different genres and how various disciplines reflect various ways of knowing. (Subsequent chapters, especially Chapters 5 and 7, cover these differences of genres and disciplines in more detail.)

Children Have Sustained Time for Systematic and Reflective Inquiry on a Range of Topics

Reflective inquiry requires sustained time.

Children's learning during the preschool years is developed in contexts in which they focus on topics and things that interest them. By engaging in activities with others who sustain and extend these interests, children acquire amazing linguistic, cognitive, and social abilities. Schooling, thus, should plan and provide for more and more of these contexts of concentrated effort. In most traditional classrooms, however, the entire school day is fragmented into small time slots during which teachers and children alike are on a treadmill to get it done and move along. Rather than this "cha-cha-cha curriculum," children in an integrated language classroom have time—ample blocks of time—to explore and think and change their minds, to consider and evaluate different points of view, to decide on their questions and how to resolve them, to read and reread, to write and revise. Because they have regular chunks of time, they have opportunities to study a range of topics in depth, and their inquiries are systematic and reflective.

Gamberg, Kwak, Hutchings, & Altheim (1988); Wells (1986)

Donald Graves is responsible for this apt term "cha-cha-cha curriculum" (according to Calkins, 1986).

TEACHERS

The characteristics that we have described for children can be realized in the classroom only when teachers take on certain roles. Thus, it is necessary to examine what these roles are and show how they are related to the characteristics of children as learners in an integrated language classroom. Just as it was the case for the children's categories, the teacher categories or roles are not mutually exclusive. You will notice that they are quite interrelated and connected.

Teachers Use a Collaborative Style of Teaching

A collaborative teaching style is used.

Because collaborative meaning-making is so successful and efficient in the development of children's learning in the preschool years, it is critical to find ways to achieve such an approach in the classroom. For this reason, probably the most important teacher characteristic from an integrated language perspective is a collaborative style of teaching. Remember that individual children's present understandings are based on their existing schemas; consequently, interactions with children truly have to be based on where they now are.

Wells (1986)

Recall that learning language and learning through language go hand in hand. Conversation is an important medium for instruction in the classroom as well. Wells provides four general suggestions for teachers that encourage children to initiate conversations and that make those conversations easy and enjoyable enough for children to be able to sustain them:

1. Assume that children attempt to communicate because they have something important to say, and then act accordingly.
2. When children's utterances seem unclear, first try to understand children's intentions before responding.

3. When responding, confirm or check children's meaning first—that is, attempt to achieve intersubjectivity—and then either extend the topic, or invite children to do so themselves.
4. Try to have your contributions at, or just beyond, children's current understandings.

Teachers have to keep these principles in mind especially when teaching children who come from a variety of linguistic and cultural backgrounds. An appreciation of children's different "ways with words" enables teachers to capitalize on children's individual approaches to communicating (in both oral and written form) and to learning in general. For example, children may have different ways or styles of storying. Some may recount or tell of a personal experience by expressing a series of implicitly associated topics, whereas others may relate their personal narrative by focusing on a single, more explicit topic. Or children may have different ideas about what is meant by staying on the subject (there are different rules for relevance or offering contributions in discussions in different communities), or taking their turn to talk (there are different expectations in different communities regarding the signals for when it's okay to talk), or have different orientations to public performance in the classroom (there are different personal and cultural factors that influence whether children are eager to perform verbally in front of a group or whether such individual performance is uncomfortable), and so forth. Teachers must accept a wide range of language behaviors as appropriate.

Heath (1983); Lindfors (1987)

Cazden (1988); Michaels (1981)

See Cazden (1986, 1988) and Lindfors (1987) for the most recent detailed accounts of various "ways with words."

In the traditional classroom, the teacher-controlled initiate-respond-evaluate (IRE) pattern characterizes much of the so-called discussion. When using the IRE pattern, the teacher *initiates* a sequence by calling a child to share or respond, then the nominated child *responds* to the initiation or questions posed by the teacher, and then the teacher *evaluates* what the child has said before calling on the next child, and on and on. The IRE is avoided in integrated language classrooms where teachers provide a range of participation structures that better enable collaboration and negotiation to occur. Too many whole-group, teacher-led situations tend to constrain flexibility and cut down on opportunities for teachers to interact with individual children. In integrated language classrooms, children work individually, in pairs, or in small groups, and consequently teachers can engage in more face-to-face encounters with their children.

Cazden (1986, 1988)

Inherent in a collaborative style of teaching is teachers' capacities to decenter—their ability to take the child's perspective. While children are busy in their activities or projects, teachers are careful to ask and respond to questions—authentic questions—so that they can be informed about, and be helpful in, children's endeavors and better address their concerns and difficulties. The intent of the teacher's questions is not to check if children's ideas conform with the teacher's knowledge. The more teachers know a domain, the greater is the risk of their behaving egocentrically in relation to their knowledge. Egocentricity is more of a problem for teachers than for children in classrooms. A collaborative style, therefore, bridges the gap between teachers' and children's schemas so that children can create their own concepts and relationships.

Wells (1986)

Teachers Foster Problem-Solving and Risk-Taking

A climate conducive to taking risks is required.

Cambourne (1984); Lindfors (1987); Wells (1986, 1988)

As has been noted, children's schemas develop through generating and testing hypotheses about language and the world and by trying to figure out their own problems on a range of topics. For learning to continue in the classroom, teachers have to provide a climate that will further foster these children's natural learning inclinations. Rather than stressing that children discover the "correct" or "right" answer in the textbook or in the teacher's head, teachers in an integrated language classroom attempt to enhance the probability of children's own discoveries. Such an atmosphere makes children comfortable enough to put their ideas on the line, so that risk-taking is not cut off. It is okay for them to offer their own interpretation of a story, although it may be different from those of their teacher or their peers; it is all right to use invented spelling to express their good ideas when they don't know the conventional spelling of words.

Because risk-taking aims at going beyond the status quo, the modification of children's schemas—and learning—is more likely.

Teachers Demonstrate and Encourage Authentic Language for Meaningful Purposes

Authentic language is used and demonstrated by the teacher.

Authentic language is a social activity; it is language used for meaningful purposes. For speaking, listening, reading, and writing to be tools for learning instead of ends in and of themselves, teachers demonstrate how something is actually done by *using* language in integrated language classrooms. They use real books that would be found in homes, libraries, and bookstores, and they suggest ways that particular books may be useful for particular activities or projects. When they share these books with children, they read with interest, get children to predict what will happen next, wonder about an author's choice of words. During sustained silent reading time, they themselves read their own books, and then they frequently share with their students the funny or sad parts. They let children in on strategies that they themselves use in reading—for example, skip what they don't know, read more of the surrounding text to figure out or clarify an unknown word, substitute words that maintain meaning for parts of a text, reread a passage, or when they can't understand a text, even drop it altogether and get another book on the same topic, and so forth. They write letters, notes, and messages to children, parents, and colleagues. They write reminders to themselves, they label articles and places in the classroom so it is easy for all to use available resources. They are genuine responders—they acknowledge when they don't understand something children have said or written so that children are given opportunities to rephrase or revise to make their intentions clearer. In sum, teachers use authentic language, and in doing so, they encourage children to see how things are done with language. Authentic language fosters children's learning about its various registers and their awareness of how language can be used for their own purposes to learn about the world.

Calkins (1986); Newman (1985a, 1985c); Harste & Short (1988)

Lindfors (1987)

Teachers Provide Activities and Projects So That Children Can Integrate Speaking, Listening, Reading, and Writing

Activities are provided so that the integration of language is possible.

Authentic language use is language that is integrated. It occurs naturally when children have many contexts in which to explore and study a range of topics, when they have many activities and projects to engage in. For example, when a teacher provides several animals for observation and study in the classroom, children in small groups have to work together on their projects. The teacher may initially provide a range of activity cards listing open-ended questions for them to consider regarding these animals to start their inquiries (activity cards are discussed in more detail in Chapter 8). The teacher may also place a broad spectrum of books regarding these animals near the animal centers to support the children's investigations.

Church (1985); Kwak & Newman (1985); Newman (1985d)

Because teachers offer activities that are child-centered or -guided, they are then available to provide specific feedback to children themselves regarding all aspects of the children's projects. Children may follow up on a question or comment a teacher has made in their journals by reading several books and then discussing them with the teacher. Teachers are also free to facilitate interaction among the children; they can guide them to consider their peers as sources of help and support in deciding if their organization of material on their topic seems to be clear and interesting to others, and so forth. In such situations, therefore, children have many opportunities to take turns offering and listening to each other's ideas about what needs to be done, and how to do it. When a child writes a report on a particular subtopic that is related to a topic another child has chosen, they become interested conversational partners. They share their resources, pointing out parts of books they have come across in their own re-

Hyde & Bizar (1989); Wells (1986, 1988)

search that may be useful for their peers on their own projects. When teachers offer meaningful activities and projects for children, the need for integrated language—the use of authentic language—naturally arises.

Teachers Expect and Understand Children's Approximations in Language and Learning

Approximations help teachers understand children's hypotheses or schemas about the world.

Because teachers view children as active learners who have constructed their own knowledge, they expect children's approximations in their theories about the world and about the rules of language use. Approximations are the result of risk-taking and are the result of children's hypotheses. These approximations are reflected in everything they do—how they think a machine works, why people acted the way they did years ago, what they believe an author means, how to express and revise the information they found on a topic in their research reports, how to spell a word, how to figure out a word they encounter in their reading. Because approximations are based on their existing schemas and are important indicators of children's present understandings, teachers in an integrated language classroom are careful observers of how children make sense of language and the world.

Lindfors (1987)

Goodman (1985); King (1985); Newman (1985a)

Integrated language teachers are *kid watchers* and evaluate children's learning while the children are actually using language in their activities and projects. Approximations are guideposts by which teachers can assess individual children's strategies and knowledge. Teachers realize that the logic by which children learn may not be the same logic as that used by adults. Consequently, they monitor children's approximations so that they know how to respond to children to further foster, sustain, and extend their present efforts. They document children's approximations made in various contexts and across time so that they have a valid means of accountability.

Teachers Foster Children's Choices and Ownership of Their Activities and Projects and Promote Children's Autonomy and Control of Their Learning

Providing choices is critical to fostering ownership.

Harste & Short (1988); Newman (1985a); Hyde & Bizar (1989); Wells (1986)

Inherent in the collaborative approach is a certain management style. Rather than being in control of everything that is done in the classroom, teachers in an integrated language classroom share with their students control of what happens. They do that by providing many choices—by letting children decide what topic to pursue, what questions to pose and resolve, what ways to relate what they have learned, and so forth. By accepting children's approximations, they help children represent problems to themselves, and they foster children's intellectual autonomy. When teachers allow children to be in charge of their learning, when they allow children to have ownership of their activities and projects, children's feelings of self-respect are developed and they become confident in what they know. Moreover, the model that teachers have provided for children means that children learn how to treat their peers in the same way.

Teachers Provide Feedback that Facilitates Children's Self-Regulation of Their Schemas

Useful feedback helps children to develop existing schemas.

Bruner (1983, 1986); Goodman (1985); Halliday (1982); Lindfors (1987); Newman (1985a); Vygotsky (1962)

A collaborative style of teaching gives teachers many opportunities to provide critical feedback to children as they engage in activities and projects. Teachers go in close and listen to understand. They take children's problems seriously and attempt to address their intentions. Their questions and suggestions are related to these intentions, and then children are left on their own to consider these possibilities. Teachers lead from behind, they track what children are trying to do, and then provide the support that enables children to stretch and go beyond their own limits. These interactions provide the kind of assistance children need to modify their theories and self-regulate their schemas. As teachers interact with children in this way, children internalize their teachers' response modes and begin to interact with their peers in a similar manner. Children become coaches, asking for and giving useful feedback to one another.

Teachers Provide Opportunities to Integrate Language across the Curriculum

Various curricular areas and disciplines deal with various content and domains that are expressed by varying language patterns and language registers. Consequently, providing opportunities to use language across the curriculum fosters communicative competence in a natural way but yet at a sophisticated level. It is one thing to know mathematical facts, but how should these data be reported in a survey that has been completed, or be expressed in a report on an experiment that has been conducted? As another example, information about the Aztecs has been obtained through reading nonfictional history texts and some stories in which Aztecs are characters. How should this information about the Aztecs be presented to the class? Should it be expressed by writing a piece of historical fiction, or should it be explained by an informational report? Maybe poetry should be considered? What is best? What are the advantages and disadvantages of selecting one form over the others? When children are given opportunities to use language across the curriculum, the choices abound, and the decisions to be made seem endless. However, in the process, children better appreciate various ways of knowing and become aware of the generative, creative potential of language.

Many ways to use language across the curriculum are provided.

Hyde & Bizar (1989); Lytle & Botel (1988)

Halliday (1978)

Teachers Can Plan and Implement Thematic Units So That Children Have Sustained Time for Systematic and Reflective Inquiry on a Range of Topics

The use of thematic units has many advantages. It provides both depth and breadth. Recall the LET'S EAT, EXPLORATIONS, and DIGGING UP THE PAST thematic units briefly introduced in the "Introduction." (Many more thematic units are illustrated throughout this book, especially in Chapters 3, 4, and 7.) A thematic unit has a central theme or concept that provides overall coherence. At the same time, it provides opportunities for children to explore in depth specific topics and domains. Because these individual and group projects are related to the theme, however, many more connections are made. Learning has a richness and a significance that are rarely seen when basals and textbooks determine the course of study.

Thematic units also allow for choices for children. Moreover, they provide the sustained time children need to pursue their topics of study. Teachers and peers can better interact and support children in their activities and projects. Having time for systematic inquiry on topics of one's choice leads to reflective thinking. There is a constant relating of what one already knows to something new. Because the children know what's familiar and what's new, new routines and connections evolve and become apparent. Children actually become more consciously aware of these new interpretations. They move into what are called *disembedded modes of thought.* That is, they are able to reflect on their language and thinking in abstraction. This is the metalinguistic and metacognitive awareness that was discussed in an earlier section of this chapter.

Thematic units provide sustained time for projects and inquiries.

Gamberg, Kwak, Hutchings, & Altheim (1988); Wells (1986)

Donaldson (1978); Hyde & Bizar (1989)

Teachers Are Learners and Committed Professionals

Teachers in an integrated language classroom see themselves as learners. As children construct their knowledge, teachers learn about their own discoveries. Children become experts on particular topics and share their knowledge with the teacher. Teachers collaborate with children who have different ways with words and learn about the ethnic and cultural complexity of our world. When teachers include books and materials to implement their thematic units, some resources may be unfamiliar to them or be known only in a superficial way. Consequently, teachers learn more about content, learn more

Teachers are learners and researchers of their own practice.

Lindfors (1987); Goswami & Stillman (1987)

about how that content is expressed in written language, and so forth. Teachers then see themselves as researchers of their own practice.

Unlike teachers in traditional classrooms who believe their job is to implement others' programs and curriculum, teachers in integrated language classrooms see themselves as professionals who own and develop their own programs. Children operate from their own schemas and, consequently, travel different routes in learning. Thus, curriculum in some prepackaged form that has been broken down into small steps or pieces and arranged in a linear sequence to be followed by each child is not considered very useful because it has been made for *unidirectional transmission;* that is, where bits or "facts" from the material are delivered *one way* straight to the presumed empty mind of the child who is considered to have no influence in learning. Instead, teachers view knowledge in integrated language classrooms as an active reconstruction that is constantly being negotiated. What happens in the classroom, therefore, must be done in a collaborative way.

Hyde & Bizar (1989); Wells (1986, 1988)

THE CULTURE OF THE CLASSROOM

What does it mean to say that each classroom represents a culture of its own? It means that norms are established regarding cooperation for the use of space and time, for the use of resources, and for valuing and behaving in certain ways. At the beginning of this century, Dewey wrote: "From the standpoint of the child, the great waste in school comes from his inability to utilize the experiences he gets outside of school in any complete and free way; while, on the other hand, he is unable to apply in daily life what he is learning at school" (p. 75). Unfortunately, this description still characterizes many of our schools. In an integrated language classroom, norms are developed and realized in such a way that life in school is not so different from life out of school. Children can readily apply what they have learned at home in school, and what they have learned in school can also be used at home.

Dewey (1956)

As you have seen in this chapter, the nature of learners, language, and knowledge when viewed from this perspective means that teachers have certain roles. However, the agendas of teachers and children alike are considered and negotiated. The classroom culture is one in which teaching and learning are a collaborative enterprise!

How can such a classroom culture be realized? How are the norms or behavior patterns in such a classroom culture established? What exactly are thematic units? How can teachers develop plans around themes that provide choices for children that foster the use of integrated, authentic language across the curriculum? How are thematic units implemented on a day-by-day basis? Chapters 3 and 4 will address these kinds of basic questions so that you can better visualize how these ideas can be translated into the classroom.

REFERENCES

Bruner, J. S. (1983). *Child's talk: Learning to use language.* New York: Norton.

Bruner, J. S. (1986). *Actual minds, possible worlds.* Cambridge, MA: Harvard University Press.

Calkins, L. M. (1986). *The art of teaching writing.* Portsmouth, NH: Heinemann.

Cambourne, B. (1984). Language, learning and literacy. In A. Butler & J. Turbill, *Towards a reading-writing classroom.* Portsmouth, NH: Heinemann.

Cazden, C. B. (1986). Classroom discourse. In M. C. Wittrock (Ed.), *Handbook of research on teaching,* 3rd ed. (pp. 432–463). New York: Macmillan.

Cazden, C. B. (1988). *Classroom discourse: The language of teaching and learning.* Portsmouth, NH: Heinemann.

Church, S. (1985). The war of the words. In J. M. Newman (Ed.), *Whole language: Theory in use* (pp. 153–162). Portsmouth, NH: Heinemann.

Dewey, J. (1956). *The child and the curriculum and the school and society* (combined edition). Chicago: University of Chicago Press.

Donaldson, M. (1978). *Children's minds.* Glasgow: William Collins Sons.

Duckworth, E. (1987). *The having of wonderful ideas and other essays on teaching and learning.* New York: Teachers College Press.

Dunn, J. (1988). *The beginnings of social understandings.* Cambridge, MA: Harvard University Press.

Edelsky, C. (1986). *Writing in a bilingual program: Habia una vez.* Norwood, NJ: Ablex.

Gamberg, R., Kwak, W., Hutchings, M., & Altheim, J. (1988). *Learning and loving it: Theme studies in the classroom.* Portsmouth, NH: Heinemann.

Genishi, C. (1985). Observing communicative performance in young children. In A. Jaggar & M. T. Smith-Burke (Eds.), *Observing the language learner* (pp. 131–142). Newark, DE: International Reading Association.

Goodman, Y. M. (1985). Kidwatching: Observing children in the classroom. In A. Jaggar & M. T. Smith-Burke (Eds.), *Observing the language learner* (pp. 9–18). Newark, DE: International Reading Association.

Goswami, D., & Stillman, P. R. (1987). *Reclaiming the classroom: Teacher research as an agency for change.* Portsmouth, NH: Boynton/Cook.

Graves, D. (1983). *Writing: Teachers and children at work.* Portsmouth, NH: Heinemann.

Halliday, M. A. K. (1975). *Learning how to mean: Explorations in the development of language.* London: Edward Arnold.

Halliday, M. A. K. (1978). *Language as a social semiotic: The social interpretation of language and meaning.* London: Longman.

Halliday, M. A. K. (1982). Three aspects of children's language development: Learning language, learning through language, and learning about language. In Y. Goodman, M. Haussler, & D. Strickland (Eds.), *Oral and written language development research: Impact on the schools* (pp. 7–19). Urbana, IL: National Council of Teachers of English.

Harste, J. C., & Short, K. G. (1988). *Creating classrooms for authors: The reading-writing connection.* Portsmouth, NH: Heinemann.

Harste, J. C., Woodward, V. A., & Burke, C. L. (1984). *Language stories and literacy lessons.* Portsmouth, NH: Heinemann.

Heath, S. B. (1983). *Ways with words: Language, life, and work in communities and classrooms.* Cambridge: Cambridge University Press.

Holdaway, D. (1979). *Foundations of literacy.* Sydney, Australia: Ashton Scholastic.

Hyde, A. A., & Bizar, M. (1989). *Thinking in context: Teaching cognitive processes across the elementary school curriculum.* White Plains, NY: Longman.

Jaggar, A. M. (1985). On *observing the language learner:* Introduction and overview. In A. Jaggar & M. T. Smith-Burke (Eds.), *Observing the language learner* (pp. 1–7). Newark, DE: International Reading Association.

King, M. L. (1985). Language and language learning for child watchers. In A. Jaggar & M. T. Smith-Burke (Eds.), *Observing the language learner* (pp. 19–38). Newark, DE: International Reading Association.

Kwak, W., & Newman, J. M. (1985). Activity cards. In J. M. Newman (Ed.), *Whole language: Theory in use* (pp. 137–144). Portsmouth, NH: Heinemann.

Lindfors, J. W. (1987). *Children's language and learning.* Englewood Cliffs, NJ: Prentice-Hall.

Lytle, S. L., & Botel, M. (1988). *PCRP II: Reading, writing and talking across the curriculum.* Harrisburg, PA: Pennsylvania Department of Education. (To be published in 1990 as *Frameworks for Literacy* by Heinemann Boynton/Cook.)

Michaels, S. (1981). "Sharing time": Children's narrative styles and differential access to literacy. *Language in Society, 10,* 423–442.

Newman, J. M. (1985a). Insights from recent reading and writing research and their implications for developing whole language curriculum. In J. M. Newman (Ed.), *Whole language: Theory in use* (pp. 7–36). Portsmouth, NH: Heinemann.

Newman, J. M. (1985b). Introduction. In J. M. Newman (Ed.), *Whole language: Theory in use* (pp. 1–6). Portsmouth, NH: Heinemann.

Newman, J. M. (1985c). Using children's books to teach reading. In J. M. Newman (Ed.), *Whole language: Theory in use* (pp. 55–64). Portsmouth, NH: Heinemann.

Newman, J. M. (1985d). Mealworms: Learning about written language through science activities. In J. M. Newman (Ed.), *Whole language: Theory in use* (pp. 145–152). Portsmouth, NH: Heinemann.

Smith, F. (1982). *Understanding reading.* 3rd ed. New York: Holt, Rinehart and Winston.

Vygotsky, L. S. (1962). *Thought and language.* Cambridge, MA: MIT Press.

Wells, G. (1981). *Learning through interaction: The study of language development.* Cambridge: Cambridge University Press.

Wells, G. (1986). *The meaning makers: Children learning language and using language to learn.* Portsmouth, NH: Heinemann.

Wells, G. (1988, April). *Developing literate minds.* Paper presented at the annual meeting of the American Educational Research Association, New Orleans, LA.

3

Planning Thematic Units

The preceding chapters have shown how children are active constructors of knowledge. In the years before entering school, children tackle tremendously complex processes not only with determination but also with enthusiasm. This learning occurs in many social contexts when the child uses language for a variety of purposes to express and communicate a variety of ideas and feelings. Once children enter school, learning should build on these same foundations.

Thematic units reflect patterns of thinking, goals, and concepts common to bodies of knowledge. They link together content from many areas of the curriculum and depict the connections that exist across disciplines. Thematic units provide a framework for a community of learners in which all children can continue to learn language and to construct knowledge.

Chaplin (1982); McClure (1982); Moss (1984); Norton (1982)

The topics chosen for thematic units are broadly based to take advantage of different ways of knowing that individual children bring to the classroom. Thematic units also provide children with many choices about how to pursue their learning. They come to feel a powerful sense of ownership as they initiate some activities and engage in others suggested by their teachers. Moreover, as children work alone or in groups, sharing and discussing their work and the results of their projects, the classroom becomes a community of learners—a classroom culture—that shares ownership of a body of knowledge and understanding that has been jointly created.

Such a classroom culture is created by identifying themes or topics that may be common to many or all subject areas. The theme of HOUSES developed for younger children, for example, could include information about houses in the community as well as houses around the world, imaginary houses, animal houses, or even environments for microorganisms. A theme of JOURNEYS might involve older children in a study of the age of exploration or the American westward movement. They could also learn about the "journeys" of molecules or nutrients at the same time that they think about journeys in their own lives or in the lives of characters in their books. In both themes, language, the arts, mathematics, science, and the social studies become vehicles for thorough exploration.

Themes provide a central focus for linking many subject areas.

In this book we focus on broadly based thematic units that may last for many weeks. However, it is possible to have units with a more concentrated focus—for example, a unit on cumulative stories, horses, one aspect of a country, a specific kind of literature such as poetry, the works of one author or illustrator, or even a unit on a

Thematic units can be planned to last for several days or for many weeks.

Wells (1986)

single novel. Whatever the topic or length of study, the aim of any thematic unit is to provide a supportive context for meaning-making.

CHOOSING A THEME

Thematic units evolve in a variety of ways.

There is no single "right" way to develop or plan a thematic unit. We present here methods for planning that can be adapted to individual teachers, classrooms, and children. These methods are guides, suggestions, recipes to be tried and modified just as a good cook learns to improve combinations of ingredients to improve the flavor of a dish.

The topic of thematic units can be chosen in a variety of ways. You will want to consider broad areas of study that link content areas called for in district and state curriculum guidelines. In addition to considering the content of the year's instruction, however, think of children as partners in the learning that is to come, and plan with their interests and enthusiasms in mind.

Topics come from the curriculum, yet consider children's interests.

You may want to begin the year by taking full responsibility for choosing and organizing the themes, and then allowing children a more active role in planning as the year progresses. But even from the beginning, be open to the ways in which you can tie in concepts to be taught with your students' natural curiosity and excitement about the world around them. For example, a second grade teacher found that on the first day of school one of the children had brought in a lovely seashell from her vacation to show the class. The other children were so fascinated by it (some had never traveled from their landlocked state to visit the ocean) that the teacher began a unit on THE SEA, a theme she had planned to cover later in the year. Another teacher had wanted to explore water and water systems with her third and fourth graders. She wasn't sure how to organize the unit until one of her students reported that his house was being remodeled. "They're tearing out the walls, and there's all these pipes!" he exclaimed. The unit then proceeded with the children studying WATER SYSTEMS in the school and neighborhood, diagramming cross sections of water fountains and fire hydrants, studying physical properties of flush toilets and water wheels, mapping the school's water systems, interviewing roofing (and gutter) and municipal water companies, and completing research reports on a water system (see Figure 3.1).

Children's experiences help to shape the direction of the unit.

In choosing a topic for a thematic unit, pick one that is broad enough to incorporate many types of books, resources, and activities but not so broad that children lose sight of the connections that exist among areas to be explored. The topic of nutrition, for example, is likely to be required at many grade levels. It is, however, too narrow for a good thematic unit. There are few (if any) works of good fiction that would fit that topic, and much as we might hope otherwise, few children would leap to study such a topic.

Topics should allow the use of many types of resources.

Nutrition may, on the other hand, be explored as part of a unit of health, but health is such a broad area that it would be difficult to cover the vast amount of material in a way that builds strong schemas or domains of knowledge related to the topic. We would prefer to choose a theme like FOOD or EATING, such as the one described in Chapter 4. Such a topic has considerable child appeal, but it does not sacrifice intellectual content.

WEBBING

Choosing a topic is the first step in planning thematic units. What follows is a multifaceted method of planning. There is no one "correct" way to proceed or one single avenue of exploration. Figure 3.2 is an overview of the major components involved in planning and developing a thematic unit. Notice that the planning is a dynamic process. As the first top "diamond" of Figure 3.2 suggests, selecting materials leads to choosing activities, and vice versa. This process sometimes influences the nature of the theme itself. Recasting of the theme may then lead to changes in materials and activities, and so forth. Once be-

Figure 3.1

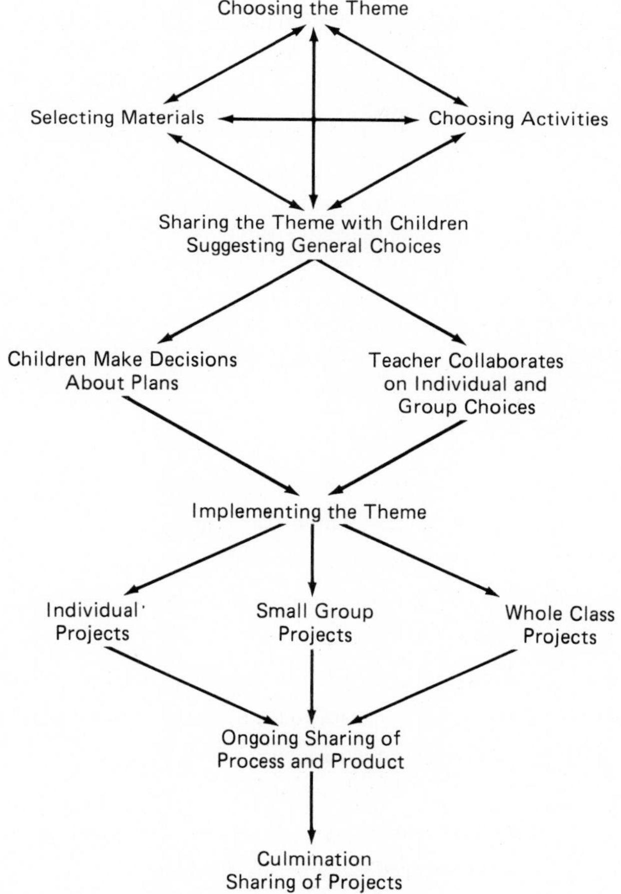

Figure 3.2 Planning for Thematic Units

gun, the process develops as indicated by the figure, and components may be reshaped or changed as the theme is refined and executed.

Corwin, Hein, & Levin (1976); Huck, Hepler, & Hickman (1987)

Webbing is a schematic technique, the realization of a brainstorming process. A WEB is a semantic map, a mental representation of concepts and relationships. Webbing allows you to extend a theme in many meaningful directions, fleshing out the topic by choosing meaningful categories and subcategories. In addition, the WEB provides an overview of the many books, props, resources, and activities that are possible avenues of exploration for the theme.

To get the webbing process started, you may want to do some free-associating and simply list everything that comes to mind in connection with a chosen theme. Doing this with a colleague or with children opens up alternative possibilities and prevents you from becoming locked into traditional ideas. As you generate lists or ideas, you will begin to see how many ideas can be grouped together in related categories. From these, other categories or connections begin to emerge. As you brainstorm, try to keep in mind titles of books and other print resources with which you are familiar, props or manipulable materials that could give children hands-on experience with the theme, and community resources or resources in the arts that could be incorporated.

Brainstorm topics with friends.

The ideas in Figure 3.3 were generated by a group of teachers in one such brainstorming session on the theme of TIME. Although the idea of thematic units was new to them, they had little trouble producing many ideas as part of their brainstorming. This was especially true once one person leaped beyond more traditional ideas of time (clocks, schedules, early, late) by thinking about time in music, and another group member recalled Madeleine L'Engle's Newbery Award–winning *Wrinkle in Time.*

L'Engle (1962)

As teachers looked over the list, they began to see how many of the items mentioned could be grouped together into subcategories of the main theme. Categories such as "changes over time," "time in nature," "personal time," "playing with time," "time passing," and "measuring time" emerged, which in turn helped them to consider other concepts, well-known books, and other resources. Eventually, a preliminary sketch of a WEB helped shape further planning and finally evolved into the more complex form shown in Figure 3.4.

The first WEB is a sketch that changes as the unit progresses.

Many teachers new to webbing think that once they pick a topic they should categorize activities and resources into traditional subject areas such as science, social studies, poetry, or writing. This type of planning tends to lead back to the traditional compartmentalizing of subject areas that we want to avoid. The diagram in Figure 3.5 illustrates how the content areas can be included and integrated throughout the many logical avenues for exploring the theme of TIME. As you plan your own thematic units, establish the subcategories that seem to be appropriate parts of the larger domain you have chosen. Then con-

clocks watches tardy 24 hours time period hurry up

slow down

schedules sundial sunset sunrise time tables times tables

time is relative theory of relativity sundial deadlines

metronome

measure rhythm time zone earth's rotation seasons life cycle

"Hickory Dickory Dock" "Back to the Future" A Wrinkle in Time

The Time Machine biological time "As Time Goes By"

"Minute Waltz"

childhood middle age sleepy time sandman

"Mr. Sandman Bring Me A Dream"

day month year

Figure 3.3 Initial Brainstorming for a Theme of TIME

sider how each of those areas may represent or incorporate subject matter or understandings from the various content areas.

SELECTING RESOURCES

One of the aims of a thematic unit is to provide children with wide experience with a range of resources for learning. Three major types of resources are incorporated in units. First, a thematic unit includes a variety of genres of children's literature, as well as other sources of printed information—newspapers and magazines, diaries, letters, and other primary sources. Second, thematic units employ many manipulable materials—artifacts, props, equipment, and so forth. Third, units use resources from the community and the wider world—people, animals, and places that contribute to children's understanding of a theme. The arts can also contribute to the theme through the use of paintings, sculpture, crafts, music, the theatre, films, and other media.

Printed Resources

Anderson, Hiebert, Scott, & Wilkinson (1984)

Research has shown that in an effort to meet state requirements for readability and content, today's textbooks are often dry, uninteresting, and even poorly written. A thematic unit allows the teacher to make selective use of textbook materials but also to include many of the excellent works of fiction, information books, and periodicals published for children. These resources not only allow for more critical reading on a subject but also accommodate the many reading abilities found in a heterogeneous classroom. In addition, these well-written works provide children with excellent models for their own writing.

The next steps in planning a thematic unit, then, may be those that lead to the school or municipal library or archives. One of the best sources of information for gathering materials is the librarian or media specialist. These professionals are familiar with good children's books and other new materials. They can also direct you to the many good indexes to children's materials, to archival materials, and to other data sources.

Hopkins (1987); Huck, Hepler, & Hickman (1987); Kobrin (1988)

Many indexes survey children's literature and other materials. (See "Selecting Books and Media for Children" on pages 60–61.) These indexes often group titles together thematically or are themselves organized around a theme. In making use of these sources, it is a good idea to consult subject headings first, but it may also be helpful to skim through the list of titles and annotations to find materials that could help children explore a theme in unusual ways.

Monson (1985)

In planning a theme of FOOD, for example, a logical place to start would be under the subject guide listings in an index such as *Adventuring with Books,* in which you can consult the subsection under "Social Studies" titled "Food, Clothing and Shelter," the subsection of the "Sciences" titled "Human Health and Development," and the listing under "Crafts and Hobbies" for the section on "Cooking." In addition, skim through the list of titles and annotations in the fiction section, where you will find books such as *Cloudy with a Chance of Meatballs, How to Eat Fried Worms, The Chocolate Touch, Strega Nona, Stone Soup,* or *The Magic Porridge Pot.* Notice that these titles are listed under the subheadings of "humorous stories" or "folktales" rather than "food" in the table of contents. You would not have found them through the usual research techniques. Therefore, finding titles often requires some digging beneath the surface of indexes or tables of content.

Barrett (1978); Rockwell (1973); Catling (1979); de Paola (1975); Brown (1947); Galdone (1976)

Because we want to make more children be critical readers and to foster their learning the various registers of written language, it is best to try to include a balance of fiction and nonfiction materials in a thematic unit. If, as you begin collecting titles, you find that there are not enough types of material to provide for the broad range of reading abilities and interests in your class, you may want to broaden the topic of your unit. Research on the unit of RODEO, for example, may reveal a limited amount of suitable literature. If the topic were expanded to AMERICAN WESTWARD EXPANSION, a wealth of materials could be found.

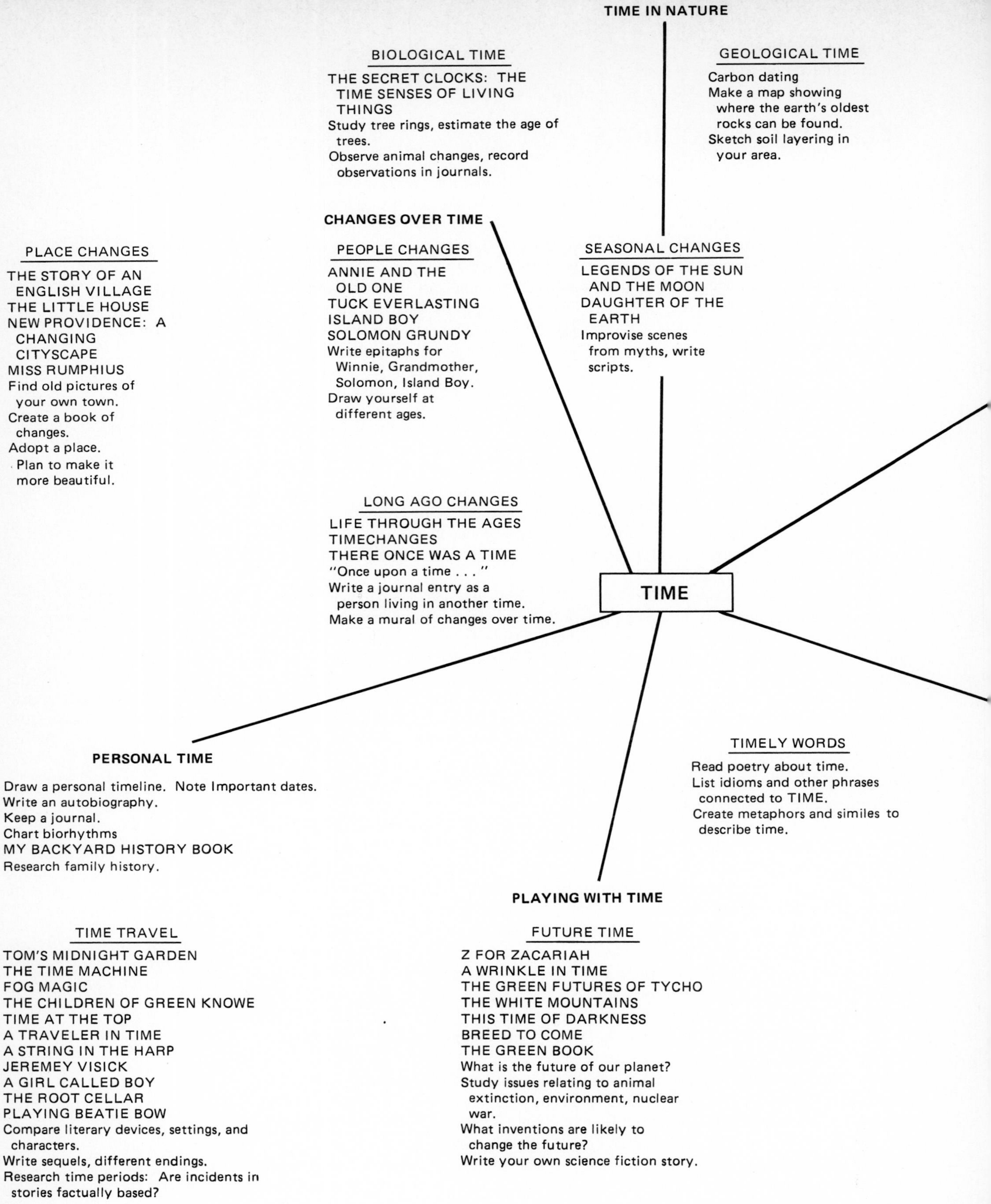

TIME IN NATURE

BIOLOGICAL TIME

THE SECRET CLOCKS: THE TIME SENSES OF LIVING THINGS
Study tree rings, estimate the age of trees.
Observe animal changes, record observations in journals.

GEOLOGICAL TIME

Carbon dating
Make a map showing where the earth's oldest rocks can be found.
Sketch soil layering in your area.

SEASONAL CHANGES

LEGENDS OF THE SUN AND THE MOON
DAUGHTER OF THE EARTH
Improvise scenes from myths, write scripts.

CHANGES OVER TIME

PLACE CHANGES

THE STORY OF AN ENGLISH VILLAGE
THE LITTLE HOUSE
NEW PROVIDENCE: A CHANGING CITYSCAPE
MISS RUMPHIUS
Find old pictures of your own town.
Create a book of changes.
Adopt a place. Plan to make it more beautiful.

PEOPLE CHANGES

ANNIE AND THE OLD ONE
TUCK EVERLASTING
ISLAND BOY
SOLOMON GRUNDY
Write epitaphs for Winnie, Grandmother, Solomon, Island Boy.
Draw yourself at different ages.

LONG AGO CHANGES

LIFE THROUGH THE AGES
TIMECHANGES
THERE ONCE WAS A TIME
"Once upon a time . . ."
Write a journal entry as a person living in another time.
Make a mural of changes over time.

TIME

PERSONAL TIME

Draw a personal timeline. Note Important dates.
Write an autobiography.
Keep a journal.
Chart biorhythms
MY BACKYARD HISTORY BOOK
Research family history.

TIMELY WORDS

Read poetry about time.
List idioms and other phrases connected to TIME.
Create metaphors and similes to describe time.

PLAYING WITH TIME

TIME TRAVEL

TOM'S MIDNIGHT GARDEN
THE TIME MACHINE
FOG MAGIC
THE CHILDREN OF GREEN KNOWE
TIME AT THE TOP
A TRAVELER IN TIME
A STRING IN THE HARP
JEREMEY VISICK
A GIRL CALLED BOY
THE ROOT CELLAR
PLAYING BEATIE BOW
Compare literary devices, settings, and characters.
Write sequels, different endings.
Research time periods: Are incidents in stories factually based?

FUTURE TIME

Z FOR ZACARIAH
A WRINKLE IN TIME
THE GREEN FUTURES OF TYCHO
THE WHITE MOUNTAINS
THIS TIME OF DARKNESS
BREED TO COME
THE GREEN BOOK
What is the future of our planet?
Study issues relating to animal extinction, environment, nuclear war.
What inventions are likely to change the future?
Write your own science fiction story.

Figure 3.4

TIME PASSING

FROM DAY TO DAY

WHAT MAKES DAY AND NIGHT
Compare and contrast the use of time in these books.
Make a cartoon or film strip to show the passage of time.
THE HOUSE FROM MORNING TO NIGHT
MORNING, NOON AND NIGHTTIME TOO
DAWN
FOG DRIFT MORNING
DUSK TO DAWN
NIGHT IN THE COUNTRY
Sketch or paint your favorite time of day. Choose music to capture your mood.

THE WAY TO START A DAY
WHEN THE SKY WAS LIKE LACE
Write rules for your favorite time of day.
PORCUPINE STEW
HILDILID'S NIGHT
GRANDFATHER TWILIGHT
Write about a magical event.

OPENING NIGHT
NIGHT GHOSTS AND HERMITS
NIGHT MARKETS
Interview someone who works at night.
View night creatures at the zoo.

FROM SEASON TO SEASON

THE REASONS FOR SEASONS
MY FAVORITE TIME OF YEAR
SUGARING TIME
TIME OF WONDER
OX-CART MAN
Survey peoples' favorite times of year.
Compare hours of daylight and dark at different times of year.

TIME IN MUSIC

Grofé, "Sunset" and "Sunrise" from Grand Canyon Suite
Ravel, "Day Break" from Daphnis et Chloe
Prokofiev, "Midnight Waltz" from Cinderella
Vivaldi, The Four Seasons

TIME IN ART

French Impressionists
Monet
Sunset Impressions, Haystacks
Sisley, June Morning
American Luminists—Heade, Twilight, Spouting Rock Beach
Church, Morning in the Tropics

Other Artists—
Van Gogh, Starry Night
Turner, Norham Castle, Sunset
Constable, Clouds
Hopper, Night Hawks, Night Shadows

MEASURING TIME

MUSICAL CLOCKS

metronomes
notation system

SIMPLE CLOCKS

Make sundials,
sand clocks,
water clocks.
13 CLOCKS
MS. GLEE WAS WAITING
CLOCKS
THIS BOOK IS ABOUT TIME
CLOCKS AND MORE CLOCKS
CLOCKS AND HOW THEY GO
Make a graffiti wall of time words.
Compose accompaniment for TIME poems.
THE IDEAS OF EINSTEIN
IT'S ALL RELATIVE
Study the theory of relativity.

MECHANICAL CLOCKS

Bring time pieces from home, sketch and describe them.

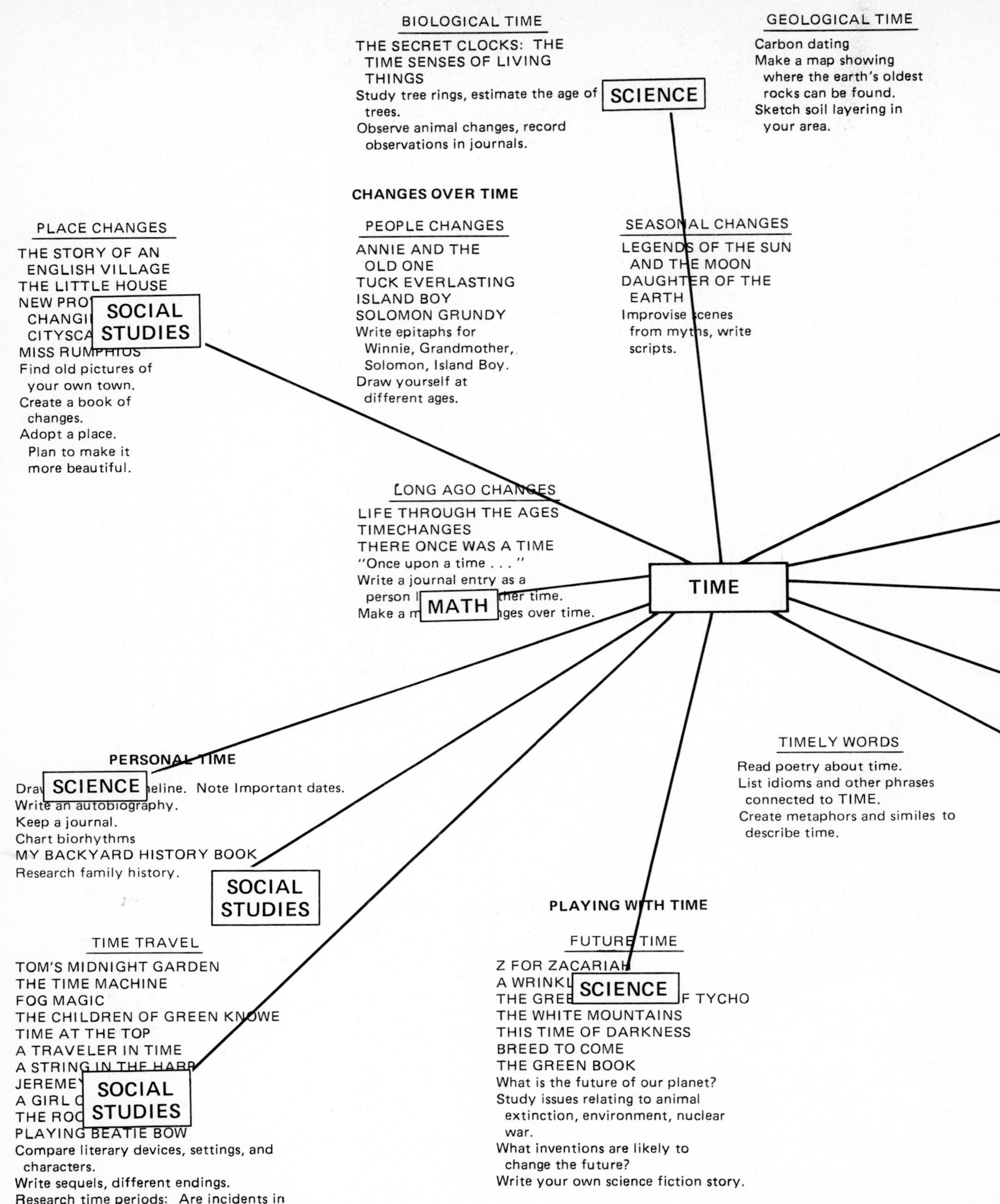

TIME IN NATURE
BIOLOGICAL TIME
THE SECRET CLOCKS: THE TIME SENSES OF LIVING THINGS
Study tree rings, estimate the age of trees.
Observe animal changes, record observations in journals.
SCIENCE
GEOLOGICAL TIME
Carbon dating
Make a map showing where the earth's oldest rocks can be found.
Sketch soil layering in your area.
CHANGES OVER TIME
PLACE CHANGES
THE STORY OF AN ENGLISH VILLAGE
THE LITTLE HOUSE
NEW PRO
CHANGI
CITYSCA
MISS RUMPHIUS
Find old pictures of your own town.
Create a book of changes.
Adopt a place. Plan to make it more beautiful.
SOCIAL STUDIES
PEOPLE CHANGES
ANNIE AND THE OLD ONE
TUCK EVERLASTING
ISLAND BOY
SOLOMON GRUNDY
Write epitaphs for Winnie, Grandmother, Solomon, Island Boy.
Draw yourself at different ages.
SEASONAL CHANGES
LEGENDS OF THE SUN AND THE MOON
DAUGHTER OF THE EARTH
Improvise scenes from myths, write scripts.
LONG AGO CHANGES
LIFE THROUGH THE AGES
TIMECHANGES
THERE ONCE WAS A TIME
"Once upon a time . . ."
Write a journal entry as a person l ther time.
Make a m ges over time.
MATH
TIME
PERSONAL TIME
SCIENCE
Dra eline. Note Important dates.
Write an autobiography.
Keep a journal.
Chart biorhythms
MY BACKYARD HISTORY BOOK
Research family history.
SOCIAL STUDIES
TIMELY WORDS
Read poetry about time.
List idioms and other phrases connected to TIME.
Create metaphors and similes to describe time.
TIME TRAVEL
TOM'S MIDNIGHT GARDEN
THE TIME MACHINE
FOG MAGIC
THE CHILDREN OF GREEN KNOWE
TIME AT THE TOP
A TRAVELER IN TIME
A STRING IN THE HARP
JEREME
A GIRL C
THE RO
PLAYING BEATIE BOW
Compare literary devices, settings, and characters.
Write sequels, different endings.
Research time periods: Are incidents in stories factually based?
SOCIAL STUDIES
PLAYING WITH TIME
FUTURE TIME
Z FOR ZACARIAH
A WRINKL
THE GREE F TYCHO
SCIENCE
THE WHITE MOUNTAINS
THIS TIME OF DARKNESS
BREED TO COME
THE GREEN BOOK
What is the future of our planet?
Study issues relating to animal extinction, environment, nuclear war.
What inventions are likely to change the future?
Write your own science fiction story.

Figure 3.5

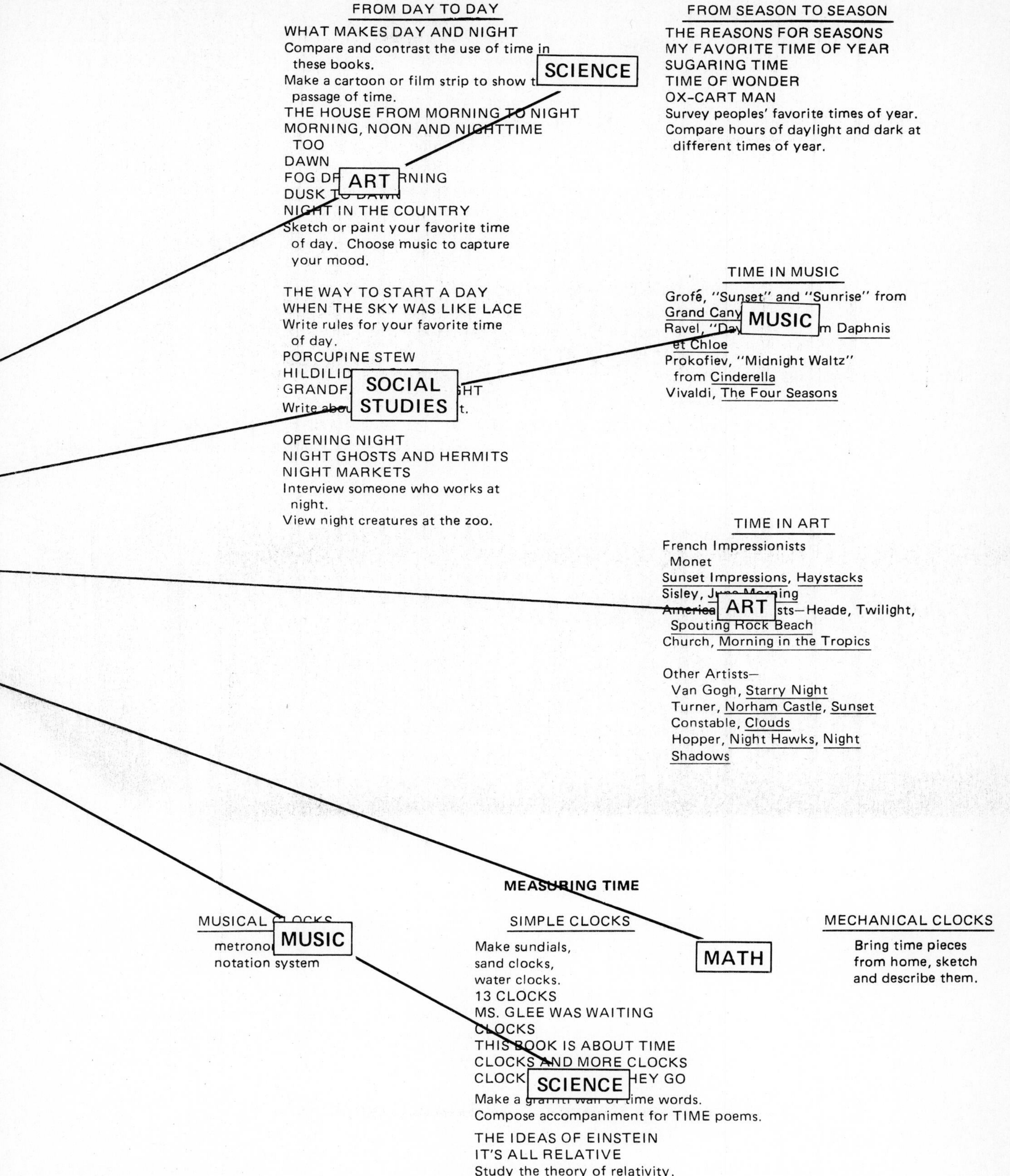

TIME PASSING
FROM DAY TO DAY
WHAT MAKES DAY AND NIGHT
Compare and contrast the use of time in these books.
Make a cartoon or film strip to show t passage of time.
THE HOUSE FROM MORNING TO NIGHT
MORNING, NOON AND NIGHTTIME TOO
DAWN
FOG DR RNING
DUSK TO DAWN
NIGHT IN THE COUNTRY
Sketch or paint your favorite time of day. Choose music to capture your mood.
THE WAY TO START A DAY
WHEN THE SKY WAS LIKE LACE
Write rules for your favorite time of day.
PORCUPINE STEW
HILDILID
GRANDF HT
Write t.
OPENING NIGHT
NIGHT GHOSTS AND HERMITS
NIGHT MARKETS
Interview someone who works at night.
View night creatures at the zoo.
SCIENCE
ART
SOCIAL STUDIES
FROM SEASON TO SEASON
THE REASONS FOR SEASONS
MY FAVORITE TIME OF YEAR
SUGARING TIME
TIME OF WONDER
OX-CART MAN
Survey peoples' favorite times of year.
Compare hours of daylight and dark at different times of year.
TIME IN MUSIC
Grofé, "Sunset" and "Sunrise" from Grand Cany
Ravel, m Daphnis et Chloe
Prokofiev, "Midnight Waltz" from Cinderella
Vivaldi, The Four Seasons
MUSIC
TIME IN ART
French Impressionists
Monet
Sunset Impressions, Haystacks
Sisley, ing
sts—Heade, Twilight,
Spouting Rock Beach
Church, Morning in the Tropics
Other Artists—
Van Gogh, Starry Night
Turner, Norham Castle, Sunset
Constable, Clouds
Hopper, Night Hawks, Night Shadows
ART
MEASURING TIME
MUSICAL
metrono
notation system
MUSIC
SIMPLE CLOCKS
Make sundials, sand clocks, water clocks.
13 CLOCKS
MS. GLEE WAS WAITING
CLOCKS
THIS BOOK IS ABOUT TIME
CLOCKS AND MORE CLOCKS
CLOCK HEY GO
Make a ime words.
Compose accompaniment for TIME poems.
THE IDEAS OF EINSTEIN
IT'S ALL RELATIVE
Study the theory of relativity.
SCIENCE
MATH
MECHANICAL CLOCKS
Bring time pieces from home, sketch and describe them.

If, on the other hand, you find yourself overwhelmed by titles, you may want to narrow the focus of your theme or let specific categories define the scope of a unit. A primary unit on animals might be narrowed to a unit on BEARS or PETS. Or subcategories of the ANIMALS theme, "Animals at Work," "Animals in the Neighborhood," and "Animals Just for Fun" may make the unit more manageable.

As you plan a thematic unit, you may wonder how many titles are enough. We like to think that, as with chocolate, you can never have enough books. Many teachers who have been teaching through thematic units for many years work with between four and five hundred books; their classroom libraries are supplemented by school and municipal collections. We suggest that rather than setting a specific number of titles, you plan to collect the following *types* of materials:

Choose the best works of literature to read aloud.

Materials to Read Aloud. Reading aloud is an opportunity for teachers to share the best works of children's literature with their students. You may also choose to share books (or other materials) that children might not (initially) read on their own. Poetry, information books, biography or autobiography, and picture books for all grades, and chapter books or longer novels can also be used. These read-alouds may be works that call for careful and sensitive discussion on important issues to be explored within the theme, or they may have intricacies of plot or characterization that demand careful guidance.

See Huck, Hepler, & Hickman (1987) for criteria for choosing books for children.

Materials for Group Activities. If these materials are books, you should choose them with literary qualities in mind, but they should also be good candidates for small group activities that don't require your direct attention. You can often find multiple copies of paperbacks that fit your theme. A MYSTERIES theme for fifth graders might see four or five children in a group reading such novels as *The Secret Garden, The Children of Green Knowe, The House of Dies Drear,* and *From the Mixed-Up Files of Mrs. Basil E. Frankweiler;* information books such as *Lost Lands and Forgotten People, Where Did They Come From? Mysterious Origins of Ancient People, Mysteries of Nature Explained and Unexplained,* and *Into the Unknown: Nine Astounding Stories;* or articles concerning mysteries found in current periodicals or newspapers.

Burnett (1962); Boston (1958); Hamilton (1968); Konigsburg (1967); Cornell (1978); Caras (1979); Mooser (1980)

Jackdaws, or collections of primary source materials, which could include such printed sources as journals, letters, maps, old newspapers or advertisements, and photographs, could provide another focus for group work (see Chapter 8 for further information on assembling jackdaw-like packets). When these types of materials are the focus of group projects, children will naturally be involved in activities that particularly require analysis and evaluation.

Additional Reading Materials for Personal Exploration. Reading interests of individual children in any classroom vary and should be catered to by including many other titles that may be chosen for personal enjoyment or individual research. Children involved in the MYSTERIES theme can read some of the more popular series books such as "Encyclopedia Brown," science-oriented books such as the "Einstein Anderson" series, or books about mysterious phenomena such as the Bermuda triangle.

Sobol (1980); Simon (1980)

Primary Source Materials. Primary source materials include originals, copies or facsimiles of such printed resources as letters, journals, maps, photographs, newspapers, magazines, advertisements, ledgers, account books, mail-order catalogs, and any other artifacts that give us firsthand information about real people who lived in other times or other places, or about the community of which we are a part today. Primary source material also includes notes of observations, transcriptions of interviews, and the like.

Hands-on Resources—Artifacts, Equipment, and Props

Objects that are products of human culture—tools, machinery, and so on—or natural objects and other materials can be useful features of thematic units. These hands-on resources can provide a focus for wondering, speculating, hypothesizing, or reconstructing events concerning people's lives, both past and present. Consider how old pottery shards, Indian arrowheads, ceremonial masks, costumes, toys, and household items could serve as an entry into another time or another culture. Plan to collect headgear, footwear, and other items of clothing; shells, seeds, rocks, and other natural objects; clocks, watches, irons, toasters, pipes, hammers, beakers, test tubes, and other equipment such as tools and simple machines as a means of extending and exploring the theme.

An old washboard, washtub, and scrub brush, for example, might be part of a unit called WASH AND WEAR (Chapter 4). It could serve as a focus for creative dramatics; a springboard for comparing different methods of cleaning clothes, both past and present; a vehicle for exploring the changing roles of women in society; or as an entry into stories such as *Mrs. Wishy-Washy, The Wild Washerwoman*, or *Washday on Noah's Ark*.

Cowley & Melser (1980); Yeoman (1979); Rounds (1985)

Community Resources

Learning is not confined within the walls of the classroom but extends into the community. When children are involved in a thematic unit, they just naturally connect events and experiences in their lives outside the classroom to things that are happening in school. In addition, plan specifically to make full use of community resources—people, places, animals, and other living things—that can help strengthen children's understanding of the theme.

Bring the community into the classroom.

The children themselves are sometimes the best source of information on a topic. Some may have had experiences that can broaden other children's awareness. Others may have unique viewpoints or understandings that shed new light on familiar ideas. Parents and other family members may also have much to contribute in the way of experience, cultural knowledge, or expertise. Plan also to include professionals, specialists, business people, and others in the community who could contribute through classroom visits, interviews, or field trips.

Children and their families are important resources.

Animals and other living things are sources of information that seem to be especially appealing to children. Many thematic units can include small animals, fish, reptiles, or insects as part of the classroom environment for short periods without harm. Plants also make excellent classroom resources. Zoos, aquariums, farms, arboretums, and other such facilities, as well as the natural environments of forest, park, tidal pools, ponds, or even playgrounds, can provide the children with a wealth of learning experiences and activities.

Places in the community can become classrooms as part of the thematic unit. Museums of all types and historical sites often have organized presentations and special exhibits that can be part of, or even trigger, a thematic unit. The city streets, country village, even a cemetery can provide less formal, but no less exciting, learning possibilities.

To see how you can make use of community resources in a thematic unit, consider how Sara's schema of spiders and insects (discussed in Chapter 1) could have been further extended during a thematic unit on BUGS. Children could collect insects from home and neighborhood in "bug" jars. Various insects are sketched in different positions and, with a detailed written description, placed in a classroom display. Other children keep a daily journal of their observations of caterpillars that have spun cocoons and have been placed in a see-through box to await their metamorphosis to butterflies. You can invite several persons from the community who have an interest in insects to speak to the class. These could include one child's grandparent who collects butterflies, a local beekeeper who brings honey for the children to taste, an exterminator who arrives in a truck with a model of a huge roach perched on the top, and a local farmer who talks about the ways in which insects can help or hinder crops. The children take notes in their journals and later write up these visits in the class newspaper or use the information in research reports they are writing. Children then elect to do follow-up interviews. Some ask family members about interests or hobbies concerning insects. Others interview farmers about their favorite and least favorite insects. Still others call local pest control companies to find out the biggest pest control problem. Results of these interviews are then written up and displayed on bar graphs. The children visit a special exhibit on insects at the museum of natural history where an entomologist conducts a special hands-on tour. While in the museum, they have some time to do some thought ramblings in a field trip booklet (that leads to their writing a variety of poetry and short descriptive pieces), as well as interview other professional staff. Finally, as a culminating event of the unit, the children present research reports on insects to the rest of the class. Sara, or course, has chosen to do hers on arachnids.

The Arts

Include the arts as resources and as vehicles for exploring themes.

Another category of resources for use in thematic units involves the arts—painting, sculpture, or architecture; the decorative arts; the graphic arts; crafts; musical arts; theater, television, and film. These arts provide important visual, auditory, tactile, and kinesthetic experiences that can give rise to important understandings about a theme. (Chapter 7 provides a wider discussion of art and music in thematic units.)

The arts can be involved in, for example, a unit on WHAT MAKES YOU LAUGH. Children would certainly want to make use of their favorite cartoons and comic strips, and the teacher might find old silent movies or radio broadcasts to share with the class. The school music teacher might contribute recordings of music with a comic element or show how instruments can produce sounds that evoke laughter or a happy sound. The art teacher might help gather resources from the world of painting and sculpture. For example, seventeenth-century Dutch painter Franz Hals is well known for his scenes of people in situations ripe with laughter, and his portraits such as "The Laughing Cavalier" have a wonderful exuberance. French Impressionist, Pierre-Auguste Renoir, is also known for his pictures of people enjoying themselves, whereas eighteenth-century English artist William Hogarth is best known for such biting satire as "The Rake's Progress." In this century comic art has taken many forms, from the painting and sculpture of French artist Jean Dubuffet to the clean, spontaneous linear designs of such well-known cartoonists as Edward Gorey and William Steig.

The theatre department of a local college or a little theatre group might present comedies for the children's entertainment, or a mime might be invited to perform for the class. Children could also study differing forms of comedy throughout the world, such as the Punch and Judy puppet shows from England and France or shadow puppets from Indonesia. The use of masks in ancient Greek comedies could be of interest to children.

Experiencing these various art forms can lead children to use the arts to further explore the theme of laughter. They may want to create their own comic art or sculpture, comic strip or cartoon; to present a puppet show, or to video tape a silent movie; to try pantomime, to write a comedy for theatrical presentation or a script for radio theatre; and to compose or find music to accompany these efforts. Table 3.1 lists a range of resources for selecting books and media for children.

TABLE 3.1 Selecting Books and Media for Children

A to Zoo—Subject Access to Children's Picture Books (1985). Ed. Carolyn W. Lima. Ann Arbor, MI: R. R. Bowker.

Adventuring with Books, A Booklist for Preschool–Grade 6, 1981 Edition. Diane Monson, ed. Urbana, IL: National Council of Teachers of English.

Best Science Books for Children: Selected and Annotated (1983). Kathryn Wolfe et al., eds. American Association for the Advancement of Science.

Bibliography of Books for Children (1984). Sylvia Sunderling, ed. Washington, DC: The Association for Childhood Education International (revised every three years).

A Bicultural Heritage: Themes for the Exploration of Mexico and the Mexican American Culture in Books for Children and Adolescents (1978). Metuchen, NJ: Scarecrow Press.

The Black Experience in Children's Books (1984). Barbara Rollock, selector. New York Public Library.

The Bookfinder: Volume 3: When Kids Need Books: Annotations of Books Published 1973–1982 (1985). Sharon Spredmann Dreyer. Circle Pines, MN: American Guidance Service.

Booklist Magazine. The American Library Association, 50 E. Huron St., Chicago, IL 60611 (periodical).

Books for You: A Booklist for Senior High Students (1988). Richard F. Abrahamson and Betty Carter, eds. Urbana, IL: National Council of Teachers of English.

Books on American Indians and Eskimos: A Selection Guide for Children and Young Adults (1977). Mary Jo Lasswoodin, ed. Chicago, IL: American Library Association.

Children's Mathematics Books: A Critical Bibliography (1979). Margaret Mathias and Diane Thiessen. Chicago, IL: American Library Association.

Choices: A Core Collection for Young Reluctant Readers (1984). Carolyn Flemming and Donna Schatt, eds. Evanston, IL: John Gordon Burke Publishers.

Educational Media Yearbook (annual). James W. Brown and Shirley N. Brown, eds. Littleton, CO: Libraries Unlimited.

Girls Are People Too!: A Bibliography of Nontraditional Female Roles in Children's Books (1982). Joan E. Newman. Metuchen, NJ: Scarecrow Press.

Growing Up with Science Books, 9th ed. 1977. R. R. Bowker

Hey Miss! You Got a Good Book For Me?: A Model Multi-cultural Resource Collection (1981). Joanna E. Chambers, ed. Austin, TX: Austin Bilingual Language Editions.

A Hispanic Heritage: A Guide to Juvenile Books About Hispanic People and Cultures (1980). Isabel Schon. Metuchen, NJ: Scarecrow Press.

The Horn Book (periodical). 31 St. James Ave., Boston, MA 02116.

Index to Children's Songs (1979). Carolyn Sue Peterson and Ann D. Fenton. Bronx, NY: H. W. Wilson.

Index to Fairy Tales, 1949–1972. Including Folklore, Legends and Myths in Collections (1973). Norma Olin Ireland. Metuchen, NJ: Scarecrow Press.

Index to Poetry for Children and Young People: 1976–1981 (1984). John E. Brewton, ed. Bronx, NY: H. W. Wilson.

Index to Young Reader's Collective Biographies (1979), *2nd ed.* Judith Silverman, ed. Ann Arbor, MI: R. R. Bowker.

Literature by and About the American Indian: An Annotated Bibliography (1979). Lee Stensland. Urbana, IL: National Council of Teachers of English.

More Notes From A Different Drummer: A Guide to Juvenile Fiction Portraying the Handicapped (1984). Barbara H. Baskin and Karen H. Harris. Ann Arbor, MI: R. R. Bowker.

The Museum of Science and Industry Basic List of Children's Science Books (1985). Bernice Richter. Chicago, IL: American Library Association.

Reading for Young People Series: *The Great Plains; Kentucky, Tennessee, West Virginia; The Middle Atlantic; The Northwest; The Rocky Mountains; The Southeast; The Upper Midwest* (published during the years 1979–1985). Chicago, IL: American Library Association.

Reading Ladders for Human Relations, 6th ed. (1981). Eileen Tway, ed. Urbana, IL: National Council of Teachers of English.

Subject Guide to Children's Books in Print (annual). Ann Arbor, MI: R. R. Bowker.

The WEB: Wonderfully Exciting Books. The Ohio State University, 200 Ramseyer Hall, Columbus, OH 43210 (periodical).

World History in Juvenile Books: A Geographical and Chronological Guide (1973). Seymour Metzner, ed. Bronx, NY: H. W. Wilson.

Your Reading, A Booklist for Junior High and Middle School Students (1988). James E. and Hazel K. Davis, eds. Urbana, IL: National Council of Teachers of English.

PLANNING ACTIVITIES

When you collect books and other materials for the thematic unit, consider also the many types of activities and projects with which children can choose to explore the theme. These activities will, in turn, suggest other books and materials; the unit may seem to be taking on a life of its own. In planning for these experiences, consider not only language but also math, social studies, the sciences, and the arts as vehicles for exploring the ideas and concepts within the scope of the thematic unit. As you consider the many experiences that could be part of a thematic unit, you will note that language will be an important component of any activity. The prototypes in Chapter 4 illustrate the kinds of projects that can be planned to include these curricular domains. In addition, Chapter 7 covers important ideas and concepts in these different disciplines in more detail and provides further support for integrating language across the curriculum.

Halliday (1975)

It is important to ensure that children extend their communicative competency to the fullest extent possible. During their development as competent communicators in their preschool years, children used language for many purposes in learning how to mean. They desired, demanded, socialized, personalized, wondered, imagined, and informed. If they are to continue to grow beyond the confines of their neighborhood into the context of the wider world, these activities must extend into the world of print as well as encompass the many situations in which oral language is used in that world. A strong curriculum, therefore, must allow children to continue to express their own personal ideas.

As you select books and other resources for the theme and the WEB begins to take shape, make sure that topics are explored through a variety of purposeful oral and written activities. A balance of these and a balance of materials are more likely to develop competent communicators *and* critical thinkers. These experiences help children to express personal feelings through discussion, journals, editorials, reviews, and debates; to interact through letters and interviews; to inform through directions, descriptions, records, and reports; to wonder through experiments, observations, and theses; and to imagine through drama, poetry, and story.

Plan discussion and activities that lead children back into the book.

Planning for activities such as these can occur in several ways. Activities can serve as springboards that lead children to books and other resources as they did in the WASH AND WEAR, BUGS, and WHAT MAKES YOU LAUGH? themes briefly described earlier. At other times, a book can serve as the focus for meaningful activities, some that lead children back to the book and others that connect to other books or experiences that are part of the thematic unit.

Allen (1986); de Paola (1975)

Although we illustrate this kind of planning in Chapter 4, it is helpful at this point to provide an example of the scope of possibilities and extensions that are possible within the covers of a single book. Tomie de Paola's story of *Strega Nona* illustrates ways of planning some of these experiences.

In this delightful story, Big Anthony, an apprentice to the good witch, Strega Nona, tries to work a spell on a magic pasta pot to cook pasta. He cannot turn the pot off; as a result pasta threatens to overrun the town. Fortunately, Strega Nona returns in time to save the day, and Big Anthony receives a punishment that fits the crime—he has to eat up the overflow of pasta. Following the reading of the book (which can be used in a thematic unit on FOOD or MAGIC), you can first develop the following activities that focus attention on the book and help children to think more deeply about events, characters, settings, and themes in the story:

1. Retell the story using stick puppets or a flannel board.
2. Make a *Strega Nona* board game that incorporates key events or sequence. Write directions for play.
3. Make a *Strega Nona* mural or collage.
4. Choose character roles. Conduct an "interview" by asking characters about their roles in the story.
5. Write a "Help Wanted" ad for Strega Nona.
6. Write a "Situation Wanted" ad for Big Anthony.
7. Write a front page headline for a newspaper, plus an article that details the events in the story.
8. Interview classmates about their favorite part of the story.

Rose (1976); Galdone (1976)

9. Read *Akimba and the Magic Cow: A Folk Tale from Africa* as retold by Anne Rose and *The Magic Porridge Pot* by Paul Galdone. Make a comparison chart, and compare and contrast the three books.

Then, in addition to leading children back into a book through such activities, you can also plan experiences, such as those in the following list, that extend beyond the covers of a single book:

1. Create a magic object museum. Collect objects from other folk tales and display them.
2. Read poems like Shel Silverstein's "Spaghetti," Eve Merriam's "A Round," and Jack Prelutsky's "Spaghetti, Spaghetti."
3. Create a choral reading for Silverstein's poem.
4. Sing the Prelutsky poem to the tune of "Greensleeves."
5. Write additional verses for Merriam's "A Round."
6. Make and cook pasta from scratch. Measure the ingredients and weigh the dough. Then measure the noodles and graph your findings.
7. Write the recipe for making pasta.
8. Categorize types of pasta according to size, color, and shape.
9. Choose a pasta and write a description. Then display all types of pasta, and let other children match the written descriptions with the correct pasta.
10. Have a pasta party. Plan the menu. Write invitations. Set the tables, figuring the number of place settings needed for the total number of guests.
11. Write about the pasta party for the social column of the class newspaper.
12. Listen to the scherzo by Paul Dukas called the "Sorcerer's Apprentice." Choreograph the story of *Strega Nona* to this music.

Silverstein (1974); Merriam (1986); Prelutsky (1980)

Notice that these experiences allow children to use many reading strategies (comparing and contrasting, sequencing, recalling details, making inferences about characters), involve them in writing, speaking, and listening for many purposes, and engage them in the arts, mathematical problem-solving, and concepts of science as well. If all these experiences can grow out of one book, it is not difficult to imagine the many exciting experiences that are possible during the course of an entire thematic unit.

ORGANIZING THE CLASSROOM

The classroom layout can facilitate learning.

Because the thematic unit presents children with many possibilities for exploring the theme and asks that you play many roles, it is important that the physical setup of the classroom facilitate the implementation of the unit. Whether you find yourself in a self-contained or an open classroom, whether you take responsibility for the whole day or are in a departmentalized program, your use of space can facilitate implementation and organization of the unit.

Take time with students at the beginning of the year to discuss the setup of the classroom and how to use the space effectively and comfortably. Children should be made to feel ownership of the classroom and should take responsibility for its uses as well as contribute suggestions concerning its organization. However that organization finally evolves in your classroom, some features we consider important to the integrated language program in general and thematic units in particular are discussed in the following pages. Figure 3.6 shows a floor plan of a classroom that incorporates many of these suggestions. Amenities such as sinks and computers are not available in many classrooms, but the other factors such as centers can be achieved with minimum outlay as long as desks and furniture can be moved around.

Materials and Equipment

We have already mentioned the importance of an extensive classroom library supplemented by volumes from the school or municipal library as new themes are planned. In addition, the thematic unit determines the many other types of resources that are collected and displayed within the classroom at any given time. A variety of materials

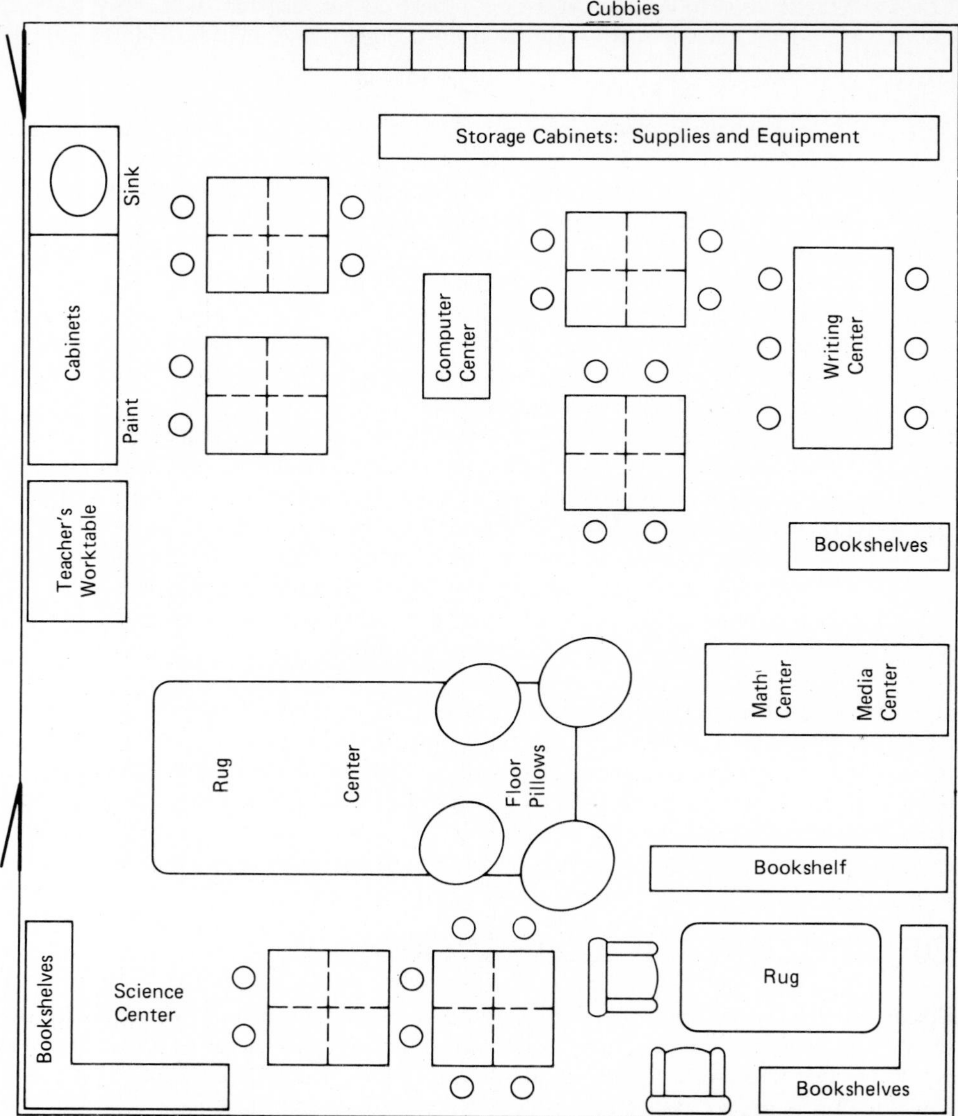

Figure 3.6

Donations of furniture and materials can come from parents and other community members.

for writing and art activities are always desirable. These need not eat up the supply budget but can be culled from community or family sources. We have seen books on which children have written on the backs of wallpaper samples or used computer printouts. Beautiful collages and sculpture have been created from scrap paper, fabric scraps, feathers, sequins, beans, macaroni, paper-towel tubes, and other "found" materials.

Desks, chairs, and tables should be movable so that centers can be reorganized according to the demands of a particular unit or activity. Comfortable chairs, pillows, and an old couch or area rugs can further define space and indicate quiet corners. (One lucky teacher found an old porcelain bathtub. Filled with throw pillows, it became the focal point of the reading center.) Easels, walls, and movable bulletin boards on which children's work can be displayed are essential. Rooms should be filled with children's writing, art, and other projects. Bookcases, including the type that can display books cover forward, along with storage cabinets for art supplies, science equipment, math manipulables, and other materials are also important features. Additional materials and equipment can be added according to the needs of each unit and the realities of the school budget.

Centers

Once furniture and equipment are gathered, they can be arranged into centers that suit the needs of a particular unit. Consideration should be given to the need for quiet places for individual activities such as reading, writing, teacher-child conferencing, and to centers where activities might result in more bustle. Space should be kept clear for large group gatherings and creative dramatics or movement.

Both permanent and temporary centers are created in the classroom.

Some centers are permanent. The classroom library, the reading loft, the listening post, the writing center where paper, writing implements, and other materials for publishing are stored, and the art center where art supplies are found and used remain unchanged across thematic units during the whole year. Other centers have a temporary, short-term life. Tables are moved to certain places in the room so that children have access to the specific resources to be used and explored during a particular thematic unit. For example, places are set up where animals, insects, or plants can be observed and studied; where equipment to conduct experiments is situated; where a classroom restaurant or museum can be established, and so forth. When an individual thematic unit is over, much of what had been found in these temporary centers is dismantled and new centers begin to support the activity and exploration of the next thematic unit.

IMPLEMENTING THE UNIT

Although the thematic unit is more a planning scheme for teachers, the general nature of it should be shared with children so they are aware of their choices regarding activities and also of the contributions they might make. The thematic WEB should thus be shared with children at the outset of the unit, and their own suggestions for topics and books should be incorporated whenever possible.

Once you begin implementing the unit, ensure that children have the opportunity to explore the theme in ways that will expand domains of knowledge. That is, a thematic unit is a tentative and flexible framework. Changes can be easily made as children's own ideas for projects and activities evolve. Part of this flexibility is accepting even a child's tangential interest. To this end, an initial agreement about what projects are to be carried out as part of the thematic unit is a useful planning and organizing tool. These agreements, which can be realized in many different ways, are means by which children and teacher are able to keep track of what children are doing. They can also provide valuable information about children's processes of learning and serve as sources for accountability. (See Chapters 8 and 9.)

Agreements serve to help organize and facilitate the ongoing work of the unit.

Initial expectations about children's work should be general in nature. Specific projects and dates are then negotiated and become more clearly defined as children have the opportunity to engage in a variety of activities that require reading and writing in a range of genres, that require using language to discuss and organize learning in various areas of the curriculum, and that require participation in various ways of knowing.

It is important that children, or the teacher, have the opportunity to renegotiate agreements. Perhaps a child becomes excited about a particular topic and wants to do additional research. One of the other activities can be dropped to allow the time needed. Or, if a topic or an assigned book has proven too difficult, a more suitable one can be substituted. This flexibility encourages children to take risks but also to become aware of their capabilities.

At the outset of each unit, you may decide on several activities that could be major avenues for exploring the theme. Each child would be expected to choose one of these projects and to choose whether to work alone or with a small group. At this time, you may want to consider children's past choices and ask them to consider an alternative

A diorama is a three-dimensional view of a scene, often constructed in a shoebox.

activity. For example, if a child has made only dioramas as extensions of books read, or writes only stories or reports, you may suggest other options to ensure that throughout the year all children have the opportunity to use language for a variety of purposes while engaged with a wide range of resources.

For a theme of TIME, for example, ask children to choose from the following projects:

1. Study the use of time in literature. Read nighttime and daytime stories, and make a comparison chart of the books.
   Or, read and compare time fantasies by constructing dioramas that depict these fantasies. Write about your study and what you have found.
2. Observe and chart the daily changes in the growth of a plant or animal in a journal. Illustrate and write up findings.
3. Investigate ways in which time has been measured over the centuries, using information books and other sources. Create a time line depicting various time pieces. Write about the ways of telling time.
4. Use interviews and primary sources to investigate changes in your community over time. Create a mural depicting changes. Write up the results of your study for the class newspaper.

Additional choices can then be made available that meet interests and enthusiasms of individual children. The ideas in the following list represent only a few of the many additional experiences that are possible as part of a TIME theme and that individual children can select as part of their agreement:

Zubrowski (1988)

1. Plan creative dramatics or Reader's Theatre in response to a time story or myth.
2. Build a water clock following the directions in *Clocks: Building and Experimenting with Model Timepieces.*
3. Visit the art museum and make a list of paintings that show times of the day or the year. Write about your favorite painting.
4. Interview classmates about favorite times of the day or year. Write results for class newspaper.
5. Read TIME poetry. Write a poem about a favorite time of day.
6. Try doing a thought rambling in your journal while listening to music depicting times of day.
7. Visit a clock shop and interview the owner about the business aspects of time.
8. Identify time zones on a world map. Select major cities from various parts of the world, and figure how many hours difference there is between each city and your own locale. Chart the mileage between your home and those cities. How long would it take to get there if you were walking (or swimming) at 500 miles per hour?

At this time, in consultation with each student, you can assign each child a book that is to be read in small groups. This book could be one of a set of multiple copies available or one of many individual books grouped together by theme or type. Ensure that children select from a wide range of genres and that they do not work with the same group of classmates all the time. This is much less likely to happen when children are grouped according to interest in a particular topic or project rather than according to so-called reading levels.

Agreements are designed to help you and students plan and to help children know what is expected of them. Due dates can be placed on the agreement to help children become self-monitoring and to aid you in pacing. There may be times when you want children to move through activities at approximately the same pace so that all of them are introduced to some aspect of the theme at the same time, or so that everyone is working on a research paper at the same time. In other units this may not be crucial, and children can decide which activity to complete first.

CONCLUSION

Through the course of a unit, children have many opportunities to share process and products concerning ongoing activities with other classmates (and with the wider community). This collaboration happens in the course of daily discussions and when children's work is presented, published, and displayed. As domains of knowledge are constructed and expanded, integrated language classrooms truly become *communities of learning.* Children not only pursue their own projects with enthusiasm, but they are also aware of and interested in the projects of their classmates. When the thematic unit culminates in the sharing of final projects, children can be encouraged to look back and reflect on their own learning and also consider the ways in which the classroom culture constructed a body of knowledge together. This joining of effort and understanding is the essence of collaboration and is perhaps the most satisfying and enriching aspect of teaching and learning through thematic units.

It may seem that thematic units require an inordinate amount of work. You need to remember, however, that *all* teaching takes time; the integrated language/thematic unit approach only means that time is used differently. Implementing any new approach takes additional time initially, but eventually teaching this way becomes second nature.

In her delightful book, *A House Is a House for Me,* poet Mary Anne Hoberman contemplates the simple idea of a house and then begins to reshape the concept of houses into new and unusual formats. This poem reflects the processes that are involved in webbing, planning, and implementing thematic units.

Hoberman (1978)

Perhaps I have started farfetching . . . .
Perhaps I am stretching things some . . . .
A mirror's a house for reflections . . . .
A throat is a house for a hum . . . .
But once you get started in thinking,
You think and you think and you think.
How pockets are houses for pennies
And pens can be houses for ink; . . .
And once you get started in thinking this way,
It seems that whatever you see
Is either a house or it lives in a house,
And a house is a house for me!

However you approach thematic units, the goal is to open for children the many possibilities that exist in even the simplest of ideas such as "houses" and to help move them to new and exciting insights and understandings. We believe that once *you* start thinking in terms of thematic units, it's likely that whatever you see in the curriculum you will see in terms of meaningful connections. The integrated language approach will become not just another way of teaching but an exciting and enriching way of living in the world.

Chapter 4 describes eight prototype thematic units to illustrate in more detail how theory from this perspective gets put into action in the classroom. You will revisit Ruby, Carol, and Caitlin, the teachers you briefly met in the "Introduction," and you will encounter other teachers who use this approach at various grade levels in the elementary school.

REFERENCES

Allen, V. G. (1986). Developing contexts to support second language acquisition. *Language Arts, 63*(1), 61–66.

Anderson, R. C., Hiebert, E., Scott, J., & Wilkinson, I. (1984). *Becoming a nation of readers.* Washington, DC: The National Institute of Education.

Chaplin, M. T. (1982). No more reading "reading." *Reading World, 21,* 340–346.

Corwin, R., Hein, G. E., & Levin, D. (1976). Weaving curriculum webs: The structure of nonlinear curriculum. *Childhood Education*, 248–251.

Halliday, M. A. K. (1975). *Learning how to mean: Explorations in the development of language.* London: Edward Arnold.

Hopkins, L. B. (1987). *Pass the poetry please.* New York: Harper & Row.

Huck, C. S., Hepler, S., & Hickman, J. (1987). *Children's literature in the elementary school.* New York: Holt, Rinehart and Winston.

Kobrin, B. (1988). *Eye openers: How to choose and use children's books about real people, places and things.* New York: Penguin Books.

McClure, A. A. (1982). Integrating children's fiction and informational literature in a primary reading curriculum. *The Reading Teacher, 35*(8), 784–789.

Monson, D. (Editor). (1985). *Adventuring with books; A booklist for pre-K through grade 6.* Urbana, IL: National Council of Teachers of English.

Moss, J. F. (1984). *Focus units in literature.* Urbana, IL: National Council of Teachers of English.

Norton, D. E. (1982). Using a webbing process to develop children's literature units. *Language Arts, 59*(4), 348–356.

Wells, G. (1986). *The meaning makers: Children learning language and using language to learn.* Portsmouth, NH: Heinemann.

CHILDREN'S LITERATURE

AKIMBA AND THE MAGIC COW by A. Rose. Four Winds, 1976.

ANNIE AND THE OLD ONE by M. Miles. Illustrated by P. Parnall. Little, Brown, 1971.

BREED TO COME by A. Norton. Viking, 1972.

THE CHILDREN OF GREEN KNOWE by L. M. Boston. Harcourt Brace, 1955.

THE CHOCOLATE TOUCH by P. S. Catling. Morrow, 1979.

CLOCKS AND HOW THEY GO by G. Gibbons. Crowell, 1979.

CLOCKS AND MORE CLOCKS by P. Hutchins. Penguin, 1970.

CLOCKS: BUILDING AND EXPERIMENTING WITH MODEL TIMEPIECES by B. Zubrowski. Illustrated by R. Doty. Morrow, 1988.

CLOUDY WITH A CHANCE OF MEATBALLS by J. Barrett. Illustrated by R. Barrett. Atheneum, 1978.

DAUGHTER OF THE EARTH: A ROMAN MYTH by G. McDermott. Delacorte Press, 1984.

DAWN by U. Shulevitz. Farrar, Straus & Giroux, 1974.

DUSK TO DAWN: POEMS OF NIGHT. Selected by H. Hill and others. Illustrated by A. Brugess. Crowell, 1981.

EINSTEIN ANDERSON SHOCKS HIS FRIENDS by S. Simon. Viking, 1980.

ENCYCLOPEDIA BROWN CARRIES ON by D. Sobol. Four Winds, 1980.

FOG DRIFT MORNING by D. K. Ray. Harper & Row, 1983.

FOG MAGIC by J. Sauer. Viking, 1943.

FROM THE MIXED-UP FILES OF MRS. BASIL E. FRANKWEILER by E. L. Konigsburg. Atheneum, 1967.

A GIRL CALLED BOY by B. Hurmence. Clarion, 1982.

GRANDFATHER TWILIGHT by B. Berger. Philomel, 1984.

THE GREEN BOOK by J. P. Walsh. Farrar, Straus & Giroux, 1982.

THE GREEN FUTURES OF TYCHO by W. Sleator. Dutton, 1981.

HILDILID'S NIGHT by C. D. Ryan. Illustrated by A. Lobel. Macmillan, 1986.

THE HOUSE FROM MORNING TO NIGHT by D. Bour. Kane Miller, 1985.

A HOUSE IS A HOUSE FOR ME by M. A. Hoberman. Illustrated by B. Fraser. Viking, 1978.

THE HOUSE OF DIES DREAR by V. Hamilton. Macmillan, 1968.

HOW TO EAT FRIED WORMS by T. Rockwell. Franklin Watts, 1973.

THE IDEAS OF EINSTEIN by D. E. Fisher. Illustrated by G. Brodkin. Holt, Rinehart, and Winston, 1980.

INTO THE UNKNOWN: NINE ASTOUNDING STORIES by S. Mooser. Lippincott, 1980.

ISLAND BOY by B. Cooney. Viking, 1988.
IT'S ALL RELATIVE: EINSTEIN'S THEORY OF RELATIVITY by N. H. Apfel. Illustrated by Y. Kondo. Lothrop, 1981.
JEREMY VISICK by D. Wiseman. Houghton Mifflin, 1981.
LEGENDS OF THE SUN AND MOON by E. and T. Hadley. Illustrated by J. Nesbitt. Cambridge, 1983.
LIFE THROUGH THE AGES by G. Caselli. Grossett & Dunlap, 1987.
THE LITTLE HOUSE by V. L. Burton. Houghton Mifflin, 1942, 1969.
LOST LANDS AND FORGOTTEN PEOPLE by J. Cornell. Sterling, 1978.
THE MAGIC PORRIDGE POT by P. Galdone. Clarion, 1976.
MISS RUMPHIUS by B. Cooney. Viking Penguin, 1982.
MORNING NOON AND NIGHTTIME, TOO. Compiled by L. B. Hopkins. Illustrated by N. Hannans. Harper & Row, 1980.
MRS. WISHY WASHY by J. Cowley and J. Melser. The Wright Group, 1980.
MS. GLEE WAS WAITING by D. Hill. Illustrated by D. Dawson. Atheneum, 1978.
MY BACKYARD HISTORY BOOK by D. Weitzman. Illustrated by J. Robertson. Little, Brown, 1975.
MY FAVORITE TIME OF YEAR by S. Pearson. Illustrated by J. Wallner. Harper & Row, 1988.
THE MYSTERIES OF NATURE: EXPLAINED AND UNEXPLAINED by R. Caras. Harcourt Brace Jovanovich, 1979.
NEW PROVIDENCE: A CHANGING CITYSCAPE by R. von Tscharner and R. L. Fleming. Illustrated by D. Orloff. Gulliver/Harcourt Brace Jovanovich, 1987.
NIGHT IN THE COUNTRY by C. Rylant. Illustrated by M. Szilagyi. Bradbury, 1986.
NIGHT MARKETS: BRINGING FOOD TO THE CITY by J. Horwitz. Crowell, 1984.
NIGHT OF GHOSTS AND HERMITS: NOCTURNAL LIFE AT THE SEASHORE by M. Stolz. Illustrated by S. Gallagher. Harcourt Brace Jovanovich, 1985.
OPENING NIGHT by R. Isadora. Greenwillow, 1984.
OX-CART MAN by D. Hall. Illustrated by B. Cooney. Viking, 1979.
PLAYING BEATIE BOW by R. Park. Atheneum, 1982.
PORCUPINE STEW by B. Major. Illustrated by E. Ingraham. Morrow, 1982.
THE REASONS FOR SEASONS: OR THE GREAT COSMIC MEGAGALACTIC TRIP WITHOUT MOVING FROM YOUR ARMCHAIR by L. Allison. Little, Brown, 1975.
THE ROOT CELLAR by J. Lunn. Scribner, 1983.
"A Round" in A SKY FULL OF POEMS by E. Merriam. Dell, 1986.
THE SECRET CLOCKS: TIME SENSES OF LIVING THINGS by S. Simon. Illustrated by J. Brett. Viking, 1979.
THE SECRET GARDEN by F. H. Burnett. Lippincott, 1962.
SOLOMON GRUNDY by S. R. Haguet. Dutton, 1986.
"Spaghetti" in WHERE THE SIDEWALK ENDS by S. Silverstein. Harper & Row, 1974.
"Spaghetti, Spaghetti" in RAINY RAINY SATURDAY by J. Prelutsky. Greenwillow, 1980.
STONE SOUP by M. Brown. Scribner, 1947.
THE STORY OF AN ENGLISH VILLAGE by J. Goodall. Atheneum, 1979.
STREGA NONA by T. dePaola. Prentice-Hall, 1975.
A STRING IN THE HARP by N. Bond. Atheneum, 1976.
SUGARING TIME by K. Laskey. Photographs by C. G. Knight. Macmillan, 1983.
THERE ONCE WAS A TIME by P. Ventura. Putnam, 1986.
THE THIRTEEN CLOCKS by J. Thurber. Illustrated by M. Simont. Simon & Schuster, 1950.
THIS BOOK IS ABOUT TIME by M. Burns. Illustrated by M. Weston. Little, Brown, 1978.
THIS TIME OF DARKNESS by H. M. Hoover. Viking, 1980.
TIME AT THE TOP by E. Ormondroyd. Houghton Mifflin (Parnassus), 1963.
TIME OF WONDER by R. McCloskey. Viking, 1957.
TIMECHANGES: THE EVOLUTION OF EVERYDAY LIFE by G. Trease. Kingfisher, 1985.
TOM'S MIDNIGHT GARDEN by P. Pearce. Lippincott, 1959.

A TRAVELER IN TIME by A. Uttley. Viking, 1964.

THE TREASURE OF GREEN KNOWE by L. M. Boston. Harcourt Brace, 1958.

TUCK EVERLASTING by N. Babbitt. Farrar, Straus & Giroux, 1975.

WASHDAY ON NOAH'S ARK by G. Rounds. Holiday, 1985.

THE WAY TO START A DAY by B. Baylor. Illustrated by P. Parnall. Scribner, 1978.

WHAT MAKES DAY AND NIGHT by F. M. Branley. Illustrated by A. Dorros. Crowell, 1961, 1987.

WHEN THE SKY IS LIKE LACE by E. L. Horwitz. Illustrated by B. Cooney. Lippincott, 1975.

WHERE DID THEY COME FROM? MYSTERIOUS ORIGINS OF ANCIENT PEOPLE by J. Cornell. Sterling, 1978.

THE WHITE MOUNTAINS by J. Christopher. Macmillan, 1967.

THE WILD WASHERWOMEN by J. Yeoman. Illustrated by Q. Blake. Greenwillow, 1979.

A WRINKLE IN TIME by M. L'Engle. Farrar, Straus & Giroux, 1962.

Z FOR ZACARIAH by R. O'Brien. Atheneum, 1975.

4

Prototypes for Integrated Language Classrooms

Now that you have organized possible activities, projects, and resources in your WEB, how does your thematic unit get off the ground? First steps are often the most difficult to plan and to take; once an activity begins and confidence builds, things tend to fall into place. So it is with implementing a thematic unit in an integrated language classroom. Those first few moments and first few activities set the stage for what is to come and can either generate interest, enthusiasm, and learning or create difficulties that are hard to overcome. The stage must be set with *meaning-full* work for children to do if they are to be engaged as meaning-makers.

STARTING A THEMATIC UNIT

Reflective Inquiry

The creation or discovery of a problem to solve can lead students to create and test hypotheses, explore variations on an initial problem, and study a theme in depth. *Reflective inquiry* is the term given to this process, and it is a crucial factor in the development of a thematic unit. Reflective inquiry is more than the acquisition of knowledge and skill—they are the *tools* of inquiry. Reflective inquiry involves the following:

Barr, Barth, & Shermis (1977)

1. The ability to encode information—that is, to understand what information is relevant (or irrelevant) to solving a problem.
2. The ability to combine pieces of information, even though those pieces may at first seem unrelated.
3. The ability to compare the problem with problems previously encountered and to use those skills and concepts previously employed.

Ryan and Ellis describe the process of inquiry as recognizing a problem, selecting appropriate data sources, processing the data, and making inferences from the data. One teacher begins with a black-box problem. He asks students to watch carefully as he places a black cardboard box with tripod legs on a desk. There are several buckets immediately below the desk, and a jar of clear liquid is next to the box. The box itself has a rubber spigot spouting from the bottom front and a funnel in the center top. A

Ryan & Ellis (1974)

student is asked to pour the liquid from the jar into the funnel, while another student monitors the spigot end. As the liquid pours into the funnel, red liquid begins to pour from the spigot—and pours and pours—until the bucket and part of another on the floor are full.

Before discussion begins, the teacher asks students to think carefully about what they have seen and then to draw a picture of what they think is in the black box. Over the next several days, students bring pictures to share and set up possible systems to test, which are all displayed in a center with a sign that reads "How Does It Work?" Another center has reference books about the "insides" of all sorts of machines. Some students ask to build their own black boxes and set them up for their peers to figure out. Stories of inventions are shared, new inventions are proposed, and all are used to spark student writing.

Inquiry can spark student writing.

In sum, an initial problem provided the catalyst for a wide variety of learning experiences that might have been less effective if students had simply been assigned the text reading on machines. The inquiry into the problem and sufficient time to reflect on possible solutions, to discuss them, and to test hypotheses also presented a model for problem-solving. So did the teacher's refusal to open the black box. Throughout the year, even after the unit was over, students continued to construct possible machines to make the box work. Their continued reflection would have been shut off if the teacher had revealed a single "right" answer. Instead, he encouraged a form of speculation similar to that used by scholars investigating all manner of "black boxes"—human cognition, prehistory, and quarks, for instance.

In the foregoing example, the teacher introduced the problem and provided some of the data sources that students examined. The students then reflected on that data through discussion and the generation and testing of hypotheses. Such teacher-generated problems encourage students to engage in a wide variety of investigations that might not arise naturally in the classroom. It is important to note, however, that inquiry need not begin with a contrived problem. Students can use an inquiry approach to deal with a variety of problems. In one primary classroom, a classmate's playground accident led children to pose their own question: "How can we make a safer playground?" They decided what data they would need, organized to gather it, and worked together to interpret the results of their study. Finally, they presented a plan to the principal and worked on an implementation committee.

Both types of reflective inquiry encourage student interaction and can generate ideas for thematic units. They have the additional advantage of also providing a model that can be used in seeking solutions to other problems. The following ideas can be used to begin thematic units that are based on inquiry.

Begin with Children's Interests

As already noted in Chapter 3, children's interests can be used to inspire a thematic unit. Sometimes a vacation trip can spark interest in a study. One teacher sets up an interest center based on the seashells, sand, and seaweed brought back from a child's trip to the shore. She also arranges a selection of informational books, poetry, and fiction in the center. Among these resources, she places several cards with different questions for children to consider. The children then choose a line of inquiry, using the resources, and that starts the children on a LIFE IN AND NEAR THE WATER thematic unit.

Support inquiry with a variety of literary genres.

In another classroom, children become interested in a rhododendron branch that has been wilting in a corner. When they start asking questions about the dying plant, the teacher decides to use this interest as the beginning point for a WEB on the effect of water on living things. Students conduct experiments to chart changes caused by dehydration, they study the uses of dried plants, they measure plant growth, and so forth.

A butterfly cocoon brought into a third grade class has similar results, serving as the beginning point for the teacher's WEB. Throughout the thematic unit, children observe the cocoon and use reference books to help make inferences about what may emerge. The culminating activity of the unit includes the excitement of seeing the cocoon hatch, and then the ceremony accompanying the butterfly's release into the wild.

In each of these instances, children's ideas and interests provided a theme for further study and elaboration. The children's initiative generated interest and motivated in-depth inquiry around the original theme.

Begin with an Artifact

Another way to begin a thematic unit is to present students with an artifact or to use one brought in by a student or community member, so that curiosity is aroused and speculation begins. One teacher introduces a unit on Japan by gathering her class in a semicircle about her and pulling a wooden mask out of a bag. As the children pass the mask around the circle and peer through its oddly shaped eyes, the teacher asks students to share their observations. On small sheets of paper, the children then write a few lines—poetry for some, simple thought ramblings for others—about who this character might be. Several of these observations are shared, and then all are mounted and displayed with the mask. Next, the teacher records the students' questions about the mask on a large piece of paper. She then tells the children that she is going to share a book with them that comes from the same part of the world as the mask.

Record student questions on chart paper to encourage continued reference.

The teacher leads the class to discover a topic of interest by focusing children's attention on an unusual object and by maintaining its mystery while she draws children into another culture. Any artifact—from a fossil to a painting—can serve as the first step in implementing a thematic unit.

Begin with a Book

Literature is a rich source of ideas and starting points for thematic units. Another teacher uses Barbara Cooney's *Miss Rumphius,* for instance, to spark interest in a thematic unit on MAKING THE WORLD MORE BEAUTIFUL. In Cooney's book, little Alice Rumphius wants to travel to distant places and come home to a house by the sea. Her grandfather tells her that that is all very well but that the last, most difficult thing she must do is to make the world more beautiful. How Miss Rumphius manages to accomplish this last, most difficult thing leads to a discussion of the ways people have made the world more beautiful and of the ways in which people sometimes destroy the world's beauty. Following their discussion, the class takes a walking tour of the neighborhood to find evidence of both beautiful and ugly things. They return to share their findings in many ways, including plans for beautification projects and studies of art, architecture, gardens, music, and literature. They make a museum of beautiful things created by students—and on and on.

Cooney (1982)

Provide many opportunities for children to share their work with peers.

Begin with Drama

Creative dramatics, role-playing, and simulation can lead children to explore a theme by establishing a context for the investigation and a need for research. A fifth grade unit on AMERICA'S WESTWARD MOVEMENT begins when students are assigned the roles of family members on a New England farm who must decide whether to head for land in Kansas. To resolve the family conflict raised in the role-play, students need more information. They list some of the things they need to know: How much can they get for their present land? How much will the trip cost? How can they get to Kansas? What supplies will they need? Who else might be going? What crops can be grown there? Are there Indians already living on the land?

Clements, Tabachnik, & Fielder (1966)

These questions form the backdrop for organizing student inquiry and lead to the use of the computer simulation "Oregon," to questions about the politics of pioneering across times and places, and to exploration of the body of literature about pioneers. At different points throughout the unit, dramatic techniques are used to focus on such

Oregon Trail (1985)

issues as Native American rights, the power of the railroads and industry, establishment of free and slave states, and suffrage for women.

Empowering Teachers and Children

Each of the teachers described here assumed that one of a teacher's roles is that of motivator and facilitator of learning. Teachers in the classroom know both the curriculum and the children. They can link both in such a way that children are more likely to develop schemas for understanding the world, not just as it is in their immediate experience but as it was in the past, is in other places in the present, and could be in the future. The intent is to empower children by creating a learning environment in which content, process, and intellectual excitement are connected. By encouraging reflective inquiry, the processes of learning are not separated from the content learned. Instead, processes are linked to specific contents, or domains of knowledge. As children debate whether to move west, for instance, they use data sources specific to history—primary documents such as diaries or letters written by actual pioneers, or census information. To evaluate these sources, they learn such historical processes as cross-documentation. Is this information supported by other documentation? Are there documents that give a contrary point of view? Whose perspective is gained? Whose is missing?

Blake (1981); Shaftel & Shaftel (1982); Feshback (1975)

By role-playing or participating in a simulation, they also gain skill in perspective taking, an important element in developing historical as well as global understanding. As in the "black-box" experience, they practice careful observation, inference, making and testing hypotheses, and scientific speculation. In short, children learn research skills by using them as they were intended to be used—as a way to better understand the world. The prototypes that follow provide one way of looking at this process.

PROTOTYPES IN ACTION

The first steps are taken, the unit initiated, and then . . . what? Prototypes—excerpts from integrated language classrooms in action—provide an overview of what happens when teachers and children work together to explore themes and engage in the various activities that make up a school day. Eight prototypes offered in this chapter demonstrate the versatility and flexibility of this approach while spanning grade levels:

Prototype	Grade	Theme
1	K	SPACES
2	K	WASH AND WEAR
3	1	CHANGES
4	1	EXPLORATIONS
5	2	LET'S EAT
6	2/3	GIANTS
7	4/5	EXPLORATIONS
8	6	DIGGING UP THE PAST

There are samples taken from self-contained, family-grouped, and departmentalized settings, from thematic units that begin in different ways, and from teachers with very different styles for engaging children.

Each of the eight prototypes contains five parts:

* A WEB demonstrating the range of choices available to the teacher(s) and students.
* A schedule demonstrating how time is used in the classroom.
* An "Into the Classroom" component that follows children and teacher(s) through one entire day and portions of two other days.

* A summary pointing out particular features of the prototype.
* A bibliography of books and resources that are referred to in the WEB in each prototype.

What to Look for in Prototypes— Tips on How to Read Them

The prototypes are provided in a chronological order. There are some advantages in reading all the prototypes in the order they have been presented. It enables you to compare and contrast the various features illustrating different prototypes, and you can better observe and abstract developmental characteristics. However, the prototypes have been written so that you can skip around to read individual prototypes by focusing on a particular grade level, a certain classroom feature (e.g., family grouping or departmentalization), or a specific theme.

It is important to point out two features ahead of time so that you can read the prototypes more easily. First, the information in the component called "Into the Classroom" is presented in tables with two columns. The first column, "Children," describes the activities that children are engaged in, according to the time allotments depicted in the "Schedule" section of that prototype. The second column, "Teacher," then highlights teacher roles, showing what the teacher does during children's activities at the same periods.

The second point is that various classroom routines such as Comparison Charts*, Sustained Silent Reading (SSR)*, Big Books*, and so on, which are mentioned in these tables and elsewhere, may be unfamiliar to you. These routines are those that are marked with an asterisk (e.g., Big Books*). The asterisk means that the routine so marked is explained in more detail in Chapter 8, the how-to chapter.

Prototype 1: Half-Day Kindergarten—Spaces

SPATIAL RELATIONS

Movement exploration, bubble gum bubble, other activities.
Buried body, bottomless bottles, video viewing, the gate game, and other games
WHERE'S SPOT?
LOOK OUT HE'S BEHIND YOU
GUINEA PIGS FAR AND NEAR
INSIDE, OUTSIDE, UPSIDE DOWN
SNAKE IN SNAKE OUT
BECCA BACKWARD, BECCA FRONTWARD
BIG AND LITTLE
BIG WORLD, SMALL WORLD
FROM WHERE YOU ARE
Look at things from different perspectives. Describe them.
Label classroom locations.
Plan an obstacle course and map it. Tell directions for getting through it successfully.
Dance the Hokey Pokey.

YOUR OWN SPACE

A PLACE FOR BEN
EVAN'S CORNER
Write a letter inviting a friend to visit your special place.
Measure your place.
SOPHIE'S HIDEAWAY
YOUR OWN BEST SECRET PLACE
SECRET PLACES
"Solitude"
Draw a picture of a secret place.
Make a list of things to keep in your secret place.
Write a poem about your secret place.

CROWDED SPACES

MR. GUMPY'S MOTOR CAR
MR. GUMPY'S OUTING
MUSHROOM IN THE RAIN
WHO SANK THE BOAT?
TROUBLE IN THE ARK
HOW MANY ARE IN THIS OLD CAR?
IT COULD ALWAYS BE WORSE
SHEEP IN A JEEP
MILLIONS OF CATS
ALWAYS ROOM FOR ONE MORE
"The Old Woman Who Lived in a Shoe"
How many is too many? Count the characters in each story. Compare the numbers. Show the different sets on a graph. Which story had the most characters? The least?
Make a mural of crowded stories.
Make a clay model.
Act out one of the stories.
Find out which story your classmates like best.
"I Know an Old Lady Who Swallowed a Fly"
Make up new verses to the song.

INSIDE SPACES

ALFIE GETS IN FIRST
THE CAT IN THE HAT
I UNPACKED MY GRANDMOTHER'S TRUNK
Play the unpacking game.
WHAT'S INSIDE THE BOX?
Hide something in a box. Have others guess what's inside.
THE INSIDE-OUTSIDE BOOK OF NEW YORK CITY
THE INSIDE-OUTSIDE BOOK OF WASHINGTON, D.C.
THE HOUSE FROM MORNING TO NIGHT
Draw your house inside and out.
Play with a doll house.
Make a list of things you find inside and things you find outside.
THE WILD INSIDE
A HOUSE IS A HOUSE FOR ME
Think up other houses for things.
Make a tent. Play inside.

ANIMALS INSIDE

SNAIL IN THE WOODS
THE SNAIL'S SPELL
INSIDE TURTLE'S SHELL
TURTLE AND SNAIL
TURTLE WATCH
Pretend you are an animal that lives inside something. Tell what it is like.
Why do some animals need protective shells?
Make a hermit crab home in a glass aquarium.

INSIDE LIVING THINGS

A BOOK ABOUT YOUR SKELETON
SKELETON
THE SKELETON INSIDE YOU
THE SKELETON BOOK: AN INSIDE LOOK AT ANIMALS
DINOSAUR BONES
A CAT'S BODY
Invite a doctor or a vet to show you X-rays.
Have a classmate trace your body on large brown paper. Draw what you think your X-ray would look like.

OVER, UNDER, AND THROUGH

On a water and sand table, play with pipe constructions, observing water run through and come out.
OVER, UNDER AND THROUGH AND OTHER SPATIAL CONCEPTS
OVER, UNDER AND ALL AROUND
TUNNELS
Make an obstacle course.

THE VERY HUNGRY CATERPILLAR
ACROSS THE STREAM
OVER IN THE MEADOW
"The Bear Went Over the Mountain"
TEN IN A BED
"Roll Over, Roll Over"
Sing the songs. Make up new verses.
ROSIE'S WALK
Play hide and go seek. Tell whether you hid under, over, behind, or inside something.

Figure 4.1

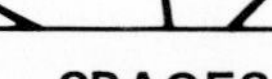

IT'S DARK INSIDE

A DARK DARK TALE
IN A DARK DARK HOUSE
Make pictures for a big book.
Retell the story. Use sound effects.
THE FAT CAT
THE TERRIBLE TIGER
THE GREEDY PYTHON
Play with nesting dolls.
Make a sock puppet. Have the puppet eat all the characters in the story.
WHAT'S HATCHING OUT OF THAT EGG?
Make a classroom incubator. Keep a calendar of observations.

UNDERNEATH SPACES

UNDERGROUND
CHIPMUNK SONG
THE HIDDEN WORLD: LIFE UNDER A ROCK
HOW TO DIG A HOLE TO THE OTHER SIDE OF THE EARTH
Pretend you are in a space ship or a submarine. Radio back to the surface and tell what you see or how you are feeling.
THERE'S AN ALLIGATOR UNDER MY BED
What hides under <u>your</u> bed?
THE THREE BILLY GOATS GRUFF
Build a bridge for the ogre. Tell the story from the ogre's point of view.

OUTSIDE SPACES

SPOT'S FIRST WALK
Pretend to be Spot. Look behind, go through, and look under things.
THE PARK BOOK
PLAYGROUND
IN MY GARDEN
MY BACKYARD
Visit an outdoor place. Tell what you see. How is it different from indoors?
OUTSIDE OVER THERE
Recreate the story in pantomime as the teacher reads aloud.

UP ABOVE SPACES

HIGHER ON THE DOOR
HOW HIGH IS UP?
UP GOES THE SKYSCRAPER
SKYSCRAPER GOING UP
A GREAT DAY FOR UP
UP AND UP
UP, UP AND AWAY
ON TOP
THE CROSS COUNTRY CAT
Pretend you are taking a balloon ride. Tell how the world looks from above.
BLOWN SKY HIGH
THE EMPEROR AND THE KITE
THE DRAGON KITE
Make a kite and have a kite flying festival.
THE TURNAROUND WIND
Draw "turnaround" people.
THE CLOUD BOOK
Make a chart of different kinds of clouds.
DREAMS
Imagine what shapes and creatures you see in the clouds. Make them in soft sculpture.
SKY SONGS
SPACE SONGS
Read other space poetry.

OUTER SPACE

A SPACE STORY
Interview an astronaut. Design a mission patch for your class.
EARTH, OUR PLANET IN SPACE
THE PLANETS IN OUR SOLAR SYSTEM
Compare the number of laps it takes to reach each planet.
Make a solar system on your own football field.
Learn planet order chart.
Use vegetables and dried beans as models for planets.
WHAT THE MOON IS LIKE
THE MOON
LET'S FIND OUT ABOUT THE MOON
Play "moon buggy."
JOURNEY INTO A BLACK HOLE
Plan a space mission, make props, and blast off. Tell about your trip when you return.
Dress up in many layers of clothes. Why do astronauts need so much protection? How does it feel to move?
ROCKETS AND SATELLITES
Watch "The Secret City." Build a classroom space lab.
LET'S FIND OUT ABOUT THE SUN
COMETS
LOOK INTO THE NIGHT SKY
THE SKY IF FULL OF STARS
Make star viewers. List the steps it took.
THE LEGEND OF THE MILKY WAY
HER SEVEN BROTHERS
Compare stories.
IS THERE LIFE IN OUTER SPACE?
SPACE CASE
Interview the alien for TV. Find out how it feels to be on another planet far from home.
Write secret messages from the alien to its spaceship.

Schedule

The SPACES thematic unit is a half-day kindergarten, a time frame typical of many school districts around the country. Beth Busch's classroom is self-contained and organized into centers. There is a large open area for creative dramatics, dance, music, and reading. There is a library filled with books and comfortable places to read. Many of the books are on shelves, but many more are displayed cover forward on wooden racks or tables or are lined up along the floor where children have easy access to them. There is an art corner with a sink, supply cupboards, table, and several easels. A building or construction corner with large wooden blocks, a playhouse made out of plastic pipes, and sand and water tables provide many opportunities for dramatic play and scientific exploration. The classroom looks like a place where exciting things are happening. The children's art work, writing, and projects, their shared and dictated writing are displayed in every available space.

The thematic unit on SPACES began because Beth wanted to develop a unit that would allow her five- and six-year-olds to explore the world around them and their relationships to it, particularly in terms of spatial relationships. She felt that an understanding of different perspectives and the concepts relating to spatial relationships are important in language, mathematics, science, and geography, as well as for social development. The theme of SPACES also enabled her to capitalize on children's fascination with outer space and gave many opportunities for dramatic play.

As Beth's planning developed, she also began to think about "inner" spaces such as hiding places, spooky houses, tunnels, and submarines. As Beth looked through several of the indexes to children's books, she found other titles that helped her further develop categories for the WEB. Many of the print materials, songs, and finger plays were chosen because they included and often repeated words such as *in, into, inside, out, behind, in front of, above, below, under, over, through, high, low, up, down, bottom,* and *top.*

Activities were planned to give children occasions to explore these relationships at firsthand, to use the words orally in meaningful ways, and to see these words in print. *Dinosaur Bones* by Aliki, a book featured in a library display, opened up another category of "Inside Spaces"—those inside animals and inside animal eggs. Eventually the hatching of baby chicks from a classroom incubator provided the children with one of the most rewarding experiences of the entire year because it helped them to take on the perspective of another living thing when they tried to imagine what it is like to live inside an egg.

Table 4.1 shows a typical weekly plan for Beth's half-day program. The outdoor time is often used for free play, but during this unit Beth sometimes planned more focused activities—trips to a municipal park and other special community spaces, obstacle courses, and solar system walks, for example. The presence of an aide and frequent parent and other family volunteers allows Beth to work regularly with individual children or small groups.

Into the Classroom

The unit began with a favorite song and dance, "The Hokey Pokey." This and other songs that incorporate movement ("The Bear Went over the Mountain," "Roll Over, Roll Over," and "Put Your Hands up on Your Head") were an ideal beginning point for active kindergarteners and gave them concrete experiences for talking about directional and spatial terms. In the ensuing weeks, the children had a variety of experiences that helped them further explore and refine their understanding of spatial relationships, their own space and that of others. These experiences provided them with a range of perspectives for looking at and talking about their worlds.

The children enjoyed the building that went on in the block corner. A space ship, submarines, and space stations were planned for and constructed so that they could "live in" these places through their imagination. They were busy engaged in the experiments and activities occurring at the sand and water tables and in the constructive

TABLE 4.1 Weekly Schedule, Beth Busch's Half-Day Kindergarten

Time	Monday	Tuesday	Wednesday	Thursday	Friday
8:00	Arrival				
8:10	Center. Teacher reads books or tells story, leads singing or finger play. Children prepare to go to activities.				
8:30	Activity time. Water or sand table, building, library, art, or writing corner. Teacher works with small groups or individuals.				
9:40	Snack time				
9:50	Outdoor play	Obstacle course	Walk to local park	Solar system race	Outdoor play
10:35	Activity time. Book reading, Big Book*, or shared writing activities with small or large groups. Children working with teacher or in centers.				
11:35	Clean-up and evaluation				
11:55	Dismissal				

play that these experiences promoted. They laughed at the antics of the characters in "crowded" stories, stories in which too many characteristics gathered in too small a space, and they delighted in acting out these situations or writing their own versions. They liked finding out about animals and insects that lived inside something or underground. Joanne Ryder's stories, *The Snail's Spell* and *Chipmunk Song,* were particularly good in helping children visualize the world from the perspective of the animal, and Mary Ann Hoberman's delightful poem *A House Is a House for Me* (p. 67) gave children new ways to think about things that contain other things. Children also enjoyed the delicious scariness of such stories as *A Dark Dark Tale* and frequently retold or acted these out. They were also intrigued with seeing normally scary skeletons in a new light when local veterinarians and doctors visited to show X rays of animal and human skeletons.

Beth wove these activities throughout the unit, but she also planned them in such a way that children moved from more familiar experiences to more unfamiliar, difficult concepts. The full descriptions of Day 1 and of portions of Days 4 and 15 in Table 4.2 illustrate how carefully Beth orchestrated these experiences for her children. You can see how the outer space activities and books were planned to occur at the end of the unit so that children could become more familiar with spatial concepts and orientation in their immediate environment before they had to deal with those on a more distant plane. Note also how responsive Beth was to the needs and interests of the children during these activities.

Summary

Children learn through play and active participation.

Beth's classroom is a place where children have the opportunity to be children and to explore their environments and spaces in ways that make sense to them. She believes that the kindergarten is a place where children learn best through play and through active participation rather than through teacher-directed formal lessons. To this end, Beth is a facilitator. She observes carefully and listens closely, trying to understand how it is that her students are constructing knowledge. Then she attempts to respond to what they are trying to do. She demonstrates and collaborates as a fellow—and more experienced—learner. The language that accompanies children's experiences involves and engages them in many language modes and registers. Beth believes that they are already readers and writers when they enter her classroom, so she gives them many opportunities to use written language in natural, authentic ways. As they share reading and writing with each other and with other adults, they are thus able to refine and further build on the emergent literacy understandings that had been developed before they came to school.

TABLE 4.2 Detailed Schedule, Half-Day Kindergarten

DAY 1 (SPACES)

Time	Children	Teacher
TEACHER ARRIVAL 7:30		Beth and Sandy, her aide, arrive to set up new centers, take care of paperwork.
CHILDREN ARRIVE 8:00	Children come in; put away. Many move to centers. Some go to talk to Beth or Sandy.	Beth greets the children, talking informally with several.
CENTER 8:10	The children gather in the open areas of the classroom.	
	Some children have trouble sorting right from left. All enjoy the active movement.	Beth leads the children in a favorite dance, "The Hokey Pokey." She observes children's sense of direction, knowledge of body parts, and spatial orientation. The activity gives her a good idea of children's strengths. She encourages children to watch her if they get confused. After they have sung the song several times, Beth invites them to sit on the rug. She asks them to recall the action of the game. Where did they put their hands, legs, and so on?
	Several children remember "in," "out," and, "all about."	
	Children respond with chairs, desks, TVs, people, pets for inside; cars, trees, grass, flowers, birds for outside.	Beth asks them to think of other things that are inside and outside. As they volunteer ideas, she makes a list on a large sheet of chart paper divided into two columns. She reads each word as she writes it.
	One child knows that birds can be found inside and outside because he has a pet parakeet. Others recall their pet dog or cat that goes outside.	She then asks children if there are some things found both inside and outside. She reads back through the list pointing to each word and reading it. "Could we find birds inside and outside?" When the children respond "yes," she marks it with a star.
	The children are unsure about this concept.	She explains that inside and outside are names we give to spaces. "What other names do we have for spaces?" she asks. She prompts children by asking about birds. "Where are spaces birds might be?"
	The child with the pet parakeet replies, "In a cage." Another child says outdoors. "Up in a tree," "In the sky," "On the ground," volunteer others.	"Where outdoors?" Beth asks.
		Beth responds, "*Up in* the tree, *down on* the ground. These are words that tell about places and spaces. We're going to start a unit today that's all about spaces. We'll find out about spaces that are inside and outside, up above and down under, over and through and *all about*."
	"All about" says one child. "That's where we shook all about."	"Who can think of some special spaces right here in our classroom?"
	The children name the block corner, art corner, housekeeping corner.	Beth explains that for the next several weeks they will find

many activities in these centers that will help them explore many different spaces. She suggests that this morning, the block corner may be a good place to build a space ship to go to outer space. She has set up a special activity at the sand table and a game called "the gate game" at another center. She points out several books that show insides and outsides and sets them in the reading corner. After children have looked at these, they may want to draw pictures of their houses inside and outside, or play with the dollhouse she has brought in. She asks each child what he or she plans to do during activity time. She reminds four children that they are helpers during snack time.

ACTIVITY TIME 8:45

Children move to centers. Four children enthusiastically enter the building center and begin to pull out blocks to build a space ship. They exchange suggestions for how big and how long it ought to be. One child begins to make blast-off noises as he puts bricks together. Other children are in the reading center looking at Roxie Munro's "Inside, Outside," books about New York City and Washington, DC. Two children reading together begin to chant "inside, outside" as they turn the pages. Another child is excited by the skeleton views of a large house in *The House from Morning to Night.* She takes it to the children who are playing with the doll house to show them the different rooms. Several children play the "gate" game. They soon realize that to roll a ball through cardboard gates or arches, to knock over the objects placed there, they have to reposition their bodies in space.

Beth's aide, Sandy, stands by to reposition objects behind the arches each time they are knocked down. She purposefully moves the objects so that the children have to move their bodies to aim at the objects. She helps the children articulate what they are doing.

Some of the children were intrigued by the activity at the sand table and moved to play at that center.

Beth joins the children at the sand table and tells them she is going to dig down deep. Beth asks Michelle what she has found.

Several children begin to imitate Beth, and one uncovers a paper drawing. Michelle is not sure at first what is under the sand, and a friend helps her move more sand away. They discover a hand. One child guesses that the bottom of the table is under the sand. Others begin to move sand away from the paper hand. Eventually the children uncover a life-size doll.

Beth asks the children what they think is under the sand.

Beth talks with the children as they make predictions about what they are doing and uses words like "covered over," "under," "bottom," "top." She asks the children what the doll might be able to see.

Several children think the doll is looking at them. Another puts his

(Continued on next page.)

TABLE 4.2—Continued

DAY 1 (SPACES) Time	Children	Teacher
	head down near the doll's and looks up at the ceiling.	
9:25	Four children move to help prepare snacks. Each child counts out snacks for six children.	Sandy takes out Fig Newtons, peanuts in shells, and olives. She asks the children what is inside each of the snacks.
SNACK TIME 9:40	Children enjoy eating snacks and begin to name other foods that have something inside. They then expand to talking about foods with outsides, like apples with skin or sandwiches with bread outside.	Beth and Sandy help the children think about insides and outsides of food.
OUTDOOR PLAY TIME 9:50	Children enter into the imaginary bubbles and move carefully to Beth's directions.	Beth takes the first part of outdoor time to do some movement exploration. She asks the children to crouch down on the ground and imagine they are chewing a big piece of bubble gum. They are then to imagine that they blow a gigantic bubble and step inside it. Once inside, they can gently touch the inside of their bubbles. Then she tells them that they can move slowly to the right but that their bubble cannot touch anyone else's bubble or it will burst. She leads them in various movements inside their bubbles. If anyone bumps, he or she must leave the group.
ACTIVITY TIME 10:30	The children enjoy chiming in and predicting where the snake will go next. Some of the children want to play snake.	Beth reads *Snake In, Snake Out.*
	Children enjoy being leader and followers.	Beth helps the children to line up and hold each other's waists so that the line is like a snake. She then gives children directions in a "Simon says" manner. "Snake go around the art table. Snake go through the reading center. Snake step over the block bridge." She then invites children to take turns at giving directions to the snake.
		When the game is finished, Beth asks the children to help her label positions in the classroom. She writes out oak tag labels with words "under," "over," "up," "down," "front," "back," and gives them to children to place around the room.
	Several children have trouble with some of the positions like "front" and "back." A lively discussion ensues.	Beth is interested in the children's thinking. This will give her insights into the ensuing activities she plans.
CLEAN-UP AND	Children clean up centers and put away materials.	Beth asks children to think about more inside/outside things and

EVALUATION 11:35		foods for tomorrow. She ends by leading the children in a favorite song, "I Know an Old Lady Who Swallowed a Spider."

DAY 4

Time	Children	Teacher
OUTDOOR PLAY 9:50		Beth and the P.E. teacher have set up an obstacle course on the playground using old tires and the standard playground equipment. She walks children through the course verbally,
	Children proceed through the obstacle course one by one. When they have finished, they ask to do it again.	telling them to step into the first tire, run around the tire tower, crawl under the cargo net, climb up the ladder, and slide down the slide. She, her aide, and the P.E. teacher station themselves along the course. All give directions to the children.
		After the children have completed the race several times, Beth asks different children to serve as leader and give directions.
ACTIVITY TIME 10:30	Children work in centers with activities begun earlier in the week. In addition, several children have taken a large cardboard box and decorated it as a car. They are acting out *Mr. Grumpy's Motor Car.* In the reading center, children are playing school with a Big Book* version of *Where's Spot?* The teacher has printed the words and glued flaps over the hidden animals, and the children have created the pictures.	
		Beth works with a small group to write a version of a song they learned the previous day, "The Bear Went Over the Mountain."
	The children decide they want the bear to change directions in their version. They suggest that he go under a bridge, climb up a tree, and run into a cave.	
		Beth makes the process of composition explicit. She tells the children where she would begin writing and says each word as she writes it on a large sheet of oak tag. She stops to ask the children's opinion about word choices and reminds them of the pattern of the original song. She suggests they add adjectives so that their sentences better fit the rhythm of the song ("the bear ran into a dark cave"). She writes each verse on a separate sheet of oak tag and gives pairs of children verses to illustrate.

(Continued on next page.)

TABLE 4.2—Continued

DAY 4

Time	Children	Teacher
	Several children have difficulty remembering which verse they are to illustrate.	Beth asks if there are any clues to help them figure out the words.
	Susan remembers the labels they placed around the room. She can match up the label with a word in the written text. She knows the order of the words they composed and can match the words in her head to the words on the page until she comes to the word "under." "The bear went . . . ." She and Richard look at the labels and find the same word on a label under the table. Richard looks at the word "under." "There's an 'R' there," he points out. "That's in my name."	Beth asks if they had any other clues.

DAY 15 (SPACES)

Time	Children	Teacher
ACTIVITY TIME 8:30	The children are working in centers. Several are creating a collage mural of crowded story characters. Others are busy decorating kites. Some are building a space station in the block corner. In an open area, three children are playing with a moon buggy. The buggy has a large seat, a metal frame, and casters that rotate. The children are seated facing outward and have to cooperate to get the buggy to move in any one direction. They have decorated the buggy with tin foil, flags, and "antennas" and are wearing space paraphernalia they have made.	Beth moves from group to group. Beth's aide works with the group to help them understand how to move the vehicle.
SNACK TIME 9:40	The children are intrigued by the sizes of the objects. They seem to have trouble with the representations of large sizes with small objects.	Beth has set out a "Solar System" salad. A dried pea represents the moon, a fresh pea is Pluto, walnuts represent the Earth and Venus. Beans stand for Mars and Mercury and cabbages for Jupiter and Saturn. An orange stands for Neptune and a small grapefruit for Uranus. She places them in order on the snack table then serves children a mixture cut up earlier. Beth suggests they think about the dollhouse and the smaller scale of objects and people. She suggests that the children look at several of the information books in the library, especially *The Planets in Our Solar System.*

OUTDOOR PLAY
9:50

Beth selects children to represent the inner planets. She hangs a name and picture label on each child and gives them the appropriate vegetable, fruit, or nut from the snack table. She then leads the children to the school track. The aide has placed planet signs around the track at intervals that correspond to miles in the solar system. She helps children find their stations.

Terrestrial planet children (Mars, Venus, Mercury, and Earth) match their name cards to the signs on the track.

Beth asks the children to imagine they are on a journey from Earth to all the planets in the solar system. She then leads them on a walk around the track where a yard equals 211,265 miles. Imagining that the beginning is the sun, they will have to walk 2/5 of a lap to reach Mercury, 3/4 of a lap to reach Venus, 1 lap to reach Earth, and 1 1/2 laps to get to Mars. The journey to the outer planets would require many more laps: 5 1/2 laps to get to Jupiter, 9 1/2 laps to Saturn, 19 1/5 to get to Uranus, 30 laps to Neptune, and 39 2/5 to Pluto. She suggests that bicycles might be needed to complete the rest of the journey.

The children enjoy imagining that they are on space ships as they "walk" the solar system.

The children who have been planets want to take the walk, too. They place their fruit at the foot of the planet sign and join the aide in a walk of their own.

Several children who live near the school volunteer to bring their bikes tomorrow so they can complete the solar system trip.

Beth agrees to set up signs for the outer planets on the following day and help the children count off laps.

Children's Literature, SPACES

ABOVE AND BELOW STAIRS by J. Goodall. Atheneum, 1983.

ACROSS THE STREAM by M. Ginsburg. Illustrated by N. Tafuri. Greenwillow, 1982.

ALFIE GETS IN FIRST by S. Hughes. Morrow, 1981.

ALWAYS ROOM FOR ONE MORE by S. N. Leodhas. Illustrated by N. Hogrogian. Holt, 1965.

"The Bear Went Over the Mountain" in IF YOU'RE HAPPY AND YOU KNOW IT: EIGHTEEN STORY SONGS SET TO PICTURES by N. Weiss. Greenwillow, 1987.

BECCA BACKWARD, BECCA FRONTWARD: A BOOK OF CONCEPT PAIRS by B. McMillan. Lothrop, 1986.

BIG AND LITTLE: A BEGINNING CONCEPT BOOK by J. Satchwen. Random House, 1984.

BIG WORLD, SMALL WORLD by J. Titherington. Greenwillow, 1985.

BLOWN SKY HIGH: KITES FOR THE CLASSROOM by M. Greger. Illustrated by J. Slattery. Logan Grove Press, 1977.

"Boa Constrictor" in WHERE THE SIDE WALK ENDS by S. Silverstein. Harper & Row, 1974.

A BOOK ABOUT YOUR SKELETON by R. B. Gross. Illustrated by D. Robinson. Hastings House, 1979.

THE CAT IN THE HAT by T. Geisel (Dr. Seuss). Random House, 1957.

A CAT'S BODY by J. Cole. Photographs by J. Wexler. Morrow, 1982.

CHIPMUNK SONG by J. Ryder. Dutton/Lodestar, 1987.

THE CLOUD BOOK by T. de Paola. Holiday, 1984.

COMETS by F. M. Branley. Illustrated by G. Maestro. Crowell, 1984.

CROSS-COUNTRY CAT by M. Calhoun. Illustrated by E. Ingraham. Morrow, 1979.

A DARK DARK TALE by R. Brown. Dial, 1983.

DINOSAUR BONES by Aliki. Harper & Row, 1988.

THE DRAGON KITE by N. Luenn. Illustrated by M. Hague. Harcourt Brace Jovanovich, 1982.

DREAMS by P. Spier. Doubleday, 1986.

EARTH, OUR PLANET IN SPACE by S. Simon. Four Winds, 1984.

THE EMPEROR AND THE KITE by J. Yolen. Illustrated by E. Young. Philomel, 1988.

EVAN'S CORNER by E. S. Hill. Illustrated by N. Grossman. Holt, 1967.

FANCY THAT by P. Allen. Orchard, 1988.

THE FAT CAT: A DANISH FOLKTALE by J. Kent. Parents, 1971.

FROM WHERE YOU ARE by J. Wakefield. Illustrated by T. Dunnington. Children's Press, 1978.

A GREAT DAY FOR UP by T. Geisel (Dr. Seuss). Random House, 1974.

THE GREEDY PYTHON by R. Buckley. Illustrated by E. Carle. Picture Book Studio, 1985.

GUINEA PIGS NEAR AND FAR by K. Duke. Dutton, 1984.

HER SEVEN BROTHERS by P. Goble. Bradbury, 1988.

THE HIDDEN WORLD: LIFE UNDER A ROCK by L. Pringle. Macmillan, 1977.

THE HOUSE FROM MORNING TO NIGHT by D. Bour. Kane Miller, 1985.

A HOUSE IS A HOUSE FOR ME by M. A. Hoberman. Illustrated by B. Fraser. Viking, 1978.

HOW HIGH IS UP? by B. Kohn. Illustrated by J. Pyk. Putnam, 1971.

HOW MANY IN THIS OLD CAR?: A COUNTING BOOK by C. and J. Hawkins. Putnam, 1988.

HOW TO DIG A HOLE TO THE OTHER SIDE OF THE EARTH by F. McNulty. Illustrated by M. Simont. Harper & Row, 1979.

I KNOW AN OLD LADY WHO SWALLOWED A FLY. Adapted by N. Bernard. Joy Street, 1981.

I UNPACKED MY GRANDMOTHER'S TRUNK by S. R. Hoguet. Dutton, 1983.

IN A DARK DARK ROOM by A. Schwartz. Illustrated by D. Zimmer. Harper & Row, 1984.

IN MY GARDEN by R. Maris. Greenwillow, 1987.

THE INSIDE OUTSIDE BOOK OF NEW YORK CITY by R. Munro. Dodd, Mead, 1985.

THE INSIDE OUTSIDE BOOK OF WASHINGTON, D.C. by R. Munro. Dodd, Mead, 1987.

INSIDE OUTSIDE UPSIDE DOWN by S. and J. Berenstain. Random House, 1968.

INSIDE TURTLE'S SHELL by J. Ryder. Illustrated by S. Bonners. Macmillan, 1985.

IS THERE LIFE IN OUTER SPACE? by F. M. Branley. Illustrated by D. Madden. Crowell, 1984.

IT COULD ALWAYS BE WORSE by M. Zemach. Farrar, Straus & Giroux, 1976.

JOURNEY INTO A BLACK HOLE by F. M. Branley. Illustrated by M. Simont. Crowell, 1986.

THE LEGEND OF THE MILKY WAY. Retold by J. M. Lee. Holt, Rinehart and Winston, 1982.

LET'S FIND OUT ABOUT THE MOON by C. and M. Shapp. Illustrated by S. Later. Franklin Watts/Random House Sound Film Strip.

LET'S FIND OUT ABOUT THE SUN by M. and C. Shapp. Illustrated by S. Later. Franklin Watts/Random House Sound Film Strip.

LOOK OUT, HE'S BEHIND YOU by T. Bradman. Illustrated by M. Chamberlain. Putnam, 1988.

LOOK TO THE NIGHT SKY: AN INTRODUCTION TO STAR WATCHING by S. Simon. Viking, 1977.

MILLIONS OF CATS by W. Gag. Putnam, 1928, 1988.

THE MOON by S. Simon. Macmillan, 1984.

MR. GUMPY'S MOTOR CAR by J. Burningham. Crowell, 1973.

MR. GUMPY'S OUTING by J. Burningham. Holt, Rinehart and Winston, 1970.

MUSHROOM IN THE RAIN by M. Ginsberg. Illustrated by J. Aruego and A. Dewey. Macmillan, 1974.

MY BACKYARD by A. and H. Rockwell. Macmillan, 1981.

ON TOP by M. MacGregor. Morrow, 1988.

OUT AND ABOUT by S. Hughes. Lothrop, 1988.

OUTSIDE OVER THERE by M. Sendak. Harper & Row, 1981.

OVER, UNDER AND ALL AROUND: RELATIONSHIPS IN SPACE by S. Tester. Child's World, 1977.

OVER IN THE MEADOW by E. J. Keats. Scholastic, 1971.

OVER, UNDER AND THROUGH by T. Hoban. Macmillan, 1973.

THE PARK BOOK by C. Zolotow. Illustrated by H. A. Rey. Harper, 1944, 1972.

A PLACE FOR BEN by J. Titherington. Greenwillow, 1987.

THE PLANETS IN OUR SOLAR SYSTEM by F. M. Branley. Illustrated by D. Madden. Crowell, 1981.

PLAYGROUND by G. Gibbons. Holiday, 1985.

ROCKETS AND SATELLITES by F. M. Branley. Illustrated by G. Maestro. Crowell, 1987.

"Roll Over, Roll Over" in IF YOU'RE HAPPY AND YOU KNOW IT: EIGHTEEN STORY SONGS SET TO PICTURES by N. Weiss. Greenwillow, 1987.

ROSIE'S WALK by P. Hutchins. Macmillan, 1968.

SECRET PLACES by B. Brodsky. Lippincott, 1979.

SHEEP IN A JEEP by N. Shaw. Illustrated by M. Apple. Houghton Mifflin, 1986.

SKELETON by S. Parker. Knopf, 1988.

THE SKELETON BOOK: AN INSIDE LOOK AT ANIMALS by M. Livaudis and R. Dunne. Walker and Co., 1972.

THE SKELETON INSIDE YOU by P. Balestrino. Illustrated by T. Kelley. Crowell, 1989.

THE SKY IS FULL OF STARS by F. M. Branley. Crowell, 1981.

SKY SONGS by M. C. Livingston. Illustrated by L. E. Fisher. Holiday, 1984.

SKYSCRAPER GOING UP by V. Cobb. Illustrated by J. Strejan. Crowell, 1987.

SNAIL IN THE WOODS by J. Ryder and H. S. Feinberg. Illustrated by J. Polseno. Harper & Row, 1979.

THE SNAIL'S SPELL by J. Ryder. Illustrated by L. Cherry. Frederick Warne, 1982.

SNAKE IN, SNAKE OUT by L. Banchek. Crowell, 1978.

SOPHIE'S HIDEAWAY by R. Kozikowski. Harper & Row, 1983.

SPACE CASE by J. Marshall. Dial, 1980.

SPACE SONGS by M. C. Livingston. Illustrated by L. E. Fisher. Holiday House, 1988.

A SPACE STORY by K. Kuskin. Illustrated by M. Simont. Harper & Row, 1978.

SPOT'S FIRST WALK by E. Hill. Putnam, 1981.

TEN IN A BED by M. Rees. Joy Street, 1988.

THE TERRIBLE TIGER by J. Prelutsky. Illustrated by A. Lobel. Macmillan, 1970.

THERE'S AN ALLIGATOR UNDER MY BED by M. Mayer. Dial, 1987.

THE THREE BILLY GOATS GRUFF by P. C. Asbjornsen and J. E. Moe. Illustrated by M. Brown. Harcourt, 1957.

TROUBLE IN THE ARK by G. Rose. Bodley Head, 1985.

TUNNELS by G. Gibbons. Holiday, 1984.

THE TURNAROUND WIND by A. Lobel. Harper & Row, 1988.

TURTLE AND SNAIL by Z. O'Neal. Illustrated by M. Tomes. Lippincott, 1979.

TURTLE WATCH by G. Ancona. Macmillan, 1987.

UNDERGROUND by D. Macauley. Houghton Mifflin, 1976.

UP AND UP by S. Hughes. Lothrop, 1979.

UP GOES THE SKYSCRAPER by G. Gibbons. Four Winds, 1986.

UP, UP AND AWAY by M. Hillert. Follett, 1982.

THE VERY HUNGRY CATERPILLAR by E. Carle. Philomel, 1983.

WHAT THE MOON IS LIKE by F. M. Branley. Illustrated by T. Kelley. Crowell, 1986.

WHAT'S HATCHING OUT OF THAT EGG? by P. Lauber. Crown, 1979.

WHAT'S INSIDE THE BOX? by E. and L. Kessler. Dodd, Mead, 1976.

WHERE'S SPOT? by E. Hill. Putnam, 1980.

WHO SANK THE BOAT? by P. Allen. Putnam, 1985.

THE WILD INSIDE; SIERRA CLUB'S GUIDE TO THE GREAT INDOORS by L. Allison. Sierra Club/Little, Brown, 1988.

YOUR OWN BEST SECRET PLACE by B. Baylor. Illustrated by P. Parnall. Scribner, 1979.

Prototype 2: All-Day Kindergarten—Wash and Wear

MAKING CLOTHES

THE CRANE WIFE
DAWN
"Arachne"
Resource People
weaver with small hand loom
spinner and spinning wheel
garment factory visit
THE WEAVER'S GIFT
PICKING AND WEAVING

Sewing Center
toy sewing machines and small looms
Make potholders.

RUMPLESTILSKIN
DUFFY AND THE DEVIL
Make hand puppets.
Present a puppet show.
JENNY'S HAT
Make hats with paper plates and found materials.

NATURAL FIBERS

CHARLIE NEEDS A CLOAK
WOOL GATHERING: SHEEP RAISING IN OLD NEW ENGLAND
THE STORY OF WOOL
Learning Center
Match samples of cloth to their raw form and then to pictures of their origin. Include wool, cotton, linen, silk, raw wool, raw cotton, flax (available from a florist), silk cocoon.
Invite someone with a knowledge of textiles to talk about fibers for different climates.

SELLING CLOTHES

GENERAL STORE
THE STORE KEEPER
DEPARTMENT STORE
Visit a department store, and draw a map of the store.
Measure the sizes of clothing, hats, shoes.
Create a classroom store
collect old clothes, price them, and play store.
ON MARKET STREET
Create a collage of unusual clothing.

WASH AND WEAR

DECORATING CLOTHES

DANDELION
EASY COSTUMES YOU DON'T HAVE TO SEW
Have a T-shirt party.
Write invitations. Ask people to bring a T-shirt and to decorate them with fabric paint, sequins, applique, or tie-dye.
Write or draw the steps you followed.
Make grocery bag vests and decorate.

HISTORY OF CLOTHES

Collect old mail order catalogs. Cut out and make a display or time line.
Make and cut out clothes for paper dolls of today and yesterday.
Visit an art museum. Look at costume exhibits or costumes in painting.
NEW CLOTHES: WHAT PEOPLE WORE—FROM CAVEMEN TO ASTRONAUTS

FROM HEAD TO TOES

CAPS FOR SALE
THE ADVENTURES OF CHARLIE AND HIS WHEAT STRAW HAT
THE 500 HATS OF BARTHOLEMEW CUBBINS
A THREE HAT DAY
THE HAT HUNT
LITTLE RED CAP
YOU'LL SOON GROW INTO THEM TITCH
Collect some of your old clothes. Measure and compare them to the sizes you wear now.
LITTLE BEAR'S TROUSERS
MARY WORE HER RED DRESS
Write another version, sing it to the same tune.
THE WALKING COAT
THE PURPLE COAT
LITTLE RED RIDING HOOD
TATTERCOATS
SHOES
THE SHOEMAKER AND THE ELVES
BIRD'S NEW SHOES
TWO PAIRS OF SHOES
PUSS IN BOOTS
CINDERELLA
Comparison charts, retellings
Write a new version.
Story problems
Shoe sorting activity
Practice tying shoes in a learning center.
"The Old Woman Who Lived in the Shoe"
Act out the story.
"Shoes"
"The Rain Has Silver Sandals"
Choose a shoe from the shoe center. On large strips of butcher paper draw the person to go with the shoe.
Make moccasins from patterns.

Figure 4.2

REASONS FOR CLOTHES

Learning Center Matching Game
Categorize pictures of types of clothing with their function (decoration or communication) or with climate (hot or cold). Create math sets.

"Wendy in Winter"
"The Muddy Puddle"
"Winter Clothes"
Pantomime the action in poems.

Invite resource poeple to wear national costumes or special uniforms to class.
Keep old clothes in a costume corner, ask a Little Theater group to bring costumes.
Play dress-up.
HATS HATS HATS
HATS, CAPS AND CROWNS
MARTIN'S HATS
WHOSE HAT?
WHOSE HAT IS THAT?
WHOSE SHOES ARE THESE?
Try on hats, shoes, and guess what kind of worker might wear each one.
GOGGLES
Collect items of clothing worn for personal safety, and categorize them as to type.
ANIMALS DEFINITELY SHOULD NOT WEAR CLOTHING
Write reasons why animals should not wear clothing.

DRESSED AND UNDRESSED

BEAR GETS DRESSED
GETTING DRESSED
Dressing Up Learning Center
Practice zipping, buttoning, snapping, buckling, and dressing dolls.
HOW DO I PUT IT ON?
Tell your own version of the right way and the wrong way to put on clothes.
JESSIE BEAR, WHAT WILL YOU WEAR?
"The New Vestments"
List all the things you can wear besides clothes.
SUNSHINE, MOONLIGHT
Draw a comic strip showing how you get dressed in the morning, or undressed at night.
Find music that could accompany a film of your family getting dressed every morning and going to bed each night.
THE PHILHARMONIC GETS DRESSED
THE DALLAS TITANS GET READY FOR BED
Make a list of the items of clothing or pieces of equipment that football players wear.
Graph the number of people wearing each item.
Listen to a recording of the Philharmonic.
Try on a football uniform.
"Summer"
"Jonathan Bing"
THE EMPEROR'S NEW CLOTHES
Design an outfit for the emperor.

CLEANING UP

THE WILD WASHERWOMEN
WASHDAY ON NOAH'S ARK
THE DAY JIMMY'S BOA ATE THE WASH
Clothesline sequencing activity.
MOLLIE'S NEW WASHING MACHINE
"Swish Swash Washing Machine"
"Our Washing Machine"
Make up other noises for washing machines.
Write a washing machine poem.
"Laundromat"
Visit a Laundromat, and learn how to use a washing machine.
Thought ramble, or describe sounds and sights around you.
Write directions for washing clothes.

MRS. WISHY-WASHY
Shared reading
Collect washday implements—washboard, brush, wash tub.
Dramatize washday routines.
Make washtub music.
KEEPING CLEAN
Compare other ways of washing around the world or in the past.
Make soap, and note the chemical changes.
Collect different bars of soap, and experiment with them on a water table.
Which float? Graph the results.
Collect soap boxes and wrappers.
Make an environmental print collage.
"Soap Bubble"
SOAP BUBBLE MAGIC
Make soap bubbles, experimenting with different kinds of bubbles. Try other experiments.
Make a foil boat go with soap power.
Make colored soap bubble designs.
LET'S FIND OUT ABOUT WATER

Schedule

The following plans are suggested as part of an all-day, self-contained kindergarten classroom. The idea for the theme began with a Big Book* entitled *Mrs. Wishy Washy* that was a great favorite with Peter Williams' kindergarteners. Peter happened across several other books about washing, among them *Mollie's New Washing Machine* and *Washday on Noah's Ark,* and soon began to think about combining the ideas of "washing" and "clothes." He was well aware of five-year-olds' enthusiasm for messing about with water, and also their special delight with clothes and the sense of mastery they felt in being able to dress themselves. He began to collect more books, poems, and nursery rhymes and to think of other resources that might be incorporated into activities and centers. Although there were not a great many information books on clothes written for this level, Peter did know Tomie de Paola's *Charlie Needs a Cloak,* which explains all the steps in making a cloak—from sheep shearing, to weaving, to sewing, to wearing. This led him to think of centers on fibers and for making and decorating clothes. Planning a field trip to a local department store could provide the focus for many social studies and math activities, as well as dramatic play in the classroom. He also decided that he could incorporate a mapping activity by making a simple puzzle from the map depicting the large areas of major departments of the store. Children could have a chance to play with this puzzle map before the visit and then have fun "walking" through their map on the day of the field trip. Other ideas for centers that allowed children to consider reasons for clothing and that provided many more opportunities for children to be involved in math projects and science experiments also emerged in Peter's mind. Peter was delighted at how the unit seemed to be blossoming on its own accord—thinking of "Wash and Wear" was moving him naturally to subthemes like "Weather" (from raincoats and snowshoes to swimsuits) to "Machines and Tools" (from washing machines to scrub brushes), and was helping him consider how washing could lead into "Baths," "Car Washes," or "Water" in general.

Table 4.3 shows how Peter modified his typical schedule to reflect the centers, resources, and activities he came up with for this WASH AND WEAR thematic unit.

Into the Classroom

The unit began with a math activity to teach graphing, a skill that Peter wanted the children to use often during the year. Peter first asked all the children to take off one of their shoes, and together they decided how the shoes could be sorted into categories. They considered attributes such as string laces or velcro closings, right or left shoes, tennis shoes or other kinds of shoes, and colors of shoes. Peter created a large grid on the floor with masking tape, and once they decided on categories the children placed the shoes on the grid according to category. Peter helped them to summarize the results of their survey by counting and labeling each category. The children then filled in smaller wall charts by cutting shoe shapes out of construction paper.

When the activity was finished, Peter read the book *Shoes.* This rhyming story later became a Big Book* for shared reading, but at the beginning it was a good way to introduce children to the theme of WASH AND WEAR and to discuss activities and centers planned for the following few days (see Table 4.3).

A closer look at the bustle of activity in this kindergarten classroom reveals careful planning and organization on Peter's part. Table 4.4 traces this orchestration on three days—Days 6, 7, and 13—following the introduction of the theme and the shoe graphing activity. On Day 6 children are busy in various learning centers. For example, in the decorating center, some children are decorating paper bag vests, while others sort pictures of articles of clothing corresponding to the functions of clothing items—protection, communication, and decoration. Later in the day a class visitor shares wool at various stages. The children see a videotape on Renaissance clothing and listen to *Rumpelstiltskin.* During the afternoon, there is integrated work time, with children again working in centers. Some children select Reading Buddies*. Children "play school" using the Big Book* version of *Shoes,* the book introduced on the first day of the unit.

TABLE 4.3 Weekly Schedule, Peter Williams's All-Day Kindergarten

Time	Monday	Tuesday	Wednesday	Thursday	Friday
9:00	Preparation. Children arrive, go to centers or meet informally with teacher.				
9:10	Circle time. Teacher reads book or tells story. Goes over daily schedule and individual plans.				
9:30	Integrated work time. Children at centers. Teacher circulates or works with individuals or small groups. Choices might include experiments at the water table, dress-up at the costume box, art activities at the decorating or weaving center, play in the classroom store.				
10:45	Snack				
11:00	Recess				
11:15	Library	Math. Graphing activity with shoes.	Music. Washboard rhythms.	Science. Soap film experiments.	Physical Education
		Whole group involved in activity and discussion with teacher.			
11:45	Clean-up				
12:00	Lunch and outdoor play				
12:45	Nap or rest period. Some children engaged in bookreading or quiet play.				
1:15	Book time. Teacher reads or works with Big Book*.				
1:30	Snack time				
1:45	Integrated work time. Children work in centers. Teacher works with small groups or individuals. Choices include writing corner, reading corner, listening post, dictated writing.				
2:30	Clean-up				
2:45	Whole group time. Children engaged in music, creative dramatics, movement.				
3:05	Discussion of day's events, plans for tomorrow.				
3:15	Dismissal				

They take turns being student and teacher in repeated reenactments of the book. Others are involved in other activities—dictating and then reading to their peers stories on how to make cloth and working in the classroom department store.

Some of these activities and projects are further extended during the morning of Day 7. In a center, for example, children examine natural fibers other than wool. They also explore more about the clothing of the past by recalling yesterday's videotape and looking at the illustrations from *Rumpelstiltskin.* Day 13 has children getting ready for their own production of *Rumpelstiltskin* in the costume corner and conducting "experiments" with soap and water.

Summary

This classroom is one that supports both the child as learner of language and learner of the world. It is filled with exciting and worthwhile experiences that incorporate many opportunities for children to expand oral language competencies and also to be readers and writers. Print can be found everywhere—in books and other resources (including "environmental" print), print that the teacher has written, and many examples of the children's own writing.

The child is a learner of language and of the world.

In Peter's school, some of the youngest children attend class only in the mornings. As a result, Peter arranges the kind of introductory literacy experiences most needed

(Summary continued on page 97.)

TABLE 4.4 Detailed Schedule, All-Day Kindergarten

DAY 6 Time	Children	Teacher
TEACHER ARRIVAL 8:30		Peter arrives, takes care of paperwork and messages, and begins to set up centers. He chooses some of the books about clothes from the book shelves and displays them on the table in the reading corner.
ARRIVAL 9:00	Children begin arriving at school and move to centers after they have put away their coats and lunches. Others go to the reading corner where they browse through the books on display.	Peter greets the children and is available to talk informally. He checks off attendance and notes lunch count as children enter the room.
CIRCLE 9:10	Children assemble on the braided rug in the open area for story time. Following the reading, they help Peter make a list of things they could wear besides clothes. Children discuss plans for integrated work time.	Peter reads *Jessie Bear, What Will You Wear?,* inviting the children to make comments, predict, and join in on familiar refrains. On a sheet of chart paper, he lists the children's suggestions for unusual things to wear (Jessie wears such items as "juice from a pear and rice in my hair" and "bear hugs from you and three kisses too"). Following this activity, he checks briefly with each child as to which centers he or she will visit during work time, making suggestions when children have difficulty deciding.
INTEGRATED WORK TIME 9:30	Children move to centers. Several have chosen to work in the decorating center cutting and pasting materials on paper bag vests. Three work in the center with pictures of articles of clothing. They are to decide which function the item of clothing serves—protection, communication, or decoration—and sort the pictures into appropriately labeled shoe boxes. Several are working in the dressing corner practicing shoe lacing and tying, or dressing and undressing dolls. Some are in the drama corner trying on costumes for their version of "The Old Woman Who Lived in a Shoe." Others are in the "store" categorizing items of old clothes and writing prices on tags. They are looking at department store ads they have cut out of the newspaper.	Peter moves from group to group, talking with children about their work and dealing with any difficulties. He spends most of his time with the children who are sorting pictures of clothing into categories. These children may require some help in thinking about the purposes for wearing clothes (such as for communication, for protection, or for decoration). Ultimately Peter will respect the choices of the children, realizing that categorization at this age may be highly idiosyncratic. He sees the activity as an opportunity for him to gain insight into children's thinking rather than impose his own adult structures on the children. He also gives extra attention to the group working in the Department Store center, helping children look through the newspaper ads he has collected and suggesting other places in the environment where they will see prices written.
SNACK 10:45	Children clean up and put away materials. They then move to the snack table where today's helpers have helped Peter prepare the snacks.	As Peter and his helpers make peanut butter and celery snacks, he reminds them of how Jessie Bear "wore" his lunch.

RECESS 11:00	Most of the children choose to go outside to play. Several who were involved in the earlier activity choose to remain inside to continue working.	Since an aide monitors children on the playground during recess, Peter can stay in the classroom with the children who want to continue working. Today he wants to be in the classroom to greet the visitor who has come to talk with the children. Joan Ward is a member of a local weaver's guild. She has brought her spinning wheel and a small loom. While she gets set up, Peter brings out paper bags that he has filled with wool in various stages from its raw form to woven cloth.
GROUP TIME 11:15	The children assemble on the rug for a class visitor. They pass around paper bags that contain samples of wool in various stages. They feel inside their bag and try to guess what is inside by feeling. They then collect the samples and line them up on a low table as Joan tells them the sequence in which raw wool becomes a woven coat. Following Joan's demonstration, they each help card the raw wool and work the spinning wheel.	When the children have settled themselves on the rug, Peter reminds them of the book they read the previous day called *Charlie Needs a Cloak.* He helps them read through a picture chart they made showing the steps in making Charlie's cloak. He introduces Joan, and together they pass out a paper bag to pairs of children. Each child is asked to feel inside the bag and guess what is inside. Following discussion, the class arranges the samples in the proper sequence. Then Joan demonstrates the steps in making yarn from wool and weaving on a loom. She lets the children try their hand. Peter then introduces children to a new learning center with potholder looms and other simple materials for weaving and sewing.
CLEAN-UP 11:50	The children put away supplies and any materials that won't be used in the afternoon.	
LUNCH 12:00	Lunch and outdoor play.	
NAP TIME 12:45	All the children are asked to rest for half an hour. Those who don't sleep go to the book corner or engage in quiet play until the others awake.	
BOOK TIME 1:15	The children gather back on the braided rug to watch a videotape of a "Reading Rainbow" program. In this episode Lavar Burton visits a Renaissance Festival and watches cloth being woven. Then the book *Rumpelstiltskin* is read on the program.	Peter sets up a videotape player. After they see the *Rumpelstiltskin* tape, Peter draws their attention to the types of clothes worn by people long ago. He shows them copies of the book read on the show and other versions of the tale, such as *Duffy and the Devil*, which he places in the reading corner. He promises to read these to the children at a later date.
SNACK TIME 1:35	Helpers put out the afternoon snack as children prepare to select activities for the afternoon work time.	

(Continued on next page.)

TABLE 4.4—Continued

DAY 6

Time	Children	Teacher
INTEGRATED WORK TIME 1:45	Children work in centers. Some select the reading corner for Buddy Reading* while others move to an easel with a teacher-made Big Book* version of *Shoes* to play "school." Each one takes a turn as teacher and leads the others in reading the story with a pointer. Others draw pictures and write about Joan Ward's visit. Several dictate individual reports about how to make cloth. They will illustrate these and later read them to at least three of their classmates. Children in the Department Store center are measuring clothes, shoes, gloves, and hats and deciding on a sizing system.	Peter often focuses afternoon work time on emergent reading and writing activities. Because many of these activities allow children to function independently as readers and writers, Peter can sit down with individual children to take dictation. He makes sure the child can see him write and says each word aloud as he prints. After the short piece of writing is finished, Peter invites the child to read it back to him and together they explore various features of print. While he is working with one child, other children are drawing pictures in anticipation of their dictated texts.
CLEAN-UP 2:30	Children put away all materials and set aside books or projects that will go home at the end of the day.	
GROUP TIME 2:45	The children listen to *Mary Wore Her Red Dress*, predicting what each character will wear by looking at the picture. They then sing along to the music and help compose new verses.	Peter has brought a guitar and after he reads the story he leads the children in singing to the tune printed in the back of the book. He then lets children take turns composing new verses using names of children in the room, additional colors, and other items of clothing.
WRAP-UP 3:05	Children tell about the activities they participated in that day and make plans for tomorrow.	Peter uses the final minutes of the day to let children share their experiences and feelings about what they have done and learned. He also alerts them to a project they will do the following day using cut-out construction paper shapes and a clothesline. He finishes by reading a poem by Edward Lear titled "The New Vestments" in which an old man wears some highly unusual items of clothing.
DISMISSAL 3:15		

DAY 7

Time	Children	Teacher
CIRCLE TIME 9:10	Children assemble on the rug and join in reading *Mary Wore Her Red Dress.* Then they discuss the order in which you might put on items of clothing like underwear, shoes and socks, shirt and pants, sweater, coat, and mittens. They help Peter sequence the items of clothing on the clothesline with clothespins.	As the children come to the rug, Peter takes out his guitar and leads them in singing another round of *Mary Wore Her Red Dress.* He then brings out large colored construction paper shapes that represent items of clothing. He has strung a clothesline in one corner of the room and asks children to help

		him hang up the items of clothing in the order in which they might be put on. As they do this Peter uses words like "first," "next," "then," "last." He then introduces them to a new center where he has set out construction paper, scissors, and clothespins. He suggests that when children visit the center they choose colors and cut out items of clothing. Then they can work together to sequence the items of clothing on the clothesline in the center.
INTEGRATED WORK TIME 9:45	The children move to centers. In addition to the previous day's choices, children can also select the clothesline sequencing activity, the weaving center, and a third center in which, in addition to wool in various stages, other samples of natural fibers have been placed. The children are asked to sort through these and match up the sample with the finished fabric in the proper sequence. Cotton, for example, is represented by a branch from a cotton plant, ginned cotton, and cotton cloth.	Peter moves from center to center. He makes sure that children are able to work with the potholder looms and then moves to a center with samples of different fibers to help the children with this activity.
GROUP TIME 11:15	The children recall how clothing in the book *Rumpelstiltskin* and at the Renaissance Festival was different from their clothes. They then make suggestions about clothing of the past as they look at the pictures Peter has assembled. They talk about clothing for different climates and clothing for different purposes.	Peter has assembled pictures of clothing from different time periods. These have been culled from old catalogs, photographs, magazine ads, and the art teacher's file of reproductions. He shares these with the children and asks them to speculate on how old the clothes are and what uses the clothing may have had. He has mounted the pictures and put numbers on the bottom that correspond to centuries. These will be placed in a center and children asked to place them on a timeline.
INTEGRATED WORK TIME 1:45	Many of the choices available are those from the previous day. Children select alternative activities today. Several elect a new activity. They will create the illustrations for a Big Book* version of *Mary Wore Her Red Dress,* which has been placed in the art center.	Peter circulates among groups as he did on the previous day, taking dictation from a new group of children. In addition, he has written the text of *Mary Wore Her Red Dress* on large pieces of poster board and placed these in the art corner. He has placed a copy of the book close by in case children making the pictures for the Big Book* need to check the sequencing of pages or want to match pictures to print.

DAY 13 (WASH AND WEAR)

Time	Children	Teacher
CIRCLE TIME 9:10	The children listen and make sound effects for the story, *Mollie's New*	Peter encourages children to enjoy the literary aspects of the story and

(Continued on next page.)

TABLE 4.4—Continued

DAY 13 (WASH AND WEAR) Time	Children	Teacher
	Washing Machine and poems Peter reads about washing machines. They suggest other sounds that washing machines might make and Peter writes these on a Graffiti Wall*.	the two poems, but he also wants to draw their attention to words used for their unusual sounds, words that represent sounds and ways in which letters represent sound and can be joined together to make words. He thus allows children to join in on the nonsense refrains in *Mollie's New Washing Machine* and repeat sounds like swish, swash, bubble, spin, whissity, whirr, grrr, and click from the poems, "Our Washing Machine" by Patricia Hubbell and "Swish Swash Washing Machine" by Eve Merriam. Writing these sound words (onomatopoeia) on large chart paper he calls a Graffiti Wall* may help some children to make the connection between spoken sounds and printed symbols.
INTEGRATED WORK TIME 9:30	The children move to centers. Some are working on the clothesline sequencing activity. Others are in the costume corner getting ready for a production of *Rumpelstiltskin.* Several are in the art corner drawing comic strips that show how they get up and get dressed in the morning or get undressed for bed at night. Others are making puppets for a puppet show of *The Day Jimmy's Boa Ate the Wash.* Three children are comparing the sizes of shoes in the shoe box.	Peter moves from center to center working with the individuals and small groups. He monitors the group working with a collection of different size shoes and when they have finished their sorting and measuring activity, he unrolls long sheets of brown wrapping paper and invites them to choose one shoe and to draw the person who would go with that shoe.
GROUP TIME 11:15	Children volunteer hypotheses as Peter performs experiments with bubbles and water.	Peter has selected experiments from Seymour Simon's book, *Soap Bubble Magic.* He performs these to encourage children to make hypotheses and to talk about properties of air and water.
BOOK TIME 1:15	Children respond to *The Wild Washerwoman.* They join in on familiar refrains.	Peter has chosen to read *The Wild Washerwoman* by John Yeoman and Quentin Blake because it fits in with the clothes-washing theme and also because of some of the repeated refrains and delightful use of words. He suggests that some of the children will want to act this story out using some of the clothes in the dress-up corner as props.
INTEGRATED WORK TIME 1:45	The children have the opportunity to read *Mrs. Wishy Washy,* a Big Book*, or to write washing machine poems. An aide is available today	Peter has transferred the two poems about washing machines to overhead transparencies. He will work with several children who

to take dictation. The children can choose to tell about the science experiments that morning or to continue their own experiments with water and soap. Several children work with Peter on identifying and filling in words and letters from the washing machine poems. Two children are Buddy Reading* with Peter Spier's book of noises, *Crash, Bang, Boom.*

have begun focusing on the graphic information in printed text. They will "play" with these poems, underlining short vowel sounds, initial consonants, or word endings. On a piece of large chart paper, Peter has written the poems, leaving key words or letters blank. As he prepares to move to another group, he invites these children to fill in the blanks on their own.

(Summary continued from page 91.)

by these children in the morning. More focused literacy activities needed by the older children are generally planned for the afternoon. But no matter what the time of day or what activity, there are materials to read and things to write about in purposeful ways. Peter recognizes the importance of play in the young child's learning and knows that as children play at being cooks, kings, storekeepers, or stevedores, they can use reading and writing as part of their imaginary worlds.

Children's Literature, WASH AND WEAR

THE ADVENTURES OF CHARLIE AND HIS WHEAT STRAW HAT by B. Hiser. Illustrated by M. Szilagyi. Dodd, Mead, 1986.

ALLIGATOR SHOES by A. Dorros. Dutton, 1988.

ANIMALS DEFINITELY SHOULD NOT WEAR CLOTHING by J. Barrett. Illustrated by R. Barrett. Atheneum, 1970.

"Arachne" in BOOK OF GREEK MYTHS by I. and E. P. D'Aulaire. Doubleday, 1962.

BEAR GETS DRESSED—A GUESSING GAME STORY by H. Ziefert. Illustrated by A. Lobel. Harper & Row, 1986.

BIG SHOE, LITTLE SHOE by D. Cazet. Bradbury, 1984.

BIRD'S NEW SHOES by C. Riddell. Holt, Rinehart and Winston, 1987.

BUBBLES: A CHILDREN'S MUSEUM ACTIVITY BOOK by B. Zubrowski. Illustrated by L. Bourke. Little, Brown, 1988.

CAPS FOR SALE by E. Slobodkina. Harper & Row, 1987.

THE CAT IN THE HAT by T. Geisel (Dr. Seuss). Random House, 1957.

CHARLIE NEEDS A CLOAK by T. de Paola. Simon & Schuster, 1974.

CINDERELLA OR THE LITTLE GLASS SLIPPER by C. Perrault. Illustrated by E. LeCain. Bradbury, 1973.

THE CRANE WIFE by S. Yagawa (translated by K. Paterson). Illustrated by S. Akaba. Morrow, 1981.

THE DALLAS TITANS GET READY FOR BED by K. Kuskin. Illustrated by M. Simont. Harper & Row, 1986.

DANDELION by D. Freeman. Viking, 1964.

DAWN by M. Bang. Morrow, 1983.

THE DAY JIMMY'S BOA ATE THE WASH by T. H. Noble. Illustrated by S. Kellogg. Dial, 1980.

DEPARTMENT STORE by G. Gibbons. Crowell, 1984.

DUFFY AND THE DEVIL by H. Zemach. Illustrated by M. Zemach. Farrar, Straus & Giroux, 1973.

EASY COSTUMES YOU DON'T HAVE TO SEW by G. T. Cherroff. Four Winds, 1977.

THE EMPEROR'S NEW CLOTHES by H. C. Andersen. Adapted and illustrated by J. Stevens. Holiday, 1985.

THE FIVE HUNDRED HATS OF BARTHOLEMEW CUBBINS by T. Geisel (Dr. Seuss). Vanguard, 1938.

GENERAL STORE by R. Field. Illustrated by N. W. Parker. Little, Brown, 1988.

GETTING DRESSED by V. Cobb. Illustrated by M. Haffner. Lippincott, 1989.

GOGGLES by E. J. Keats. Macmillan, 1969.

THE HAT HUNT. Translated by A. Barnett-Lindberg. Illustrated by S. Nordquist. Farrar, Straus & Giroux, 1988.

HATS, CAPS AND CROWNS by L. S. Kenworthy. Julian Messner, 1977.

HATS, HATS, HATS by A. Morris. Photographs by K. Heyman. Lothrop, 1989.

HOW DO I PUT IT ON? by S. Watanabe. Illustrated by Y. Ohtomo. Putnam, 1980.

I CAN GET DRESSED by N. Rubel. Macmillan, 1984.

JENNIE'S HAT by E. J. Keats. Harper & Row, 1966, 1985.

JESSIE BEAR, WHAT WILL YOU WEAR? by N. W. Carlstrom. Illustrated by B. Degen. Macmillan, 1986.

"Jonathon Bing" by B. C. Brown in THE RANDOM HOUSE BOOK OF POETRY. Compiled by J. Prelutsky. Illustrated by A. Lobel. Random House, 1983.

KEEPING CLEAN by V. Cobb. Illustrated by M. Haffner. Lippincott, 1989.

"Laundromat" by D. McCord in CLICK RUMBLE ROAR. Compiled by L. B. Hopkins. Photographed by A. H. Audette. Crowell, 1987.

LET'S FIND OUT ABOUT WATER by M. and C. Shapp. Illustrated by C. Nicklaus. Franklin Watts/Random House Sound Film Strip.

LITTLE BEAR'S TROUSERS by J. Hissey. Philomel, 1987.

LITTLE RED CAP by J. and W. Grimm. Translated by E. Crawford. Illustrated by L. Zwerger. Morrow, 1983.

LITTLE RED RIDING HOOD by J. and W. Grimm. Retold by T. S. Hyman. Illustrated by T. S. Hyman. Holiday, 1983.

MARTIN'S HATS by J. W. Blos. Illustrated by M. Simont. Morrow, 1984.

MARY WORE HER RED DRESS AND HENRY WORE HIS GREEN SNEAKERS by M. Peek. Clarion, 1985.

MOLLIE'S NEW WASHING MACHINE by L. Geringer. Illustrated by P. Mathers. Harper & Row, 1986.

MOONLIGHT by J. Ormerod. Lothrop, 1982.

MRS. WISHY WASHY by J. Cowley and J. Melser. Illustrated by E. Fuller. Wright Group, 1981.

"The Muddy Puddle" by D. Lee in THE RANDOM HOUSE BOOK OF POETRY. Compiled by J. Prelutsky. Illustrated by A. Lobel. Random House, 1983.

"My Tall Silk Hat" in IF YOU'RE HAPPY AND YOU KNOW IT by N. Weiss. Greenwillow, 1987.

NEW CLOTHES: WHAT PEOPLE WORE—FROM CAVEMEN TO ASTRONAUTS by L. Weill. Atheneum, 1987.

A NEW COAT FOR ANNA by H. Ziefert. Illustrated by A. Lobel. Knopf, 1986.

"The New Vestments" by E. Lear in THE RANDOM HOUSE BOOK OF POETRY. Compiled by J. Prelutsky. Illustrated by A. Lobel. Random House, 1983.

"Old Woman in the Shoe" in TOMIE DE PAOLA'S MOTHER GOOSE by T. de Paola. Putnam, 1985.

ON MARKET STREET by A. Lobel. Illustrated by A. Lobel. Greenwillow, 1981.

"Our Washing Machine" by P. Hubell in CLICK, RUMBLE, ROAR: POEMS ABOUT MACHINES. Compiled by L. B. Hopkins. Photographs by A. H. Audette. Crowell, 1987.

THE PHILHARMONIC GETS DRESSED by K. Kuskin. Illustrated by M. Simont. Harper & Row, 1986.

PICKING AND WEAVING by B. Le Tord. Four Winds, 1980.

THE PURPLE COAT by A. Hest. Illustrated by A. Schwartz. Four Winds, 1986.

PUSS IN BOOTS by C. Perrault. Illustrated by M. Brown. Scribner, 1952.

"The Rain Has Silver Sandals" by M. Justus in THE RANDOM HOUSE BOOK OF POETRY. Compiled by J. Prelutsky. Illustrated by A. Lobel. Random House, 1983.

RUMPELSTILTSKIN by J. and W. Grimm. Retold and illustrated by P. Zelinsky. Dutton, 1986.

THE SHOEMAKER AND THE ELVES by C. and W. Birrer. Lothrop, 1983.

SHOES by E. Winthrop. Illustrated by W. Joyce. Harper & Row, 1986.

"Shoes" in FRESH PAINT by E. Merriam. Macmillan, 1986.

"Soap Bubble" in ALL THE SMALL POEMS by V. Worth. Illustrated by N. Babbitt. Farrar, Straus & Giroux, 1987.

SOAP BUBBLE MAGIC by S. Simon. Illustrated by S. Ormai. Morrow, 1985.

THE STOREKEEPER by T. C. Pearson. Dial, 1988.

THE STORY OF WOOL by G. Patterson. Andre Deutsch, 1987.

"Summer" by F. Asch in THE RANDOM HOUSE BOOK OF POETRY. Compiled by J. Prelutsky. Illustrated by A. Lobel. Random House, 1983.

SUNSHINE by J. Ormerod. Lothrop, 1981.

"Swish Swash Washing Machine" in BLACKBERRY INK by E. Merriam. Illustrated by H. Wilholm. Morrow, 1985.

TATTERCOATS by A. F. Steele. Illustrated by D. Goode. Bradbury, 1976.

A THREE HAT DAY by L. Geringer. Illustrated by A. Lobel. Harper & Row, 1985.

TWO PAIRS OF SHOES by P. L. Travers. Illustrated by L. and D. Dillon. Viking, 1980.

THE WALKING COAT by T. de Paola. Simon & Schuster, 1987.

WASHDAY ON NOAH'S ARK by G. Rounds. Holiday, 1985.

THE WEAVER'S GIFT by K. Laskey. Photos by C. G. Knight. Fred Warne, 1981.

"Wendy in Winter" by K. Starbird in THE RANDOM HOUSE BOOK OF POETRY. Compiled by J. Prelutsky. Illustrated by A. Lobel. Random House, 1983.

WHOSE HAT? by M. Miller. Greenwillow, 1988.

WHOSE HAT IS THAT? by R. Roy. Illustrated by R. Hausherr. Clarion, 1987.

WHOSE SHOES ARE THESE? by R. Roy. Illustrated by R. Hausherr. Clarion, 1988.

THE WILD WASHERWOMAN by J. Yeoman. Illustrated by Q. Blake. Crown, 1979.

"Winter Clothes" by K. Kuskin in THE RANDOM HOUSE BOOK OF POETRY. Compiled by J. Prelutsky. Illustrated by A. Lobel. Random House, 1983.

WOOL GATHERING: SHEEP RAISING IN OLD NEW ENGLAND by E. Gemming. Coward, McCann, 1979.

YOU'LL SOON GROW INTO THEM, TITCH by R. Hutchins. Greenwillow, 1983.

Prototype 3: First Grade—Changes

**ANIMAL CHANGES—
FROM ONE STAGE TO ANOTHER**

EVOLUTION
SPHINX: THE STORY OF A CATERPILLAR
AMAZING WORLD OF BUTTERFLIES AND MOTHS
BUTTERFLY AND MOTH
THE BUTTERFLY CYCLE
Observe caterpillars spin cocoons. Note the changes in daily log.
Talk to a butterfly collector.
Examine butterfly specimens, and classify them by size and color.
Make a butterfly mobile.
THE VERY HUNGRY CATERPILLAR
Retell the story with hand puppets or on a flannel board.
THE CATERPILLAR AND THE POLLIWOG
BULLFROG GROWS UP
SALAMANDERS
JUMP, FROG, JUMP!
FROGS
A FROG'S BODY
COMMON FROG
Visit a pond in the spring.
Collect tadpoles. Construct a class aquarium and observe changes.

**RIDICULOUS CHANGES—
FROM ONE FARCE TO ANOTHER**

FISH IS FISH
"YOU LOOK RIDICULOUS," SAID THE RHINOCEROS TO THE HIPPOPOTAMUS
THE MIXED UP CHAMELEON
Write another version of the stories.
Paint a picture of an animal you make up.

**IMAGINARY CHANGES—
FROM ONE VIEW TO ANOTHER**

GRAHAM OAKLEY'S MAGICAL CHANGES
ROUND TRIP
REFLECTIONS
CHANGES CHANGES
Study optical illusions.
MOUSE PAINT
LITTLE BLUE AND LITTLE YELLOW
Experiment with changes in color mixing.

CHANGES

FROM LITTLE TO BIG

HOW PUPPIES GROW
TWO KITTENS ARE BORN: FROM BIRTH TO TWO MONTHS
WATCHING THEM GROW: INSIDE A ZOO NURSERY
LET ME TELL YOU ABOUT MY BABY
Compare the rate of change in animals and humans.

FROM DAY TO NIGHT

WHAT MAKES DAY AND NIGHT
SUN UP, SUN DOWN
THE NEW MOON
THE MOON SEEMS TO CHANGE
Make a calendar showing phases of the moon.
LIGHT
GRANDFATHER TWILIGHT
Paint the same place at different times of day.

FROM ONE COLOR TO ANOTHER

Study coloration changes in the animal world.
THE MIXED UP CHAMELEON

FROM SEASON TO SEASON

WONDERS OF SEASONS
Study a globe.
Make a model of the earth's rotation and revolution.
WHERE DO ALL THE BIRDS GO?
Study a map of bird migration. What other animals migrate? Create a calendar showing migration times.

Figure 4.3

FROM YOUNG TO OLD

HOW DOES IT FEEL TO BE OLD?
I HAVE FOUR NAMES FOR MY GRANDFATHER
GROWING OLDER
ANNIE AND THE OLD ONE
Interview older persons. Help make a scrapbook of their favorite memories.
WHEN PEOPLE DIE
THE DEAD BIRD
THE TENTH GOOD THING ABOUT BARNEY
Plan a funeral ceremony

WEATHER CHANGES—FROM FAIR TO FOUL

THE CLOUD BOOK
WILL IT RAIN?
TORNADO
TORNADO! POEMS
FLASH, CRASH, RUMBLE, AND ROLL
HURRICANE WATCH
DREAMS
Study barometers.
Keep a journal of weather changes.
Make a terrarium.
Watch steam collect on a glass plate above a steam kettle.
EVENING GRAY MORNING RED
Predict the weather.
Give a TV weather broadcast.
Interview a meteorologist.
WHEN THE WIND BLEW

MAGICAL CHANGES

THE DONKEY PRINCE
THE HEDGEHOG BOY
THE UGLY DUCKLING
THE FROG PRINCE
THE FROG PRINCESS
DAWN
THE CRANE WIFE
Make a comparison chart.
Interview the changelings.
Make a mural showing all the characters before and after.

CHANGES IN MATTER FROM ONE STATE TO ANOTHER

Boil water, then freeze it.
Make bread.
Make jello.
POPCORN
THE POPCORN BOOK
Cook and observe the changes.
WHAT HAPPENS TO HAMBURGER
MESSING ABOUT WITH BAKING CHEMISTRY
Conduct experiments. Hypothesize results.

FROM SEED TO PLANT

FROM FLOWER TO FRUIT
OAK AND COMPANY
HOW THE FOREST GREW
Plant seeds, and chart the daily growth.
Experiment with different light and nutrient conditions.

CHANGES IN THE LANDSCAPE FROM ONE VIEW TO ANOTHER

THE LITTLE HOUSE
THE STORY OF AN ENGLISH VILLAGE
NEW PROVIDENCE: A CHANGING LANDSCAPE
Study old photographs of your community. Make a book showing the changes.

CHANGES IN ME—FROM ONE ME TO ANOTHER

ONE MORNING IN MAINE.
"Change"
TITCH
HIGHER ON THE DOOR
SOMEONE NEW
Collect baby pictures in an album.
Interview a family member about things you used to do.
Collect toys and clothes that you used to wear. How have your interests and sizes changed?

Schedule

George Kim teaches a first grade in an open area school. In this school organization, grades are grouped together in pods that are separated from other grades by walls but open to other classes in the same grade level. The teachers in the first grade pod work together to organize space, blocking off areas with bookcases and bulletin boards that can easily be rolled around. They have also found that cardboard cutting boards (available in fabric stores) and old appliance boxes can be cut into folding display panels to help organize space and allow for the display of work at the perfect eye level for first graders. The teachers in the first grade pod also work well as a team, and although each takes responsibility for his or her own class, they sometimes plan themes together. They also make sure to schedule quiet times when all the teachers read aloud or all children are involved in Sustained Silent Reading (SSR)*.

George planned the theme of CHANGES as a spring unit. He knows that first graders are very much aware of their new grown-up status and also understands that changes for them can sometimes be hard to deal with. He also knows that spring (in most areas of the country) is a time when changes in the outside world are most evident. He has planned experiences designed to deal with the traumas and triumphs of the first grade as well as to cover elements of the first grade curriculum in math, science, social studies, and health. Table 4.5 shows the weekly schedule for George Kim's first grade classroom.

Into the Classroom

The charts for this prototype, CHANGES, begin with Day 5 when children explore change in many ways. For example, during integrated work time, a small group of children go outside and begin to track changes in their own shadows by tracing them on large pieces of paper. They place their paper on the ground and then take turns tracing each others' shadows. Their first tracing is done around 9:30 in the morning, and they collect two more, at noon and at 2:00 in the afternoon. They will be asked to reflect on and to write their observations and pose possible explanations for the changes they have seen. To support these hypotheses and understandings, George has given them two books—*Round Trip* and *Reflections*—to read and discuss among themselves.

On this day, George has planned with his friend, Mrs. Martinez, for a bread-baking experience. Four children work with Martinez to make bread. Besides noting how the bread dough changes as it rises, she involves the children in writing the bread recipe. She has already written the ingredients on the board, plus the first step of the directions. Later the children dictate to her the other directions or steps they observe during the bread-making process. During the last integrated work time, all the children get to eat the fresh bread they have baked.

Also on this day two children are working on a puppet show derived from *The Very Hungry Caterpillar.* On the next day, Day 6, these children give the show to the children during morning group time. Children who baked bread with Mrs. Martinez work together to write up the changes noted in making bread. The shadow tracers share their tracings from the day before, and George reads *What Makes Day and Night* to the class.

Then, on Day 10, the class begins to observe live caterpillars. They will keep daily records of their observations of the caterpillars and note the changes in their Learning Logs*.

Summary

The concept of change is basic to all curricular areas and one that children will encounter and reencounter throughout their school years and for the rest of their lives. It is important that George Kim know this, but it is equally important that he know first graders so well that he can make this concept vital for them. George's knowledge of content,

TABLE 4.5 Weekly Schedule, George Kim's First Grade Classroom

Time	Monday	Tuesday	Wednesday	Thursday	Friday
8:00	Teacher preparation time				
8:25	Children arrive, put down chairs, get supplies, work on assignments, or read a book.				
9:00	Group time. Discuss ongoing projects, introduce new assignments, introduce new materials, or share completed work.				
9:20	Integrated work time. Children work on individual or group projects. Teacher meets with small groups or has individual conferences.				
9:45	Recess				
10:00	Book time. Read book or poem to class. Discuss or follow up with an activity.				
10:20	Integrated work time. Continue with projects begun earlier or inspired by read-aloud.				
10:50	Clean-up. Put away materials, supplies, projects, and assignments in storage areas.				
11:00	Sharing. Children share work with class or George shares information relevant to the unit.				
11:15	Lunch and outdoor play				
12:15	Art	Music	Library	Art	Music
12:55	Sustained Silent Reading (SSR)*. (George conferences with individual children.) Twice a week children have Buddy Reading* with second graders.				
1:35	Group time. George reads aloud or focuses on special activity.				
1:55	Recess				
2:10	Integrated work time				
2:45	Clean-up. Pass out papers. Evaluate the day.				
3:00	Dismissal				

curriculum, and children enables him to plan effectively in ways no teachers' manual could replicate.

George Kim is also an able collaborator with other adults, inviting them into the classroom to share their expertise with his first graders. He knows when to step aside, as he does with Mrs. Martinez, and he knows when to reenter to move children in new directions. You can see the practiced interplay of capabilities that constitute teaching in an integrated language classroom. George Kim and the other teachers you meet in this book constantly refine these skills and learn to be expert kid-watchers in the process.

Integrated language teachers are good collaborators.

Children's Literature, CHANGES

AMAZING WORLD OF BUTTERFLIES AND MOTHS by L. Sabin. Illustrated by J. Helmer. Troll, 1982.

ANNIE AND THE OLD ONE by M. Miles. Illustrated by P. Parnall. Little, Brown, 1971.

BULLFROG GROWS UP by R. Dauer. Illustrated by B. Barton. Greenwillow, 1988.

BUTTERFLY AND MOTH by P. Whalley. Knopf, 1988.

THE BUTTERFLY CYCLE from Oxford Scientific Films. Photographs by J. Cooke. Putnam, 1977.

THE CATERPILLAR AND THE POLLIWOG by J. Kent. Simon & Schuster, 1982.

"Change" in RIVER WINDING by C. Zolotow. Harper & Row, 1978.

CHANGES, CHANGES by P. Hutchins. Macmillan, 1971.

COMMON FROG from Oxford Scientific Films. Photographed by G. Bernard. Putnam, 1979.

THE CRANE WIFE by S. Yagawa. Translated by K. Paterson. Illustrated by S. Akaba. Morrow, 1981.

(References continued on page 107.)

TABLE 4.6 Detailed Schedule, First Grade Classroom

DAY 5 (CHANGES)

Time	Children	Teacher
TEACHER ARRIVAL 7:50		George arrives to set out special supplies. He takes time to look through children's work folders.
CHILDREN ARRIVE 8:25	Children arrive and begin putting away lunches. Many go to the reading corner. Several bring things in from home to share with George.	George greets the children and prepares the lunch count'and takes attendance. Mrs. Martinez also arrives to help with a project later.
GROUP TIME 9:00	Several have brought items from their baby days. Others have brought toys they now play with. Several have brought in baby pictures.	George introduces Mrs. Martinez to the children. He calls on children who want to share something with the rest of the class. George sets out the children's memorabilia on a display table marked "I'm Changing." He invites children to write about the items they have brought. He suggests that the children might want to display the baby pictures without names to let other children guess who is who.
INTEGRATED WORK TIME 9:20	Children move to work area, stopping to get supplies they need from their dishtubs (stored on shelves). Two are working on a puppet show for *The Very Hungry Caterpillar*. Several are working on illustrations for a Big Book* version of *Jump, Frog, Jump!* Six children take large brown sheets of paper George has provided. With a parent volunteer, they take these out on the playground and in pairs, take turns tracking their shadows on the paper. They will come back at 12:00 and 2:00 and do the same. Then they will write about the changes they observe and why they think this happened.	George asks each child what he or she will be doing during integrated work time. Many are involved in ongoing projects. He asks for volunteers to make "shadow" drawings, and a group who will participate in a shared writing experience. He sends four children to work with Mrs. Martinez. He writes the ongoing activities on the blackboard.
	Four children help Mrs. Martinez. They hand her the ingredients, help mix them together and then take a turn at kneading dough. They then help her write a recipe. Several recall a favorite story about breadmaking, *The Little Red Hen*.	Mrs. Martinez assembles the ingredients to bake bread. While they wait for the yeast to set, she writes the ingredients she is using on a large chart paper. Then she writes in the first step. Following the dough preparation, she will ask children to help her with the rest of the directions.
	The children want to call their story "The Very Hungry Kittycat." They remember another favorite story called *The Fat Cat*.	George works with a group of children to write a first draft of a version of *The Very Hungry Caterpillar*. They negotiate the new text as George demonstrates the process of composing.

STORY TIME 10:00	Children enjoy hearing the story about losing teeth. Several recall their own summer vacations. Others think of animals they know who have lost teeth.	George reads *One Morning in Maine.* He asks how many have lost teeth. He has cut out simple tooth shapes and hands these to children, one for each tooth lost. He invites each child to glue these in the spaces on the chart by his or her name. He then shows the children some teeth he has collected, including one of his own and a shark's tooth. He sets these on a sheet of colored paper in front of the chart.
INTEGRATED WORK TIME 10:20	Children continue with projects begun earlier.	George gives Ann Jonas's *Round Trip* and *Reflections* to the children who have done the shadow tracings. He asks them to look through the books and talk about them with each other.
	The children who helped with "The Very Hungry Kittycat" begin work on illustrations for the draft they helped George write.	George will type up the text pages for their book and children will glue them on their illustrations.
CLEAN-UP 10:50		
11:00	Children share the work they've been involved in.	
LUNCH 11:15		George reminds children to do another shadow drawing after lunch. He tells them to stand in the same spot as before and note the time on their drawing.
MUSIC 12:15	The children respond to the teacher's hand signals to change voices from high to low, fast and slow, soft to loud.	The music teacher introduces the children to the idea of changes in pitch, tempo, and volume. She leads them in several sounds, signaling when to change their voices in various ways.
SSR 12:55	Children Buddy Read* with members of a second grade class. Each child has brought a book to read aloud to the other children.	George holds individual conferences with three children. He listens to them read, and takes dictation or reads their writing with them.
GROUP TIME 1:35	Children volunteer memories.	George reads *Someone New* and asks children to help him fill in a chart divided into two columns: "When I Was Little" and "Now That I'm Bigger."
RECESS 1:55	Shadow tracers do one last tracing, noting time of day and place.	
INTEGRATED WORK TIME 2:10	Children return to activities begun earlier. Children enjoy the fruits of their labors.	George helps the shadow tracers to line up their drawings sequentially from early morning to afternoon. Mrs. Martinez sets out freshly baked bread and jam for the children.
CLEAN-UP 2:45	Children put away supplies and join the group.	George asks each child what project was worked on during the day and

(Continued on next page.)

TABLE 4.6—Continued

DAY 5 (CHANGES)

Time	Children	Teacher
		whether it was completed. He notes children who are finished with a project and suggests some choices they might like to consider the following day.

DAY 6 (CHANGES)

Time	Children	Teacher
GROUP TIME 9:00	The children who have worked on the puppet show from *The Very Hungry Caterpillar* present the show to the rest of the class.	
	Several more children have brought baby things or pictures to class.	George invites the children to talk about the puppet show or to share other information.
INTEGRATED WORK TIME 9:20	Many children are involved with ongoing projects. Children who baked bread help write a recipe. Then they fill in the blanks of the simplified version. Independently, they write about the changes they noted. Several children in the art corner are working with color paints and mixing them to change colors. Other children elect to be involved in the activities previously done by other groups.	Mrs. Martinez writes the steps for making bread as dictated by the children.
		George gets children started in measuring each other and noting height through simplified measures.
	The children compare heights through addition and subtraction. (John is ______ blocks or inches taller than Peter. Peter is ______ shorter than John.) They can also bring in measurements from previous years and compare their own changes.	
BOOK TIME 10:00	Children hypothesize about the reasons for the changes.	George asks all the children to look at the shadow tracings done by children the day before. He reads *What Makes Day and Night* and demonstrates the book's information using simple props.

DAY 10

Time	Children	Teacher
GROUP TIME 9:00		George has ordered live caterpillars, nutrients, and a large box with cellophane windows from a science

	Children help George set up the experiment and volunteer hypotheses. Many of them guess that the caterpillar will turn into a butterfly. Some think it will spin a cocoon first. They think this because they recall *The Very Hungry Caterpillar.*	supply center. He has helpers place nutrients in small plastic containers and then passes out a container to each child. He has given them markers to label the lids to the containers. He then passes out a caterpillar to each child. He asks children what they think will happen to the caterpillars once they have eaten the nutrient. He suggests some of them might like to write about their hypotheses in their Learning Logs* and to keep a daily record of observations of the caterpillar's changes.
INTEGRATED WORK TIME 9:20	Several children are working with books about changes from day to night and trying experiments with props. Some are in the reading corner, working with a Big Book* version of *Jump, Frog, Jump!* A small group is making a Comparison Chart of frog stories.	George is conferencing with individual children. George suggests the children fill in categories like "title," "frogs real or make-believe," "colors in illustrations."
BOOK TIME 10:00		George reads *The Little House* by Virginia Lee Burton. He asks children to help him make a list of the changes they noticed in the book. He gives the book to one child who wants to read it again. He shows children John Goodall's *The Story of An English Village* and suggests that during afternoon work time several children might want to look at it and make a list of things that change.

(CHANGES *references continued from page 103.)*

DAWN by M. Bang. Morrow, 1983.

THE DEAD BIRD by M. W. Brown. Illustrated by R. Charlip. W. R. Scott, 1958.

THE DONKEY PRINCE by J. M. Craig. Illustrated by B. Cooney. Doubleday, 1977.

DREAMS by P. Spier. Doubleday, 1986.

EVENING GRAY, MORNING RED by B. Wolff. Macmillan, 1976.

EVOLUTION by J. Cole. Illustrated by Aliki. Crowell, 1987.

FISH IS FISH by L. Leoni. Pantheon, 1970.

FLASH, CRASH, RUMBLE AND ROLL by F. M. Branley. Illustrated by B. and E. Emberley. Crowell, 1985.

THE FROG PRINCE by W. Gag. Coward, McCann, 1936.

THE FROG PRINCESS by E. Isele. Illustrated by M. Hague. Crowell, 1984.

FROGS by G. Tarrant. Illustrated by T. King. Putnam, 1983.

A FROG'S BODY by J. Cole. Photographed by J. Wexler. Morrow, 1980.

FROM FLOWER TO FRUIT by A. O. Dowden. Crowell, 1984.

GRAHAM OAKLEY'S MAGICAL CHANGES by G. Oakley. Atheneum, 1979.

GRANDFATHER TWILIGHT by B. Berger. Philomel, 1984.

GROWING OLDER by G. Ancona. Dutton, 1978.

THE HEDGEHOG BOY by J. Langton. Illustrated by I. Plume. Harper & Row, 1985.

HIGHER ON THE DOOR by J. Stevenson. Greenwillow, 1987.

HOW DOES IT FEEL TO BE OLD? by N. Farber. Illustrated by T. S. Hyman. Dutton, 1979.

HOW PUPPIES GROW by M. Selsam. Photographed by E. Bubley. Four Winds, 1971.

HOW THE FOREST GREW by W. Jaspersohn. Illustrated by C. Eckart. Greenwillow, 1980.

HURRICANE WATCH by F. M. Branley. Illustrated by G. Maestro. Crowell, 1985.

I HAVE FOUR NAMES FOR MY GRANDFATHER by K. Lasky. Illustrated by C. G. Knight. Little, Brown, 1979.

JUMP, FROG, JUMP! by R. Kalan. Illustrated by B. Barton. Greenwillow, 1981.

LIGHT by D. Crews. Greenwillow, 1981.

LITTLE BLUE AND LITTLE YELLOW by L. Lionni. Astor-Honor, 1960.

THE LITTLE HOUSE by V. L. Burton. Houghton Mifflin, 1942, 1969.

MESSING ABOUT WITH BAKING CHEMISTRY by B. Zubrowski. Illustrated by S. Hanson. Little, Brown, 1981.

THE MIXED UP CHAMELEON by E. Carle. Crowell, 1984.

THE MOON SEEMS TO CHANGE by F. M. Branley. Illustrated by B. and E. Emberley. Crowell, 1987.

MOUSE PAINT by E. S. Walsh. Harcourt Brace Jovanovich, 1989.

THE NEW MOON by H. S. Zimm. Morrow, 1980.

NEW PROVIDENCE: A CHANGING CITYSCAPE by R. von Tscharner and R. L. Fleming. Illustrated by D. Orloff. Gulliver/HBJ, 1987.

OAK AND COMPANY by R. Mabey. Illustrated by C. Roberts. Greenwillow, 1983.

ONE MORNING IN MAINE by R. McCloskey. Viking, 1952.

POPCORN by M. Selsam. Photographs by J. Wexler. Morrow, 1976.

THE POPCORN BOOK by T. de Paola. Holiday, 1978.

REFLECTIONS by A. Jonas. Greenwillow, 1987.

ROUND TRIP by A. Jonas. Greenwillow, 1983.

SALAMANDERS by C. W. Billings. Dodd, Mead, 1981.

SOMEONE NEW by C. Zolotow. Illustrated by E. Blegvad. Harper & Row, 1978.

SPHINX: THE STORY OF A CATERPILLAR by R. M. McClung. Illustrated by J. Helmer. Troll, 1982.

THE STORY OF AN ENGLISH VILLAGE by J. Goodall. Atheneum, 1979.

SUN UP, SUN DOWN by G. Gibbons. Harcourt Brace Jovanovich, 1983.

THE TENTH GOOD THING ABOUT BARNEY by J. Viorst. Illustrated by E. Blegvad. Atheneum, 1971.

TITCH by P. Hutchins. Macmillan, 1971.

TORNADO by F. M. Branley. Illustrated by G. Maestro. Crowell, 1988.

TORNADO! POEMS by A. Adoff. Illustrated by R. Himler. Delacorte, 1977.

TWO KITTENS ARE BORN: FROM BIRTH TO TWO MONTHS by B. Schilling. Holt, Rinehart and Winston, 1980.

THE UGLY DUCKLING by H. C. Andersen. Illustrated by T. Locker. Macmillan, 1987.

THE VERY HUNGRY CATERPILLAR by E. Carle. Philomel, 1983.

WATCHING THEM GROW: INSIDE A ZOO NURSERY by J. Hewitt. Photographs by R. Hewitt. Little, Brown, 1979.

WHAT HAPPENS TO A HAMBURGER by P. Showers. Illustrated by A. Rockwell. Crowell, 1985.

WHAT MAKES DAY AND NIGHT by F. M. Branley. Illustrated by A. Dorros. Crowell, 1961, 1987.

WHEN PEOPLE DIE by J. E. Bernstein and S. V. Gullo. Photographs by R. Hausherr. Dutton, 1977.

WHEN THE WIND BLEW by M. W. Brown. Illustrated by G. Hayes. Harper & Row, 1977.

WHERE DO ALL THE BIRDS GO? by T. Lewis. Dutton, 1988.

WILL IT RAIN? by H. Keller. Greenwillow, 1984.

WONDERS OF THE SEASONS by K. Brandt. Illustrated by J. Watling. Troll, 1982.

"YOU LOOK RIDICULOUS," SAID THE RHINOCEROS TO THE HIPPOPOTAMUS by B. Waber. Houghton Mifflin, 1966.

Prototype 4: First Grade—Explorations

EXPLORING THE NATURAL WORLD

OBSERVING

DAWN
A POCKETFUL OF CRICKET
A WALK THROUGH THE WOODS
"Poem to Mud"
"To Look at Anything"
A CRACK IN THE PAVEMENT
SECRETS IN STONES
HOW DOES IT FEEL TO BE A TREE?
HOW TO BE A NATURE DETECTIVE
Take a listening walk.
Record sounds of nature.
Make a seed mosaic.
Make a collage of natural materials.
Take a blind walk.
Describe smells, textures.
Display natural colors.
Weave with natural objects.

CLASSIFYING

ONCE WE WENT ON A PICNIC
A FIRST LOOK AT INSECTS
BENNY'S ANIMALS AND HOW HE PUT THEM IN ORDER
WILD GREEN THINGS IN THE CITY
A FIRST LOOK AT LEAVES
Make a leaf print with ink, crayon, or sunprint.
Make a museum of "100" collections. Label them.

EXPLORING BIG AND LITTLE

DINOSAURS AND THEIR YOUNG
MAIA
WILD AND WOOLY MAMMOTHS
JUNGLEWALK
IF YOU MADE A MILLION
SMALL THINGS CLOSE UP
BUGS
THE WEB IN THE GRASS
ALL UPON A SIDEWALK
ALL UPON A STONE
Cut lengths of string to the size of the biggest animals in the past and present.
Make a list of the biggest things in different categories (biggest dinosaur, insect, mountain).
Where do big things live? Locate on a world map and display the map.
Look at a drop of water under a microscope.
List the smallest things you can think of.
Write a story from a bug's point of view.

PEOPLE IN THE ENVIRONMENT

ABC OF ECOLOGY
SAVE IT! KEEP IT! USE IT AGAIN!
ABEL'S ISLAND
ANNA'S GARDEN SONG
BLACKBERRY INK
MY SIDE OF THE MOUNTAIN
Make a collage of litter from the playground.
Make a conservation scrapbook.
Plant a garden.
Devise a way to keep track of time using natural items.

EXPLORING THE IMMEDIATE ENVIRONMENT

UP GOES THE SKYSCRAPER
BIG CITY PORT
MILK
AIR
GERMS MAKE ME SICK
A YEAR IN THE COUNTRY
TOPS: BUILDING & EXPERIMENTING WITH SPINNING TOYS
CLOCKS: BUILDING & EXPERIMENTING WITH MODEL TIMEPIECES
Make a survey of all the people-made objects in the environment.
Chart their uses, where they are found, and so on.
Pick one category of things (boats, buildings, and the like), and see how many different types of that thing you can identify.
Pick an everyday sort of thing (air, germs, milk), and find out how they affect you.

EXPLORING THE WORLD OF PEOPLE

EXPLORING THE FUTURE

HOW DOES IT FEEL TO BE OLD?
GRANDMA GETS GRUMPY
SAYING GOODBYE TO GRANDMA
GRANDPA'S FACE
Invite older students to tell about what it is like to be in upper grades.
Make a list of the best things about getting older; the worst.
Invite adults of all ages to class and add their comments to "best" and "worst."
Write a poem about growing up, using information from lists.
Write a poem about best and worst parts of being a kid.

EXPLORING NEW PLACES

ROUND TRIP
FREIGHT TRAIN
OX-CART MAN
MISS RUMPHIUS
STRINGBEAN'S TRIP TO THE SHINING SEA
List reasons for going to new places.
Invite a traveler to share his/her travels.
Compare the travels in each book.
Make a roundtrip book to a place you'd like to visit.

EXPLORING AROUND THE WORLD

PEOPLE
HOW MY PARENTS LEARNED TO EAT
A NORSE LULLABY
THE STORY OF WALIDAD
POSSUM MAGIC
VILLAGE OF ROUND AND SQUARE HOUSES
FACES (magazine)
BREAD, BREAD, BREAD
HATS, HATS, HATS
Invite guests from other places to share their customs.
Locate their countries on a map and learn to say "hello" in their language (see FACES).
Share something from your culture with your guests.
What happens on Sunday? Find out what other people do on Sunday. Chart the results.
Write to pen pals. Exchange a "culture" package.
Trace your ancestors. Mark all the places on a world map. Make displays for the countries your class's ancestors came from. Use PEOPLE as a model for a book about ancestors.

EXPLORING YOUR OWN PLACE

MY PLACE
OVER BY THE RIVER
MOJAVE
MY SECRET PLACE
Ask your family to take you on a family history exploration. What things do you have in your home that come from past generations? Are there things family members have made? List all the "heirlooms" you can find.
Put together a "trunk" full of things that go back a generation or two. Try on old clothes, hats, and other items.
Write a story about when grandma or grandpa was your age. Illustrate it.

Figure 4.4

EXPLORATIONS

EXPLORING WITH NUMBERS

ANNO'S COUNTING HOUSE
1 HUNTER
WORLD OF WONDERS: A TRIP THROUGH NUMBERS
GOING UP! A COLOR COUNTING BOOK
Think of all the reasons you might need numbers. List.
Make up a game where the clues use numbers.
Collect 100 of something that can fit in a plastic bag. Mark off 100 days on the calendar and have a 100th day party.
Have a 100s Olympics.
Make up math problems whose answer is 100.

EXPLORING WITH LANGUAGE

RIDDLES AND JOKES

GIANTS: A RIDDLE BOOK
GOING BANANAS
LAUGHING TOGETHER
Collect favorite riddles and jokes.
Survey classmates.
Survey adults and make a comparison chart, or "history of jokes" book.
Make riddles based on "explorations."

NONSENSE AND MADE-UP WORDS

OUNCE DICE TRICE
JABBERWOCKY
THE SCROOBIOUS PIP
WHEN THE SKY IS LIKE LACE
Make up words that sound like the things they describe.
Find words in the dictionary that no one in the class has ever heard, and play a "pick the definition" game.
Make a list of favorite funny words.

CODES AND SPECIAL LANGUAGES

ALVIN'S SECRET CODE
Learn American sign language.
Make up a poem in sign language.
Make up a coded message and see who can break the code.

POETIC SOUNDS

"The Pickety Fence"
"Jug and Mug"
RHYTHM ROAD
Write lines of poetry that use onomatopoeia or alliteration.

LITERAL AND FIGURATIVE LANGUAGE

TEACH US, AMELIA BEDELIA
THE KING WHO RAINED
A CHOCOLATE MOOSE FOR DINNER
Illustrate everyday sayings literally.
Find a better way to say it. Make a list of cliches and come up with better ways to describe things.

EXPLORING THE ARTS

ART

Select autobiographies of illustrators.
Make art out of found objects.
Visit an art museum or gallery.
Make a class gallery.
Survey the uses of art in school and neighborhood.
Study illustrations in books. Explore illustrators' media.
Experiment with mixing colors. Chart the results.

MOVEMENT

A VERY YOUNG DANCER
Play a variety of music and create movements to match.
Invite a dancer to class to discuss the language of dance.
Learn dances from some of the countries you have learned about.

MUSIC

Create your own instruments.
Make a display of different kinds of instruments. Classify them.
Experiment to make different sounds. Record your results.
Learn songs from other countries.
Share music with another class.

IMAGINARY EXPLORATIONS

MYTH, FOLK AND FAIRY TALES

ST. GEORGE AND THE DRAGON
LITTLE RED RIDING HOOD
SLEEPING BEAUTY
SNOW WHITE
The same illustrator has done each of these books. What things do they have in common? Why do you think the illustrator picked them? What kind of explorations are they?
Find other illustrations of each of these tales. Make a comparison chart.
DEEP IN THE FOREST
JIM AND THE BEANSTALK
What stories do you need to know in order to understand each of these books?
Write a version of another folk or fairy tale.
Collect other variations.

WISHES AND DREAMS

WHERE THE WILD THINGS ARE
THERE'S A NIGHTMARE IN MY CLOSET
GORILLA
POLAR EXPRESS
WYNKEN, BLYNKEN AND NOD
COULD BE WORSE
THE GORILLA DID IT!
Make up an imaginary exploration using "Could be Worse" as a pattern.
Study these stories and decide which are wishes and which dreams.
What things in each story let you know that this is imaginary?

Schedule

Ruby Antoncic's first grade room opens onto a commons area and adjacent hallway. Her room is separated from two other first grades by folding walls and bookcases. Ruby and her two fellow teachers join efforts for many activities, but this is essentially a self-contained, heterogeneously grouped classroom, stuffed with children, animals, books, and all the material Ruby has collected over the years.

Ruby's schedule is arranged to include more whole-class activity than is done in most of the other prototypes. She uses this time to build more communal support for these young children, many of whom are categorized as being at risk. Nonetheless, there is considerable opportunity for a range of individual and small group activities, some of which run concurrently with larger group projects. Ruby also brings visitors of all types into the classroom and takes children into the community on a regular basis. Ruby works very hard to bring parents into the classroom to listen to children read, to share in children's successes, and to tell stories, discuss occupations, or help with a particular project. This means that the schedule is as flexible as the needs and interests of participants in the classroom require. Few days go quite as scheduled, but all involve children so intensely that the bell at the end of the day almost always comes as a surprise and interrupts children who are reluctant to leave the task at hand.

Into the Classroom

Ruby tells children that they enter first grade as explorers setting out to conquer new worlds, and she tells them about her own expeditions into new areas—trying to learn to water ski and learning to live in a rural part of Tanzania as a Peace Corps volunteer. She jokes about her attempts to do it right, and how grateful she was for the friendly people who tolerated her attempts and helped her become more comfortable and competent. She then engages children in a discussion of areas they would like to explore, and she suggests that the class keep a log of explorations—attempts made to learn new things, things learned from failures, new things to explore. In a sense, then, "exploration" is a year-long, everyday theme. The EXPLORATIONS WEB indicates one period of concentrated study to acquaint children with some of the domains open for exploration, and it encourages children to try new things, to take on new challenges, or to reconquer old ones. This approach fosters intellectual risk-taking, but it also encourages children to see themselves as able partners in the enterprise of making sense of the world. Problems are challenges, not stumbling blocks, and teachers are partners in the business of exploration.

Exploration is a joint student and teacher venture.

A playfulness runs throughout this theme. As you read through the charts of chil-

TABLE 4.7 Weekly Schedule, Ruby Antoncic's First Grade Classroom

Time	Monday	Tuesday	Wednesday	Thursday	Friday
7:50	Sharing time	Art	Sharing time	Sharing time	Sharing time
8:00	Whole class		Music	Whole class	
9:15	Individual time			Physical Education	Individual time
9:45	Recess				
10:00	Centers				Library
11:20	Literature				
12:00	Lunch				
12:45	Math				
1:30	Individual time or whole group, depending on needs				
2:00	Clean-up and evaluation of day				
2:15	Dismissal				

dren's and teacher's activities, you will observe a joint enthusiasm for the possibilities inherent in language—in jokes and riddles, in limericks and nonsense words, in secret codes and alliterative poetry. Language is a tool for intellectual play as well as the more serious, if not less enjoyable, job of communication.

Ruby's class is also a place where imagination is invited, and is not restricted to the arts. Notice the "Wishes and Dreams" subtheme that allows children to use literary patterns as a vehicle for expressing hopes and fears. Children use *Could Be Worse* as a pattern for their own classroom version of a series of accidents that could have happened at school or out in their neighborhood and that gets resolved in unusual ways.

Look for the various ways in which Ruby entices children into using all their senses to explore their world and the ways in which sensory explorations lead children into literature and writing and into a richer range of language with which to express themselves. Ruby also uses art and drama to further sensitize children to the ways in which to communicate.

Finally, you will notice that Ruby is aware that not all children may participate in the same way in each activity. Even though the rest of the class, for instance, is involved in dramatizing *Where the Wild Things Are,* Walter is off by himself, reading a biography of George Washington. Walter is engrossed in a project on the presidency, and his reading capabilities are such that he is more interested in pursuing his research independently than in joining his classmates' "wild rumpus." Walter volunteers later to go to the cafeteria to pick up the snack that will end the rumpus and so participates in the way in which he is most comfortable.

As you move through the prototypes, you will notice that the theme of explorations is revisited in a fourth/fifth grade setting, and that some of the same areas are explored but in different ways. Ruby and the team teachers of these older children share enthusiasm for encouraging children to work in ways that foster a sense of efficacy and of adventure in learning.

Summary

Although Ruby anticipated a number of avenues of exploration as she developed the thematic WEB, there were things suggested by the children that Ruby encouraged them to pursue but that did not appear in her initial planning. The children's fascination with Joey's father, for instance, led to involvement with the language of Cameroon that Ruby had not foreseen. In fact, the children were so charmed by the possibility of speaking in another language that they all took names from other countries and made dictionaries of useful terms in several languages. They invited Joey's father back to class several times and participated with him in an African meal.

Ruby was able to accommodate these interests and adjust her plans accordingly, and she enjoyed the directions suggested by the children at least as much as they did. She was also pleased with the children's enthusiasm for working with the hearing-impaired children in the school. As a result of the class's first performance of *Where the Wild Things Are,* an exchange program was set up that lasted all year and involved plenty of practice in all forms of communication. It also involved inviting the class's new friends to the African feast.

In few other first grade classes would children have this many opportunities to really study another culture. Yet there is evidence that stereotyped notions of "others" harden as early as fourth grade and that young children of first grade age are more open and accepting than they will probably ever be again. Ruby's introduction of cross-cultural experiences and the variety of cultures represented in her own class provided an excellent opportunity to build more world awareness and to lay the foundation for understanding as children encounter the wider world.

Stone (1986)

Children's Literature, EXPLORATIONS 1

ABC OF ECOLOGY by F. Wosmek. Davenport, 1982.

ABEL'S ISLAND by W. Steig. Farrar, Straus & Giroux, 1976.

(References continued on page 117.)

TABLE 4.8 Detailed Schedule, First Grade Classroom

DAY 3 (EXPLORATIONS 1)

Time	Children	Teacher
OPENING EXERCISES 7:50	Children come into room and greet teacher and peers. They go immediately to jobs, and to check on the bird feeder outside the widow, and the parakeet in the animal center.	Ruby checks attendance and fills out lunch forms; makes sure everyone has had something to eat and drink. (School provides breakfast for many children; Ruby keeps juice and cereal in the room for anyone who wants it.)
BOOK TIME 8:00	Children discuss "mischief" and what happens when they get into mischief.	Ruby gathers children around a chair and three cloth bags. She asks children if they have ever dreamed of being far away from home and if they've ever made mischief.
	Children are familiar with story and read parts along with Ruby.	Ruby reads *Where the Wild Things Are.*
	Children pick instruments to represent different parts of the story and play as their part of the story is read. Some of the children play their instruments while others move to the music, and several others read the story again.	Ruby opens one bag and pulls out musical instruments. "What kind of sounds would Max make? The Wild Things?" "How would wild things move in a wild rumpus?"
	Walter volunteers to go get the supper that "was still warm" in the story—a snack from the cafeteria. Until this point, Walter has been reading on his own, only sometimes looking up to see what his classmates are doing.	Ruby invites Walter to share the snack and to tell the class what he has discovered in his reading of a biography of George Washington.
WHOLE CLASS ACTIVITY 8:30	Children dictate description and then copy their story into their exploration logs.	Ruby acts as transcriber as children dictate a description of what they have done this morning. Asks children what kind of exploration Max was making.
	Children discuss nonverbal ways of communicating. Some have heard of sign language and suggest that. They practice sign language.	Ruby asks how children would communicate with Wild Things. Ruby introduces the special education teacher who knows sign language. This teacher asks a hearing-impaired child in the class to help teach sign language.
	One group decides to tell *Where the Wild Things Are* through sign language. Rest of group decides to accompany the sign language with instruments and dance used during story time.	Special education teacher invites children to visit her class and share their story. Ruby helps plan for an appropriate time. Asks other teacher how children
	Children suggest that they make masks for the Wild Things. Walter asks if he can make a George Washington mask and tell about	

	Washington in sign language. Other children agree. A committee forms to go to the library and find more information to share with the class.	could find out more about sign language.
	Children help each other figure out jokes in sign language. Two children volunteer to work on comedy exploration.	Special education teacher "signs off" with a joke. Ruby pulls *Going Bananas* off the shelf and asks if some children would like to work on a comedy exploration.
INDIVIDUAL TIME 9:15	Most children work on ideas generated during whole group time. A small group shares their logs with Ruby and each other. Two children work on a computer program to practice math.	Ruby works with individual children and listens to them read. They are sharing "wishes and dreams" stories including *There's a Nightmare in My Closet, The Gorilla Did It,* and *Could Be Worse.* Each child may select a book to take home to read.
RECESS 9:45		
CENTER TIME 10:00	As children enter the room after recess, they move into centers: —**Smallest things.** Work on creating a catalogue of smallest things. Use *The Web in the Grass, All Upon a Sidewalk,* and *All Upon a Stone.* Use materials collected on walk on previous day. —**Biggest things.** Use *Guinness Book of World Records* as model for reporting their study of big things—dinosaurs, elephants, tarantulas, and so on. —**Writing.** Children work with finding words and expressions that describe big and small. Others work on writing about learning sign language. Children put "Super Words" in their logs. They will try to use their words during this week.	Ruby works with children in centers, helping them as they make decisions about how to share their work. Ruby walks around the room and awards "Super Words" for particularly interesting work. These are slips of tagboard with interesting words relevant to the current study.
LITERATURE TIME 11:20	Listen to story and discuss how nature is used for survival.	Ruby reads third chapter of *My Side of the Mountain.*
LUNCH 12:00		
MATH 12:45	Children work in small groups arranging bottle caps to add up to one hundred, and recording the results of their "Exploring 100" project. Share projects.	Ruby walks through class checking student work and offering help as needed. Puts "100" problems on the board, and works through them with the class.

(Continued on next page.)

TABLE 4.8—Continued

DAY 3 (EXPLORATIONS 1)

Time	Children	Teacher
WHOLE CLASS ACTIVITY 1:30		Ruby gathers children in large circle on the floor and pulls out her second bag of "surprises"—full of blindfolds.
	Sighted child leads blindfolded child on a "sensory walk." Switch places midway and return to the classroom.	Ruby pairs children, and blindfolds one child in each pair.
	Discuss other senses.	Ruby transcribes descriptions of the blind walk, emphasizing sensory responses and a vocabulary to match.
	How could they explore using their senses?	
	Help plan for a "texture walk."	Plans with children for tomorrow's walk.
CLEAN-UP 2:00		

DAY 4 (EXPLORATIONS 1)

Time	Children	Teacher
BOOK TIME 8:00	Children participate in group portions of the story and ask Mr. U. plenty of questions about Cameroon.	Joey's father, Mr. U., is visiting today from Cameroon. He shares stories from his country.
WHOLE CLASS ACTIVITY 8:30	Mr. U.'s visit has sparked much discussion and interest.	Ruby helps children locate Cameroon on a map. Shares *The Village of Round and Square Houses*, a story set in Cameroon.
	Children express interest in building a Cameroon village and in learning more about this part of the world.	Ruby agrees to ask the music and art teachers to help and sends several children to the library to locate informational books. She uses a large piece of chart paper and labels it "Exploring Languages."
	Discuss how men and women communicate in the story's village.	
	Children suggest putting sign language first on the list. They add the forms of communication used in the village. As they add to the chart, the children try speaking in the different languages mentioned.	Ruby asks Joey if he can share something in the language of his father's country. She then shows the children a copy of *Faces Magazine* and shares the section on how to say "hello" around the world.
	They learn to say "hello" in other languages and begin to categorize the kinds of communications they have learned about.	
INDIVIDUAL WORK TIME 9:15	Two children work on math at the computer. Most read books on Africa. Walter is completing his project on U.S. presidents.	Ruby has collected a range of books on African countries and has set up a computer exercise based on an African counting game that involves a variety

Time	Children	Teacher
		of mathematical manipulations. She sets two girls to work at the computer and encourages the other children to find books on Africa.

DAY 12 (EXPLORATIONS 1)

Time	Children	Teacher
SHARING TIME 8:00	Each group has made a model of a village or small town in a different part of the world. The first group has also done a picture book based on *People* that shows the ways in which small communities are alike and different.	Several groups are ready to report on the project that originated with interest in Cameroon. Ruby has cleared an area in the room where their work can be displayed.
	A second group has prepared a mural of work people do in small communities.	
	A third group has collected words that describe small communities and categorized them as positive, negative, and in between.	
	Several children are interested in finding out if there are big cities in the places they have studied and if they are like the city in which the children live.	Ruby participates in the discussion of small communities and asks how these places differ from big cities.
BOOK TIME 9:30	Children listen to *Little Red Riding Hood* and discuss what they expected Little Red Riding Hood to look like.	Ruby shares two versions of *Little Red Riding Hood.* She draws the students into a careful look at the illustrations in each book and asks if the children have any other versions of this story that they could bring to class.
PHYSICAL EDUCATION 10:00	Children learn to dance a Norwegian circle dance.	After talking with Ruby, the physical education teacher has planned to work with international village or folk dances.
MATH 11:00	Children work in small groups to experiment with ways of working with parts and wholes.	Ruby has brought a variety of manipulatives to use in helping children understand part/whole relationships. This is a follow-up to the children's explorations with the concept of "100."

(EXPLORATIONS 1 *references continued from page 113.)*

AIR by A. Webb. Watts, 1987.
ALL UPON A SIDEWALK by J. George. Dutton, 1974.
ALL UPON A STONE by J. George. Crowell, 1971.
ANNO'S COUNTING HOUSE by M. Anno. Putnam, 1982
BIG CITY PORT by B. Maestro and E. DelVeccio. Macmillan, 1983.
BLACKBERRY INK by E. Merriam. Dell, 1987.

BUGS by N. Parker and J. Wright. Greenwillow, 1987.

A CHOCOLATE MOUSSE FOR DINNER by F. Gwynne. Prentice-Hall, 1987.

COULD BE WORSE by J. Stevenson. Greenwillow, 1977.

A CRACK IN THE PAVEMENT by R. Howell. Photographs by A. Strong. Atheneum, 1970.

DAWN by U. Shulevitz. Farrar, Straus & Giroux, 1974.

DEEP IN THE FOREST by B. Turkle. Dutton, 1976.

DINOSAURS AND THEIR YOUNG by R. Freedman. Illustrated by L. Morill. Holiday, 1983.

FACES MAGAZINE published by Cobblestone Press.

A FIRST LOOK AT INSECTS by M. Selsam and J. Hunt. Walker, 1974.

A FIRST LOOK AT LEAVES by M. Selsam. Illustrated by H. Springer. Walker, 1972.

FREIGHT TRAIN by D. Crews. Penguin, 1985.

GERMS MAKE ME SICK by M. Berger. Harper & Row, 1986.

GOING BANANAS: JOKES FOR KIDS by C. Keller. Treehouse, 1975.

GORILLA by A. BROWNE. Julia MacRae, 1983.

THE GORILLA DID IT by B. S. Hazen. Macmillan, 1974.

GRANDMA GETS GRUMPY by M. Berger. Harper & Row, 1986.

GRANDPA'S FACE by E. Greenfield. Putnam, 1988.

HOW DOES IT FEEL TO BE A TREE? by F. Morse. Illustrated by C. Watson. Parents Press, 1976.

HOW DOES IT FEEL TO BE OLD? by N. Farber. Illustrated by T. S. Hyman. Dutton, 1979.

HOW MY PARENTS LEARNED TO EAT by I. Friedman. Illustrated by A. Say. Houghton Mifflin, 1984.

HOW TO BE A NATURE DETECTIVE by M. Selsam. Harper & Row, 1988.

JABBERWOCKY by L. Carroll. Illustrated by K. Buckley. Harper & Row, 1985.

JIM AND THE BEANSTALK by R. Briggs. Coward, MacCann, 1970.

JUNGLEWALK by N. Trufari. Greenwillow, 1988.

THE KING WHO RAINED by F. Gwynne. Simon & Schuster, 1970.

LITTLE RED RIDING HOOD by W. and J. Grimm. Illustrated by T. S. Hyman. Holiday, 1982.

LITTLE RED RIDING HOOD by W. and J. Grimm. Illustrated by S. Moon. Creative Education, 1983.

MAIA: A DINOSAUR GROWS UP by J. Horner and J. Gorman. Illustrated by D. Henderson. Courage, 1987.

MILK by D. Carrick. Greenwillow, 1985.

MISS RUMPHIUS by B. Cooney. Viking, 1983.

MOJAVE by D. Siebert. Harper & Row, 1988.

MY PLACE by N. Wheatley and D. Rawlins. Collins, 1987.

MY SECRET PLACE by G. Gibbons. Science of Mind, 1975.

A NORSE LULLABY by M. L. VanVorst. Illustrated by M. Tomes. Lothrop, 1988.

OVER ON THE RIVER by J. Jackson. Illustrated by G. Ancona. Lothrop, 1980.

OX-CART MAN by D. Hall. Illustrated by B. Cooney. Viking, 1979.

PEOPLE by P. Spier. Doubleday, 1980.

A POCKETFUL OF CRICKET by R. Caudill. Illustrated by E. Ness. Holt, Rinehart and Winston, 1964.

POLAR EXPRESS by C. Van Allsburg. Houghton Mifflin, 1985.

POSSUM MAGIC by M. Fox. Illustrated by J. Vivas. Abingdon, 1987.

THE RANDOM HOUSE BOOK OF POETRY. Compiled by J. Prelutsky. Illustrated by A. Lobel. Random House, 1983.

REFLECTIONS ON A GIFT OF WATERMELON PICKLE by S. Dunning et al. (Eds.). Lothrop, 1966.

ROUND TRIP by A. Jonas. Greenwillow, 1983.

SAINT GEORGE AND THE DRAGON. Retold by M. Hodges. Illustrated by T. S. Hyman. Little, Brown, 1984.

SAYING GOODBYE TO GRANDMA by J. Thomas. Illustrated by M. Sewell. Tichnor & Fields, 1988.

THE SCROOBIUS PIP by E. Lear. Illustrated by N. Burkert. Harper & Row, 1987.

SECRETS IN STONES by R. Wyler and G. Ames. Four Winds, 1972.

SELF-PORTRAIT: TRINA SCHART HYMAN by T. S. Hyman. Addison-Wesley, 1981.

SLEEPING BEAUTY by C. Perrault. Illustrated by T. S. Hyman. Little, Brown, 1974.

SMALL THINGS CLOSE UP by L. Grillone and J. Gennaro. Crown, 1978.

SNOW WHITE AND THE SEVEN DWARFS by W. and J. Grimm. Illustrated by N. Burkert. Farrar, Straus & Giroux, 1987.

SNOW WHITE by W. and J. Grimm. Illustrated by T. S. Hyman. Little, Brown, 1974.

THERE'S A NIGHTMARE IN MY CLOSET by M. Mayer. Dial, 1976.

TYRANOSAURUS WAS A BEAST by J. Prelutsky. Illustrated by A. Lobel. Greenwillow, 1988.

UP GOES THE SKYSCRAPER by G. Gibbons. Macmillan, 1986.

A VERY YOUNG DANCER by J. Krementz. Dell, 1986.

VILLAGE OF ROUND AND SQUARE HOUSES by A. Grifalconi. Little, Brown, 1986.

THE WEB IN THE GRASS by B. Freschet. Illustrated by R. Duvoisin. Scribner, 1972.

WHEN THE SKY IS LIKE LACE by E. Horwitz. Illustrated by B. Cooney. Harper & Row, 1987.

WHERE THE WILD THINGS ARE by M. Sendak. Harper & Row, 1963.

WILD AND WOOLY MAMMOTHS by M. Aliki. Harper & Row, 1983.

WYNKEN, BLYNKEN AND NOD by E. Field. Illustrated by S. Jeffers. Dutton, 1982.

Prototype 5: Second Grade—Let's Eat!

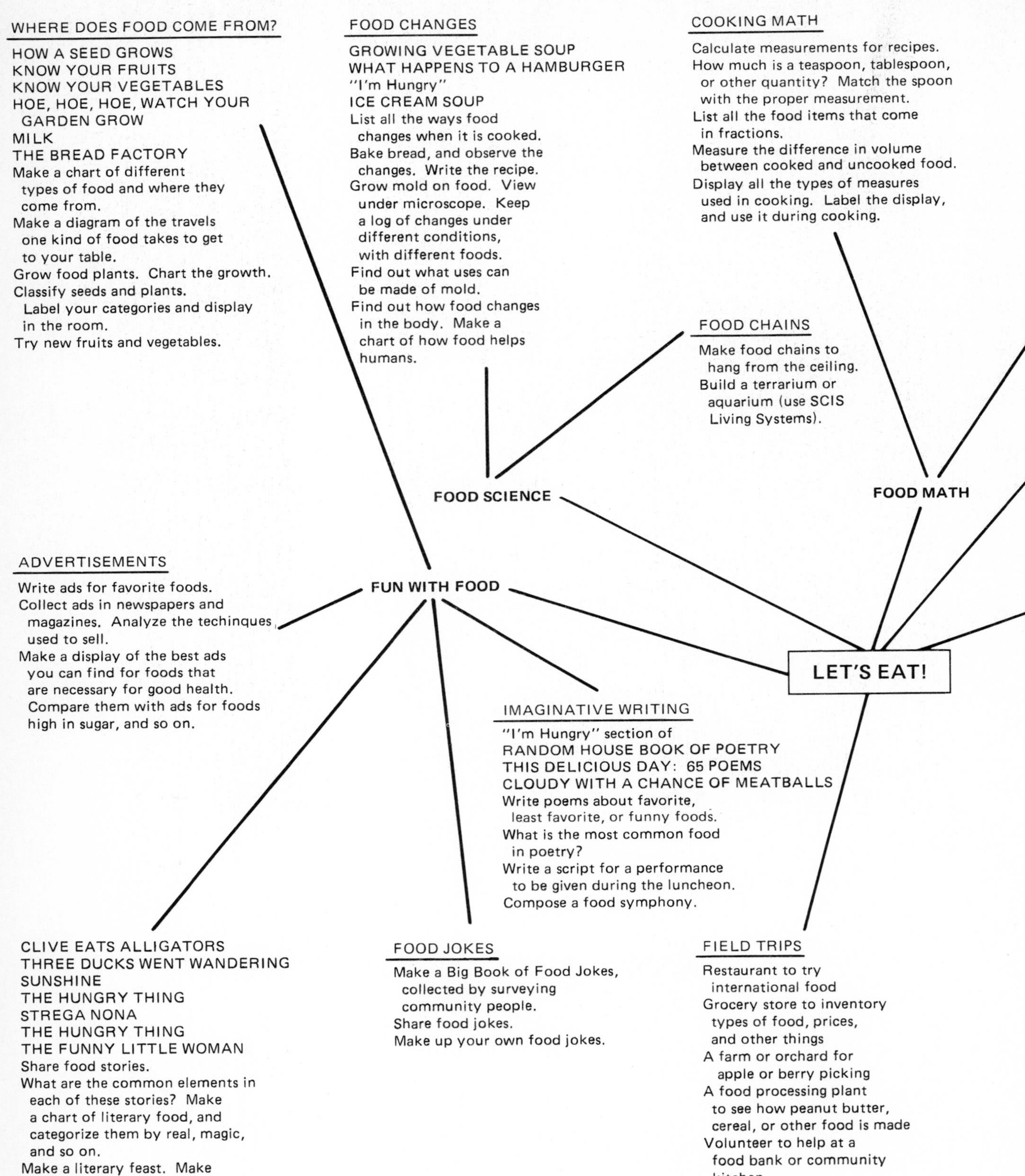

WHERE DOES FOOD COME FROM?
HOW A SEED GROWS
KNOW YOUR FRUITS
KNOW YOUR VEGETABLES
HOE, HOE, HOE, WATCH YOUR GARDEN GROW
MILK
THE BREAD FACTORY
Make a chart of different types of food and where they come from.
Make a diagram of the travels one kind of food takes to get to your table.
Grow food plants. Chart the growth.
Classify seeds and plants. Label your categories and display in the room.
Try new fruits and vegetables.
FOOD CHANGES
GROWING VEGETABLE SOUP
WHAT HAPPENS TO A HAMBURGER
"I'm Hungry"
ICE CREAM SOUP
List all the ways food changes when it is cooked.
Bake bread, and observe the changes. Write the recipe.
Grow mold on food. View under microscope. Keep a log of changes under different conditions, with different foods.
Find out what uses can be made of mold.
Find out how food changes in the body. Make a chart of how food helps humans.
COOKING MATH
Calculate measurements for recipes.
How much is a teaspoon, tablespoon, or other quantity? Match the spoon with the proper measurement.
List all the food items that come in fractions.
Measure the difference in volume between cooked and uncooked food.
Display all the types of measures used in cooking. Label the display, and use it during cooking.
FOOD CHAINS
Make food chains to hang from the ceiling.
Build a terrarium or aquarium (use SCIS Living Systems).
FOOD SCIENCE
FOOD MATH
ADVERTISEMENTS
Write ads for favorite foods.
Collect ads in newspapers and magazines. Analyze the techinques used to sell.
Make a display of the best ads you can find for foods that are necessary for good health. Compare them with ads for foods high in sugar, and so on.
FUN WITH FOOD
LET'S EAT!
IMAGINATIVE WRITING
"I'm Hungry" section of RANDOM HOUSE BOOK OF POETRY
THIS DELICIOUS DAY: 65 POEMS
CLOUDY WITH A CHANCE OF MEATBALLS
Write poems about favorite, least favorite, or funny foods.
What is the most common food in poetry?
Write a script for a performance to be given during the luncheon.
Compose a food symphony.
CLIVE EATS ALLIGATORS
THREE DUCKS WENT WANDERING
SUNSHINE
THE HUNGRY THING
STREGA NONA
THE HUNGRY THING
THE FUNNY LITTLE WOMAN
Share food stories.
What are the common elements in each of these stories? Make a chart of literary food, and categorize them by real, magic, and so on.
Make a literary feast. Make foods described in stories (such as pasta, rice balls).
THE LITTLE PIG'S COOKBOOK
FOOD JOKES
Make a Big Book of Food Jokes, collected by surveying community people.
Share food jokes.
Make up your own food jokes.
FIELD TRIPS
Restaurant to try international food
Grocery store to inventory types of food, prices, and other things
A farm or orchard for apple or berry picking
A food processing plant to see how peanut butter, cereal, or other food is made
Volunteer to help at a food bank or community kitchen.

Figure 4.5

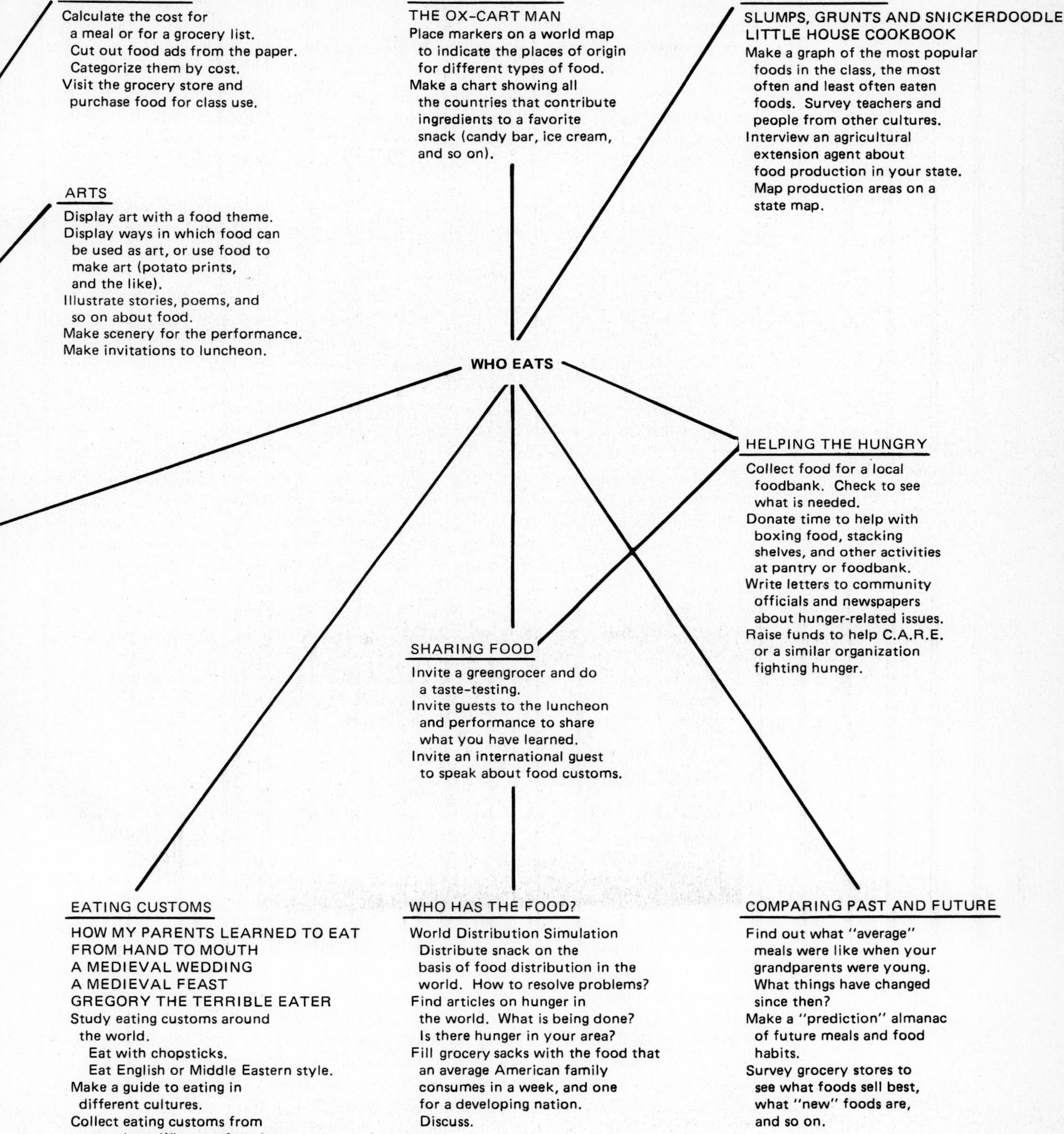

GROCERY MATH
Calculate the cost for a meal or for a grocery list.
Cut out food ads from the paper.
Categorize them by cost.
Visit the grocery store and purchase food for class use.
FOOD GEOGRAPHY
THE OX-CART MAN
Place markers on a world map to indicate the places of origin for different types of food.
Make a chart showing all the countries that contribute ingredients to a favorite snack (candy bar, ice cream, and so on).
WHO EATS WHAT?
SLUMPS, GRUNTS AND SNICKERDOODLES
LITTLE HOUSE COOKBOOK
Make a graph of the most popular foods in the class, the most often and least often eaten foods. Survey teachers and people from other cultures.
Interview an agricultural extension agent about food production in your state.
Map production areas on a state map.
ARTS
Display art with a food theme.
Display ways in which food can be used as art, or use food to make art (potato prints, and the like).
Illustrate stories, poems, and so on about food.
Make scenery for the performance.
Make invitations to luncheon.
WHO EATS
HELPING THE HUNGRY
Collect food for a local foodbank. Check to see what is needed.
Donate time to help with boxing food, stacking shelves, and other activities at pantry or foodbank.
Write letters to community officials and newspapers about hunger-related issues.
Raise funds to help C.A.R.E. or a similar organization fighting hunger.
SHARING FOOD
Invite a greengrocer and do a taste-testing.
Invite guests to the luncheon and performance to share what you have learned.
Invite an international guest to speak about food customs.
EATING CUSTOMS
HOW MY PARENTS LEARNED TO EAT
FROM HAND TO MOUTH
A MEDIEVAL WEDDING
A MEDIEVAL FEAST
GREGORY THE TERRIBLE EATER
Study eating customs around the world.
Eat with chopsticks.
Eat English or Middle Eastern style.
Make a guide to eating in different cultures.
Collect eating customs from your class. What are favorite foods, special celebration foods, and other food-related themes?
WHO HAS THE FOOD?
World Distribution Simulation
Distribute snack on the basis of food distribution in the world. How to resolve problems?
Find articles on hunger in the world. What is being done?
Is there hunger in your area?
Fill grocery sacks with the food that an average American family consumes in a week, and one for a developing nation.
Discuss.
COMPARING PAST AND FUTURE
Find out what "average" meals were like when your grandparents were young.
What things have changed since then?
Make a "prediction" almanac of future meals and food habits.
Survey grocery stores to see what foods sell best, what "new" foods are, and so on.

Schedule

The schedule for Prototype 5 is based on activity in a self-contained, integrated-day, primary classroom. As the WEB indicates, there is an activity planned to involve parents and other adults from outside the school. Although this technique is not always necessary, it can be an important way in which to involve other adults in the school and to build interest in and support for the school program.

The theme in this classroom fits with a common primary health/science unit on nutrition and attempts to put the concept of nutrition into a broader context than the traditional four food groups by looking at cultural contexts for eating, problems of hunger and malnutrition, and ways in which children can be problem alleviators even in the primary grades.

The teacher, Carol Hagihara, introduces the theme with a piece of literature, *The Hungry Thing* by Slepian, a humorous story about hunger and communication that is enjoyable for young children and that easily leads into a variety of extension activities. Table 4.9 shows how Carol blocks class time for the week. Note that Carol's schedule allows for movement from whole group to small group to individual activities throughout the day and allows for quieter times—poetry sharing, for instance—to follow more active periods such as physical education. Carol has also organized the integrated work time around activity centers. Children rotate through groups over the course of the day or week, but not every child will spend time in each center, nor will every child spend the same amount of time in each center. Instead, Carol plans with the children for individual, group, and whole class responsibilities.

Parent involvement can provide flexibility for teachers.

Carol also uses a parent volunteer in one center for this thematic unit. Although this is not necessary for every theme, it is certainly a worthwhile involvement of an interested parent, and it allows Carol to use a cooking experience in a small group that might have been awkward to arrange otherwise. Carol's school also has an outdoor education program that culminates in a fifth grade overnight and a sixth grade four-day camping trip. As a result, Carol has responsibility for planning outdoor experiences (one block of time on Fridays) to prepare her children for the overnight and camping trips when they are older. On Monday through Thursday, however, her children go to classes in art, music, and physical education, and Carol has a fifty-minute planning period on each of those days.

Finally, Carol has established a Reading Buddies* program in which older students are matched with children in her class and are allotted time in which to read together.

Into the Classroom

The schedule is simply the bare bones of Carol's planning. Stepping into her classroom and following both Carol and the children through portions of a thematic unit allow us to see how time and activity are shared in this second grade classroom. In Table 4.10, the entire first day of the thematic unit is outlined, along with portions of the second and fifteenth days of the unit. Notice how much activity is generated on the first day and how Carol concentrates that focus during sharing and whole group times on the second day. She uses writing—a child-constructed Big Book* on eating customs in the United States and Japan—to move into a discussion of the mechanics of punctuation, and she asks children to attend to this feature of their writing. Carol also uses the second day's activities to help children to focus on the concept of "fairness" relative to problems of food distribution and to consider issues of hunger. Instead, however, of simply telling children there are problems of hunger, she encourages them to think of ways they can make a difference in the larger community outside the school. This provides the impetus for the integrated work time that follows.

Between Day 2 and Day 15, children will have worked through a number of activities suggested and depicted on the WEB, as well as working with their Reading Buddies*, having Sustained Silent Reading (SSR)* each day, and going to their regularly

TABLE 4.9 Weekly Schedule, Carol Hagihara's Second Grade Classroom

Time	Monday	Tuesday	Wednesday	Thursday	Friday
7:35	Opening exercises. Attendance, lunch count, sign-ups.				
8:05	Sharing time. Projects, writing, solutions to work-related problems, planning, progress report.				
8:25	Whole group activity. Theme introduction, simulation, guest speaker, Reader's Theatre*.				
9:00	Integrated work time. Move between centers, work in small groups.				
9:45	Recess				
10:00	Art	Music	Physical Education	Library	Outdoor Education
10:50	Poetry time. Teacher shares poetry, children share poetry.				
11:00	Integrated work time. Rotate groups.				
11:30	Lunch				
12:10	Integrated work time				
12:30	Sustained Silent Reading* and individual conferences				
12:55	Literature time	Reading Buddies*	Writing workshop	Reading Buddies*	Author's Chair*
1:30	Integrated work time				
2:15	Evaluation and clean-up				

scheduled art, music, physical education, and library classes. Day 15 is selected for a luncheon and theme-related performance for invited guests. This sharing brings together other strands from the WEB—celebrating food, the communal importance of eating, and the children's literary and artistic endeavors related to the theme. Notice that Carol has rescheduled the day to accommodate this activity, and the children involve themselves in decorating the room with examples of their work. A book written and illustrated by the children to represent the various types of experiences they have had is placed near each visitor's seat. There are chapters on where food comes from, favorite foods around the world, the use of food in literature, and so forth. A glance at the WEB indicates the projects children might represent in their book.

Day 15 also begins with a report on the food pantry that the children have "adopted" as one response to their study of the problems of hunger. There are also quiet times just before and after the guests come. This helps Carol and the children to cope with the excitement of performance and guests without resorting to harsher disciplinary tactics. Carol has also worked with children so that they take on the responsibilities of hosts, including appropriate behavior.

As children move through centers and engage in various activities, Carol works with them on particular center projects. In one case (Day 1), after checking to ensure that everyone understands the morning's work, Carol meets with a small group needing extra assistance in math. Carol subsequently leaves the math group and moves in and out of small and individual encounters with other children as they work.

Summary

Over the course of this thematic unit, Carol strove to balance individual and small and whole group activities. She provided for vigorous movement, discussion, and quiet, reflective time. Each part of the day was planned to incorporate a wide variety of language use. There was reason to practice oral reading and plenty of time for pleasurable,

Seek a balance among individual, small, and whole group activities.

(Summary continued on page 128.)

TABLE 4.10 Detailed Schedule, Second Grade Classroom

DAY 1 (LET'S EAT!)

Time	Children	Teacher
TEACHER PREPARATION 7:25		Carol checks setups for class, writes announcements on board, and checks mail in office.
OPENING EXERCISES 8:55	Children arrive and fill in attendance and lunch count, drop forms in appropriate box. Several sign up for Sharing Time.	Carol greets children as they enter, makes sure forms are filled in, and makes announcements.
SHARING TIME 8:05	Two groups share projects from previous unit. Peers ask questions and comment on work done.	Carol invites children to sharing area. She shares a limerick as an introduction to Sharing Time, and then monitors time and participates in the group discussion.
UNIT INTRODUCTION 8:25	Children stay in sharing area, listen to story, and discuss. They read along with the Big Book* version of the story.	Carol introduces a new story, *The Hungry Thing.* Leads discussion of hunger, "What might happen if no one could figure out what you wanted?"
	Children take different parts to read, and all recite the Hungry Thing's lines.	Carol uses the Big Book* and reads it along with the children. She points out features of the text and of individual words and phrases. As children suggest additional things to feed the Hungry Thing, Carol adds lines to the Big Book* text.
	Several children suggest activities for a class work chart.	Carol introduces the new unit on eating, solicits children's suggestions, and goes over some possible activities.
	Children help plan their work for integrated work time. Planning sheets are checked off, and work assignments made.	
INTEGRATED WORK TIME 9:00	Children move to work areas throughout the room:	Carol moves between groups, helping children get started on their work.
	—**Grocery list.** Children locate advertisements for luncheon foods and figure math problems related to serving a luncheon. A grocery store in the area provides practice in careful shopping, making change, adding money, and checking work with a calculator. Finished work is put in a folder for the teacher to review.	
	—**Food measures.** This group works with an assortment of measuring devices and dry foods to measure. They work to establish equivalencies and make a chart to use in cooking activities.	Carol works with a small group who have been having difficulty with previous math activities. The children then work in pairs to check their work.

	—**Growing food.** Assorted seeds and reference books help children with sorting and matching seeds to full-grown plants. Children set up experiments to observe root growth and chart development of different types of food plants.	Carol leaves the math group and joins the children who are planting seeds. She shares part of *Hoe, Hoe, Hoe, Watch My Garden Grow* and discusses types of plants children have decided to grow. She asks children for a report on their progress during today's evaluation time.
	—**Food in fiction.** Children select books from the reading center to read to each other. Each child picks a book to read during individual conferences.	
	—**Eating around the world.** Children listen to the story, and try to use chopsticks. They discuss the experience and try to find interesting words to describe it. They locate Japan and the United States on their inflatable globes and on the Peter's Projection world map. In pairs, they create directions for eating in America and in Japan.	A parent volunteer (prepared by Carol) is working in this area today. She has a pot of Japanese noodles bubbling in a corner, and *How My Parents Learned to Eat* in hand. She shares the story and invites children to eat the noodles with chopsticks. In between helping children manage the chopsticks, she records the descriptive words and phrases the children use to describe this experience. These will be added to children's Learning Log* and used in their writing.
RECESS AND SPECIAL CLASSES		
POETRY 10:50	Children recite their favorite poems after the teacher shares some poetry. A child suggests illustrating Shel Silverstein's "Adelaide" and several other children decide to put together a book of eating poems and illustrations.	Carol shares several "eating" poems from *The Random House Book of Poetry.* Carol points out other books of poetry in the reading center and suggests asking the librarian for help, too.
INTEGRATED WORK TIME 11:00	Children rotate groups or move to writing tables to complete projects begun earlier in the day.	Carol works with a child who is ready for an "editor" for part of "How to Eat in Japan and the United States." She also checks with the poetry group to see that they have themselves organized for work.
LUNCH FOLLOWED BY A THIRD INTEGRATED WORK TIME		
SUSTAINED SILENT READING* 12:30–12:55	Children read selections of their choice.	Carol has conferences with individual children or with small groups to hear them read and to discuss their reading.

(Continued on next page.)

TABLE 4.10—Continued

DAY 1 (LET'S EAT!)

Time	Children	Teacher
LITERATURE 12:55	After discussing food preferences, children decide to survey a grocery store to find out what foods are best sellers. They select a committee to work with the teacher in developing a survey.	Carol shares *Gregory the Terrible Eater* and leads discussion of favorite and least favorite foods.
	Children retrieve *How My Parents Learned to Eat* to find parts that refer to American eating customs. They reread some parts.	Carol asks children to share what was learned about Japanese food and customs. What part of the story helped them to understand how complicated American-style eating was? She invites several children to share parts of the story by reading them aloud.
INTEGRATED WORK TIME 1:30	Complete work for today's projects and plan for next day.	Carol works with the survey committee to get them started, and then moves between groups to help children decide on future directions, or bring closure to a project.
EVALUATION AND CLEAN-UP 2:15	Children put work in notebooks and begin end-of-day jobs.	Carol asks children to survey food products at home and to see if they can find two foods that did not come from the United States.

DAY 2 (LET'S EAT!)

Time	Children	Teacher
SHARING TIME 8:05	One group shares their Big Book* of eating customs in the United States and Japan. Children discuss punctuation in the Big Book* as the group explains that they had some difficulty in this area. Several children read sentences as if other punctuation had been used (i.e., question marks rather than an exclamation mark or a period). They begin to construct some helpful hints for punctuation. Several children come to the board to put punctuation marks in sentences and to see if their hints are really helpful.	Carol points out interesting words and ideas, comments on their careful attention to punctuation, and asks the class why they think certain choices were made. Carol writes some sentences on the board and asks children to use their new helpful hints to punctuate them. "Let's see if we can use these hints to make our writing more interesting. Why don't you bring some examples of good use of punctuation to 'group' today?"

WHOLE GROUP ACTIVITY 8:25	Children match passports from a previous activity to country names posted in the room and sit in those areas.	Once children are seated by country, Carol distributes snack based on food distribution in the countries represented.
	Children quickly note that the snack is not "fairly" distributed.	Carol asks them to outline the problem and then offer possible solutions.
	Discuss as a class how to solve the problem. Rank order solutions. Pick one, and act on it.	"How do we decide which solution to pick?" Compare to problems in the world. "Can we think of possible solutions to some of these problems?"
	Discuss ways to help hungry people. Select several possibilities to work on.	Divide class into groups based on the suggestions and student interests.
INTEGRATED WORK TIME 9:00	Work in groups to plan for hunger projects (see WEB).	Carol helps make plans workable and serves as recorder.
	Share plans and make a schedule for accomplishing them.	

DAY 15 (LET'S EAT!)

Time	Children	Teacher
SHARING TIME 8:05	A committee that went to the food pantry reports on the need for cardboard boxes. The class decides to collect boxes and deliver them the following week.	Carol participates in the discussion that is led by the committee of students.
DRESS REHEARSAL 8:25	Run through the play, poems, and other readings planned for guests.	Organize a runthrough of the program, including play adapted from *The Funny Little Woman.*
ROOM ARRANGEMENT 9:00	Put final touches on decorations, and organize food.	Work with children on room decoration.
RECESS AND SPECIAL CLASSES 9:45		
LITERATURE 10:50	Gather quietly for story.	Share *Bon Appetit, Mr. Rabbit.*
SPECIAL PROGRAM 11:00	Children greet guests and show them to seats. They introduce program and put on performance.	Carol also greets guests. She assists and directs as necessary and makes sure guests receive books made for them.
	Children serve luncheon (all planned and made by children).	
	Bid guests goodbye.	
	After all guests leave, everyone goes out for recess.	
CLEAN-UP 12:15	Everyone helps put room back into working order.	
SUSTAINED SILENT READING* 12:55	Read book of own choosing.	Read book of own choosing.

private reading, as well as listening when the teacher shared books. There were opportunities to talk and to listen, to organize thoughts in writing, to express ideas in art, charts, graphs, and action. Children made choices, as when they decided to adopt the food pantry and to collect food and volunteer time there. With Carol's guidance, children were engaged in activities that allowed them to participate in the community beyond the school. They learned in graphic ways about a community's responsibility to help to feed its members. They were also involved in learning the content and concepts of such subject areas as science and social studies when they compared cross-cultural patterns of food use or tried raising their own food crops. Carol's role as facilitator helped children to see the connections between these domains more clearly.

Certainly Carol's placement in a self-contained setting and her school's interest in integrated-day planning supported her move toward an integrated language curriculum. But other settings—for example, the following second/third grade family grouped setting—can also support such integrated language programs at this same elementary level.

Children's Literature, LET'S EAT

THE BAKERY FACTORY by A. Jenness. Crowell, 1978.

BON APPETIT, MR. RABBIT by C. Boujon. M. K. McElderry, 1987.

CHOCOLATE FEVER by R. K. Smith. Dell, 1978.

A CHOCOLATE MOUSSE FOR DINNER by F. Gwynne. Prentice-Hall, 1987.

THE CHOCOLATE TOUCH by P. S. Catling. Bantam-Skylark, 1981.

CLIVE EATS ALLIGATORS by A. Lester. Houghton Mifflin, 1986.

CLOUDY WITH A CHANCE OF MEATBALLS by J. Barrett. Macmillan, 1978.

FROM HAND TO MOUTH, OR HOW WE INVENTED KNIVES, FORKS, SPOONS AND CHOPSTICKS AND THE TABLE MANNERS TO GO WITH THEM by J. C. Giblin. Crowell, 1987.

THE FUNNY LITTLE WOMAN by A. Mosel. Illustrated by B. Lent. Dutton, 1972.

GOING BANANAS: JOKES FOR KIDS by C. Keller. Treehouse, 1975.

GREGORY THE TERRIBLE EATER by M. Sharmat. Illustrated by J. Aruego and A. Dewey. Four Winds Press, 1987.

GROWING VEGETABLE SOUP by L. Ehlert. Harcourt Brace Jovanovich, 1987.

HOE, HOE, HOE, WATCH MY GARDEN GROW by M. Daddona. Addison-Wesley, 1980.

HOW A SEED GROWS by H. J. Jordan. Harper & Row, 1960.

HOW MY PARENTS LEARNED TO EAT by I. Friedman. Illustrated by A. Say. Houghton Mifflin, 1984.

THE HUNGRY THING by J. Slepian and A. Seidler. Scholastic, 1967.

ICE CREAM SOUP by F. Modell. Greenwillow, 1988.

KNOW YOUR FRUITS by S. S. Bose. Jules Books, 1988.

KNOW YOUR VEGETABLES by S. S. Bose. Jules Books, 1988.

LITTLE HOUSE COOKBOOK by B. Walker. Harper & Row, 1979.

THE LITTLE PIGS' COOKBOOK by C. N. Watson. Little, Brown, 1987.

MEDIEVAL FEAST by M. Aliki. Harper & Row, 1983.

MERRY EVER AFTER by J. Lasker. Viking, 1976.

MILK by D. Carrick. Greenwillow, 1985.

OX-CART MAN by D. Hall. Illustrated by B. Cooney. Viking, 1979.

POSSUM MAGIC by M. S. Fox. Illustrated by J. Vivas. Abingdon, 1987.

THE RANDOM HOUSE BOOK OF POETRY. Compiled by J. Prelutsky. Illustrated by A. Lobel. Random House, 1983.

REFLECTIONS ON A GIFT OF WATERMELON PICKLE by S. Dunning et al. (Eds.). Lothrop, 1966.

ROUND TRIP by A. Jonas. Greenwillow, 1983.

GIANT FUN

Take on character roles from the giant stories. Conduct a TV talk show interview with the characters.
Plan a giant party. Write invitations. Plan a menu based on giant stories.
Determine the relative size of giants in all the giant stories. Make a progressive size chart from smallest to largest on long sheets of butcher paper.
Brainstorm the list of places a giant could not go because of his/her size.
Design a home for a giant.
Create a giant museum. Collect objects found in giant stories and display them. Write descriptions for museum viewers.
Create a graffiti wall of words that describe giant things or giant feelings.
Grow "giant" bean stalks. Plant bean seeds in different soils and treat them under different light, food, and moisture conditions. Hypothesize about which conditions will produce the biggest plant. Keep a daily log of observations.
Interview your classmates about their favorite giant story, their favorite real life giant, and their favorite animal giant. Show the results on a bar graph.

TALL TALES

PAUL BUNYAN
PECOS BILL
Present a one-minute TV news bulletin about one of these amazing events.
Read other American tall tales about characters that are larger than life: John Henry, Slue Foot Sue, Old Stormalong, and Joe Magarac.
Make a mural of tall tale characters.
TALL TALES AND OTHER LIES FROM AMERICAN FOLKLORE
Interview family members or friends for their best tall tales. Collect these in a book.
Write your own tall tale.

"Paul Bunyan"
Write a "giant" poem.

GIANT APPETITES

THE BOY WHO ATE MORE THAN A GIANT AND OTHER SWEDISH FOLKTALES
" 'I Want My Breakfast', the Giant Said"
GUSTAVE, THE GOURMET GIANT
"Ol' Paul and His Camp"
Read a recipe for "flapjacks." Measure and weigh the ingredients, then cook them.
Multiply the ingredients so that you could feed Paul Bunyan or another giant.
WHAT'S ON YOUR PLATE?
What foods will help you grow into a giant?
Write more giant food riddles.

UP AGAINST A GIANT

THE GIANT'S APPRENTICE
THE BRAVE LITTLE TAILOR
NORSE GODS AND GIANTS
HARALD AND THE GIANT KNIGHT
THE GIANT WHO SWALLOWED THE WIND
INSIDE MY FEET: THE STORY OF A GIANT
DAVID AND GOLIATH
THE VALIANT LITTLE TAILOR
THE DRAGON, GIANT AND MONSTER TREASURY
Retell a giant story using stick puppets.
Write a Giant Newspaper. Include front page stories and headlines, want ads, sports page, and editorials.
Tell the story from the giant's point of view.
"The Towering Giant"
Plan a choral reading of the poem.

GIANTS

GIANTS OF THE HEART

Marion Anderson
Martin Luther King
Jackie Robinson
Cesar Chavez
Roberto Clemente
Jim Thorpe
Phyllis Wheatley
Harriet Tubman
JUAREZ, MAN OF LAW
SHARK LADY: TRUE ADVENTRUES OF EUGENIE CLARK
Read about these or other people who were giants of the heart. Why is this a good description for these people?
Dress up as your character and tell about yourself.
Draw a picture of your "giant" and write a biography.

GIANTS ALL AROUND

THE MYSTERIOUS GIANT OF BARLETTA
FINN M'COUL: THE GIANT OF KNOCKMANY HILL
THE GOOD GIANTS AND THE BAD PUKWUDGIES
THE BFG
GIANT POEMS
Make a comparison chart of giants. Include categories for personality, physical appearance, job, habitat, hobbies, friends, and so on.
Make a giant board game. Write directions for how to play it.

GIANTS UP A (BEAN) TREE

JACK AND THE BEANSTALK
Make a map showing the sequence of action and places in the story.
Write a letter from the giant to Jack asking for the return of his magic harp and his magic goose.
Write a lost and found ad for the giant's property.
JIM AND THE BEANSTALK
Write a sequel to another giant story.
JACK AND THE WONDER BEANS
JACK AND THE BEAN TREE
Make a giant drawing of one of the giants. Label the parts of the giant's body with poetic phrases from the books ("Feet like cornsleds").
Compare styles of language in the different versions. Write a version using phrases from your own region or using modern slang.
Read other "Jack tales."

Schedule

Estella Esquivel teaches a second/third grade family grouped class. This situation is common in many schools, sometimes out of necessity but often out of choice. Family grouping has many pluses. Children of various backgrounds and abilities can work together successfully. Older children benefit from helping younger children and from acting as their tutors. They are often more familiar with the classroom organization and can help initiate the younger members into the routine of the thematic unit approach. This type of grouping more readily accommodates children with a variety of language and literacy capabilities and gives them plenty of time to develop as readers and writers.

In this particular class, the teacher is responsible for teaching all subject areas except art, music, health, and physical education. The school staff believes in cooperative planning, however, and specialists in these subject areas enjoy extending classroom themes through their particular areas of expertise.

The GIANTS theme grew out of Estella's awareness of the children's strong interest in dinosaurs and other giant animals. She also knew that the seven- to nine-year age span is when an interest in fairy tales and folk tales is at its height. The longer tales about giants were perfect for children who were becoming fluent readers but who were perhaps not quite ready for longer novels. In addition, her science curriculum required that she deal with animal life, and the social studies guide called for a look at neighborhoods and communities of the past and present. Because the school was part of an urban system, tall buildings, monuments, and museums made the theme of GIANTS especially appealing.

TABLE 4.11 Weekly Schedule, Estella Esquivel's Second/Third Grade Family Grouping Classroom

Time	Monday	Tuesday	Wednesday	Thursday	Friday
7:30	Teacher preparation time				
8:00	Children arrive, put away coats, prepare lunch count, and take attendance.				
8:10	Group time. Teacher reads poetry, story, or information book. Plans for the day are discussed.				
8:30	Integrated work time. Children work in small groups or individually. Teacher works with small groups or has individual conferences.				
10:00	Recess				
10:15	Art	Music	Health	Art	Music
10:45	Math				
11:45	Group meeting. Teacher and students discuss morning's work. Several students share their writing or other projects.				
12:00	Lunch and outdoor play				
1:00	Sustained Silent Reading*				
1:20	Book talk. Several children talk about the books they have been reading.				
1:30	Integrated work time. Children continue work time, or teacher works with whole class.				
2:15	Physical Education				
2:35	Clean-up				
2:45	Read-aloud. Teacher reads or asks children to read from their work.				
3:00	Dismissal				

Into the Classroom

As you enter Estella Esquivel's classroom and watch the interactions between members of the classroom community, you will note that the use of folk and fairy tale literature helps to set the stage for a wide variety of activities, including growing plants, studying enormous creatures, and playing with the language of enormity. Concepts such as "giant," "big," and "little" have great appeal in the elementary years, as evidenced by children's enduring enthusiasm for such books as the *Guinness Book of World Records*. You will recall that the concepts of "big" and "little" were also subthemes in the EXPLORATIONS WEB (Prototype 4). Sometimes such subthemes develop into full-length thematic units. In other cases, they provide a base of experience for later in-depth study. In either case, they motivate enough interest and offer enough rich possibilities to support a second encounter.

Another feature of this prototype is Estella's excellent support from the art teacher. Mr. Herchenroether—Mr. H, the children call him—consults with Estella and then introduces a sequence of activities that encourage children to experience "giant" art. They get to respond to abstract expressionism, as well as to art in the public and outdoor environment. He then involves the children in creating a giant piece of art for the schoolyard. Mr. H's willingness to extend classroom themes into the art class provides Estella and her students with an additional expertise and a richer variety of theme-related experiences.

Table 4.12 samples the first day of the GIANTS theme and provides an overview of how Estella draws children into planning activities, how she works with the art specialist, and how she shares books with her students. Day 3 describes a particular response to theme-related literature—a Comparison Chart*—and, finally, Day 16 shows the class's shift in emphasis from fiction to informational literature, and from story writing to the beginnings of a research report.

Summary

The opportunity to work with like-minded and cooperative colleagues is certainly a plus for Estella Esquivel. It is also representative of her approach to teaching and learning that her collegial relationships benefit her students. Estella does not pretend to know everything there is to know about each theme introduced in the course of a year. Instead, she embarks as a learner—albeit a more expert one—with her students. As a learner, she taps resources just as her students do and asks for help in constructing new knowledge as they do. Together, Estella, her students, and her peer teachers elaborate on the initial theme and make it more meaningful to all involved.

Children's Literature, GIANTS

THE BFG by R. Dahl. Illustrated by Q. Blake. Farrar, Straus & Giroux, 1982.

THE BIG BEAST BOOK: DINOSAURS AND HOW THEY GOT THAT WAY by J. Booth. Illustrated by M. Weston. Little, Brown, 1988.

THE BIG BOOK OF REAL SKYSCRAPERS by G. Ingoglia. Illustrated by T. LaPadula. Grosset/Dunlap, 1988.

"Boa Constrictor" in WHERE THE SIDE WALK ENDS by S. Silverstein. Harper & Row, 1974.

THE BOY WHO ATE MORE THAN A GIANT AND OTHER SWEDISH FOLKTALES by V. Lofgren. Collins, 1978.

THE BRAVE LITTLE TAILOR by J. and W. Grimm. Translated by A. Bell. Illustrated by S. Otto. Larousse, 1979.

"Brontosaurus" by G. Kredenser in THE RANDOM HOUSE BOOK OF POETRY. Compiled by J. Prelutsky. Illustrated by A. Lobel. Random House, 1983.

BUILDING, THE FIGHT AGAINST GRAVITY by M. Salvador. Illustrated by S. Hooker and C. Rogers. Atheneum, 1979.

(References continued on page 139.)

TABLE 4.12 Detailed Schedule, Second/Third Grade Family Grouping

DAY 1 (GIANTS)

Time	Children	Teacher
TEACHER ARRIVAL 7:30		Estella arrives to complete paperwork, get materials ready for children. Today she sets out folktales about giants in the reading corner.
ARRIVAL 8:00	Children come in, put away coats and lunches. Several are assigned to take lunch count and attendance. Others move to the reading center and browse through books about giants.	Teacher takes time to chat with individual children.
GROUP TIME 8:10	Children respond to book with comments about the illustrations and story. Many remember the familiar tale and join in on the refrain "Fee, fi, fo, fum."	Estella announces the beginning of new thematic unit. She begins by reading Jack Prelutsky's poem "The Towering Giant." Then she reads Lorinda Bryan Cauley's version of *Jack and the Beanstalk.*
INTEGRATED WORK TIME 8:30	Children volunteer ideas. These include scary giants, monsters, nice giants. Several suggest words to describe giants—"huge," "big," "monstrous." When one child mentions dinosaurs, another thinks of whales, another the great white shark.	Since this is the beginning of a new theme, Estella takes time with the whole group to introduce them to the whole unit. She begins with a large sheet of craft paper and asks the children to brainstorm the idea of GIANTS. She writes their ideas on the paper Graffiti Wall*. After they are done, she invites children to add to the wall as they find new ideas or new words about giants. She then explains that the unit will involve them in activities connected to giants they may already know about but may also help them to think about giants in a new way. She summarizes some of the activities they will be involved in during the course of the unit. Then she introduces folktales with giants as characters. She has grouped the books together and takes volunteers for each of the groups, explaining the basic theme of each group of stories.

9:15	Children volunteer for "Giants Up a Tree," "Giants All Around," "Up Against a Giant," or "Tall Tales." Each group of six to eight gathers together. Children look through the selections available, and each child chooses a story to read.	Estella has collected more than enough books or anthologies for each group. She groups the children together and allows them to choose from the 10 to 12 stories available for each type of giant story. She then asks children to work together in groups of 3 or 4. Estella explains that after the children finish their story, they are to meet with their group and tell the rest of the group about the story they read. As each person tells about the story, children are asked to think about how their own story is similar and different. Then they will decide on categories in order to construct a Comparison Chart*.
	Children read silently. As some finish before other members of their group, they jot down details in their Learning Logs*. Several get art paper and draw a picture from their story. Several groups begin telling each other about their stories.	Estella monitors silent reading, stopping to listen to several children who want to read to her. As groups begin discussion, she moves from group to group and observes the children at work. She suggests that one member in each group jot down details that seem to be alike in the stories.
ART 10:15	Children attend art class with a special teacher. Children use straws to blow paint in various designs over and across surface of the paper.	Keith Herchenroether, the art teacher, has been alerted to the GIANTS theme by Estella. He decides to use his time to introduce the children to the idea of size in paintings. He shows them pictures of paintings in art books and reproductions. He then uses an opaque projector to show the children the actual size of paintings. He selects several that are of a familiar size and then some recent art by painters Jackson Pollack, Mark Rothko, and Franz Kline and explains a bit about abstract expressionism. He gives the children a chance to try Pollack style paintings on small surfaces. He moves from child to child dropping colors of watered-down tempera paint on construction paper rectangles. When these are dry, they will be mounted side by side to form one giant painting for the hallway of the school. On subsequent days he will look at other giant art such as the Land sculpture of Christo and monumental sculpture in the community, with a planned visit to several famous sculptures, and a design for a schoolyard piece of giant art.

(Continued on next page.)

TABLE 4.12—Continued

DAY 1 (GIANTS)

Time	Children	Teacher
MATH 10:45	Children manipulate rods in pairs and write equations to represent their findings. Children are given sheets of graph paper squared to a quarter inch, with square inches squared in blue. Working in pairs, they choose pictures from a shoebox and draw them to a scale of 1 inch to 1 foot. They then cut these out and arrange them on a line from shortest to tallest.	Estella wants the children to be aware of relative sizes as they explore the GIANTS theme. She distributes cuisinaire rods and asks the children to think about concepts of "larger than" and "how much larger than." She then shows the children how graph paper can allow them to draw objects, making the same types of comparisons. She has placed pictures of different sized objects with the average height in feet written underneath. She demonstrates how she could draw a 5-foot person on the graph paper, and then asks children to try. She moves from pair to pair monitoring work and checking progress.
GROUP MEETING 11:45	Children share their sized drawings and speculate about the size of graph paper needed to depict objects taller than 11 feet.	
LUNCH 12:00		
SUSTAINED SILENT READING* 1:00	Children read silently, selecting from books and magazines about giants or finishing their giant folktale.	Estella reads an autobiography by Beverly Cleary.
BOOK TALK 1:20	Several children volunteer information about the books they are reading. Some who are finished with a book give it to a friend to read.	Estella talks about her reasons for wanting to read Cleary's book and how she likes it so far.
INTEGRATED WORK TIME 1:30	Children prepare bean seeds by soaking them on wet paper towels. Each child takes three paper cups and writes labels for three growing conditions to observe. These are placed in and on shoeboxes. Finally, each child personalizes his or her shoebox with drawings from *Jack and the Beanstalk.*	Estella explains that they will try to grow giant beanstalks. She asks the children what conditions might provide the biggest plants. She reminds children that plants need soil, water, light, and food to grow and asks children to decide on three combinations of soil, water, light, and food for growing their bean plants.

PHYSICAL EDUCATION 2:15		
CLEAN-UP 2:35		
READ-ALOUD 2:45	Children listen to book. Some write in their Response Journals* or make sketches to go with the story.	Estella reads chapter one of *The BFG,* a giant story by Roald Dahl.
DISMISSAL 3:00		Estella reminds them that tomorrow they will continue their Comparison Charts*.

DAY 3 (GIANTS)

Time	Children	Teacher
GROUP TIME 8:10	Children enjoy hearing the silly stories Schwartz has collected. Several ask to have the book to read later.	Estella reads from Alvin Schwartz's *Whoppers: Tall Tales and Other Lies from American Folklore.* She suggests some children might like to compare their own collections by interviewing their friends. She writes the phrases: It was so cold that . . . It was so big that . . . on the board. She asks children to try writing their own "tall" phrases.
	Several children report on the progress of their comparison charts.	Before the children move to work centers, she asks for group progress reports.
INTEGRATED WORK TIME 8:30	Children continue work on Comparison Charts*. The groups have finished the discussion of their stories, and each child is working on writing details from his or her book on pieces of paper, one for each category. These will later be glued on a large piece of craft paper. Some are making illustrations from their book with which to decorate their chart. Several are writing about the activity and what they found. One person from each group will do special lettering for the chart.	Estella moves from group to group talking with children about their categories. This often provides a focus for some teaching about motifs in folktales or asking questions to uncover understandings the children may have gained. Estella also takes time to conference individually with several children.
HEALTH 10:15	The children write their own nutrition riddles.	Estella has invited the health and physical education teacher, Mr. Marks, to talk with the children about human growth. Mr. Marks suggests foods that are especially important for growing tall. He reads nutrition riddles from *What's On Your Plate?* by Norah Smaridge.

(Continued on next page.)

TABLE 4.12—Continued

DAY 16 (GIANTS)

Time	Children	Teacher
GROUP TIME 8:10	The children enjoy looking at the pictures of the giant animals and buildings. They recognize how artists have used scale to show relative size, especially in *Giants of Land, Sea and Air.*	Estella reads from the books *Giants of Land, Sea and Air: Past and Present* and *Grand Constructions* and *Farm Giants.*
8:30	Children volunteer topics and begin thinking about one that might interest them. They browse through information books, magazines, and other materials and talk with each other about possible topics.	Estella tells the children they will each write a research report on real-life giants. She asks them to brainstorm giant animals, plants, buildings, and machines. She explains that today they will have an opportunity to look at many resources and to begin thinking about a topic that might interest them. These reports will be grouped together into class books about giants. Estella circulates, talking with children about possible topics.
INTEGRATED WORK TIME 9:10	Children return to individual and group activities. Some are working on a "Giant" museum and labeling cards for exhibits. Others are painting a mural of giants from the many stories they have read. Some are writing a "giant" newspaper. Two children are doing interviews of favorite giant stories. Several have written sequels or their own original giant books. The ideas for research topics will incubate overnight, and children will begin making decisions the following day.	Estella monitors groups and meets with individuals for writing.
MUSIC 10:15	The children listen to music and compare sounds of different types of instruments.	Miss Martinez plays excerpts from several musical recordings. She lets the children hear sounds made by different instruments and asks them to categorize "giant" and "tiny" sounds according to dynamics.

CASTLES by D. Macauley. Houghton Mifflin, 1977.

CATHEDRAL: THE STORY OF ITS CONSTRUCTION by D. Macauley. Houghton Mifflin, 1973.

CESAR CHAVEZ by R. Franchere. Crowell, 1970.

"Chant of the Awakening Bulldozers" by P. Hubbel in CLICK, RUMBLE, ROAR: POEMS ABOUT MACHINES. Compiled by L. B. Hopkins. Photographs by A. H. Audette. Crowell, 1987.

"Construction Job" by M. C. Livingston in CLICK, RUMBLE, ROAR: POEMS ABOUT MACHINES. Compiled by L. B. Hopkins. Photographs by A. H. Audette. Crowell, 1987.

CRICTOR by T. Ungerer. Harper, 1958.

THE DAM BUILDERS by J. E. Kelly and W. R. Park. Illustrated by H. E. Lake. Addison-Wesley, 1977.

DAVID AND GOLIATH by B. S. deRegniers. Viking, 1965.

DESERT GIANT: THE WORLD OF SAGUARO CACTUS by B. Basa. Sierra Club/Little, Brown, 1989.

THE DRAGON, GIANT AND MONSTER TREASURY. Selected by C. Royds. Illustrated by A. Spenceley. Putnam, 1988.

FARM GIANTS by R. Olney. Atheneum, 1982.

FINN M'COUL: THE GIANT OF KNOCKMANY HILL by T. de Paola. Holiday, 1981.

FLYING GIANTS OF LONG AGO by J. Kaufman. Crowell, 1984.

"Garbage Truck" by M. Ridlon in CLICK, RUMBLE, ROAR: POEMS ABOUT MACHINES. Compiled by L. B. Hopkins. Photographs by A. H. Audette. Crowell, 1987.

GIANT DINOSAURS by E. Rowe. Illustrated by M. Smith. Scholastic, 1973.

THE GIANT DINOSAURS: ANCIENT REPTILES THAT RULED THE LAND by D. Eldridge. Illustrated by N. Nodel. Troll Associates, 1979.

GIANT POEMS by D. Wallace. Illustrated by Holiday, 1974.

THE GIANT WHO SWALLOWED THE WIND by J. Cunliffe. Illustrated by F. Jaques. Dutton, 1980.

THE GIANT'S APPRENTICE by M. K. Wetterer. Illustrated by E. Primavera. M. K. McElderry, 1982.

GIANTS OF LAND, SEA AND AIR: PAST AND PRESENT by D. Peters. Knopf, 1986.

THE GOOD GIANTS AND THE BAD PUKWUDGIES by J. Fritz. Illustrated by T. de Paola. Putnam, 1982.

GRAND CONSTRUCTIONS by G. P. Ceserani. Illustrated by P. Ventura. Putnam, 1983.

GUSTAVE THE GOURMET GIANT by L. A. Gaeddert. Illustrated by S. Kellogg. Dial, 1976.

HARALD AND THE GIANT KNIGHT by D. Carrick. Clarion, 1982.

HARRIET TUBMAN: THE ROAD TO FREEDOM by L. Johnson. Troll, 1982.

" 'I Want My Breakfast,' the Giant Said" in BLACKBERRY INK by E. Merriam. Illustrated by H. Wilheim. Morrow, 1985.

INSIDE MY FEET: THE STORY OF A GIANT by R. Kennedy. Illustrated by R. Himler. Harper & Row, 1979.

JACK AND THE BEAN TREE by G. E. Haley. Crown, 1986.

JACK AND THE BEANSTALK by L. B. Cauley. Putnam, 1983.

JACK AND THE WONDERBEANS by J. Still. Illustrated by M. Tomes. Putnam, 1977.

JACKIE ROBINSON by K. Rudeen. Illustrated by R. Cufari. Crowell, 1971.

JIM AND THE BEANSTALK by R. Briggs. Coward, McCann, 1970.

JIM THORPE by T. Fall. Illustrated by J. Gretzer. Harper & Row, 1970.

JONAH: AN OLD TESTAMENT STORY by B. Brodsky. Lippincott, 1977.

JONAH AND THE GREAT FISH by W. Hutton. M. K. McElderry, 1983.

JUAREZ, MAN OF LAW by E. B. de Trevino. Farrar, Straus & Giroux, 1974.

LILI: A GIANT PANDA OF SICHUAN by R. M. McClung. Illustrated by I. Brady. Morrow, 1988.

LITTLE GIANTS by S. Simon. Illustrated by P. Carroll. Morrow, 1983.

MARION ANDERSON by T. Tobias. Illustrated by S. Shimin. Crowell, 1972.

MARTIN LUTHER KING, JR.: FREE AT LAST by D. A. Adler. Illustrated by R. Casilla. Holiday, 1986.

MEET THE GIANT SNAKES by S. Simon. Illustrated by H. Springer. Walker, 1979.

MONARCHS OF THE FOREST: THE STORY OF THE REDWOODS by A. E. Brown. Dodd, Mead, 1984.

MONSTER TRUCKS AND OTHER GIANT MACHINES ON WHEELS by J. Bushey. Carolrhoda, 1985.

MYSTERIOUS GIANT OF BARLETTA by T. de Paola. Harcourt, 1984.

NORSE GODS AND GIANTS by E. and I. d'Aulaire. Doubleday, 1962.

"Ol' Paul and His Camp" in OL'PAUL, THE MIGHTY LOGGER by G. Rounds. Holiday, 1949, 1976.

PAUL BUNYAN by S. Kellogg. Morrow, 1984.

PECOS BILL by S. Kellogg. Morrow, 1985.

PHYLLIS WHEATLEY: AMERICA'S FIRST BLACK POETESS by M. Fuller. Garrard, 1971.

"The Power Shovel" by R. Bennett in CLICK, RUMBLE, ROAR: POEMS ABOUT MACHINES. Compiled by L. B. Hopkins. Photographs by A. H. Audette. Crowell, 1987.

PYRAMID by D. Macauley. Houghton Mifflin, 1975.

REDWOODS ARE THE TALLEST TREES IN THE WORLD by D. A. Adler. Illustrated by K. Mizumura. Crowell, 1978.

ROBERTO CLEMENTE by K. Rudeen. Harper & Row, 1974.

SEA MONSTERS OF LONG AGO by M. E. Selsam. Illustrated by J. Hamberger. Four Winds, 1977.

SHARK LADY: TRUE ADVENTURES OF EUGENIE CLARK by A. McGovern. Illustrated by R. Chew. Four Winds, 1978.

SKYSCRAPER GOING UP by V. Cobb. Illustrated by J. Strejan. Crowell, 1987.

THE STORY OF JONAH. Retold by K. Baumann. Translated by J. Curle. Illustrated by A. Reed. North South, 1987.

"The Towering Giant" in THE HEADLESS HORSEMAN RIDES TONIGHT: MORE POEMS TO TROUBLE YOUR SLEEP by J. Prelutsky, Illustrated by A. Lobel. Greenwillow, 1980.

UP GOES THE SKYSCRAPER by G. Gibbons. Four Winds, 1986.

THE VALIANT LITTLE TAILOR. Retold by V. Ambrus. Oxford, 1980.

WHALE SONG by T. Johnston. Illustrated by E. Young. Putnam, 1987.

WHALES: GIANTS OF THE SEA by K. D. Marko. Illustrated by B. R. Beach. Abingdon, 1980.

WHALES: GIANTS OF THE DEEP by D. H. Patent. Holiday, 1984.

WHAT'S ON YOUR PLATE? by N. Smaridge. Illustrated by I. Kudrna. Abingdon, 1982.

WHOPPERS: TALL TALES AND OTHER LIES FROM AMERICAN FOLKLORE by A. Schwartz. Illustrated by G. Rounds. Lippincott, 1975.

Prototype 7: Fourth/Fifth Grade—Explorations

EXPLORING WITH LANGUAGE

EXPLORING THE ARTS

PERSONAL EXPLORATION

WORD ORIGINS

WORDS FROM THE MYTHS
WORD PEOPLE
IS THAT MOTHER IN THE BOTTLE?
Make a dictionary of word origins for new terms in science and social studies. Illustrate your dictionary.
List all the suffixes and prefixes you can discover and categorize by use and meaning.
Make a chart of confusing "word additives" (such as non-flammable/inflammable).
Make a current slang dictionary.
Use the DICTIONARY OF AMERICAN SLANG for ideas.

EXPLORING DIALECTS/ACCENTS/REGIONALIEMS

JACK AND THE WONDER BEANS
BRAIDS
THE PEOPLE THEY COULD FLY
Make a list of regional expressions.
Collect regional ways of naming or pronouncing certain words (such as all the words for a submarine sandwich).
Tell a story from your region. How would someone from another region tell it? Compare regional versions of common stories ("Jack and the Beanstalk," "The Night Before Christmas").
Invite a storyteller to class who can use dialect effectively.
Make a comparison chart of similarities and differences in regional story versions.
Locate language/dialect regions on a U.S. map. Where does "standard English" come from?
Survey TV or radio for use of dialect/accent/regional expressions.

UNDERSTANDING TIME

Make a display of all the ways time can be measured.
Make a sundial and compare it with digital clock time.
How are time zones calculated? What happens at the international Time Line? All of China is on one time. List problems and advantages of this system.
A WRINKLE IN TIME
Compare the time travel in L'Engle's book with other time fantasy. Is there a scientific basis for wrinkles in time?
Make a model showing how a clock works.

CODES AND SPECIAL LANGUAGES

OVER SEA, UNDER STONE
HANDTALK
Review sign language. Work with hearing impaired children in school as a learning buddy.
Tell a story in sign language.
Read a story in several different languages.

EXPLORING THE FUTURE

THE GREEN FUTURES OF TYCHO
THE WHITE MOUNTAINS
What might lead to the futures depicted in these books? Make a future wish list of things we need to do to ensure a better future. Write to find out what is being done to make a good future.
Make a predictions chart, listing things you think are likely to happen.
20,000 LEAGUES UNDER THE SEA
What things did Jules Verne predict accurately?
Write a history of your time as if you were living 100 years from now.

FIGURATIVE LANGUAGE

WHITE SNOW, BRIGHT SNOW
IT DOESN'T ALWAYS HAVE TO RHYME
REFLECTIONS ON A GIFT OF WATERMELON PICKLE
Go on an adverb and adjective hunt. Collect descriptive words for environmental phenomena.
Collect beautiful ways of saying things from poems or other literature.
Create metaphors and similes to describe a favorite place, or event.
Make an anthology of favorite poems that use interesting language.

Poetic Exploration

INVENTIONS THAT CHANGED MUSIC

Make a display showing the earliest known instruments.
Make a time line showing the history of musical instruments.
Listen to recordings of ancient instruments.
Listen to different styles of music over time. What inventions changed musical styles? Prepare a demonstration of electronic music (new age music). Compose and play own electronic music.

ARTISTIC BREAKTHROUGHS

ON THE FRONTIER WITH MR. AUDUBON
WINSLOW HOMER
MY STORY: TRINA SCHART HYMAN
Create a museum of different art styles. Make a guide to the museum and invite others to visit.
Write to a variety of artists and survey them on questions of interest.
Visit a print shop to see how art is reproduced.
Make a survey of the uses made of art in the community. Create a guide to community art.
Raise money to buy a piece of art for the school.
Explore different artistic mediums. Use art to share findings from other investigations.

NEW DANCE FORMS

What is the language of dance? Make a dictionary of dance.
A VERY YOUNG DANCER
Create a photo-essay to illustrate your dictionary.
Find out how dance is used in other cultures. Learn a dance from another culture. Compare ways you use dance.
Create a dance to represent the theme "exploration."

INNER JOURNEYS

ON MY HONOR
A FINE WHITE DUST
IOU'S
THE ELEPHANT IN THE DARK
Make a life line of important events in your life. What makes an event good or bad?
What makes a good person? Make a list of characterisitcs of a good person. Make a comparison chart of literary and real characters using your list of characteristics.
Discuss what each character in A FINE WHITE DUST and IOU'S is involved in exploring.
Write a tentative plan for things you want to accomplish this year, in the next 3 years, and so on.

Figure 4.7

EXPLORING TIME

Time Travel
TOM'S MIDNIGHT GARDEN
THE FORGOTTEN DOOR
THE TIME MACHINE
THE ROOT CELLAR
A CONNECTICUT YANKEE IN KING ARTHUR'S COURT
Make a display that illustrates the ways in which characters travel in time.
Show "Back to the Future." Discuss the use of the travel in movie. Compare to literature.
Write "Rules for Time Travelers."
Write "If I could Visit the Year ———."

EXPLORING THE MICROSCOPIC

SMALL WORLDS CLOSE UP
GERMS MAKE ME SICK
Research the discovery of microbes and the microscope. Make a time line of important medical discoveries in the twentieth, nineteenth, and other centuries. What are current explorations?
Use microscopes to look at life in raindrops, mold from hands, and other places.

EXPLORING AIR AND SPACE

NEBULAE
SATURN
JUPITER
Research the history of flight. Create a gallery of famous pilots and astronauts. Write a brief caption for each. Make an aerospace museum. Visit flight-related agencies, and interview workers. Explain how a plane works. Demonstrate jet propulsion with a balloon, string and straw. Set up a jet-propelled race and a paper airplane race. Analyze effective designs for carrying cargo, smooth landings, etc.
Find out how recent unmanned explorations of distant planets has changed what we know about the universe.
Invite an astronomer to class to discuss recent discoveries related to planets, nebulae, etc. Construct a mural of the known universe, incorporating recent discoveries.
Write a story of travel to Saturn or Jupiter.

SCIENTIFIC EXPLORATIONS

EXPLORING UNDER THE SEA

MONSTERS OF THE DEEP
KON TIKI
Make a time line of underwater exploration.
Experiment with the cartesian diver.
Make a display of the benefits of undersea exploration.
Debate: Should the Titanic be left alone or artifacts removed?
Watch Cousteau films. Trace his voyages on maps of the world and of the ocean floor.
Locate the deepest trenches and tallest mountains in the seas.
Compile a bibliography of stories and legends related to the seas.
Sink or float. Use SCIS unit.

EXPLORING LIFE HISTORIES

HARRIET AND THE RUNAWAY BOOK
"Mother to Son"
PETER THE GREAT
LIFT EVERY VOICE
Make time lines of life stories.
Write a biography.
Study the biography as a genre.

EXPLORING TIME

EXPLORATION

HISTORIC EXPLORATIONS

POLITICAL EXPLORATIONS

SEARCHING FOR FREEDOM
NORTH TO FREEDOM
THE NIGHT JOURNEY
JOURNEY OF THE SHADOW BAIRNS
EXIT FROM HOME
IMMIGRANT KIDS
HOW MANY DAYS TO AMERICA
THE ROAD FROM HOME
WESTMARK
What forms of government did explorers bring to the world?
Play the simulation games "Powderhorn" and "Dangerous Parallel."
Invent a "good government." What rights and responsibilities would people have? Compare your system with the constitutions of several countries. What did you leave out? Add?
"Who Should Be President?" (see resources list)
Research other people's ideas of ideal societies—utopias.
ZOAR BLUE
A GIFT FOR SARA BARKER
Collect news articles about issues of human rights, a just society.
Set up a classroom government.
Debate: Reparations for Japanese-Americans who were interned during WWII.

THE AGES OF EXPLORATION

I, CHRISTOPHER COLUMBUS
MARCO POLO
LIFE THROUGH THE AGES
THE DOUBLE LIFE OF POCAHONTAS
CONSTANCE: A STORY OF EARLY PLYMOUTH
FOOTSTEPS IN THE SAND
Make a time line all around the room and place noteworthy explorations on it.
On large world map (floor map) trace exploration of Magellan, Henry the Navigator, Eric the Red, and other explorers.
Make a comparison chart showing positive and negative effects of explorations.
Collect maps showing how different people viewed the world over time.
Compile a list of explorers; categorize by fact/fiction, century, age, goals, and so on.
Role play a discussion at an early settlement of how to deal with the native population. Reverse, and role play from native perspective.
SING DOWN THE MOON
LET THE CIRCLE BE UNBROKEN
BEYOND THE DIVIDE
SAVE QUEEN OF SHEBA
A LANTERN IN HER HAND
What provisions would you take on one of these trips? What one luxury item would you bring?
Write a journal of a journey of your own.
Explore the history of forced journeys.
ONLY THE NAMES REMAIN
SLAVE DANCER
JOURNEY TO TOPAZ
VALLEY OF THE SHADOW
Turn one of these tales into an epic poem or ballad.
Tell a story of Columbus' coming from the Native American viewpoint. Research to make your story more accurate.
Pick one exploration to study in depth. Share your findings with peers.
Write a newspaper report or editorial about one of the forced journeys.

EXPLORING CAREERS

Invite people to come and talk about their work.
Visit selected worksites and conduct an inventory of necessary skills.
What are the most needed jobs? What are the most common jobs around the world?

WISHES AND DREAMS

Where do dreams come from? Gather information on dreams and share them with the class.
Survey the ways in which dreams are used in literature. Compare picture books.
WHERE THE WILD THINGS ARE
THERE'S A NIGHTMARE IN MY CLOSET
POLAR EXPRESS
And novels:
THE MOON AND THE FACE
THE BLUE SWORD
TOM'S MIDNIGHT GARDEN

Schedule

These plans are based on activity in a departmentalized fourth/fifth grade family grouping situation. This arrangement is becoming fairly common in intermediate classrooms, and especially when middle school settings include fifth and/or sixth grades. Integrating curriculum in such a condition necessitates joint planning by the entire grade-level faculty, along with faculty from special classes such as art, music, and physical education.

The topic EXPLORATIONS is an adaptation of the required curriculum at both fourth and fifth grade levels in many states—regional studies in fourth grade and national history in fifth—and can be adjusted accordingly to meet such local requirements. It is also an example of a broad thematic approach that encourages children to study explorations at different periods and across disciplines. This theme helps children to link past, present, and future, and it broadens the scope of history to include past developments in the sciences, math, and language. Children study past explorations in comparison to modern times (e.g., the European exploration of the Americas compared to the exploration of space by the United States and the USSR), and then they speculate about and make plans for the future—their future.

The WEB for this unit was initially planned around topics rather than curricular areas. In a departmentalized situation, teachers may then allocate parts of themes to the separate disciplines for which they are responsible. Planning emphasizes the connectedness of the various disciplines, however, and an effort is made to help children see that many of the discipline categories are artificial divisions that separate what is rarely separated in the real world.

The schedule shown in Table 4.13 shows four groups of children and four teachers working together. Each teacher is responsible for a homeroom of twenty-five children, has lead-teacher responsibility for one content area, and is a team teacher for at least one other area. Team planning is scheduled during the blocks of time when students are in art, music, physical education, and library classes. Group sizes in classes vary, and schedules are frequently adjusted to accommodate special programming, single or multiple teacher involvement, or small group needs.

Into the Classroom

To show how this thematic unit would operate in a departmentalized setting, the tables that follow are designed to depict the fairly typical pattern that a child might follow through several days of the unit. Other children might take these classes in a different order, or with a different team teacher, but the activities would be basically the same. Thus, the charts here are different from those found in the other prototypes in that they describe the activities of different groups of children and teachers within the same several team settings. As a result, under the column headed "Teacher," activities are those of the teacher in charge of that period.

The team teachers arranged this unit to begin with a broad overview of some of the myriad ways in which exploration occurs. The Day 1 table shows some of the ways in which this is done. Excerpts from Days 14 and 20 then outline students' movement into more focused and intensive study—their use of primary source materials, role-playing, and reflective inquiry. Children are expected to share this work with their peers and to participate in other activities depicted on the WEB or developed on the basis of student interests.

You will notice that a life-story strand runs throughout most of the classes on the first day. This strand involves children in exploring other lives through reading poetry, biography, autobiography, and historical fiction, and through writing a "fictionalized" biography, through role-playing, and so forth.

A second strand centers around exploration as problem-solving and is carried out by activities in math and art by role-playing, student writing, and experiments in magnification. These activities are intended to draw student attention to the nature of problems in various domains, as well as to the procedures and resources used to solve those problems. Day 20 moves students into contemplating possible futures.

TABLE 4.13 Weekly Schedule, Departmentalized Fourth/Fifth Grade Family Grouping

Time	Monday	Tuesday	Wednesday	Thursday	Friday
8:00	Homeroom, opening exercises, attendance, lunch count.				
8:10	Language Arts or Math			Art or Physical Education (8:10–9:00)	
9:50	Social Studies or Science		Music or Library	Social Studies or Science	
10:50	Recess				
11:05	Social Studies or Science		Art or Physical Education	Social Studies or Science	
12:05	Lunch and recess				
12:40	Language Arts or Math				Music or Library (1:30–2:30)
2:30	Homeroom and dismissal				

Some classes are shortened when art, music, physical education, and library are scheduled. This adjustment is distributed across the classes, so that no part of the curriculum is regularly shortchanged. In addition, state requirements for time in reading and language arts are met, not by cutting out science or social studies, as is so often the case in elementary schools, but by making language activities integral to all the curriculum. Literature is used across the curriculum, and social studies and science offer content for communication (e.g., America's westward expansion provides data for the creation of fictionalized biographies).

Summary

Clearly, this type of teaming requires considerable cooperation on the part of all team members. It also requires a theme that is broad enough to cross disciplinary lines. Sometimes, however, a theme may be selected that more actively involves, say, social studies but not mathematics. In this case, team members make the necessary adjustments and adapt to a more domain-specific type of instruction for this period.

Team meetings facilitate planning thematic units and build community.

Generally, however, regular team meetings allow teachers to build on activities in other classes or to introduce a topic from one perspective that another teacher will deal with from a different disciplinary perspective. Thus, when students began work on writing biographies, they used primary resources in language arts, but they also gained background material from their research for the role-playing situation in social studies. It was expected that they would cross disciplines in using their sources and that they would work cooperatively in acquiring information. Learning in this team setting is seen as a collaborative venture for teachers and students. Teachers model collaboration as they plan and work together. Students then take responsibility, along with the teachers, for constructing meaning out of the diverse sources of information provided in their classrooms. A sense of community emerges that supports speculation, problem-solving, and intellectual risk-taking.

Thus, one advantage of this team arrangement is the potential for teachers to develop areas of content expertise that are sometimes more difficult to manage when a single teacher is responsible for the entire curriculum. The lead teacher for a curricular area can be the team expert and can focus his or her energies on collecting resources, keeping up with the developments in a field, and so forth. The advantages of

(Summary continued on page 151.)

TABLE 4.14 Detailed Schedule, Departmentalized Fourth/Fifth Grade Family Grouping

DAY 1 (EXPLORATIONS 2)

Time	Children	Teacher
HOMEROOM 8:00	Children fill in attendance and lunch count, engage in quiet conversation with friends; prepare for first two classes; change classes.	Homeroom teacher greets children as they enter, checks lunch and attendance count, and makes announcements.
LANGUAGE ARTS 8:10	On large sheets of paper, children draw lifelines and mark important events in their lives (that they are willing to share).	Teacher displays biography and autobiography in library area. Bulletin board with questions and quotes is arranged to spark curiosity.
	Discuss what makes an event positive or negative. Students tally positive and negative items on class lists. Discuss what they have in common (classification). What things on the lists are unique?	Teacher introduces idea of lifeline.
	Children write memorable event and then use this as the basis for writing a story. Several students share their drafts.	Teacher asks children to take five minutes to write a brief description of a memorable event in their lives, and then to use that description as the basis for a story.
	Children select books to read after teacher has read. Most read for 15 minutes, several work with teacher in individual conferences.	Finished stories are collected to display with lifelines, and the teacher introduces genres of biography and autobiography, shares the beginning of *Harriet and the Runaway Book*, notes copy of *Uncle Tom's Cabin* in the reading area.
	Children try different ways to read "Mother to Son," by changing pacing, emphasis, intensity. With teacher's help, they arrange the poem as a Reader's Theatre* piece.	Teacher conducts individual reading conferences. Ends SSR* by sharing Langston Hughes's "life-story" poem, "Mother to Son." Passes out copies of the poem.
		Helps orchestrate the poetry reading. Agrees that this would be a good poem to share with other classes.
	Record homework assignment.	Gives homework: Select a biography or autobiography, and read the introductory chapter. Note how the author begins the story, and how the reader is drawn into the tale. Make notes for class discussion tomorrow.

SOCIAL STUDIES 9:50	Children discuss trips in small groups and write names of places they have visited on small flags. They try to locate the places they have visited on the map given to their group.	A variety of maps are displayed around the room, including traditional Mercator projections, a Peter's Projection, a fifteenth-century world map, a U.S. map, and state and local maps. Each desk has a supply of flags and a smaller world map. The teacher begins by asking children to work in small groups to describe the most memorable or interesting trips they have ever taken.
	Discuss changes in countries and accuracy of maps. Are there places left to explore? How might one explore them?	Each group has been assigned a different type of map, and the teacher anticipates that they will have some difficulty locating their trip destinations. "What has happened to change the world from one map to another?" Writes EXPLORATION on the board and leads discussion of what that term means.
	Students list types of explorations, and then decide which might be interesting to pursue.	Divides class into exploration teams and passes out "Exploration Guide," a research aid for each group.
	Groups go over study guide and plan direction of study, possible resources. Groups are responsible for submitting a work plan by the second class period.	Teacher moves between teams, makes suggestions on resources and strategies, helps negotiate work loads, and allocates time. A portion of class time for the next two weeks will be devoted to team explorations of such subthemes as "Exploring Time," "Ancient Explorations," "Finding New Worlds," and so forth.
RECESS 10:50		
SCIENCE 11:05	As children enter and receive their observation guide, they follow directions to the pictures around the room and attempt to identify what they see.	Pictures of ordinary objects greatly magnified are hung all around the room. The teacher greets students at the door and distributes an observation guide and directions.
	Students participate in guided observation and discuss the difference between observation and inference.	The teacher assembles the class for discussion of their observations and calls attention to *Small Things Close Up,* a book of magnified "small things." Lights are dimmed, and a slide show begins a second guided observation.

(Continued on next page.)

TABLE 4.14—Continued

DAY 1 (EXPLORATIONS 2)

Time	Children	Teacher
	Students set up their laboratory books for work in each station. Stations involve students in learning to use a microscope and to do careful observations. Students create a list of benefits of microscopics. What impact on individual life stories has the microscope had? Several students select books to use for their language arts assignment.	Teacher assigns students to stations around the room and then moves between stations, keeping a check sheet of problem areas for later discussion or activity. Students are drawn back into the central area to discuss the impact of microscopic observation. Teacher suggests reading about scientific explorers, including Van Loewenhoek, Pasteur, and others. Calls attention to books displayed for student use.
LUNCH AND RECESS 12:05		
ART 12:40	Student monitors pass out materials. Class moves outside to work with watercolors of natural objects in the environment.	Biographies and autobiographies of artists are on display, with the caption "Explorations in the Arts." The teacher begins by sharing samples of the art of Winslow Homer and a small section of *The Island*, in which a boy experiments with watercolors.
MATH 1:40	For the first ten minutes of class, students work on "challenge problems" involving calculations of the length of voyages of exploration.	Teacher puts challenge problems on the board for immediate attention. For the next ten minutes, works with a small group who had difficulty with homework.
	Discuss possible solutions to the challenge problems and explain how their answers were arrived at.	Teacher records possible solutions and asks for proof. Participates in resulting discussion.
	Make up three problems that use the operations practiced in homework and exchange problems. Work in small groups to solve the problems.	Teacher asks students to construct three problems, and then distributes the problems for solutions or adjustments.
HOMEROOM 2:40	Clean-up, collect supplies needed for homework. Listen to end-of-day announcements. Perform class jobs.	

DAY 14 (EXPLORATIONS 2)

Time	Children	Teacher
LIBRARY 8:10	Browsing time. Children return books, pick new ones. A few children work in listening center.	Librarian has displayed historical fiction set in the United States and emphasizing themes of exploration. The listening

	Gather in story area to share favorite parts of books read since last week. Listen while librarian gives a Book Talk* on *The Double Life of Pocahontas.*	center has a tape and filmstrip interview with children's author Jean Fritz discussing her works of biography and historical fiction.
	Take home strips of tagboard to write quotes on. The children decide to make this a guessing game bulletin board titled "Who said it?"	Librarian gives a Book Talk* on Fritz's biography of Pocahontas. Draws children's attention to *Abraham Lincoln: A Photobiography* by Freedman and reads several quotes from the end of that book. Asks children to find quotable quotes in the biographies that they are reading.
LANGUAGE ARTS 9:10	Children participate in discussion, adding information gathered from library class. Help make tentative set of criteria for writing historical fiction. Children work in small groups with Primary Source Material related to a person from the U.S. westward movement. Over the next five days, this information will form the basis for student writing.	Large wall chart shows student-generated list of criteria for biography and autobiography. Teacher reviews these with students and asks if any will work for historical fiction. Discuss historical fiction and what an author might need in writing it. As children make suggestions, teacher serves as recorder. She then introduces the Primary Source Material* and divides the class into small groups.
	Begin developing a primary source vocabulary.	Teacher leads discussion of problems with source material. "What information can a document give us? What can't it tell us? How do you suppose an author uses this material?"
SOCIAL STUDIES 9:50	Children enter and seat themselves in a semicircle in front of a table and five chairs. A wall poster behind the table announces land for sale in Kansas. Children read poster and list salient points of information (i.e., date, location of land, conditions of sale).	Teacher refers to character introduced in language arts. Where is this person going? How would students feel if suddenly faced with such a move. Calls attention to the "Land For Sale" poster. Teacher asks children to read the poster carefully, and then to list all the information given on the poster that could help a person decide whether to buy this land.
	As children participate in the role-play, they discover that they need more information to make decisions. Questions are listed, and committees formed to find answers. They break into groups to get necessary information. (This information will be used in writing their biographies in	Teacher passes out role cards involving a New England family's decision to buy land in Kansas and move west. Teacher suggests reconvening the role-play as a town meeting where information can be shared and discussed. She points out reference works located in the room and helps

(Continued on next page.)

TABLE 4.14—Continued

DAY 14 (EXPLORATIONS 2)

Time	Children	Teacher
	language arts as well as for the role-play.)	students divide into committees based on the questions raised during the role-play.
RECESS 10:50		
SCIENCE 11:05	Children report latest observations of living systems.	Teacher begins with groups reporting on aquaria and filling in class observation charts.
	Watch video on ocean exploration.	Introduces the video and suggests specific things to look for related to the just-completed group reports.
MATH 12:40	Children work on challenge problems related to time and as a follow-up to work on the discovery of time. Students then work with math partners on calculating time differences between different points on the globe.	Teacher works with individual student who is working with metric problems. As students move into math partner work, teacher refers them to charts on writing mathematical "sentences," and then moves between groups checking to see how students are formulating their problems, and guiding their work.

DAY 20 (EXPLORATIONS 2)

Time	Children	Teacher
LANGUAGE ARTS 8:10	Author's Chair*. Students share their completed biographies.	
	Discussion centers on how sources were used and whether authors slipped into "presentism" or included anachronisms in their writing.	Teacher asks if historical fantasy could be a literary genre. Asks for examples of fantasy in historical writing. "How is fantasy used? Why might an author choose that medium to tell a story?"
	Students discuss historical fantasies they have read.	Teacher introduces *Playing Beatie Bow.*
	Sustained Silent Reading (SSR)*	
	Children work in small groups or individually on several projects related to their reading, including Plot Profiles* and Character Sociograms*. Several children go to a primary classroom as Reading Buddies* for children there. They check their plans with the teacher before they leave.	Teacher meets with individuals and small groups for reading conferences.

SOCIAL STUDIES 9:50	Children have participated in the simulation "Powderhorn" on the previous day. As a three-tiered society was created, the students in the bottom "class" planned a rebellion, and today they create a document of protest. The other two groups prepare responses. Students decide to interview parents and other adults about their ideas of a just society. Two students volunteer to write to the governor and local congressional representatives to ask for their ideas.	The simulation begun the previous day has reached the point of rebellion. The teacher posts the documents and responses and then passes out several documents that outline a just society (Declaration of Independence, Bill of Rights, Declaration of Human Rights). Each "class" is asked to analyze how each answers the concerns of their "class." What is left out? What does the document include that was not in the documents prepared by the students? Teacher suggests inviting the mayor to class to talk about her view of a good and just society.
SCIENCE 11:05	Students work on individual and small group projects including: —Developing a book of experiments on altering the flight of paper airplanes. —Creating a board game based on efforts to clean water supplies. —Designing clay boats that will carry different arrangements of cargo, and then writing up the results. —Creating a display of undersea geography. —Preparing a presentation on women in science.	Teacher works with individuals and groups as needed. Most of these projects are well under way and need only some help in organizing for presentation.

(Summary continued from page 145.)

teaming, however, do not mean that a teacher in a self-contained intermediate classroom cannot develop expertise in relevant domains, as you will see in the next prototype.

Children's Literature, EXPLORATIONS 2

ABRAHAM LINCOLN: A PHOTOBIOGRAPHY by R. Freedman. Clarion, 1987.

BEYOND THE DIVIDE by L. Lasky. Macmillan, 1983.

THE BLUE SWORD by R. McKinley. Greenwillow, 1982.

A CONNECTICUT YANKEE IN KING ARTHUR'S COURT by M. Twain. Illustrated by T. S. Hyman. Morrow, 1988.

CONSTANCE: A STORY OF EARLY PLYMOUTH by P. Clapp. Penguin, 1986.

DAWN WIND by R. Sutcliff. Walch, 1961.

THE DOUBLE LIFE OF POCAHONTAS by J. Fritz. Illustrated by E. Young. Putnam, 1983.

THE ELEPHANT IN THE DARK by C. Carrick. Illustrated by D. Carrick. Tichnor & Fields, 1988.

A FINE WHITE DUST by C. Rylant. Bradbury, 1986.
THE FORGOTTEN DOOR by A. Key. Scholastic, 1986.
GERMS MAKE ME SICK! by M. Berger. Harper & Row, 1986.
THE GIFT OF SARAH BARKER by J. Yolen. Viking, 1981.
THE GREEN FUTURES OF TYCHO by W. Sleator. Dutton, 1981.
HANDTALK by R. Charlip and M. Beth. Macmillan, 1980.
HOMESICK: MY OWN STORY by J. Fritz. Illustrated by M. Tomes. Putnam, 1982.
HOW MANY DAYS TO AMERICA? A THANKSGIVING STORY by E. Bunting. Illustrated by B. Peck. Tichnor & Fields, 1988.
I, CHRISTOPHER COLUMBUS by L. Weil. Macmillan, 1983.
IMMIGRANT KIDS by R. Freedman. Dutton, 1980.
IOU'S by O. Sebastyen. Dell, 1986.
THE ISLAND by G. Paulsen. Orchard Books, 1988.
JOURNEY OF THE SHADOW BAIRNES by M. J. Anderson. Knopf, 1980.
JOURNEY HOME by Y. Uchida. Atheneum, 1978.
JOURNEY TO TOPAZ by Y. Uchida. Atheneum, 1976.
JUPITER by S. Simon. Morrow, 1988.
THE LAND I LOST by H. Q. Nhuong. Harper & Row, 1982.
A LANTERN IN HER HAND by B. Aldrich. Appleton, 1932.
LET THE CIRCLE BE UNBROKEN by M. Taylor. Dial, 1981.
THE MOON AND THE FACE by P. A. McKillip. Berkley, 1986.
MY SIDE OF THE MOUNTAIN by J. George. Dutton, 1988.
NEBULAE by N. Apfels. Lothrop, 1988.
THE NIGHT JOURNEY by K. Lasky. Macmillan, 1982.
NORTH TO FREEDOM by A. Holm. Peter Smith, 1984.
ON MY HONOR by M. Bauer. Tichnor & Fields, 1986.
ON THE FRONTIER WITH MR. AUDUBON by B. Brenner. Putnam, 1977.
ONLY THE NAMES REMAIN: THE CHEROKEES AND THE TRAIL OF TEARS by A. Bealer. Illustrated by W. S. Bock. Little, Brown, 1972.
OVER SEA, UNDER STONE by S. Cooper. Harcourt Brace Jovanovich, 1966.
THE PEOPLE COULD FLY: AMERICAN BLACK TALES by V. Hamilton. Knopf, 1985.
PLAYING BEATIE BOW by R. Park. Macmillan, 1980.
POLAR EXPRESS by C. Van Allsburg. Houghton Mifflin, 1985.
REFLECTIONS ON A GIFT OF WATERMELON PICKLE by S. Dunning et al. (Eds.). Lothrop, 1966.
THE ROAD FROM HOME: THE STORY OF AN ARMENIAN CHILDHOOD by D. Kherdian. Greenwillow, 1979.
THE ROOT CELLAR by J. Lunn. Macmillan, 1983.
SAVE QUEEN OF SHEBA by L. Moeri. Dutton, 1981.
SATURN by S. Simon. Morrow, 1988.
SELF-PORTRAIT: TRINA SCHART HYMAN by T. S. Hyman. Addison-Wesley, 1981.
SING DOWN THE MOON by S. O'Dell. Houghton Mifflin, 1970.
SLAVE DANCER by P. Fox. Bradbury, 1973.
SMALL THINGS CLOSE UP by L. Grillone and J. Gennaro. Crown, 1978.
THE TIME MACHINE by H. G. Wells. Raintree, 1983.
THERE'S A NIGHTMARE IN MY CLOSET by M. Mayer. Dial, 1976.
TO BE A SLAVE by J. Lester. Dial, 1968.
TOM'S MIDNIGHT GARDEN by P. Pearce. Harper & Row, 1984.
TWENTY THOUSAND LEAGUES UNDER THE SEA by J. Verne. Airmont, 1964.
VALLEY OF THE SHADOW by J. Hickman. Macmillan, 1974.
WESTMARK by L. Alexander. Dutton, 1981.
WHERE THE WILD THINGS ARE by M. Sendak. Harper & Row, 1963.
THE WHITE MOUNTAINS by J. Christopher. Macmillan, 1967.

WHITE SNOW, BRIGHT SNOW by A. Tresselt. Illustrated by R. Duvoisin. Morrow, 1947.
WINSLOW HOMER by E. Goldstein. Garrard, 1982.
WIZARD OF EARTHSEA by U. LeGuin. Parnassus, 1968.
WRINKLE IN TIME by M. L'Engle. Farrar, Straus & Giroux, 1962.
ZOAR BLUE by J. Hickman. Macmillan, 1976.

Prototype 8: Sixth Grade—Digging Up the Past

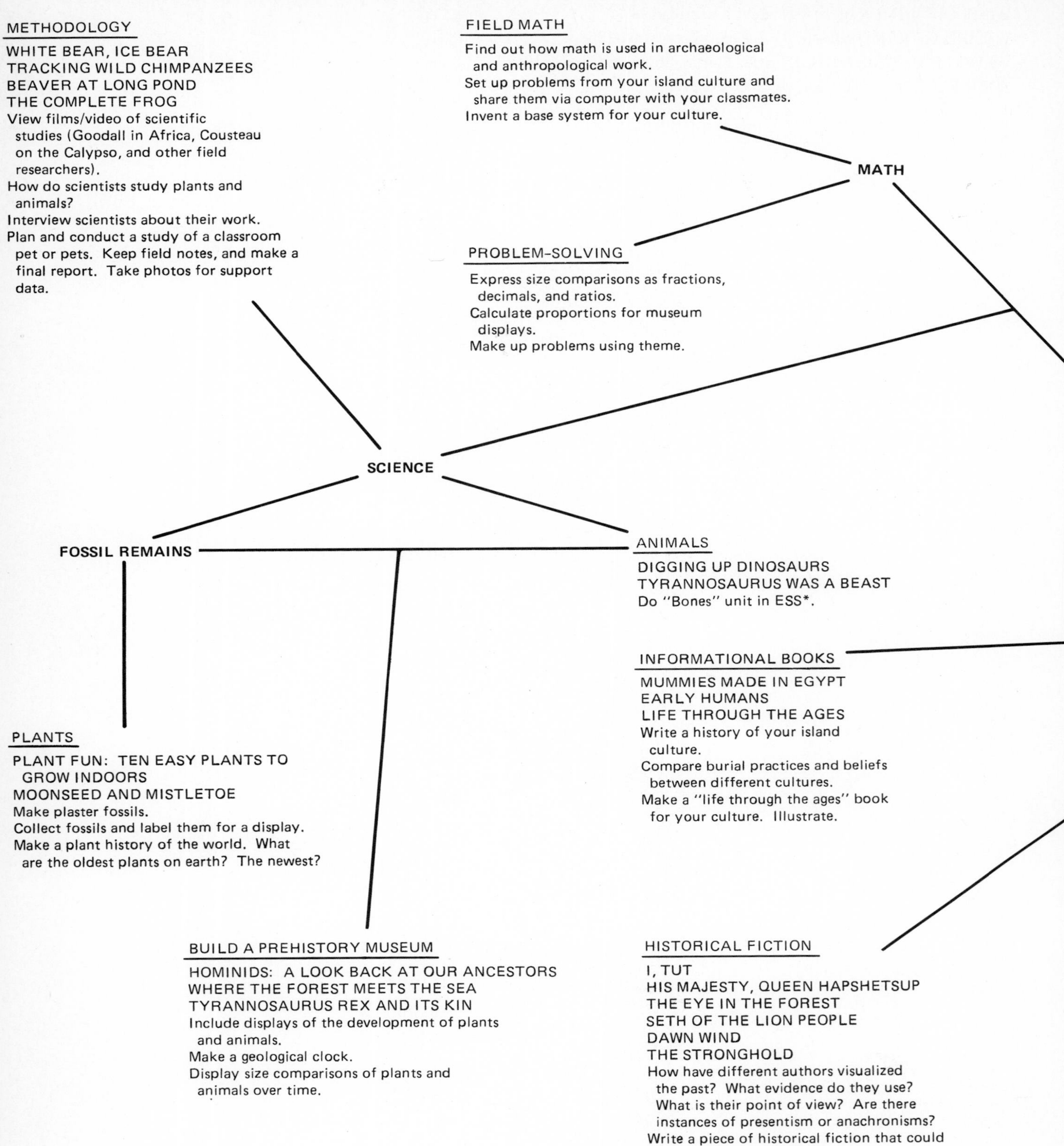

METHODOLOGY
WHITE BEAR, ICE BEAR
TRACKING WILD CHIMPANZEES
BEAVER AT LONG POND
THE COMPLETE FROG
View films/video of scientific studies (Goodall in Africa, Cousteau on the Calypso, and other field researchers).
How do scientists study plants and animals?
Interview scientists about their work.
Plan and conduct a study of a classroom pet or pets. Keep field notes, and make a final report. Take photos for support data.
FIELD MATH
Find out how math is used in archaeological and anthropological work.
Set up problems from your island culture and share them via computer with your classmates.
Invent a base system for your culture.
MATH
PROBLEM-SOLVING
Express size comparisons as fractions, decimals, and ratios.
Calculate proportions for museum displays.
Make up problems using theme.
SCIENCE
FOSSIL REMAINS
ANIMALS
DIGGING UP DINOSAURS
TYRANNOSAURUS WAS A BEAST
Do "Bones" unit in ESS*.
INFORMATIONAL BOOKS
MUMMIES MADE IN EGYPT
EARLY HUMANS
LIFE THROUGH THE AGES
Write a history of your island culture.
Compare burial practices and beliefs between different cultures.
Make a "life through the ages" book for your culture. Illustrate.
PLANTS
PLANT FUN: TEN EASY PLANTS TO GROW INDOORS
MOONSEED AND MISTLETOE
Make plaster fossils.
Collect fossils and label them for a display.
Make a plant history of the world. What are the oldest plants on earth? The newest?
BUILD A PREHISTORY MUSEUM
HOMINIDS: A LOOK BACK AT OUR ANCESTORS
WHERE THE FOREST MEETS THE SEA
TYRANNOSAURUS REX AND ITS KIN
Include displays of the development of plants and animals.
Make a geological clock.
Display size comparisons of plants and animals over time.
HISTORICAL FICTION
I, TUT
HIS MAJESTY, QUEEN HAPSHETSUP
THE EYE IN THE FOREST
SETH OF THE LION PEOPLE
DAWN WIND
THE STRONGHOLD
How have different authors visualized the past? What evidence do they use? What is their point of view? Are there instances of presentism or anachronisms?
Write a piece of historical fiction that could come from your island culture.

Figure 4.8

ARTS AND CRAFTS

Try crafts from culture studies.
Make a display of crafts indigenous to the cultures you study.
List all the ways you can find that art is used in your own culture.

MUSIC AND DNACE

Learn music and dance from other cultures.
Invite guests to help.

ARCHITECTURE AS A TIME LINE

UNBUILDING
CATHEDRAL
CITY
MILL
PYRAMID
THE CHANGING CITY
THE CHANGING COUNTRYSIDE
PROVINCETOWN
See if you can unravel the mysteries behind the building of the pyramids, Stonehenge, or the ancient Mayan buildings. Think of an interesting way to share your discoveries.
Make a display of distinctive architectural features for different cultures.
Use either of Muller's books, and trace the history of one feature of the changing landscape.
Write a story about a person living in any of the places you've read about in these books.

THE ARTS

DIGGING UP THE PAST

LITERATURE

INTERPRETING CULTURES

SHAKA, KING OF THE ZULUS
DAWN WIND
THE STRONGHOLD
LOST AND FOUND
THE LAND I LOST
HOMESICK
Make a catalogue of ways in which cultures take care of necessities.
Create a traveler's guide to a culture. Be sure to let the traveler know about customs that could cause misunderstandings.
Make a survey of common perceptions people have of other cultures.
Write a set of "Laws for Cross-Cultural Travelers."

SOCIAL STUDIES

TRADITIONAL LITERATURE

IN THE BEGINNING
Compare folktales, myths, and legends for other cultures.
Hypothesize a type of folktale for a culture (such as an island culture might have water spirits). Check your hypothesis.
Write a catalogue of common themes, characters, and so on in traditional literature.
Write a tale that would fit your island culture.

STUDYING HUMAN ARTIFACTS

"HISTORY LESSONS"
MOTEL OF THE MYSTERIES
DIGGING TO THE PAST
Do the activities in the MATCh unit, "The House of Ancient Greece."
Construct an island culture. Prepare geographic and historic reports, decide on government, and so on.
Write documents, laws, create art, literature, music, communicate, and trade with others.
Interview an anthropologist about their work.

Schedule

This unit begins with a simulated experience—an archaeological dig—and uses the "unearthing" of artifacts to draw children into an exploration of the processes used to define and resolve problems in various domains. The unit is designed to incorporate the world studies curriculum typical of sixth grade programs into a larger unit on the interpretation of human, plant, and animal remains. It builds on the foundation of independent reading and research begun in earlier years, with the intent to help children further develop their understanding that knowledge is a human construction subject to change and interpretation, and that we all—students and teachers alike—participate in making and interpreting knowledge.

The unit also makes use of a commercial simulation, "The House of Ancient Greece" (a unit developed by the Boston Children's Museum) and "Bones" [an Elementary Science Study (ESS) science program]. Although commercial materials are not necessary to the theme, they do provide otherwise unavailable or difficult to obtain resources.

Two "digs" introduce this unit. The first is a wastebasket excavation that introduces children to the process of excavation and interpretation of data. The second is the simulated excavation of a house in ancient Greece. These activities take approximately one week, with about 45 minutes to an hour per day being devoted to the digs.

Although it has become common to departmentalize at sixth grade, the teacher in this class, Caitlin Cooper, works in a self-contained sixth grade in a school noted for its integrated language curriculum. Her schedule is given in Table 4.15.

Into the Classroom

Caitlin's use of integrated work times is similar to that in Carol Hagihara's second grade (Prototype 4). Students move among work centers distributed throughout the room and a central grouping of tables and chairs arranged for projects using reading and writing. We begin on Day 6, after children have worked with the excavations. Caitlin uses most of the morning on this day to establish the idea of interpretation of artifacts and to set the stage for the later introduction of the "Bones" unit and a study of fossils and geological interpretation.

Invite guests to serve as consultants for student work.

Caitlin's plans also call for inviting an anthropologist to class. The traditional task of the guest expert is to deliver a speech of some sort (with short discussion afterward) and then leave. In this case, however, Caitlin has asked the guest to talk a bit about the concept of culture and then to serve as consultant to the children as they develop their own island cultures. Caitlin may be the only teacher assigned to this classroom, but she regularly invites other people in to provide other points of view, different types of expertise, and a range of audiences for children's work. During this unit guests include, in addition to the anthropologist, an architect, a storyteller, several parents who have traveled to the areas being studied, a dancer, and international students from a nearby university.

Another project that involves students in interpreting data and communicating their results is the development of a museum of prehistory and the creation of artifacts and documents related to a student-developed culture. In each case, children are actors in a simulation of the activity of experts in a domain. They have recourse to some of the same data that an expert might have, and they can consult experts as they develop their ideas. They make approximations in their interpretations in the same ways that they use approximations in other forms of communication. This intellectual risk-taking is encouraged when Caitlin shares literature, such as Ray Bradbury's short story, "History Lesson," in which the tentative nature and possibility of error are pointed out in humorous fashion.

Between Days 6 and 10, students worked on constructing an island culture using a teacher-constructed simulation and began reconstructing plant and animal histories. Portions of the schedule of Day 20 highlight the continued development of the theme as children prepare to share their findings.

TABLE 4.15 Weekly Schedule, Caitlin Cooper's Sixth Grade Classroom

Time	Monday	Tuesday	Wednesday	Thursday	Friday
8:00	Opening exercises				
8:10	Forum. Children gather to share work, group plan, and learn about activity choices for the day.				
8:30	Integrated work time. Children sign up to work in various areas, participate in special projects (i.e., digs). Opportunity for problem-solving, creative thinking, self-expression, communication, and content engagement.				
9:50	Special classes: Art, Music, Physical Education, Library				
10:30	Recess				
10:45	Integrated work time				
12:00	Lunch				
12:45	Sustained Silent Reading (SSR*)				
1:00	Forum. Whole group experiences that include introducing new material, guest speakers, writing/editing workshops, math reviews, and the like.				
2:00	Integrated work time				
2:30	Clean-up, announcements, dismissal				

Summary

Departmentalized teaching requires careful team planning and coordination of efforts by an entire team of teachers, but a teacher in a self-contained classroom, such as Caitlin, must also use her planning periods wisely. She must be constantly alert to student interests and possible extensions. She makes extensive use of the school librarian and of the surrounding community for human and material resources. She also works with the art, music, and physical education teachers to enrich her themes. Caitlin also spends time carefully organizing her room and thinking about what her students most need as they work. Thus, she uses a variety of methods and media. She especially uses videotapes. Sometimes children watch prepackaged programs; often they make their own. In this way, Caitlin capitalizes on early adolescents' fascination with the video media to promote careful observation and to support their inferences, as well as to help them recognize and appreciate the perspective of the filmmaker.

The advantage of this type of self-contained, integrated approach of study is the ease with which Caitlin and her students can cross and relate disciplinary categories. Time is as flexible as the class's inclinations and the requirements of their studies.

Children's Literature, DIGGING UP THE PAST

BEAVER AT LONG POND by W. T. George and L. B. George. Illustrated by L. B. George. Greenwillow, 1988.

THE BONE WARS by K. Lasky. Morrow, 1988.

BORN FREE by J. Adamson. Random, 1974.

CATHEDRAL by D. Macaulay. Houghton Mifflin, 1977.

THE CHANGING CITY by J. Muller. Atheneum, 1977.

THE CHANGING COUNTRYSIDE by J. Muller. Atheneum, 1977.

CITY by D. Macaulay. Houghton Mifflin, 1974.

THE COMPLETE FROG: A GUIDE FOR THE VERY YOUNG NATURALIST by E. A. Lacey. Illustrated by C. Santoro. Lothrop, 1988.

A CONNECTICUT YANKEE IN KING ARTHUR'S COURT by M. Twain. Illustrated by T. S. Hyman. Morrow, 1988.

DAWN WIND by R. Sutcliffe. Walck, 1962.

DIGGING TO THE PAST: EXCAVATIONS IN ANCIENT LANDS by W. J. Hackwell. Scribner, 1986.

(References continued on page 160.)

TABLE 4.16 Detailed Schedule, Sixth Grade Classroom

DAY 6 (DIGGING UP THE PAST)

Time	Children	Teacher
FORUM 8:10	Children make chart of what can be known/inferred from artifacts. Use digs and slides of Viking dig as data.	Caitlin shares parts of *Digging to the Past.* What other digs do they know of? Shows slides of Viking excavation, Yorvik, at York, England.
INTEGRATED WORK TIME 8:30	Select a settlement location on Mystery Island. List factors influencing their decisions. Break into groups based on location, and discuss what it would take to survive in their group's area. Each group takes a clan name, and begins to plan for the kind of civilization they will be able to develop in that area.	Caitlin distributes map of an uninhabited island and asks children to select a location where they could survive. Each group is then given a list of supplies they will have to work with. After students have worked in groups, Caitlin leads a discussion of problems encountered, ideas tried, and so on. She calls on a student to record some of the considerations each clan must deal with. This is posted in the room for student reference throughout this activity.
LITERATURE 9:50	Listen to story and discuss connections to interpreting artifacts.	Caitlin shares "History Lesson," and participates in discussion.
INTEGRATED WORK TIME 10:15	Children try to identify artifacts from their state's prehistory and to infer their use.	A specialist from the local museum brings artifacts to class and leads a discussion of how the museum staff reconstructs the past and builds displays based on fragments from the past.
WHOLE GROUP ACTIVITY 11:00	Children observe slides and discuss the observations that led to the archaeologist's misinterpretations of the artifacts in the slides.	Caitlin follows up the guest talk with a slide show based on *Motel Mysteries,* a spoof of artifact interpretation.
INTEGRATED WORK TIME 11:20	Children return to their "clans" and work on developing their culture, using some of the ideas gathered during the earlier part of the morning.	Caitlin moves among groups asking questions and listening to students' discussions.
FORUM 1:00	Children work in pairs to identify groups of bones. They measure bones and calculate the possible size of the creature.	During this period, Caitlin introduces a new type of artifact—bones—using the ESS unit, "Bones."
INTEGRATED WORK TIME 2:00	Children work in pairs or individually on: —Comparing traditional literature from ancient cultures. —Investigating arts and crafts common to ancient cultures. —Using *Tyrannosaurus Was a Beast* as a model for writing poems about the creatures reconstructed during Forum. —Making size comparison charts of features of Mystery Island.	Caitlin works with small groups for part of this period and conducts several Reading Conferences* for the rest of the time.

DAY 10 (DIGGING UP THE PAST)

Time	Children	Teacher
FORUM 8:10	Listen to story.	Caitlin reads portion of *The Bone Wars.*
INTEGRATED WORK TIME 8:30	Children listen to and talk with guest. They then move into centers including: —Mystery Island. Present part of their culture to the anthropologist and use expert help in solving problems.	Guest anthropologist speaks about what a "culture" is, and responds to student questions. The anthropologist then works with small groups as they rotate into the Mystery Island center.
	—Plants. Organize a plant history that connects plants and agriculture with human culture.	Caitlin works with the plant history group as they organize data.
	—Literature. Create a comparison of "origin" stories from different cultures. Note how plants and animals are explained in these stories.	Caitlin brings a pomegranate and copy of *Daughter of Earth* to share with this group. After everyone tastes the seeds, and discusses whether they were worth the months in Hades, Caitlin calls students' attention to several other "origin" myths, and to Hamilton's *In the Beginning,* a collection of creation stories from around the world.
	—Animal observations. View video on Jane Goodall's work and begin to read *Born Free.*	Caitlin enters this area as the video ends, and talks with the students about careful observation of live animals. Introduces *Born Free.*
ART 9:50	Children construct mosaics in the fashion of those used in The House of Ancient Greece (MATCh unit), except that they use symbols representing different aspects of their island culture.	An art specialist works with this class, and plans some of her activities to coincide with units that Caitlin has developed.
RECESS 10:30		
INTEGRATED WORK TIME 10:45	Children rotate between groups.	Caitlin continues as during first integrated work time.
FORUM 1:00	Students working with a base 5 number system present their work to the class, including giving the rest of the class some base 5 problems. Three students share their most recent writing.	Caitlin helps as students do base 5 problems. Congratulates those who figure it out: "Look as if you're ready to try another base system!" She also joins in the discussion of the writing presented, uses overhead to answer questions about quotations and paragraphing in dialogue.
INTEGRATED WORK TIME 2:00	Students work in centers.	Caitlin works with small groups, holds a Reading Conference* on *The Stronghold* and *Dawn Wind.*
CLEAN-UP AND DISMISSAL 2:30–2:40		

DAY 20 (DIGGING UP THE PAST)

Time	Children	Teacher
FORUM 8:10	A small group reports on their ten-day study of Ethel, the	Caitlin encourages other animal studies. When two children

(Continued on next page.)

TABLE 4.16—Continued

DAY 20 (DIGGING UP THE PAST)

Time	Children	Teacher
	classroom guinea pig. They have made charts of growth and a video of Ethel's behavior. The class discusses the study and compares it to the video on Goodall and to *Born Free.* They decide that several comparison studies would be useful and begin to plan how to conduct them.	suggest a study of sixth-graders, she tells them to think about what their questions might be to guide the study, how they would collect data, and how they would protect their "subjects' " privacy. She suggests they submit a plan to the class for discussion and approval.
INTEGRATED WORK TIME 8:30	Several new groups have grown from previous work, including: —Museum group. Construction is under way on a diorama-type museum of the prehistoric world. Students have designed exhibits to compare interpretations of what the prehistoric world was like. —Architecture. After working with the art teacher, students are preparing a report on the "Bones of Buildings," and using *Unbuilding* as a model for planning their report.	
	—Human culture. Three groups have each looked at a different culture and are now collaborating on a way to share the results of their studies.	Caitlin works carefully with this group in planning how to share their findings.
	—Leaders. After questions of leadership arose in the Mystery Island activity, a group of students decided to study the influence of different types of leaders in history, and are preparing a news conference with Shaka Khan, Mao Zedong, Saladin, Henry VIII, and Franklin D. Roosevelt.	
FORUM 1:00	Author's Chair*—students share some of their writing with peers.	Caitlin participates in listening to and discussing each author's work.

(DIGGING UP THE PAST *references continued from page 157.*)

DIGGING UP DINOSAURS by Aliki. Crowell, 1981.

DINOSAURS AND THEIR YOUNG by R. Freedman. Illustrated by L. Morill. Holiday, 1983.

THE EYE IN THE FOREST by W. and M. Steele. Dutton, 1975.

FROM MAP TO MUSEUM: UNCOVERING MYSTERIES OF THE PAST by J. Anderson. Photographs by G. Ancona. Morrow, 1988.

HIS MAJESTY, QUEEN HATSEPSHUT by D. S. Carter. Lippincott, 1987.

"History Lesson" by R. Bradbury. In TRANSFORMATIONS II: UNDERSTANDING AMERICAN HISTORY THROUGH SCIENCE FICTION. Fawcett Crest, 1974.

HOMINIDS: A LOOK BACK AT OUR ANCESTORS by R. Sattler. Illustrated by C. Santoro. Lothrop, 1988.

I, TUT: THE BOY WHO BECAME PHAROAH by M. Schlein. Four Winds, 1979.

IN THE BEGINNING by V. Hamilton. Illustrated by B. Moser. Harcourt Brace Jovanovich, 1988.

IN THEIR OWN WORDS by M. Meltzer. Crowell, 1964.

LIFE THROUGH THE AGES by G. Caselli. Putnam, 1987.

LOST AND FOUND by J. P. Walsh. Andre Deutsch, 1985.

MAIA: A DINOSAUR GROWS UP by J. Horner and J. Gorman. Illustrated by D. Henderson. Courage, 1987.

MILL by D. Macaulay. Houghton Mifflin, 1983.

MOONSEED TO MISTLETOE: A BOOK OF POISONOUS WILD PLANTS by C. Lerner. Morrow, 1988.

MOTEL OF THE MYSTERIES by D. Macaulay. Houghton Mifflin, 1980.

MUMMIES MADE IN EGYPT by Aliki. Crowell, 1979.

PLANT FUN: TEN EASY PLANTS TO GROW INDOORS by A. H. Soucie. Four Winds, 1974.

PYRAMID by D. Macaulay. Houghton Mifflin, 1975.

SETH OF THE LION PEOPLE by B. Pryor. Morrow, 1988.

SHAKA, KING OF THE ZULUS by D. Stanley and P. Vennema. Illustrated by D. Stanley. Morrow, 1988.

THE STRONGHOLD by M. Hunter. Harper & Row, 1974.

TRACKING WILD CHIMPANZEES by J. Powzyk. Lothrop, 1988.

TRACES OF LIFE by K. Lasky. Illustrated by W. Powell. Morrow, 1989.

TYRANNOSAURUS REX AND ITS KIN by H. R. Sattler. Illustrated by J. Powzyk. Lothrop, 1988.

TYRANNOSAURUS WAS A BEAST by J. Prelutsky. Illustrated by A. Lobel. Greenwillow, 1988.

UNBUILDING by D. Macaulay. Houghton Mifflin, 1983.

WHERE THE FOREST MEETS THE SEA by J. Baker. Greenwillow, 1988.

WHITE BEAR, ICE BEAR by J. Ryder. Illustrated by M. Rothman. Morrow, 1988.

CONCLUSIONS

Each of the teachers visited in the eight prototypes in this chapter is a unique individual in strength, interests, and enthusiasm. Some of them are more likely to think initially in disciplinary or curricular categories when planning; others prefer to follow a theme across categories first and attend to disciplinary or curricular requirements at a later stage in the planning. Some of them work well in teams or in open classrooms; others enjoy the flexibility of self-contained or family grouped settings. Despite these and other differences, there are also commonalities among them that identify these teachers' classrooms as integrated language environments. To begin with, these classes are distinguished by the joint participation of adults and children in meaning-making. Ruby Antoncic makes that point most specifically when she invites children on a journey of exploration and uses herself as an example of that process. But other teachers also invite collaboration. Estella Esquivel, for instance, regularly involves children in brainstorming at the outset of a thematic unit so that children see themselves as active participants, not just in learning about something or someone but in selecting what to learn about.

Distinguishing features of integrated language classrooms

A related feature of these integrated language classrooms is a different view of error. Children hypothesize, make approximations, develop theories, and test them against new data. Their hypotheses and theories may not be supported by these new data, and their approximations may be refined as they learn more, but that is the nature of learning. Hypothesis-making requires risk, and these classes provide a context within which intellectual risk-taking is encouraged, supported, and expected. Caitlin Cooper depicts this perspective as her students first develop the tools of archaeological observation and inference and then use those tools to construct their own civilization. Peter

Teachers and children in these classes develop a different view of "error" and intellectual risk-taking.

Williams also encourages hypothesizing in the soap bubble experiments so closely tied to a rich array of literature.

Teachers become child developmentalists rather than technicians.

Teachers in integrated language classrooms see themselves as child developmentalists rather than as teacher technicians. They are professionals responsible for developing a child-centered curriculum that has solid intellectual content. Child developmentalists know that content and context are inseparable. They strive to arrange the kind of context that fosters student engagement in their process of building theories about the world. These classrooms were full of participants, not recipients. They were the active makers of meaning.

These classroom contexts are filled with a range of materials, but they are not expensive resources. Rather, they are gathered from many sources, including materials donated by or borrowed from families, friends, acquaintances, and other members from the community. Books and print resources are easily obtained from libraries. Recall our references in Chapter 3 to the fact that experienced integrated language teachers frequently use approximately four to five hundred books during a thematic unit. Because of the space constraints on the prototypes we provided, we were not able to list that many books on the WEBs. Consequently, the WEBs in this chapter included only a portion of the books that are available on these themes.

Integrated language classrooms are content-rich and community oriented.

Related to this feature of resources is the way that the community serves as a resource for the classrooms described in the chapter. An important characteristic of the integrated language classrooms you have seen here is how frequently the boundaries between the community and the classroom were crossed. Time after time, the community was brought into the classroom to provide expertise or help. Parents and friends and children from other classes joined class participants to celebrate and support children's efforts. Children went on field trips into the community to gain important information and data for their projects. Through this two-way process, the classroom culture was enlarged and expanded, and bridges were constructed to span the gulf between the school and the world at large.

Finally, the various classroom and teaching arrangements depicted here are not specific to a particular grade or age. A teacher working on a seventh or eighth grade team in a middle school setting, for instance, would be more likely to use patterns such as those suggested in the fourth/fifth grade departmentalized setting than those in the sixth grade self-contained model. Obviously, ideas from one prototype can be used in others, and activities set up for younger children can often be adapted for use with older students, and vice versa. Classrooms, as with any human community, change over time. The crucial factor in these classrooms is that each of these teachers constantly seeks to make changes that will enrich children's lives by making them more interested and able learners.

REFERENCES

Barr, R., Barth, J., & Shermis, S. S. (1977). *Defining the social studies.* Bulletin 51. Washington, DC: National Council for the Social Studies.

Blake, D. W. (1981). Observing children learning history. *The History Teacher, 14,* 533–549.

Clements, M., Tabachnik, R., & Fielder, W. (1966). *Social study.* New York: Bobbs-Merrill.

Feshback, N. D. (1975). Empathy in children: Some theoretical and empirical considerations. *Counseling Psychologist, 4,* 25–30.

"Oregon Trail" (1985). Minnesota Educational Computer Consortium.

Ryan, F., & Ellis, A. (1974). *Instructional implications of inquiry.* Englewood Cliffs, N.J.: Prentice-Hall.

Shaftel, F. R., & Shaftel, G. (1982). *Role playing in the curriculum, 2nd ed.* Englewood Cliffs, N.J.: Prentice-Hall.

Stone, L. C. (1986). International and multicultural education. In V. Atwood (Ed.), *Elementary social studies: Research as a guide to practice* (pp. 34–54). Bulletin 79. Washington, DC: National Council for the Social Studies.

CHILDREN'S LITERATURE REFERENCES

MISS RUMPHIUS by B. Cooney. Viking, 1983.

OTHER RESOURCES

"Bones," Elementary Science Study (1974). New York: McGraw-Hill.

Kresse, F. H. (1969). "The House of Ancient Greece," Materials and Activities for Teachers and Children. A MATCH unit. Boston: American Science and Engineering.

5

Learning More about Written Language

Chapter 1 provided a preliminary review of the theoretical foundation of the integrated language perspective.

The following three major interrelated principles were emphasized:

- Children (all humans) are active, constructive learners.
- Language is organized in different ways, in different patterns or registers because it is used for different purposes in different social contexts.
- Knowledge is organized and constructed by individual learners through social interaction.

This chapter builds on and extends the second principle that has to do with the variation of language by focusing more on the nature of written language and the processes—reading and writing—of using it. Although this chapter concentrates on the second principle, the other two principles are involved in our discussion, too, because all three principles are interrelated and cannot really be separated.

REGISTERS OF WRITTEN LANGUAGE

What Is a Genre?

The range of written genres is limitless.

In the previous chapters in this book we have argued that it is important for children to have many opportunities to use a range of written genres in the classroom. We have argued that a major advantage of the use of a thematic unit is that such an approach provides a means to accomplish this. But what is really meant by the term *genre?* You probably have met this term in English literature courses during which you have read and studied various written genres such as short stories, odes, sonnets, novels, novellas, plays, and so forth. We will use *genre* much more broadly, not only to include these literary genres but also to incorporate the potentially limitless number of written texts available in our culture.

There are many spoken genres, too.

Although we focus mostly on written texts in this chapter, our meaning of genre also includes a similar limitless range of spoken texts. Our culture consists of a variety of structured activities occurring in a range of contexts of situation. When the particulars in these situations are similar, the spoken texts constructed by participants end up being similar and having a similar form or organization. When the factors in situations are different, the spoken texts related to these contexts result in different forms, different organizations. Think of the kinds of texts, the types of discourse patterns, that are used when people participate in service encounters—when they go shopping in stores or markets, buy stamps or send packages at post offices, buy tickets at travel agencies. Contrast these texts with the kind of spoken language employed when people visit a doctor, consult with a lawyer, or perhaps seek advice from a university academic advisor. Now consider the language patterns that are likely to occur in very different activities—when people attend a party, go to a restaurant to have lunch with friends, participate in a religious service, conduct a public meeting, and on and on. Were you able to "visualize" the variation of spoken language—the different registers of language—in these examples? Can you "sense" similarities or commonalities and differences in these examples? Certain texts appeared to be similar or go together into certain sets or categories because they seemed to be part of certain socially ordered activities serving similar purposes. For example, the texts in the service encounters might resemble each other even though different "goods"—groceries, stamps, plane tickets, and the like—might be bought and sold in these interactions. Moreover, this set of texts would be somewhat different from the discourse patterns in which we seek a service from a professional such as a physician or lawyer. And both of these sets would be very different from the text registers of a party or going to a restaurant with friends. We can call these various categories of texts—these similar sets, ways, or registers of using language—*genres.*

Christie (1987); Collerson (1988); Halliday & Hasan (1985); Himley (1986); Martin, Christie, & Rothery (1987)

A genre is a conventional way of using language.

Just as there are numerous kinds of spoken genres, there are numerous types of written genres. Besides the literary ones already mentioned, there are mysteries, western stories, fantasies, science fiction, historical fiction, romances, biographies, poems, how-to manuals, editorials, advertisements, information books, commentaries, business letters, reviews of books, films, and movies, newsletters, recipes—the list can go on and on.

However, genres—spoken or written—have two characteristics that at first glance appear to be contradictory. First, genres are *stable.* They have fixed elements or patterns: A story is organized in a different way from an essay, which is, in turn, different from a recipe. These different genres are stable because they do certain jobs in our culture. When we need to, we can choose from this system of language, this range of genres, to communicate our intentions.

Genres are stable patterns of language use.

Although they are stable, genres always involve *change.* They change because we put together various available options from different genres in a different way or borrow elements or features from different genres in new, novel ways; we create new subgenres. Because we frequently have new language goals or purposes to be accomplished in everyday life, aspects of the patterns of genres are altered. Genres are *evolved* and *evolving systems.* The generic characteristics of stability and change lead to predictable and creative texts. A particular text is always a new, creative instance of some genre, but at the same time it is always predictable, being in some sense "old hat" for its users.

Genres reflect change in patterns of language use.

Stability in generic patterns leads to predictability in texts; change in generic patterns leads to creativity in texts.

The Organization of Written Genres

The predictability and creativity, or novelty, of written texts belonging to particular genres is owed to their linguistic organization. Authors do not simply sequence words, sentences, paragraphs, and so on in a random, helter-skelter fashion. Instead, they structure their texts in particular ways that are influenced by the purposes they want the language to accomplish. In doing so, they draw on their knowledge of the linguistic conventions of various genres.

Genres consist of organized linguistic schemes.

The organization of genres is related to how language is used for social processes.

The Textural Patterns of Written Texts

Wildsmith (1971); Gibbons (1984)

Let's consider again the story *The Owl and the Woodpecker* and the information book *Tunnels* that were discussed in Chapter 1. Each of these texts represents a *typical* example of its respective genre—that is, everyone would agree that *The Owl and the Woodpecker* is a storybook and that *Tunnels* is an information book. We have already observed (in Chapter 1) that each possesses different linguistic patterns—what are called *textural* differences. That is, the story has linguistic patterns (identity chains) to refer to the *same* characters or objects (woodpecker, owl, woodpecker's tree, for example) in the text, whereas the information book includes patterns (co-classification chains) in which the same *classes* of objects or animals (tunnels, ants, and worms, for example) are referred to in the text. Other aspects of texture were mentioned—the use of the past verb tense in the story versus the present tense in *Tunnels,* and the fact that this information book contains many more descriptive constructions than does the story.

Hasan (1985a)
Texture involves meaning relations.

If we looked at these two texts from these two genres and at other texts that are typical examples of the genres, we would probably notice even more linguistic differences. Now, you surely were aware of these linguistic differences in stories and information books even before you read this textbook, but you probably have never examined them in any explicit way. This chapter points out other linguistic patterns of a range of written genres, patterns that you already know about in a tacit or subconscious way, so that they become more explicit, so that you will be more aware of the nature of written genres. This awareness enables teachers to know how to select books of various genres for children to read in the classroom and to know how to respond to children as they attempt to read and write in various genres.

The Global Structure of Written Texts

Genres are also organized in global ways.

Pappas (1985)

Besides textural differences, texts of written genres are structured in a more global way. That is, texts are also organized into big "chunks," and these chunks are different for different genres. Each genre has a shape, or global structure, of its own. For example, stories are typically formed into elements according to what many researchers call a *story grammar.* Although researchers have described and labeled the components of these global frameworks in different ways, the schemes are very similar. We use the framework (and terminology) developed by the linguist Ruqaiya Hasan, who has studied the language of bedtime stories in depth.

Hasan (1984, 1985b)

Storybook genre
Hasan (1984)

According to Hasan's scheme, there are chunks or elements that every story has to have to be considered a story, and there are optional elements that a particular story may or may not include. The elements she calls the Initiating Event, Sequent Event, and Final Event are the necessary (or obligatory) elements in this framework; the Placement, Finale, and Moral are the optional elements. Remember, these elements are not just one sentence or event but big chunks of text that may include many events or sentences. These elements are described and illustrated by the story *The Owl and the Woodpecker* (Table 5.1); see if you can recognize them in other stories that you know.

Bruce (1980, 1984)

Stories have to do with interpersonal understandings—how characters' goals interrelate, how their plans to achieve these goals mesh or clash. This genre shapes its message so that inferences about human beliefs, purposes, or motives can be expressed. In contrast, the information genre does not involve specific characters and their goals, personal motives for action, and the like. As a result, just as a different texture exists, the information book genre has a different global structure or a different "grammar." We use Pappas's scheme to describe this genre, which, like Hasan's story framework, has both necessary global chunks, or elements, that every information book has to include and optional elements that particular information books may or may not express. *Tunnels* (refer to Table 1.6 in Chapter 1) is used to illustrate the global elements in this genre (see Table 5.2).

Information book genre

Pappas (1986, 1987, 1988)

These two generic schemes—for stories and for information books—are provided

TABLE 5.1

Description of the Global Elements	Examples from *The Owl and the Woodpecker*
Placement—an author may introduce or "place" characters on "stage" in the story, provide time or locale information, relate what characters habitually do, or talk about certain attributes of characters, and so on (optional).	"Once upon a time" information, as well as something about the locale—"in a forest, far away"—and about the habitual behavior of the woodpecker character—"lived in a tree in which he slept all night and worked all day"—are included.
Initiating Event—the conflict or problem of the story emerges.	The owl, who has sleeping and working habits that are the opposite of those of the woodpecker, moves into a nearby tree. The woodpecker's daily tapping keeps the owl awake, and he becomes so bad-tempered that something has to be done.
Sequent Event—a recount of characters' attempts to resolve the problem or conflict.	Other animals in the forest have a meeting and decide that the owl has to leave, since the woodpecker was there first. They try one night, while the owl is out hunting, to push down his tree, but have no success.
Final Event—resolution of the problem/conflict.	The tree is blown down by a terrible storm. However, fortunately the owl, who had been sound asleep and was not aware that he was in danger, is saved by the woodpecker's tapping before the tree crashes to the ground.
Finale—a restoration of the habitual or normal state of affairs (optional).	The woodpecker helps the owl find a new home/tree in another part of the forest so that the owl is not disturbed by the woodpecker's tapping, and the owl and the woodpecker remain "good friends all the rest of their lives."
Moral—a moral statement or claim is made (optional).	Not realized in this book. Can you think of a story in which it is included?

to illustrate how two genres are organized, how they differ with respect to their global patterns. These schemes also have other organizational features. For example, each generic text structure has rules for how the global elements are ordered, whether some elements have a fixed order, and how others can have more flexibility with respect to their order. For example, the Moral story element, if it is included in a story, must always follow the Final Event of the story; however, if the story also includes the Finale global element, the Moral element can come either before or after the Finale. The Placement (if it is included in a particular text), the Initiating Event, the Sequent Event, and the Final Event have a fixed order, following one another as they have been listed.

Part of a genre's organization is the order of its elements.

The order of elements can be fixed or variable.

The generic scheme for information books also has fixed and variable aspects of order. The Topic Presentation is always the first element, but the next three elements shown in Table 5.2—Description of Attributes, Characteristic Events, and Category Comparison—can be variable in their order. The Summary Statement (if it is included in a text) always follows all of these, and the Afterword (again if it is included) always ends the book.

Another characteristic of generic schemes is whether certain elements can be discrete, separate chunks or whether they can be interspersed in other elements. Both of the generic schemes we have discussed have such features. The story scheme allows for the possibility that in certain stories Placement information can be interspersed in the Initiating Event. The information book generic scheme permits even more interspersion. The Topic Presentation can be interspersed in any one of the three elements

Certain elements of a generic scheme can be discrete or interspersed.

TABLE 5.2

Description of the Global Elements	Examples from *Tunnels*
Topic Presentation—the topic of the text is presented or introduced.	The topic, tunnels, is presented.
Description of Attributes—a description of the attributes of the class or topic the book is about.	That tunnels are long and short, that they are underground or under water holes, and so on are described.
Characteristic Events—characteristic or habitual or typical processes/events are expressed.	How tunnels are built or made by digging, by blasting through rock, and so on and how tunnels are used—to walk through, to drive through, and the like.
Category Comparison—compares or discusses different members of the class or topic that a book is about (common, but optional).	Different types of tunnels—tunnels made by animals and people, or the rock, soft ground, underwater, and cut-and-cover tunnels, and so on—are explained.
Final Summary—summary statements are made about the information covered in a book (common, but optional).	Animals and people have many uses for tunnels.
Afterword—extra information about the topic is included (optional).	Extra specific details about tunnels are added—for example, the fact that cavemen dug tunnels to connect their caves, facts about the first manmade tunnel in the United States, the Seikan Tunnel in Japan, the five tunnels that go through the Alps, and so on.

just mentioned regarding variable order—Description of Attributes, Characteristic Events, and Category Comparison—and any of these three can be interspersed in each other.

Learning about various generic schemes helps readers and writers.
Smith (1988)

Again, you already know about this structure, or organization, of storybooks and information books, although the organization of these two written genres and many others may seem complicated when it is described in this explicit way. Nevertheless, these generic text structures provide a sense of stability. Knowledge of these schemes makes texts more predictable and comprehensible to readers. Reading a range of written genres to children and providing many opportunities for children themselves to read texts of various genres helps children internalize knowledge of the shape, rhythm, and flow of the various registers, or genres, of written language. Moreover, experiences with various genres provide for children a wide range of models to draw on in their own writing.

Although generic schemes have structure, order, and specificity, at the same time they allow for the creation of new texts that show variation and novelty. We have noted how creativity in particular texts can occur through the inclusion of certain optional elements, changes in their order, or through interspersion of information of some elements in others. The potential for creativity in written texts is even greater than that, however. Creativity in written texts can be best understood and appreciated by examining some other texts from other written genres and by developing a general model of genres.

A GENERAL MODEL OF WRITTEN GENRES

The Owl and the Woodpecker and *Tunnels* are *typical* examples of their genres.

We have already mentioned that the story *The Owl and the Woodpecker* and the information book *Tunnels* are typical texts from their respective genres. That is, in reading or reviewing them, no one would disagree that the former is a story and the latter is an information book. However, many texts are not so clear-cut, not so typical. There are many "fuzzy," or atypical, texts. Let's consider two texts, *Mouse* by Sara Bonnett Stein and *Panda* by Susan Bonners, to illustrate the notion of "fuzziness." Table 5.3 shows the first part of each text.

Some texts are "fuzzy" examples of genres.

Stein (1985); Bonners (1978)

Review the texts in Table 5.3 with these questions in mind: Are these texts information books? Are they stories? Left of the two excerpts are the abbreviations of possible global elements from the story and information book genres described earlier (see the key at the bottom of Table 5.3 that explains the abbreviations). The dashed lines mark pages in the books. First, approach each as an example of the story genre. The first four pages of *Mouse* seem like a Placement. A mouse is introduced, and the actions of the mouse—where she lives, how she makes her nest—could be considered as habitual behavior. Then the last page of that excerpt could be seen as the beginning of the Initiating Event in which a baby is born. A similar case regarding global structure can be made for *Panda.* A sort of Placement can be established for the first three pages of the excerpt in which a panda is introduced and habitual information is included. The Initiating Event also begins with the birth of an offspring. Moreover, in each text identity chains for the mouse and panda can be established, a textural feature of the story genre.

Now consider each text as an instance of the information book genre. The first page of each book seems to be a Topic Presentation, each presenting the topic—mouse and panda, respectively. Then the second page of each book begins the second global element. In *Mouse* the second element is the Characteristic Event, whereas in *Panda,* the element could be either Description of Attributes with information from the Characteristic Event in it, or the other way around. Although it seems that identity chains are involved in each, neither book has the theme about "human" conflict that characterizes stories. However, *Mouse* is in the present tense—a textural feature of the information book genre, and *Panda* begins with the present tense but switches to the past tense.

TABLE 5.3

	Mouse
P? TP?	A mouse lives in a dark closet where the family never sees her.
CE?	She makes her nest of soft things she finds in the closet—white stuffing, blue wool, red cloth.
	The outside of the nest is round, with a hole just big enough for a mouse to get through.
	The inside of the nest is hollow, just the right size for the mouse and her babies.
IE?	When the nest is finished, the mouse is ready to have her babies. Her belly tightens. She pushes out a wet, pink baby in a thin wrapper.
	Panda
P? TP?	In a mountain forest of southwestern China, a giant panda sits in a birch tree.
DA/CE?	Snowflakes fall on her black and white fur, but she does not look for shelter. She has lived in snow most of her life.
IE?	Early one autumn, she found a den in a rocky mountainside. There she made a nest out of broken bamboo stalks. While frosty winds blew through the forest, she gave birth to her cub.

KEY: From the Story Genre:
P = Placement Global Element
IE = Initiating Event Global Element
From the Information Book Genre:
TP = Topic Presentation Global Element
DA = Description of Attributes Global Element
CE = Characteristic Events Global Element

Source: Stein (1985).

Mouse and *Panda* include features from the storybook and information book genres.

Thus, these are "fuzzy" or atypical texts because they do not fit clearly in either genre. They seem to have some story features and some information features. They lie where the boundaries of these genres overlap. We need to visualize these typical and atypical, overlapping texts of genres. Figure 5.1 tries to do this by using genre "curves" or "mountains." It depicts both typical texts of each genre that we have already discussed (*The Owl and the Woodpecker* and *Tunnels*) and the more atypical or fuzzy texts, *Mouse* and *Panda.*

An atypical text can be coherent, comprehensible, and of high quality.

The fact that a text is atypical does not mean that it is necessarily less coherent or comprehensible or of low quality. It is because authors have knowledge of the structure and features of various genres that they are able to select and write a text that is creative, novel, and interesting. Thus, we need a model of genres that can deal with such creativity.

Typical texts are found in the "peaks" of genre mountains.

Atypical texts are found in the "slopes" or "valleys" of genre mountains.

Genres do not have absolute boundaries, as Figure 5.1 shows. Real texts are not the result of all-or-nothing formulas. Instead, some texts are typical of particular genres; they lie in the shaded part of the genre mountains—at the peaks—and are very distinctively different from typical texts of other genres. Other texts reflect degrees of atypicality and are less distinctive; they lie on the nonshaded slopes of the genre mountains, or where the genre mountains overlap and interact.

Consequently, our model of genres has to depict these characteristics of texts that are a matter of degree. We cannot go into every type of text in this chapter, but let's try to extend Figure 5.1 to consider other genres. First, how should we treat the genres of poetry and how-to manuals? We add these genres to the story and information book genres by placing them in multidimensional space. Figure 5.2 depicts this by adding two new genre mountains.

Siebert (1988)

Now, let's consider two atypical texts that show overlap between genres. The first is the book, *Mojave,* by Diane Siebert (1988). The first four pages of this book about the Mojave Desert, an area that covers thousands of square miles of southern California, southern Nevada, and small portions of Utah and Arizona, are reprinted here.

Mojave

I am the desert.
I am free.
Come walk the sweeping face of me.

Through canyon eyes of sandstone red
I see the hawk, his wings outspread;
He sunward soars to block the light
And casts the shadow of his flight

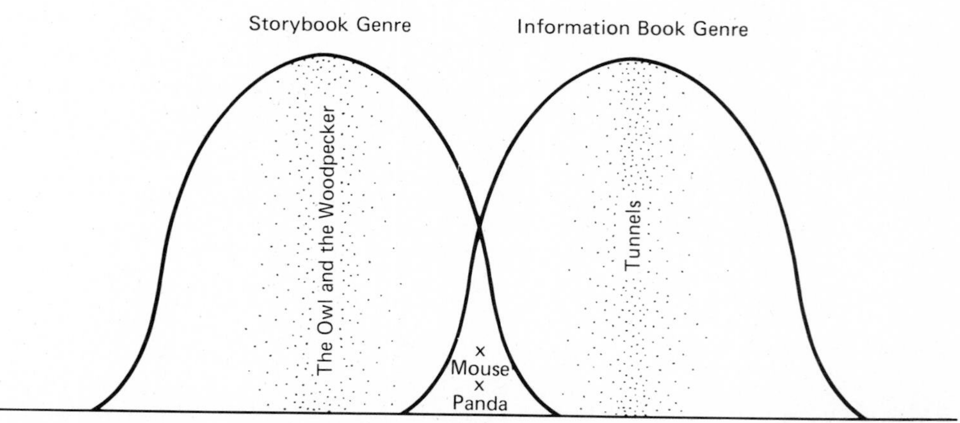

Figure 5.1

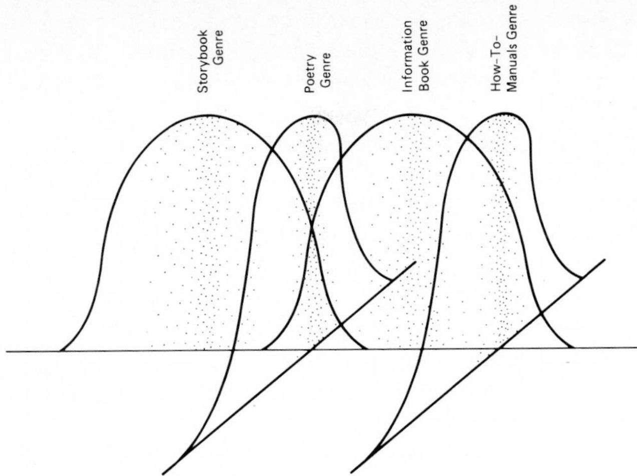

Figure 5.2

Upon my vast and ancient face,
Whose deep arroyos boldly trace
The paths where sudden waters run—
Long streams of tears dried by the sun.

- -

I feel the windstorm's violent thrust;
I feel the sting of sand and dust
As bit by bit, and year by year,
New features on my face appear.

- -

Great mountain ranges stretch for miles
To crease my face with frowns and smiles.
My lakes are dry and marked by tracks
Of zigging, zagging, long-eared jacks.
Dust devils swirl and slowly rise;
They whistle, whirling to the skies,
While tossed and blown in great stampedes
Are stumbling, bumbling tumbleweeds.

- -

I feel the tread of tiny feet
As lizards dart in swift retreat
To hide in shadows, safe, unseen,
Beneath the yucca's spears of green.
Here Joshua trees, in mighty stands,
Spread twisted arms and sharp, green hands
Above the tortoises who sleep
Within the shade, then slowly creep
Across my rocks, in armored domes,
To crawl inside their burrowed homes;
And snakes with lovely, patterned skin
Go gliding, hiding deep within
My rocky face, far from the light,
Protected, cool, and out of sight.

Can you see how this text is atypical? In what ways is it "fuzzy"? It is like an information book because it provides information about the Mojave desert, the creatures that live there, the vegetation, the sand and sun, and how the desert changes with the seasons. However, this information is expressed by lyrical prose, by a poetic register. Thus,

Mojave includes features from the information book, poetry, and personal narrative genres.

there is an overlap of information book features and poetry features. We could even make the case that *Mojave* also has some features of yet another genre—that of the personal narrative (a genre that we have not included in Figure 5.2). That is, the message seems also to be communicated through the experiences of an "I"—in this case, the "I" being the desert.

Haldane (1984)

Another book, *The See-Through Zoo: How Glass Animals Are Made,* by Suzanne Haldane (1984) also shows fuzziness. Excerpts from this book follow. Unlike excerpts from the other books we have included in this chapter, this excerpt does not start with the first page; it also skips to other parts of the book.

The See-Through Zoo:
How Glass Animals Are Made

Glass is made from materials that could be found in any backyard: sand, soda, ash, and lime. Yet from these familiar ingredients, objects both ordinary and unique have been fashioned for many thousands of years.

The Egyptian glass pig on the left is over two thousand years old. And his companion on the right was made fifteen hundred years ago, in the Roman Empire. (p. 8)

- -

In this French drawing, from an eighteenth-century encyclopedia, a glassmaker sits at his workbench. Glass is made much the way it was centuries ago.

Today's glassmakers use the same simple tools. (p. 9)

- -

In a large open area, several paces from where the craftsmen work, the furnace is fired up to the melting temperature of 2600°F—more than ten times the heat needed to boil water.

At night, while the glassmakers are home sleeping, the batch is cooked. During the ten to twelve hours it takes to fuse—melt and blend—the ingredients, the intense heat must be kept constant, or the furnace will be damaged and the glass ruined. . . .

Too hot ever to touch, the molten glass, now referred to as "metal," is ready to be worked.

Two people are needed to turn metal into animals. One is the teacher, the other the pupil.

The master craftsman is called the gaffer, from an old English word meaning grandfather. He has had years of experience and familiarity with glass. Guided only by his imagination, he pulls and pushes the glass into the shapes of more than fifty different animals, using a variety of tools.

His helper, called a gatherer because he collects or gathers the glass, assists and learns from the master. (p. 15)

- -

The gatherer starts the process. . . .

While the gatherer does all of his work standing up, the gaffer needs to sit at a bench to do his. . . . (p. 16)

- -

The two artisans must work fast. They are always racing against time, because glass cools rapidly, and below a certain temperature it can no longer be shaped.

Tiny animals may be pulled and pinched into shape in a matter of seconds. But larger animals, especially those composed of several pieces of metal, must be reheated before the addition of each piece, because hot glass will only stick to hot glass. . . . (p. 18)

An animal starts as a ball of molten glass. The gaffer begins most animals at either the head or tail. Cats, horses, and unicorns begin at the head; dolphins, sharks, and seals at the tail.

When making an elephant, however, the gaffer begins with the body. . . . (p. 19) (Haldane, 1984)

The See-Through Zoo includes features from the information book and how-to manual genres.

These parts of the text were included to illustrate that the book is like an information book in that it provides an account of what glass is made of, how it is made, and so forth. It also includes features of a how-to manual in that it describes the step-by-step work of a master glassmaker (the gaffer) and his assistant (the gatherer) in fashioning glass animals in general and a glass elephant specifically. Thus, this text seems also to overlap genres.

Authors create typical texts of particular genres, as well as atypical texts that reflect overlapping genres. As a result, our model of genres has to have a multidimensional perspective to explain both the typicality *and* the overlap, or atypicality, of texts in a range of genres.

Classifying all texts into two large genres is too simplistic.

Discussions of genres are frequently simplified by depicting them as two large all-or-nothing categories, such as fiction and nonfiction or narrative and expository. Unfortunately, many texts do not fit easily into these categories. Although most fiction is narrative, a personal narrative is not fiction. What about biography? Or letters? Newspaper stories? They are narrative, but they are factual or nonfiction. Two major categories or general types of genres cannot account for the complexity and the range of the genres present in our culture.

When we consider the subgenres, it is clear that no two-category model will work. Are mysteries, fantasies, westerns, science fiction, historical fiction, and so on part of the story genre? Or are they genres on their own? What is the distinction between biographies and historical fiction? How do they overlap? How do recipes and reports of science experiments overlap with the information book genre and how-to manuals? How do epics, sonnets, and odes relate? Where should letters—personal, business, thank-you notes, and invitations—fit? Figure 5.3 tries to depict what such a model of genres would look like. (Suggested Activity 1 at the end of the chapter can help you to explore more about the multidimensional, overlapping, aspects of written genres.)

Summary

Genres are products of social processes.

Written genres are *products* of our culture, but these products are the result of various social *processes* that have certain purposes or goals. Genres are organized to provide both *stability* (they have certain fairly predictable elements and an accepted sequence, and so forth) and *change* (although they are somewhat "fixed," they reflect new versions of structure and sequence elements in novel and creative ways). *Typical texts* of a particular genre reflect that genre as a whole; they are exemplars for which consensus can be found. However, many *atypical* texts exist as well; they are borderline cases or instances of subgenres that contain features of one or more other genres. Because of

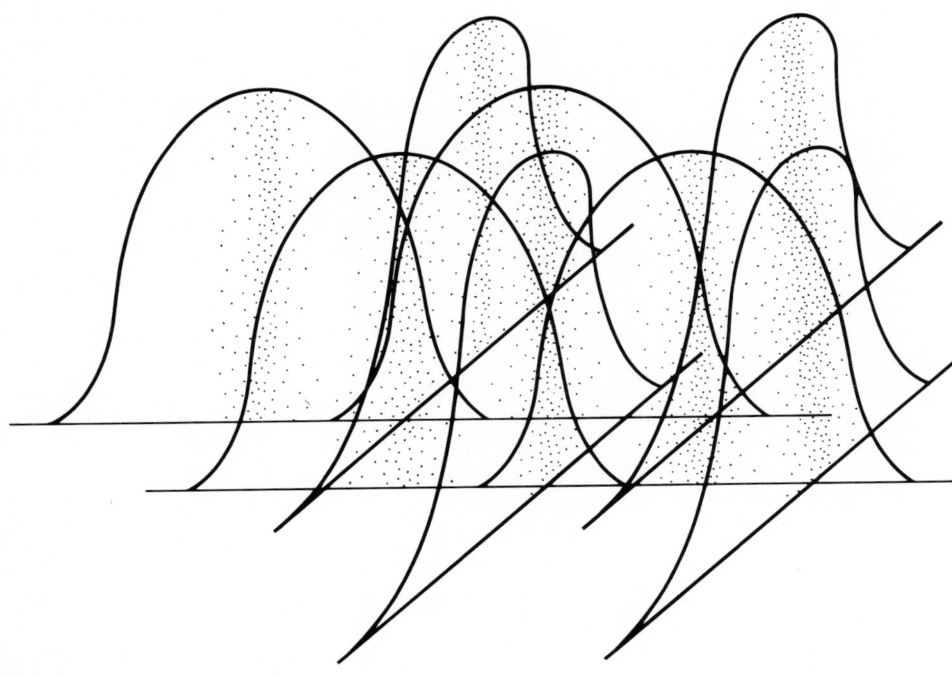

Figure 5.3

the complexity of written genres, their structural patterns (just like every aspect of language patterns, spelling patterns, sentence patterns, paragraph patterns, etc.) cannot be taught in direct, formal ways; otherwise, children will be misled, given only part of the story. They will miss out and never understand the creativity, limitless options, or the potential of language. However, if teachers have an awareness of the various conventions of a range of written genres, they can support and foster children's processes of reading and writing them. They can provide many examples of the genres (both typical and atypical texts), point out and compare elements and features in them, and facilitate children's comprehension and composing of texts of a variety of genres.

THE READING AND WRITING PROCESSES

In Chapter 1 we discussed the involvement of the reader-writer contract in processing or using written texts. It was emphasized that both reading and writing are meaning-making processes—that is, both readers and writers bring meaning (based on their schemas) to texts. In this chapter, we extend and expand on these important ideas by looking further into each side of the contract, the reading process and then the writing process, and then we reconsider again the connections between them.

The Reading Process

Goodman (1967); Smith (1988)

Reading is a constructive, problem-solving process. Readers pose problems or ask questions about the text. Inherent in this process is *prediction,* a set of reader expectations. Readers predict what print means—reading consists of informed guesses. They confirm their predictions or they resolve or answer the problems they pose, or they disconfirm their initial predictions and have to set new hypotheses or consider new questions or problems about the meaning of the text. In this process, readers understand or partially comprehend the text.

Goodman & Burke (1985)

de Beaugrande (1980); Nystrand (1986)

Transaction

Lytle & Botel (1988); Rosenblatt (1978); Weaver (1988)

Using a variety of strategies, readers use the linguistic clues or "cues" provided by the author (the type of genre the author has chosen is a particular source of these clues). Readers employ these clues to build or construct their own useful, personal world of the text. They structure their own knowledge or schema regarding that text. Thus, from the reader's point of view, meaning is not in the text itself. Instead, meaning arises during the interaction—or what many researchers call the *transaction*—between the written words of the text and the reader. Let's try to get an idea of what this transaction with text is like by considering the following passage about Rocky, and then we'll examine some important issues regarding it.

Anderson, Reynolds, Shallert, & Goetz (1977)

> Rocky slowly got up from the mat, planning his escape. He hesitated a moment and thought. Things were not going well. What bothered him most was being held, especially since the charge against him had been weak. He considered his present situation. The lock that held him was strong but he thought he could break it. He knew, however, that his timing would have to be perfect. Rocky was aware that it was because of his early roughness that he had been penalized so severely—much too severely from his point of view. The situation was becoming frustrating; the pressure had been grinding on him for too long. He was being ridden unmercifully. Rocky was getting angry now. He felt he was ready to make his move. He knew that his success or failure would depend on what he did in the next few seconds.

Well, who is Rocky? Most readers answer, "a wrestler" or "a prisoner" (or "a convict"). How did you respond? This passage has been used in research studies in which some subjects were asked, before reading, to take the perspective that Rocky is a wrestler, and some were asked to consider Rocky as a prisoner. Then, after the reading, they were asked to answer questions about the passage. The subjects answered the same questions differently, depending on the perspective they adopted. In another study, the researchers did not ask the subjects to take a particular perspective ahead of time, yet they got similar findings. Subjects again responded differently to the same questions. In this study the subjects were college students majoring in either physical education or sociology. What was so interesting about these findings was that the ways the subjects answered the questions corresponded to their major. Without being asked to do so, most of the physical education majors took the perspective that Rocky was a wrestler, whereas the sociology students most frequently viewed Rocky as a prisoner.

Carey, Harste, & Smith (1981)

Different readers had different interpretations of "Rocky."

How can we account for these different reader responses? These readers read the same text, the same words, so the meaning cannot be said to reside totally in the text. Instead, individual readers had different transactions with the text. Some readers with whom we have shared this passage have also reported that Rocky was a horse or a dog. We have even gotten the answer "a kindergartener" from a teacher in a recent workshop with early elementary teachers. In this setting, we were discussing and evaluating how much the bits of language (letters, sounds, words, etc.) were emphasized in the reading lessons in the basal readers used in their schools. Take a kindergartener's point of view, and read the passage again.

Spiro (1980)

This "Rocky" passage was constructed by researchers for a particular experiment. If it were found in any other context, we would probably not consider it complete. It seems to be the beginning of a story in which an author may possibly include many flashbacks to fill in important circumstances or pertinent events in Rocky's life. If it is a story, the subgenre is unclear from the passage as it stands; maybe it's a mystery.

Nevertheless, by using this passage, several important points can be made about the reading process. First, readers use their own prior knowledge or experience about the world and language to construct a meaning of the text. In other words, they construct a meaning of the text by bringing meaning to it. Notice that individual words from the passage—"mat," "escape," "charge," "lock," and so forth—have different meanings depending on whether a wrestler or prisoner (or horse, dog, or kindergartener) perspective is taken. The same is the case for the individual sentences. That is, different readers were concerned with different predictions and different questions and answers before, during, and after reading the Rocky passage. This means that, although people might *think* that reading proceeds in a bottom-up or part-to-whole (from letters to words to sentences, etc.) process, the opposite is the case. Because reading is more of a top-down, whole-to-part process, comprehension of texts is a relative, not an absolute all-or-nothing phenomenon; more than one interpretation is possible in transactions with texts. Second, although varied responses are possible for a particular text, it is not the case that everything goes. No one, in reading the Rocky passage, would say that Rocky is a beautician or a florist. The language of the text, the way the text is organized, is more like a "blueprint." The text offers openness, but it also provides control or certain constraints. We know, for example, that the Rocky passage is not the beginning of a text that belongs to the poetry, informational, or how-to manual genres. Third, readers' transactions and interpretations are influenced by factors of social context. These factors include the background of the reader (cultural, economic, gender, personal, and so on) as well as the actual situation in which the reading occurs. Remember how the researchers set up the task for the subjects in the study, asking different ones to take on different roles for Rocky? Remember how the sociology and the physical education majors responded to the task without having been asked to take a specific perspective? What personal *and* situational factors were affecting the teacher's response to the Rocky passage?

Readers use prior knowledge to understand texts.

Smith (1982a); Weaver (1988)

The comprehension of texts is a relative phenomenon.

Rosenblatt (1978)

The characteristics of a text affect readers' interpretations of that text.

Personal and immediate situational factors affect readers' interpretations of texts.

These three characteristics, or influences on readers' responses, are summarized by Figure 5.4. A reader's transactions with text are the result of (1) the characteristics of the reader (knowledge, attitudes, skills, values, etc.), (2) characteristics of the text (the genre, text structure, the content or topic, etc.), and (3) the characteristics of the social context (the immediate situational context—perhaps a certain context in a certain classroom—*and* the broader social-cultural contexts—school, home, neighborhood, town/city, state, region, nation, culture).

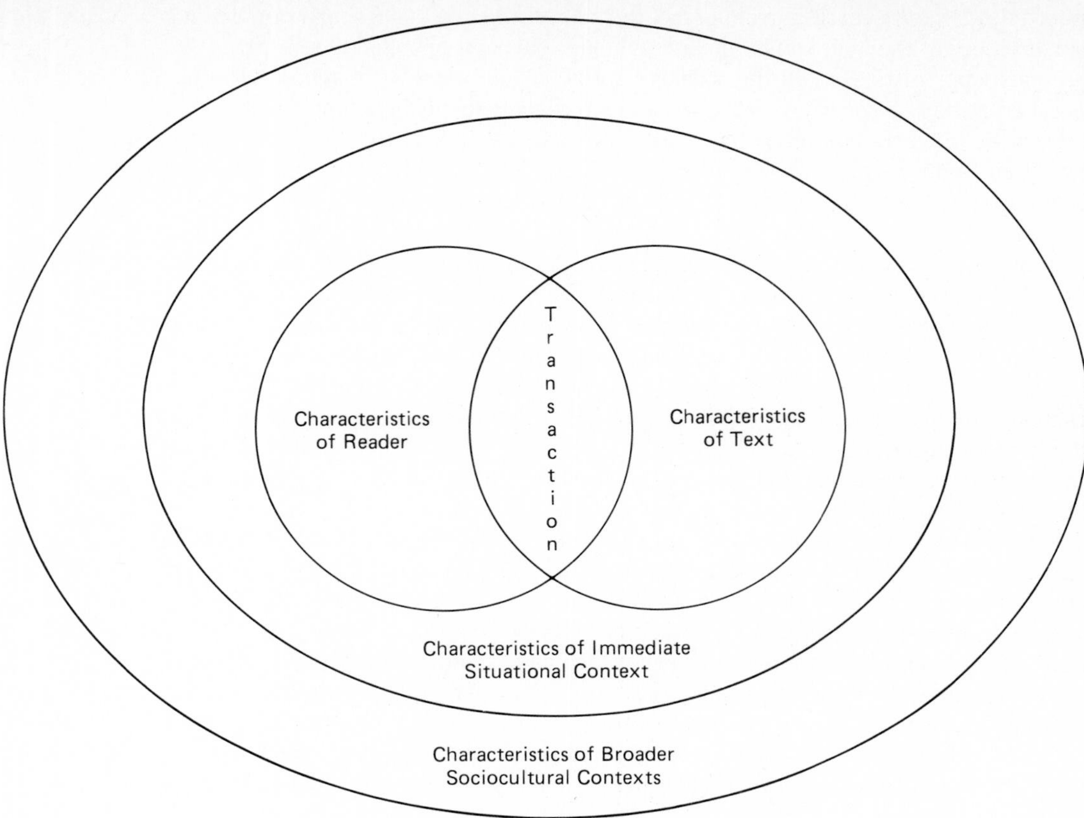

Figure 5.4 Reading as Social Reader-Text Transactions

Reading involves social reader-text transactions.

The term *transaction* thus emphasizes the active meaning-making flavor of the reading process, how readers experience or "evoke" the text. When children learn to read or use written texts across the curriculum, they acquire the conventions of genres of particular disciplines, the different "ways of knowing," the various domain-specific rules of evidence for history, science, math, art, and so forth. At the same time, they develop some general approaches to reading across the curriculum, a range of types of transactions with text. Table 5.4 outlines these types of transactions.

Heath (1983); Hyde & Bizar (1989); Lindfors (1987)

A range of transactions is possible in reading.

These transaction categories have been taken from Lytle & Botel (1988).

Emotional, experiential, and autobiographical transactions

Connective transactions

Descriptive and analytic transactions

Interpretive and elaborative transactions

Evaluative transactions

Self-evaluative transactions

These transactions reflect the ways in which children engage with, and respond to, texts before, during, and after reading. One type of transaction is the *emotional, experiential, and autobiographical* responses of readers—what stands out or is salient for them when they read particular texts. *Connective* transactions have to do with readers making links with prior knowledge of experiences and texts when they read texts, connect with ideas within texts, and fit in new ideas with their present schemas about various topics or experiences. *Descriptive and analytic* transactions are those in which features of texts are noted, where authors' actual structures or wordings—their specific linguistic choices expressed in texts—are examined. *Interpretive and elaborative* transactions deal with the sense-making, problem-solving strategies readers employ to predict, consider, infer, explain, ponder, and question ideas to decide what texts mean for them. *Evaluative* transactions are considerations of appropriateness regarding texts. Readers assess authors' ideas and arguments and their effectiveness in relating or expressing their messages. Readers decide whether particular texts are "good" or not. Finally, *self-reflective* transactions involve readers' noting and monitoring their own processes of reading.

Thus, in reviewing Table 5.4, you will note that these types of transactions involve

TABLE 5.4 Types of Transactions with Text

Types	Definitions	Sample Questions
Emotional, experiential, and autobiographical	Initial response, showing involvement with the text; identifying and/or empathizing. Experiencing the text by using mental/sensory imagery.	What stands out for me? How do I feel about this?
Connective	Linking text with prior experiences, with attitudes and ideas and similar texts, other ideas within the text; making analogies.	What does this text make me think of? remind me of? How does this text fit with what I already know about this subject?
Descriptive and analytic	Noticing features of the text, e.g., choice or function of particular words, syntax or length of sentences; functions of sentences or paragraphs in the text; characters and events; tone; type of discourse; style; use of metaphor or other figures of speech; author's arguments.	How does this text work? What's going on here? What does it say?
Interpretive and elaborative	Using reasoning or problem-solving strategies to construct meaning, resolve doubts, and make sense of text; hypothesizing; making predictions, asking questions; using evidence to confirm or disconfirm a hypothesis or prediction or to answer own question. Explaining, exploring, making inferences, questioning and defining intentions, problems, themes, symbols. Creating, revising, and adding to text. Pondering implications of ideas, including incongruities, discrepancies, ambiguities, omissions.	What does this text mean? What might be added here? omitted? changed? Where can I apply these ideas? How valid/reliable is this argument?
Evaluative	Evaluating the text according to criteria related to appropriateness, effectiveness, difficulty, relevance, importance of content or form.	Does this make sense? How [good] is this? What do I agree/disagree with?
Self-reflective	Noticing one's own processes of reading; monitoring or keeping track of current understandings of words, sentences, or discourse level meanings; noticing conflicts between text and own knowledge and beliefs.	What am I doing as I read? What questions do I have? What do I understand? Not understand?

Source: Lytle & Botel, 1988.

a range of reader experiences and a variety of reader questions. These questions can be either at a tacit or subconscious level or at the level of a more explicit awareness. They will depend on readers' purposes for reading—whether they are reading for pleasure at Sustained Silent Reading time (see Chapter 8), whether they are reading (skimming) quickly to decide if a particular book will provide useful information for a project they are doing, whether they are reading books to get answers to specific questions for a report, or to participate in a discussion with peers, and so forth. Thus, there is no hierarchy or order in these transactions in reading. Many of them occur simultaneously; they overlap, affecting each other. Some transactions predominate in reading particular genres—in reading a story versus a biography versus a how-to manual. Some happen because of specific contextual factors.

Reader questions about a text can be tacit or explicit.

Many transactions can occur at the same time.

Transactions are influenced by the genre involved.

Summary

Reading is an active, constructive, social meaning-making process. It consists of a range of transactions with a range of texts during which readers ask their own questions, monitor their understanding or partial understanding of particular texts, and take control of their reading processes. Transactions such as these foster abilities to question the authority of texts and to read critically and creatively. Moreover, when children are monitoring and evaluating their own reading, they think or reflect about their own thinking. Metacognitive awareness is enhanced.

The Writing Process

Lytle & Botel (1988)

The writing process is also an active, constructive, social, meaning-making enterprise. Drawing on their own schemas (which include their knowledge of the language system, the conventions of a range of written genres) writers create texts for readers to use. Because they have to decide what to include in their texts and how to express their messages, the writing process itself engenders in writers new ideas and insights, new meanings, a deeper thinking.

There are just as many misconceptions about the writing or composing process as there are about the reading process. As a result, instruction in writing has persisted in emphasizing the mechanics of the *product* and the language *parts* (the formation of letters, spelling of words, grammatical relationships among words, etc.) rather than the *whole* of the writing *process* (that is, writers' efforts at meaning-making in the creation of texts). To become writers, children need many opportunities from the beginning to write a range of meaningful, authentic texts, rather than being kept busy with the isolated assigned exercises to "practice writing" that are found in many traditional classrooms.

Calkins (1986); Graves (1983); Smith (1982b)

Current views of writing emphasize the process of writing.

Current research in writing has changed to emphasize the process of writing, to describe how real writers go about constructing texts. That does not mean that the product and parts of language are ignored. Instead, the product is considered *within* the process.

Writing activities or experiences are dynamic and interactive.

The writing process has been described (but sometimes in different terms) as consisting of prewriting, drafting, revising, editing, and publishing. These five activities are not to be seen as linear, discrete steps or stages of a single composing process. Instead, just as reading involves interacting, simultaneously occurring, transactions or experiences, these activities or experiences of writing are also dynamic, and frequently they simultaneously affect and interact with one another. Thus, to counteract the idea that composing is a single, neat, lock-step sequence act or process, we consider these five activities as different dimensions, aspects, or *experiences of writing* for constructing or creating texts.

Experiences of Writing

Prewriting experiences (sometimes called rehearsal experiences)

Prewriting Experiences. A prewriting experience is more than just what precedes or motivates writing. Instead, prewriting includes almost anything and everything. In some sense, writers' schemas, all their experiences, can be seen as prewriting. Prewriting is generating and exploring ideas, recalling and rehearsing ideas, relating and probing ideas, planning, thinking, deciding, and so forth. Prewriting experiences occur when we talk and listen (during discussions, presentations, written passages read aloud, brainstorming sessions, etc.). They happen while we read, skim, research, observe experiments or demonstrations, and see films and videotapes. Drawing and sketching—especially for young children—constitute prewriting experiences. Moreover, prewriting experiences consist of writing itself—jotting down notes or questions, sketching out patterns or connections among ideas, constructing semantic maps on a topic, charting or outlining commonalities and differences in observations, transcribing others' talk, and so on. Thus, prewriting is an ongoing experience, not some distinct period of writing. It can occur and interact simultaneously with the other writing experiences yet to be described.

Drafting experiences

The word *drafting* implies tentativeness.

Drafting Experiences. Drafting involves attempts to create or construct a whole text. Unlike the language fragments jotted down during brainstorming, discussion, or observations, drafting consists of spontaneous experiences in producing connected discourse. *Drafting* is a better term than *writing* because it reflects the tentative nature of the text so constructed. It is a matter of trying to get the ideas down, frequently quickly because the mind is always faster than the pen (or the keys of the typewriter or computer). Leaving blanks when the "right" word doesn't pop immediately to mind or periodically suspending concerns about audience sometimes enables a writer to deal with this time factor. Also, during drafting, the writer tries not to worry too much about spelling and punctuation, knowing that the text produced will be reconsidered, crossed out, changed, rearranged, and elaborated on. Drafting can be interrupted by prewriting experiences; it can also occur concurrently with revising experiences.

Revising experiences

Revising consists of the "re-vision" of a writer's meanings.

Revising Experiences. Revising experiences have to do with attempts of re-vision. They are occasions to re-think, re-view, re-see, re-make, re-construct, and re-create the text. Revising is also an ongoing activity. It can happen during prewriting: At the same time ideas are being generated, they are revised or reexamined. It can occur during drafting: While ideas are being put down, they are reconsidered, so that certain wordings are chosen or selected over others.

Revising experiences also frequently occur subsequent to, or interspersed with, drafting experiences; that is, revising exists after, or in between, the production of sections of text. Revision is an effort to stand back to interact with the text. The writer becomes a reader when the text is reread and reconsidered to find out what it means, to decide whether the writer's intentions or message has been expressed clearly. This is also when other readers (the teacher and peers) may interact—or transact—with the text and provide specific information and feedback about its effect on them. Readers' expectations and questions about the text may lead to more drafting as well as more prewriting experiences.

Chapters 6 and 8 cover conferences in more detail.

Editing experiences

Editing Experiences. Editing experiences are those that are intended to "clean up" the draft of a text so that its message is stated in the most comprehensible way, using the most appropriate language possible. Editing involves shaping the message, perhaps changing sentences, condensing them, deleting, or combining them. It can involve replacing one word with another to make it "fit" better or be more vivid. In addition, the tone or style of the text, as well as spelling, punctuation, and grammar, are checked during editing. Teachers and children may set up different rules or systems for editing experiences. Peer groups and/or self-editing procedures are frequently established. The important point about editing is that it is done in the context of children's own writing, not as a separate, isolated exercise.

Chapters 6 and 8 cover editing in more detail.

Editing concerns are addressed *within* the context of the child's writing.

Publishing experiences

Publishing Experiences. Publishing consists of sharing. The publishing of final drafts takes various forms in the classroom (and differs from classroom to classroom). It is different in the nature of the final product that is shared and in how the sharing is done. With respect to the product itself, some publishing experiences require only that the children rewrite their texts in their best handwriting. Other publishing means having the final draft typed (by the teacher, by a parent volunteer, by the student). It may have a special cover, or it may be placed in a special format for display. Sometimes the publishing of final drafts ends up in classroom, school, community (or even national) newspapers and magazines.

Publishing is sharing.

Because publishing has to do with sharing in general, publishing experiences are not limited to the publishing of final drafts only. Thus, any of the children's writing experiences can be "published." Prewriting experiences—plans for projects, questions to be investigated, semantic mappings on a topic from small group brainstorming sessions—can be shared; drafts and edited copies can be responded to by peers, teacher, and/or the whole class. Moreover, as indicated for final drafts, publishing experiences can occur with a range of audiences within the classroom or beyond (with other classes of the school, with others in the community, etc.).

Summary

Ownership is an important feature of the writing process.

Writing is an active, constructive, social meaning-making process that consists of a range of writing experiences in the construction of texts from a variety of genres. Writing entails ownership. Writers are given opportunities to take control of the composing process: They decide on their own topics, for what purposes their writings are to accomplish, through which genres their texts are to be formed, and for which audiences their messages are to be expressed. In the writing experiences described, the text as a product is a concern, but the *process* of the construction of that text, as well as thinking about that process, is also emphasized.

THE READER-WRITER CONTRACT RECONSIDERED

Now that we have looked at reading and writing separately, it is important to consider again the relationships or connections between the two processes. In Chapter 1, we emphasized that *both* readers and writers construct texts, and in doing so, they are aware of one another in the reader-writer contract. We learn to read by reading and to write by writing, but we also learn to read by writing and to write by reading. There are similarities in the reading and writing processes, *and* the reading and writing processes assist each other.

Similarities exist in the reading and writing processes.

Hyde & Bizar (1989); Nystrand (1986); Smith (1982b); Tierney & Pearson (1984)

These are adapted from Butler & Turbill (1984).

First look at some of the commonalities of the two processes. Both readers and writers use their schemas—what they know about the world and language—to *compose* (i.e., *transact,* from the reader's point of view, and *construct,* from the writer's point of view) the text. Tables 5.5 to 5.7 cover the kinds of things that readers and writers do that are in common before, during, and after reading and writing.

Similarities *before* reading and writing

As Table 5.5 shows, BEFORE READING AND WRITING, readers' and writers' expectations and prior knowledge of the topic or content and how it is expressed through the language of the text affect the way they approach their tasks. Thus, prewriting experiences affect both the reading and writing processes. What and how transactions are realized in reading and what and how constructions are expressed in writing are determined by the readers' and writers' questions or hypotheses. Purpose is inherent in both processes.

Similarities *during* reading and writing

There are similarities in reading and writing during their respective acts as well, as shown in Table 5.5. As you can see in Table 5.6, DURING READING AND WRITING, both readers and writers must draft, revise, and edit. In drafting, they directly deal with the text at hand. Revising occurs in re-reading and re-writing—when initial purposes, questions, and hypotheses are re-examined, re-evaluated, changed, and clarified. Finally, editing is accomplished in reading and writing when medium-related aspects of print—spelling, punctuation, and so on—are examined and corrected if necessary.

Similarities *after* reading and writing

Table 5.7 depicts what readers and writers do after reading and writing. What happens *after* reading and writing are like "publishing" experiences. Responses to and

TABLE 5.5 Prewriting

What Readers Do *Before* Reading	What Writers Do *Before* Writing
The proficient reader brings and uses knowledge: • about the topic (semantic knowledge) • about the language used (syntactic knowledge) • about the sound-symbol system (graphophonic knowledge)	The proficient writer brings and uses knowledge: • about the topic (semantic knowledge) • about the language to be used (syntactic knowledge) • about the sound-symbol system (graphophonic knowledge)
The proficient reader brings certain expectations to the reading cued by: • previous reading experiences • presentation of the text • the purpose for the reading • the audience for the reading	The proficient writer brings certain expectations based on: • previous writing experiences • previous reading experiences • the purpose of the writing • the audience for the writing

Adapted from Butler & Turbill (1984).

TABLE 5.6 Drafting, Revising, Editing

What Readers Do *During* Reading	What Writers Do *During* Writing
The proficient reader is engaged in: • draft reading — *skimming and scanning* — *searching for sense* — *predicting outcomes* — *re-defining and composing meaning*	The proficient writer is engaged in: • draft writing — *writing notes and ideas* — *searching for a way in, a "lead"* — *selecting outcomes* — *re-reading* — *revising and composing meaning*
• re-reading — *re-reading parts as purpose is defined, clarified, or changed* — *taking into account, where appropriate, an audience* — *discussing text, making notes* — *reading aloud to "hear" message*	• re-writing — *re-writing text as purpose changes or becomes defined, clearer* — *considering readers and the intended message* — *discussing and revising text* — *re-reading to "hear" the message*
• using writer's cues — *using punctuation to assist meaning* — *using spelling conventions to assist meaning*	• preparing for readers — *reading to place correct punctuation* — *proofreading for conventional spelling* — *deciding on appropriate presentation*

Adapted from Butler & Turbill (1984).

TABLE 5.7 Publishing

What Readers Do *After* Reading	What Writers Do *After* Writing
The proficient reader: • responds in many ways (e.g., talking, doing, writing) • reflects on it • feels success • wants to read again	The proficient writer: • gets response from readers • gives to readers • feels success • wants to write again

Adapted from Butler & Turbill (1984).

reflections about the meanings expressed in the text are made by the reader or writer. Moreover, attitudes and motivations are developed in readers and writers, which lead to more and more successful reading and writing.

Besides these commonalities in the two processes, reading and writing influence and aid each other. Table 5.8 outlines the kinds of things the reader and writer learn about the writing and reading processes while engaged in these respective processes.

This is adapted from Butler & Turbill (1984).

The reading and writing processes assist each other.

Physical presentation/layout features

As Table 5.8 indicates, to read like a writer and write like a reader involve learning about three major aspects of texts. Learning the physical presentation or layout—with certain layout features frequently corresponding to specific genres—is the first aspect listed. Contracts, jokes, advertisements, menus, recipes, and so on all look different. Where and how words are physically placed and presented has to do with a text's purpose. A reader learns that through writing, and a writer through reading.

TABLE 5.8

What We Learn *About Writing* While Involved in the Reading Process	What We Learn *About Reading* While Involved in the Writing Process
Physical Presentation/Layout	
The reader learns:	**The writer learns:**
• the way it is done in different sorts of print matter, in which purpose can be determined by layout, e.g., advertisements, poems, recipes, etc.	• to expect different purposes as indicated by presentation/layout
• that symbols and other patterns of stress or emphasis are used to add impact and meaning to writing	• to use all the other information on the page, e.g., symbols, pictures, size or boldness of print, etc.
Register/Genre	
The reader learns:	**The writer learns:**
• that text should follow a logical sequence so it makes sense	• to expect text to follow a predictable sequence in order to make sense
• that different registers/genres follow different sets of conventions	• to appreciate and notice conventions authors use in registers/genres
• that there needs to be sufficient information to allow readers to follow what is happening and make predictions about what might be coming	• to predict likely outcomes based on information given in the text
• that there are different registers and generic forms for different purposes and different audiences	• to expect particular registers and generic forms appropriate to purpose and audience
• that there are beginnings, endings, sequencing of ideas, events, etc., appropriate to different registers/genres	• to expect certain beginnings, endings, sequencing of ideas, events, etc., according to different registers/genres
• that writers use "cohesive ties" (e.g., pronouns, to refer to specific and general persons, objects, places, etc.; conjunctions; repetitions and synonyms of lexical items; etc.) to knit text together (in different genres) so readers can follow it	• to expect the range of "cohesive ties" used to knit text together in different genres
Surface/Medium Features	
The reader learns:	**The writer learns:**
• directional principles of print	• to expect a certain direction of lines of print
• the function of punctuation in text	• to expect punctuation to guide us in our reading
• spelling conventions, i.e., how words *look* in print	• letter-sound relationships, i.e., how spoken words can be represented in print
• other print medium conventions, e.g., spacing, use of hyphens, abbreviations, paragraphs, etc.	• to expect other print medium conventions to guide us in our reading

Adapted from Butler & Turbill (1984).

The second category of Table 5.8 in which reading and writing assist each other has to do with how meaning is realized in texts, how the linguistic messages are organized or patterned. These are global and textural features of various registers or genres that we discussed in the first section of this chapter.

Register/genre features

The third category has to do with medium aspects of print—how we learn to use spelling and punctuation to make sense of, or express, the wordings that constitute the text—as well as the other conventions of the print medium.

Surface/medium features

SUMMARY

This chapter began by examining the nature of written genres. All genres—spoken and written—emerge in a culture as conventional responses to particular and recurrent situations. They come about because particular texts are accomplishing some social action. We have emphasized written genres in this chapter, and we have discovered that genres are organized in various ways because they serve different jobs in our culture. To understand both the stability and change inherent in genres, a general model of genres that included both typical and atypical texts was presented.

Then, the processes of using written texts were examined. First reading, and then writing, was addressed. Reader interactions with texts—transactions—were examined, and the writing experiences constituting the writing process were covered. It was emphasized that both reading and writing are constructive, meaning-making, social processes.

Finally, although writing and authors were alluded to in the section on the reading process, and reading and readers were acknowledged to be part of the writing process, the last section more explicitly examined the reader-writer contract that exists between the two processes. Both commonalities of the two processes and the ways the processes assist each other were covered. Because of this reader-writer contract, Figure 5.4 has to be expanded and modified because it showed only the reader-text transaction. Figure 5.5 adds the other side of the process of the contract—the writer-text composition.

Two other features are included in Figure 5.5. First, notice the arrows around the top and bottom of the text circle. The interaction of the reader and the writer—the reader-writer contract—is by way of the text. There are similarities in the ways by which both readers and writers activate the semantic potential of the text. In addition, readers always learn about writing when they read; the opposite is also the case, namely, that writers learn about reading when they write. When children understand that writers write on the premises of having readers, and readers read on the premises of having writers, coherent communication is developed. Thus, these arrows are included to reflect the bridges between the reader and writer, that is, to emphasize the connections between the reading and writing processes.

Speaking and listening are *integrated* with the reading and writing processes.

The other feature added in Figure 5.5 has to do with the role of speaking and listening in our reconsideration of the reader-writer contract. In our discussion of the reading and writing processes, speaking and listening were apparent and significant. Sharing readers' responses to a range of texts with others in whole class or small group discussions, brainstorming a particular topic with peers (as a prewriting experience), listening to authors' published final drafts read aloud, and so forth are examples that illustrate that speaking and listening are integral to the reading-writing processes in the classroom. This integration of speaking and listening (depicted in Figure 5.5 through a dotted, shaded area surrounding the reader-writer contract) with reading and writing is the essence of what is meant by an *integrated* language perspective. You may want to review again how that integration was realized in the classroom prototypes in Chapter 4. (Activity 2 at the end of this chapter can help you to become more aware of this integration in the prototypes.)

In subsequent chapters, more examples and specific suggestions to facilitate connections between reading and writing and the integration among all the language processes in the classroom are provided.

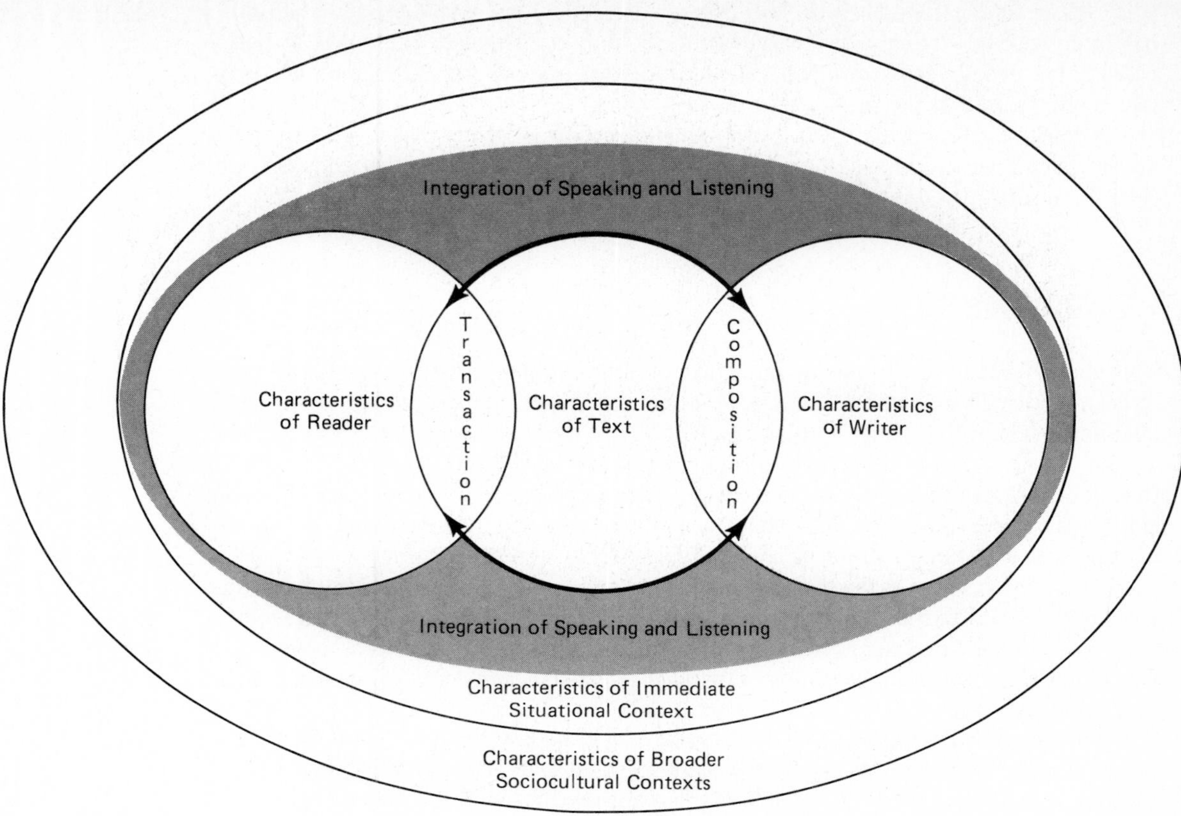

Figure 5.5 Reader-Writer Contract Reconsidered

SUGGESTED ACTIVITIES

1. To help you explore more about the multidimensional, overlapping nature of written genres, collect a range of written genres with the help of classmates. Choose texts from many sources, from books, magazines, newspapers, and so on. Put your texts in two piles, one having typical texts, the other having atypical or fuzzy texts. (This activity is similar to Suggested Activity 4 in Chapter 1 where you collected stories and information books. Here, however, you are not limiting your examination of texts to only two genres.)

   See if you can identify typical texts of genres, those that everyone would agree belong to a particular genre. Discuss why you think they are typical. Try to look at the language patterns—both the global chunks and the textural organizations—that seem to be involved. Now, consider your atypical or fuzzy texts. How are they atypical? What is the nature of the overlap—that is, what genres seem to be involved in the language patterns?
2. To help you make more explicit the integration of speaking, listening, reading, and writing processes in classroom contexts, review again the prototypes in Chapter 4. Try to identify instances in which integration occurred. See if you can classify these experiences of integration.

REFERENCES

Anderson, R. C., Reynolds, R. E., Schallert, D. L., & Goetz, T. E. (1977). Frameworks for comprehending discourse. *American Educational Research Journal, 14,* 367–381.

Bruce, B. C. (1980). Plans and social actions. In R. J. Spiro, B. C. Bruce, & W. T. Brewer (Eds.), *Theoretical issues in reading comprehension: Perspectives from cognitive psychology, linguistics, artificial intelligence, and education* (pp. 367–384). Hillsdale, NJ: Erlbaum.

Bruce, B. C. (1984). A new point of view on children's stories. In R. C. Anderson, J. Osborn, & R. J. Tierney (Eds.), *Learning to read in American schools: Basal readers and content texts* (pp. 153–174). Hillsdale, NJ: Erlbaum.

Butler, A., & Turbill, T. (1984). *Towards a reading-writing classroom.* Rozelle, Australia: Primary English Teaching Association.

Calkins, L. M. (1986). *The art of teaching writing.* Portsmouth, NH: Heinemann.

Carey, R., Harste, J., & Smith, S. (1981). Contextual constraints and discourse processes: A replication study. *Reading Research Quarterly, 16,* 201–212.

Christie, F. (1987). Learning to mean in writing. In N. Stewart-Dore (Ed.), *Writing and reading to learn* (pp. 21–34). Rozelle, Australia: Primary English Teaching Association.

Collerson, J. (1988). What are these genres, anyway? In J. Collerson (Ed.), *Writing for life* (pp. 12–22). Rozelle, Australia: Primary English Teaching Association.

de Beaugrande, R. (1980). *Text, discourse, and process: Toward a multidisciplinary science of texts.* Norwood, NJ: Ablex.

Goodman, K. S. (1967). Reading: A psycholinguistic guessing game. *Journal of the Reading Specialist, 6,* 126–135.

Goodman, Y. M., & Burke, C. (1985). *Reading strategies: Focus on comprehension.* New York: Richard C. Owen Publishers.

Graves, D. (1983). *Writing: Teachers and children at work.* Portsmouth, NH: Heinemann.

Halliday, M. A. K., & Hasan, R. (1985). *Language, context, and text: Aspects of language in a social-semiotic perspective.* Victoria, Australia: Deakin University Press.

Hasan, R. (1984). The nursery tale as a genre. *Linguistic Circular, 13,* 71–102.

Hasan, R. (1985a). The texture of a text. In M. A. K. Halliday & R. Hasan, *Language, context, and text: Aspects of language in a social-semiotic perspective* (pp. 70–96). Victoria, Australia: Deakin University Press.

Hasan, R. (1985b). The structure of a text. In M. A. K. Halliday & R. Hasan, *Language, context, and text: Aspects of language in a social-semiotic perspective* (pp. 52–69). Victoria, Australia: Deakin University Press.

Heath, S. B. (1983). *Ways with words: Language, life and work in communities and classrooms.* Cambridge: Cambridge University Press.

Himley, M. (1986). Genre as generative: One perspective on one child's early writing growth. In M. Nystrand (Ed.), *The structure of written communication: Studies in reciprocity between writers and readers* (pp. 137–157). Orlando, FL: Academic Press.

Hyde, A. A., & Bizar, M. (1989). *Thinking in context: Teaching cognitive process across the elementary school curriculum.* White Plains, NY: Longman.

Lindfors, J. W. (1987). *Children's language and learning.* Englewood Cliffs, NJ: Prentice-Hall.

Lytle, S. L., & Botel, M. (1988). *PCRP II: Reading, writing and talking across the curriculum.* Harrisburg, PA: Pennsylvania Department of Education. To be published in 1990 by Heinemann-Boynton Cook as *Frameworks for Literacy.*

Martin, J. R., Christie, F., & Rothery, J. (1987). Social processes in education: A reply to Sawyer and Watson (and others). In I. Reid (Ed.), *The place of genre in learning: Current debates* (pp. 58–82). Victoria, Australia: Deakin University Press.

Nystrand, M. (Ed.) (1986). *The structure of written communication: Studies in reciprocity between writers and readers.* Orlando, FL: Academic Press.

Pappas, C. C. (1985). The cohesive harmony and cohesive density of children's oral and written stories. In J. Benson & W. S. Greaves (Eds.), *Systemic perspectives on discourse: Selected applied papers from the 9th international systemic workshop* (pp. 169–186). Norwood, NJ: Ablex.

Pappas, C. C. (1986). *Exploring the global structure of "information books."* ERIC Document No. ED 278 952.

Pappas, C. C. (1987). *Exploring the generic shape of "information books": Applying "typicality" notions to the process.* ERIC Document No. 299 834.

Pappas, C. C. (1988, January). *Exploring the textual properties of information books: A sociopsycholinguistic perspective.* Paper presented at the 1988 Ohio State University Children's Literature Conference, Columbus, OH.

Rosenblatt, L. M. (1978). *The reader, the text, the poem.* Carbondale, IL: Southern Illinois University Press.

Smith, F. (1982a). *Understanding reading.* New York: Holt, Rinehart and Winston.

Smith, F. (1982b). *Writing and the writer.* New York: Holt, Rinehart and Winston.

Smith, F. (1988). *Understanding reading,* 4th ed. Hillsdale, NJ: Erlbaum.

Spiro, R. J. (1980). Constructive process in prose comprehension and recall. In R. J. Spiro, B. C. Bruce, & W. F. Brewer (Eds.), *Theoretical issues in reading comprehension: Perspectives from cognitive psychology, linguistics, artificial intelligence, and education* (pp. 245–278). Hillsdale, NJ: Erlbaum.

Tierney, R. J., & Pearson, P. D. (1984). Toward a composing model of reading. In J. M. Jenson (Ed.), *Composing and comprehending* (pp. 33–45). Urbana, IL: ERIC Clearinghouse on Reading and Communication Skills.

Weaver, C. (1988). *Reading process and practice: From socio-psycholinguistics to whole language.* Portsmouth, NH: Heinemann.

CHILDREN'S LITERATURE

MOJAVE by D. Siebert. Illustrated by W. Minor. Crowell, 1988.

MOUSE by S. B. Stein. Illustrated by M. Garcia. Harcourt Brace Jovanovich, 1985.

THE OWL AND THE WOODPECKER by B. Wildsmith. Oxford University Press, 1971.

PANDA by S. Bonners. Delacorte, 1978.

THE SEE-THROUGH ZOO: HOW GLASS ANIMALS ARE MADE by S. Haldane. Pantheon Books, 1984.

TUNNELS by G. Gibbons. Holiday House, 1984.

6

Learning Kid-Watching Procedures and Techniques

This chapter describes certain procedures and techniques to help you become a good kid-watcher. Teachers in integrated language classrooms have certain views regarding learners (and learning), language, and knowledge (see Chapters 1 and 2). They believe that children's language and concepts (knowledge) are related to the kinds of experiences they have in a range of contexts. Consequently, most typical traditional ways to assess or evaluate children's development or learning are rarely useful. For example, completed ditto sheets, besides not being examples of meaningful use of language, are frequently misleading because they cannot capture the *process* of what children are actually doing or learning. That is, "wrong" answers can reflect children's intelligent thinking or reasonable hypotheses, whereas "right" answers can be based on misunderstandings or misconceptions. There is no way for the teacher to check which is the case when using these materials; they offer little reliable information for making appropriate teaching decisions.

The assessment of products without regard to process is usually unreliable.

Thus, integrated language teachers need to have alternative means for assessment and evaluation. They have to have techniques for learning about children's ways with words, how children learn to use a variety of language registers in a variety of contexts, how they apply what they know in a range of activities and projects. Teachers need to gain information about what children say (and/or write) and do to understand how the children's schemas are being modified in various domains. This information is necessary to guide, extend, and support children's learning—to become an effective teacher. This information is also critical for documenting teaching effectiveness; it provides a means for accountability (see Chapter 9).

This kid-watching chapter is organized into two major sections. The first section covers schemes for assessing and evaluating children's strategies and understandings in reading, writing, and producing certain oral language "compositions" (e.g., dictations and retellings). We call these kid-watching procedures *literacy assessments*. The second section describes several *general observation schemes* for gathering information about how language and concepts are developed across the curriculum. Both sets of observation systems may initially seem formal because they are new and unfamiliar. However, with practice, these kid-watching procedures or techniques become internalized by teachers so that they can use them to evaluate children's learning and language *informally* while children are actively engaged in a range of meaningful activities in the classroom.

LITERACY ASSESSMENTS

Three kinds of literacy procedures are covered: (1) those that focus on reading and writing (Modified Miscue Analysis and Writing schemes); (2) those that evaluate the literacy understandings of emergent learners (Concepts About Print, Approximations To Text, and Dictations); and (3) a way to evaluate children's retellings of a text.

Modified Miscue Analysis (MMA)

Goodman (1973); Goodman, Watson, & Burke (1987)

Miscues are constructions.

Miscues reflect the reading process in action.

The MMA taps readers' strategies.

Miscue analysis was originally developed by Ken Goodman to provide a window on the reading process. A *miscue* is defined as a deviation or difference between a reader's production and the text when the reader is reading aloud. Miscue analysis is based on two major assumptions: (1) Miscues are not random but have a variety of causes. Miscues are the result of readers' *constructions* of the linguistic message. They are based on readers' present oral language development, their knowledge of the topic of the reading passage, their purpose for reading, their familiarity with the register or genre of the text, and so on. Because reading is a constructive process, everybody makes miscues when they read aloud. (2) Miscues reflect how readers are actually using the reading process. Besides pragmatic cues (e.g., reasons or purposes for reading), reading is the integration of three major cues: *graphic cues* (some people term these graphophonemic cues), which deal with the set of relationships between sounds and the written forms to represent those sounds in texts; *syntactic cues,* which deal with interrelationships of words, sentences, paragraphs, and so on; and *semantic cues,* which deal with the meaning of texts.

There are many variations of miscue analysis. We present a Modified Miscue Analysis (MMA) that classroom teachers have found easy to use. Briefly, the MMA is a procedure by which a child's miscues (made while reading a text aloud) are qualitatively and quantitatively assessed to gain insights into the child's reading strategies. Part of the procedure is asking the child to retell the text subsequent to the oral reading.

Selection of Material. It is best to use a piece of literature (avoid basal passages) for the reading passage. It can be a story, an informational piece, a magazine article, or a chapter of a book. The selection should be entirely new to the student, but at the same time it should incorporate concepts and situations that the reader can comprehend. The length of the selection should be such that it can be read in ten to fifteen minutes. It is important that the student read an entire selection even if only a portion of the miscues are later coded and analyzed. The selection must be difficult or challenging enough for the student so that miscues will be made, but it should not be so difficult that the reader will not feel comfortable reading it. (If you do not know the child well—for example, at the beginning of a school year—a useful way to determine appropriate material is to bring several selections to the MMA session and ask the child to read silently a little of each selection. After the child has read each text, ask the child if it seemed easy or hard to read. Don't use a text the child says is "easy" or "hard"; instead choose the text that the child describes as "sort of easy and sort of hard.") A selection must generate a minimum of 25 miscues to be used. (It is possible to have a sample of fewer miscues, but it will be a less reliable sample of the child's reading behavior.)

Taping the Oral Reading and Retelling. The child reads from the printed text while the teacher marks on a specially prepared copy of the selection called a *worksheet.* The whole session is tape-recorded. The worksheet should retain the physical characteristics of the book from which the student reads. That is, it should be an exact line-for-line copy; moreover, there should be sufficient space between the lines of the text so that all miscues can be clearly noted. However, many teachers use a clear photostat copy of the text to save time typing a separate worksheet.

The taping should take place in a quiet atmosphere with no distractions. Directions include: (1) Students are told why they are being asked to read—namely, that the teacher wants to understand how they read something that they have never read or seen before. (2) Students are told that they are to read the entire text aloud and that they will be asked to retell and talk about it at the end. (3) Students are informed that they cannot be given any help during the reading. Consequently, if they come to a word that they don't know, they should just do their best, just do what they normally do while reading.

After the reading, students are simply asked to retell the text in their own words. If the retelling is a sparse one, the reader can be asked about a favorite or interesting part. (It is normal for a reader to give only a brief retelling here because the reader knows that the teacher knows the text. When retellings are short in this situation, it is important not to jump to the conclusion that the reader does not comprehend the text.) Follow-up questions can be prepared ahead of time as well (questions can be constructed to correspond to the types of transactions listed in Chapter 5) to complement the retelling, and more extemporaneous questions may be asked as appropriate.

Marking the Worksheet. While the reader is reading, the teacher identifies miscues and marks them on the worksheet according to the system described by Table 6.1. Thus, the first decision to be made when a miscue occurs is what kind of deviation it represents. There are four kinds of miscues: substitutions, omissions, insertions, and reversals. These are mutually exclusive categories, and the teacher must decide *which one* more accurately categorizes each deviation. *Substitutions* involve replacing other words for those in the text. *Omissions* occur when words are dropped by the reader. There are two possibilities regarding omissions. Some omissions are fluent in that they are made without hesitation; others occur only after readers hesitate and inspect the text. Young children (e.g., kindergarteners and first graders) frequently make a lot of the second type, and therefore marking both types may provide useful information regarding their reading development. For older elementary readers, such a distinction may not be necessary. *Insertions* are words included by the reader that are not in the text. Finally, *reversals* occur when wordings of the text are reversed during the reading. Table 6.1 explains how these four types of miscues are marked and noted on the worksheet (i.e., the copy of the text that is read).

There are four categories of miscues.

Reader attempts to self-correct miscues are also identified and marked on the worksheet. (Nothing is noted on the worksheet if the reader does not try corrections.) Attempts can be successful or unsuccessful and are noted accordingly. These notations are explained and illustrated on the bottom of Table 6.1.

There are four other considerations to keep in mind in identifying miscues, as follows:

Miscues that are repeated throughout the text are coded the first time if the miscue is *exactly* the same each time (e.g., *Steve* for *Sven* miscued more than once). However, different miscues for the same word are each coded at their first occurrence (e.g., *Steve* for *Sven,* then *Seven* for *Sven*).

A related series of miscues can be coded as one miscue (e.g., *At first he saw* for *I first saw*). This can occur with a phrase or a clause.

"Nonsense" word substitutions are coded as miscues, but incomplete attempts are not (e.g., *glod* for *glad* is a miscue, but *gla-* then *glad* for *glad* is not).

Slight dialect differences (e.g., *pin* for *pen*) are not usually coded as miscues. Judgments of acceptability should depend on what is acceptable in that dialect.

Summary. Some teachers who have had lots of experience in doing MMAs mark the worksheet as children read. Others (even those who are experienced) mark the worksheet later because they find it distracting to the reader to mark during the reading. Novices can also do the latter. In addition, novices find it useful simply to indicate (with a pencil) places on the worksheet where there are deviations or possible miscues when they first hear the tape of the child's reading; they then listen to the tape a second time to mark the miscues with the appropriate designations.

Figure 6.1 shows the miscues made of a nine-year-old boy, Mike, reading the

TABLE 6.1 Instructions for Marking the MMA Worksheet

1. *SUBSTITUTIONS:* Write the substitution above the appropriate part of the text.

Example: He ran down the street. (road)

2. *OMISSIONS:* Circle the *word(s)* left out. (If a reader reads "sing" for "singing," treat it as a substitution, not an omission of "ing.") Two types are possible:
   (a) *Omission without Inspection (w/o I):* Just circle the omission. These are "fluent" omissions.

Example: John drank his milk, too. Then he left the table.

   (b) *Omission with Inspection (I):* Circle the omission and place an "I" next to it. These are omissions where the reader hesitates and inspects a word in the text, and then omits it.

Example: He usually walked home alone.

3. *INSERTIONS:* Place an insertion sign (carat) at the point it occurs, and then write the insertion above the line.

Example: The hat blew ^ into the tree. (up)

4. *REVERSALS:* Use the commonly used symbol ( ).

Example: "Hit the ball," yelled Pete.

ATTEMPTS AT CORRECTION:

   (a) *Attempted and Successful:* Mark C next to the miscue. Write each unsuccessful attempt above the word.

Example: He watched the ships in the harbor. (shops C)

   (b) *Attempted but Unsuccessful:* Mark UC next to the miscue. Write each unsuccessful attempt above the word.

Example: Tommy never heard that noise before. (hurt UC, hard)

   (c) *Changed Something Already Read Correctly* (rare): Mark AC next to the miscue. Write the change above the word.

Example: The hat blew into the tree. (flew AC)

Wilder (1953)

beginning of Wilder's *Farmer Boy*. Most of his miscues are substitutions, but examples of the other three types of miscues (an omission, two insertions, and a reversal) are also present. In Mike's dialect, *bar* for *bare* is a miscue, but in some regional dialects, *bar* would be an acceptable pronunciation of *bare* and would not be considered to be a miscue. Note that *Elissa* for *Eliza* is counted as a miscue the first time, but the subsequent same renditions of the name are not.

Completing the Coding Sheet. After the miscues have been noted and numbered on the worksheet, they are transferred to the coding sheet. For each miscue, certain judgments are made. That is, miscues are not like errors, which are treated in an all-or-nothing fashion. Miscues represent the predictions, confirmations, and disconfirmations of readers; thus, miscues have to be examined qualitatively. Some miscues represent good, effective reading strategies; others may not. Table 6.2 illustrates an MMA coding sheet and provides the instructions for completing it.

On the coding sheet, each miscue is evaluated with respect to its acceptability—that is, whether it is reasonable grammatically speaking, and whether it makes sense. Substitution miscues are also judged by their graphic similarity to the text. Moreover, a reader's attempts to correct are examined. Finally, each uncorrected miscue is evaluated to see if it resulted in significantly changing the meaning of the author's message. Table 6.3 illustrates how Mike's miscues would be transferred on the coding sheet. Notice that *maple* (for *maples*) and *sister* (for *sisters*) are treated as substitutions, not as omissions of the plural morpheme "s." All but one of Mike's miscues are marked as being syntactically and semantically acceptable. *Boughts* for *boughs* is an interesting miscue. It is marked with a "?" under Column 9, because many teachers would mark this miscue as being syntactically acceptable because it retains the plural morpheme.

"School Days"

0101 It was January in northern New York State,

0102 sixty-seven years ago. Snow lay deep every-

(1) bar (C) (2) maple

0103 where. It loaded the bare limbs of oak and maples

(3) went over (4) boughts (5)

0104 beeches, it bent the green boughs of cedars

0105 and spruces down into the drifts. Billows of snow

0106 covered the fields and the stone fences.

0107 Down a long road through the woods a little

0108 boy trudged to school, with his big brother Roy-

(6) sister (C) Elissa (7)

0109 al and his two sisters, Eliza Jane and Alice. Royal

Elissa Jane (8)

0110 was thirteen years old, Eliza was twelve, and

0111 Alice was ten. Almanzo was the youngest of all,

0201 and this was his first going-to-school, because

0202 he was not quite nine years old.

0203 He had to walk fast to keep up with the oth-

had had had (UC) (9)

0204 ers, and he had to carry the dinner-pail.

0205 "Royal ought to carry it," he said. "He's big-

0206 ger than I be."

(10) (C)

0207 Royal strode ahead, big and manly in boots, and

0208 Eliza Jane said:

0209 "No Manzo. It's your turn to carry it now,

0210 because you're the littlest."

0211 Eliza Jane was bossy. She always knew what

(11)

0212 was best to do; and she made Almanzo and Alice

0213 do it.

Figure 6.1 Mike's Reading of "School Days"

Analyzing the Oral Reading Miscues. Using the data on the coding sheet, five major questions about oral reading miscues can be considered. Answers to these questions tell how a child is using the cueing systems. The result is quantitative data, that is, percentages (ranging from 0 to 100) that reflect certain reading strategies. Table 6.4 lists these questions and explains how to compute the percentages on the basis of counts taken from the coding sheet.

What Do These Percentages Mean? These percentages (and the retelling data to be described in the following section) provide useful information about readers' strategies. *The first set of questions regarding substitutions* tells us whether a reader is integrating all three cueing systems or is overrelying on one or two of them. Consider first 1A: What percentage level would you expect from a hypothetical fluent reader? You would expect it to be high because effective reading integrates all sources of redun-

TABLE 6.2 How to Complete the MMA Coding Sheet

Column	
1	*NO.* (1–25). The number of the miscue from the worksheet.
2	*TEXT.* Write the correct word or phrase that was miscued.
3	*READER.* Write the precise miscue that the reader made. If the reader makes more than one attempt at a word or phrase, code the *first* attempt.
4	*SUBS. (SUBSTITUTION).* Check (√) if the miscue is a substitution.
5	*GRAPHIC SIMILAR. (GRAPHIC SIMILARITY).* Coded only for substitutions. Check (√) if the miscue is similar. A miscue is considered graphically similar to the text if: (1) both the first and last letters of the miscue match the first and last letters of word(s) of the text, *OR* (2) either the first letter *or* the last letter *and* a majority of the remaining letters of the miscue match the letters and their position in the text.
6	*OMISSIONS w/o I* (without Inspection). Check (√) if the reader maintains reading and fluency, reacting as if the word was not there.
7	*OMISSIONS w I* (with Inspection). Check (√) if the reader obviously spends some time studying the word before omitting it.
8	*OTHER.* Check (√) if the miscue is other than a substitution or an omission, namely, an insertion or a reversal.
9	*SYNTAC. ACCEPT. (SYNTACTIC ACCEPTABILITY).* Check (√) if the miscue is syntactically acceptable. A miscue is considered syntactically acceptable when the resulting sentence is acceptable according to its syntax (i.e., acceptable part of speech, acceptable word order, etc.) regardless of its meaning. Also, in evaluating the acceptability of a miscue, you must consider previous and subsequent miscues in the sentence (final attempts, successful or unsuccessful).
10	*SEMAN. ACCEPT. (SEMANTIC ACCEPTABILITY).* Check (√) if the miscue is semantically acceptable. A miscue is considered semantically acceptable when the resulting sentence is acceptable according to its meaning (i.e., it makes sense) regardless of its syntax. However, because meaning and syntax are so closely related, it is unlikely that many syntactically unacceptable sentences will retain an acceptable meaning. Again, in evaluating the acceptability of a miscue, you must consider previous and subsequent miscues in the sentence (final attempts, successful or unsuccessful). Also, consider how the reader is making sense of previous text through the miscues.
11	*CORRECT.(ION): ATT. (ATTEMPTED).* Check (√) if the reader made any attempt to correct.
12	*CORRECT.(ION): SUCC. (SUCCESSFUL).* Check (√) if the reader's attempt to correct was successful.
13	*MEANING CHANGE.* Check (√) if the miscue represents a *significantly* different meaning from that intended in the text *and* if the miscue was not successfully corrected.
TOTAL	Number of checks in each column on the coding sheet.

dancy—graphic, syntactical, and semantic. And you would expect that a hypothetical fluent reader's percentages of 1B and 1C to be low and about the same. In other words, such a reader would not rely on one cue (e.g., graphics, or letter-sound relationships) over the others (syntactic and semantic cues).

Consequently, by contrasting percentages of such a hypothetical reader with those of a particular reader, a teacher can decide on appropriate instruction. For example, if a child such as Mike has percentages in 1A, 1B, and 1C similar to our hypothetical fluent reader, it would indicate that the child is integrating all three cueing systems effectively. If a child has a low percentage in 1A and 1B but a relatively high percentage in 1C, however, it would suggest that the child is focusing too much on graphics, or letter-sound relationships, and is missing meaning altogether (especially if the percentage of question 4 about meaning change is high). The teacher might then conduct some CLOZE mini-lessons (see Chapter 8), for example, to help the child to consider using more of the co-text in identifying words, or other lessons that emphasize meaning, not the accurate decoding of words (e.g., "Say Something" and "Readers' Theatre" activities—see Chapter 8).

TABLE 6.2a MMA Coding Sheet

Col.	1	2	3	4	5	6	7	8	9	10	11	12	13
					Graphic	Omissions			Syntac.	Seman.	Correct.		Meaning
	No.	Text	Reader	Subs.	Similar.	w/o I	w I	Other	Accept.	Accept.	Att.	Succ.	Change
	1												
	2												
	3												
	4												
	5												
	. . .												
	25												
	TOTALS												

TABLE 6.3 MMA Coding Sheet for Mike

Col.	1	2	3	4	5	6	7	8	9	10	11	12	13
					Graphic	Omissions			Syntac.	Seman.	Correct.		Meaning
	No.	Text	Reader	Subs.	Similar.	w/o I	w I	Other	Accept.	Accept.	Att.	Succ.	Change
	1	bare	bar	✓	✓				✓	✓	✓	✓	
	2	maples	maple	✓	✓				✓	✓			
	3	bent	went	✓	✓				✓	✓			
	4	—	over					✓	✓	✓			
	5	boughs	boughts	✓	✓				?				✓
	6	sisters	sister	✓	✓				✓	✓	✓	✓	
	7	Eliza	Elissa	✓	✓				✓	✓			
	8	—	Jane					✓	✓	✓			
	9	he had	had had	✓	✓				✓	✓	✓		
	10	in	—			✓			✓	✓	✓	✓	
	11	best to do	to do best					✓	✓	✓			
	. . .												
	25												
	TOTALS												

Table 6.4 Questions Regarding Patterns of Miscues

1. The first question deals with *substitutions only* and has three parts:

A. To what extent is the reader integrating all cueing systems (i.e., graphic, syntactic, and semantic) when making substitutions?

$$\frac{\text{number of miscues having a check in Cols. 5 \& 9 \& 10}}{\text{total number of substitutions (Col. 4)}} \times 100 = \_\_\_\_\_\_$$

B. To what extent is the reader using syntactic/semantic information *only* in making substitutions?

$$\frac{\text{number of miscues having a check in Col. 4, no check in Col. 5, but a check in Cols. 9 \& 19}}{\text{total number of substitutions (Col. 4)}} \times 100 = \_\_\_\_\_\_$$

C. To what extent is the reader using graphic information *only* in making substitutions?

$$\frac{\text{number of miscues having a check in Col. 5, and no check in Cols. 9 \& 10}}{\text{total number of substitutions (Col. 4)}} \times 100 = \_\_\_\_\_\_$$

2. To what extent are the miscues syntactically and semantically acceptable?

$$\frac{\text{number of miscues having a check in Cols. 9 \& 10}}{\text{total number of miscues (25)}} \times 100 = \_\_\_\_\_\_$$

3. To what extent is the reader successful in the corrections he or she attempts?

$$\frac{\text{total number of Col. 12 (succ. corr.)}}{\text{total number of Col. 11 (att. corr.)}} \times 100 = \_\_\_\_\_\_$$

4. To what extent does the reader leave meaning changes?

$$\frac{\text{total number of Col. 15}}{\text{total number of miscues (25)}} \times 100 = \_\_\_\_\_\_$$

5. To what extent is the reader stopping and inspecting text before it is omitted?

$$\frac{\text{total number in Col. 7 (w I)}}{\text{total of Cols. 6 \& 7}} \times 100 = \_\_\_\_\_\_$$

Question 2 looks at the acceptability of all the miscues, not just substitutions. It tells whether what the reader reads sounds like language and makes sense. Again, Mike's percentage (computations not included) is high, indicating that his reading is meaning-driven. A low percentage for question 2 indicates that the reader is not reading with meaning. Lessons (similar to those suggested earlier) can be created to enable the reader to have that focus.

Question 3 gets at self-correction, an important feature of effective reading. Mike had a high percentage here. If a low percentage occurs here, however, lessons can be constructed to help the reader be more successful in correcting miscues. Or a teacher may note that the reader does not self-correct very much in general (even though there is a high percentage of meaning change) and may provide activities to motivate the reader to reread texts and/or self-evaluate initial responses in reading.

Question 4 involves significant meaning changes. Mike had a low percentage on this question, but if the percentage here is high for a particular reader, then again the teacher would try to get the child to focus more on meaning, perhaps by including him or her in small response groups in which members share their interpretations of a book or text (Chapter 8), or by providing other experiences that require the reader to reevaluate and justify miscues.

Question 5 provides useful information for evaluating the reading progress of children who are in transition from emergent reading to more independent reading. Children in this stage do a lot of inspecting of text because they are beginning to integrate the graphics with syntactical and semantic cueing systems. The results in this question, therefore, can document this development. The teacher can skip this last question for older elementary readers such as Mike.

In sum, the miscue patterns can provide important information for the teacher in two ways: deciding on specific instructional activities to meet the needs of the reader, and documenting a reader's strategies over time. Doing MMAs on children's reading of a variety of genres provides even more useful information for instruction and accountability. Once teachers do one or two MMAs in the formal sense we have described, they know how to "listen" to children read and they can take anecdotal records on their oral reading more informally (that is, without *taping* children's reading).

Analyzing the Retelling. The retelling and discussion subsequent to the oral reading provide more information about the child's understanding of the text. Four general questions can be asked about this part of the MMA to complement the oral reading data analyzed in the preceding section:

1. What was the nature of the reader's retelling? Did the retelling include essential information expressed in the text? That is, did the reader adequately understand the major ideas, the gist, of the message expressed in the text?
2. If the reader gave a sparse retelling (remember, it is normal to produce a brief response in such a social situation) and was asked to recount a favorite or interesting portion, were there aspects of this account that indicated comprehension of the text?
3. How did the reader respond to any questions asked about the selection?
4. Compare individual miscues when the reader had meaning changes (see Column 13 on the MMA Coding Sheet, Table 6.2) with the retelling (and other) responses. Were there cases when the reader left a meaning change miscue, yet seemed to understand the author's message in these subsequent responses? That is, are there miscues that might have been self-corrected in the reader's mind?

Summary. Miscue analysis must seem very complicated from the foregoing description, and indeed it is until it is tried a few times formally by examining the miscues and retellings of real readers. However, it is only through doing MMAs that teachers can know *how* to observe, to listen to, the strategies and interpretations children use in oral reading in more informal contexts. Inherent in using this kid-watching technique is a new appreciation on the part of the teacher of the constructive nature of reading. Teachers learn to wait, or be more patient and not intervene too soon or too much, when children do not read the actual words of the text with absolute accuracy. They learn that a reader may put in a reasonable substitution or may self-correct when something does not make sense. Thus, through these informal MMAs, teachers can collect useful ongoing information to document children's progress in reading, and they can decide what instruction or intervention is appropriate to support and extend children's present understandings and efforts. (See the Reading Activities and Experiences section in Chapter 8 for more information regarding informal reading assessments.)

Writing

The view of writing described in Chapter 5 is sometimes termed a *process-conference approach.* It emphasizes the process of writing in which writers engage, and it uses teacher (and peer) conferences to evaluate and support this process. Teacher interactions and conferences occur while children are engaged in any of the types of writing experiences (prewriting, drafting, revising, editing, and publishing) described in Chapter 5. Here, however, we focus on conferences in which the teacher confers with children on drafts that children plan to revise or edit. An analysis scheme for evaluating children's writing is presented, and on the basis of that analysis, suggestions for ways teachers can conduct conferences to support revising and editing are covered.

Atwell (1987); Calkins (1986); Graves (1983); Turbill (1983)

This assessment assumes that the teacher has obtained a draft written by a child on a topic the child has chosen. If observation during the drafting process is also possible, the teacher can jot down notes about the ways children do the following:

Use space (how they start to write, the direction of writing, whether they leave spaces between "words"), punctuation, capitalization, paragraphing, and so on.
Form letters and words.

Correct or change what they write.
Comment on what they write.

It may be necessary for young children who use invented spellings—that is, spelling approximations that are constructed by them on the basis of what they have learned about the orthographic system—to read their text right after they have finished so it can be deciphered by the teacher (although experienced teachers, who have had lots of practice "cracking the code" of a range of young writers, usually can figure out these invented spelling patterns without having children read them beforehand). In integrated language classrooms, approximations are encouraged, so teachers need to know the general developmental changes in spelling. Table 6.5 outlines general characteristics of these changes. We will go into these more when writing samples are reviewed.

Henderson & Beers (1980); Temple, Nathan, Burris, & Temple (1988)

Analyzing a Writing Sample. In analyzing a draft, consider both message (content) aspects (items listed under Register/Genre in Table 5.8) and medium aspects (items listed under Surface/Medium Features in Table 5.7). Teachers usually have separate conferences regarding these two aspects of children's writing. That is, they have content conferences with children to deal with the message of a text, and they have editing conferences to address medium issues *after* children have revised their text. Chapter 8 discusses ways to implement these conferences in the classroom, but here we concentrate on the analysis scheme and review the types of questions teachers may ask by considering several writing samples from a range of elementary age children. Thus, we will be treating message *and* medium concerns at the same time.

Content conferences deal with message aspects of a writer's text; editing conferences deal with medium aspects of a writer's text.

The analysis of children's writing consists of asking questions about the message and medium aspects of their texts. See Table 6.6 for a list of these questions.

TABLE 6.5 Developmental Changes in Spelling

Prephonemic Spelling

Characteristics: Prephonemic spellers know a lot about language; they know how letters are formed and that they somehow represent language. However, they string letters (mostly consonants) together in an unsystematic fashion because they have not as yet discovered the phonetic principle, that is, that letters represent the speech sounds or phonemes in words. Prephonemic spellers usually have not as yet learned to read.

Examples: BMKGTO (candy) MBRRDRGC (cat)

Early Phonemic Spelling

Characteristics: Early phonemic spellers have discovered the phonetic principle and attempt to represent phonemes in words with letters—they have begun to figure out how spelling works. Although they try to represent letters for sounds they hear in words, their products are sparse. That is, they usually just put down letters for only one or two sounds (and then may finish with random letters). This is because they usually do not have a stable concept of what a word is, so they can't keep words in "their minds" long enough to match sounds of words with letters. Early phonemic spellers are usually not reading as yet.

Examples: P (piano) N (engine)

Letter-Name Spelling

Characteristics: Letter-name spellers are able to break down a word into its phonemes and represent them with letters, but they work on a rule of one-to-one correspondence—that is, one sound is represented by one letter. They are called letter-name spellers because they frequently use the sounds of the *names* of letters to stand for respective phonemes in words. Letter-name spelling is in many ways the most complex set of spelling approximations and is therefore the most challenging system for teachers to decipher. The examples below reflect some of the major rules children rely on in their letter-name spelling. Letter-name spellers are often not readers, but they have a stable concept of word and are beginning to develop a sight vocabulary. When they begin to read, they will read conventional spelling but will write words in letter-name spelling (which sometimes leads to confusion when they try to read their own writing).

Examples: HARE (cherry). A good example of the use of letter-names and the one-to-one rule. Thus, consonant digraphs—e.g., *ch, sh, th, ph*—are represented by only one letter.

LAP (lamp) YET (went) (Nasals (*n, m*) are dropped near medial vowels.)

SOPR (supper) LETL (little). When vowels occur in syllables that are unstressed, they are said to be "reduced." In these cases, only the consonant (R and L, respectively) is provided by the child.

BAT (bet) PAT (pet) (front middle)
FEH (fish) HEM (him) (front high), etc.

Lax or "short" vowels are represented by letter-name vowels that have the same tongue positions when produced. That is, the tongue's position is in the front, middle part of the mouth when the lax "e" in "bet" and the tense "a" in "bait" are made.

Transitional Spelling

Characteristics: Transitional spellers have gone beyond the one-to-one correspondence between sounds and letters. They have learned many features of conventional spelling (they include many conventional spellings), but these understandings are employed uncertainly or are overextended. Transitional spelling *looks like* English and is easy to read. Frequently, transitional spellers may have all the correct letters of a word but not in the right order. Transitional spellers are readers.

Examples: NIHGT (night) DAER (dear). Correct letters but in the wrong order.
PUTT (put) DINNIGE (dining). Overextension of "double" consonants and "silent e" vowel pattern.

Derivational Spelling

Characteristics: Derivational spelling is very similar to transitional spelling. Derivational spellers rely on the *morphophonemic* nature of the English spelling system. That is, through their spellings, they demonstrate that they are aware that the spelling of a particular word reflects, or is derived from, a "core" meaning.

Examples: EXPLAINATION (explanation) JUDGEMENT (judgment). Spellings reflect the meaning of "explain" and "judge," respectively.

Conventional Spelling

Characteristics: Correct spellings are used.

The best sources for learning about developmental changes of spelling are: Temple et al. (1988). *The Beginnings of Writing* (2nd edition); Henderson & Beers (1980). *Developmental and Cognitive Aspects of Learning to Spell.*

TABLE 6.6 Analysis Scheme for a Writing Sample

Use the following questions to evaluate children's texts:

Message Questions	Medium Questions
1. What genre is the child attempting to write? How successful is the child? Are there certain beginnings, endings, sequences used to indicate a certain genre?	1. Does the child show knowledge of the directionality principles of the writing system? How about the spacing principle? Layout features? Paragraphing? etc.
2. Is the text complete according to the genre the child is attempting? If complete, is it sparse, or are relevant details and elaborations included?	2. Does the child show that (s)he has a stable concept of letter/word/sentence?
3. Does the child use an interesting vocabulary? Is it appropriate to the genre attempted? Does the child use cohesive ties to knit the text together? Does the child use any words that are unclear or ambiguous—e.g., pronouns with uncertain antecedents?	3. How does the child use punctuation, capitalization, and so on?
4. Are there any gaps of information or "missing links" in the text? Does the child order information to make sense?	4. What does the child know about the orthographic (spelling) system? At what developmental level do you think the child is? (Give examples.)
5. Does the child appear to have audience or reader "sense"?	5. How does the child control various grammatical structures—e.g., noun and verb agreement, parallel constructions, and the like?

FACILITATING THE REVISING AND EDITING OF A WRITING SAMPLE

On the basis of this analysis, teachers then decide how to conference with children about their texts. As you may have noted, an important distinction is made between helping children learn to *edit* and to *revise* their writing. Editing involves medium changes, things that an editor, teacher, or someone else can change: spelling, punctuation, noun and verb agreement, for example. Most instruction and feedback in writing have traditionally emphasized editing. In the process-conference approach, these editing aspects are considered, but they are done differently.

Revising, on the other hand, has to do with changes of the message of a text. Only writers can revise, because only they know what they are intending to express. Although little instruction or feedback is given in the revision of writing in most traditional classrooms, it is the most important for it will help children be better writers. Facilitating revising helps children become readers of their own writing; it sensitizes them to the requirements of other readers of their writing so that their writing is comprehensible.

The reader-writer contract is emphasized.

The following general guidelines are useful in conferences:

1. Have children read their writing first and note any spontaneous changes they make.
2. Point out any changes children make in reading their texts aloud that they did not note on their actual text.
3. Address only one or two message issues and only one medium concern in each conference.
4. Be positive and show interest in what children are trying to express.
5. Start by responding to a strength or positive feature of the texts.
6. Don't tell children what to do, but use questions to support them in finding their own answers.
7. Leave the pencil in children's hands. That is, all changes, additions, and so on—all writing—should be left under children's control and ownership.
8. When asking a question, be sure that children are given time to respond. Have a long "wait time."
9. Try to make your questions and responses as specific as possible.
10. End each conference by asking children what they will do next.

To get an idea of the kinds of specific questions teachers may ask, we'll consider the writing samples of K to 6 children. For each child, we'll have a "conference" in which we pretend we're the teacher.

Amber, Megan, Mike: Kindergarteners

Amber, Megan, and Mike are kindergarteners. We have to be careful in our conferences with young writers. We want to encourage them to see themselves as writers, to use their own approximations for conventional forms. If we stress revising or editing too much or too soon, we can give them the message that we do not value their efforts.

Addressing revising and editing concerns in very young, emergent writers must be done with great caution.

Amber's and Megan's texts were the result of a MONSTERS unit, and Mike's was a sign he wrote as the result of a classroom accident.

Amber

Amber's text (Figure 6.2) is short and is about the Cookie Monster of *Sesame Street* fame.

Message Analysis. The most prevalent issue in very young writers' texts involves trying to understand what genre they are attempting to tackle (see Message Question 1, Table 6.6). This is partly because their texts are usually short; there isn't very much information on which to base a reliable decision. This seems to be the case for Amber's text. What form is she trying? Is it a personal narrative? Or is she attempting a story?

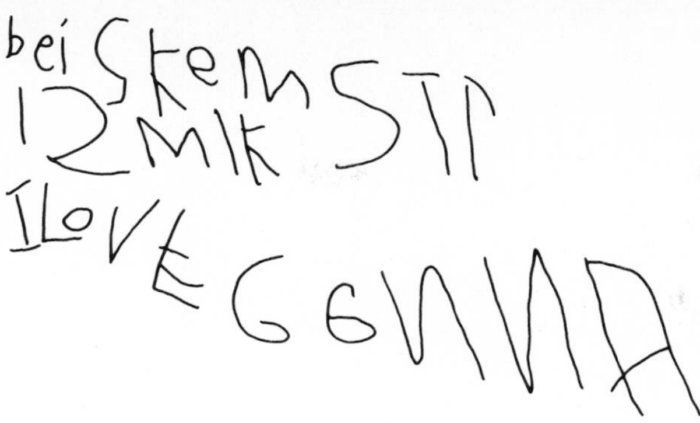

(Amber I saw Cookie Monster. I saw him again. I love Genna.)

Figure 6.2 Amber's Text

And how does the last line fit with the rest of the text? Thus, a teacher might first ask a question to address this genre issue: "Amber, is this a pretend story about Cookie Monster, or are you writing about your actually seeing Cookie Monster?" Any subsequent questions would then depend on how Amber answers. For example, if she says that it was a pretend or make-believe story, then the teacher may ask about what Cookie Monster is going to do in the story and, perhaps, if Genna is going to do something with Cookie Monster. In contrast, if Amber indicates that her text is a personal narrative, then questions about what Cookie Monster did when she saw him would be appropriate. Frequently, revisions for young children like Amber are mostly talking more about their texts. The teacher may not expect Amber actually to rewrite her text. Instead, the teacher may invite Amber to add those things she has related to her text, realizing that Amber may or may not be able to do so at this time.

Revising for young children consists of their *talk* about their texts.

Medium Analysis. Most of the spellings in this text indicate that Amber is an early phonemic speller. (Her last line consists entirely of conventional spellings, but she probably has learned these words as "wholes.") "Genna" is Amber's friend; the first two letters of her text, "be," are part of Amber's name. Amber shows that she is aware of direction of print, but she does not seem to have a concept of a word (there is no spacing between words). She uses no capitalization or punctuation. At this point, the teacher would not say anything to Amber about editing. If the text is going to be published—perhaps typed and then illustrated by Amber—then the teacher may edit it during the typing. Amber's progress in spelling will be facilitated by developing a stable concept of a word, so the teacher will engage her in many activities to facilitate this development—example, Dictations (see this section later in the chapter), Group Composed Writing, Big Book, and so on (see Chapter 8)—as well as provide many other opportunities for her to write.

Megan

Figure 6.3 is Megan's text on dinosaurs in the form of a small, stapled four-page booklet.

Message Analysis. It is not clear from Megan's short text what genre she is attempting. Is it an information book about dinosaurs? Or is it an attempt to write a story? Consequently, the major issue to resolve is to help Megan decide which is the case. The teacher can begin by asking if this is a pretend story about dinosaurs or if it is an information book (notice that she uses present tense verbs). If Megan says it is a story, then the teacher can ask her more about what exciting things the dinosaurs are doing or how they got to be friends. If Megan says it is an information book, then the teacher can get Megan to tell what else she has learned about dinosaurs that she could add to her book. Again, the teacher's expectations consist of encouraging only. Most revisions involve talking about revisions, rather than actually more writing or rewriting. The teacher may suggest that Megan unstaple her booklet and add pages, and that could be Megan's revision.

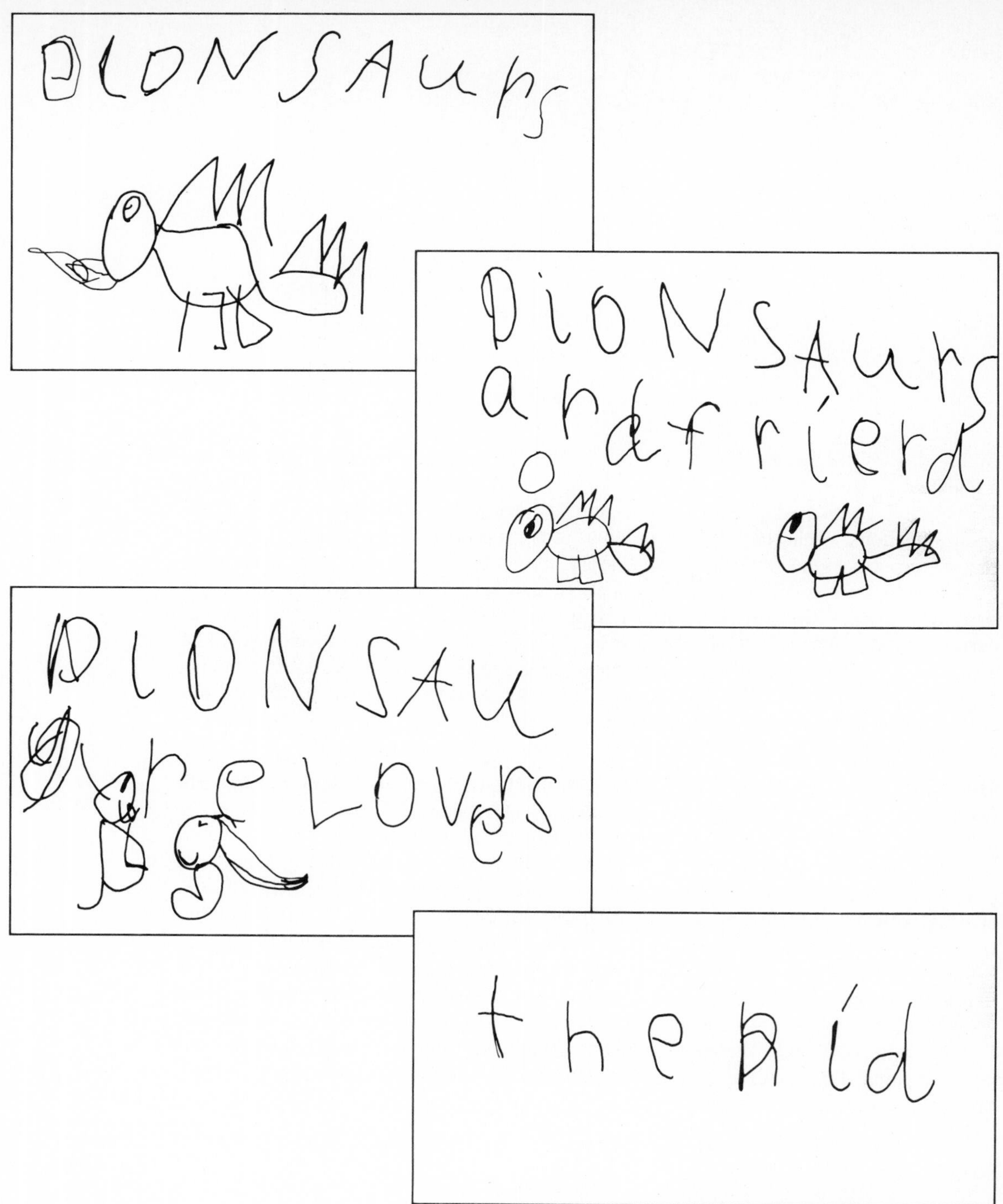

Figure 6.3 Megan's Text

Medium Analysis. Although there is not much to work on in her short text, Megan does have a better grasp of medium aspects of written language than Amber does. She has a better sense of space and seems to know what a word is. Megan is a letter-name speller, although her text indicates that she may be more advanced than that. She incorrectly copied the word "dinosaurs" from a big display in the classroom, and her peers helped with "friends" (also incorrect) and "lovers." Thus, the teacher would not do anything regarding editing.

Mike

Mike's text arose as the result of a classroom accident. The children were studying guppies and other fish, and the water tank was placed on a low shelf. One day a child lost her balance and accidentally sat down in the tank. At evaluation time at the end of the day, Mike argued that something should be done about the water tank so no one else would fall in it. The teacher asked him if he wanted to make a sign to put next to the tank. With her help, he wrote, "Dont pus," and then he finished it on his own (Figure 6.4).

Message Analysis. There is no doubt about Mike's genre. Notice how he has incorporated the grammatical structures appropriate to signs: "Don't push . . .," "Be careful," "Read this. . . ." It is an amusing sign, of course, very few signs include the admonition to read it. The teacher did not suggest that Mike change that last line, because Mike was the youngest of several siblings, and he was reluctant to use invented spelling at all because he was afraid he might be wrong. So this was an important breakthrough for Mike, and the teacher merely confirmed and shared his delight of accomplishment. They published it by hanging it on the wall near the tank, and the teacher and the children frequently reread it to remind themselves about it.

Medium Analysis. Mike has some early-phonemic inclinations (his spelling for "careful" perhaps), but he is mostly a letter-name speller with respect to this text. He relies on letter names to spell "any" (N E) and the beginning of "water" (Y). It's not clear whether he has a stable concept of a word; sometimes he has spaces between words and sometimes he runs his words together, as in the last line. The teacher does no editing because she doesn't want to risk doing anything to harm his new confidence.

Annie and Robbie: First Graders

First graders, Annie and Robbie, are attempting to write stories (see Figures 6.5 and 6.6).

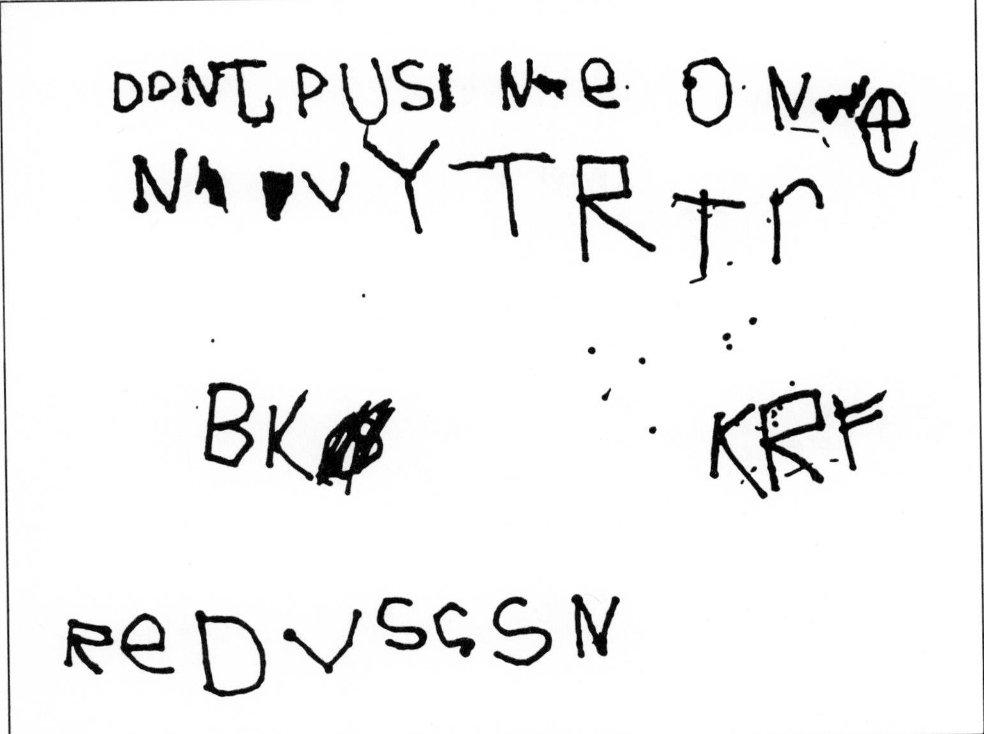

(Don't push anyone in the water tank. Be careful! Read this sign!)

Figure 6.4 Mike's Text

I Bildid a snow man

1

I Bildid a snow man bot thin It was tim
To ete and thin it wus tim to gowroBed It wasn

2

then I woc up and got drest and I atebrefist
and then I wint uot sid and mi snow men was
mel tid and I crid and cisd Him

and then He cam bacto Lif and weplad

18
8
The End
We Lifd Haple efr aftr
3

Figure 6.5 Annie's Text

Oncs a Pon there was a
forg. Hwo liked to jump a Lot.
One day he Siad to himself. I will
go to my Mom's Pond. whrer she
Livs. So he Pakt. He jumt there.
When he got there. He kocked on the
Lily Pad. his Sistr ansrd. She Siad hi
Can I hlep you. borther. is Mom here. yes. can talk to hr Sistr
you can So he cam in. His Mom was yes
Siting Down in hr favrit cheir. She siad
hi forgy. He said hi Momy.

the
End

Figure 6.6 Robbie's Text

Annie

Calkins (1986); Dyson (1987); Graves (1983)

Message Analyses. Drawing is an important prewriting experience for Annie. She frequently draws (with lots of colors, which are lost in copying) on each page of her draft first and then writes what is going on in her picture. This is a complete but bare-bones story. Annie's story deals with everyday experiences—eating, going to bed, waking up, and getting dressed—but also incorporates the "fantastic" feature of having a snow man coming back to life (perhaps influenced by "Frosty the Snow Man" TV specials; she wrote her story in January of her first grade year). The teacher would probably address this latter aspect of her text because it is not clear. For example, the teacher may ask: "I'm not sure about this part of your story. Did the girl's crying on the snow man *cause* him to come back to life? Tell me more about this." In this way, the teacher gives Annie an opportunity to clarify the reader's confusion and to elaborate on her story to make it more comprehensible and credible.

Robbie

Robbie is also attempting a story, but it seems to lack certain essential parts. Like Annie, Robbie is using information about everyday experiences. He includes what he knows about parents having favorite chairs, and about visiting by including dialogue with the frog's sister. However, we don't know what has happened that has caused the frog to go to his mom's—that is, we don't know why he has decided to live alone no longer—or how the fact that the frog liked to jump a lot is related to the story line. Consequently, the teacher would address questions to these facets of the story. "Why is the frog living alone and now deciding to go back home? Does the fact that the frog jumps a lot have to do with his decision?" By thinking about the teacher's reaction to his story, Robbie can begin to think of ways to revise his text to fill in pertinent details, thereby clarifying his intentions.

Annie and Robbie

Medium Analyses. Both texts reflect letter-name and transitional spellings, but Annie seems to be more of a letter-name speller, whereas Robbie appears to be more of a transitional one. Words like "cam (came)," "bac (back)," and especially those words that incorporate the *ed* past tense morpheme [e.g., "drest" (dressed), "meltid" (melted), and "plad" (played)] follow letter-name rules. However, Annie does have some spellings that reflect more transitional understandings [e.g., "ete" (eat), "gow" (go)].

Robbie also uses letter-name spellings for *ed* words—"pakt" (packed), "jumt" (jumped), and "ansrd" (answered)—but he does include the conventional spelling of the morpheme in "kocked" (knocked) and "liked." Many of his words have all the correct letters, but they are in the wrong order, and there is evidence that he has gone beyond the letter-name one-to-one rule—"whrer" (where) and "cheir" (chair), for example.

The teacher could address some spelling issue for each child: Both of them spelled a high-frequency word inconsistently. Annie spelled "then" conventionally and as "thin," and Robbie spelled "said" correctly once at the end of the story, but all the other times he used "siad." The teacher could point out the errors in an editing conference. The teacher also could help Robbie understand the function of quotation marks; it is hard to follow the dialogue in his story without them. By having him mark those places (with his two index fingers) where someone is saying something, Robbie will begin to understand the role of quotation marks in a meaningful way.

Katy and Russell: Second Graders

Katy

Katy's text (Figure 6.7) was some writing done as part of a unit ANIMALS—LARGE AND SMALL in which children described their pets (those children who didn't have a pet, described those they would like to have).

Message Analysis. Katy doesn't really give much description of her hamster, focusing mostly on an event in the hamster's life when he broke his leg. Two facets could be addressed. First, Katy goes on about how cute her hamster is, yet she doesn't tell why she feels that way. Thus, in conference, the teacher could say, "You talk a lot about how cute your hamster is, but you don't tell why. What can you add here to explain why it is so cute?" The second feature that could be discussed with Katy could

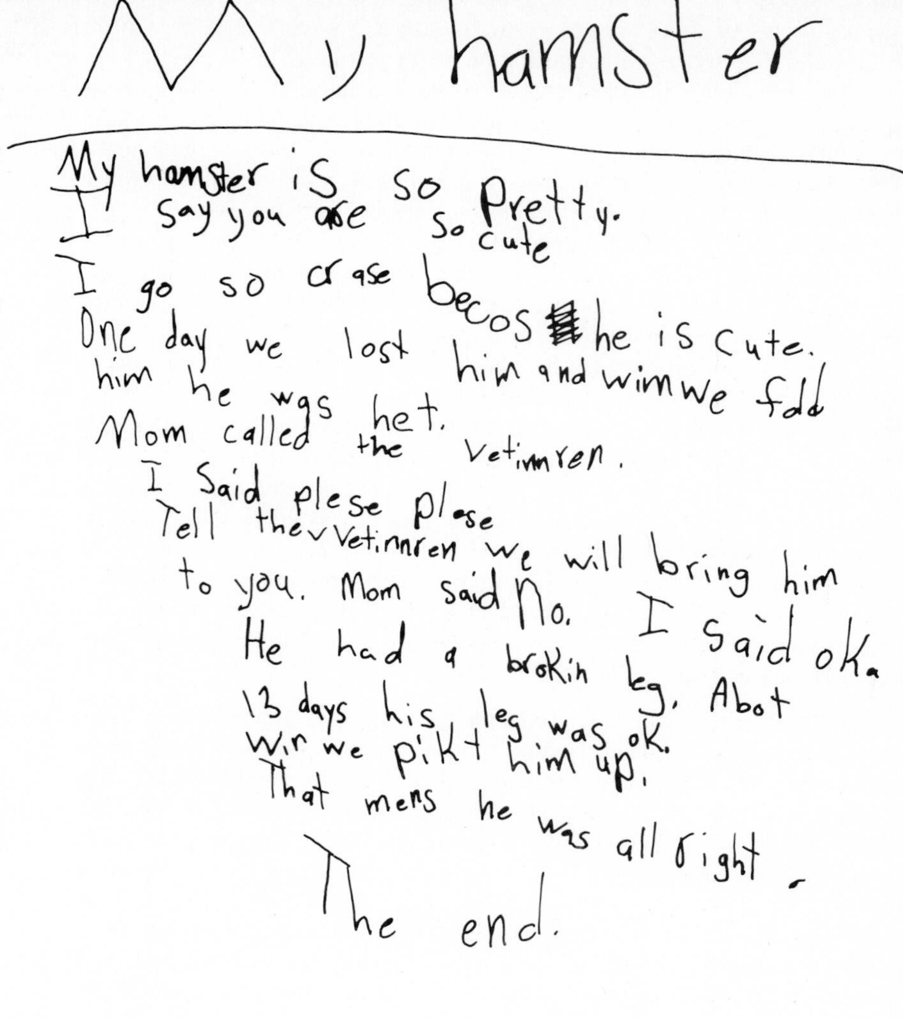

My hamster

My hamster is so Pretty.
I say you are so cute
I go so crase becos he is cute.
One day we lost him and win we fdd
him he was het.
Mom called the Vetinnren.
I Said plese please
Tell the Vetinnren we will bring him
to you. Mom said no. I said ok.
He had a brokin leg. Abot
13 days his leg was ok.
Win we pikt him up.
That mens he was all right.
The end.

my hamsters name is Peewee

Figure 6.7 Katy's Text

be the confusion involved in calling the veterinarian: "Katy, I'm not clear about when your mom called the vet when your hamster was hurt. Is it important to include this telephone call, and what does this part—'Mom said no. I said ok.'—mean?" Thus, the teacher's questions are posed both to help Katy elaborate and to give reasons for her statements about her hamster, and to get her to think more about the relevance and clarity of part of her text.

Medium Analysis. Katy is in between being a transitional speller [she has many conventional spellings, plus spellings like "plese" (please)] and a letter-name speller [she has many spellings that are letter-name, like "crase" (crazy), "win" (when), "abot" (about), "pikt" (picked)]. She has a better control of punctuation than do most of the children we have met so far, but the teacher could address the role of quotation marks in the place where Annie asks her mom to call the vet. Of course, if the child decides that the whole conversation about telephoning the vet is not necessary (see message analysis), then something else could be picked for Katy's attention (maybe the spelling of "when" since that is such a frequent word and would have a big payoff in editing in future pieces).

Russell's text (Figure 6.8) appears to be a story about the adventure of a little fish. **Russell**

Message Analysis. Russell has a very elaborate Placement (see Chapter 5). In fact, it is more than half of his text. It is almost as if he spent so much energy on this first part that he had little left to include the other essential parts of his story. Thus, Russell's conference should try to help him to sustain such a good beginning. The teacher's comments could be: "Russell, I really liked the beginning of your story because I could really picture what the little goldfish was like, and I can sort of figure out the end where the fish ends up in the jail and her parents help her get out. But, I don't understand the middle part—what is zone a? I think your readers will want to know more about this part of the fish's adventure. This is the really exciting part, isn't it?" The teacher tries to point out how an important part of the story may be missing or not clear and

Once there was a little fish who wanted to be biger and braver, but even a pollywog wold frittn her. She was alittle goldfish, had a BIG amaganation sometimes she wold pretent she was a shark but most of the time she wold wish and wish and sometimes she wold bump into some one. And once she even went into SONE a and got cault and had to goto jail. For a day intell her mom and Dad called and told them that she was wishing and that she Didn't see what thay were doing.

Sone a

Jail

ring

Figure 6.8 Russell's Text

encourages Russell to revise by mentioning that this is the part that readers will likely find most exciting.

Medium Analysis. Russell has mostly transitional (and conventional) spellings. Spellings like "cault" (caught), "intell" (until), and "thay" (they) show that he has gone beyond the one-to-one rule of letter-name spellers. He seems to have a fairly good control of the use of commas, but he is inconsistent in his use of periods. Because he does demonstrate that he has some sense of a sentence, the teacher may extend this understanding by reading through Russell's text, pausing only when periods are there and getting him to hear how it sounds that way. Then the teacher could have Russell go through the story again (with the teacher's help) and reconsider his use of periods.

Bryan and Carla: Third and Fourth Graders

Bryan

Bryan, a third grader, has been studying kangaroos and has written a report (Figure 6.9) on what he has learned.

Message Analysis. Bryan's text is a typical example of the information book genre. He does a good job in relating the typical behavior of kangaroos, where they live, and so on and is consistent in using the present tense of this genre. What Bryan seems to need help on is the organization of his information. Teacher comments could direct his attention to this issue: "You certainly have some useful information here, but I was somewhat confused about how you have ordered it. There seem to be three major subtopics here—do you agree? But, sometimes you have mixed up this information, and that makes it not so clear." The teacher could then help Bryan to identify these three subtopics: where kangaroos live (in Australia and where there is green grass and water), how they protect themselves, and how they give birth. Perhaps the teacher could demonstrate the technique of semantic mapping (having three major branches—see Chapter 8) to help him organize his data. This might provide him with a framework on which to revise.

Medium Analysis. Bryan is a typical transitional speller. Look, for example, at his overextension of the terminal "e" in "greene" (green) and "enouge" (enough) and his understanding of vowel digraphs in "Allstrailya" (Australia) and "a nouther" (another). However, in editing, the teacher would probably address the concept of paragraphs with him. Because Bryan is working on three major points about kangaroos, this is a good time for the teacher to show him how to use paragraphs to signal this organization of his information. That is, he will get the idea of paragraphs more easily because in his writing it can be tied so nicely to function.

Carla

Figure 6.10 is the text written by Carla, a fourth grader, at the beginning of the year. As part of a HOUSES unit, Carla and some of her classmates had recently taken a tour through a house bus. Carla and her small group decided to come up with different versions of alternative housing and describe them to their classmates.

Message and Medium Analyses. Carla had told the teacher that she was trying to describe her ideas on alternative housing by writing a poem but that she was having trouble. Both the message and medium aspects of Carla's text are being discussed together, because the structure or form of her poem and the physical layout of that poem were integrally linked. Both Carla and the teacher looked at a variety of poems, commenting on the possibilities. Then the teacher asked Carla to see if she could structure her individual sentences (that is, could she find a pattern in her text that she could follow?) and then if she could group her sentences as if they were sort of stanzas. Carla thought that she liked her first two sentences: "The first one sort of tells what my dream house is." She also liked the pattern she had in the second sentence: "for a light I would . . . when it's night time I would . . . ." Carla noted that her second sentence started okay—"And for a special thing . . ."—but that she wasn't consistent with the verb. She used "I'll" instead of "I would." The teacher helped her go through a few more sentences and then let her try revising the others on her own. The teacher sug-

Kangaroos live in Allstrailya.
They are born alive. They
fight for thier componyons. They
use thier feet for fighting.
Thier feet have sharp clows.
Thier feet could tear open
thier components skin. When
they fight they put thier
heads back to pretect thier
eyes. Kangaroos can jump very
high. They use thier strengh
to jump fast enouge to
get away from preditors like the
coyote, and the wolf. Theese
animals eat meat. Kangaroos
live where the gras is greene and
on the lands where water is. Becass
They eat grass. They give live birth.
The babies stay in a pouch for
about 6 mounths in a row
when geting bigger their mothers
pouch gets to littil and her musels
have to loosen up for her babey

to get out. The babby
gets bigger and its on its own.
Meanwile the mother gives
birth to a nouther Kungurov
and this repeats twice.

Figure 6.9 Bryan's Text

gested that the places where she wrote about water and food, and so on, could go together and be in a different stanza in her verse from the first set of sentences. Again, Carla was given the job to try to consider that, and to evaluate the rest of her poem in that light. Thus, grammatical structure and genre format were both incorporated into this conference.

```
MY DREAM HOUSE

I would like to live in a floating house on the
beach.  For a light I would cut some squares on the
roof and when it's night time I would pin some
square cloths on top of my roof windows and turn
on my lamps.  And for a special thing I'll cut a
square on the floor in my bedroom and put a square
glass between the cut wood and look at the
fish before I go to bed.  As for water, I'd open
my back door and scoop up water from my pail and
clean the water in my Water Cleaner machine that
I invented.  As for keeping my food cold I have
two big Ice boxes.  And for cooking food I have
a electric stove.  As for furniture there nailed to the
ground.  To keep me company I have a big television
and some books to read.  And when I need more
food I climb into my little boat witch is tighten to
my Boat House.  And when I'm board of the
same place I'm at, I have a Big motor in the
end of my house and can go iney were I want.

THE END
```

Figure 6.10 Carla's Text

David and Eileen: Fifth and Sixth Graders

David and Eileen are students in a fifth/sixth grade classroom. Their texts were the result of a HEROES unit. Both wrote a biography of two heroes they had studied. These texts are quite long, so only excerpts can be provided here. Both texts were second drafts—that is, both David and Eileen had already had conferences with their teacher on their first drafts.

David

David, a fifth grader, wrote on Amelia Earhart (see Figure 6.11).

Message Analysis. David starts his text by describing the search for Amelia Earhart when she disappeared, and then he uses the flashback technique to talk about her life before then. The excerpt includes the first part of his text and the last few paragraphs. David attempted a sort of fictionalized biography in this text. For example, in relating the episode about the small girl on the sled, he was attempting to show the type of woman Earhart was, that she was a woman who "thrived on excitement." Thus, he tried to provide a "story" about the girl/woman Earhart was, based on the facts he discovered about her. Sometimes he was not consistent in his efforts to do this, and most of the teacher's initial conference addressed this issue. His second draft was much better, but he still had difficulty in expressing the transitions between the different episodes he chose to highlight. He chose times in Earhart's life that appeared to be

AMELIA EARHART

8:45 A.M. Amelia Earhart's voice came over the microphone giving her position. Little did she know that this would be her last message. Somewhere around tiny Howland Island her plane would disappear.

A giant search party consisting of the battleship Itasca, four destroyers, a minesweeper and an aircraft carrier and all its planes began to embark on a sixteen day search . . . . . .

A small girl on a boy's sled came whistling down an icy slope, her hair flying behind her. At the end of the slope the junk man and his old horse and buggy were slowly plowing through the snow. If she kept going on her present course she would surely collide with him! She held tight and hoped. She couldn't yell because the junk man was deaf, and the horse had blinders.

Closer and closer she came! She held her breath! She shot like a bullet right underneath the horse's belly, and out through the other side without a scratch!

Another time Amelia tried to build a contraption somewhat like a roller coaster. She fell off, almost breaking her leg, and rubbed her chin raw. To her this was fun.

She thrived on excitement.

.
.
.
.

March 17, 1937: the beginning of a journey from which she and her navigator, Fred Noonan would never return.

They had made many previous stops. Now, they were heading toward Howland Island.

Their plane was circling around Howland Island. They should have landed two hours ago. Then her last message was heard.

There is much speculation on what happened at 8:45 that day.

Figure 6.11 David's Text

significant in her decision to become a pilot, and the teacher helped him to figure out how to express the chronological events so that they were coherent and not just a listing of isolated events in time. The teacher also asked David if he thought he might include what the "speculation" about what happened to Earhart consisted of at the end of his text. In other words, he was asked to consider if a discussion of the various hypotheses about her disappearance might be a useful addition.

Medium Analysis. Both David and Eileen helped each other with peer editing, so this second draft was very polished already. David was, for the most part, a conventional speller and had a good control of conventional grammar and punctuation. The teacher pointed out that there were two instances where David did not use commas appropriately regarding appositives, so he noted them for his final draft.

Eileen

Eileen's text was entitled "Thurber Years." Figure 6.12 is an excerpt of the first part of her text (which consisted of five chapters). Eileen is a sixth grader.

Message Analysis. As already mentioned, Eileen's text on James Thurber is a second draft. Eileen's text represented a more typical biography in one sense, but it was unusual in that she attempted to relate Thurber's life by "cloning" his style of writing. Her initial conference mostly addressed the difficulties she had in being consistent in doing this. This second conference reexamined places in which revisions had been made and where Eileen had rethought others. The teacher asked Eileen to consider places in which Eileen tells what she is doing in reporting on Thurber's life. For example,

Thurber Years

CHAPTER ONE

In Which We Meet James

Thurber Country, The Thurber Album, Lanterns and Lances, These and More. Sound familiar? It should. Many has been the person who has recited these titles "Who are they by?" asks the naive child. This is where I come in. I feel that it is about time that someone else wrote about him, instead of him doing all of the writing. "But who is he?" you ask. I reply with "I think that everyone should be acquainted with James Thurber and his works." In this biography, I will be telling why. Also, I will tell some of his escapades during his career life.

"What other books did he write?" you could probably be wondering. Well, you asked for it. Is Sex Necessary, The Seal in the Bedroom, Arms and Diversions, and Let Your Mind Alone, are all of his works. "Are they good?" you might ask. I'll be contented to leave that to you.

.

.

.

.

Figure 6.12 Eileen's Text

Eileen begins her second chapter: "Now I'm going to tell you about his Ohio Life." The teacher asked, "Now, have you included this sentence because you think Thurber would have written it this way as part of his style, or because you think this is appropriate for a biography?" The teacher attempted to help Eileen decide to distinguish style versus genre issues.

Medium Analysis. Eileen is also a conventional speller and has control of conventional grammar and punctuation. However, as with David, the teacher addressed a punctuation issue in the editing conference. Eileen did not always put commas or periods within the quotation marks when she listed stories written by Thurber, so the teacher pointed out how to do this on this second draft.

Summary

In conferences, teachers address message and medium issues of individual writers. The foregoing examples describe the kinds of problems children tackle in their developmental writing and the ways teachers can support and extend their efforts through their questions and comments in conferences. Writing conferences are discussed again in Chapter 8.

KID-WATCHING PROCEDURES FOR EMERGENT LEARNERS

Before children are able to read in a conventional sense (that is, before they have acquired a sight word vocabulary or are able to figure out and use the graphic or graphophonemic cues afforded by written language), they can engage in experiences that demonstrate their present literate understandings. Some of these were covered in the preceding section when children's invented spellings and other principles and concepts of writing were discussed. This section examines three other literacy activities involving emergent learners. When teachers know kid-watching techniques such as these, they are able to document and support the early stages of reading and writing more effectively. The first scheme involves examining what young children know about the medium aspects of written language as they help the teacher read a book. The second evaluates children's repeated reenactments of a book. The third focuses on teachers' observations while taking down children's dictations.

See also Genishi & Dyson (1984) for other good ideas for assessment of emergent and primary age learners.

Concepts About Print Assessment

The "Concepts About Print" (CAP) assessment was developed by Marie Clay. To find out what young children already know about medium aspects of written language (e.g., directional principles, concepts of first, last, word, letter, various punctuation), Clay developed two little books (*Sand* and *Stones*) to share with children. Each book is altered in certain ways. For example, a picture is inverted, lines of print are reversed and upside down, words and letters in words are switched around, and so on. Teachers read the book as if the alterations do not exist, and as they do, they ask children to help them: "How should I put the book down for me to read it?" "Where should I start to read?" "Which way should I go?" "What's this for (pointing to a comma, period, etc.)?" "Show me the first part I should read on this page?" Thus, this book-sharing experience represents an inquiry situation for children to show what they already know about the concepts and conventions of the medium aspects before they can read conventionally from print.

Clay (1979a)

Clay (1972, 1979b)

Many teachers use *Sand* in the beginning of the year and *Stones* at the end (or vice versa) to assess and document children's understandings. Others, following the format of these books, design and write their own books to use with their children.

Another alternative is to apply the ideas in *Sand* and *Stones* in a regular book, which is what we illustrate here. Keep the following four book features in mind when choosing a book to use:

1. Select a book that, when it is open, has some pages that have print on both the left and right pages.
2. Select a book that has several types of punctuation.
3. Select a book that has one page with only one line of print (that is a complete sentence).
4. Select a book that has one page with three lines of print.

Rockwell (1984)

Figure 6.13 covers the instructions for sharing *Our Garage Sale* by Anne Rockwell.

Not all the concepts are included in the Clay books (they have twenty-four items,

Before starting, thoroughly familiarize yourself with this test. Paginate the book (pencil in numbers in the corners of each page). Use instructions similar to the ones suggested below. Use the CAP scoring sheet (see Figure 6.14) to remind yourself of these instructions and to score the child's responses.

Begin by saying to the child: "I'm going to read you this book, but I want you to help me." (Note: You will read the whole text but will ask questions on only some of the pages.)

COVER

Item 1 Test: For orientation of book. Pass the book to the child holding the book vertically by the outside edge, spine toward the child.
Say: "Show me the front of this book."
Score: 1 point for each correct response.

GO TO...

Pages 2/3

Item 2 Test: A left page is read before a right page.
Say: "Where do I start reading?"
Score: 1 point for left page indication.

GO TO...
Page 8

Item 3 Test: Capital and lower case correspondence.
Say: "Find a little letter like this." Point to the capital "S" and demonstrate by pointing to "Ss" if the child does not succeed. Then say, "Find a little letter like this." Point to capital "W" and "O" in turn.
Score: 1 point if *both* 'Ww' and 'Oo' are located.
Test: Three types of punctuation.
Read the text.
Say: "What's this for?"

Item 4 Point to the period or trace it with a pencil.
Score: 1 point for a functional definition (e.g., "It tells you that it's done, or to stop").

Item 5 Point to the comma or trace it with a pencil.
Score: 1 point for an acceptable functional definition.

Item 6 Point to the quotation marks or trace with a pencil.
Score: 1 point for an acceptable functional definition.

GO TO...
Page 12 Test: For directional rules.

Item 7 Say: "Show me where to start."
Score: 1 point for top left.

Item 8 Say: "Which way do I go?"
Score: 1 point for left to right.

Figure 6.13 Instructions for the Concepts About Print (CAP) Test on *Our Garage Sale* by Anne Rockwell (1984)

Item 9 Say: "Where do I go after that?"
Score: 1 point for return sweep to left.
(Score items 7–9 if all movements are demonstrated in one response.)

Item 10 Test: Word-by-word pointing on one page.
Say: "Point to the words while I read." (Read slowly but fluently.)
Score: 1 point for exact matching.

Pages 14/15

Item 11 Test: Word-by-word pointing on left and right pages.
Say: "Point to the words while I read." (Read slowly, but fluently.)
Score: 1 point for exact matching.

Pages 16/17

Item 12 Test: A left page is read before a right page. (This incorporates features of Item 2 and Items 7–9. However, here the lines of print on each page in this book are placed in the same place on the page, so it would be easy for the child to indicate to read the rest of the first line on page 16 and then to the first line of page 17, then to the second line of page 16, etc.)
Say: "Where do I start reading?"
"Which way do I go?"
"Where do I go after that?"
Score: 1 point for left page indication.

GO TO...
Page 20

Item 13 Test: Concept of first and last applied to text.
Say: "Show me the first part to read on this page."
"Show me the last part on this page."
Score: 1 point if *both* are correctly indicated.

Read the rest of the book. Then go back to:

Page 18 Have two small index cards (3 × 5) that the child can hold and slide easily over the line of text to cover words and letters. To start, lay the cards on the page but leave all print exposed.

Item 14 Test: Letter concepts.
Say: "This page says, 'It didn't rain on Saturday.' I want you to push the cards across the page like this until all you can see is one letter." (Demonstrate the movement of the cards, but do not do the exercise.)
"Now show me two letters."
Score: 1 point if *both* are correct.

Item 15 Test: Word concept.
Say: "Show me just one word."
"Now show me two words."
Score: 1 point if *both* are correct.

Item 16 Test: First and last letter concepts.
Say: "Show me the first letter of a word."
"Show me the last letter of a word."
Score: 1 point if *both* are correct.

Item 17 Test: Capital letter concept.
Say: "Show me a capital letter."
Score: 1 point if letter is correctly located.

Back

Item 18 Test: Back of book.
Say: "Show me the back of the book."
Score: 1 point for correct response.

Top/Bottom

Item 19 Test: Top and bottom of book.
Say: "Show me the top and the bottom of the book."
Score: 1 point for correct responses.

whereas the *Our Garage Sale* example has only nineteen), mostly because in a real book there are no inverted pages and print. It is useful to develop a scoring sheet to administer the assessment. Figure 6.14 has been developed for that purpose and illustrates how Amanda (a kindergartener) responded.

The first column indicates the page of the book involved, the second column lists the concept or principle involved, and the third column lists the items. The large column notes the behavior of the child that leads to a point for each item. The information in the parentheses are reminders for the teacher who administers the assessment. The last column reflects the score for each item.

You will see that the teacher jotted down some extra information on some of Amanda's responses. For example, item 16 has children indicate the first letter of a word and the last letter of a word on the line of print found on page 18: "It didn't rain on Saturday." Amanda indicated these correctly by revealing the "I" (of "It") and the "y" (of "Saturday"), but the fact that she showed only the beginning and end of the sentence indicates that she may be just beginning to understand these concepts of first and last. The teacher will note in subsequent observations if she indicates first and last letters in the same word, which will suggest greater control on her part of these concepts.

Thus, the CAP assessment gives a score, but more importantly it pinpoints those concepts that individual children already have and those that need to be fostered. Amanda, for example, knows orientational features of books, directional rules, first and

Child ______________________ Date ____________ Score ____________

Concepts About Print Test for: OUR GARAGE SALE (by Anne Rockwell)
(Keep book jacket on book)

Page	Concept/Prin.	Item	Child's behavior for giving points (Reminder for admin.)	Score
cover	front	1	Indicates front of book (Show me the front of book)	/
2/3	left page	2	Indicates that lft. page precedes rt. (Where do I start)	/
8	capital/lower case	3	Locates two capital & lower case letter pairs (Ww & Oo)	/
↓	punctuation	4	Indicates meaning of period (What's this for)	—
↓	↓	5	Indicates meaning of comma (What's this for)	—
↓	↓	6	Indicates meaning of quotation marks (What're these for)	—
12	direction	7	Points at top left page (Show me where to start)	/
↓	↓	8	Indicates left to right (Which way do I go)	/
↓	↓	9	Indicates return sweep to left (Where do I go next)	/
↓	one-to-one same pg.	10	Word by word pointing/matching (Point while I read) almost	—
14/15	one-to-one lft. tort. pg.	11	Word by word pointing/matching (Point while I read) almost	—
16/17	all lft. pg.	12	Indicates all of lft. pg. read before rt. (Where do I, etc.)	/
20	first/last text	13	Indicates first & last of text (Show me the first/last)	/
GO BACK 18	letter/word	14	Locates one and two letters (Show me one/two letter(s))	/
C A	↓	15	Locates one and two words (Show me one/two word(s))	—
R D	first/last ltr of wd	16	Locates first & last letter of word (Show me first/last) ends	/
S	capital ltr	17	Locates a capital letter (Show me a capital letter) Saturday d	—
back	back	18	Indicates the back of book (Show me the back of book)	/
top/bottom	tp/bottom	19	Indicates the top & bottom of book (Show me tp/btm of bk)	/

Figure 6.14 Scoring Sheet

last concepts, and so on. However, she does not have a stable concept of word—she could not locate one and two words (items 15) or indicate word-by-word pointing—nor does she seem to know the functions of punctuation. Thus, the teacher will need to provide experiences to help her develop these concepts. Involving Amanda in Big Book and Group Composed Writing activities (see Chapter 8), as well as providing many opportunities for her to write her own texts, will foster these concepts and extend Amanda's present understandings about written language. Again, once teachers have had experience in doing CAP assessments in the more formal way described here, they will be able informally to evaluate children's present understandings and then to intervene to guide their development of new concepts.

Approximations To Text Assessment

Holdaway (1979); McKenzie (1977); Pappas & Brown (1989)

The Approximations To Text (ATT) assessment is also appropriate for emergent learners. It is based on research (and the observations of many parents and preschool teachers as well) which indicates that after young children have been read books, they spontaneously "reenact" or role-play "reading" them on their own. As adults repeatedly share these books, children repeatedly "pretend read" their favorite texts, and each time their renditions get closer and closer to the actual wordings until they have learned them by heart. In the process, children develop an awareness of the nature of registers of written language. Their acquisition of "book language" is a gradual, constructive process. Subsequently, they begin to integrate the graphic cueing system with what they know about the syntactic/semantic patterns of the message. Thus, ATT attempts to tap the reading process for children who cannot be evaluated through an MMA assessment.

The procedure consists of reading an unfamiliar book to a child three times (usually on consecutive days) and on each occasion inviting the child to take his or her turn to "read" or "pretend read" it. Each reading is audiotaped and then transcribed.

The teacher then compares the child's approximations to those of the book and to the ways the child's texts change across the three times. Analyses usually focus on the following four major areas:

1. *Children expand and elaborate on the message of the book across the three readings.* Children may initially give a bare-bones rendition of the text, but as they hear the text being read again and have opportunities to take their turns to read it again, they begin to fill in and add more of the author's message.
2. *Children acquire certain vocabulary used in the book.* They may provide a synonym or make up their own word for certain vocabulary in early readings, but in subsequent readings, they may begin to incorporate the actual wordings of the author.
3. *Children incorporate the author's grammatical structures.* Written language uses various kinds of grammatical constructions (more use of relative clauses, passive voice, etc.) that are not as typical in oral language, so children frequently create their own versions of these structures and then gradually begin to include structures similar to those of the author in the subsequent readings.
4. *Children's elaborations based on the illustrations change across the readings.* In early readings children rely on the illustrations of a book to construct and sustain the message of the book, but then these elaborations usually drop out or are somehow incorporated or expressed more in terms of the linguistic message in later readings.

Figure 6.15 shows a form that might be used to document these four types of approximations.

Teachers respond to any child initiation or question about the message, pictures, or print of the book during the ATT sessions. At the bottom of the form (Figure 6.15),

Child's Name ____________ Date ____________ Book ____________

	Reading #1	Reading #2	Reading #3
Important message ideas and details included			
Strategies in learning vocabulary			
Strategies in learning grammatical constructions			
Changes in elaborations based on illustrations			
Interesting questions, comments made			

Figure 6.15 ATT Analysis Sheet

the teacher might jot down interesting questions or comments the child might have had.

Children's questions, such as "What's this word?" or "Is this word ______?," are answered unless the child asks about every other word. If it is clear, after a page or so, that the child is unwilling to follow the "pretend route," then the teacher may consider an alternative procedure. This alternative procedure consists of reading page by page—that is, the teacher reads one page, and then the child takes a turn to "read" that page. The fact that some children are reluctant to "pretend read" is normal. It indicates that these children have acquired a lot about the graphic or medium aspects of written language and are more motivated to tackle the print realization of the message now. An MMA scheme could be applied to the children's readings in these cases instead of the form illustrated by Figure 6.15.

Like the MMA assessment, the ATT procedure is initially complicated and time-consuming. Again, the advantage of using it is that it enables teachers to internalize ways of informally observing young children's approximations. It also helps teachers to appreciate children's constructive process of reading at the very early stages, and to be aware of the kind of strategies children employ in learning "book language." It encourages teachers to provide opportunities in the classroom for children to reenact or "pretend read" books from a range of genres—reading Big Books, doing Book Talks, participating in Buddy Reading activities, and the like (see Chapter 8).

Dictations

Genishi & Dyson (1984); Temple, Nathan, Burris, & Temple (1988)

Dictations and Retellings (to be described in the next section) are oral compositions. Although teachers are constantly encouraging children to write on their own, dictation experiences are also useful in fostering the composing process because they give children opportunities to concentrate more on creating their message, leaving the scribing work to the teacher. That is, as children focus on orchestrating their discourse, the teacher takes on the mechanical task of writing and the concerns about spelling and punctuation. Dictations, therefore, provide important information about a child's potential in the composition process that would not be available if only their own writings were considered. Figure 6.16, which provides examples of two stories composed

DICTATION:

Once upon a time there was a little boy. And he was trying to go to sleep, but he heard a noise in the closet. So he sat up in bed. He opened the door of the closet and he looked in. There was a monster. And so he says, "Are you a scary monster?" And the monster said, "No." And so he says, "Will you play with me?" The monster says, "Of course." And so the boy called in his sister, and he said, "Here, I have a friend. He is a monster." The little girl said, "You do?" because she liked monsters. So the little boy said, "Yes." And so he asked the monster to play games with them. The monster won every game. And in London Bridges they couldn't fit their arms around him. In Hide-and-Go-Seek he had two heads so he could tell where they were going. Then the little boy asked him, "Why were you in the closet?" He said because he was looking for candy. The little girl said, "Well, I have some candy." The monster said, "You do?" And the little girl said, "Yes." And so she got him a piece, and he ate it up. But then he said, "Yuk!" He didn't like peppermint. And so he said, "Well, now I have to hunt in the closet for more candy." And so he did. And the little boy woke up and he found out that it was all a dream.

WRITING: (Note: spelling and punctuation have been corrected.)

Once there was a girl and a boy.
The girl said, "Let's play!"
So they played and played.
They turned and turned.
They got dizzy.
They stopped.
The room went around.

Figure 6.16 Janet's Dictation and Written Texts

around the same time (mid-October) by a first grader, illustrates this fact. Janet's dictation (on the top) is much more complex than her written story (on the bottom).

Dictation experiences provide a means to assess both the product *and* process of children's composing process. That is, by means of the message criteria discussed earlier, the dictation text as product can be evaluated. However, other information about children's participation in the process can also be assessed. For example, what is the delivery style of the child's dictation? Does the child dictate the message at a pace that is easy for the teacher to take down? Or does the child seem to be unaware of constraints on the writing process, rattling on and on and having to be stopped repeatedly so the teacher can keep up? Does the child pay attention to what the teacher is scribing? For example, does the child seem to read along as the teacher writes down the text? Does the child comment on or take notice of the spelling or punctuation aspects of the text? Does the child initiate any repairs (or revisions) of the message during the dictation process? Figure 6.17 summarizes the kinds of things that can be assessed during dictation. Figure 6.17 also indicates the context in which a particular dictation occurred. For example, Janet's dictation came about because children were creating a classroom story anthology. At the bottom of the form shown in Figure 6.17, instructional ideas, based on the dictation activity, can also be noted.

A more formal dictation assessment has teachers keep their interactions with children at a minimum. Other than stopping children when unable to keep up with their dictation, teachers avoid commenting on or drawing the children's attention to message or medium aspects of the text being composed because the teachers want to have a clearer view of children's understanding. Then, on the basis of the data gained in these formal contexts, teachers know what to focus on when they interact with children in subsequent dictations (as well as what other activities may be appropriate for them).

Thus, there are many reasons to use dictations in the early elementary grades. Children's sight vocabulary is fostered through dictations; children are very successful in identifying the words of texts when they are *their* words. Moreover, many demonstrations of medium aspects of written language (directionality, spacing, spelling, use of punctuation, etc.) are available for children during the dictation process. Teachers can also demonstrate the revising and editing processes during dictation. Finally, once

Child:________________________________ Date:____________

Context	
How well does the child control the genre being attempted? Are there certain beginnings, endings, sequences present to indicate a certain genre?	
Is the text complete? Are details or elaborations included?	
Interesting vocabulary used? Use of cohesive ties? Ambiguous terms?	
Any missing information? Is information ordered to make sense?	
Interesting repairs used?	
Attention to transcription of medium aspects of text?	
Delivery pace or dictating style?	

INSTRUCTIONAL IDEAS:

Figure 6.17 Dictation Sheet

teachers have experience in assessing dictations in a formal way, they know how to evaluate dictations informally in the classroom. As Figure 6.17 shows, they can document the contexts in which dictations arise and can note instructional ideas to foster and extend children's present efforts. Dictating can serve as important sources of evaluation and accountability (see Chapter 9).

Retelling Assessment

Like dictations, retellings are a type of oral composition. However, they differ from dictations as well. First, they aren't "original" compositions. That is, here children are retelling or reconstructing someone else's message, not their own. Second, dictations are usually used in the early primary grades (although certain versions of dictation can be used with older elementary age children—e.g., see Group Composed Writing activities in Chapter 8). In contrast, retellings can occur at any grade level.

The retelling assessment procedures consist of either reading to children or having them read themselves a text and then inviting them to retell it to someone who does not know it (usually other children in the class who haven't heard or read the text). The fact that children retell the text to naive listeners is a critical factor, because it provides a social context that requires children to produce a complete linguistic message. The assessment then addresses children's strategies to provide such a text.

Thus, such retellings are very different from the retellings in the MMA assessment where the listener has knowledge of the text being read.

Retellings are audiotaped and then transcribed in more formal versions of the procedures. After reading the text to be retold, most teachers have the children go through it again by letting them see the pictures again (if the text is illustrated), or by discussing or commenting on any questions children might have regarding the text before they do the retelling. Because reading is a construction of meaning, retellings are viewed as "new" versions of the author's message. That is, retellings may be organized in ways that are different from the published text and may reflect interpretations different from those of the teacher.

Retellings are constructions of an author's message.

Figure 6.18 shows an analysis sheet that could be used to document retellings from

Child's Name ______________________ Date __________

Was the child provided the "essential" information? Is there anything significant missing?	Has the child included interesting elaborations (extra information not expressed in the text)?	Has the child provided substitutions of wording which represent similar ideas or meanings?	Are there aspects that are unclear? Is it clear as to who is doing/going; what is being discussed, etc.?

Figure 6.18 Analysis Sheet for Retelling

such a perspective. In the first column, the teacher considers whether the essentials of the text have been included in the retelling and notes any significant information that seems missing. The second and third columns provide places to document the interesting elaborations and substitutions children may have used. In the last column, the teacher jots down any places where children's retellings may have been unclear, may have used ambiguous pronouns, and so on, making the retelling text not cohesive. Thus, the analysis sheet can assess children's comprehension of a particular text, and at the same time it can document the constructive nature of retelling by capturing various "ways with words," or styles, in the retelling process. As an oral composition, the retelling provides a means to evaluate children's strategies in creating and organizing a text for others.

Cazden (1988); Heath (1983); Lindfors (1987); Michaels (1981)

Like the other assessments in this chapter, once teachers have practice in assessing retellings in the formal way described here, they can use their internalized framework to evaluate children's retellings in more informal contexts—for example, when they retell a story using props (flannel board characters, e.g.), retell sections of a text in a response group, or share texts in buddy reading (see Chapter 8).

GENERAL OBSERVATION SCHEMES

The schemes discussed in the preceding sections focused specifically on certain literacy events, but teachers need the means to evaluate how children are using language and developing concepts as they interact with others in a variety of activities across the curriculum, too. In an integrated language perspective, skills cannot be discerned in isolation from the culture or settings in which they appear. That is, valid kid-watching procedures and evaluation must include observation and documentation of children's understandings as they emerge in the natural and familiar settings of the classroom. We need to see how children are constructing concepts in particular domains, how they become experts in various topics. We need to be able to see children's learning over time because it develops slowly and in different patterns for different children. Because development is socially influenced, we need to discover how children act with partners and peers in small group and whole class interactions. Finally, we need to be able to find out children's working styles, how individual children approach, initiate, and sustain their work and inquiry. To meet these needs, three types of observation schemes or approaches are covered: target-child(ren) observation; roving anecdotal observation; and other miscellaneous observation ideas.

Johnston (1987a, 1987b); Goodman, Goodman, & Hood (1989); Wexler-Sherman, Gardner, & Feldman (1988)

Target-Child(ren) Observation

Sylva, Roy, & Painter (1980)

The first observation approach is a modification of the kid-watching ideas developed by Bruner and his colleagues to document young children's sustained attention in activities in preschool playgroups and nursery schools. This scheme involves selecting a target child on whom to do repeated short, ten-minute observations. Teachers decide on a few children to follow each day, and using a recording sheet, they take notes on what these children do and say. See Figure 6.19 for an example of the recording sheet.

At the top of the form, the teacher writes the name of the child, the date, and time of the observation. The procedure consists of several ten-minute observations done at different times of the day to capture a variety of experiences and interactions. The first half-minute of each minute is spent observing; the last half of the minute is spent summarizing the child's activities and language (jotted down under the headings "Activity Record" and "Language Record," respectively). As Figure 6.19 shows, information about the context, activity, or task and any participants involved with the target child is also included on this form. At the bottom of the form, the teacher jots down any instructional ideas that may come to mind on the basis of the ten-minute observation. These ideas are conclusions based on observations, reminders for subsequent intervention, or suggestions that pertain to the child observed. Teachers try to be

Name(s):		Date and Time Observed:	
ACTIVITY RECORD	LANGUAGE RECORD	CONTEXT/TASK	OTHER PARTICIPANTS
1			
2			
3			
4			
5			
. . .			
10			
Instructional Ideas:			

Source: Sylva, Roy & Painter (1980). Reprinted with permission.

Figure 6.19 Target-Child(ren) Observational Sheet

unobtrusive during the ten-minute observations. Most teachers set up a signal system (e.g., wearing a certain hat or scarf) in their classroom so children know that they are not to interrupt while the observations are occurring.

Describe, don't interpret yet.

It is important to write down *what the child does* in the "Activity" column, not an interpretation of the behavior, or what can be concluded about the child on the basis of what has been seen (as indicated above, conclusions can be noted under "Instructional Ideas" on the bottom of the form). Information about materials or objects is also incorporated in this activity record if relevant. Under the "Language" column, everything that the child says and what other children say to the child is noted. It is frequently impossible to write all the exact words spoken, but the gist of comments can be recorded. Short-cut abbreviations can be used to help in the recording. Most teachers initially find it difficult to record observations, but with practice, the observations get to be second nature.

Sylva, Roy, & Painter (1980)

Part of observation is to document how children sustain their attention in an activity or project, so after the writing is done, the record is gone over for coherent *themes* in the child's behavior. A *theme* is defined as a continued stream of activity during which the child seems to be following a thread. The theme may be based on the materials that the child is using or on the children the child is participating with, but it does not coincide with a shift of activity per se. For example, a child named Joey may finish reading a particular book and go over to the writing center for some paper and markers. He may then glance over the book again as he chats with a peer about some of the illustrations, and then begin a "sketch to stretch" activity (see Chapter 8). He tells his friend that he's going to finish the drawing later this afternoon, but before he joins everyone in a whole class sharing session, he notes in his learning log his ideas for the drawing so he doesn't forget them. Thus, although the foregoing is only a summary of the child's behavior (i.e., it doesn't include the details a real observation record would have), it illustrates the fact that a particular theme can integrate several activities and several places over several minutes. Themes are noted on the observation sheet by drawing double lines across the page of the sheet to indicate where one theme ends and another begins.

The same form can be used to record observations of small group activities. For example, when stable small groups are established to work on special projects in a thematic unit, teachers can document the course of their inquiries. Instead of one child, a target group of children is the focus. After these observations, teachers record relevant instructional ideas that could be helpful to support the group work. Perhaps a question to ask the group or a book or other resource to suggest is noted.

Roving Anecdotal Observation

Roving observation has many features of target-child(ren) observation, but it has a broader focus in the sense that teachers may not have a particular child or group in mind when they begin to observe. However, it does have a narrower focus as well, in that teachers gather briefer, specific "spot" information as they rove around the room to interact with individuals and small groups who are busy engaged in activities or projects.

Anecdotal observations are made to gain valuable information about children's particular strengths, needs, strategies, and interests in the natural social life of the classroom. There is a range of experiences to be recorded, so each particular observation needs to be focused to be of much use for understanding individual children and for providing or generating appropriate instructional strategies. Categories of interesting behavior that such observations could concentrate on follow. A particular note could include (but not be limited to):

Interactions with Peers

Strategies for joining and departing groups
Responses to initiations from others
Negotiation strategies
Examples of abilities to take the perspective of others
Instances of leadership or responsibility
Examples of peer support, empathy
Cooperation strategies
Examples of turn-taking abilities

Strategies and Processes

Process of problem-solving with people
Process of problem-solving with objects, materials
Creative use of resources to tackle problems
Strategies for accomplishing tasks
Unusual use of objects or materials beyond conventional roles
Unusual combination of objects, resources, materials
Representational and imaginary object use

Oral Language Samples

Interesting quotations
Sophisticated vocabulary
Unusual working definitions of words
Examples of explanations and descriptions
Examples of metalinguistic awareness (using language as an object)
Instances of register or code switching

Literacy Samples

Use of books as a resource to help solve problems
Strategies used in reading aloud
Strategies used in various writing experiences (prewriting, drafting, revising, editing, publishing)

Creative book extensions
Spontaneous use of reading and writing
Unusual or interesting use of reading and/or writing in projects

Miscellaneous

Examples of sustained attention and focusing
Self-correction strategies
Examples of reflective behavior
Examples of autonomous or self-management behavior
Examples of interesting working styles

These are only a few examples of the range of strategies and understandings that can be made visible through anecdotal observations. More possibilities will become apparent as you learn more about specific curricular content (Chapter 7) and about how to implement a variety of activities and experiences in thematic units (Chapters 7 and 8).

Some teachers write down their observations on index cards. We like Post-it notes because later the teacher can easily transfer these notes to a separate page for each child (that can, in turn, be placed in the child's learning portfolio—see Chapter 9). These sheets can then be easily copied to share with parents, who enjoy reading these "snapshots" of their child in the classroom.

The following guidelines are important to keep in mind while writing anecdotal observations:

Include the child's name (underlined), date, and perhaps where the child was observed, if relevant.
Try to confine one piece of anecdotal information to one Post-it page.
Try to confine information to *one* child's reactions or responses. If other children are involved, write additional notes for the other participants.
Confine comments to what is being observed that particular day; don't refer to behavior on previous days.
Include a description of problem-solving processes.

Teachers who are just beginning to write anecdotal observations sometimes find the last point the most difficult. However, it is critical that these notes include *how* a child accomplishes a task, rather than recording *that* a child has done something. Figure 6.20 contrasts notes that provide helpful information than those that do not. As these examples illustrate, the more helpful, informative notes capture the process and strategies that children actually employed, not just a statement that something occurred or that a task was accomplished.

Describing the *process* of what the child is doing is emphasized.

In the target-child(ren) scheme, teachers have to avoid interacting with children to concentrate on the ten-minute observations. In roving anecdotal observation, however, teachers move about the room to visit children as they engage in individual and small group activities during integrated work time. The advantage of this type of observation, therefore, is that teachers can easily interact with children while they are observing. Thus, if teachers ask a question or make a comment about children's behavior or activities, they are able to document the responses to suggestions or input. Children can also be encouraged to contribute their own observation notes when they think they have done something interesting that may have been missed by the teacher.

Miscellaneous Observation Ideas

Teachers can modify the ideas that we have discussed to come up with their own kid-watching systems of observation. For example, they can develop schemes for particular purposes, and they can come up with checklists of various kinds. By using the same list several times over the year, teachers can document children's progress toward certain goals. Teachers can also construct checklists for certain types of activities that occur during the ongoing flow of the classroom. Checklists are timesavers and can

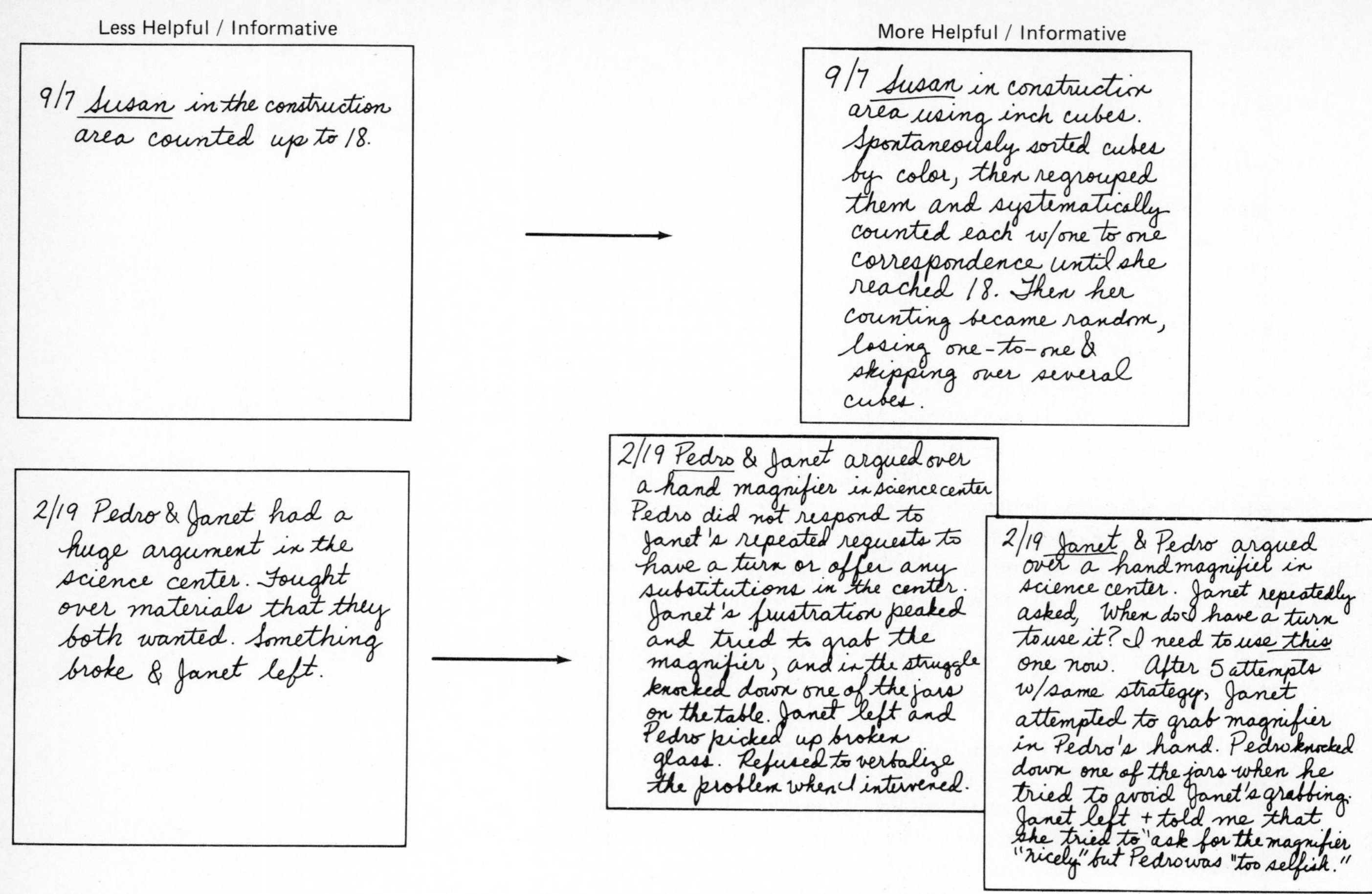

Less Helpful / Informative
More Helpful / Informative
9/7 Susan in the construction area counted up to 18.
9/7 Susan in construction area using inch cubes. Spontaneously sorted cubes by color, then regrouped them and systematically counted each w/one to one correspondence until she reached 18. Then her counting became random, losing one-to-one & skipping over several cubes.
2/19 Pedro & Janet had a huge argument in the science center. Fought over materials that they both wanted. Something broke & Janet left.
2/19 Pedro & Janet argued over a hand magnifier in science center. Pedro did not respond to Janet's repeated requests to have a turn or offer any substitutions in the center. Janet's frustration peaked and tried to grab the magnifier, and in the struggle knocked down one of the jars on the table. Janet left and Pedro picked up broken glass. Refused to verbalize the problem when I intervened.
2/19 Janet & Pedro argued over a hand magnifier in science center. Janet repeatedly asked, When do I have a turn to use it? I need to use this one now. After 5 attempts w/same strategy, Janet attempted to grab magnifier in Pedro's hand. Pedro knocked down one of the jars when he tried to avoid Janet's grabbing. Janet left + told me that she tried to "ask for the magnifier "nicely" but Pedro was "too selfish."

Figure 6.20

provide useful information, but they cannot provide an adequate picture of progress unless they are complemented by more detailed observations, such as those described in the preceding sections in this chapter.

Almy & Genishi (1979)

Vignettes are also useful for assessing progress. A vignette is an account of a particularly meaningful event of a child's classroom life. Vignettes represent a significant milestone or "aha" phenomenon for a certain child. They are similar to anecdotal observations, but, perhaps relying on these observations, are more detailed and are usually written up later by the teacher. Many teachers like to include at least one vignette per thematic unit or per grading period to share with parents and to become part of the child's learning portfolio (see Chapter 9).

Specific observation sheets for specific centers or activities can be created. For example, a teacher may have some snails in the classroom for children to study as part of a thematic unit. A special observation sheet can be quickly drawn up to capture what is going on at that center and to document the kinds of hypotheses children are generating, the language they use to talk about what they see, and so forth. Figure 6.21 illustrates what such an observation form might be like. Using this form (a clean copy for each day), the teacher tries to observe daily what is happening at the snail study center. In the first few days of the study, most of the teacher's notes probably center on questions 1 to 5, but as children's questions become better articulated, observations for questions 6 to 8 are filled in. By reviewing these forms during the course of the study, the teacher is able to document who was involved, the process by which children found their answers, what they produced as the result of their study, how they relied on one another and written resources to support their inquiries, and the like.

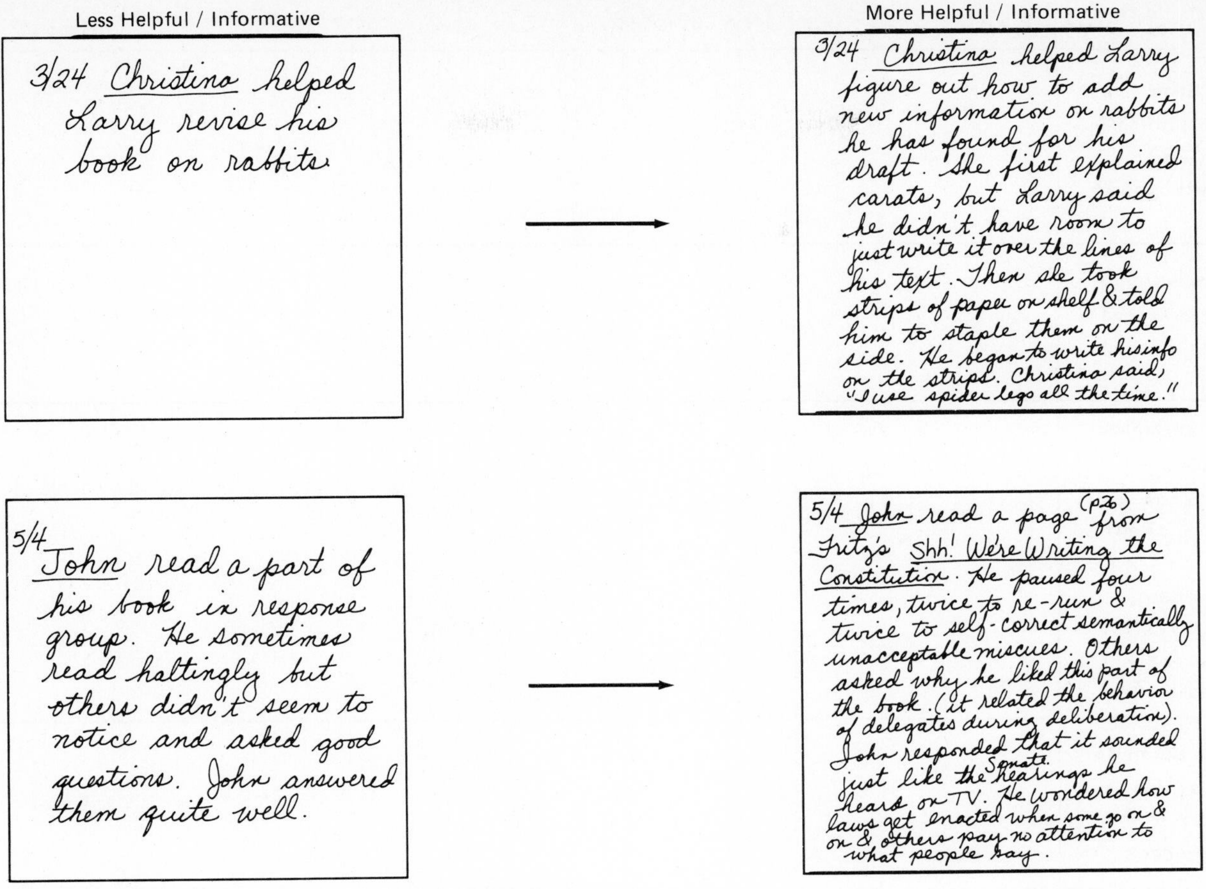

Less Helpful / Informative
More Helpful / Informative
3/24 Christina helped Larry revise his book on rabbits.
3/24 Christina helped Larry figure out how to add new information on rabbits he has found for his draft. She first explained carats, but Larry said he didn't have room to just write it over the lines of his text. Then she took strips of paper on shelf & told him to staple them on the side. He began to write his info on the strips. Christina said, "I use spider legs all the time."
5/4 John read a part of his book in response group. He sometimes read haltingly but others didn't seem to notice and asked good questions. John answered them quite well.
5/4 John read a page (p26) from Fritz's Shh! We're Writing the Constitution. He paused four times, twice to re-run & twice to self-correct semantically unacceptable miscues. Others asked why he liked this part of the book. (It related the behavior of delegates during deliberation). John responded that it sounded just like the Senate hearings he heard on TV. He wondered how laws get enacted when some go on & on & others pay no attention to what people say.

Figure 6.20 (continued)

CONCLUSIONS

Evaluation in context

We want children continuously to encounter novel and interesting problems. We want to encourage them to hypothesize and seek comprehension of their problems on the basis of what they presently know. We want them to use their interactions with others in the classroom community as sources for learning. Consequently, we need kid-watching techniques that are in-process assessments that let us evaluate what children are understanding about content as they are actually experiencing it. The kid-watching schemes presented in this chapter do this: The first set of procedures focused on ways to examine children's strategies in a range of literacy assessments, and the last set provided more general schemes to capture the content and process of their ongoing experiences occurring in individual and small group activities or projects.

The approaches described here are not an exhaustive list but are offered as ways to learn how to become a kid-watcher, to learn how to acquire (and internalize) new ways of observing children's strategies as they go about using language and developing concepts or constructing their knowledge. In subsequent chapters, we go into various curriculum content in more detail. These chapters include examples of ways to integrate the disciplines into thematic units (Chapter 7), and they cover a variety of experiences and activities for implementing an integrated language theory into practice (Chapter 8). Thus, other kid-watching procedures and ideas emerge. Other issues related to kid-watching and evaluation are addressed in Chapter 9.

Snail Study Center	Children involved: Date:
① What are some of the hypotheses (or questions) Cs construct about snails?	
② What conclusions (or answers) about the snails do Cs come to?	
③ What are examples of Cs' using their "own language" to find out about snails? ④ How does their language reflect their own feelings about snails?	
⑤ What are examples of joint action + cooperation in the learning process?	
⑥ How did books support Cs inquiries on snails?	
⑦ What writing resulted regarding Cs' study of snails?	
⑧ What other activities resulted from snails study (e.g. drawing, math, constructing, etc.)	

Figure 6.21

REFERENCES

Almy, M., & Genishi, C. (1979). *Ways of studying children.* New York: Teachers College Press.

Atwell, N. (1987). *In the middle: Writing, reading, and learning with adolescents.* Portsmouth, NH: Boynton/Cook.

Calkins, L. M. (1986). *The art of teaching writing.* Portsmouth, NH: Heinemann.

Cazden, C. B. (1988). *Classroom discourse: The learning of teaching and learning.* Portsmouth, NH: Heinemann.

Clay, M. (1972). *Sand—The concepts about print test.* Portsmouth, NH: Heinemann.

Clay, M. (1979a). *The early detection of reading difficulties: A diagnostic survey with recovery procedures.* Portsmouth, NH: Heinemann.

Clay, M. (1979b). *Stones—The concepts about print test.* Portsmouth, NH: Heinemann.

Dyson, A. H. (1987). Individual differences in beginning composing: An orchestral vision of learning to write. *Written Communication, 4,* 411–442.

Genishi, C., & Dyson, D. H. (1984). *Language assessment in the early years.* Norwood, NJ: Ablex.

Goodman, K. S. (1973). Miscues: Windows on the reading process. In K. S. Goodman (Ed.), *Miscue analysis: Applications to reading instruction* (pp. 3–14). Urbana, IL: ERIC Clearinghouse on Reading and Communication Skills.

Goodman, K. S., Goodman, Y. M., & Hood, W. J. (1989). *The whole language evaluation book.* Portsmouth, NH: Heinemann.

Goodman, Y. M., Watson, D. J., & Burke, C. L. (1987). *Reading miscue inventory: Alternative procedures.* New York: Richard C. Owen Publishers.

Graves, D. (1983). *Writing: Teachers and children at work.* Portsmouth, NH: Heinemann.

Heath, S. B. (1983). *Ways with words: Language, life, and work in communities and classrooms.* Cambridge: Cambridge University Press.

Henderson, E. H., & Beers, J. W. (Eds.) (1980). *Developmental and cognitive aspects of learning to tell.* Newark, DE: International Reading Association.

Holdaway, D. (1979). *The foundations of literacy.* Sydney, Australia: Ashton Scholastic.

Johnston, P. (1987a). Teachers as evaluation experts. *The Reading Teacher, 40,* 744–748.

Johnston, P. (1987b). Assessing the process, and the process of assessment, in the language arts. In J. R. Squire (Ed.), *The dynamics of language learning: Research in reading and English* (pp. 335–357). Urbana, IL: ERIC Clearinghouse on Reading and Communication Skills.

Lindfors, J. W. (1987). *Children's language and learning.* Englewood Cliffs, NJ: Prentice-Hall.

McKenzie, M. (1977). The beginnings of literacy. *Theory Into Practice, 16,* 315–324.

Michaels, S. (1981). "Sharing time": Children's narrative styles and differential access to literacy. *Language in Society, 10,* 423–442.

Pappas, C. C., & Brown, E. (1989). Using turns at story "reading" as scaffolding for learning. *Theory Into Practice, 28,* 105–113.

Sylva, K., Roy, C., & Painter, M. (1980). *Childwatching at playgroup and nursery school.* Ypsilanti, MI: The High/Scope Press.

Temple, C., Nathan, R., Burris, N., & Temple, F. (1988). *The beginnings of writing.* Boston: Allyn and Bacon.

Turbill, J. (1983). *Now, we want to write!* Rozelle, Australia: Primary English Teaching Association.

Wexler-Sherman, C., Gardner, H., & Feldman, D. H. (1988). A pluralistic view of early assessment: The project spectrum approach. *Theory Into Practice, 27,* 77–83.

CHILDREN'S LITERATURE

FARMER BOY by L. I. Wilder. Illustrated by G. Williams. Harper, 1953.

OUR GARAGE SALE by A. Rockwell. Illustrated by H. Rockwell. Greenwillow, 1984.

7

More Ideas to Integrate Curricular Areas

Two major characteristics of the integrated language perspective are the use of oral and written language across the curriculum and the integration of the various curricular areas. Chapters 3 and 4 explain how this integration is accomplished through thematic units. This chapter provides more specific details and ideas to help teachers integrate language and content in five curricular areas: social studies, science, mathematics, art, and music. In each curricular area, there are two major emphases. First, a brief overview of current views, principles, and concepts in the particular curricular area or discipline is presented. Second, more ideas or suggestions for ways to integrate language within that particular area (and across other curricular areas) are provided.

SOCIAL STUDIES

What Is Social Studies?

See also Barr, Barth, & Shermis (1977) for a discussion of the implications of differing definitions of social studies.

Ellis (1986)

Social studies connects children to the world.

Gamberg, Kwak, Hutchings, & Altheim (1988)

Social studies is an integration of content, concepts, and generalizations from several disciplines.

We see social studies as the integration of the processes of learning about people as they arrange to live together in groups, and the content of history and the social sciences as they relate to these human activities. How children learn and what they learn are both fundamental parts of social studies. In the social studies, children learn to recognize and evaluate social data, build causal theories, draw conclusions, and make generalizations about human behavior. This means that the basic subject matter and constant focus of the social studies is people. Social studies connects children to the world, whether by studying family history, looking at the influences of the Nile River on Egyptian society and how Egyptians have attempted to control those influences, or by studying the economic, social, and political impact of urbanization in a Third World nation. In our perspective, social studies is often the core of what children do in an integrated curriculum, for it provides powerful themes for study and offers opportunities for children to see themselves as responsible, reflective citizens of a number of human communities. Social studies, along with science, is also one of the most powerful contexts within which children use all the forms of language we have discussed in previous chapters.

Like science, social studies is not a single discipline but an integration of content, concepts, and generalizations from a number of disciplines. Social studies generally draws on history, geography, anthropology, sociology, political science, and psychology. The intent in combining these disciplines is to encourage children to see the way in which these forces combine to influence human activity. Figure 7.1 shows the way content from several disciplines can pose different questions to be used in exploring a single theme.

Maxim (1987)

The integrated nature of social studies, however, makes it a bit more complicated to define than science. Part of the problem in defining social studies as a field has to do with the multiple perspectives or purposes that can be attributed to this curricular area. Do we include this area in the curriculum to educate "good" citizens, or to educate students in the structures of the various disciplines? Do we propose to educate students as reflective inquirers, or do we challenge them to grapple with the "closed"—or controversial—aspects of our society?

Barr, Barth, & Shermis (1977); Stodolsky (1988)

In addition to these obviously sensitive questions, social studies is frequently the part of the curriculum assigned the task of dealing with such issues as race, class, gender, and ethnicity. One can see why this very exciting area of study can be intimidating to a teacher who must also deal with all the other areas of the elementary curriculum. It also explains, at least in part, why social studies is too often reduced to its least interesting and least controversial aspects. In too many classrooms, social studies is little more than perfunctory studies of such topics as "community helpers" or "transportation," without any real attention to the human consequences of social studies content. (See also 1989 NCSS Position Statement, "Social Studies for Early Childhood and Elementary School Children Preparing for the 21st Century: A Report from NCSS Task Force on Early Childhood/Elementary Social Studies," for further discussion of this issue.) In the context of an integrated curriculum, however, social studies is defined in particular ways and gains an importance that it often lacks in the traditional classroom.

NCSS Position Statement (1989)

Building the Social Studies Context

Linking Process and Content. As we have already mentioned, social studies involves integrating the *processes* of learning about history and the social sciences, with content drawn from each of these domains. This is a crucial idea in understanding the

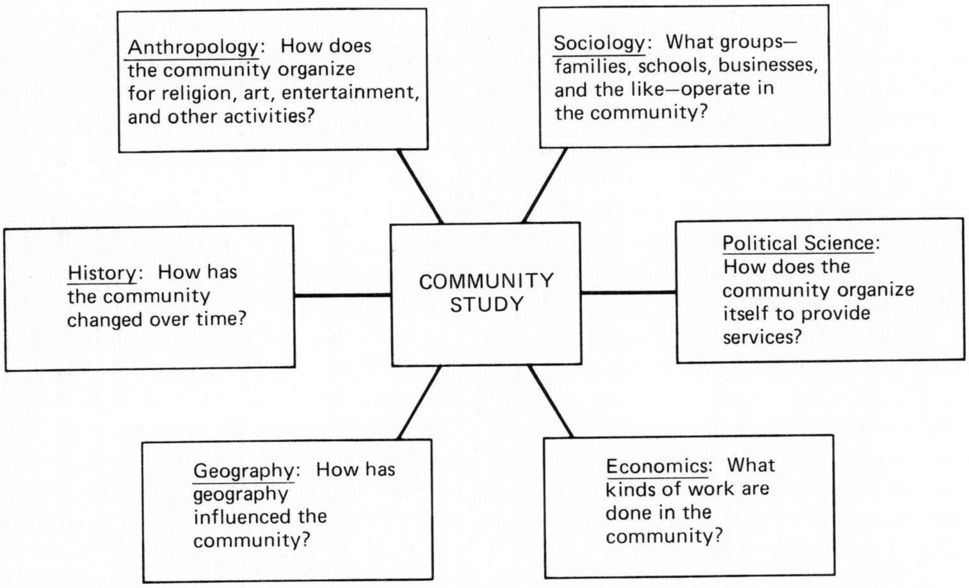

Figure 7.1

place of social studies in an integrated curriculum. If developing understanding is domain-specific, as we have already suggested, then students need plenty of opportunity to study the content of a particular domain. But they also need to learn *how* knowledge is acquired in that domain. The way knowledge is constructed in a domain such as history, for instance, is quite different from the way in which scientists understand chemistry. A scientist can observe the way in which hydrogen combines with oxygen to produce water and can generate laws based on this observation. A historian can never observe the phenomena under investigation. Instead, history is constructed from the partial residue of the past. The historian constructs a plausible explanation of how that residue fits into the past but cannot construct laws to explain this phenomenon. History is particularistic and resists our attempts to construct a full account of the past. These are very different ways of thinking about evidence, hypotheses and proofs. For children to develop understanding in these different domains, they need to understand these differences, too. In social studies, this means that children need experience in using and interpreting various kinds of social data from the domains that constitute the social studies. Yet, process alone is not social studies. No matter what processes are used, there is always a subject of study—the substance or content under investigation. And not all subjects are equally worthy of study. Given the limited amount of time and the almost infinite variety of topics that can be studied in any school year, part of the teacher's obligation is making sure that the topics studied are worth the time spent.

Downey & Levstik (1988); Levstik & Pappas (1987); Wilson & Wineberg (1988); Wineberg & Wilson (in press)

"Knowing" in a domain is more than remembering discrete "facts."

History is interpretation based on the residue of the past.

Gamberg, Kwak, Hutchings, & Altheim (1988)

A month spent investigating Valentine's Day, for instance, may not seem worthwhile in terms of content, despite some possibilities for helping children learn to use the processes of gathering and analyzing data or communicating findings. On the other hand, consider the possibilities from both process and content perspectives when second grade children study a problem in their community.

No More Litter

Harlan Elementary School, Harlan, KY (1986)

Children study an authentic problem.

Children in a mountainous rural district were engaged in a thematic unit centered on their community (see Figure 7.1 for some of the content involved in this unit). After taking a tour of the community, they began discussing a real problem in their area: illegal dumping of trash and garbage. They thought that something ought to be done about the garbage that littered their hillsides, but they were not sure what that could be or if children could make any difference in any case. Their teacher suggested that they investigate, and collect data to help them decide if there was anything that could be done about the problem. She then arranged a series of field trips to garbage collection sites: illegal dumps, the county landfill, and a recycling center. The children planned interview questions and wrote these collectively. They recorded their observations and interviews and then set about analyzing their data. Their teacher encouraged them to express their findings in a variety of ways. Soon the classroom was full of captioned artwork detailing what had been found. Some children made a mural showing how the plants and animals might feel about all the garbage. The trees and birds—even the sun—commented on how awful the litter was. Only germs, maggots, and rats had good things to say about the garbage. The children had been researching in informational books, and they shared their findings about the relation of germs, maggots, and rats to garbage.

Children record their observations.

Next, the class decided to begin a recycling campaign. Their trip to the recycling center had convinced them that this would have several benefits. Not only would it clean up the environment; they could also earn money to pay for the videotapes they were using. The second grade sponsored a can-collecting contest in the school, and they soon were recycling huge amounts of aluminum cans. They also began writing a play about a community where it was illegal *not* to litter. They made up songs and dialogue and constructed props as a way to convince the rest of their school to participate in an anti-litter campaign.

Children participate in alleviating a problem.

The next step was to visit their local government representatives to find out what was being done about the litter problems. They discovered that their county had begun an adopt-a-spot campaign to encourage a sense of responsibility and ownership about the environment. The class decided to adopt their school yard and to educate others in the community about their responsibility to the environment. Before long, the children had edited their tapes, selected artwork and writing, as well as musical background, and produced a videotape called "No More Litter." The tape was used at parent-teacher meetings, and it encouraged adults to join the adopt-a-spot program.

Consider what these children accomplished in terms of the goals of social studies:

Accomplishing the goals of social studies

1. The topic had power and reality for them. It dealt with how people lived together and managed their environment (geography, sociology, and economics).
2. The unit allowed the children to find ways in which they could be part of alleviating a real problem in their community (citizenship, political science).
3. They learned something about the community services available to help people take care of such basic problems as the disposal of garbage and the recycling of wastes (economics, political science, sociology).
4. They discovered that there were elected officials who shared their concerns and were willing to work with the community to solve problems (political science).
5. They learned what resources could be used to investigate a problem and how to effectively communicate their findings to other people (reflective inquiry).

At the end of this unit, children had a sense of efficacy rather than defeat. They had discovered a powerful motivation for using their writing and reading skills, and as a result, they improved the very skills that had caused them problems in their previous schooling. Finally, this thematic unit broke down the walls between school and the world surrounding the school.

Little of this would have happened if the children had not had time to study in depth and then to reflect on what they had learned, ask new questions, and select ways to respond to their findings.

Depth. For children (and adults) to come to understand a particular cognitive domain, they need enough time to study in such depth that they begin to build theories about how knowledge in a particular domain is used. They need to see how particular *information* fits in the larger context of a knowledge domain. How is information used in geography, for instance? How does one piece of information—the location of a mountain range—relate to another—a low density of population? What can one understand about people by knowing this information—by developing understanding in this domain? Providing context means providing an *opportunity to study something in depth,* as the second grade children studied the problem of litter in their community. There are two parts to the concept of depth. The first is the idea of *extensiveness.* In other words, a topic is rich enough to generate subtopics, activities, and interest. The second part, *study,* is equally important in that it encourages the kind of thinking that relates to theory-building in a domain. As a result, social studies is not just the accumulation of information in a particular content area. Rather, it is a way of asking questions about a subject and a way of answering and understanding the answers. This usually means that some incongruity or anomaly must strike children as they encounter the social studies. Read the following account of a classroom, and think about how the teacher uses incongruity to involve children in thinking about interpretation in the social studies.

Carey (1985a, 1985b); Keil (1984)

Context can facilitate depth.

Hyde & Bizar (1989)

Social studies is a way of asking and answering questions.

Immigrant Children

Using incongruity

As part of a thematic unit on MIGRATIONS, Mr. Kowalsky brought a selection of books on U.S. immigration into his fifth grade classroom. He hoped to generate interest in a recurrent theme in American history and a current topic of debate in the surrounding community. He brought one of his favorite books, *Immigrant Children* by Russell

Freedman (1980)

Freedman, to share orally. As he read to the class, he pointed out the photographs illustrating the text. One picture of a child bathing in a metal sink generated a good deal of discussion; children noted how difficult it would be to keep clean and how little privacy families would have had in the tenement pictured. Some days later, as Mr. Kowalsky shared *Watch the Stars Come Out* by Rikki Levinson, one of the children called attention to Diane Goode's illustration of a child bathing in a metal sink in a New York tenement—clearly based on the photograph they had seen earlier. The children were amazed at the difference between Goode's soft pastel treatment of the same scene that the photographer had captured in all its squalor. At this point, Mr. Kowalsky saw an opportunity to help children look at the interpretive nature of historical reporting. He gathered other examples of authors and illustrators treating issues of immigration in varying ways. For instance, he brought to the classroom Milton Meltzer's *In Their Own Words,* a compilation of the memories of Black slaves, and Belinda Hurmence's *A Girl Called BOY,* historical fiction based on slave narratives. He also located copies of the slave narratives preserved at his State Historical Society, so that a group of students could study the source material for Meltzer's nonfiction and Hurmence's fiction. He located collections of pictures of the ethnic and poor neighborhoods of Manhattan that were taken by Jacob Riis at the turn of the century and published in *How the Other Half Lives.*

Levinson (1987)

Looking at history as interpretation

Meltzer (1964)
Hurmence (1982)

Teachers gather resources.

Riis (1971)

Children share findings.

Students also located reference material in the school and public library and in their textbooks and set to work analyzing the varying interpretations in the sources they had collected. One group developed charts to show such things as the following:

Children chart results.

The sources for information used by authors and illustrators.
The ways in which illustrations were used to help interpret information.
The types of interpretations authors used.
Specific information selected for inclusion or omission.

Soon, these fifth graders were developing criteria for evaluating informational books and historical fiction (see Figure 7.2).

Children create their own texts.

The children went on to create their own informational books and historical fiction based on their studies and the criteria they had developed. One of the texts they wrote was entitled *How to Read History.* As a result of their study, these children had learned a great deal about the interpretive nature of history, as follows:

1. They were engaged in comparing and contrasting interpretations that would help them to understand the history of immigration but that would also serve them well when they studied other history and read historical literature.

Criteria	Biography	History	Historical Fiction
Conversation	Not invented.	Must have evidence.	Invent only for fictional characters.
Order of events	Can't change—if it's true.	Definitely can't change.	Only for made-up events.
Invented actions	Not for real people.	Never. Infer with support.	Yes, as long as it doesn't change history.
Invented people	No. Maybe disguise identity of real people.	No. Must be based on evidence.	Yes. Put invented people in real situations.

Figure 7.2

2. They learned to look for certain types of errors, bias, and misinterpretation—an important part of understanding history and the social sciences.
3. They learned some of the ways in which historical information can be "mythologized" and misunderstood.

Avoiding Social Studies Mythologies

Helping children see the ways in which history and the social sciences use social data and the kinds of problems that can arise in these domains is an important way to help children recognize mythologized information. Unfortunately, the tendency to simplify complex subject matter for children has often resulted in a social studies curriculum that is little more than an accumulation of myths and misunderstandings. Children learn little more about such a complex figure as Abraham Lincoln than that he freed the slaves (not only the slaves in the rebelling states), split rails as a boy, and grew to be a very tall man in a stovepipe hat. As with so many other national figures, Lincoln is lost as a person. One of the purposes of social studies in an integrated curriculum is recapturing the humanity of such people, which is not a matter of presenting children with historical "dirty linen." Rather, it is an attempt to connect children with real people so that they can better understand the nature of their nation's and the world's past, present, and possible future. Few people are entirely heroic or completely unassailed by doubts—whether they are children or famous adults. Social studies can provide a context in which to look at the decisions both good and bad that people have made, and to see how they responded to the challenges life offered them.

Freeman & Levstik (1988)

Oversimplification leads to misunderstanding.

Egan (1979)

Connect children with real people.

Provide a context for studying human decision-making.

One of the most popular units in Mrs. Mott's third grade class is MEETING CHALLENGES. Mrs. Mott and her third graders interview people in the community selected by the students as people who meet challenges in a variety of ways. Firefighters and police officers talk about the challenges of their jobs; news reporters talk about the challenges of accurately reporting the news; people who have met physical challenges come and work with the children. In addition, Mrs. Mott sets up a History Roundtable in which children learn about figures from the past, with an emphasis on the challenges they met (e.g., Should Mr. Lincoln abolish slavery? Should Washington be king?). Children come to the Roundtable in character, prepared to talk to each other and to classmates about how they might respond to these historical challenges. They use a variety of literature as background material and often end by asking very interesting questions. One boy, for instance, found George Washington most admirable. But, he wondered, why had Washington continued to own slaves? The class discussed the possibility of a person being heroic in some ways but not in others. Could such a person still be a hero, they debated, and they concluded that most people probably were not heroic all the time.

Encourage children to see history as the story of people meeting challenges.

These children chose their heroes and heroines not because they were presented with myths but because they were beginning to understand the strengths and weaknesses of the people they admired. Aside from this being a more accurate view of history as well as of human nature, it also means that children can better imagine themselves meeting challenges and overcoming weaknesses.

Encourage children to see themselves as able to meet challenges.

Exploring the Border Areas of Human Behavior

Social studies is not only concerned with others. It is also the part of the curriculum that helps children understand themselves as members of a number of human communities. It should provide a safe context for the exploration of the areas of human experience that are important concerns of children of elementary age. Particularly for older children, this involves an exploration of the border areas of human experience. The border areas can best be characterized as the "unwished-for worst" and the "hoped-for best" of which humans are capable. In a study of sixth graders involved in a literature-based introduction to history (which included a study of historical fiction, biography, autobiography, and informational pieces on historical topics), Levstik found that

Hardy (1978)

Levstik (1986, 1989)

students reported being moved, inspired, and sometimes angered by what they read, and they frequently added that they had learned something they labeled "the truth." The frequency with which children described their need to know about various topics in history was remarkable. Reading appeared to allow them to test themselves and their own potential for good or evil against characters in literature. They willingly read challenging books and vigorously participated in discussions. In their discussions, they compared literary characters in historical fiction with themselves and with choices they might have made under similar circumstances. As one child said, "I loved this book because it sees through the eyes of this person. I never knew how hard people had it. This book is so real."

Children express a need to know about the past.

Social studies in the integrated curriculum should make people in other times, places, and circumstances real to children. It should present people as complex beings who share many of the students' hopes and fears, and it should provide opportunities for children to discuss and debate as well as to research human behavior.

Provide for discussion and debate.

Richter (1987)
Greene (1973)
Reiss (1972)
Yolen (1988)

Sixth graders reading Holocaust literature, for instance, can be exposed to Richter's *Friedrich* and Greene's *The Summer of My German Soldier* as well as to Reiss' *The Upstairs Room,* and Yolen's *The Devil's Arithmetic.* They then meet in small groups to share what they have been reading and to discuss their personal responses as well as their analyses of the books as literature and as history. How does their understanding of the Holocaust and of Germans change as they read each of these books? What is the nature of prejudice in each of these contexts? Students need opportunities to express their responses through writing and artwork, investigations of primary and secondary sources, and interviews and field trips.

Provide opportunities to express responses in many ways.

Again, depth is necessary to provide adequate background for understanding and to guard against the myths that too easily arise when a subject is presented in too cursory a fashion.

Attending to the Language of Social Studies

Hyde & Bizar (1989)

All the examples of social studies describe language use in the content areas that constitute the social studies. A teacher in an integrated language classroom seeks ways to use language across the curriculum, but that means attending to the uses of language peculiar to many knowledge domains. What is the language of geography, for instance? How are symbol systems used on maps and globes to transmit geographic information and a sense of place? What do place names tell us about human geography?

A short activity using one symbol system—maps—may point out the way language shows the interconnectedness of our world. You need only a map of your state. Any state will do, actually. Lay the map out, and begin to look for names borrowed from other places. In one small section of central Kentucky, for example, you can locate Paris and Versailles. Ohio has Lima and Cadiz and Schoenbrun. Where in the world did the place names in your state come from? What parts of the world predominate? Are there also names borrowed from Native Americans? You may want to try this with a map of Australia. What could account for this geographic phenomenon?

Part of the teacher's job is to help children learn to use the vocabulary of history and the social sciences intelligently. This means that there should be opportunities for children to express what they are learning in charts, graphs, and maps and in informational genres. They should have experience taking surveys and talking about the limitations of survey methods. (Did the survey really ask the right questions? Who answered the survey? Are they representative?) When children use the data sources common to each of these fields in their investigations, they can use these sources as models for communicating the results of their own studies. Children studying immigration produce maps of migration patterns and create bar graphs comparing immigration from and to different parts of the world. They may collect historic photographs from their own community and create a history of local immigration that includes a table of contents and bibliography. In other words, they use the language of historians and social scientists to talk about these domains of knowledge.

Teacher as Learner

With seven areas (history, geography, anthropology, sociology, political science, economics, and psychology) to consider, the elementary teacher may not have a great deal of background in any single field related to social studies. Although this is often seen as a disincentive for teaching social studies, it is also an opportunity to try a role other than that of dispenser of information. Traditionally, many elementary teachers rely on the textbook to delineate the curriculum and to form the boundaries of knowledge. The teacher's role in that case is to help children acquire the information that is within those boundaries. The teacher and the children share the same source of information, and the teacher has the "answers" at least insofar as the text and teacher's guide provide them. However, an integrated approach to the curriculum proposes a different way of looking at the teacher's role. There is no way a teacher can know everything there is to know about the topics that can come up in the course of a thematic unit. As a result, the teacher expects to study the topics with the children and assumes the role of fellow learner. The teacher is a more sophisticated learner and probably has more background knowledge to bring to bear in trying to understand a new area, but the task is a joint endeavor by students and teacher. This dramatically alters the teacher's stance, as the following examples demonstrate. Think about a teacher as one who engages in the following four activities.

Teachers are both decision-makers and fellow learners.

1. Arranges opportunities for children to think critically about the content of social studies. Observe how this fourth grade teacher leads children to clarify their understanding of the geographic concept of "desert" through a Sketch to Stretch* exercise.

Fourth graders studying about the desert begin by drawing what they imagine a desert to look like. Most of the children include sand (yellow), snakes, lizards, and cactus. One child draws a tent strung between two saguaro cactus plants and surrounded by people in turbans and long robes. After the class discusses what features they think most deserts have in common and list some of the places where they are not sure of their information, the teacher records the results on chart paper as a Semantic Map* (see Figure 7.3). She also asks that they save their pictures until the end of the investigation.

During the next class session, a guest from Yemen shares slides of the deserts and other features of Yemen. The children are surprised by pictures of corrugated tin houses surrounded by a brown, stony, and arid landscape. They have many questions to ask, and later they add to and amend their semantic map considerably (see Figure 7.4).

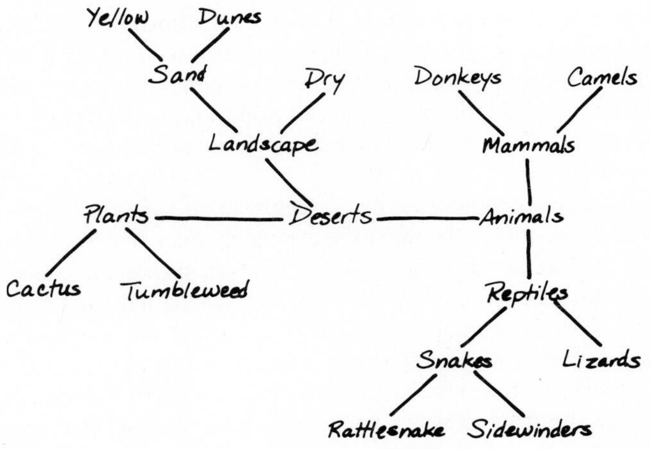

Figure 7.3

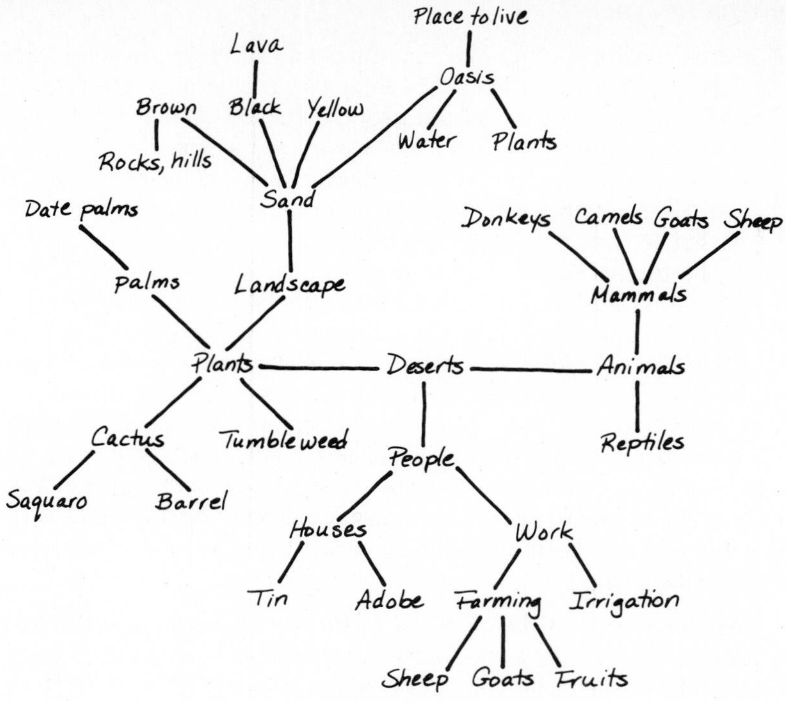

Figure 7.4

Teachers learn to elicit student questions.

The teacher has a short filmstrip that shows the high tableland in the desert sections of Arizona and Nevada. The children express surprise at the difference between the black hills of Nevada and the red landscape of Arizona. As they add more information to their semantic map, they become involved in a debate about whether saguaro cactus grow in all deserts. The teacher asks them to work in groups to construct questions that still need to be asked about deserts. She suggests that they think about the pictures they drew on the first day of their discussion. What questions would help them to make their pictures more accurate?

After the small groups have developed their questions, the teacher leads a debriefing session, during which the children share their work and begin to organize the questions they have and to consider the sources they can use to find answers.

Teachers learn to arrange for incongruities.

2. Provides challenges to assumptions. Most of us prefer to let our assumptions go unchallenged, and we work hard to fit new information into old schemas. For children to enrich their schemas relative to social studies, some entrenched ideas must be challenged and other possibilities presented. The teacher must find out what children know about a topic and what assumptions, or schema, they already have in place. The teacher in the foregoing example did this by asking children to draw their ideas of a desert. The teacher's next task is to deal with the anomalies, or incongruities, things that do not fit with the children's existing schema.

A fifth grade teacher found that his students were sure that the work of men on the frontier was much more strenuous and difficult than that done by women. The teacher did not tell students that their information was inadequate. Instead, he brought in diary excerpts describing a day's work done by a young mother on the Oregon frontier. He also brought in several artifacts—kitchen implements necessary for meal preparation and reproductions of period clothing borrowed from a costume shop. These artifacts caused children to question their assumptions because it became clear that household work on the frontier was considerably more taxing than they had assumed.

Children learn to distinguish between observation and inference and between supported and unsupported claims.

3. Helps children formulate questions and generate opinions. As children confront discrepant events or anomalies and begin to think about problems and issues to explore, the teacher helps them to formulate their questions so that when it is time to communicate findings and draw meaning from their study, children will be able to make supported claims and to understand the claims made by others. One simple activity that helps older children distinguish between observing data and drawing inferences based on those data involves the concepts of "developed" and "underdeveloped" countries. The teacher introduces the terms and asks for student response in listing the characteristics, or properties, of each classification (thus establishing existing schema). Next, a series of eight to ten slides showing scenes in countries generally considered to be developed (e.g., United States, England, Germany, Soviet Union) and underdeveloped (e.g., Rwanda, Indonesia, Kampuchea, Yemen) are shown, but the slides contradict the stereotypes. Thus, a U.S. slide shows a poor rural area without electricity or indoor plumbing, and an Indonesian slide pictures a large, modern city, and so forth. Children are asked to quickly classify the scene in each picture as either developed or undeveloped. After they have done so, the slides are shown again and discussed so that the problems with these common terms are demonstrated and students are forced to think differently about how parts of the world are categorized.

4. Organizes resources for student inquiry. As topics are chosen for investigation, the teacher must also be prepared to search out multiple sources at a variety of levels for student use. This is not as daunting a task as it may seem at first. A number of organizations are anxious to help teachers provide good materials for social studies. The National Geographic Society, for instance, has launched an extensive program to improve the instruction of geography, including their National Geographic Kids Network Project from Technical Education Research Centers, Inc. State Councils On Economic Education and the American Bar Association provide materials, activities, and support for teachers who want to include more economic and law content in their social studies programs. Historical agencies provide suggested activities and materials for use in classrooms. Some colleges and universities have programs that link international students with area classrooms so that students can meet and talk with people from other cultures. The resources are there; teachers are the vital link between resources and students.

Links with colleges and universities can match classrooms with international students studying in the United States.

Obviously, no single book can suggest everything there is to do in a field as diverse as social studies. The activities suggested here are just to get you started in thinking about how to use a field such as social studies as the context for integrating across the curriculum.

SOCIAL STUDIES REFERENCES

Barr, R., Barth, J., & Shermis, S. S. (1977). *Defining the social studies.* Bulletin No. 51. Washington, DC: National Council for the Social Studies.

Carey, S. (1985a). *Conceptual change in childhood.* Cambridge: MIT Press.

Carey, S. (1985b). Are children fundamentally different kinds of thinkers and learners than adults? In S. B. Chipman, J. W. Segal, & R. Glaser (Eds.), *Thinking and learning skills: Research and open questions.* Vol. 2 (pp. 485–517). Hillsdale, NJ: Erlbaum.

Downey, M. T., & Levstik, L. S. (1988). Teaching and learning history: The research base. *Social Education, 52,* 336–342.

Egan, K. (1979). What children know best. *Social Education, 43* (2), 130–139.

Ellis, A. (1986). *Teaching and learning elementary social studies.* Boston: Allyn-Bacon.

Freeman, E., & Levstik, L. (1988). Recreating the past: Historical fiction in the social studies curriculum. *Elementary School Journal, 88* (4), 329–337.

Gamberg, R., Kwak, W., Hutchings, M., & Altheim, J. (1988). *Learning and loving it: Theme studies in the classroom.* Portsmouth, NH: Heinemann.

Hardy, B. (1978). Narrative as a primary act of mind. In M. Meek, A. Warlow, & G. Barton (Eds.), *The cool web: The patterns of children's reading.* New York: Atheneum.

Harlan Elementary School (1986). "No More Litter." Videotape made by Third Grade Class. Harlan, KY.

Hyde, A. A., & Bizar, M. (1989). *Thinking in context: Teaching cognitive processes across the elementary school curriculum.* White Plains, NY: Longman, 1989.

Keil, F. C. (1984). "Mechanisms of cognitive development and the structure of knowledge." In R. J. Sternberg (Ed.), *Mechanisms of cognitive development.* New York: Freeman.

Levstik, L. S. (1986). The relationship between historical response and narrative in a sixth-grade classroom. *Theory and Research in Social Education, 14,* 1–15.

Levstik, L. S. (1989). Historical narrative and the young reader. *Theory Into Practice, 28* (2), 114–119.

Levstik, L. S., & Pappas, C. C. (1987). Exploring the development of historical understanding. *Journal of Research and Development in Education, 21,* 1–15.

Maxim, G. W. (1987). *Social studies and the elementary school child (3rd ed.).* Columbus, OH: Merrill.

NCSS Position Statement (1989). "Social Studies for Early Childhood and Elementary School Children Preparing for the 21st Century: A Report from NCSS Task Force on Early Childhood/ Elementary Social Studies," *Social Education, 53* (1), 14–23.

Riis, J. (1971). *How the other half lives.* New York: Dover.

Stodolsky, S. S. (1988). *The subject matters.* Chicago: University of Chicago Press.

Wilson, S. M., & Wineberg, S. S. (1988). Peering at history through different lenses: The role of disciplinary perspectives in teaching history. *Teachers College Record, 89,* 525–539.

Wineberg, S. S., & Wilson, S. M. (in press). Subject matter knowledge in the teaching of history. In J. E. Brophy (Ed.), *Advances in research on teaching.* Greenwich, CT: JAI.

CHILDREN'S LITERATURE, SOCIAL STUDIES

THE DEVIL'S ARITHMETIC by J. Yolen. Viking Kestral, 1988.
FRIEDRICH by H. Richter. Penguin, 1987.
A GIRL NAMED BOY by B. Hurmence. Clarion, 1982.
IMMIGRANT KIDS by R. Freedman. Dutton, 1980.
IN THEIR OWN WORDS by M. Meltzer. Crowell, 1964.
THE SUMMER OF MY GERMAN SOLDIER by B. Greene. Dial, 1973.
THE UPSTAIRS ROOM by J. Reiss. Crowell, 1972.
WATCH THE STARS COME OUT by R. Levinson. Illustrated by D. Goode. Dutton, 1987.

SCIENCE

What Is Science?

Sagan (1978)
Science encompasses many domains.

Carin & Sund (1985); Kyle, Bonnstetter, Gadsden, & Shymansky (1988); Labinowicz (1980)

Sciencing implies active participation in investigations.

Carl Sagan suggests that human beings are predisposed by intellect, emotional makeup, and evolution to be interested in those things we label *science.* Science is a categorical label used to encompass such domains as biology, chemistry, physics, geology, and the like. Most significantly, science is a way of knowing. In fact, some people prefer to talk about "sciencing" rather than "science." Advocates of "sciencing" want to emphasize that science is more than a collection of facts and formulas. Science is a way of dealing with and ordering experience, usually by rigorous investigation of physical and biological phenomena. Because experience rarely arranges itself tidily into discrete disciplines, much of modern science crosses disciplinary boundaries. You are probably familiar with biochemistry as a cross-disciplinary category, but you may be less used to thinking about the "science" of social science—the search for the patterns and processes that influence the way in which people think and behave. Much of the preceding chapters' discussion of how children think and learn is drawn from scientific studies of such cross-disciplinary phenomena. Some of the newer science programs being designed for elementary schools recognize the intersection between fields of study. One of these, the Biological Sciences Curriculum Study (BSCS), explains its stance this way:

Bybee, Ellis, Muscella, & Robertson (1988)

Learning science includes making informed choices about health and technology.

> Children should learn about science, technology, and health as they need to understand and use them in their daily life and as future citizens. Education in the elementary years

should sustain the natural curiosity of children, allow exploration of their environments, improve explanations of phenomena in their world, develop understanding and use of technology, and contribute to informed choices in their personal and social lives.

Science as a Way of Knowing

Perhaps it will help to think about teaching and learning science as having four major elements.

Science as a way of thinking. Science offers a unique way of looking at the world and of asking questions, gathering and interpreting data, and explaining findings. Scientific thinking involves particular attitudes that include making judgments based on adequate data, striving to be rational and analytical, and maintaining a sense of wonder at the complexity and beauty of the universe. You have probably learned to call this process the *scientific method.*

Learning science involves maintaining a sense of wonder.

Components of sciencing

Science draws on and constructs the body of facts, principles, laws, and theories that attempt to explain physical, biological, and behavioral phenomena. This body of scientific knowledge forms the framework for understanding and thinking while engaged in the processes of science and is also the "product" of the sciencing process.

Science includes a technological component. Technology uses knowledge from science to accomplish tasks and to solve problems. Sometimes, too, technology creates new problems, and people are faced with moral and ethical dilemmas. Children as well as adults must learn to examine the benefits and risks of this aspect of sciencing and to understand the relationship between science, technology, health, and society.

Science involves a behavioral component. Science can help us to understand certain phenomena, but knowing is not always doing. We can know that certain foods are bad health risks, yet eat them anyway. Part of science education, then, is linking knowing and behaving. Thus, children learn to adopt and maintain healthy behaviors.

You may have noticed that there are some similarities between this definition for science and the previous definition of social studies. Both fields stress the integration of process and content, of a way of thinking about the world and of observing and making inferences about what we observe. Both emphasize the recognition of problems to study and possibly resolve. As we have already mentioned, there is "science" in the social sciences, and there are social issues in the sciences. There are also differences that make it useful to consider separately these two ways of thinking.

Hyde & Bizar (1989)

Science is essentially a search for explanatory laws and principles—something rarely possible in history and not always possible in the social sciences. Gravity operates according to laws that do not respond to changing social conditions, political upheavals, or economic trends. Little in social studies can be said to be subject to such laws. Science attempts to control social factors so that results can be generalized beyond a specific instance; history and the social sciences often seek to understand and explain specific instances. There are places where these two parts of the curriculum intersect—in ecology, for instance—but each also offers a particular way of knowing that can challenge children to think in increasingly more mature ways. Think about the difference in approach taken in the "No More Litter" example, which used a social studies theme, and the following example.

Science looks for generalizations; history studies the particular.

Water Cleanup

McShane (1988)

A sixth grade class in Iowa became concerned about pollution in their community's water supply. Their reading had led them to conclude that suds and phosphates were a contributing factor to the pollution of waterways. In class discussions, the children hypothesized that laundry detergents must be putting the suds into the streams and rivers. Several had seen evidence of suds at the water treatment plant, and others had observed overflowing washers and rinse water full of suds going into drains. They wanted to find out if there were some detergents that did not make so many suds.

Building hypotheses

Testing hypotheses

The enterprising teacher of this class arranged for the donation of a washing machine, and a parent set up a suds collector. The class then made arrangements with the school janitor to use white cotton cleaning cloths, all of equal size. Students decided that they would need to test the cleaning power of detergents as well as the suds production, especially if they later wanted to be able to convince others to use lower suds detergents. With this in mind, they decided that they would test a variety of stains: catsup, mustard, motor oil, salad dressing, lipstick, marker, ballpoint pen ink, tea, coffee, chocolate, soil, and blood.

Controlling variables

The next steps involved setting up procedures for testing and recording results. The students were most concerned about the importance of using scientific methods and procedures. They tried to keep their work accurate by maintaining the same brands for making stains and ensuring that the same amount of the staining substance was used in each trial. They set up a data sheet for recording each trial that included information about the water temperature, brand of detergent, type of stain, amount of suds in the wash and rinse cycles, and results of a litmus test.

Studying community impact

Interviews with a representative from the local sewage treatment plant helped students to understand some of the social and environmental problems that resulted from excessive sudsing and phosphates. Interviews with parents helped them to understand the consumer's dilemma when there is a choice between better cleaning power in a detergent and less pollutants in the public's water. Finally, the children shared their results with the community, letting others know how each of the detergents in their study had fared and how clean the low-suds detergents got laundry.

Meeting the goals of sciencing

Consider what these children accomplished in terms of the goals of sciencing:

1. Clearly, this topic had power for these children, as the litter study had for the younger children. It, too, dealt with how people managed their environment, especially in making decisions about the uses of technology versus protecting the environment (technology, ecology).
2. The methods used in designing the study, establishing hypotheses, gathering and analyzing data, and reporting results engaged children in learning and using the scientific method that is so essential to sciencing.
3. As part of their study, children drew on content from various sciences. They investigated the impact of suds and phosphates on water environments and on the humans who used the water (biology). The children studied the action of detergents as they interacted with water, stains, and cloth (chemistry). They also learned something about the machinery used to conduct the experiments (physics).
4. They learned that problems in science do not always have simple, clear-cut solutions. This is a point of intersection with social studies, where human interests conflict and problems are not easily resolved.

Seeing science as a feature of living

5. They learned that the process of solving one problem in science frequently raises other questions, so that sciencing is a continuous feature of living.

Making cross-curricular connections

Throughout this study, students had opportunities to use a variety of language. They wrote letters, set up their experiments, wrote descriptions of observations, and wrote reports of their data. They referred to other sources: library references, technical material from manufacturers, expert testimony. They cooperated with people in the community: the companies that donated goods and services, the parent who helped set up the suds gauging machine, and their peers. For eight weeks, these children conducted a rigorous, controlled study into a real problem in their community. This scientific investigation could also have been integrated into a larger study of the community or of ecology, or it could spur a series of investigations looking at water purity historically, culturally, and scientifically.

Depth. As you have probably gathered by now, understanding in a cognitive domain requires depth. The children investigating detergent pollution spent eight weeks on their study. Their teacher knew that such a study would require enough time to really think about the investigation, plan carefully, and conduct accurate tests. At the end of eight weeks, the children knew a great deal more than which low-suds detergent was the most effective cleaning agent. It might have been possible to give them that information based on EPA tests. What they had learned, however, was how to "know" in science. They were building the scaffolding that would support future learning in science and that would also help them to evaluate other scientific claims. Imagine, for instance, that these children were watching a commercial for a detergent that got clothes "whiter than white." What problems might they have with such claims? What questions might they have about supporting evidence? How might they understand such issues of water quality as the salt content in rivers and streams? They are likely to think very differently about these issues because they have had an opportunity to think in depth about related issues and to build a framework for understanding new information. Depth also allows children to understand the connections between "pure" science and the applications of science that we term "technology."

Hyde & Bizar (1989); Wassermann & Ivany (1988)

Connecting "pure" science to its applications

Science and Technology

We all take much of science for granted, especially as it relates to technology. One primary teacher, inspired by David Macaulay's *The Way Things Work,* decided to try a thematic unit built around MACHINES. She remembered as a child wondering how a pencil sharpener worked and what made the toaster pop. She was sure from watching her young students that they shared her interest in the way things work. To begin the unit, the teacher gathered a number of machines that could be easily dismantled and that were safe for small children to experiment with. She arranged a Machine Center in the room and laid out a manual meat grinder, pencil sharpener, coffee grinder, egg beater, flour sifter, and pepper mill. She then gathered the children around her in a circle on the floor and introduced the concept of the wheel. While children experimented with moving objects of various shapes across the floor, the teacher asked questions. Why is it easier to move the toilet paper roll and the ball than the cracker box and the block? How could you use the roll or ball to move the box? As children made suggestions, the teacher put several wheeled vehicles in the circle. Were there any shapes like the paper roll on these vehicles? Children quickly identified the wheels and proceeded to load the wagons and trucks with boxes and blocks.

Macaulay (1988)

Establish an interest center.

Encourage initial exploration and experimentation.

Use questions to move explorations in new directions.

At this point, the teacher shared the section of Macaulay's book about wheels with the children. Over the next several days, children kept track of all the ways in which they could observe wheels being used. They also used construction toys (e.g., Erector sets and LEGOS) to build wheeled vehicles. They drew pictures of new uses for wheels and collected pictures from magazines to make wheel collages.

Introduce informational books as a resource.

Their teacher pointed out that many of the things they had worked with were machines. She asked the children to separate some of the things that used wheels into two categories: one to include wheels used as machines and the other to include wheels that were not machines (e.g., a single disc attached to nothing). There was much discussion as children tried to decide what constituted a machine. With help from the teacher and from *The Way Things Work,* they wrote this definition: "A machine does work. Some parts of machines move."

Provide practice with examples and nonexamples.

Help children to construct definitions.

With this definition written on chart paper, the students set to work listing all the machines they could find in their classroom. For homework, they decided to make lists of all the machines they could find in one room at home. Before long, children began bringing in samples of machines to add to the collection in the Machine Center. As this unit progressed, students tried using a variety of machines. They took apart machines and tried to figure out how they worked. They used information books to help them understand machines, built machines to do various simple tasks, and drew machines for doing work in the future. They wrote and talked about and experimented with machines. Their teacher left messages for them in the center, asking them to think about such questions as: How is an eggbeater like a meat grinder? or Can you find a machine that uses a ratchet?

Maintain excitement and enthusiasm. Themes need not just disappear.

See also Lind & Milburn (1987) for another good example of a primary unit on machines.

If children are engaged in the kind of sciencing just described, it soon becomes clear that they are, as Carl Sagan suggests, disposed to be curious about the area we label *science*. This also means that sciencing is motivating and can be an excellent context for integrating across the curriculum.

SCIENCE REFERENCES

Bybee, R., Ellis, J. D., Muscella, D., & Robertson, W. C. (1988). *New designs for elementary school science: A study conducted by the Biological Sciences Curriculum Study (BSCS)*. Biological Sciences Curriculum Study. The Colorado College, Colorado Springs, CO.

Carin, A. A., & Sund, R. B. (1985). *Teaching modern science*. Columbus, OH: Merrill.

Hyde, A. A., & Bizar, M. (1989). *Thinking in context: Teaching cognitive processes across the elementary school curriculum*. White Plains, NY: Longman.

Kyle, W. C., Bonnstetter, R. J., Gadsden, T., & Shymansky, J. (1988). What research says about hands-on science. *Science and Children, 25* (7), 39–40, 52.

Labinowicz, E. (1980). *The Piaget primer: Thinking, learning, teaching*. Reading, MA: Addison-Wesley.

Lind, K. K., & Milburn, M. J. (1987). Mechanized childhood. *Science and Children, 25* (5), 322–333.

McShane, J. B. (1988). The mean machine. *Science and Children, 26* (3), 19–21.

Sagan, C. (1978). Address given at the National Science Teachers Association's 26th Annual National Convention, Washington, DC.

Stodolsky, S. S. (1988). *The subject matters*. Chicago: University of Chicago Press.

Wassermann, S., & Ivany, J. W. G. (1988). *Teaching elementary science. Who's afraid of spiders?* New York: Harper & Row.

CHILDREN'S LITERATURE, SCIENCE

THE WAY THINGS WORK by D. Macaulay. Houghton Mifflin, 1988.

MATHEMATICS

Recent research in mathematics gives validity to the language integration perspective in the classroom regarding helping children to learn math. Having opportunities to use math as a tool, as an aid to tackle a problem to be examined, or the means to accomplish a project within a thematic unit of study is consistent with what we know about how children learn mathematical understandings during the preschool years and how they form mathematical knowledge in out-of-school activities in general.

Emergent mathematicians

Gelman & Gallistel (1978); Hughes (1986); Saxe (1988); Saxe, Guberman, & Gearhart (1987)

Besides being emergent readers and writers, it is clear now that young children during the preschool years are also emergent mathematicians. For example, preschoolers engage in a variety of everyday activities involving number, including playing games of parents' and children's invention, such as counting stairs; using store-bought games involving number; watching educational television shows (e.g., "Sesame Street"); helping their parents on shopping trips; discussing the number of hours till supper or that it takes to get to grandma's house; noting how many floors yet to go in an elevator to get to the doctor's office in a building having many floors; and so forth. Moreover, numbers depicting the cost of products, miles to places, speed limits, and the like are frequently incorporated into the public print of the signs and labels found in our culture. As a result of these experiences, even two- and three-year-olds have considerable competence in counting objects. By the age of four, most children extend their early counting knowledge to comparing and reproducing sets and to addressing simple arithmetic problems with small sets. When kindergarteners begin school, they have already constructed important mathematical understandings; they have considerable arithmetic prowess on which to build and extend.

In this new view of the emergent mathematician, language plays an important role. In fact, the origin of numbers can be traced to one of the earliest uses of language by the child. There is ample evidence to show that babies' early utterances of "up," "more," "all gone," and so on represent functional expressions that also serve as precursors of numbers in children's subsequent language. In addition, relying on the number-words (and numerals) found everywhere in their world, as well as repeatedly used in interactions with themselves and others, children try to make sense of what they see and hear by employing their versions of "counting" to answer their own questions of "how many?" or "how much?" That is, the development of mathematical understandings is also learning through language. Thus, the view that children learn mathematics principally through math lessons in school, and only when they enter what Piaget has described as the concrete operational stage of development, has been questioned by cognitive developmentalists, mathematicians, and mathematics educators alike.

Language is integrally related to early understanding of math.

Nesher (1988)

Piaget (1952, 1953)

Donaldson (1978); Gelman & Gallistel (1978); Hughes (1986); Nesher (1988)

A critical aspect of the recent views on the development of mathematical understandings is the importance of sociocultural influences on the process. That parents and others engage young children in everyday activities and games involving mathematical concepts, and that these interactions support the children's efforts in learning math suggests that similar collaborative experiences are needed in the classroom to strengthen and extend these understandings. Another important related issue in this current view on mathematics is the movement from the performance of techniques to a more reflective way of knowing. Rather than emphasizing a curriculum in which children practice or perform techniques to get "right" answers, a curriculum is envisioned in which children develop an understanding and critical awareness of how and when to use mathematical techniques, as well as why they work and how they are developed. Such a curriculum requires personal interpretation and invention and opportunities to read, talk, and write about others' views and opinions on mathematical problems and issues. In this view, then, controversy, ambiguity, doubt, and risk-taking all play important roles not only in the children's development of mathematical understandings but also of their attitudes and the value of mathematics as a discipline, as a certain way of knowing.

Social-cultural factors affect mathematical development.

Carraher, Schliemann, & Carraher (1988); Hatano (1988); Lave, Murtaugh, & de la Rocha (1984); Saxe (1988); Saxe, Guberman, & Gearhart (1987)

Shift from performance techniques to reasoning and thinking about math.

Bishop (1988); Cobb, Yackel, & Wood (1989); Hiebert (1984); Siegel, Borasi, & Smith (1988); Stigler & Perry (1988)

This new view can be seen in the key goals that the National Council of Teachers of Mathematics (NCTM) has recently set for mathematics instruction in the 1990s:

1. To learn to value mathematics.
2. To become confident in their ability to do mathematics.
3. To become mathematical problem solvers.
4. To learn to communicate mathematically.
5. To learn to reason mathematically.

National Council of Teachers of Mathematics (1989)

These goals are radically different from what is found in traditional classrooms, but they are consistent with those fostered in integrated language classrooms. The following section covers more ideas for integrating mathematics in thematic units, and the last section suggests ways in which mathematics can be incorporated in language and literacy activities in units in the classroom.

Using Mathematics in Projects in Thematic Units

Like any symbolic system, mathematics involves both pure and applied aspects. The pure aspects have to do with the abstractions of the symbolic language of mathematics, its concepts, its principles, its theories. The applied aspects refer to the variety of ways in which we use mathematics to explain the physical world around us and to help us in various everyday social interactions. These pure and applied aspects are not separate. In fact, in the history of mathematics, new abstract formulations of mathematics have almost always been developed because specific situations or problems had to be addressed. Then these new pure mathematical notions have frequently found applications to many other situations or problems. Before coming to school, children have acquired their knowledge of mathematics in a dynamic, interactive way; their no-

See Hughes (1986) for a readable account of young children's math abilities with useful practical teaching suggestions.

Carraher, Schliemann, & Carraher (1988); Ginsburg & Asmussen (1988); Hatano (1988); Hiebert (1984); Hyde & Bizar (1989); Saxe (1988)

See also Cordeiro (1988) for an example of a sixth grade unit on infinity.

See Baratta-Lorton (1976) for a useful discussion of graphing.

Graphing opportunities should be planned for, but many can also emerge spontaneously.

See Chapter 8 for more information on graphing.

Cooking measurement

tions of pure math have been anchored in applied circumstances. Unlike traditional classrooms, where frequently only pure or abstract math is emphasized, integrated language classrooms incorporate both aspects of math. In various thematic units, children continue to learn the abstract aspects of math *within* meaningful contexts that facilitate their understanding of, and thinking about, mathematical concepts.

Math consists of many concepts: number sense, numeration, and number systems; fractions and decimals; measurement, geometry, and spatial sense; estimation; statistics and probability; algebra; and so forth. Only a hint of the possibilities can be provided here. Mathematizing—mathematics as reasoning and as active problem-solving—is an integral feature of all the suggestions presented.

Graphing. Graphing can be used in practically any and every thematic unit and by children at any level in the elementary school. In developing graphs, children compare, count, add, and subtract. Other mathematical operations, such as multiplying and dividing, are also possible in organizing data in a systematic way to discover patterns. Graphs can be the result of surveys that children have conducted on a range of topics or issues. Graphs may come about when children have opportunities to observe data accumulation in the course of a thematic unit—for example, when they gather specific information in particular scientific experiments.

In the WASH AND WEAR prototype in Chapter 4, we saw how Peter and his children graphed types of shoes. Similar activities can easily be incorporated in any of the prototypes. In the SPACES unit, graphing can show how children get from one space to another—how many children in the class go to school by walking, by car, or by bus. Older elementary children in a SPACES unit could collect this information for the whole school and/or expand the number of space categories—besides school, spaces such as stores, entertainment places, and the like could be added. In the CHANGES WEB, children plant various kinds of seeds and chart daily growth. Graphs showing and comparing growth patterns for the plants could be constructed. The CHANGES unit also has children collecting old toys and clothes that they used to wear. The information on toys and clothes could be organized and displayed through a graph.

Older children are able to develop more complex graphs. Instead of depicting only frequencies that may rely mostly on adding and subtracting, graphs can reflect percentages, averages, and so on that incorporate more complex mathematical operations. For example, in a fourth grade version of the LET'S EAT thematic unit, children could keep journals of their food consumption for a week and plot their average number of calories for each day of the week and/or contrast the average number of calories consumed through nutritious food versus "junk" food. In the fourth/fifth departmentalized EXPLORATIONS WEB, children collect slang expressions for a dictionary as part of their study of word origins in the subtheme "Exploring with Language." Besides this dictionary, they could document the percentage of use of certain slang expressions used in the different grades. Or, in that same unit, in the subtheme "Exploring Careers," graphs reflecting percentages could emerge as the result of children's inventory of the necessary skills required at the various worksites they visit.

In sum, graphs can be incorporated in many ways in any thematic unit. Teachers can consider graphing activities as part of planning a WEB. For example, you could review the prototype WEBs in Chapter 4 and brainstorm a range of other possibilities that are not now depicted. However, some of the most valuable graphs are those that evolve spontaneously. Recognizing the natural opportunities in the classroom allows for an integration of math with every curricular area. A pollywog graph can be developed when children notice some pollywogs with developed feet and others with less developed feet. Contrasting the books that have been read on various topics within a unit, charting miles traveled by various explorers, depicting types of foods eaten by people in various regions or countries, and so on all incorporate various graphing activities that require meaningful mathematical experiences for children across the curriculum.

Measurement. Limitless possibilities for measurement exist in thematic units. Only a few ideas can be presented here. Various cooking activities, which can be incorporated in most units, readily incorporate measurement of ingredients: liquids such as milk, water, and oil; solids such as butter or shortening; particles of "matter" such as flour and sugar. As children follow various recipes, they begin to understand fractions and comparable amounts. The doubling or tripling of recipes requires estimating and confirming equivalences of particular ingredients. Writing a cookbook for giants in the GIANTS prototype requires children to consider measuring ingredients in a big way; liquids have to be computed in terms of quarts and gallons instead of cups or pints.

In the WASH AND WEAR prototype, many water activities are incorporated that could have children measuring liquids. Various containers could be available so that water could be measured by containers having both cup and milliliter markings. Comparing English and metric liquid and dry measurements could be included in the LET'S EAT unit. Children could bring in weight information for various packaged and canned goods from the grocery store and then try to represent these weights (in terms of pounds and grams) by using scales and a range of objects in the classroom.

Contrasting English and metric systems

As you may have already noted, measurement is usually an initial step of graphing, especially so when linear measurement is involved. Measuring the growth of plants from seeds, for example, is a prerequisite to graphing plant differences in the CHANGES unit. It is important that children have opportunities to use both the English and metric systems in linear measurements. In a SPACES unit, for example, children could measure their favorite spaces at home (the length and width of their room, their bed, etc.) in inches, feet, and yards *and* in centimeters and meters. Older children could consider the notion of perimeter by figuring out the perimeters of objects in the various spaces in the classroom.

"Body Spaces" could also be explored in both the SPACES and EXPLORATIONS thematic units (as well as other units such as TAKING CARE OF MY BODY). Children's heights, as well as lengths and widths of various body parts, could be measured. For older children, the concept of circumference could be explored by measuring the circumferences of children's waists, heads, wrists, thighs, and so on.

Time measurement

Measurement of time can frequently be incorporated in a range of thematic units. In a FLIGHT unit, children, using a stopwatch, can chart the time it takes their miniature parachutes—attached to objects of various weights—to land from the top of the playground equipment. A study of some of the timed events from the *Guinness Book of World Records* can lead to children keeping track of their own everyday events to identify their own records. In a thematic unit on TIME, encouraging children to determine the time elapsed by noting both the hands on a clock as well as digits on a digital clock helps them to begin a study of the ways people have described time.

Many scientific experiments involve the measurement of time. In a unit on DISAPPEARING ACTS, older elementary students studied a range of topics—various magic tricks and magicians such as the famous Houdini, certain aspects of pollution (many materials are not easily biodegradable and are therefore *not* good disappearing acts), famous missing persons such as Amelia Earhart. They also timed the evaporation rates of various liquids (water, oil, alcohol, and soapy water). Another scientific activity possible in such a unit could be the exploration of the disappearing acts (the "demise" of soapy bubbles) and why certain bubbles lasted longer than others. Measuring various transformations is frequently an integral aspect of the careful observation required in the process of sciencing. In sum, measurement can be easily incorporated in various ways in thematic units. Just as in graphing, possible measurement ideas should be considered ahead of time in planning WEBs, but more natural opportunities emerge frequently if the teacher is alert enough to spot and support them.

Fostering Geometrical and Spatial Sense. In traditional elementary classrooms, geometry content is usually limited to children learning the labels of various geometric shapes, and in the older grades, sometimes memorizing formulas to compute the area of various shapes. However, when engaged in activities and experiences in various thematic units, children can be encouraged to think about and analyze the shapes in more meaningful ways. For example, when children are asked to measure the area of

Pappas & Bush (1989)

the construction paper "rug" necessary to cover the bottom (and perhaps also the top and sides) of a diorama children construct as an extension of a book they have read, the formula to compute the area of a rectangle is much more understandable. Other such constructions—making Strega Nona's house (found in de Paola's *Strega Nona, Big Anthony and the Magic Ring,* and *Strega Nona's Magic Lessons*) or the houses of the three little pigs—require that children visualize the third-dimensional nature of geometrical figures. As part of a fourth, fifth, or sixth grade SPACES unit, children's attempts to construct accurate scaled-down versions of their favorite spaces at home fostered a concentrated effort to understand geometrical and spatial sense. This project also meant that children had to employ a range of measurements, deal with ratios, apply certain algebraic expressions, and so forth. Children gained similar understandings when, after having architects and city planning personnel come to visit the classroom in a HOUSES thematic unit, they decided to design and construct a model of a town depicted in a story they were all reading.

de Paola (1975, 1979, 1982)

In a thematic unit such as DESIGNS AND PATTERNS, children are able to explore geometrical figures in depth. Besides studying the symmetrical patterns of plant and animal organisms and of various crystal formations, children examine all kinds of patterns and geometrical designs. Children construct many patterns and designs by using a range of material (pennies, buttons, seeds, small sticks, attribute blocks, LEGO blocks, etc.) and then describe them in writing or through illustrations so others can try to replicate them. Musical patterns are examined, patterns of three in stories are compared, quilts are designed using various geometric shapes. Children use rubber bands to construct shapes on student-made or commercially made geoboards, circles are made by using the compass, various triangle designs are constructed, as well as pentomino or hexomino puzzles. Dot or centimeter paper is used to make hexagons or equilateral triangles for tessellating patterns. Geometry circuit boards are set up to show various geometric shapes; they are arranged so that when a match is made, a bell rings. Thus, geometrical understandings can be fostered in many meaningful ways in thematic units such as DESIGNS AND PATTERNS in which geometrical sense is a major focus. They can also be fostered in many other units when teachers are aware of the possibilities.

See Larke (1988) and Van de Walle & Holbrook (1987) for good classroom examples in geometrical and pattern units.

Other Miscellaneous Ideas for Integrating Math. As already noted, only some of the possibilities for integrating meaningful math activities in the classroom can be suggested here. There are many everyday routines in which children can use math in the classroom. Having children being responsible for various routine tasks such as taking roll, keeping track of lunch or milk money or book orders, distributing materials, and so on fosters mathematical understandings.

Understanding of decimals is developed when real money is computed and handled for real purposes. There are many opportunities to deal with money in thematic units as well. Money can be exchanged in grocery stores or restaurants that are set up in the classroom in units such as LET'S EAT. Children can trade and sell stocks in hypothetical accounts as part of a DISAPPEARING ACTS unit. Commercially and student-made games (games are discussed in the next section as well) also provide many opportunities for developing the concept of number and other mathematical principles.

See Kamii (1985) for examples of using games in a first grade classroom.

Having many manipulatives available for children to use encourages many kinds of mathematical understandings. We know of a kindergarten teacher who fosters the idea of number sets by having children tell how many sets (of ten, three, four, etc.) of blocks they will be counting out when they choose to work in the construction area each day. The teacher observes the strategies the children employ in their counting of blocks and intervenes to support their efforts or to point out how peers' sets are different or equivalent. By the end of the year, most of these children know that two sets of ten blocks are equivalent to four sets of five blocks, and so forth.

Many ways to use math are possible in the classroom no matter what the thematic unit is at a particular time. More ideas that integrate language and literacy more directly are suggested in the following pages.

Language, Literacy, and Mathematics

Integration of Oral Language. Speaking and listening are naturally integrated in children's discussions that involve mathematical concepts. As they compare information they have obtained or accumulated as part of projects they are engaged in, mathematics as a way of knowing is fostered. In small groups or as a whole class, they debate how, when, and why certain mathematical operations are appropriate for the issues being investigated. Addition, subtraction, multiplication, division, fractions, decimals, and so on are not pursued as separate subjects of math. In real-life situations, problems frequently require solutions that integrate several techniques. Consequently, children have to talk about and consider others' views when they decide which mathematical operations are necessary.

Discussion of math problems fosters math understandings.

Integrating Literacy. Many opportunities for reading and writing about math are also possible in an integrated language classroom. Reading and writing occur when children jot down the data of their surveys or organize their various calculations in projects in their Learning Logs*, and then share these notes with others. The construction of graphs also incorporates reading and writing. Reading and writing reports of scientific experiments or other investigations include opportunities to express and comprehend mathematical data. Constructing and playing games, as extensions of books read and studied in class, can also provide meaningful occasions to apply and use math. Board games may depict important significant events of a story or a biography, or stages of transformation in an experiment or animal and plant growth, and so forth. As children decide on and write their directions so others can play, particular mathematical operations are considered and clarified. Players then develop these mathematical understandings as they try to comprehend and follow the directions of the game.

Fulwiler (1980, 1982)

Many wonderful books have mathematical concepts in them. There are numerous excellent counting books in children's literature that can be included in thematic units at the early elementary grades. Other types of books that include mathematical concepts are also available. Several books are discussed here to suggest the possibilities.

In *One, Two, Three, and Four. No More?,* Catherine Gray's verses and Marissa Moss's illustrations depict various animals in combinations of the first four numbers, thereby providing a delightful introduction of simple sequence, addition, and subtraction for young mathematicians.

Gray (1988)

Besides reading these verses over and over, children can extend the book in many ways. They can make stick or other animal puppets and dramatize these arithmetical operations. They can also write their own verses using other animals and having mathematical operations that involve numbers over four. Older elementary children can try writing similar verses (or verses using other kinds of poetic structures, or focusing on objects or people rather than animals) that use other operations, such as multiplication and division. Writing verses incorporating mathematical notions can be part of children's Learning Logs* as they engage in various projects in thematic units throughout the year.

Another book, *The King's Chessboard* by David Birch (illustrated by Devis Grebu), is a story that takes place in ancient India. The King of Deccan is so pleased with his wise man's service that he wishes to give him a reward. The wise man does not think he needs a reward, but the King is insistent. The wise man reflects, and then noting the King's chessboard, asks the King for the following:

Birch (1988)

> Tomorrow, for the first square of your chessboard, give me one grain of rice; the next day, for the second square, two grains of rice; the next day after that, four grains of rice; then, the following day, eight grains for the next square of your chessboard. Thus for each square give me twice the number of grains of the square before it, and so on for every square of the chessboard.

Because the King isn't sure how much rice would be necessary to cover sixty-four squares and because he is too proud to let on to anyone that he doesn't know, he grants the wise man's request as his reward. With only half the squares accounted for, however, the royal granaries are nearly bare from meeting the requirements of the reward. As children discover how the King finds a way to save face over being outwitted by the wise man, they begin to reflect on the mathematical power of a simple request. Extensions of this book could include children posing other "simple" requests that require different kinds of mathematical patterns—adding ten or some other number for each chessboard square, for example. These could be incorporated in stories or expressed by short descriptions of various patterns [e.g., on day 1 there are ten pennies (or whatever); on day 2, twenty; day 3, fifteen; day 4, twenty-five; then thirty-five; thirty; and so forth] for other classmates to figure out. Possible mathematical abstractions can be considered by children because the abstractions began in a meaningful way and are initiated and controlled by the children.

Nozaki & Anno (1985)

Anno has several books incorporating various mathematical concepts. Two are mentioned here. In *Anno's Hat Tricks,* Anno and Nozaki introduce to children the deductive reasoning that is the basis of binary logic. As the hatter encourages Shadowchild (the reader) to play tricks about red and white hats, the power of "if" is explained in the way it is used by computer programmers, mathematicians, and other scientists. Children enjoy making their own hats to dramatize the book, or writing plays to illustrate other examples of the process of elimination and binary logic.

Anno & Anno (1983)

In *Anno's Mysterious Multiplying Jar,* Mitsumasa Anno and his son, Masaichiro, illustrate the concept of factorials in a manner that children who have a beginning understanding of multiplication can grasp. Like a cumulative folktale, the authors present an island in a sea, and on that one island, two countries exist; and in each country, three mountains; and so on up to ten jars. How many jars altogether? Well, there were 10! jars. As children discover a new function of the exclamation mark, they begin to realize how it signals a special kind of numerical relationship. That "!" means that the number it follows stands for the product of that number multiplied by the next smaller number, multiplied by the next smaller number, and so forth all the way down to 1. Extensions can consist of children trying to figure out other real-life scenarios that depict factorials (e.g., showing the possible arrangement for the desks of four students). In addition, because the Anno book is like a cumulative tale, a study of some of these folktales leads children to discover how the part-whole relationships in these tales compare with the relationships having to do with the mathematical factorial idea. Sometimes this investigation can result in children writing a new genre—"cumulative factorial" tales.

Konigsburg (1967)

In Konigsburg's *From the Mixed Up Files of Mrs. Basil E. Frankweiler,* Claudia, aged eleven, decides to run away to the Metropolitan Museum of Art in New York City. She's given up hot fudge sundaes for three weeks, but she still has saved only $4.18, so she invites her younger brother, Jamie, to go along because he can help bankroll the expedition. This book is filled with story problems for children to figure out, and more can be constructed as extensions. For example, children can compare the amount of Claudia's allowance with theirs, and they can figure out how much money Claudia and Jamie have left for meals after paying train fare. Moreover, children can also determine the rate of inflation by comparing how much things cost in 1969 (the year the book was published) with how much things cost now. This book can also encourage children to write their own books that are filled with real-life mathematical problems.

Burns (1975)

An informational book that children love is *The I Hate Mathematics! Book* by Marilyn Burns (illustrated by Martha Hairston). A range of activities convinces children that math can be fun and that there is more to math than arithmetic. For example, topology (the study of surfaces) is examined in "A Topological Garden," exponential growth is introduced in "Doing Dishes," a palindrome is discovered in "The Perfect Palindrome." Children can reenact in the classroom many of the tricks and games described in the book. Trying them out on unsuspecting others in other classes or at home can lead to writing up reactions to be shared in class. Because the activities are frequently illustrated in a cartoon fashion, children are sometimes spurred to express through cartoons other math tricks they have discovered.

One of the best ways children can make mathematics meaningful is to write their own story problems. These can be constructed and collected in every thematic unit throughout the year, perhaps in a special journal designated for this purpose. Ideas are generated as the children read a range of genres and investigate problems across the curriculum. For example, they can incorporate their mathematical data by spinning a yarn using the characters and episodes in a story they are enjoying. Problems can be expressed by describing the behaviors of animals or by relating historical events. As writers, children begin with a solution and then work backward to construct an interesting problem. As readers of their peers' problems, they do the opposite—that is, they begin with trying to figure out the problem, working toward the solution. These reading and writing experiences and the spirited discussions surrounding them are invaluable mathematical problem-solving activities.

Children can also be authors of mathematics books. By writing their own book for children in other classes or for children next year, children have opportunities to display and reflect on what they know about math. Math again becomes meaningful—even for kindergarteners—as they try to explain and illustrate mathematical concepts and procedures they know so that other children can understand them. Children come up with interesting and novel ideas by sketching classroom and real-world scenarios to show these mathematical understandings.

See Van den Brink (1987) for a good classroom example of the writing and illustration by first graders of their own arithmetic books.

In summary, in an integrated classroom, problem-solving is emphasized across the curriculum. Both pure and applied aspects of mathematics are integrated. Math is concrete and meaningful because it has to do with real-world problems and scenarios. As children discuss the process of mathematical operations or techniques, they examine why they are appropriate; risk-taking is fostered when they consider and evaluate alternative methods. Teachers will need to demonstrate mathematical operations or approaches to problems in Mini-Lessons* (see Chapter 8) or have regular sessions in which math is the focus. However, rather than spending a lot of rote practice on many problems, children tackle a smaller number but in depth. In doing so, children develop an appreciation of the coherence of what is involved in problems and what the process is in attempting to solve them. Math is seen as a powerful way of knowing, and children see themselves as confident mathematicians.

Hughes (1986)

The *coherence* of problems in meaningful contexts is emphasized.

REFERENCES

Baratta-Lorton, M. (1976). *Mathematics their way.* Menlo Park, CA: Addison-Wesley.

Bishop, A. (1988). *Mathematical enculturation.* Dordrecht, The Netherlands: Kluwer Academic Publishers.

Carraher, T. N., Schiemann, A. D., & Carraher, D. W. (1988). Mathematical concepts in everyday life. In G. Saxe (Ed.), *Children's mathematics* (pp. 71–87). New Directions for Child Development, No. 41. San Francisco: Jossey-Bass.

Cobb, P., Yackel, E., & Wood, T. (1989, April). *Young children's emotional acts while doing mathematical problem solving.* Paper presented at the annual meeting of the American Educational Research Association, New Orleans, LA.

Cordeiro, P. (1988). Playing with infinity in the sixth grade. *Language Arts, 65,* 557–566.

Donaldson, M. (1978). *Children's minds.* Glasgow: William Collins Sons.

Gelman, R., & Gallistel, C. R. (1978). *The child's understanding of number.* Cambridge, MA: Harvard University Press.

Ginsburg, H. P., & Asmussen, K. A. (1988). Hot mathematics. In G. Saxe (Ed.), *Children's mathematics* (pp. 89–111). New Directions for Child Development, No. 41. San Francisco: Jossey-Bass.

Fulwiler, T. (1980). Journals across the disciplines. *English Journal, 69,* 14–22.

Fulwiler, T. (1982). Writing: An act of cognition. In C. W. Griffin (Ed.), *Teaching writing in all disciplines* (pp. 15–26). New Directions for Teaching and Learning, No. 12. San Francisco: Jossey-Bass.

Hatano, G. (1988). Social and motivational bases of mathematical understanding. In G. Saxe (Ed.), *Children's mathematics* (pp. 55–70). New Directions for Child Development, No. 41. San Francisco: Jossey-Bass.

Hiebert, J. (1984). Children's mathematics learning: The struggle to link form and understanding. *Elementary School Journal, 84,* 497–513.

Hughes, M. (1986). *Children and number: Difficulties in learning mathematics.* New York: Basil Blackwell.

Hyde, A. A., & Bizar, M. (1989). *Thinking in context: Teaching cognitive processes across the elementary curriculum.* Oxford: Longman.

Kamaii, C. K. (1985). *Young children reinvent arithmetic: Implications of Piaget's theory.* New York: Teachers College Press.

Larke, P. J. (1988). Geometric extravaganza: Spicing up geometry. *Arithmetic Teacher, 36,* 12–16.

Lave, J., Murtaugh, M., & de la Rocha, O. (1984). The dialectic of arithmetic in grocery shopping. In B. Rogoff & J. Lave (Eds.), *Everyday cognition: Its development in social context* (pp. 67–94). Cambridge, MA: Harvard University Press.

National Council of Teachers of Mathematics (1989). *Curriculum and evaluation standards for school mathematics.* Reston, VA: National Council of Teachers of Mathematics.

Nesher, P. (1988). Precursors of number in children: A linguistic perspective. In S. Strauss (Ed.), *Ontogeny, phylogeny, and historical development: Human development,* Vol. 2 (pp. 106–124). Norwood, NJ: Ablex.

Pappas, C. C., & Bush, S. (1989). Facilitating understandings of geometry. *Arithmetic Teacher, 36,* 17–20.

Piaget, J. (1952). *The child's conception of number.* London: Routledge & Kegan Paul.

Piaget, J. (1953). How children form mathematical concepts. *Scientific American, 189,* 74–79.

Saxe, G. B. (1988). Candy selling and math learning. *Educational Researcher, 17,* 14–21.

Saxe, G. B., Guberman, S. R., & Gearhart, M. (1987). Social processes in early number development. *Monographs of the Society for Research in Child Development, 52* (2, Serial No. 216).

Siegel, M., Borasi, R., & Smith, C. (1988, December). *A critical review of reading in mathematics instruction: The need for a new synthesis.* Paper presented at the annual meeting of the National Reading Conference, Tucson, AZ.

Stigler, J. W., & Perry, M. (1988). Mathematics learning in Japanese, Chinese and American classrooms. In G. B. Saxe (Ed.), *Children's mathematics* (pp. 27–54). New Directions for Child Development, No. 41. San Francisco: Jossey-Bass.

Van den Brink, J. (1987). Children as arithmetic book authors. *For the Learning of Mathematics, 7,* 44–47.

Van de Walle, J. A., & Holbrook, H. (1987). Patterns, thinking, and problem solving. *Arithmetic Teacher, 34,* 6–12.

CHILDREN'S LITERATURE, MATHEMATICS

ANNO'S HAT TRICKS by A. Nozaki & M. Anno. Philomel, 1985.

ANNO'S MYSTERIOUS MULTIPLYING JAR by M. Anno & M. Anno. Illustrated by M. Anno. Philomel, 1983.

BIG ANTHONY AND THE MAGIC RING by T. de Paola. Harcourt Brace Jovanovich, 1979.

FROM THE MIXED UP FILES OF MRS. BASIL E. FRANKWEILER by E. I. Konigsburg. Atheneum, 1967.

THE I HATE MATHEMATICS! BOOKby M. Burns. Illustrated by M. Hairston. Little, Brown, 1975.

THE KING'S CHESSBOARD by D. Birch. Illustrated by D. Grebu. Dial Books, 1988.

ONE, TWO, THREE, AND FOUR. NO MORE? by C. Gray. Illustrated by M. Moss. Houghton Mifflin, 1988.

STREGA NONA by T. de Paola. Prentice-Hall, 1975.

STREGA NONA'S MAGIC LESSONS by T. de Paola. Harcourt Brace Jovanovich, 1982.

ART AND MUSIC

Langer (1942, 1978)

Language and the arts are our human vehicles for constructing and conveying meaning. Suzanne Langer has argued that whereas language is linear and the arts nonlinear, both are branches of the same root. Language is a way of naming, and the arts a way of knowing. Gardner suggests that through language and the arts the human mind creates, revises, transforms, and "recreates wholly fresh products, systems and even worlds of meaning" (p. 5).

Gardner (1982)

In Western mainstream cultures, the attention of educators has been on the acquisition of verbal language and the teaching of "literacy." We cannot afford, however, to ignore the potential of the arts for constructing and representing ourselves and our particular culture, what Rudolf Arnheim has called the neglected "gift of comprehending through our senses" (p. 1). The arts seem to be integrally entwined with children's need to make sense of themselves and their world through symbols. Very young children quickly pick up the intonation or musical patterns of various registers of language. They sing little rhymes to themselves, savoring the sounds and patterns of words. They create metaphors and tell stories as they go about the business of exploring their world. They exhibit an astonishing creative artistry in the manipulation of the elements and principles of the visual arts. We know, too, that artistic expression seems to enable children in the creation of oral and written texts.

Arnheim (1974)

Dyson (1986)

Thus, there is good reason to include the arts as natural vehicles for exploring the topics in thematic units. We need, argues Gardner, "to acknowledge forms and intensities of thought *other* than" those traditionally valued by our school systems (p. 214). Yet too often education in the arts has been considered a frill and is the first to be eliminated in the face of budget cuts. Or the study of the arts in the elementary school is limited to the production of art and music (that is, students engaged in *making* art or *making* music), and this takes place only once a week for twenty minutes to an hour in a room apart from the day-to-day business of the classroom.

Gardner (1982)

In recent years, however, a broadening and redefining of arts education curricula has occurred. In visual art education, the result is an approach called *Discipline Based Art Education.* Growing out of a collaboration between Elliott Eisner and the Getty Center for Education in the Arts, these programs call for experiences in four major areas: art making, art history, art criticism, and aesthetics. According to Eisner, these are the four things people do with art, "they make it, they understand it, they make judgments about it and they appreciate it" (p. 7). He suggests that when children make pots out of clay coils, for example, they should have the opportunity to think about proportion and technique, to consider the feelings conveyed when pots are delicate or heavy, and to make connections to the uses and forms of pots in other times and other cultures.

Arts curricula have been reexamined.

Aesthetics raises the question, "What is art and what is my response to it?" Brandt (1988a)

A complementary approach has developed out of the work of Howard Gardner and his colleagues at Harvard Project Zero, a group that has had major influence on arts research and education. This approach focuses on the arts as alternative ways of knowing, and it emphasizes artistic *production* as a central focus of the curriculum with strands of *perception* (discrimination) and *reflection* (introspection and critical analysis about productive and perceptual endeavors) interwoven.

Brandt (1988b)

Historical, critical, and aesthetic understandings should be developed as children create and reflect on art.

Gardner's work has been especially helpful in understanding how teachers can respond to the child's artistic development in ways that are similar to their response to the child's development of language systems. He suggests, for example, that across cultures the years from two to about seven are spent "coming to grips with the world of 'symbols.'" During this time "the child's capacity to use, manipulate, transform and comprehend various symbol systems matures at a ferocious pace" (pp. 211–212). These young children should be given full opportunity to explore media and forms of expression in a way that allows natural processes to unfold. Older children, however, become increasingly aware of the culture in which they live and become occupied with the rules and standards of those around them. Thus, the type of experimentation with art forms and the lack of conformity they exhibit before formal schooling begins give way to a period of wanting to know how to make a drawing look "real" or a song sound "right." At this point, a teacher can step in with experiences that help children to gain mastery of various techniques and media at the same time they introduce them to questions and concepts regarding standards and criticism. Giving the preteenager a knowledge of techniques and a familiarity with various media should make it less likely that during the critical years of adolescence, when teens begin to recognize the range

Gardner (1980, 1982)

Gardner (1982)

of the finest art and performance that exist, they do not give up because they cannot measure up. If, instead, they feel that their own work is generally competent or acceptable, it is more likely that they may remain willing participants in the arts throughout their lives.

The arts are resources and vehicles for learning.

We have already explored the arts as resources in thematic units in Chapter 3. The TIME WEB included aspects of rhythm and meter in art and music as well as the study of paintings and musical compositions in which artists and composers sought to portray times of day and night. We also noted how a theme of humor could incorporate resources from art, drama, dance, and music. In Chapter 4, the GIANTS theme illustrated the collaboration among art and music specialists and the classroom teacher in developing understanding of size relationships in painting and sculpture and of dynamics in music. Because of the limitations of space in this book, we cannot deal with the wide range of genres that exist within the scope of the disciplines called "the arts." In Chapter 8, we look at the language-related arts of drama and literature. In the remainder of this section, however, we look more closely at two of the arts, visual art and music, as vehicles for exploring and responding to the content in thematic units and as domains of knowledge in their own right.

McFee & Degge (1980)

Because the arts often require special skills or talents as well as specialized knowledge, you may feel a bit intimidated by developing experiences that involve children with techniques used in art and music production or in discussing critical, historical, or aesthetic dimensions of art and music. There are many excellent resources that will boost your own confidence and suggest practical methods for developing art and music activities. Some of these resources are included in a bibliography in Table 7.1, along with books that can engage children in various ways of thinking and experiencing these art forms.

Consider also the artists within your own community as resources. Many school districts now have artist-in-residence programs that can provide children with a valuable firsthand look at the creative process inherent in the production of a work of art. In the light of our new understanding about children's conceptions of the arts and the call for developing their critical and aesthetic awareness, it seems especially important that children see this process evolve over time rather than simply examine or listen to a finished product.

Specialists are resources and team members.

Don't hesitate to enlist the support of your school or district's art and music specialists. They have expertise in developing critical, aesthetic, and historical perspectives for children in these respective fields, and you should enlist them as team members and resource persons for all thematic units. They can suggest composers, musicians, and musical compositions or art and artists from many historical periods that can be incorporated into the units. They may also have libraries of recordings or art reproductions, or know of other sources, that they would be willing to share with the children. They themselves may be practicing artists or know of artists who can share their work and processes with the children.

At other times, a theme may suggest some important critical or aesthetic factors to the specialists on which they can expand during their time with the children. Such was the case in Estella Esquivel's GIANTS unit when the art teacher helped children to consider size as a factor in art appreciation, and the music teacher concentrated on critical factors such as dynamics and crescendo in music.

Themes can also provide specialists with the opportunity for developing experiences with special techniques. A theme of SPACES for older children can provide the opportunity for teaching different techniques in two- or three-point perspective so that they could represent views of a scene or an object from below or above.

Art or music can often serve as the focus of a classroom study (a WEB on the books of a particular illustrator or on exploring art or music through books) or as a springboard to a classroom unit. We know a fifth grade teacher who used the study of oriental art conducted by the art teacher to begin a study of Japan, and a middle school music teacher who helped classroom teachers to develop a unit for studying American history through American music.

TABLE 7.1 Books for Looking at Art and Music

Making Art

Arnosky, J. (1982) *Drawing from nature.* New York: Lothrop
Bolognese, D. & Thornton, R. (1983) *Drawing and painting with the computer.* New York: Franklin Watts
Graham, A. (1976) *Fossils, ferns and fish scales: a handbook of art and nature projects.* Illustrated by D. Stoke. New York: Four Winds
Weiss, H. (1974) *Pencil, pen and brush, drawing for beginners.* New York: Scholastic
Weiss, P. (1976) *Simple printmaking.* Illustrated by S. Gralla. New York: Lothrop
Zaidenberg, A. (1971) *How to draw and compose pictures.* New York: Harper

Art History and Appreciation

Behrens, J. (1977) *Looking at beasties.* Chicago, IL: Children's Press
Behrens, J. (1977) *Looking at children.* Chicago, IL: Children's Press
Bjork, C. (1985) *Linnea in Monet's garden.* Illustrated by L. Anderson. New York: R&S
Brown, L. K. & Brown, M. (1986) *Visiting the art museum.* New York: Dutton
Ceserani, G. P. & Ventura, P. (1983) *Grand constructions.* New York: Putnam
Conner, P. (1982) *Looking at art: people at home.* New York: Atheneum
Conner, P. (1982) *Looking at art: people at work.* New York: Atheneum
Craft, R. (1975) *Brueghal's the fair.* New York: Lippincott
Cummings, R. (1979) *Just look: a book about paintings.* New York: Scribner
Cummings, R. (1982) *Just imagine: ideas in painting.* New York: Scribner
Fine, J. (1979) *I carve stone.* Photos by D. Anderson. New York: Crowell
Gates, F. (1982) *North American Indian masks: craft and legend.* New York: Walker
Glubok, S. (1972) *The art of the new American nation.* Illustrated by G. Nook. New York: Macmillan
Goffstein, M. B. (1983) *Lives of the artists.* New York: Harper
Highwater, J. (1978) *Many smokes, many moons: a chronology of American Indian history through Indian art.* New York: Lippincott
Holmes, B. (1979) *Enchanted worlds: pictures to grow up with.* New York: Oxford University Press
Holmes, B. (1980) *Creatures of paradise: pictures to grow up with.* New York: Oxford University Press
Janson, H. W. & Janson, A. F. (1987) *History of art for young people.* New York: Abram's
Kennet, F. & Measham, T. (1979) *Looking at paintings.* New York: Van Nostrand, Reinhold
Macauley, D. (1973) *Cathedral: the story of its construction.* Boston, MA: Houghton Mifflin
Munthe, N. (1983) *Meet Matisse.* Illustrated by R. Kee. Boston, MA: Little, Brown
Price, C. (1977) *Arts of clay.* New York: Scribner
Proddow, P. (1979) *Art tells a story: Greek and Roman myths.* New York: Doubleday
Provensen, A. & M. (1984) *Leonardo Da Vinci.* New York: Viking
Raboff, E. (1988) *Henri Matisse.* New York: Lippincott
Ventura, P. (1984) *Great painters.* New York: Putnam
Waterfield, G. (1982) *Looking at art: faces.* New York: Atheneum

Art in ABC's, Counting and Wordless Picture Books

Anno, M. (1975) *Anno's alphabet.* New York: Crowell
Anno, M. (1980) *Anno's Italy.* New York: Putnam
Azarian, M. (1981) *A farmer's alphabet.* Boston, MA: David Godine
Fischer, L. E. (1978) *Alphabet art: thirteen ABC's from around the world.* New York: Four Winds
Fischer, L. E. (1982) *Number art: thirteen 1 2 3's from around the world.* New York: Four Winds
Mayers, F. C. (1986) *ABC: the museum of fine arts, Boston.* New York: Abrams
Nygren, T. (1988) *The red thread.* New York: Farrar, Straus
Oakley, G. (1979) *Magical changes.* New York: Atheneum

Art as a Theme

Picture Books

Agee, J. (1988) *The incredible painting of Felix Clousseau.* New York: Farrar, Straus
Canning, K. (1979) *A painted tale.* New York: Barron's
Carrick, D. (1985) *Morgan and the artist.* New York: Clarion
Cohen, M. (1980) *No good in art.* Illustrated by L. Hoban. New York: Greenwillow
Craven, C. (1987) *What the mailman brought.* Illustrated by T. de Paola. New York: Putnam
de Paola, T. (1989) *The art lesson.* New York: Putnam
Ernst, L. (1986) *Hamilton's art show.* New York: Lothrop
French, F. (1977) *Matteo.* New York: Oxford University Press
Isadora, R. (1988) *The pirates of Bedford Street.* New York: Greenwillow
Kesselman, W. (1980) *Emma.* Illustrated by B. Cooney. New York: Doubleday
Lobel, A. (1968) *The great blueness and other predicaments.* New York: Harper
McPhail, D. (1978) *The magical drawings of Mooney B. Finch.* New York: Doubleday
O'Kelley, M. L. (1983) *From the hills of Georgia: an autobiography in paintings.* Boston, MA: Atlantic Monthly

TABLE 7.1—Continued

Rylant, C. (1988) *All I see.* Illustrated by P. Catalanotto. New York: Orchard
Schick, E. (1987) *Art lessons.* New York: Greenwillow
Small, D. (1987) *Paper John.* New York: Farrar, Straus
Spier, P. (1978) *Oh, were they ever happy!* New York: Doubleday
Wadell, M. (1988) *Alice the artist.* Illustrated by J. Langley. New York: Dutton

Novels

de Trevino, E. B. (1965) *I, Juan de Pareja.* New York: Farrar, Straus
Konigsburg, E. L. (1967) *From the mixed up files of Mrs. Basil E. Frankweiler.* New York: Atheneum
Paterson, K. (1979) *Bridge to Terabithia.* New York: Harper
Picard, B. L. (1966) *One is one.* New York: Holt
Sutcliff, R. (1978) *Sun horse, moon horse.* New York: Dutton

The Elements of Art

Fisher, L. E. (1986) *Look around, a book about shapes.* New York: Viking
Hoban, T. (1978) *Is it red? Is it yellow? Is it blue?* New York: Greenwillow
Hoban, T. (1984) *Is it rough? Is it smooth? Is it shiny?* New York: Greenwillow
Hoban, T. (1986) *Shapes, shapes, shapes.* New York: Greenwillow
Hoban, T. (1987) *Dots, spots, speckles, and stripes.* New York: Greenwillow
Lionni, L. (1959) *Little blue and little yellow.* New York: Astor
Walsh, E. S. (1989) *Mouse paint.* San Diego, CA: Harcourt, Brace

The Art of the Picture Book

Aliki (1986) *How a book is made.* New York: Harper
Blegvad, E. (1979) *Self portrait, Eric Blegvad.* Reading, MA: Addison Wesley
Fischer, L. E. (1986) *The papermakers.* Boston, MA: David Godine
Hyman, T. S. (1981) *Self portrait, Trina Schart Hyman.* Reading, MA: Addison Wesley
Irvine, J. (1987) *How to make pop-ups.* Illustrated by Barbara Reid. New York: William Morrow
Zemach, M. (1978) *Self portrait, Margot Zemach.* Reading, MA: Addison Wesley

The Science of Art and Music

Allison, L. & Katz, D. (1982) *Gee whiz! How to mix art and science or the art of thinking scientifically.* Boston, MA: Little, Brown
Baum, A. & J. (1987) *Opt: an illusionary tale.* New York: Viking
Branley, F. M. (1978) *Color: from rainbow to lasers.* Illustrated by H. Roth. New York: Crowell
Kettelkamp, L. (1982) *The magic of sound.* Illustrated by A. Kramer. New York: William Morrow
Simon, H. (1981) *The magic of color.* New York: Lothrop

Looking at Music Through Books

Making Music

Hawkinson, J. & Faulhaber, M. (1969) *Music and instruments for children to make.* Niles, IL: Albert Whitman
Stecher, M. (1980) *Max the music maker.* New York: Lothrop
Walther, T. (1981) *Make mine music.* Boston, MA: Little, Brown
Wiseman, A. (1979) *Making musical things.* New York: Scribner

Music History and Appreciation

Anderson, D. (1982) *The piano makers.* New York: Pantheon
Ardley, N. (1989) *Music.* Photos by D. King, P. Dowell, and M. Dunning. New York: Alfred Knopf
Arnold, C. (1985) *Music lessons for Alex.* New York: Clarion
Berliner, D. C. (1961) *All about the orchestra and what it plays.* New York: Random House
Bierhorst, J. (1979) *A cry from the earth: music of the North American Indians.* New York: Four Winds
Busnar, G. (1979) *It's rock and roll.* New York: Julian Messner
Englander, R. (1983) *Opera! What's all the screaming about?* New York: Walker
English, B. L. (1980) *You can't be timid with a trumpet.* New York: Lothrop
Fornatale, P. (1987) *The story of rock 'n' roll.* New York: Morrow
Gass, I. (1970) *Mozart: child wonder, child composer.* New York: Lothrop
Glass, P. (1969) *Singing soldiers: a history of the Civil War in Song.* New York: Grosset & Dunlap
Haskins, J. (1987) *Black music in America.* New York: Crowell
Houston, J. (1972) *Songs of the dream people: chants and images of the Indians and Eskimos of North America.* New York: Atheneum
Lasker, D. (1979) *The boy who loved music.* Illustrated by J. Lasker. New York: Viking
Monjo, F. N. (1975) *Letters to horseface: being the story of Wolfgang Amadeus Mozart's journey to Italy.* New York: Viking
Previn, A. (ed.) (1983) *Andre Previn's guide to the orchestra.* New York: Putnam

Schaff, P. (1980) *The violin close up.* New York: Four Winds
Stevens, B. (1983) *Ben Franklin's glass harmonica.* Minneapolis, MN: Carolrhoda
Suggs, W. W. (1971) *Meet the orchestra.* Illustrated by E. Arno. New York: Macmillan
Terkel, S. (1975) *Giants of jazz.* New York: Crowell
Weil, L. (1979) *The magic of music.* New York: Holiday House

Music into Stories

Aliki (1974) *Go tell Aunt Rhody.* New York: Macmillan
Bangs, E. (1976) *Steven Kellogg's yankee doodle.* Illustrated by Steven Kellogg. New York: Parents' Magazine Press
Emberley, B. (1966) *One wide river to cross.* Illustrated by E. Emberley. New York: Prentice-Hall
Hoffman, E. T. A. (1984) *The nutcracker.* Illustrated by Maurice Sendak. New York: Crown
Jeffers, S. (1974) *All the pretty horses.* New York: Macmillan
Langstaff, J. (1974) *Oh a-hunting we will go.* Illustrated by N. W. Parker. New York: Atheneum
Langstaff, J. & Rojankovsky, F. (1967) *Over in the meadow.* San Diego, CA: Harcourt Brace
Leodhas, S. N. (1965) *Always room for one more.* Illustrated by N. Hogrogian. New York: Holt
Menotti, G. C. (1986) *Amahl and the night visitors.* Illustrated by M. Lemieux. New York: Morrow
Paterson, A. B. (1970) *Waltzing Matilda.* Illustrated by D. Digby. New York: Holt
Peek, M. (1987) *The balancing act: a counting song.* New York: Clarion
Prokofoeff, S. (1982) *Peter and the wolf.* Illustrated by C. Mikolaycak. New York: Viking
Quakenbush, R. (1972) *Old MacDonald had a farm.* New York: Lippincott
Spier, P. (1970) *The Erie Canal.* New York: Doubleday
Stanley, D. (1979) *Fiddle-i-fee.* Boston, MA: Little, Brown
Stevens, J. (1981) *Animal fair.* New York: Holiday House
Zemach, M. (1976) *Hush little baby.* New York: Dutton

Music as a Theme
Picture Books and Illustrated Stories

Akerman, K. (1988) *Song and dance man.* Illustrated by S. Gammell. New York: Knopf
Baylor, B. (1982) *Moon song.* Illustrated by R. Himler. New York: Scribner
Bodecker, N. M. (1981) *The lost string quartet.* New York: Atheneum
Carlson, N. (1983) *Loudmouth George and the cornet.* Minneapolis, MN: Carolrhoda
Fleischman, P. (1988) *Rondo in C.* Illustrated by J. Wentworth. New York: Harper
Goffstein, M. B. (1972) *A little Schubert.* New York: Harper
Griffith, H. (1986) *Georgia music.* Illustrated by J. Stevenson. New York: Greenwillow
Hasley, D. (1983) *The old banjo.* Illustrated by S. Gammel. New York: Macmillan
Hill, D. (1978) *Ms. Glee was waiting.* Illustrated by D. Hill. New York: Atheneum
Isadora, R. (1979) *Ben's trumpet.* New York: Greenwillow
Komaiko, L. (1987) *I like the music.* Illustrated by B. Westman. New York: Harper
Kuskin, K. (1982) *The Philharmonic gets dressed.* Illustrated by M. Simont. New York: Harper
Lionni, L. (1979) *Geraldine the music mouse.* New York: Random House
Martin, B. & Archambault, J. (1986) *Barn dance.* Illustrated by T. Rand. New York: Holt
Monjo, F. N. (1970) *The drinking gourd.* Illustrated by F. Brenner. New York: Harper
Schick, E. (1984) *A piano for Julie.* New York: Greenwillow
Thomas, I. (1981) *Willie blows a mean horn.* New York: Harper
Walter, M. P. (1980) *Ty's one-man band.* New York: Four Winds
Weik, M. H. (1966) *The jazz man.* Illustrated by A. Grifalconi. New York: Atheneum
Williams, V. B. (1984) *Music, music for everyone.* New York: Greenwillow
Yorinks, A. (1988) *Bravo Minsky!* Illustrated by S. Egielski. New York: Farrar, Straus

Novels

Angell, J. (1982) *Buffalo nickel blues band.* New York: Bradbury
Duder, T. (1986) *Jellybean.* New York: Viking
Gilson, J. (1979) *Dial Leroi Rupert DJ.* New York: Lothrop
Hilgartner, B. (1986) *A murder for her majesty.* Boston, MA: Houghton Mifflin
Lisle, J. T. (1986) *Sirens and spies.* New York: Bradbury
MacLachlan, P. (1988) *The facts and fictions of Minna Pratt.* New York: Harper
McCaffrey, A. (1976) *Dragonsong.* New York: Macmillan
Newton, S. (1983) *I will call it Georgie's blues.* New York: Viking
Paterson, K. (1985) *Come sing Jimmy Jo.* New York: Dutton
Paulsen, G. (1985) *Dogsong.* Bradbury
Pinkwater, D. M. (1976) *Lizard music.* New York: Dodd, Mead
Showell, E. (1983) *Cecelia and the Blue Mountain boy.* New York: Lothrop
Turkle, B. (1968) *The fiddler of High Lonesome.* New York: Viking
Voigt, C. (1983) *Dicey's song.* New York: Atheneum
Weller, F. W. (XXXX) *Boat song.* New York: Macmillan

Keep in mind, then, the important role played by artists in the community and by the art and music specialist in your school. In the following section, classroom activities are suggested that can serve as foundations, easily laid by teachers, that will allow the specialists to build further expertise and understanding in the realms of art and music.

Art and Music Makers

Children learn through the languages of art and music.

Art and music are not simply tools for teaching concepts in other content areas but ways of knowing these concepts. They allow children to explore a theme, act on it, and transform it. The integrated language classroom thus provides many opportunities to create art and music and many materials and avenues of expression.

Try to make available as full a range of materials and instruments as the school budget will allow, and encourage children to consider their use as they choose ways to explore a given theme. These would include simple musical instruments and basic art supplies as well as items donated from the local community or found in the natural environment. For your someday wish list consider the use of computers and/or synthesizers that would allow children to compose, play, read, and listen to music as well as to learn notation and orchestration and to experiment with the sounds of various instruments. Or consider how interactive video disks would allow children to have immediate access to the art of the world's great museums.

Upitis (1983)

Made readily available, the simplest materials and instruments can give children the means for creating a variety of art and music in response to themes being studied. As part of "Exploring Nature" (a subtopic of EXPLORATIONS), for example, first graders may want to translate sounds and rhythms they noted on a nature walk into a symphony of sounds using natural, child-made instruments or some of the simple percussion instruments. Some children may choose to do block prints, gluing natural objects such as leaves and grasses to cardboard, inking them with a brayer (a roller used in printing), and then pressing a sheet of construction paper onto the inked surface. Others may want to do a natural hanging by suspending "found" objects from a stick with yarn, and weaving twigs, grasses, and other elements into this warp.

Walther (1981)

Graham (1976)

As part of a TIME theme, children may take a simple and familiar tune such as "Twinkle, Twinkle, Little Star" and play it on recorders. Then they may change it into a morning song, an afternoon song, a summer song, or a winter song, varying tempo, pitch, and dynamics. They can then listen to Ferde Grofé's "Grand Canyon Suite," which depicts different times of day, or listen to the variations that Mozart wrote for "Twinkle, Twinkle, Little Star."

Brandt (1988b)

Children involved in a theme of CHANGES could decide to do a painting of a local scene and want to discuss what colors or media they may choose to express changes at different times of the day, seasonal changes, or weather changes. By thinking about the ways that colors can affect feelings or the way that qualities of media such as acrylic or watercolor paints can convey meaning, children can also be led to appreciate the choices made by artists such as Claude Monet or Winslow Homer, who spent much of their careers depicting the changing light in landscapes and cityscapes.

Books often weave into a story a musical or artistic theme that suggests a musical or artistic response. Reading about "Sea Journeys" (a subtopic of JOURNEYS) may lead children to listen to the many musical interpretations of the sea, then create their own sea symphony with voice and instrument. As part of a study of "Personal Journeys," children can read Gary Paulsen's *Dogsong,* in which a young Inuit boy, Russel, braves the arctic wilderness in a search for himself and his cultural heritage. They then may seek to interpret the story through a melody and instrument that represent Russel's song or through a monochromatic painting, using shades of blue and white to represent not only the frigid arctic landscape but also to convey the mood of the character's isolation.

Paulsen (1985)

Students DIGGING UP THE PAST may want to make sketches of animal symbols found on fragments of Native American pottery, noting the abstraction of form and pattern. Then they may choose to create their own artifacts by building clay coil pots and decorating them with their own personal symbols. A group of children could create a ceramic tile mural or a mosaic of key events and understandings gleaned from their study. Others may read John Bierhorst's *A Cry from the Earth: Music of North American Indians.* The book suggests and presents Native American instruments, songs, dances, and masks that were part of music making. It could serve as a springboard for some remarkable art and music activities. These last suggestions, many of which incorporate music-making, dance, and art could serve to summarize a unit such as DIGGING UP THE PAST in ways that are every bit as effective as writing a research report.

Bierhorst (1979)

The arts can be used to summarize a unit.

However art and music making are incorporated into the integrated classroom, they provide children with a richness of expression and an added depth of understanding. Although there is not space in the present book to include detailed instructions for art and music projects, we have summarized some of the activities that would be possible as part of a thematic unit:

Music and Art as Ways of Knowing

Music

Listen to or sing theme-related music.
Do finger plays and movement exploration.
Compose music to interpret stories or poems.
Choose theme music for a story or novel.
Orchestrate poems for choral reading.
Make instruments.
Listen to sounds in nature or sounds in the city; represent pitches and rhythms on a musical scale.
Collect old song lyrics. What do these say about the time in which they were written?
Compare musical forms in your own culture.
Compare music tastes and music makers in other cultures.

Art

Weave natural objects into wall hangings.
Create a class theme quilt out of embroidered panels.
Draw a map for a work of fiction.
Make sculpture out of cardboard and plastic pipe.
Create character portraits out of clay.
Make a diorama or shoebox scene in miniature.
Paint a mural of a theme's important ideas.
Sculpt papier mâché masks.
Illustrate with watercolor collage or other media.
Sketch with charcoal or pastel chalk.
Make linoleum or meat tray prints.
Make batik or crayon-resist wall hangings.
Compare art forms in your own culture.
Compare art tastes and artists in other cultures.
Compare illustrators' media and styles.

Talking About Art and Music

When children are involved in the production of various forms of art and music, they gain control over various media such as clay, watercolor, and pastels or over such simple instruments as the human voice, recorder, and string instruments. In addition, they may begin to think about the expressive properties inherent in these art forms. Having time to explore a given instrument or medium in depth gives children opportunities to think about themselves as choice-makers as they seek to express meaning through an art form. They may come to understand that they may choose an element of art or music for its literal property (a piece of music has tempo or a painting has shapes), but that element also has expressive or metaphorical properties (a fast tempo can convey tension or the hectic pace of life or a rectangular shape can convey weight or repose).

Talk provides a focus for developing aesthetic and critical awareness or for reflecting on art forms.

Encourage children to reflect on and talk about their experiences with the arts. It is through talk that questions essential to aesthetic understandings can be raised. ("Does art have to be beautiful?" "Do we have to know what a piece of music is 'about' to enjoy it?" "Can truth be found in fiction?") Talk also provides children with the experience necessary for developing critical awareness. ("What makes this picture more effective than that?" "What criteria do I apply when I listen to a new piece of music?")

Being able to talk with children about the arts does not take expert knowledge in any of these disciplines. Teachers can ask some simple but powerful questions that will help children to think about the emotive power of art and music, another key to developing aesthetic awareness. "Why did you choose watercolor instead of tempera paint for your painting?" "Did you choose these colors for a particular reason?" "What were you thinking about as you looked at (listened to) that picture (song)?" "How did that painting (composition) make you feel?" "Why would you say that?" Young children will probably respond with idiosyncratic reasons ("I chose red because I like red"), but older children begin to understand the stylistic choices available to them and to other artists. In addition, teachers may want to use some of the critical vocabulary associated with the forms of each particular discipline in the same way they use words such as *word, sentence, character, setting, story,* or *report* in discussing the elements and forms of language. Such words or terminology help children begin to think about how artists or musicians convey meaning through a given art form, which in turn can provide fertile ground for developing aesthetic and critical awareness.

Gardner & Winner (1982)

To illustrate how this might be done, let us take an art form that is already a familiar part of integrated language classrooms and show how talking about picture books can develop an aesthetic awareness in children. It may seem surprising to think that such a familiar object as a picture book would be considered an art form, but today's picture books are part of artistic tradition dating at least as far back as 1300 B.C. to the Egyptian *Book of the Dead.* During the Middle Ages, the book illustrator or painter was held in equal esteem with the painter and sculptor, and well into the nineteenth century "the history of drawing and painting is almost exclusively devoted to the concept of pictorial narrative" (p. 215). Today with sophisticated printing techniques, book illustration is attracting many talented artists who are working in a variety of original media (the illustrator's original work may be executed in media like watercolor, pen and ink, stitchery, or collage and then reproduced by means of printing techniques).

Marantz (1989)

Marantz argues that picture books are "not literature but rather a form of visual art" (p. 154). As an *art* form the picture book is a combination of image and idea in a sequence of turning pages. When words are present, they support the pictures just as the pictures extend and enhance the meaning of the words. When we close the pages of the best picture books, we experience something that is much more than the sum of the parts.

Marantz (1983)

Studying the art of the picture book has advantages over studying reproductions of paintings or listening to recordings of a symphony. A reproduction of a painting may not be faithful to the color of the original, nor is the texture of the painting's surface accurately reproduced. More important, the size of the original may have a great impact on the viewer's response, yet reproductions are seldom faithful to a painting's original size. The picture book, on the other hand, keeps its integrity as an art object. It does not matter if we cannot see the original artwork because these originals were created so that they could be photographically reproduced and bound together within the covers of the book. Marantz explains, "What is printed on the book's pages *is* the artwork in the same sense that the printed etching (and not the metal plate) is" (p. 215).

Marantz (1989)

When you are talking with children about the art of the picture book, it may help to connect children's experiences with making choices in their own art to the choices made by the artist seeking to convey some visual meaning. Just as writers use words and sentences to create character and setting, theme and mood in the story, illustrators use line, shape, color, value, and texture to convey these same properties. As mentioned, the art elements have their objective or exemplified qualities (lines can be jagged or curving, shapes can be sharp edged or biomorphic), and they have their expressive qualities (jagged lines convey a feeling of excitement or danger, while curving lines seem restful or rhythmic). These elements are chosen and composed using the principles of design, that is, balance, rhythm, repetition, variety, unity, and eye movement: In a painting, of course, these elements and principles are present on only a single pictorial plane. In a picture book the artist can use elements and principles to unify the entire book and bring added power to the final art object.

Kiefer (1988b)

See Kiefer (1988b) for a more detailed discussion of elements of art in picture books.

An illustrator is also concerned with the technical aspects of book production. The artist's choice of original media, typeface, end pages, pictorial content, or viewpoint can add meaning and depth to the book. Likewise, illustrators may also rely on historical conventions or cultural conventions, aspects of art that have come to be identified with a particular period or culture. When adapted by an illustrator, these conventions can add to our understanding of a tale set in the past or in a distant place. Arnold Lobel, for example, used aspects of Dutch portraiture, landscape, and genre painting in *The Microscope,* the story of Anton van Leuwenhoek, who was a contemporary of Rembrandt and Vermeer. Nancy Ekholm Burkert chose elements of Oriental art to tell *The Nightingale,* Hans Christian Andersen's fantasy set in ancient China. Not only do these adaptations of historical and cultural conventions help make children more sensitive to the many choices available to an artist, but they also provide possibilities for connecting art in the classroom to art in the museum.

Kumin (1984)
Andersen (1965)

Understandings regarding style in picture books will help teachers to bring the best picture books into their classrooms and enable teachers to bring added depth to discussions about picture books. These ideas are also applicable to music and the other arts. Notice, for example, how concepts of form and composition such as movement, balance, mood, harmony, repetition, pattern, and motif are present when we talk about music and literature as well as when we talk about art. In all these areas the artist, the composer, the writer must make choices in order to convey meaning, just as children are choice makers in constructing their world.

It is not always necessary or profitable to teach these elements to children or to expect them to apply abstract stylistic labels. Instead, aesthetic understandings grow in the broader context of the integrated language classroom. While children are involved in the act of creating art, music, or writing, they may come to see how various elements convey and enhance meaning. While they are involved in talk about art, music, and literature, they acquire the words for talking about the elements and mechanics of these and other art forms. While they observe and talk with artists, musicians, and other professionals, they become more insightful about their own processes of creation. We hope they will use these understandings to broaden the scope of artistic, musical, and other forms that provide them enjoyment, and we hope also that they will become increasingly sophisticated in their search for quality in all these art forms.

Children discover style by being choice-makers.

Art and Music in the Wider World

The suggestions for using art and music in the integrated classroom are highly compatible with recent trends in arts education. The knowledge represented by art and music extends beyond the range of a single genre such as painting or choral performance to encompass broader domains. For example, notice how our understanding of domains of knowledge applies in the case of children engaged in making clay pots. In addition to producing, perceiving, and reflecting on the art of ceramics, and considering the aesthetic, historical, and critical ramifications of pottery, children can come to understand how the decoration on pottery represents accurate primary source material and gives

Children develop understandings beyond the range of a single work or single art discipline.

us access to the culture and social structure of other times, sometimes in the absence of any written history. (What legend is retold on the surface of the Greek vase? What symbols were important to Native Americans of the Southwest?) Moreover, as they create their own pottery, children must think about the object's use as a container. (Will it hold liquids or solids? Will it be used for cooking or storage?) They will gain experience with concepts of volume, mass, and density. They will have a chance to consider the object's weight in relation to its structure and form. (Will it stand up if the bottom is narrow and the top wide?) They will be able to consider the physical makeup of soils, to note changes in matter, and to think about chemical changes that may occur during the firing process. (Is it more likely to hold liquids after it is fired? Why might it explode in the kiln? What happens to the colors in glazes during the firing?) They must consider an object's placement in space and contrast three-dimensional and two-dimensional space. (When does an object have a bottom and a top but also a front and back?) Such powerful understandings are possible through musical experiences as well as the other arts and form the basis for the suggestions we have made in this chapter. These understandings show how children learn art and music as domains of knowledge. Their experience with certain media like clay or watercolor, percussion instruments or voice help them to explore more specific domains in different ways. Figure 7.5 is a visual summary of the ways in which art and music encompass and connect to many domains of knowledge.

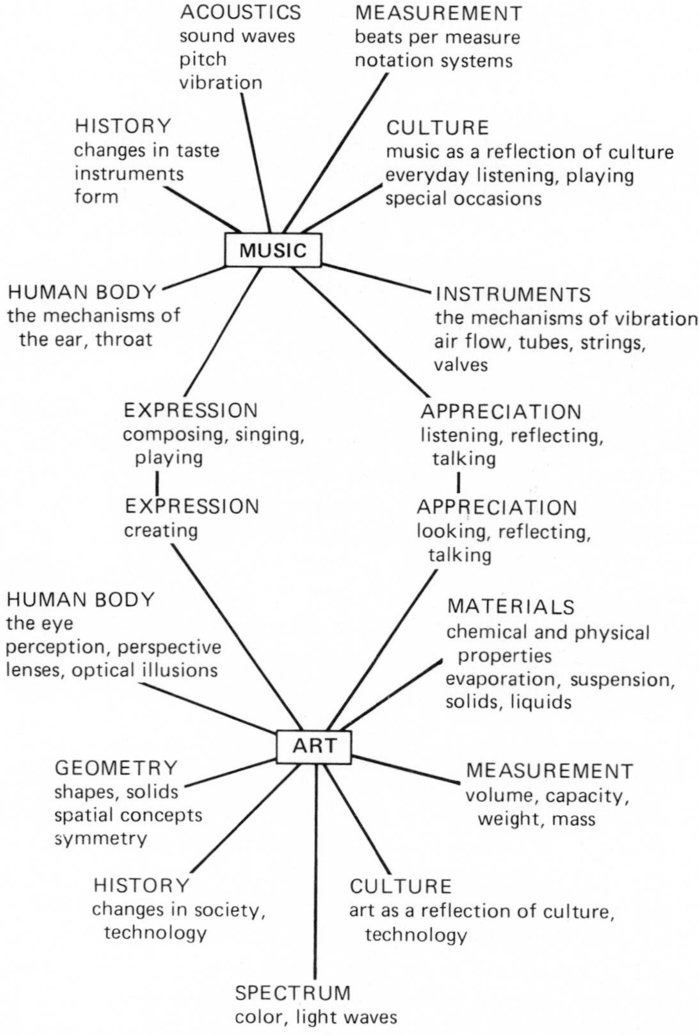

Figure 7.5 Interrelations among Domains of Knowledge in Music and Art

Moreover, part of helping children to develop an aesthetic awareness involves helping them to become sensitive to the sights and sounds in the world around them, to look and listen with a practiced eye and ear. In an integrated language classroom, the experiences children have with art and music can develop their sensitivities in a variety of subtle ways.

The arts make children more sensitive to sensory aspects of the world around them.

Sketching objects or scenes as a prelude to writing, for example, may also make children more aware of small nuances of detail, pattern, or texture that they can describe with words. Discovering the details or visual subplots that so many illustrators include in pictures, children may look more carefully at the world around them, noting, for example, subtle differences in the changes taking place in the tadpole aquarium or the textures and colors of an early spring day.

As children gain experience as makers of music, they may become more sensitive to the qualities of the human voice that they can use in reading aloud or in creative dramatics. As they listen to music, they may become aware of the subtle effects of such qualities as pitch and volume on their understandings and feelings when they listen to a sales pitch or the evening news. This attention to detail and the aesthetic qualities of the world can lead to a heightened concern with the environment (both in and out of the classroom) and with their own work. A sensitivity to musical sound, for example, can lead to greater understanding of noise in the outside world and its positive and negative effects on the emotions. Involvement with the visual arts can help to sensitize children to pollution and urban clutter.

However you and your students get involved and whatever the outcomes, art and music need to happen frequently for children of all ages. To limit children's involvement with the arts is to deprive them of powerful means of expression and understanding and to deny them the fullest opportunity for knowing themselves and their world.

ART AND MUSIC REFERENCES

Arnheim, R. (1974). *Art and visual perception: A psychology of the creative eye.* Berkeley, CA: University of California Press.

Brandt, R. (1988a). On discipline-based art education: A conversation with Elliott Eisner. *Educational Leadership, 45* (4), 6–9.

Brandt, R. (1988b). On assessment in the arts: A conversation with Howard Gardner. *Educational Leadership, 45* (4), 30–34.

Dyson, A. H. (1986). Transitions and tensions: Interrelationships between the drawing, talking, and dictating of young children. *Research in the Teaching of English, 20* (4), 379–409.

Gardner, H. (1980). *Artful scribbles: The significance of children's drawings.* New York: Basic Books.

Gardner, H. (1982). *Art, mind, and brain: A cognitive approach to creativity.* New York: Basic Books.

Gardner, H., & Winner, E. (1982). Children's conceptions (and misconceptions) of the arts. In H. Gardner (Ed.), *Art, mind, and brain: A cognitive approach to creativity* (pp. 103–209). New York: Basic Books.

Graham, A. (1976). *Fossils, ferns and fish scales: A handbook of art and nature projects.* Illustrated by Dorothea Stoke. New York: Four Winds Press.

Kiefer, B. (1988a). Images and ideas: Picture books for all the ages. *School Library Media Quarterly, 16* (4), 249–250.

Kiefer, B. (1988b). Picture books as contexts for literary, aesthetic and real world understandings. *Language Arts, 65* (3), 260–271.

Langer, S. (1942, 1978). *Philosophy in a new key.* Cambridge, MA: Harvard University Press.

Marantz, K. (1983). The picture book as art object: A call for balanced reviewing. In R. Bator (Ed.), *Signposts to criticism of children's literature.* Chicago, IL: American Library Association.

Marantz, K. (1989). Letters. *Journal of Youth Services in Libraries, 2* (3), 215.

McFee, J. K., & Degge, R. M., (1980). *Art, culture and environment: A catalyst for teaching.* Dubuque, IA: Kendall Hunt Publishing.

Upitis, R. (1983). Milestones in computer music instruction. *Music Educators Journal, 69* (5), 40–42.

CHILDREN'S LITERATURE, ART AND MUSIC

A CRY FROM THE EARTH: MUSIC OF NORTH AMERICAN INDIANS by J. Bierhorst. Four Winds, 1979.

DOGSONG by G. Paulsen. Bradbury, 1985.

MAKE MINE MUSIC by T. Walther. Little, Brown, 1981.

THE MICROSCOPE by M. Kumin. Illustrated by A. Lobel. Harper & Row, 1984.

THE NIGHTINGALE by H. C. Andersen. Illustrated by N. E. Burkett. Harper & Row.

CONCLUSIONS

An integrated curriculum is certainly organized to foster opportunities for language use across the curriculum and to help children see the connections between the various content areas that constitute the elementary curriculum, but it is also organized to capture children's interest and motivate their continued engagement in meaningful work. Although this chapter suggests only a sampling of the ways in which this engagement occurs, the research and theory behind the suggestions can facilitate a teacher's decision-making. An integrated curriculum is based on a model of teachers as learners and decision-makers as well as on research and theories about children as learners. Throughout the examples in this chapter, teachers have used their knowledge about children and about content to construct a range of interesting and challenging activities. Moreover, they have tried to diminish the barriers and make connections between schooling and the outside world. Thus, children have opportunities to go into the curricular domains in depth as well as to see the connections between those domains.

More on How-to: Ideas for Implementation in Integrated Language Classrooms

This chapter provides more how-to details of some of the routines, activities, experiences by which integrated language classrooms are realized. Traditional schooling often separates the process of learning from the content to be learned; it has generally depended on a model of information accumulation. In this model, children are expected to learn and remember information about particular subjects without necessarily understanding the nature of the information learned, how it came to be accepted as a part of a particular domain, or how to evaluate it relative to other information from that domain or any other. You probably remember classes like these. In science, perhaps, you memorized definitions for terms or formulas intended to explain *work* and *force*. Too frequently, though, you did not conduct experiments with machines that could do work, or with levers and pulleys that could lessen the force exerted to do a particular type of work. You may have been able to pass the exam, but you didn't really understand the underlying concepts related to all the terminology. Much of what you learned probably became dated before you ever had a chance to fit it into some schema to help you explain the forces that operated in the natural world. Not so very long ago, children dutifully memorized this sort of definition for *atom:* An atom is the smallest indivisible piece of matter. Not very useful in light of fission and fusion and atomic weapons beyond our wildest imaginings.

Many traditional school practices separate process from content.

Recent research on domain-specific cognition, already discussed in previous chapters, suggests that this old model of acquiring information is an inadequate way to teach and learn. Instead, there is mounting evidence that understanding processing and understanding content are inextricably bound. The schemas that provide intellectual "scaffolding" for new learning are built through experience with a particular body of knowledge in a particular context. Further experience—education—builds our repertoire of knowledge and contexts and allows us to think more abstractly and in more mature ways.

The traditional information accumulation model is outmoded.

Hyde & Bizar (1989)

It is not enough, then, simply to go through the motions of problem-solving in a sort of cookbook approach. Instead, teachers must make time for discussion and thought. It is not appropriate simply to assign children a problem for homework, collect the results the next day, and move on. Children must be guided in their research, and given appropriate resources for study. They need to work collaboratively and to have opportunities to think out loud—that is, to engage in reflection—with a responsive teacher and peer audience; they need to revise, rethink, and test ideas to learn from

Children need collaborative reflection.

and with their peers. They need to communicate with one another to consider *what all this means.* What difference does it make, for instance, if children clean up their school playground as part of an antilitter campaign? What difference does it make if children learn to recognize bias in a newspaper report? What use is that skill in their lives?

Children as adaptive experts

This is not just a "good citizen" view of education and learning. Reflection puts research and learning into the larger context of the world beyond the schoolroom walls. It is also both a communal and personal endeavor. Children build their own meanings, try them on teacher and peers, and in the process, revise and/or find ways to defend them. They are adaptive experts; they learn what it takes to argue for a position and what constitutes adequate evidence. They participate in the give and take and excitement of a community of learners where thinking is respected and good ideas are shared. The activities described in this chapter are suggestions for ways in which the development of a community of learners can be fostered. Many have already been mentioned, but they are examined in more detail here.

Hatano (1988)

Activities herein are selective.

Activities herein are suggestions.

Activities herein are interrelated and integrated.

Three interrelated caveats, however, need to be pointed out ahead of time regarding these activities. First, the activities or experiences presented do not constitute an exhaustive list. We have been selective, trying to include critical activities that show the range of implementation across the curriculum. Integrated language classroom teachers (and children) are constantly discovering new ways, new activities, to implement their own teaching and learning goals. Consequently, what is provided here should be considered only as examples of the possibilities. Second, the activities, as has already been noted, are only *suggestions* of how to manage a classroom. It is assumed that these ideas will be modified and reshaped by particular teachers and children to meet particular purposes and circumstances. Finally, we are forced in this chapter to describe these activities separately and linearly, but it is important not to conceive of them as such. In reality, most of the time these activities are incorporated into other activities, which is one of the reasons that the perspective in the book is called "integrated." In sum, the spirit of this chapter is to describe activities so you have enough information to try, or put into action in the classroom, some of the principles of the integrated language perspective.

Figure 8.1 depicts the organization of the activities in the chapter.

Some of the activities we describe are grouped together under a broad category. For example, graphic organizers is a general category consisting of four types of activities: Graffiti Walls*, Semantic Maps*, Semantic Feature Charts*, and Comparison Charts*. Two large categories include reading and writing activities and experiences, respectively. Certain experiences (e.g., Reflective Inquiry*, using Primary Sources*, and Observation/Inference*, using Graphic Organizers*) are explained first because they represent more basic or universal processes and strategies that underlie or incorporate many of the other activities. Message Board* and Mini-Lessons* are covered last because their use is more widespread in the classroom. Figure 8.1 depicts this organization and will help you locate a particular activity or experience within the chapter.

REFLECTIVE INQUIRY*

Reflective inquiry is an important way to link process and content in a meaningful context. This approach has two parts. The first sets up an inquiry or investigation into a question that has power for a particular group of children. You can see some of the ways in which this is done by reading the Prototypes in Chapter 4. Once a problem or question has been raised, children gather relevant data and use such processes as observation, inference, classification, measurement, ordering, and hypothesizing to analyze the data and propose possible solutions to problems or answers to questions. Not all problems will have single or simple solutions, and many may lead children into a variety of other explorations along the way to resolving the original concern. The processes are similar to those generally referred to as the *scientific method.*

Ellis (1986)

Arthur Ellis provides this description of an inquiry conducted by a second grade class:

Reflective Inquiry*
Primary Sources*
  Jackdaws*
Observation and Inference*
Graphic Organizers*
  Graffiti Walls*
  Semantic Maps*
  Semantic Feature Charts*
  Comparison Charts*

Reading Activities and Experiences

Reading Aloud*
Storytelling*
Sustained Silent Reading (SSR)*
Buddy Reading*
Book Talks*
Response Groups*
Book Response Journals*
Reading Conferences*
Big Books*
CLOZE*
Say Something*
General Problem-Solving
Reading Strategies*

Writing Activities and Experiences

Journals*
  Dialogue Journals*
  Thought Ramblings*
  Learning Logs*
Group Composed Writing*
Authors' Folders*
Writing Conferences*
  Content Conferences*
  Editing Conferences*
Publishing Experiences*
  Displays*
  Book Making*
  Author's Chair*

Sketch to Stretch*
Activity Cards*
Graphing*

Book Extensions*
  Story Mapping*
  Plot Profiles*
  Character Sociograms*

Drama Experiences*
  Improvisation*
  Television News Broadcasts and Talk Shows*
  Puppetry*
  Choral Reading*
  Readers' Theatre*
  Story Theatre*

Message Board*
Mini-Lessons*

Figure 8.1 Organizational Chart for Chapter 8 Activities and Experiences

One morning, members of a second-grade class were excitedly telling their teacher and each other about a near accident that had occurred at a pedestrian crossing next to the school. A primary-age child was nearly struck by a car as she was crossing the street. The students exclaimed that the intersection was dangerous, especially during the winter months when ice and snow were present. The teacher asked the students if they would like to conduct an investigation of the intersection to see how dangerous it really was and to see if they could suggest ways to make it safer. The class agreed that this would be a worthwhile project.

The class wrote a *statement of the problem* as follows: How can our school crossing be made safer? With the teacher's help, the class decided to use the following *data sources* in their research: a model of the intersection; the intersection itself; other students in the school; school staff members, including teachers, custodians, the principal, and the secretary; local residents; photographs of the intersection; and drivers who use the intersection. Working all together as well as in teams over the course of several weeks, the class *gathered data* through interviews, observation of traffic flow, timing the speed of cars near the intersection, and taking pictures of pedestrian, bicycle, and automobile traffic at peak crossing times before and after school. The students *processed their data* with a photo essay of the intersection, summaries of interviews, drawings of the intersection depicting the various problems they had discovered, and charts showing the volume of foot, bicycle, and auto traffic at peak hours.

They *made the following inferences:*

1. The crossing is dangerous, especially for younger children, and a safety awareness campaign is needed.
2. Four safety patrol students should be placed on duty rather than two, the present number.
3. Larger, more visible warning signs should be posted along the streets leading to the intersection.
4. The crosswalk lines should be repainted.

Their report was given to the school principal and to the police department. The students were pleased to see that all four of their recommendations were enacted. (pp. 197–199)

When children are engaged in this study, they create a number of documents, including surveys, graphs, and charts. Some of them may have more trouble than others with these forms. The teacher may not notice some of these problems by simple observation, but the children discuss their projects in their Learning Logs*, and the teacher can respond with suggestions and specific help. In addition, children may include some of the work from this project in a portfolio (see Chapter 9) that is shared with the teacher as part of an evaluation of their work during the study.

Hyde & Bizar (1989); Wassermann & Ivany (1988)

A second and equally crucial part of this approach is the kind of *reflection* discussed in the opening paragraphs of this chapter. Some people call this time to think and discuss *debriefing,* and we will use both terms to refer to this important aspect of reflective inquiry. In the intersection example, for instance, the teacher may debrief for ten minutes after the investigation is concluded by asking children to consider the processes used, their applicability to other problems, and the uses to which they can put their conclusions.

In addition to a final debriefing, reflection occurs throughout a study. Some teachers take five or ten minutes at the end of a work period to reflect with students about problems and successes encountered during that work time. Sometimes a spokesperson for each group working on a project will briefly report to the rest of the class; sometimes groups or individuals are encouraged to share information they have found that would be relevant to another person or group. Teachers facilitate this sharing by knowing what the children are working on, and by encouraging them to consult other students and other resources in the room.

Levstik (1986)

In one sixth grade class the teacher encourages the development of peer "experts." As the children read a variety of historical literature in preparation for selecting History Day projects, the teacher keeps track of areas where one child's study will help someone else. A child reading about medicine, for instance, came across information on Elizabeth Blackwell, a pioneer in women's entry into medicine, which was useful to another student reading about women in nontraditional occupations. The teacher organized a response group to include both these students so that they had an opportunity to share their information and expertise. At other times, when children asked the teacher questions, she referred them to a student "expert" who had been reading in that area and could be a knowledgeable resource. The teacher also encouraged children to develop particular expertise by asking them to read up on a subject that no one else seemed to know much about: "I'd like you to read this book on David Ben-Gurion. No one else seems to have discovered him, and we will need that background if we are going to discuss what's happening in the Middle East. Could you be our Ben-Gurion expert?" Soon, children looked for peer expertise without teacher suggestion and sought opportunities to develop expertise themselves.

Ellis (1986)

Reflection can also be encouraged by involving children in tackling ambiguous problems that may not be a part of a larger thematic unit, such as (1) inventing a new language and a form for writing it, (2) proving that the earth is moving, (3) designing a better human being, and (4) drawing a picture of democracy. These types of activities are exercises in divergent thinking. Children are challenged to think about multiple ways of solving problems rather than converging on a single solution. Each problem is grist for the mill of reflection and an opportunity to use a variety of symbol systems to communicate complex ideas. The activities that follow also provide opportunities for reflective inquiry across the curriculum.

PRIMARY SOURCES*

History is constructed from the residue of the past. Historians interpret and reinterpret history on the basis of the primary sources that are available to them and on the historiographic or interpretive framework in which the historian operates. The historian uses primary sources—public documents, private papers, newspapers, and artifacts produced during the period under study—and constructs a story to explain the causes and effects of past events. The historian's story, or interpretation of the past, is a secondary source.

We see the past filtered through the perspective of the historian, and so our history changes as we change. Even the way history is presented to children changes. Thus, a historical novel such as *Johnny Tremain,* written before the Vietnam War, provides a very different perspective on the American Revolution than does *My Brother Sam Is Dead,* a novel about the same era but that was written as America was just coming out of a war in Southeast Asia and was reinterpreting its past in light of that traumatic event. Such interpretations are important because they are one way in which we explain ourselves as a culture and as human beings. They provide us with a historical memory and with a record of how we have developed over time.

Forbes (1943)

Collier & Collier (1974)

Unfortunately, however, this may be the only history many of us ever encounter. We too easily assume that a secondary historical account is "the way it really was." We forget that history is interpretation and that interpretation is tentative pending new information. It is important, then, for children to understand the sources used by historians in constructing history.

A variety of primary sources are available and appropriate for use with children, especially in grades 4 and up. Local historical societies, archives, and many libraries preserve primary sources in the form of old newspapers, letters, diaries, military papers, census records, period magazines, catalogues, and so forth. Photocopying such documents is relatively inexpensive and can provide children with the raw material for doing their own historical interpretation. It is also possible to buy packaged primary source material at historical sites and museums and from commercial producers.

One of the skills children learn in working with primary source material is careful consideration of the strengths and weaknesses of various sources, possible biases, and inaccuracies. Children should be encouraged to confirm information gathered in one source by reference to other primary and secondary sources and to recognize the difference between a primary source that comes from the time being studied and a secondary source that is an interpretation of the past based on an analysis of primary sources.

One way to help older children recognize the differences between primary and secondary sources is to begin with a primary source such as Figure 8.2, a "slave narrative" or transcript of an interview with an ex-slave. (These interviews were conducted during the 1930s as part of President Roosevelt's Works Progress Administration and are a major source of firsthand accounts of slavery.)

"Slave Narrative" courtesy of the Ohio Historical Society, Columbus, Ohio

Put the slave narrative on an overhead transparency and read it with the class. After reading this document together, begin to analyze it in terms of reliability. Can this source be trusted? What things about this source might concern you if you were a historian writing about slavery? Some of the things children may notice include the age of the person interviewed (slavery ended after the Civil War; interviews were conducted in the 1930s; many of the ex-slaves were in their eighties and nineties and would have been quite young during slavery), concern with whether this person's experience was typical, who conducted the interview (if the interviewer was white—a likely possibility—would a Black person who had lived through slavery be likely to trust the interviewer?), and so forth.

Next, present students with secondary historical reports of slavery. Milton Meltz-

Meltzer (1964)

Reporter—Betty Lugabill
Editor—Harold Pugh
Supervisor—R. S. Drum

Allen County
District 10
Ex-slaves

Kisey McKimm Ex-Slave 83 Years

I was born in Bourbon County, sometime in 1853, in the state of Kaintucky where they raise fine horses and beautiful women. Me'n my Mammy, Liza'n Joe, all belonged to Marse Jacob Sandusky the richest man in the county. Pappy, he belonged to the Henry Youngs who owned the plantation next to us.

Marse Jacob was good to his slaves, but his son, Clay was mean. I remember once when he took my Mammy out and whipped her 'cuz she forgot to put cake in his basket, when he went huntin'. But that was the last time, 'cuz the master heerd of it and cussed him like God had come down from heaven.

Besides doin' all the cookin' she was the best in the county, my Mammy had to help do the chores and milk fifteen cows. The shacks of all the slaves was set at the edge of a wood, an' Lawse, honey, us chillun used to have to go out 'n gatha all the twigs 'n brush 'n sweep it jes' like a floor.

Then the Massa used to go to the court house in Paris 'n buy sheep an' hogs. Then we used to help drive them home. In the evenings our Mammy took the old clothes of Mistress Mary 'n made clothes for us to wear. Pappy, he come ovah to see us every Sunday, through the summer, but in the winter, we would only see him maybe once a month.

The great day on the plantation was Christmas when we all got a little present from the Master. The men slaves would cut a whole pile of wood for the fire place 'n pile in on the porch. As long as the whole pile of wood lasted we didn't have to work but when it was gone, our Christmas was over. Sometimes on Sunday afternoons, we would go to the Master's honey room 'n he would give us sticks of candied honey, an' Lawd chile was them good. I ate so much once, I got sick 'nough to die.

Our Master was what white folks call a miser. I remember one time, he hid $3,000, between the floor an' the ceilin', but when he went for it, the rats done chewed it all up into bits. He used to go to the stock auction every Monday, 'n he didn't wear no stockings. He had a high silk hat, but it was tore so bad, that he held the top 'n bottom together with a silk neckerchief. One time when I went with him to drive the sheep home, I heard some of the men with kid gloves call him a "hill-billy" 'n make fun of his clothes. But he said, "don't look at the clothes, but look at the man."

One time, they sent me down the road to fetch somethin' 'n I heard a bunch of horses comin', I jumped over the fence 'n hid behind the elderberry bushes, until they passed, then I ran home 'n told them what I done seen. Pretty soon they come to the house, 125 Union solders an' asked for something to eat. We all jumped round and fixed them dinner, when they finished, they looked for Master, but he was hid. They was gentlemen 'n didn't bother or take nothin'. When the war was over the Master gave Mammy a house an' 160 acre farm, but when he died, his son Clay told us to get out of the place or he'd burn the house an' us up in it, so we left an' moved to Paris. After I was married 'n had two children, me an' my man moved north an' I've been here ever since.

Figure 8.2

er's *In Their Own Words,* for instance, is a compilation of slave narratives edited and interpreted by the author. How has he used the primary sources? Which parts of Meltzer's work are primary and which interpretation? Then give the children a nonfiction narrative based on slave narratives—perhaps Julius Lester's *To Be A Slave.* How have the primary sources been interpreted here? What purpose may the author have had in writing this narrative?

Lester (1968)

Hurmence (1982)

Finally, students read Belinda Hurmence's *A Girl Called Boy,* a novel that also uses slave narratives as background research in creating a fictional tale of slavery. The children discuss the ways in which the author seems to have used the primary sources and her purposes in doing so. Can they recognize the primary parts of the novel? How has the author woven her historical information into the fictional tale of a girl who is taken back in time and mistaken for an escaped slave?

A similar procedure can be used for other types of primary sources such as photo-

Figure 8.3 A 1930s Sorghum Mill Worked by Mule

Photograph courtesy of the Kentucky Department for Libraries and Archives, Frankfort, Kentucky

graphs. After viewing the picture of a sorghum mill, children are asked to list five observations (be clear that these are observations and not inferences at this point). Working in small groups, the students try to construct three inferences that can be supported by their observations. After a debriefing in which these inferences are shared with the class, each group resumes work and makes a list of what additional information they need to confirm or disconfirm their hypotheses (inferences). At this point, the teacher can introduce further evidence, allow the children to search for further evidence, or explain that the picture shows part of a sorghum-making operation. Not every activity needs to extend for long periods. In this case, the purpose may be to provide practice in analyzing primary source material, not in initiating a study of farm technology. Children can also use primary sources to compare with descriptions in their textbooks. A text passage on the "surprise" attack on Pearl Harbor, for instance, can be compared to earlier news reports that the Japanese were preparing for just such an attack. Copies of various maps of the world can be used to initiate a discussion of what maps tell us about how people viewed the world at different times. A single coin can be analyzed as a primary source, too. If you were a person who knew nothing of American society, what could you learn by carefully analyzing a penny? Or a copy of "My Weekly Reader," for that matter. Jackdaws* provide one way to organize these and other activities using primary resources.

Jackdaws*

Jackdaws are collections of primary and secondary source material, background information, and teaching suggestions for historical and contemporary topics. Commercial Jackdaws are of this type and are generally geared for high school students. The commercial Jackdaws can be easily adapted for use in the intermediate grades and are rela-

"Jackdaw" is the commercial name for a series of primary source and activity packets covering a wide range of topics in world and U.S. history.

tively inexpensive to buy (see the item in the References at the end of this chapter). However, a teacher or the children can also construct Jackdaw-like packets.

Teacher-Made Jackdaws. A teacher can create a primary source packet modeled on the Jackdaws and geared to specific classroom needs.

Spiers (1978)

Primary Grades Source Packet. A Jackdaw for younger children might begin with a book such as Peter Spiers' *Tin Lizzie* and contain advertisements for cars from Model Ts to the present, along with road maps from different eras, pictures of gas stations, roadside merchandising such as drive-throughs, and so forth. Some secondary sources on the history of automobiles ("coffee table" books with well-done illustrations and clear captions, for instance), and suggested activities for children can help students to study the history of automotive transportation.

Intermediate Grades Source Packets. Many manuscript collections contain the papers of private individuals of historic interest. In the EXPLORATIONS 2 thematic unit, for instance, the teacher used the letters and journal of a young woman embarking on a trip West. These sources were gathered into a packet that included other primary sources related to the U.S. westward movement in the nineteenth century: descriptions of the area the young woman was leaving, copies of newspaper descriptions of western lands and eastern problems, prints from *Harper's* and *Leslie's* magazines of covered wagons, Indian raids on railroads, and so forth. The teacher also included sources about political conditions, lists of supplies recommended for travelers, a price list for some of these goods, illustrations of fashions for men, women, and children, and the like. A few guide questions were attached to each source so that children had some help in reading a document or picture. These sources were then used by the students as the raw material for constructing a biographical novel of the young woman's journey and settlement in the West. Children also had access to historical novels about the period and to fine secondary sources such as *Pioneer Women* and *Women's Diaries of the Westward Journey,* among others.

Harper's and *Leslie's* were popular illustrated magazines of the Civil War era.

Stratton (1981); Schlissel (1982)

Student-Made Jackdaws. The second type of Jackdaw is constructed by students as a way of representing what they have learned in studying a particular topic or in response to a piece of literature. After children have studied the history of automobiles, they may want to put together Jackdaw histories of their own—of washing machines, for instance, to go along with the WASH AND WEAR theme. Generally, students need some guidance in this activity. One teacher explains that children can pack a "trunk" (a cardboard box) with items to represent a particular story they have read. In a sense, these children create primary source reconstructions. A child who has read *The Cabin Faced West* by Jean Fritz makes a box that looks like an old traveling trunk and fills it with homemade dolls based on those in the story, with a diary that might have been written by the main character, parts of a letter from "back home," and so forth. Another uses an old pot to fill with "artifacts" from a trip West, similar to the one made by Meribah Simons in Kathryn Lasky's *Beyond the Divide.* It contains maps of the territories as they were in the 1840s copied from reference material in the library. There is a list of supplies recommended for the journey, which was found in a packet of materials from the local historical society. There are pictures of wagon trains and a folded piece of paper cut to the size of the interior of a typical wagon and diagramming how much room food, bedding, furniture, and clothing took up.

See also Weber (1989) for many other Jackdaw ideas.

Fritz (1958)

Lasky (1983)

Such student-created Jackdaws allow children to represent in interesting and informative ways what they have learned while accommodating children of varying strengths and interests. The Jackdaws also give the teacher feedback on the kinds of observations children are making and the accuracy of their inferences. One young boy's reconstruction of an 1867 journal, for instance, included reference to stopping off at a saloon to watch the football game on television. His teacher saw this as evidence of a lack of information on technology and made a note to introduce a unit on technology that would include timelines of inventions.

OBSERVATION AND INFERENCE*

Although most process skills seem fairly self-evident, children as well as adults have some difficulty distinguishing between observation and inference. Much of the time this is not a problem. We don't really need to distinguish between the observations and inferences that lead us to leap out of the way of a car barreling down the road in our direction. At other times, however, the distinction between what we actually *observe* and what we *infer* is crucial, particularly in social studies and science.

Observation and Inference in Social Studies

We may observe a person of another race or ethnic group as we go about our daily business. Our observation may include seeing skin color, facial features, or clothing. We may notice the aroma of perfume or aftershave or hear the sound of a different language or dialect. But we often infer a number of things that have little to do with our actual observation. Instead, our prejudices and stereotypes interfere with observation, and we may make negative inferences that are unsupported by careful observation.

Young children are as prone to leap to inferences without careful observation as any of us. As teachers, however, we have an opportunity to help hone their observation skills and insist on supported inferences. You will have noted that there are a number of activities in the Prototypes in Chapter 4 that provide children with opportunities to observe and build supported inferences, and you can see from the discussion of reflective inquiry how crucial this distinction can be.

Byrnes (1988); Sonnenschein (1988); Stone (1986); Wilson (1987)

We have evidence that as early as fourth grade children have developed specific attitudes and ideas about other races, genders, and ethnic groups. These attitudes are often the result of limited observation and experience. In the early years, however, teachers have a wonderful opportunity to build a body of observation and experience that can lead to more open-mindedness as children come in contact with a wider variety of people. Some teachers try to introduce young children to representatives from other cultures, or they do some lessons on blacks in February (Black History Month) and women in March (Women's History Week). These short-term experiences are interesting but probably do little to change stereotypes. Instead, what seems to work best is consistent, long-term experience. For instance, instead of inviting guests from six different countries for six different visits, try arranging for a person from one culture to come to class for several visits. Talk with the children about their observations after each visit. You will probably notice a change over the course of their acquaintance with your guest. In initial visits, children tend to concentrate on the most unusual features of the visitor. Over time, however, they have opportunities to observe other things—that the person enjoys soccer, or has a pesky younger sibling, or enjoys chocolate—little things that are the common denominators of human contact.

In the same way, do not limit content about minorities or experiences with gender roles to a specific month or week. Instead, provide many opportunities for children to see all sorts of people in a variety of roles and situations so that they move beyond surface differences and start searching for commonalities. When you are studying a topic like the settlement of the Americas, ask children to imagine what would be different if Native Americans wrote the history of that era. Or tell the story of the American Revolution through the eyes of a black slave or freed man in the colonies. How might a woman have written the story of the westward movement? How might a Mexican describe U.S. immigration policy?

An idea from anthropology is useful here. Anthropologists working in foreign cultures attempt to make the strange familiar. We ask you to help children make the familiar strange—to look with new eyes at the phenomena they encounter so that they can observe more carefully, infer more justifiably, and learn more richly.

Observation and Inference in Science

Careful observation is also essential to good science. It was careful observation that led Newton to infer the laws of gravity, Archimedes the laws of displacement of liquids, and Galileo to conclude that the Earth circled the sun. Before Galileo, for instance, humans had believed—inferred—that the Earth was the center of a solar orbit. Such inferences are common to children, too. Perhaps you remember thinking that the moon followed you as you drove along the highway on a clear night. Or wondering why people on the "bottom" of the world did not fall off.

When Elementary Science Study (ESS) developers tested some of their procedures while they were preparing their classroom materials and teachers' guides, they discovered that "seeing" isn't always "observing." In one third grade class, students tried to chill water with crushed ice. Their observations were intended to lead them to conclude that "there is a minimum temperature below which an ice-water mixture will not go, regardless of the quantity of ice and snow added to it." Despite several opportunities to observe that this was the case, the children persisted in thinking that the temperature would drop as more snow or ice was added. It took multiple experiences before children began to accept the evidence gathered from their experiments and to interpret that evidence so as to change their original inferences.

Alberti, Davitt, Ferguson, & Repass (1974)

The open-mindedness crucial to science obviously takes practice. In another ESS activity, children observed what happened when they put various objects on ice. Ice cubes and small objects such as pennies, chalk, paper clips, washers, and wooden cubes were distributed, and children were asked to observe what happened when these objects were placed on an ice cube. The teacher helped the children organize their observations as follows:

Didn't sink in	**Sank in a little**	**Sank in a lot**
pieces of candle	wood	money
eraser (rubber)	stone	paper clips
pieces of chalk		thumbtack
		washer

In their Learning Logs*, the children speculated about the reasons for these differences—that is, they made inferences—and then planned further experiments to see if their inferences were supported.

Other simple observation/inference activities in science include having the teacher or a student perform an activity while the other students observe carefully. For instance, the demonstrator holds up two white envelopes of equal size. The first envelope is placed against the cabinet, and it falls to the floor. The second envelope is placed against the cabinet, and it stays where it was placed. Once the observation period ends, children write down three or four observations and discuss these. Part of the discussion is separating statements of inference such as "There is glue on one envelope," from statements of observation such as "One envelope is still on the cabinet." Once the class establishes a set of observations, they begin to construct hypotheses or inferences that could explain the observations. Depending on the time available, the teacher can ask children to create envelopes that will behave as did the ones in the demonstration or can allow children to suggest further tests of inferences. They may want to see if the "sticking" envelope will also adhere to a wooden cabinet, or they may want to compare the weights of each envelope. None of the student tests should be permitted to open or destroy the envelopes.

Any number of similar activities can be constructed to help children develop their ability to make the kind of careful observations and supported inferences that are basic to understanding scientific phenomena.

GRAPHIC ORGANIZERS*

Graphic organizers are visual displays that enable children to organize and represent meanings, ideas, and concepts on a topic. They can be used for many purposes—to activate prior knowledge on a topic to be studied or read about, and then to show new concepts, connections, vocabulary, and so forth that developed as a result of an investigation on that topic; to depict (as a prewriting experience) the meanings or ideas to be included in a piece of writing; to share ideas on a topic or domain in small or whole class discussions to gain feedback; to present (or "publish") the findings of a systematic study or analysis done in an inquiry; and so forth. Just as they reflect different purposes, graphic organizers can also take on different forms. We cover four types: Graffiti Walls*, Semantic Maps*, Semantic Feature Charts*, and Comparison Charts*.

See Tierney, Readence, & Dishner (1985) for another discussion of graphic organizers.

Although graphic organizers can be realized by various forms and may fulfil various purposes, all activities involving graphic organizers have similar features. They all elicit children's *own* ideas, wordings, meanings, so that children are put into the center of their own learning. They frequently also provide a means for children to share and build on each other's ideas. Hearing others' ideas fosters divergent thinking, and children's own schemas on a topic are likely to be modified or altered. Thus, graphic organizers demonstrate ways to depict knowledge already acquired and to show directions to new learning.

Graffiti Walls*

The same urge that seems to drive people to leave some permanent record of themselves in public places can be harnessed in a positive way in the classroom through graffiti walls. Graffiti walls are free-form spaces for brainstorming or communicating key words, phrases, or ideas on a topic in a thematic unit or on the thematic unit itself. For example, at the onset of a TIME unit, the teacher may ask children to brainstorm all the words they know about time on a large sheet of butcher paper, chart paper, or newsprint. Contributions are written down in a free-form, loosely organized fashion, using Magic Markers or crayons so that the ideas can be easily seen. The teacher writes children's responses (sometimes first having children work individually or in small groups). Initially, children are likely to think of words such as *minute, hour, second, birthday, morning, evening,* and so on. As the unit unfolds, children are encouraged to add new words or phrases pertaining to time, or to illustrate interesting idioms and aphorisms such as "time flies" or "a stitch in time saves nine." At specific times during the unit, the graffiti wall can take a special focus when children are invited to write words and phrases that describe times of day (e.g., a sunset that was rose-golden) or books and poems that have time in the title (*Time of Wonder*).

Graffiti Walls focus attention on words and phrases.

McClosky (1957)

In addition to making children active searchers for new or intriguing words, the graffiti wall can serve as a class thesaurus/dictionary as children become used to consulting it to find words that enrich their writing. The teacher also returns to the graffiti wall during the course of the unit to call attention to particular features of language being used or simply to enjoy the way the display has grown.

Smaller versions of graffiti walls can be used by small groups—perhaps displaying the words, phrases, and so on that reflect initial understandings of a subtopic of a unit, and then adding ones that members are coming across in their individual reading. Once the idea of a graffiti wall is demonstrated, children can use them in many ways—showing possible topics to investigate or write on, displaying ideas to pursue in the course of a unit, keeping track of new words or vocabulary that they have learned to spell, and the like.

Semantic Maps*

Heimlich & Pittelman (1986)

Semantic maps focus on relationships among ideas and concepts.

See also Revel-Wood (1988) for a good classroom example of semantic mapping.

Semantic maps are similar to Graffiti Walls* in that they encourage children to think about what they already know and then try to build on and extend that knowledge. However, semantic maps are different from Graffiti Walls* in that they are more organized ways to call attention to the relationships among ideas of particular topics; they categorize and connect wordings and/or concepts. Semantic maps were used in Chapter 1 to illustrate schemas, our mental models of our knowledge, and to depict how Sara developed a schema of the domain of spiders. The WEBs depicted in Chapter 4 are also types of semantic maps.

To illustrate how semantic maps can be demonstrated in the classroom, let's recall Sara's increasingly complex understanding of the domain for "spider" in Chapter 1. Her teacher built on that understanding and that of her classmates by planning a thematic unit on BUGS (see the earlier discussion in Chapter 3). During the unit, Sara's teacher asks a group (or several groups, or whole class) of children to brainstorm about what they know about "spider." As they jot down ideas, the teacher encourages them to try to list those wordings that seem to go together. (Or before their brainstorming, the teacher may suggest some general categories—what spiders look like, what they do, where they are found, and so on.) Then, on the board or a large sheet of chart paper, the teacher begins listing the children's ideas about "spiders." Discussion about the words and their categories is one of the most valuable aspects of developing a semantic map while children verbalize (and perhaps argue about) their understanding of already existing schemas. Once the children's categories are all listed on the semantic map, the teacher can help them find labels for the categories. Figure 8.4 illustrates the type of semantic map that can result. Notice that many of the terms may have been contributed by children who have been doing a lot of reading and writing about spiders.

Semantic maps can be developed before children start a study—perhaps when they begin some initial observations of some spiders that have been brought into the classroom or have been seen at a local zoo. Following the discussion of the first map, children engage in some individual research and reading with the goal of enlarging and

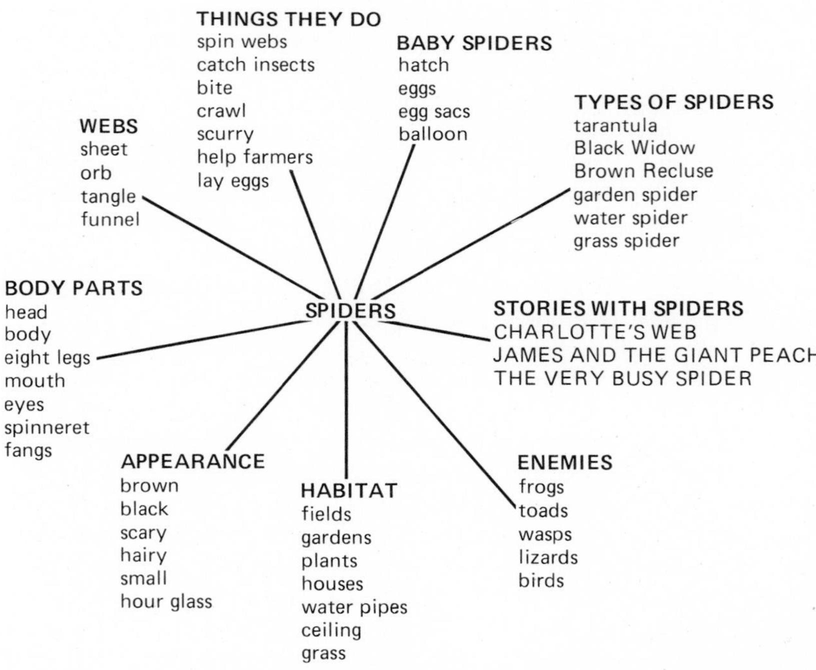

Figure 8.4 A Semantic Map on "Spiders"

extending the original map. They then construct a second map and compare the new information they have been able to add. Or instead of writing ideas down directly on the board or paper, the children can place them on brainstorming cards or strips and then organize them on a bulletin board (using thumbtacks) or a portion of the board (using masking tape "circles" on the back of the strips). As children study the topic, they write down another idea and decide where it should be placed on the map. The advantage of the strips is that children can physically place an idea in one category and then move it if they decide that it is best listed under a different (or new) category. Throughout the process, the teacher helps children find or change labels for existing categories and to distinguish subtle differences in categories and classes. Thus, the use of strips enables children to construct an ongoing semantic map in a dynamic way.

The finished map represents a summary of prior and new information.

Semantic maps can be constructed in terms of questions or key themes to be considered in an inquiry. A small group studying volcanoes as part of a unit on CHANGES, for example, may initially consider three major questions: Where are volcanoes located? Why do they erupt? What happens during an eruption? Figure 8.5 shows the type of semantic map the teacher developed for the group.

Children are asked to tell (or write down themselves) what they think they already know regarding each question. Making sure that there is plenty of space left for adding new information later, the teacher then encourages the children to read independently a range of books on the topic (e.g., Branley's *Volcanoes*) to see what else they can find out about volcanoes. The teacher also urges them to be on the lookout for new questions to consider. The children know that following their reading they will come back to the semantic map to confirm or refine their original ideas and to add new information that they have found. During their reading, they may jot down key facts or ideas in their Learning Logs* or perhaps on a smaller ditto version of the larger semantic map.

Branley (1985)

When the group comes together following their reading, they reexamine each question. First, they discuss their original ideas and determine if these were confirmed or contradicted by their reading. If confirmed, a star or asterisk is placed by that line. (Using a marker of a different color helps children to recognize the difference between prior knowledge and new information.) If an original idea was a misconception, it is crossed out. Then new information gained from the reading is added under each question. Other questions (e.g., what are the consequences of eruptions?) are also considered. The discussion surrounding semantic map activity is important. Children may have to go back to the books or text they have read to support their points of view.

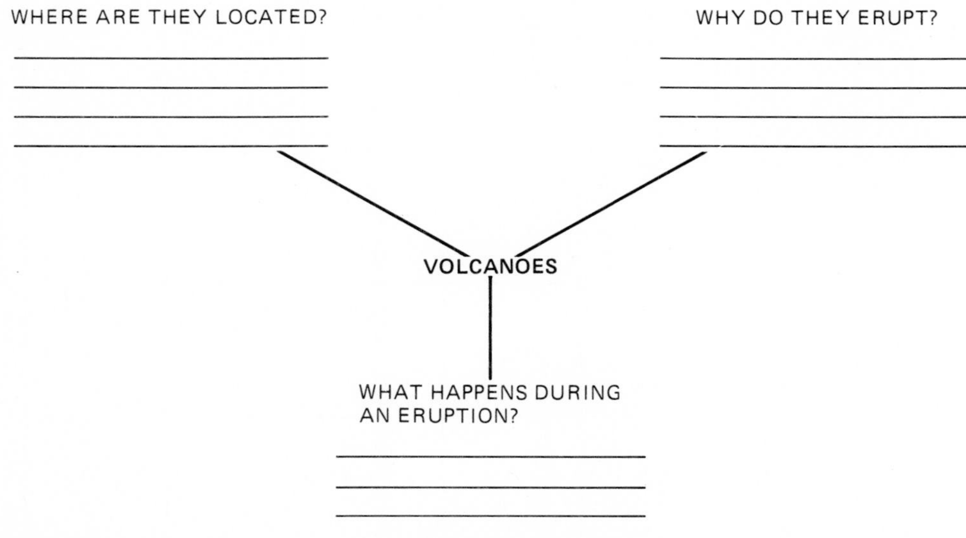

Figure 8.5 An Initial Semantic Map of Questions for the "Volcanoes" Inquiry

They must verbalize and clarify important understandings in the process of negotiating and constructing the map.

Semantic maps can be used for a range of purposes. They can be used to document and organize children's observations of snails, for example, or to note the transformations involved in a scientific experiment. They can be used as a prewriting experience or as a publication of a small group's (or individual's) study of a topic. A semantic map can be constructed for one book, rather than for a general topic on which information is acquired through reading many books and/or through other sources such as careful observation and interviewing experts. Semantic maps can also be completed for fictional stories or books in which characters, motives, actions, and outcomes are depicted.

See Heimlich & Pittleman (1986) for examples of various kinds of semantic maps.

Semantic Feature Charts*

Johnson & Pearson (1984)

Semantic feature charts focus on distinguishing features and attributes.

Semantic feature charts are designed to draw attention to more subtle characteristics of categorization, how "rules" are formulated to allocate objects (words and concepts) into categories. First, a category or class is chosen from a thematic unit, and several words within that category are listed vertically on a chart. Across the top of the chart, some of the attributes or features shared by the words or concepts are listed. Then as a result of discussion, pluses or minuses are placed in the columns under the attributes. It is important that plenty of blank spaces be provided in the matrix so that children can think of new members of the class and new attributes. Figure 8.6 shows a semantic feature chart that could have resulted from a unit on GIANTS where the focus was on animal giants. Notice that in addition to physical and biological attributes, the children may include words that describe their feelings or responses to a given label.

	Marine	Extinct	Mammal	Scales	Hair	Scary	Herbivore		
Elephant	—	—							
Gray Whale	+	—							
Tyranno-saurus Rex	—	+							
Giant Tortoise									

Figure 8.6 Semantic Feature Chart for Animal Giants

Different purposes result in different lists. Characteristics of various characters in fiction or attributes of various historical figures can be examined through this type of chart. Semantic feature charts can also be useful to analyze functions of the body parts or organs of various animals, and so forth. In addition, besides the plus/minus notation, more sophisticated systems showing the relative degree of the possession of a feature (e.g., where 1 = never; 2 = some; 3 = always) can be developed.

Tierney, Readence, & Dishner (1985)

Comparison Charts*

Comparison Charts allow children to compare and contrast ideas and information.

Comparison charts also involve examinations of likenesses and differences among ideas, events, characteristics, and so forth. Comparison charts may take a number of forms. Sometimes they may be used to focus characters, events, motifs, and themes within a single story or novel, or the characteristics, features, and attributes in informational materials. At other times, they can be useful in comparing books or events or properties within a given theme. Comparison charts give children opportunities to work individually with texts and then to pool and share details of their reading with their peers in a small group or in the class as a whole. In addition, comparison charts can give teachers a focus for looking at themes, story structure, character development, or other important features or concepts in a given work.

Figure 8.7 is an example of a comparison chart that was filled in by two kindergarten children during a thematic unit on BEARS. The teacher had told the class the story of *Goldilocks and the Three Bears* by Cauley using simple props, and many of the children had enjoyed reenacting and retelling their own versions. The teacher then brought in Brinton Turkle's *Deep in the Forest,* a wordless picture book in which a little bear enters Goldilocks's house in a reversal of the original story. The teacher drew the chart on a large sheet of construction paper and discussed the categories with two boys. These categories then provided them with a focus for problem-solving and discussion that centered on the two books. They talked about the two stories and their enjoyment of Turkle's version. There was some discussion as to who had first recognized the elements of the Goldilocks story. They also noted details that were alike and different in the two stories and spent some time talking about the illustrations. They noted the actual content of the pictures ("both of them have houses and forests and both of them show the three bowls of porridge and the three chairs"). They also noted stylistic matters—for example, that in *Deep in the Forest,* Turkle drew the background for some

Cauley (1981); Turkle (1976)

Deep in the Forest	Dad Mom little girl little bear	yellow black white brown orange	Dad Mom little girl	The little bear
Goldilocks and the Three Bears	Papa Bear Baby Bear	orange black purple white yellow blue red green	Papa Bear Mama Bear Baby Bear	Goldilocks
	List the characters in the story	What are the colors used in the illustrations?	Who lives in the house?	Who breaks into the house?

Figure 8.7 A Comparison Chart* for the Cauley and Turkle Books

pictures but in others set the figures against white paper. The chart thus served as a springboard for a rich and lengthy discussion about characteristics of the two books.

Charts can allow emergent readings to apply reading and writing strategies.

When it came time to fill in the chart, the children were able to share ideas and put into practice a variety of emergent reading and writing strategies. They could "pretend read" *Goldilocks and the Three Bears* because they knew the story so well. They could "read" *Deep in the Forest* because it was a wordless book. Together they pooled their knowledge of spelling conventions using book titles, labels on their crayons, and other data sources to fill in the columns.

Children become more critical readers when they develop their own categories.

Children are also quite capable of discovering their own categories. Again this activity provides a focus for discussion of the many elements in books or other resources. As with the other three types of graphic organizers already discussed, the finished chart is only a representation of some of the findings of children's study and analysis; it provides a means and steppingstone to writing and talking about findings with others. Charts frequently, therefore, serve as a summary of a range of reading transactions children may have had in reading books. The charts are also important prewriting experiences because many of their categories are incorporated into the stories or reports that individual children write. In a third/fourth grade classroom, for example, a group of children read four "inchling" stories, folktales that center on the tiny size of the main character. Following their reading, each child shared his or her particular story with the group. There was much discussion of themes, events, and other details as the children attempted to choose categories that would capture the features of all or most of their books, and then to decide on labels for these categories. Eventually they decided on thirteen—book title, country (of the folktale's origin), magic object, wishes, sacrifices, where did they (the parents) work and what did they work for, where did they go and why, size (of the tiny character), what did they take (on their journey), Japanese words, whom did they meet on their journey, how did they get the child, characters. Once the categories were named, the children wrote the details from each book on pieces of paper and glued them on an appropriately labeled piece of chart paper (see Figure 8.8).

Following the completion of the comparison charts, many children choose to write their own stories or to illustrate certain events in the books studied. After a study of informational texts, children may write a report on a specific animal or phenomenon

Figure 8.8 Comparison Chart for "Inchling" Stories

that has been included on a comparison chart. For example, a third grade class read many books on dinosaurs as part of a DISAPPEARING ACTS thematic unit. Comparison charts were constructed by small groups to compare dinosaur characteristics such as habitual behavior or physical features. Included in the chart was a category listing other animals that lived at the same time. Several children became interested in one of these animals, the mammoth, and as a result did more research on it. One child subsequently wrote a report on her findings, one wrote a cartoon-like saga featuring Wild Willy Mammoth (influenced by Aliki's *Wild and Woolly Mammoths*), and another child (using ideas from Joanna Cole's *Evolution*) constructed his own plaster fossil of a mammoth. In a first grade unit on FLIGHT, children in a small group completed a comparison chart on various ducks using the following simple categories: type of duck, looks, home, food, and habits. After they finished the chart, each child of the group illustrated one of the ducks and wrote a brief description of it.

Charts provide a focus or structure for further writing.

Aliki (1977); Cole (1987)

Children can also write about their experience of constructing a comparison chart for other classmates who may not be so familiar with the process, or to explain the activity for a parents' night, or include it in their learning portfolio (see Chapter 9). Figure 8.9 is an example of a ten-year-old's report of a comparison of three Japanese tales. She and a partner had both read all three tales and then decided on the categories for comparison.

Bartoli (1977); Matsutani (1968); Yagawa (1981)

Summary

Activities involving graphic organizers foster active, meaningful comprehension of ideas and concepts. The teacher's role throughout consists of acceptance of children's ideas (even if they are not "correct" according to the teacher's schema) and asking questions

My Comparison Chart Writing

I did a comparison chart with Terri. The books we compared were The Grateful Crane, The Crane Maiden and The Crane Wife.

First we looked through the books for things we could compare for example how many times the crane changed, the characters and the ending.

Then we wrote everything down on small pieces of paper in a thin black marker. We glued them down on big pieces of blue paper. We made pictures to go with it.

Some neat things I noticed was that in The Crane Wife the crane sings Tankara Tankara and in The Crane Maiden she sings riakola kinkoja.

In The Crane Maiden it doesn't look like it but the illustrator used water color and in The Grateful Crane the illustrator used a well kind of a wooden doll house and collages.

Figure 8.9

that promote problem-solving and critical thinking. Why? What do you think? How do you know? How can you find out? Risk-taking is promoted as children confirm, modify, elaborate, and relate tentative or initial understandings. Graphic organizers are a rich source for spelling, and they foster children's vocabulary in many ways. These maps and charts are means to document children's schemas; they are ways to reflect on their inquiries.

READING ACTIVITIES AND EXPERIENCES*

This section describes various activities or experiences related to reading. It is important to recall that although reading is the focus here, in an integrated language classroom, it is integrated with writing, speaking, and listening, and occurs for many purposes across the curriculum.

READING ALOUD*

Cohen (1968); Eldridge & Butterfield (1986); Wells (1986)

Hepler & Hickman (1982); Hickman (1981)

Reading aloud to children is a necessary component in integrated language classrooms. Most teachers have times when they read to the whole class; they may also read aloud to small groups during the day. Books should be selected according to children's interests and developmental background, and also to stretch their imagination, extend and spark new interests, foster an awareness of various genres, and develop an appreciation of fine writing and illustration. (Teachers who want help in selecting quality literature can turn to their librarian for advice or to award lists such as the Newbery and Caldecott winners and honor books. *Booklist* and *The Horn Book* review only books that they recommend for children and star those they judge to be outstanding. Two other professional journals, *Social Education* and *Science Teacher,* both publish a yearly list of books that are named as outstanding in the fields of social studies and science.)

Enthusiasm for the selected book, story, poem, and so on is the first ingredient of good reading aloud. Teachers should always read the text ahead of time so that they are aware of its content and so that their reading is smooth and fluent. A teacher's reading delivery depends on the text being read and that teacher's own style. Some teachers are good at doing character voices, sound effects, and physical gestures, for example, but children can also be enthralled by the quiet warmth of a gentler voice.

Reading aloud seems to work best when children are gathered on a rug or special place close to the teacher. Reading picture books with the book at shoulder level, pages facing the children and at their eye level gives them plenty of time to look at the illustrations and enables them to enter the visual as well as the verbal world of the book.

See also Huck, Hepler, & Hickman (1987) for more ideas.

Books or other texts can be introduced in various ways: by a brief discussion about the author or illustrator; by asking children to predict what the story or text is about by examining the cover and interpreting the title; by linking the topic, theme, author, or illustrator to other books children may know; and so forth. With long chapter books, teachers can begin by having children discuss the progress of the book so far and then consider what is likely to occur next.

Butler & Turbill (1984); Calkins (1986); Reardon (1988)

Teachers may also plan for places in the text to stop during reading (using small Post-it notes as reminders) to encourage children's comments or questions about what has been read or to foster predictions about what is yet to be read. It is not a good idea to ask too many questions, and the kinds of questions used should be those that help children make their own discoveries. Questions to make children aware of the craft of writing—to foster the reader-writer contract—should also be considered. For example, questions can be posed to get children to recognize the power of particular words or phrases used by the author—how they sound, how they help paint a picture, how they ask and answer certain questions of the author, and so on. We want children to appreciate authors' choices so that they become reflective of their own choices in their own writing. Many children like to sketch or write in their Book Response Journals* during the read-aloud time and should feel comfortable about initiating discussion.

After finishing reading, children may want to discuss it by relating ideas in the text to their own experiences or to other texts. Sometimes, depending on the book, it is useful to give children time to think and ponder about ideas in the text, and then to go back and reread particular passages either at the end of a reading aloud session or later in the day. It is important to note, however, that not all texts have to be discussed to be enjoyed, understood, or appreciated. It is also a good idea to frequently read whole texts aloud more than once; often it is during the second or third reading of a book that the most sensitive responses are brought to the surface. This practice also encourages *favorites,* making certain books "friends" for life.

Beaver (1982); Morrow (1988)

Holdaway (1979)

STORYTELLING*

Storytelling is an important alternative to Reading Aloud*. It is an art form that needs to be valued and perpetuated. It provides opportunities for more intimate rapport with children because no book separates the teacher and the audience. It isn't necessary to memorize stories to be a good storyteller, but careful planning is essential. The teacher needs to be familiar with the plot, the characters, and the "flavor" of the book's language. If certain chants or refrains are repeated in the text, those should be memorized. Stories such as *Goldilocks and the Three Bears* and *The Teeny Tiny Woman* are good for younger children. The use of simple props or visual aids (e.g., a flannel board or puppets) can help teachers to recall the story's key elements, and it encourages children to want to retell and reenact their own versions of the story. Bryan's West Indian story *The Cat's Purr* is a favorite of middle elementary children (7 to 9 year olds). Fifth and sixth graders also enjoy hearing a story told. Teachers' storytelling may serve as demonstrations for their own efforts to tell stories to younger children in the school, perhaps as an important part of a Buddy Reading* program. Besides the teacher, librarians, local storytellers, or parents may be happy to tell stories to children in the classroom.

Bauer (1977)

Stevens (1986); Galdone (1984)

Bryan (1985)

SUSTAINED SILENT READING (SSR)*

Sustained Silent Reading (SSR), sometimes also called USSR (Uninterrupted Sustained Silent Reading) or DEAR (Drop Everything And Read), is simply periods of quiet time set aside during the day when children read books of their own choosing. Usually, an SSR period begins with ten minutes or so and then is gradually lengthened. In many older elementary classes, forty-five-minute or longer periods may occur. In some schools, everyone (adults and visitors included) picks up a book and reads. The rationale for SSR is to demonstrate to children that adults who are important to them enjoy reading, too. Thus, as SSR fosters fluency by giving children opportunities to practice reading, it also encourages the joy of reading.

Manning & Manning (1984)

SSR for younger elementary children may involve looking at the pages and softly telling (or "pretend reading") their own versions of books or quietly reading aloud as they read to themselves. The emphasis should always be on the enjoyment of reading. A wide variety of reading materials of varied reading levels and interests is essential for SSR to work. In the beginning, especially for children who are unfamiliar with SSR time, teachers may have to guide children to books of interest or remind them to think ahead about what they will be reading during SSR so that they don't spend a lot of time just finding something to read. A timer of some sort can also be used in the beginning to mark the end of the SSR period to congratulate children on their capability to sustain a certain number of minutes of reading.

SSR fosters the enjoyment of reading.

BUDDY READING*

Many teachers implement buddy reading as an alternative to SSR*. Buddy reading acknowledges the social nature of reading by having children pair up, each with a favorite or other book of their own choosing, to read to their partner. Sometimes children take turns reading different books; sometimes they like to take turns reading pages of the same book. Buddies do not have to be at the same reading level because they are selecting their own material. Buddy reading can occur within one classroom, or children from different grade levels can read together. When older elementary children, who might be reluctant or less able readers, are paired with younger children, they have good reasons to practice the books they are to share. Self-confidence as readers is fostered. Older children also frequently enjoy experiences of Storytelling*. Making and sharing Big Books* with younger children is another feature that can be incorporated in a buddy reading program.

See Mossip (1985) for an example of buddy reading by children of different ages.

BOOK TALKS*

Bauer (1983)

Book talks are great ways to publicize good books. Frequently, teachers schedule book talk time right after SSR*. It is important, though, for teachers to model or demonstrate this activity for children, perhaps as they highlight books that will be part of a thematic unit. The first few pages can be read, or an amusing or exciting part can be recounted. Assuming the role of one of the characters is another book talk technique. Excerpts from several novels can be shared; summaries of the books found on jacket covers can be offered. Special objects that are important elements of stories (a pebble for *Sylvester and the Magic Pebble,* an old key for *The Secret Garden,* or a peach pit for *James and the Giant Peach*) can serve as foci for book talks.

Steig (1979); Burnett (1962); Dahl (1961)

Book talks should not be limited to fiction. Mentioning all the experts involved in finding and digging up dinosaurs—paleontologists, geologists, draftsmen, workers, photographers, and specialists—and what they do may be a selling point for Aliki's *Digging Up Dinosaurs.* Or showing the page where the magic school bus rises into the clouds in Cole's *The Magic School Bus at the Waterworks* may draw children to reading and finding out about water facts. Sharing some of the photographs in Freedman's *Lincoln: A Photobiography,* or relating some of the things about Lincoln in the book that were interesting to the teacher may be ways this book might be "sold." Children quickly pick up on these techniques and develop their own ways of "selling" books. It is hard to resist when a friend says, "This is the best book I ever read!" or "This was so interesting, I couldn't put it down!"

Book talks can be about books from a range of genres.

Aliki (1981); Cole (1986); Freedman (1987)

Eidman-Aadahl (1988)

RESPONSE GROUPS*

Hepler & Hickman (1982)

Response groups are opportunities for small numbers of children to discuss books in depth with one another. Frequently, these groups are organized and run by the children themselves, because they have all read the same book and want to talk about it. Or they may be reading books on a common topic or from a common genre, or they may be tackling similar problems in projects in a particular thematic unit. They may post an announcement on the Message Board* asking for interested participants. Many teachers set some time aside in integrated work time on certain days for such group interactions so that they themselves can periodically sit in on the discussions. When a teacher joins in as a member of a response group, the teacher works hard being a participant, not someone who asks all the questions or directs and controls the discussion.

The way the teacher handles discussion at Reading Aloud* sessions provides a framework that children can adopt in their own response groups. In the beginning of the year, teachers can sit in on the response groups more frequently and model ways to phrase questions or comments about texts so children get ideas about the kinds of transactions that are possible. Teachers may even have a Mini-Lesson* on the types of questions or comments that are appropriate in response group discussions.

Most teachers encourage children to come to response groups prepared, with their Book Response Journals* or Learning Logs* in hand. Using the types of transactions with text outlined in Chapter 5, teachers can conduct Mini-Lessons* on what that preparation might consist of. For example, they can suggest that children first ask themselves personal, experiential questions about the book at hand: What stands out for me? What do I feel about the ideas in this book? What are my reactions? What's my favorite part? Other questions children might also want to consider are those that connect ideas in the text under discussion with prior experiences or similar ideas in other texts. What did this book make me think of? Other questions or responses—descriptive and analytic, interpretive and elaborative, evaluative and self-evaluative responses—can be illustrated by having children brainstorm ways that they could relate to individual texts (see Chapter 5 for a review of these transactions).

Calkins (1986); Butler & Turbill (1984); Harste & Short (1988); Reardon (1988)

In these responses, comments, or explanations, the author's craft should be specifically addressed. Suggestions for questions to consider can be provided: What questions would you ask if the author were here? What sections of the text are effective in relating the setting of the story? What are the parts that are effective in explaining a particular concept or process in an informational book? Were the characters believable? What did you like about the author's style? What questions is the author answering in this book on snakes, tunnels, Lincoln, velocity, immigrants, or whatever? Are there questions that you still have that the author didn't answer?

Fostering the reading-writing contract

Response groups can also begin with children doing some dramatization or writing. For example, the teacher can ask members of the group to take the role of the townspeople in Gauch's *Thunder at Gettysburg,* maybe as they meet at a public meeting, at the beginning of the book, or after the Rebel soldiers came to town but before the Union troops arrived. Then, children can be asked to have another public meeting after the battle. Discussion may then revolve around people's changing views about the "victories" of war and what the author's view of war is and how it is communicated in the text. Children's writing responses—perhaps what Tillie, the main protagonist in *Thunder at Gettysburg,* could have written in a letter to her cousin about her experiences during the battle and about what she saw of death and destruction—can also be a focus of discussion in a response group.

Gauch (1975)

Discussion in some response groups may result in constructing a Comparison Chart* or some other kind of Graphic Organizer*. Ideas from the discussion may spark a range of writing, as well as lead children to read or reread other books on the same topic, by the same author, or in the same genre.

BOOK RESPONSE JOURNALS*

Book response journals are where children are encouraged to develop their own questions for Response Groups* and to note favorite passages and descriptions. Similar to a Learning Log*, the book response journal is a place for children to muse about personal reactions and to wonder about events, themes, and ideas in a book. Children are encouraged to include responses about everything they read—newspaper articles, information books, magazine articles, biographies, and so on, not just literary, fictional texts. In addition, many teachers use these journals to "talk" (in writing) with each child individually, sharing their own questions, feelings, and ideas about a book and making suggestions for further reading or for activities and experiences that might personalize the book for that child. Some teachers have periodic individual Reading Conferences* with children to discuss their reading specifically. A child's book response journal frequently plays a major role in such conferences.

Response journals are a source for discussion questions.

See Atwell (1987) for a good example of book response journals in action in the classroom.

READING CONFERENCES*

Because children in integrated language classrooms for the most part choose their own reading materials, reading is truly individualized. Consequently, many teachers have individual conferences with children to talk about reading. (Other teachers have many more short, less formal conferences with children when they see them reading in the classroom; then they have more general conferences with children where reading is addressed along with all their other learning—see Chapter 9.)

The two major purposes of the reading conferences are to assess and to guide: to assess children's strategies in reading; to understand their range of reading transactions and purposes; to ascertain their abilities to read critically; to determine children's reading needs and interests and their attitudes of reading in general; to suggest other books, genres, or topics to consider.

Reading conferences have four parts.

Reading conferences are usually organized into four parts: sharing, questioning, oral reading, and encouraging and guiding. Most teachers have a particular notebook or journal that they keep in which to make notes and record pertinent information gained in the conferences. They prepare for a conference by going over the information they have gathered and observed about the children's reading, so that they know what questions to ask.

See also Butler & Turbill (1984) and Hornsby & Sukarna (1988) for other ideas for reading conferences.

Sharing

Sharing. First, the children share responses about what they have been or are presently reading. They may begin by summarizing briefly what they have written in their Book Response Journals* or Learning Logs*, and then focus more on one or two texts. How and why the texts are being read can be pursued, and any information about a related book extension or activity or project in which the book is involved can be discussed.

Questioning

Questioning. The teacher asks one or two searching questions about one of the books or texts the children have read. These questions can concern the theme of the book, the author's style describing a character or setting, or they may help to explain a concept or process. Teachers may not have read all the books their children are reading, so some teachers take turns addressing a text that they know about in one conference and then asking about a text that is unfamiliar to them in the next conference. This enables teachers to acquire useful information about the children's awareness of audience.

Oral reading

Oral Reading. The teacher listens to children's reading of a short section of the text that has been chosen for sharing. Teachers usually allow children to select the part they will read aloud, but sometimes teachers may ask them to read a part discussed during sharing or questioning. The teacher notes the child's miscues (see Chapter 6)—how the child is integrating cueing systems, is self-correcting, is expressing the language of the text, and so on. (Some teachers tape this part of the conference, as well as record their impressions of children's reading strategies.)

Encouraging and guiding

Encouraging and Guiding. The teacher discusses future plans in reading. Suggestions about the selection of other books written by the same author and with the same theme or topic are made. If children are limiting their reading to one or two genres, teachers may "nudge" them to try books in other genres. Possible ideas for Book Extensions* may also be offered.

Some teachers have a reading conference with children once a week, and some may schedule one once every two weeks. As a result of the data acquired in reading conferences, teachers may organize a follow-up conference with a small number of children to foster some specific reading strategies. For example, if children seemed to overrely on grapho-phonemic cues in their own oral reading, the teacher may develop CLOZE* or other activities to get them to use syntactic and semantic cues as well (see Chapter 6 for discussion of cues). Or, if after the first set of conferences with children, teachers realize that many children demonstrate such an overreliance (perhaps as the result of instruction in the previous year), they may set up a series of Mini-Lessons* to encourage children to use more meaning-driven reading strategies.

Reading conferences can be conducted in any elementary grade. That is, teachers can have them even with kindergarteners and young first graders who may not as yet be reading from print. In these cases, children can be asked to reenact a book by approximating the text ("pretend reading") or retelling it, or by having them "read" a message they have dictated (see Chapter 6). Children show amazing progress in a very short period when they are treated as independent readers, and reading conferences are important ways to demonstrate and emphasize this independence to them.

BIG BOOKS*

Big Books are simply large-sized books containing texts written (and illustrated) on large pieces of paper or cardboard with print large enough for a group of children to see. Big Books were developed by Holdaway so that children in the classroom could interact with meaningful texts much in the same way that preschoolers interacted with them in book-sharing experiences at home with their parents (and other important literate adults). The teacher points (frequently using the handle of a wooden spoon or a ruler) to the words when reading the text in the Big Book. Then, in rereading the text, children are encouraged to join in. Later, the Big Book is placed somewhere in the classroom so that children can role-play reading the book. The original, small version of the text is available for children to practice on. Through these book-sharing and other literacy experiences, children learn to read—leading from many approximations to more competent, accurate renderings—in a self-monitoring, self-correcting manner.

Holdaway (1979)

Holdaway (1979); McKenzie (1977); Pappas & Brown (1989)

Commercially made Big Books are available, but these are usually very expensive and are sometimes also not good quality literature but just large versions of basal passages. For these reasons and because teachers want to use books having to do with a particular thematic unit, teachers usually make (with the help of their children) their own Big Books. Sometimes the books are made ahead of time by the teacher, a colleague, or parent. Teachers can make simplified drawings, or illustrations can be made by tracing pictures enlarged by an overhead projector. Teachers frequently discover that they have many friends or parents who are "closet" artists and who enjoy illustrating their Big Books.

Many teachers put in the text only and have children illustrate the books. For example, they share the text with the whole class first, and then a small group of children of varying abilities do the illustrations. The book can be constructed with small metal binders or shower hooks so that the pages can be separated for work on individual pages. Valuable discussion and rereading occur as children decide who will illustrate each page and how the illustrations should be done. Children can explore many types of media in these illustrations. The teacher usually needs to remind kindergarteners and many first graders to draw "big." Children should also be encouraged to avoid drawing pencil drafts first, for rarely do their resulting illustrations retain the initial details of the drafts. After the illustration is completed, children in the group practice the book and read it to the whole class or to children in another class. Large pieces of Plexiglas of several sizes to match varying sizes of books and with holes on the side for the binder rings make excellent book covers that stand up without an easel and are easy for young children to handle. Children's paper covers naturally adhere to the Plexiglas covers due to static electricity, so the expense of supplying sturdier paper book covers is avoided. (Large tablets from art supply stores can also be used to make Big Books.)

Children learn a lot when they are involved in illustrating Big Books*.

Plexiglas makes great Big Book covers.

Some teachers go through the whole process of making Big Books in the presence of a small group of children. Using paper or cardboard strips, the teacher writes the words of the text, having children refer to one or more copies of the book to check that mistakes are not made. As the teacher writes the words, he or she talks about

Making Big Books *with* children

the sequence of the message, mentions the characters and other aspects of the book, and refers to the spellings of some of the words and the use of some feature of punctuation (e.g., how quotation marks show the words people say). When the whole text is written, both teacher and children read the strips placed on the floor or taped on the board with masking tape. Children then pick pages to illustrate. When these are done, the group assembles the book by matching strips with illustrations and gluing them on larger pieces of paper.

Clay (1979)

Holdaway (1979)

Besides following words with a pointer, which facilitates children's understanding of one-to-one word correspondence and of the directionality of print, other aspects of written language can be facilitated through the use of Big Books. Cardboard masks (cardboard frames, having holes the width of a line of print, and a moving sliding strip) can be made to focus on certain properties of certain phrases or words (to make children be aware of repetitive refrains, or to examine various spelling patterns or graphophonemic relationships). With the use of Post-it notes, CLOZE* applications can also be made by covering particular words or parts of words to facilitate children's use of surrounding co-text to figure out or predict individual words.

Gibbons (1984); Maestro & DelVecchio (1983); Wildsmith (1974)

Patterned books (books that contain rhyme, rhythm, and/or repetition of certain language patterns) make good Big Books, but other fictional books and books of informational genres should be considered. For example, children also enjoy Big Book versions of information books such as *Tunnels, Big City Port,* and *Squirrels.* Teachers can also make their own Big Book collections of rhymes, poems, recipes, songs, and so on. Big Books foster children's beginning sight vocabulary quickly, but when children are exposed to a range of genres through Big Books, a lot more about the registers of written language is fostered. Children (with the help of their teachers) and usually in a small group can write their own Big Books, perhaps to publish the findings of a project or an in-depth study on some topic in the thematic unit.

Teachers typically use Big Books of existing literature through the second grade. Older children may want to make them for use in lower grade classrooms, however, or to use with younger children in a Buddy Reading* program.

CLOZE*

A CLOZE passage is a short excerpt (usually several paragraphs) of text in which certain words are deleted. This passage is shared with children in a problem-solving, guided reading lesson. The deletions in an otherwise complete flow of language can be provided in different ways. Usually one word out of fifteen words of text is deleted, but gaps can occur more frequently if the text seems still meaningful in that way. All the blanks in a CLOZE can be uniform, or the blanks can resemble the length of the actual word. Some of the letters for some of the deleted words can also be provided. Or CLOZE passages can be constructed so that certain kinds of words are deleted—for example, pronouns, adverbs, and adjectives.

Children apply a variety of strategies in a meaningful context.

Goodman & Burke (1985); Holdaway (1979); Routman (1988)

The discussion of strategies is more important than the "correct" answer.

The CLOZE passage can be put on a large piece of paper and taped on the board or on a transparency so children as a group can brainstorm while they try to fill in the blanks. Children can also work on their own copy individually, with a partner, or with a small group. If the beginning of a text is not chosen as the CLOZE passage, it is important to read the text up to that excerpt. In filling in the blanks, children are encouraged to predict what makes sense. An important aspect of the procedure is for children to justify or tell why their response fits and is meaningful; teachers should accept any reasonable responses. In this way, children become sensitive to the linguistic constraints operating in the co-text; they develop word attack skills and inferential reasoning. Confirming and self-correction strategies are induced when children debate among themselves as to what the most appropriate response is for a gap. Such strategies can be especially critical for children who believe that reading is merely accurately decoding each word of the text.

It is also useful to have children engage in CLOZE activities with passages from different genres so that they can become aware of the different vocabulary and language patterns realized in them.

SAY SOMETHING*

Harste & Short (1988)

Say Something activities have been designed by Harste and his colleagues to help children to develop a more functional and social view of reading. Partners read the same selection, either aloud or silently. Both read the first several paragraphs; then they stop to "say something" to their partner about what they have read. Then the second person takes a turn to "say something" about what was read. The "say something" can consist of a range of transactions: commenting on what was just read, predicting what might happen next, sharing experiences related to the ideas of the text at hand, and so forth (see Chapter 5 for the types of transactions possible). Then the partners repeat the process. They read the next several paragraphs and take turns to "say something" to each other—and so on through the text.

When most partners have finished reading the text, the teacher sets up a group discussion on it, perhaps by constructing a Semantic Map*. A central topic is placed in the middle of a large piece of paper or transparency and children are asked to offer ideas that the author expressed on the topic. These ideas are webbed off the central topic. As children contribute, they are asked to explain and justify how and why their responses are relevant concepts and ideas and how and why these ideas relate and interrelate.

GENERAL PROBLEM-SOLVING READING STRATEGIES*

See Holdaway (1979) and Routman (1988) for similar lists of strategies.

Teachers can use several general techniques to help children develop strategies that concentrate on meaning. Rather than overemphasizing word accuracy (especially at the early stages), teachers' guidance should foster *good* predicting that gets children to use all available information (see Chapter 5)—from the print (physical layout and medium aspects, etc.), from the message or register and genre of the text, from their experiences—to make an educated guess or reasoned judgment in reading. When readers get "stuck," the following teacher prompts or suggestions help children to develop their own strategies:

Re-run. Remind the child to start the sentence again when he or she stops mid-sentence. ("Try it again.") Starting again enables children to gain a refreshed feeling of how the message is structured.

Consider sense and structure. Ask the child if what has just been read made sense. ("Does that make sense?") ("Does that sound right?")

Read on. Tell the child to skip the word (by substituting "blank") and read on to the end of the sentence. ("Now, what do you think that word is?")

Predict. Encourage the child to make a good guess. ("What do you think it could be?")

Substitute. Tell the child to put in another word that fits or that means the same. ("Can you use something that means the same here?")

Picture. Ask the child to imagine what's going on. ("Can you picture what's happening?")

Placeholder. Ask the child to put in a "stand-in" for the same word recurring in text. This is especially useful for proper names for persons and places. ("Can you decide on the same 'stand-in' for this word?")

Identify. Ask the child to find that word on a previous page or paragraph. ("Where else did you see that word?")

Compare. Ask the child if it looks like a more familiar word. ("Does this word look like some word that you know?")

Inspect. Ask the child to take a careful look at the word, keeping the meaning of the text in mind. ("Could it be . . . ?" "What would you expect to see at the beginning of . . . ?" "What would you expect to see at the end of . . . ?")

Metalinguistic and metacognitive awarenesses are fostered.

No matter what prompt or suggestion teachers use in supporting children's reading, it is important that they give children time to self-monitor and self-correct. If teachers swoop in with their prompts too soon when children are stuck, children will not have opportunities to apply their own strategies or to self-correct, and the self-regulating behavior that characterizes fluent, effective reading will not be developed. It is also important for teachers to help children to be aware of their strategies. When teachers ask questions such as "How did you know?" or "Why did you think it was . . . ?" children become more conscious of the strategies they are using. They are then more likely to use them on their own and to gain independence in reading.

WRITING ACTIVITIES AND EXPERIENCES*

Hillocks (1986); Lytle & Botel (1988)

The activities and experiences we now discuss have to do with writing, but it is important to emphasize again that rarely is writing (like reading) a separate activity in integrated language classrooms. Substantial contributions have been made about how a *process-conference approach to writing* (what researchers and educators have termed current views of writing—see Chapters 5 and 6) can be implemented in the classroom. However, this approach frequently includes a "writing workshop," a certain period set aside during the day during which children write. In an integrated language classroom, writing experiences—prewriting, drafting, revising, editing, and publishing—happen all day across the curriculum. For example, children take notes during a scientific observation, jot down their responses to a book they may be reading, write questions or comments during their study of some primary materials to prepare for a small group discussion, compose an invitation asking parents or another class to come to a play they have written, write a thank-you note to a guest speaker who had visited their class, and so forth. As a result, the "formal" writing workshops suggested by Graves, Calkins, Atwell, and others are not usually implemented as such, but certain important features of these workshops are incorporated by teachers in the writing experiences for children.

Atwell (1987); Calkins (1986); Graves (1983)

Instead of a special time, teachers frequently designate a special *place* (a table or corner of the room) for drafting or for peer conferencing where children share their rough drafts to get feedback. Teachers may then drop in for informal conferences with children who may be working at that place, just as these teachers may check in and interact with children working at other projects and activities at other places in the room. Many teachers do routinely set aside some time, perhaps during a portion of the integrated work times in the daily schedule, to have more formal individual Content Conferences*. Another separate place for Editing Conferences*, where children can receive peer or teacher editing help, may also be established in the classroom.

Within such a framework, specific properties of writing workshops and other writing activities and experiences of the process-conference writing approach are discussed in more detail.

JOURNALS*

Journals can be used in the classroom in many ways. Varying kinds of journals serve varying purposes. We have already discussed Book Response Journals*, in which children write their responses, comments, and questions about the texts they are reading. Other kinds of journals have also been mentioned in this book (e.g., the math story problem journals described in Chapter 7). Keeping a specific type of journal depends on the needs of the class.

Fulwiler (1980, 1982)

Some teachers have children use private, diary-like journals (in which children record their personal feelings) with the agreement that their responses are confidential and therefore are not read, or responded to, by the teacher or peers. Most of the time, however, journals, despite their personal nature, are communications that can be shared. Three types are covered here: Dialogue Journals*, Thought Ramblings*, and Learning Logs*. Differences among these kinds of journals exist, but they are all similar in that they provide for informal writing experiences that allow for personal growth and reflection. (Sometimes teachers use only Learning Logs* and incorporate the functions of the other journals in this one kind of journal.)

Journals promote personal expression and reflection.

Dialogue Journals*

The rationale for dialogue journals is that they provide a means for children to share privately in writing their reactions, questions, and concerns about any aspect of their experiences in school and out with the teacher without any worry about evaluation. In this way, the teacher gets to know more about what each individual child is doing and thinking. Teachers also use dialogue journals to demonstrate the communicative function of writing to children, which is especially important for those children who, because of previous instruction, link writing only with evaluation. Dialogue journals encourage spontaneity in writing, which in turn fosters self-confidence and written fluency.

See also Tierney, Readence, & Dishner (1985) for a discussion on dialogue journals.

Keep the following in mind in implementing dialogue journals in the classroom:

Guidelines for using journals

1. Use a separate tablet or spiral notebook for each child. Many teachers make journals simply by stapling some paper together, perhaps using a construction paper cover that children decorate themselves. Have children date each entry. Have a special place in the classroom where the journals are stored so that children know where to get and return their journals for response.

2. Set up a schedule for the children to write in their journals. Many teachers have children write every day; others follow a Monday, Wednesday, or Friday routine, and so forth. Some teachers also discuss with children ahead of time about the times in the daily schedule that may be good times to write in their journals (e.g., immediately on coming into the classroom in the morning, after lunch, or after physical education).

3. Encourage children to write about anything they want. Many teachers have a whole class session in the beginning of the year to brainstorm possible topics for journals. It is important to assure those children who aren't sure that they have anything to write on some particular days that they can write exactly that: "I can't think of anything to write." Sooner or later children (even the most reluctant ones) do, in fact, write in their journals because they see their peers writing and getting responses from the teacher.

4. Assure children that they can use invented spelling and that their entries can be as long or short as they want. If teachers make a big deal about quantity, children are frequently reluctant to write until they have "enough" to say. In the early grades, children should be told that they can also make pictures if they don't have anything to write. It may be necessary to get kindergarten and first grade children (who may be prephonemic, early phonemic, or letter-name spellers) to read their entries to the teacher, and then have the teacher write down their responses (while saying the message aloud) right there in front of the child.

5. Respond to children's entries *frequently;* otherwise, children are likely to see writing in their journal as a drudgery rather than a dialogue.

6. Respond to the *content* of the message the child has communicated. What is wanted are two-way communications, so teachers should try not to contrive their responses to present conventional forms or grammatical structures.

Evaluations or judgmental responses should also be avoided. For those children who frequently state that they have nothing to write, the teacher can respond, "I'm sorry you can't think of something right now, but I'm sure you will think of something soon." Or teachers can include a message about something they have observed about the child. Following such a message with a specific question sometimes breaks the ice. (If children do then write in their journals, don't congratulate them; simply respond to what they have communicated.) If young children have drawn a picture, respond by commenting on the content of the illustration. (Young children also may need help in reading the teacher's responses.) Sometimes adding a question regarding their drawings leads children to try to write back.

See Unia (1985) for a good classroom example of dialogue journals.

In sum, dialogue journals can have many good effects. Teachers get to understand their children better, and children's writing fluency is fostered. Teachers' responses provide meaningful resources of the conventions of written language and even help many children, especially in the early grades, in reading. Most important, children really see themselves as writers, and they begin to feel that they can write for other purposes in the classroom.

Thought Ramblings*

Thought rambling is a way of brainstorming.

A thought rambling is a way to use writing as a tool for thinking, reflecting, and understanding. It is written for an audience of self, and it helps children to learn more about themselves and their surroundings without regard to correct form or other people's evaluation.

Thought rambling is brainstorming or putting a stream of consciousness on paper. Children are given five or ten minutes to put their ideas on paper. At the end of that time, they may find they have a page filled with phrases of feelings and sensory data. They may discover a thread of meaning or an insight. They may also find elements or themes that they might want to develop into a more formal piece of writing. Thought ramblings can serve as prewriting experiences. Thought rambling seems to work particularly well outside the usual context of the classroom when children have a chance to tune in to the sights, sounds, and other sensory aspects of their environment. For example, Figure 8.10 is a thought rambling done by a second grader after returning from a walk to a local university campus one spring day. Thought ramblings, however,

A spray of water shoots swish swish birds tweet sweetly hello
hello rocks rattle down down
every 15 minutes chimes ring out loud and clear
distant to where I am sitting I see a lamp post through the bushes
the trance of spring fever spreads
students walk on the long stone path
yellow dandylions are turning white and fluffy and leaves are
turning green
big sprouting trees reach over me branches filled with big green
leaves
bushes that are big and green
trees that fill the sky.

Figure 8.10 A Second Grader's Thought Rambling

can also occur in other contexts: after seeing a film or demonstration of some sort, after hearing a poem read aloud, after a field trip.

Learning Logs*

The major reason for having children use learning logs is to encourage them to be in control of their own learning and to promote thinking through writing. A learning log is a kind of journal that enables them to write *across the curriculum* as they plan, map, record, recall, consider, organize, assign, remember, pose, question, predict, decide, and so on in a range of projects and activities in various thematic units. Thinking with pen or pencil on paper gives children an awareness and control of their thoughts; it helps them to be constructive, reflective, and adaptive learners.

Fulwiler (1980, 1982)

Learning logs facilitate thinking and writing across the curriculum.

According to Calkins, learning logs provide a forum, an occasion for learning. The learning consists of three kinds of interrelated activities: (1) asking questions, (2) making guesses (or stating hypotheses), and (3) organizing information. The three may occur in any subject or domain. We have mentioned learning logs throughout this book, so you already have come across many examples of these three kinds of activities that learning logs promote. Following are brief summaries of these three types of activities or experiences.

Calkins (1986)

Learning logs enable children to ask questions, make guesses, and organize information.

Asking Questions. In most traditional schools, children don't ask questions but are busy answering others' questions. In an integrated language classroom, we encourage children to initiate and to ask their own questions, on the basis of their own schemas and for their own purposes. Learning logs can help to create conditions or contexts in which asking questions can happen. Children can record their own questions before, during, and after their own reading and writing. Questions can be a preparation for a small group discussion; they can serve as documentation of what children want to find out about a particular topic or theme they are studying; they can be reminders as children plan an experiment or presentation; they can be follow-up responses as a result of children's own activities or those of their peers and the teacher.

Making Guesses. If it is critical that children have opportunities to ask their own questions, then it is just as important for them to be encouraged to form their own hypotheses as answers for their own and others' questions. Rather than emphasizing "correct" answers, learning logs can help children to make educated guesses. They look for clues and connections as they read, hear their peers' ideas, see a film, engage in an experiment; they revise and reconsider as they examine others' feedback, read another book on the same topic, see a teacher demonstration; they predict, propose, and confirm in their own reading, in a class discussion or presentation, in deciding what and how to write.

Organizing Information. If learning is reconstructing knowledge, then encouraging children to be involved in searching for patterns and connections in what they know (and don't know) is crucial. Learning logs can help them to activate the process of organizing information. Categorizing their questions and guesses or possible answers can facilitate their reading and writing and their inquiries in general. Mapping on a topic ahead of time helps interactions in small group or whole class discussions and provides a framework for drafting, revising, or publishing experiences.

In summary, learning logs promote child-centered learning. They document both content and process. They provide a way for teachers to observe children's own understandings and experiences, and they are a vehicle for children's self-reflection on their own learning (see Chapter 9).

Learning logs allow children to keep track of new material they have learned, and they serve as an important source of self-evaluation.

Most teachers use spiral notebooks or three-ring binders for learning logs so that children can take only certain pages to work on at different places in the room or at other places out of school. A separate learning log might be used for each thematic unit. All entries in the log are dated. Many teachers respond to children's responses by commenting on content, asking for clarification, and providing questions for the children to consider. If children are not familiar with learning logs, teachers may do a Mini-Lesson* on the ways they can be used—perhaps using the three categories of asking questions, making guesses, and organizing information as a framework. Teacher suggestions or reminders to children in the first few days of school as they interact with them in their activities is usually enough for children to get the idea of learning logs. Learning logs are stored in a designated place in the room at the end of the day so that both teacher and children have easy access to them. The teacher can review them at the end of the day, and the children can get them at the beginning of the school day.

GROUP COMPOSED WRITING*

McKenzie (1985)

Group composed writing is a means for children to share the process of writing and to negotiate the form of various types of writing. Group composed writing can be done in two ways: (1) teacher-guided group writing, when the teacher does the transcribing and leads the composition process; and (2) peer group writing, when children contribute portions or sections of a larger piece and actually do the transcribing themselves. In both versions, children are supported in the writing process because they share the process with others; they learn from one another about the strategies they use while composing.

Teachers demonstrate the writing process.

Teacher-Led Group Composed Writing. Teacher-led group writing works well with younger children because the teacher takes over some of the mechanical aspects so that children can concentrate on the content. The idea applies to children of any age because it enables the teacher to demonstrate the thinking process involved in getting ideas into print and to make explicit the kinds of choices writers face—choices of voice, purpose, and form, as well as the medium aspects involved in creating a finished piece of writing.

Group writing can be initiated by the teacher or by children. Once children have collaborated in a group composed writing activity, they are quick to suggest their own ideas. Perhaps the teacher has just finished a particularly delightful story and has seen several children reworking or reenacting versions of the story in their art or play. Using a large sheet of chart paper or an overhead transparency, the teacher may ask for volunteers to help write a group version of the story, a first draft that will be put into book form later. The teacher begins by asking, "How should we begin our story?" Children are encouraged to draw on the ideas depicted in their drawings or play routines, and to use their own experiences with stories in general to write a new version. As the teacher writes their suggestions, he or she talks about what is happening in the transcribing process, mentioning the need for spaces between words, the use of capitalization and punctuation, and the way certain words are spelled. As the story evolves, parts are reread every so often, and questions are posed: "How does that sound so far?" "Is there anything we can change to make it better (or clearer, or exciting, or interesting, etc.)?" As children make suggestions for changes, parts can be crossed out or written in, even altered by cutting and pasting if necessary to demonstrate that first draft writing is often messy but dynamic.

Medium aspects of written language can also be referred to in teacher-led group writing.

Revising strategies are illustrated.

After children have agreed on a final version, it can be published—by simply rewriting it on a new piece of paper, by turning it into a Big Book* that children illustrate, and so on. In the following excerpt, kindergarteners used the patterns in Bill Martin's *Brown Bear, Brown Bear, What Do You See?* to write their own version using characters from *Goldilocks and the Three Bears* and other bear books they had been reading.

Martin (1983); Stevens (1986)

Papa Bear, Papa Bear, what do you see?
I see Mama Bear looking at me.
Mama Bear, Mama Bear, what do you see?
I see Paddington looking at me.

Figure 8.11 Display of Bear Characters

Each child then illustrated one of the bear characters, and their paintings were hung next to the appropriate verse on a large bulletin board display.

Group composed writing is useful with children at any age. With older children, a group writing session may center on more advanced understandings of style and form. For example, several children may have decided to create a class newspaper, but their first front-page news seems like a fictional story. By sharing the task of writing one of the newspaper accounts with the children, the teacher can help them to use a reporter's voice and present information in a more news-like genre format. They could also be shown how reading helps writing by looking at some real newspaper samples to get a sense of this style of writing and the ways it differs from other genres.

Peer-Collaborated Group Composed Writing. In peer-collaborated group writing, children do their own transcribing. It is especially useful for less proficient writers who may be overwhelmed by writing a whole book or piece on their own. Children can contribute a "chapter" in an "All About . . . Book" (on rocks, or tunnels, or dinosaurs, or bears, etc.). They can collaborate on a fairytale in which each writer composes an episode that tells how a particular character uses up one wish. They can together write up a biography of famous person, each member of the writing team concentrating on a certain period of the person's life. In peer-collaborated group writing, the teacher's role is one of helping in the coordination of the project and supporting the decision-making of the group.

Harste & Short (1988)

AUTHORS' FOLDERS*

Authors' folders are where children keep their ongoing, current writing. Frequently, the folders are part of the Learning Logs* and are kept in back of the log. [Two other folders for each child are usually kept: one in which children keep copies of final drafts that they have revised, edited, and published (children don't revise, edit, and publish everything they write), and one in which they collect other miscellaneous writings (abandoned partial drafts, prewriting notes, etc.).]

See also Atwell (1987), Calkins (1986), Graves (1983), Harste & Short (1988), and Temple, Nathan, Burris, & Temple (1988) for other ideas on authors' folders.

The organization of an author's folder

Many teachers staple or tape blank paper or forms on each of the four sides of the writing folder.

- *Outside Front.* The "Topics Sheet" is put on the outside front cover of the folder so children can jot down ideas or topics for future pieces. Some of these ideas emerge as they read, engage in various projects, or interact with other children in the classroom.
- *Inside Front.* The "Writing Log" is in the inside of the front cover of the folder. Here is where children provide some information to indicate the status of their pieces. They put in the date under the date column, and in the large column entitled "Status" (for younger children, it may be called "What I Did Today"), they note what draft they are working on, what piece they are revising, any prewriting activity they have done for a piece, what piece (and with whom) they have had a peer conference on, and the like. By reviewing this log, teachers can quickly monitor what's happening in writing for individual children. They can see if a child may be bogged down on a piece and need help. They can note when children will be ready for more formal Writing Conferences*.
- *Inside Back.* An "Evaluation Form" is kept in the inside back cover of the folder. Besides a date column, this form has two other columns entitled "Message Ideas" and "Medium Ideas." For younger children, these columns can be called "Meaning Ideas" and "Editing Ideas." Some teachers call the latter column "Spelling/Punctuation/Etc." Observations about what children have learned are written (either by children or the teacher) under the appropriate column heading. Comments about children's new strategies for forming the content or meanings in their writing are noted under "Message Ideas," and new growth regarding their use of medium aspects of written language are recorded under "Medium Ideas." This information is gathered by the teacher in everyday informal observations and interactions with children (these informal observations can be jotted down on Post-it notes or self-adhesive mailing strips and placed on the evaluation form), and by more formal Writing Conferences*. This evaluation sheet provides a means for monitoring children's writing. It is also a self-evaluation tool because children are expected to review it when they revise and edit a piece.
- *Outside Back.* The "Published Writing" form is stapled on the outside cover of the back of the folder. This is where children list their published pieces. Children frequently refer to the "Published Writing" form when they write an "About the Author" section for a book they are to publish.

Authors' folders provide sources of evaluation and accountability.

Like Learning Logs*, authors' folders are stored in a special place for easy access by both teacher and children. Most teachers go over six or so folders each night, so that they review a child's work at least once a week. Obviously, they can review more folders of younger children who usually write shorter pieces. The folders are important, for they are a means for documenting growth over time and provide an important measure of accountability (see Chapter 9).

WRITING CONFERENCES*

See also Atwell (1987), Calkins (1986), Graves (1983), Harste & Short (1988), and Temple, Nathan, Burris, & Temple (1988) for other ideas on conferences.

Like reading, children's writing is individualized in an integrated language classroom. They have had different prior writing experiences, they know different things about the registers of written language, they choose to write on different topics and genres. Therefore, as for reading, many teachers have separate individual conferences with children about their writing. And, just like reading, other teachers have many more short, less formal conferences with children as they see them writing in the classroom. They then have more general conferences with children when writing is addressed along with all their other learning (see Chapter 9).

Message aspects of language are addressed in content conferences; medium aspects of language are addressed in editing conferences.

Two major types of writing conferences are covered here—Content Conferences* and Editing Conferences*. Teachers usually address content or the message aspects of children's writing separately from the medium (spelling, punctuation, etc.) aspects—see Chapters 5 and 6. Peer conferencing is an important part of the process-conference approach, so a discussion of this topic is included in the discussion of each kind of conference.

Content Conferences*

Roving content conferences

Teacher-Student Conferences. The major purposes of conferences are to assess and guide. Teachers have roving content conferences all the time when they interact with children who are engaged in the process of writing, either at the designated writing table or at other places in the classroom. They may have jotted down information during these interactions, perhaps on Post-it notes or self-adhesive mailing strips (these might have been put on the Evaluation Form in the child's Author's Folder*, or may have been placed on sheets in his or her learning portfolio—see Chapter 9). In the more formal content conferences, teachers will have read the child's text (usually teachers schedule conferences on the basis of a sign-up sheet on which children indicate their readiness for a content conference). Children will have been expected to have already first read their text "to the wall" (so they can catch omitted words or awkward wordings themselves), and they may have also had a peer conference with another classmate (and would have revised their piece on the basis of that feedback). They will also have been expected to have revised their text according to any relevant comments on the "Evaluation Form" in their Author's Folder*.

More formal content conferences

Children prepare before having a conference with the teacher.

In the content conference, the teacher focuses on the content of the text, the way a child has organized the meanings or message of the text. (See Chapter 5, especially the register/genre section in Table 5.8, and the kid-watching writing section in Chapter 6, particularly the message questions examples.) First, it is best to comment on something positive about the writing, what the child knows and has done well. For example, a teacher may say how much information about turtles or whatever there is in the child's text. Or the teacher can remark on some writing strategy—for example, "I felt I was right there because of the way you described that place in the beginning of your story," or "That was an interesting way to conclude your text." Then the teacher asks one or two questions in a way that allows the children to retain ownership of their writing and begin to solve their own problems. Teachers try to assist children with genre or form problems and address difficulties regarding missing (or too much) information, sequencing, cohesiveness, and so on. They try to respond to children's text as an inquisitive reader. Typical questions could be: "Tell me more about *X*" or "I'm not sure that I understand *Y*." Teachers' final comments or questions concentrate on what the writer plans to do with the text as the result of the conference; they help the writer in the process of revision by asking, "What do you think you'll do next?"

A review of the message aspects of texts discussed in Chapter 5 *and* of the message questions illustrated in Chapter 6 is important for conducting successful content conferences.

Steps in conducting content conferences

At the end of the content conference, teachers and children go over what should be written under the "Status" section of the Writing Log and under the "Message Ideas" of the Evaluation Form in the Author's Folder* (usually what was discussed regarding the message aspects of the text and/or what the child has decided to work on in revision of what is summarized there).

Teachers have content conferences with even young elementary children (kindergarteners and first graders) as well, but they are very careful not to insist on too much revision too soon to avoid dampening the children's spirits regarding writing. Teachers have to show these young children that they are delighted and excited about the children's early writing efforts, so the children see themselves as writers and continue to be motivated to write. However, many young children enjoy content conferences because they like the special attention their writing gets. They also like completing the forms in the Author's Folder*.

Peer Content Conferences. Children share their writing informally all the time in an integrated language classroom, but peer content conferences are occasions to obtain more focused feedback on a finished (or partial) draft from one or two classmates. Many

Children respond to one anothers' messages during conferences.

teachers designate certain places in the classroom for peer content conferences—in a corner or in a supply closet or in the hall right outside the classroom door.

Procedures for peer conferences

Children internalize ways of acting in peer conferences through their participation in individual conferences with the teacher. Teachers also go over guidelines about how peer conferences are to be conducted. A peer conference usually consists of three parts. First, the writer reads the text aloud (older children can read the writer's text silently). Then the listener/reader makes some positive comment about it (for example, a part that was particularly exciting, interesting, or clear). Finally, the conference partner points out the place(s) that could be improved. All comments to the writer must include a reason; a remark such as "It's good" is not sufficient. After the peer conference, writers have to decide what feedback, if any, to consider in revision. Children are asked to summarize these remarks on their "Status" section of the Writing Log sheet in their Authors' Folders*. Teachers can then monitor if they are routinely dismissing useful feedback and can address this problem in their conferences with them.

Editing Conferences*

Teacher-led editing conferences

Teacher-Student Editing Conferences. After children have decided on the content of their draft, when they have done all the revision they want to do, they focus on the medium aspects of their text by editing. Teachers deal with editing in varying ways. Most teachers expect children to address editing matters themselves first, before a teacher-student conference. Some set up a special place, an editing table or corner supplied with a dictionary and thesaurus, colored pens or pencils, and perhaps specially developed checklists, where children do their editing. Children use a pen or pencil in a color that is different from that of the text and go over their text, concentrating especially on the "Medium Ideas" listed in their Author's Folder*, correcting spelling and punctuation, deleting words or phrases or inserting others to make better transitions or to improve clarity, and so on.

When the writers have finished editing, they sign up for a conference with the teacher. The teacher goes over the text with a pen of a third color, changing only medium aspects, not content. Some teachers do this editing alone and then set up an editing conference with the child; some do it with the children, explaining their changes. In either case, only one issue is usually emphasized with the children. See Chapter 6 for ideas and examples. At the end of the conference, the children record that issue under "Medium Ideas" on the Evaluation Form in the Author's Folder*.

As in Content Conferences*, teachers have to be very careful in dealing with editing matters with young emergent writers. Many teachers wait until the end of kindergarten or the beginning of first grade before talking with children about the medium aspects of their writing. Teachers want to encourage these young children to write using approximations because the children lack knowledge of many of the conventions of writing. Of course, teachers do edit the children's work when some of their texts are published (e.g., typed texts that children illustrate and then make into books). Children's attempts to read these texts that now have conventional spelling and punctuation as they illustrate them is one of the best ways to foster their reading.

Peer editing

Peer Editing Conferences. Many teachers do not edit everything children publish. Instead, they establish peer teams to play certain editing roles. Peer editing is especially useful in dealing with work that will be published through displays, charts, and so on in the classroom, and editorial boards can review classroom newspapers or literary magazines. The teacher and children together can decide what editing procedures will be followed in special class projects.

PUBLISHING EXPERIENCES*

Publishing is sharing.

In Chapter 5, we emphasized that publishing had to do with sharing. For this reason, publishing can include much more than the publishing of final drafts; any of the writing experiences discussed in Chapter 5 can be published. In this chapter, however, three aspects of publishing are covered in more detail: Displays*, Book Making*, and Author's Chair*.

Displays*

Careful display or presentation of projects helps children develop a sense of accomplishment and pride in a job well done, as well as a sensitivity to the effects their work has on others. Displays can include anything and everything—posters, charts, maps, puppets, games, dioramas, and the like.

Displays should be aesthetically pleasing.

Children are encouraged to mat finished art work and writing and to think about spacing and visual qualities in mounting their work. Mats or borders can be made by gluing the finished work to a larger sheet of construction paper. The mats can vary to include free-form shapes and multicolored backgrounds. A combination of these ideas can be used in mounting several works, thereby adding visual interest or unity to the finished products, as shown in Figure 8.12.

Teachers have several roles in displaying. They provide the materials, demonstrate and suggest some of the possibilities, support and coordinate children's decision-making regarding displays. Many teachers in traditional schools spend a lot of time and money (buying commercially made pumpkins, valentines, bunnies, etc.) to decorate their bulletin boards and classrooms. But do these classrooms reflect their children's interests or understandings? In integrated language classrooms, they do—through the displays of *children's* products, the classroom depicts the work of a community of learners.

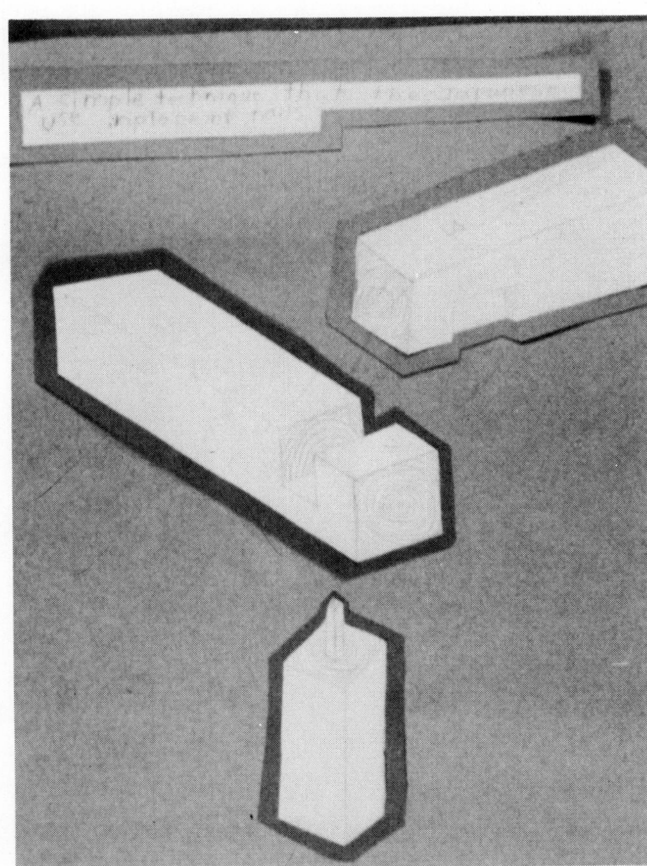

Figure 8.12 Examples of Matted Finished Artwork *(Continued on next page.)*

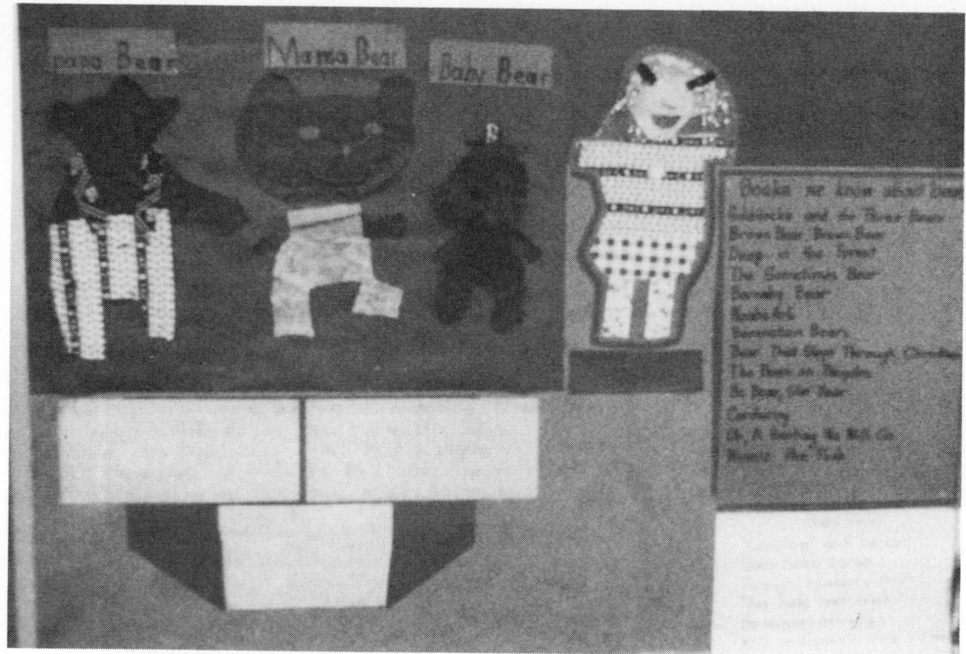

Figure 8.12 Continued

Book Making*

Publishing writing in book form lends it a sense of permanence and value. Many forms of book making by children can be used regularly throughout the year, including shape books (covers and blank paper are cut out in a special shape to tie in with a particular thematic unit); books with ring binding or binders; books with the edges stapled together with construction paper or wallpaper sample covers; books made with cloth covers (using rubber cement or dry mount tissue to glue the cover together).

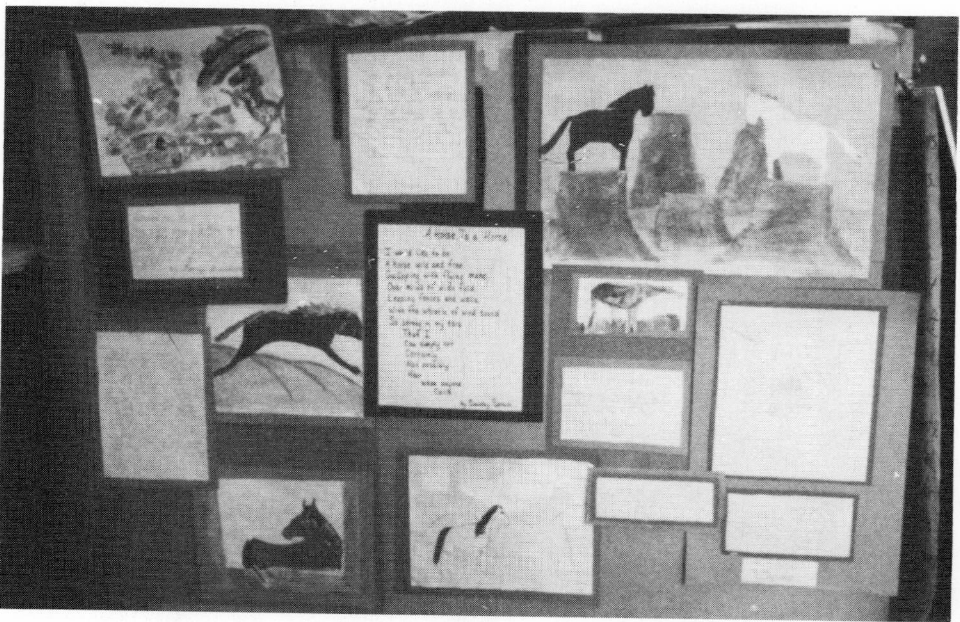

Figure 8.12 Continued

Cloth-covered books take the most time and effort, but most teachers try to provide the opportunity for children to publish this type of book several times a year. Figure 8.13 outlines instructions for such book making.

Children also enjoy experimenting with techniques for paper making and for creating decorative endpapers or cover papers. Waste paper and a kitchen blender can give a finished product that is similar to fine handmade paper (see Figure 8.14). Block, or potato printing, or other decorative techniques (see Figure 8.15) add special effects to endpapers or book covers.

See Chambers (1986) and *The Paper Makers* by Fisher (1986) for good resources on making books.

In book making, children are encouraged to include all aspects of books, such as dedications and title page. The inclusion of an "About the Author" page lets children tell some personal information about themselves as authors—their family, pets, hobbies,

Materials:

- construction paper
- cardboard (cereal boxes or old file folders are best; cardboard boxes are not good)
- rubber cement or dry mount tissue (available from photographic supply stores)
- cloth, wrapping paper, or wallpaper

Directions:

1. Measure and cut sheets of construction paper for pages. For end pages, choose 2 sheets of contrasting colored construction paper (the same size) (Figure A).
2. Fold pages and end pages in half. Keep end pages on the bottom (Figure B).
3. Sew along fold line with embroidery needles (Figure C).
4. Cut cardboard 1/4 to 1/2 in. larger than the pages for the cover.
5. Cut wrapping paper, cloth or wall paper 1″ to 2″ larger than cover.
6. Cut cover cardboard in half then trim 1/4″ off each half.
7. Lay cover paper flat, place 2 cover boards on top leaving 1/2″ between the top sheets to allow book to open and shut (Figure D).
8. a. Glue cover sheets to cover paper with rubber cement. or
   b. Place 2 sheets of dry mount tissue (cut to the same size as cover board) between coverboard and cover paper press with dry iron set on wool.
9. Fold corners in to form trianlges. Glue to cover board (Figure E).
10. Fold edges over. Glue to cover board.
11. Place pages of book on cover, end pages on bottom. Center pages on cover (Figure F).
12. Glue bottom end page to cover.

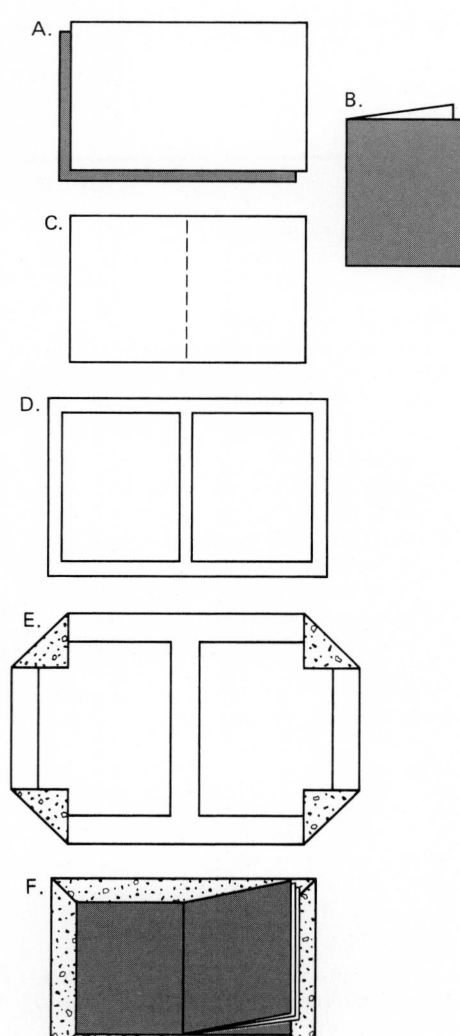

Figure 8.13 Making Books

HANDMADE PAPER

Materials:

Large container
Scrap paper (old newspaper, computer paper)
1/4 cup bleach
Sponge
Toweling
Wooden frame covered with nylon or wire screen (small mesh)
Kitchen blender
2 pieces of wooden board or masonite
Weights

Directions:

1. Tear paper into tiny pieces and add to container full of water (bleach will make paper whiter).
2. Soak overnight.
3. Add a little water to the blender. Set blender to liquify. Drop in soaked paper a little at a time. (Short pulses on the blender may be more effective.)
4. Pour mixture over screen, distributing it evenly. Let water drain off.
5. Roll pulp onto towel and press with another towel or sponge to remove water.
6. Place pulp between two boards and put weights on top.
7. Let dry.

Figure 8.14

DECORATIVE PAPERS

Chalk Dust Endpapers

Materials:

An oblong pan of water
Construction paper (The paper should have a somewhat absorbent rough texture.)
Pastel chalk (large single sticks, available in art supply stores, provide the richest color and the greatest amount of chalk dust.)

Directions:

1. Using a kitchen knife, scrape the chalk over the pan of water in random spots. A second or third color can be added.
2. Place a sheet of paper gentlv on the surface of the water, tapping it lightly to remove any air bubbles.
3. Remove the paper carefully and let it dry. When dry, the chalk dust will be bound to the paper in a delicate attractive design.
4. Repeat the process on the reverse side for the sheet of endpaper that is not glued to the cover board.

Soap Bubble Endpapers

Materials:

Oblong pan
Construction paper
Mixture of 2 parts tempera paint to 1 part liquid dishwashing soap
Plastic drinking straws

Directions:

1. Add paint mixture to the pan of water.
2. Blow bubbles in the mixture with straw.
3. Remove the straw and place paper on top of the bubbles.
4. As the bubbles break, they will produce an interesting design or "print."
5. Remove paper and dry on a flat surface. Repeat on opposite side if desired.

Figure 8.15

interests, other books they have written, and so on. Children search for and read book jackets of real books for the kinds of ideas to include. Having opportunities to write such author "blurbs" about themselves frequently serves as a motivator for some reluctant writers.

Book making is an art that extends back through the centuries and warrants special attention at some point in the elementary school years. The study of book making can include a visit to a local printing plant or to a small independent press where type is set by hand and pictures are printed from metal etchings or wood blocks. These small print shops sometimes make their own paper using old rags and handmade molds. Local artisans familiar with oriental techniques of paper making using rice paper and such natural items as pressed flowers, or craftspersons familiar with making marbleized paper for book endpapers and covers, may be available and willing to visit the classroom.

Author's Chair*

The term author's chair has both specific and general meanings in publishing. In a specific sense, the author's chair is a designated actual chair in a classroom on which writers sit when they present their own writing to peers. In a general sense, however, the author's chair represents the broad range of sharing possibilities in the classroom. It celebrates and gives value to the process of authoring. It also establishes linkages between writers and readers (and writing and reading) because it provides opportunities for peers to ask questions about what authors did or were trying to do. It helps authors to understand that readers may have different interpretations of their work; it facilitates an awareness that both readers and writers have options or choices in the process of reading and writing.

Calkins (1986); Lytle & Botel (1988)

Tierney, Readence, & Dishner (1985)

This general sense also means that publishing is more than authors reading final drafts to the class. It includes the sharing of partial drafts that need feedback and suggestions, the presenting of plans or Semantic Maps* to be explored by a small group, giving a play or puppet show, demonstrating a game, the showing of artifacts such as dioramas, topographical maps, papier-mâché tunnels or animals, and so on. Thus, the author's chair emphasizes the social dimensions of learning. It is a vehicle used by children to realize the culture of the classroom.

Many forms of sharing—or publishing—are possible.

SKETCH TO STRETCH*

Sketch to stretch activities help children to understand that meanings can be communicated through a system other than language. Through drawing children can transform or extend meanings expressed through language, or they can construct new meanings or discover insights that language alone cannot afford. Because sketch to stretch activities encourage individual responses, they also help children to understand and value variations in interpretations.

Harste & Short (1988)

Many teachers suggest sketch to stretch activities as possible responses or extensions to books that children have read or heard. For example, children can sketch what the book (or selection or text) meant to them. Or they may be given a large piece of paper folded into four or more sections and asked to draw a picture of what happened in the beginning of the story in the first section, then what happened at the end of the story in the last section, and then what happened in the middle of the story in the other sections. Children may also include short sentences or captions in each section to correspond to their drawings.

Cochrane, Cochrane, Scalena, & Buchanan (1984)

Sketch to stretch activities can be used across the curriculum. They can be used with nonfictional, informational books or topics. For example, children may draw a picture of a squirrel (perhaps also labeling its known characteristics) or a picture of what squirrels do (again including short descriptions of what they think squirrels' habitual behavior is like). They may then read or listen to *Squirrels* by Wildsmith and *The Squirrel* by Lane. Then they may create new squirrel sketches, adding, elaborating, and

Lane (1981); Wildsmith (1974)

Sketch-to-stretch activities are possible across the curriculum.

changing their initial drawings to reflect new information gained from these books. Such sketching activities can be used at the beginning of a new thematic unit by the class as a whole or to depict the initial understandings of a particular topic that members of a small group are to investigate. Children may try to sketch what they think could happen in a process in a particular science experiment, and then check their ideas by actually doing the experiment. They may illustrate the process as a way of publishing their observations of the experiment. Also recall the example of fourth graders who were investigating the geographic concept of "desert" in Chapter 7. They began by drawing what they imagined a desert to look like. Remember how children made their own math books, using illustrations to depict their own understandings of mathematical concepts and procedures. In sum, sketch to stretch activities can complement, extend, and deepen ideas, meanings, and concepts across the curriculum.

ACTIVITY CARDS*

Activity cards are invitations or suggestions for learning.

See Kwak & Newman (1985) for a good classroom example of the use of activity cards.

Activity cards encourage children to become active, independent learners by inviting them to engage in learning. The cards are not assignments giving tasks that children must follow to the letter. Instead, they list open-ended questions or suggestions for possible inquiries that can be interpreted differently by different children.

These science activity card ideas came from Wassermann & Ivany (1988).

Many teachers use activity cards to start a thematic unit. When they plan their thematic units, they come up with possible meaningful activities that children can choose from (see the activities illustrated in Chapter 3 and in the prototype WEBS in Chapter 4). They then write the activities on cards (using different sizes of index cards). Figure 8.16 illustrates activity cards that focus on science topics. Notice how these cards encourage talk and collaboration with others, and the integration of literacy. They emphasize thinking and decision-making by the children. Activity cards do not convey a specific set of expectations or level of competence; children can tackle them at their own level. Sometimes activity cards are designed for more specific support by providing, for example, some step-by-step instructions for setting up and conducting a scientific experiment, or they may give guidelines for using certain materials—for example, Jackdaws* or other Primary Materials*.

Activity cards can be modified or can spark altogether new ideas.

Because activity cards are open-ended and only suggestions, children are free to modify the ideas on the cards. The cards may even spark altogether different problems or lines of inquiry. Thus, the cards leave room for initiation and negotiation by the children regarding activities. Teachers can specifically encourage this creativity in the beginning of a unit by reading through some of the cards and then having children brainstorm modifications or elaborations of the activities on the cards, or having them try to construct new activities with the same materials at hand. Thus, teachers have a major role in the use of activity cards. They plan for choices and suggestions in the beginning, and then they support children's inquiries by raising questions or making comments that lead children to make their own decisions, and by pointing out further resources and reading materials for them to consider in their investigations.

Reading activity cards and writing modifications or new cards by the children themselves provide meaningful literacy experiences and promote other uses of reading and writing. Reviewing the activity cards at the end of a thematic unit can also help children be more aware of what the classroom community of learners has tackled and accomplished. Moreover, these cards can provide a way of documenting the kinds of learning that have been achieved—see Chapter 9.

GRAPHING*

In Chapter 7, graphing was suggested as a major way by which children could incorporate mathematical understandings in thematic units. There are three major kinds of graphs: real graphs, picture graphs, and symbolic graphs. Real graphs are especially

ACTIVITY CARD #1

* Use the materials in this center and make some observations about things that sink and things that float.
* Try as many investigations as you can think of.
* Talk with each other about your ideas.
* Then make a record of what you observed.

There may be other ways to use the materials in this center. Try some of your own investigations and see what happens.

MATERIALS: One or two large plastic basins of water. A variety of materials – sponges, chalk, Ping-Pong balls, modeling clay, aluminum foil, containers with removable lids, bits of wood, clothespins, stones, shells, styrofoam chips, plastic dishes and cups, nails, paper cups, glass jars.

ACTIVITY CARD #2

* Use the materials in this center to make some investigations with seeds.
* Make some observations and decide how these seeds might be classified. Set up some categories, and place the seeds into the category where each belongs. Then record your classification.
* Examine two kinds of seeds and compare them. How are they alike? How are they different? Find as many similarities and differences as you can, and record your findings.

You may have some other ideas for conducting investigations with these seeds. Try your ideas and see what discoveries you can make.

MATERIALS: A variety of seeds – fast-growing seeds are preferable, for example, lettuce, lima bean, mung bean, corn, alfalfa, watercress, radish. Paper towels or blotting paper, waxed paper or plastic wrap, saucers, water, sand, potting soil, small pots or other containers (e.g., milk containers) for planting, large spoons for digging.

ACTIVITY CARD #3

* Study the earthworms for a long time.
* Then, one by one, using the materials in the center, change the surfaces on which you place the earthworms.
* What observations can be made about the effect of changing the environment on the earthworm's behavior?
* Talk with each other about your observations.
* Then write about what you found.

MATERIALS: Earthworms (found in the school yard or a park, or, if necessary, purchased from a biological supply house). A variety of items with flat surfaces, such as pieces of cloth with different textures, wood, aluminum foil, plastic wrap. Some sand, water, sandpaper. Several magnifying lenses.

Figure 8.16

Real graphs

important at the lower grades because they enable children to compare groups of real objects and provide the foundation of all other graphing activities. An example of a real graph can be found in the WASH AND WEAR thematic unit in Chapter 4. Peter asked his children to compare and classify their own shoes by considering a variety of attributes—shoes with laces or velcro closings, right or left shoes, tennis shoes or other kinds of shoes, and colors of shoes. Once categories had been decided on, Peter created a large grid on the floor with masking tape, and children placed the shoes on the grid according to category. Many real graphs are possible using manipulative objects in the classroom—seeds, coins, and buttons; snack items (cookies, crackers, pieces of vegetables, etc.); blocks; and so on. Grids can be made on the floor or a table. Smaller grids can be made out of varying sizes of paper or cardboard. Grids can be made with any number of rows or categories.

Picture graphs

Picture graphs are also appropriate at the lower elementary grades. A picture graph uses pictures or models to stand for real things. Peter used a picture graph in the WASH AND WEAR prototype as well as a real graph. After children counted and labeled each category on the real shoe graph on the floor, they made smaller picture graphs using cut-out construction paper shoes to stand for the real shoes on the floor grid. The possibilities for picture graphs are also unlimited.

Symbolic graphs

Symbolic graphs, which are the most abstract level of graphs, use symbols to stand for real things. For example, a symbolic graph could have been constructed in Peter's class by having children put an "X" in the appropriate cell of the graph grid instead of the cut-out paper shoe. Symbolic graphs can then be extended to represent more and more complex patterns and relationships, and they can incorporate more and more mathematical operations. Bar graphs can be created as a result of a survey of the type of juice or fruit children prefer, or the kinds of vehicles found in the school parking lot over a week. Figure 8.17A shows how children place small paper rectangles on the graph to indicate each child's preference in fruit. Figure 8.17B depicts the average number of vehicles found in the lot over a week and involves more complex computation.

Graphs can plot frequency patterns (or patterns of averages, percentages, etc.) over time—for example, the number of vehicles observed over the different days over the week. Figure 8.18 illustrates such a graph.

See Baratta-Lorton (1976) for a good discussion of graphs.

In sum, a range of graphs of type and complexity can be incorporated into the classroom across the curriculum. Planned graphs are considered as part of planning the WEB of a thematic unit; others can emerge spontaneously while children are engaged in activities or projects related to the theme.

BOOK EXTENSIONS*

Huck, Hepler, & Hickman (1987); Johnson & Louis (1987)

Young children learn by acting on their world, transforming it through play, art, drama, music, and language into something uniquely personal. Children can also enter into the world of the book and through these same avenues, remake and reshape their experi-

Figure 8.17A

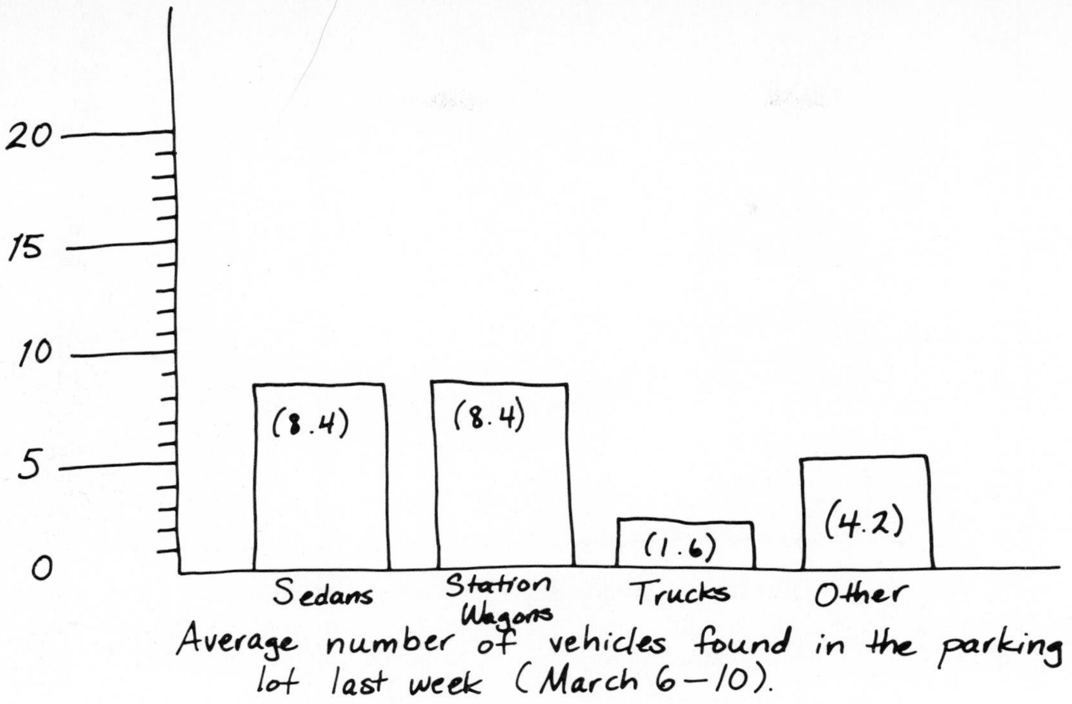

Figure 8.17B

ences with literature, making books memorable. It is through these transformations that the deepest response to books is possible.

Chapter 3 discussed ways to plan activities that would allow children to play with the characters and situations of the book *Strega Nona* in the same ways they play with people and events in real life. Activities such as these do not make workbooks out of children's literature. Instead, they represent experiences children are likely to have as language users in the real world. Children then transfer these possibilities to the world of the book. Most of these activities are designed to lead children back into the book, to have them refer to it for information, or to think more deeply about character motivation, themes, and ideas. Other activities can go beyond the book to help children to compare and synthesize information, experiences, and ideas.

de Paola (1975)

A range of book extensions—for example, Semantic Maps*, Comparison Charts*, and Sketch to Stretch* activities—has already been covered in this chapter and many others have been mentioned and illustrated in other chapters. Three kinds of book extensions suitable for fictional literature—Story Mapping*, Plot Profiles*, and Character Sociograms*—are described in more detail in following sections. Many others are possible. Figure 8.19 summarizes these possibilities.

Huck, Hepler, & Hickman (1987)

Story Mapping*

LeGuin (1968)

Story mapping helps children to visualize the physical geography that often undergirds so many stories. Think about the ways in which Ursula LeGuin's map of Earthsea helps the reader to visualize Ged's voyage, or think what fun generations of children have had in tracing Pooh's adventures on Milne's maps. Story mapping is particularly useful in visualizing created worlds in fantasy and science fiction, but think of how helpful a map can be in recreating a historical incident or following a mystery. Creating maps helps an author to keep track of the relationships between setting and action. The reader who attempts to map a literary world must delve into a literary text deeply enough to recreate those relationships in ways that are true to both text and reader.

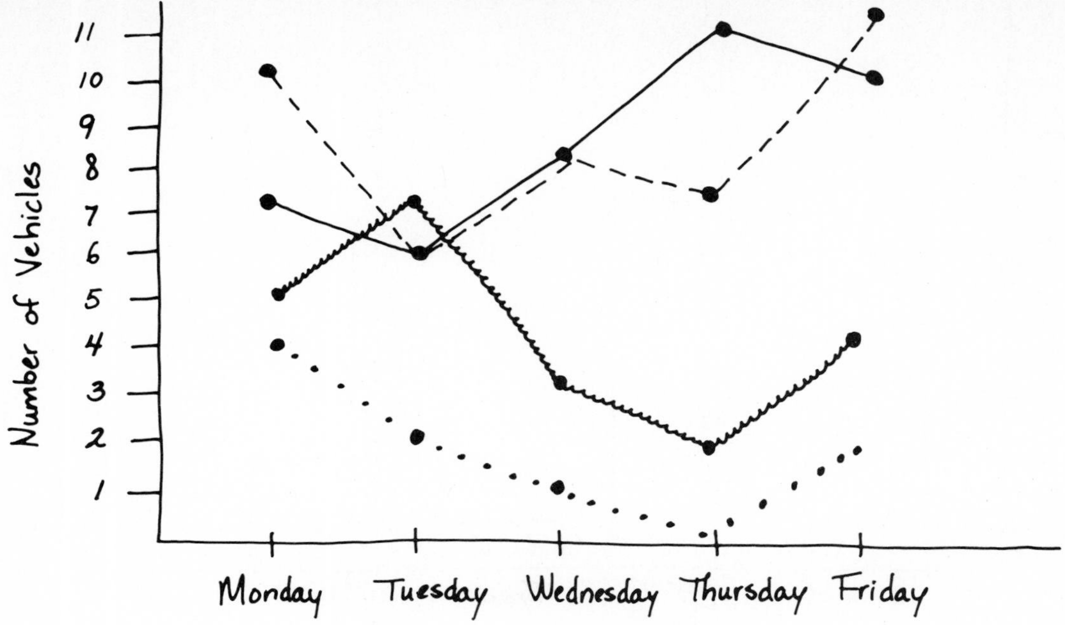

Figure 8.18

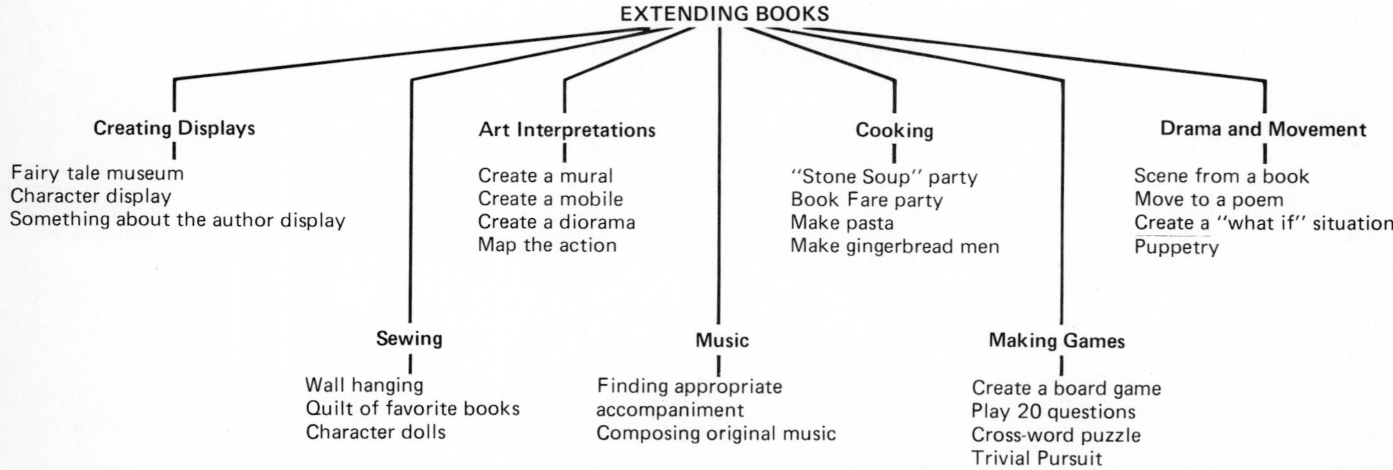

Figure 8.19 Book Extensions
Source: Huck et al. (1987).

As a result, story mapping encourages frequent rereading, as well as wrestling with spatial relationships. It also provides a glimpse of what might be called the reader's "mental geography" of a story.

A fifth grader created a map of Terabithia, the secret place across the stream in Paterson's *Bridge to Terabithia.* He struggled to represent both the magical nature of the kingdom in the woods and the menace that lay at the banks of the stream. He initially drew a map with a picture of the woods viewed from beyond the log that crossed the stream. This did not allow the student to represent Terabithia, however, and so he tried again, this time constructing a bird's-eye view of woods, stream, log, and field beyond. He added a key and a scale and labeled the map so that within Terabithia all labels were in green, the world outside was blue, and the log and stream that both protected Terabithia and took a life were red.

Paterson (1977)

The final map may not have been particularly polished, but it represented a process through which this student came to grips with (1) the ways in which maps represent physical features (e.g., bird's-eye view), (2) the emotional geography of the story (i.e., safety in green, danger in red, emotional distance in blue), and (3) the physical relationships between setting and action.

Younger children can also make story maps, but they may need a more directed experience, at least initially. After a teacher has shared a favorite story with the class, children are led to contribute to a class list of all the features that a map of this story could contain. A story map is then shown on the overhead, and the class discusses the major items included on the map. Missing features are added and labeled. Once children have had this joint experience, they can work in pairs or small groups to construct maps of other stories. The teacher may want to share a story and discuss it with the whole class, and then let small groups work on mapping that story. Or children may prefer to pick their own stories and share these as part of a later book discussion.

Although children can learn a great deal from creating their own map, story mapping can also occur when children attach story features to an existing map. Historical fiction lends itself particularly well to this activity. Children reading Lasky's *Beyond the Divide,* for instance, used a large map of the United States and attached pictures, captions, and labels to show the progress of Meribah Simon's journey from Pennsylvania to California. Other children mapped folk and fairy tales that were related to specific locales (e.g., Paul Bunyon, Pecos Bill, John Henry).

Lasky (1983)

The most challenging story maps, however, involve children in mapping stories that have only a literary geography. Sixth graders, for instance, found mapping Mary Q. Steele's *Journey Outside* particularly challenging because it moves across two planes—the underground river of the Raft People and the surface worlds through which Dilar travels after leaving the Raft People. One group constructed a two-layered map to graphically display the relationship between the river and surface worlds. They found the river world relatively easy to visualize, as it flowed in a great circle below the surface. They went back to the book many times, however, in their attempts to locate the surface worlds in their relationship to one another. Where were the mountains relative to the sea? Were they the same mountains each time? How could they represent the different landscapes using a bird's-eye view? These students decided to use a relief map to better represent their story. They then depicted Dilar's wanderings with a dotted line across the map.

Steele (1969)

Younger children may need a fair amount of practice in drawing a bird's-eye view. One way to help them is to begin the mapping activity by using models rather than flat drawings. Just as the group that made a relief map for their story found that to be a more comfortable way of representing topography, some younger children may be better able to visualize a view from above by first representing the story world in three dimensions. After the children have made a model of the story world, they can view it from the top and draw a map of what they see. The map drawn from the model can then be labeled with story features and incidents. Some teachers also encourage children to include story quotations as part of a story map.

A number of books lend themselves particularly well to story mapping. In general, any story about a journey has map-making potential. Hall's *Ox-cart Man* provides an

Hall (1979)

opportunity for children to use a map of New Hampshire and to plot a journey to Portsmouth. Steig's *Caleb and Kate* lends itself to making a map of a journey that includes an encounter with a witch. Other books encourage mapping buildings (Norton's *The Borrowers*), imaginary worlds (Engdahl's *Enchantress from the Stars*), or the inside of a pyramid (Aliki's *Mummies Made in Egypt*).

Steig (1977)

Norton (1953); Engdahl (1970); Aliki (1979)

When children work on story maps, they can develop a richer understanding in several areas relevant both to reading and to geography. First, map-making involves sequencing physical features and events. Where does the map/story begin? End? These facts are important in literary understanding, and they are also basic components of thinking in the social studies. Map-making also involves relative location and position, features that enrich literary understanding and also help children to visualize spatial relationships outside story worlds.

Mapping also requires that readers go back into the book to verify sequencing and relationships. One result of this close attention to the internal logic of a story is a richer understanding of the craft of the author. Map-making also helps the reader to understand the story in a way that is closer to the multidimensional illusion the author originally intended.

Johnson & Louis (1987)

Plot Profiles*

When children read and respond to literature, they become more informed about the structure of stories, recognizing certain clues to the kind of story they have begun (i.e., "Once upon a time" signals make-believe, whereas "It was a dark and stormy night" hints at mystery) and attending to the way in which a story rises to its climax or drops off into an ending that leaves the reader wishing for more. In integrated language classrooms, children are also authors. They write in a number of genres and so attend to literary elements from an author's as well as a reader's perspective. There are many ways to help children to think about the elements of a piece of writing. Plot profiles are one way of calling attention to the way in which an author structures a story around a plot. Plot profiles also involve children in using timelines and rating scales and plotting a graph—all skills that can be used across the curriculum.

Johnson & Louis (1987)

Plot profiles can be constructed with children of various ages. In working with younger children, however, the story should be fairly simple and have a strong, clear plot line. Folk and fairy tales work particularly well because the plot line tends to be clear and uncluttered. The children take a story such as *Goldilocks and the Three Bears* and begin an incident summary. The teacher records the children's suggestions as follows:

1. Mama Bear makes porridge.
2. The porridge is too hot.
3. The three bears go for a walk to let the porridge cool.
4. Goldilocks wanders into the Bears' house.
5. She tries the chairs.
6. She tries the porridge.
7. She tries the beds.
8. Goldilocks falls asleep.
9. The Bears come home.
10. They find the broken chair.
11. They find the empty porridge bowl.
12. They find Goldilocks.
13. Goldilocks leaps from the bed and runs away.

The teacher then shows children a time and excitement chart such as the one in Figure 8.20. The horizontal axis represents time, with number 1 being the first incident (Mama Bear makes porridge) and number 13 being the last (Goldilocks runs away). Beginning with the most exciting point (perhaps number 12, the discovery of Goldi-

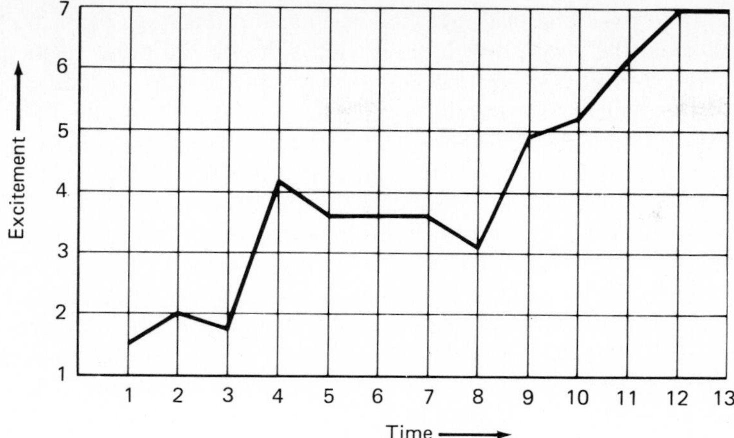

Figure 8.20 Time and Excitement Chart

locks), the children plot where that incident would fall in terms of time and excitement. Next, they plot the least exciting part (perhaps number 1, Mama Bear making porridge), and then all the points in between. After the chart is plotted, the lines are drawn, connecting the points and showing the rhythm of the story's plot.

Discussion should be encouraged throughout the plotting procedure so that the plot represents some sort of consensus. When children try this technique on other stories, they may also want to make plot profiles individually or in small groups. The profiles can be the basis of some interesting discussions when children explain why they made the decisions that led to differences between charts for the same stories.

Plot profiles for children reading more complex books can also be an interesting way to describe plot twists visually. A mystery, for instance, can have a number of rather sharp peaks as the author leads the reader from one clue to the next. These profiles can also be quite long. Sometimes a broader definition of "incident" is required to make the profile less cumbersome. For instance, a child plotting Jane Yolen's *The Devil's Arithmetic* may deal with the entire first chapter, up to the point of opening the door into the past, as one incident. Entry into the past may be a second, shorter incident, and then the period from entry until the wedding trip may be a third. *Yolen (1988)*

Illustrated plot profiles can also be created on mural paper. At each point on the chart, an illustration represents the story incident. Children work in pairs to create the illustrations, and they can select the art medium that best exemplifies the incident being pictured. A sixth grader illustrating an incident in the poem, "The Highwayman," for instance, decided that the scene where the highwayman is shot "like a dog on the highway" needed special attention. On a piece of black construction paper, he used white chalk to sketch in the moonlit highway, with trees picked out of the darkness and shadowy figures standing over the body of the highwayman. The highwayman was all in white except for the scarlet color at his throat where his life bled away across the dark road. The mural that resulted from this and other pictures, including collages, simple line drawings, and so forth, was a dramatic illustration of the students' emotional response to this piece of literature. *Noyes (1983)*

Character Sociograms*

In responding to a book she had just finished reading, one child described the power of the story this way: "It sees through the eyes of this person." In a sense, character sociograms are a way of representing the readers' understanding of what they saw through the eyes of a literary character. More than that, however, the sociograms are *Levstik (1986)* an opportunity to think and talk about the relationships between characters in stories and to think about the way in which the reader is drawn into those relationships.

It is not easy to clearly describe the processes involved in creating sociograms. It may be useful to think of a sociogram as a character web, similar to the thematic WEBS we have already talked about. The main character, then, is thought of as the center of the sociogram, just as the theme is the center of a WEB. The other characters in the story are arranged around the central character. Arrows connect the characters and show the direction and distance of the relationships. Figure 8.21 shows such a sociogram for Judith Viorst's *Alexander and the Terrible, Horrible, No Good Very Bad Day.*

Viorst (1972)

Some teachers have found that the initial steps in putting together a sociogram can be done by using movable objects and an overhead projector. For instance, the teacher sets out an array of small objects that can be used to represent each character in the story. Children identify an object with a character (this is an interesting part of the process, too!), and the teacher places each object on a transparency in relation to the main character. Pencils can be used as arrows and can be moved as discussion takes place.

Once the idea of the sociogram is generally understood, students work in pairs with either objects or paper shapes (these can be circles, squares, etc.) and arrange their sociograms so that they can write brief statements on the connecting arrows. Figure 8.22 depicts an elaborated sociogram of the relationships in the book *Alexander and the Terrible, Horrible, No Good Very Bad Day.*

As with most other activities described in this book, there is no single way to do a sociogram. Their power lies in the quality of the thinking and conversing children do as they construct them. The following guidelines are helpful in working with sociograms:

Johnson & Louis (1987)

Place the central character(s) at the center of the diagram.
Let the distance between characters reflect the perceived psychological distance between them.
Let the size of the shape representing a character vary with the importance or the power of the character.

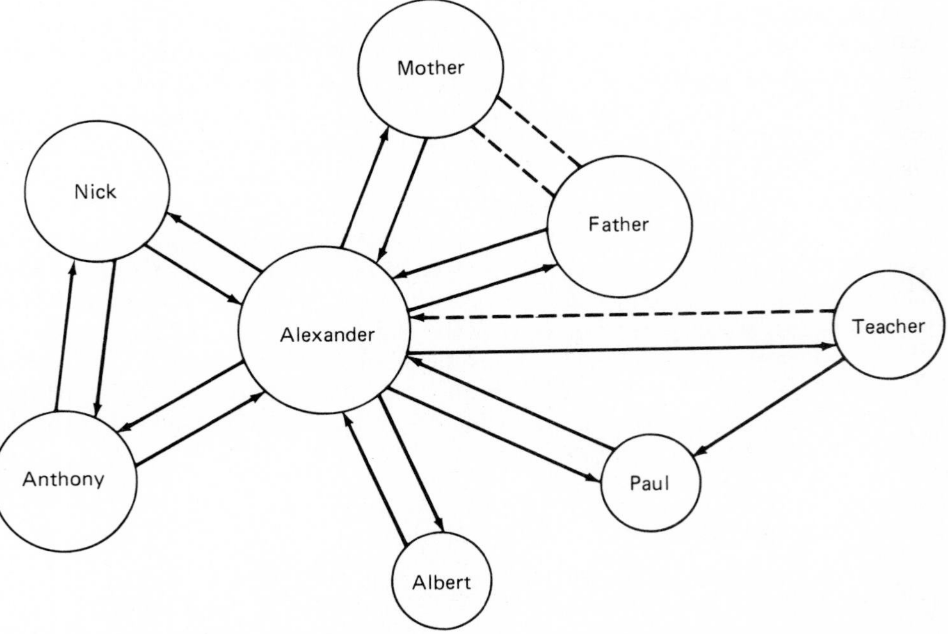

Figure 8.21 Character Sociogram for *Alexander and the Terrible, Horrible, No Good Very Bad Day*

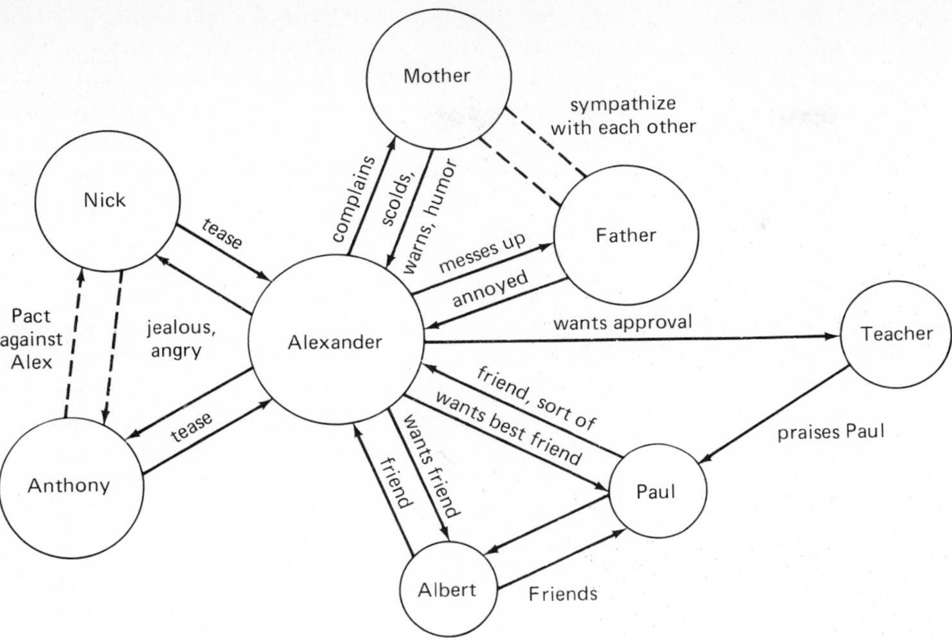

Figure 8.22 An Elaborated Sociogram of *Alexander and the Terrible, Horrible, No Good Very Bad Day*

Show the direction of a relationship by an arrow and its nature by a label.
Represent substantiated relationships with a solid line and inferred relationships with a broken line (a nice opportunity to discuss inferences!).
Circle active characters with a solid line. Circle significant absent characters with a broken line.
Place the characters who support the main character on one side of a dividing line and antagonistic characters on the other.

When character sociograms are tried, teachers and children alike invent new conventions to deal with new relationships. No single sociogram can ever entirely represent the relationships in a story, and no single interpretation of those relationships is either necessary or possible. Instead, sociograms are successful to the degree that they involve children in thinking carefully about their reading and that they support the judgments children have made (see the section on Observation/Inference*, for further discussion on this topic).

DRAMA EXPERIENCES*

Creative dramatics, like the other arts, is a way of knowing. Drama can provide a rich vein of experiences that help children to find out about themselves and others. Such insights can shape and cement children's social growth and lead to a spirit of cooperation and trust within the classroom community. Drama also allows children from a variety of cultural backgrounds to develop communicative competence by taking on many additional registers through the many characters that they choose to become.

Johnson & O'Neill (1984); McCaslin (1984); Siks (1977)

Way (1967)

Creative dramatics exists on a continuum from interpretive to improvisational activities, but it is *not* the memorization of someone else's script performed before an audience. The true value of all forms of drama lies in the *process,* not the product (or production). Teachers play important roles in providing and suggesting opportunities for dramatic experiences and in supporting the aspects of this process of drama. They offer ideas, situations, and problems to pursue in drama, and they encourage individual

O'Neill & Lambert (1982)

Process is emphasized in creative dramatics.

children to participate. Most of the time children share forms of drama with others, but they can just as well create imaginary worlds for no audience but themselves. Thus, any sets, props, or costumes should be kept simple. A Drama Corner could contain such general costumes as hats, old coats, cloaks, and paper bags that can serve many costume functions. A prop such as a yardstick can function as a sword, a scepter, or a magic wand. Several types of drama experiences are discussed in the following pages.

Improvisation*

O'Neill (1985)

Improvisation, one of the more difficult but rewarding types of drama, gives children a problem and asks them to solve it. Children can take situations from real life (past, present, or future) or rework situations they find in literature. They assume character roles and interact to solve problems confronting them as these characters. Negotiation among the participants occurs as a drama unfolds, and the finding of joint solutions is a dynamic process. The children create new situations rather than reenacting previous scenarios, yet they rely on their own experience and judgment to orchestrate these make-believe worlds.

Walsh (1982)

Improvisation from a Book. In *The Green Book,* Pattie and her family are forced to leave Earth to find a new home on another planet. They can take only a change of clothes, one or two small personal items, and one book. In a small group, children discuss what book they will take and explain their choices. A list of books that everyone agrees are important for survival on a new planet emerges.

Improvisation from the Past. As a wagon train heads west to California in the 1800s, many disasters befall the travelers. Winter is fast approaching, and the wagons must make it through the mountains before the winter blizzards hit. The sick and starving are slowing the group down. Children assume the roles of the settlers, both sick and healthy, and find a solution.

Improvisation for the Future. A group of children become part of a community that values peace and has forbidden anyone to own or use weapons. A terrible warlike people are menacing the community's border and threaten to destroy the family. What solutions are possible?

Television News Broadcasts and Talk Shows*

"Reading Rainbow" is seen on Public Broadcasting stations.

Television provides children with some models for presenting information, conducting interviews, reviewing, and editorializing. Children may assume roles of favorite news broadcasters to present the classroom news or to report on the latest information from a thematic unit. They may also give book reviews as the children on "Reading Rainbow" do. Or they can decide to become characters from history or favorite books to be interviewed in one of the many show formats.

Puppetry*

Batchelder & Comer (1956); Lynch-Watson (1980)

Puppetry is an ancient type of drama and is still enjoyed around the world in many forms. Puppets give children a comfortable vehicle for personal expression and for writing scripts or improvising stories or other scenarios on the spot. Finger puppets, shadow puppets, and puppets made of socks, gloves, sticks, or even abstract shapes allow children to focus on the drama itself rather than on the manipulation of complex forms such as marionettes. Thus, although older children of elementary age may construct and use some of these complicated puppets, most of the puppets younger children make or use should be kept simple. For example, a first grade teacher made a caterpillar out of an old brown sock and glued felt eyes to the top. She pulled it over

Carle (1969)

her hand and had it "eat" through all the items of food in *The Very Hungry Caterpillar.* When she came to the part of the book where the caterpillar spins a cocoon, she pulled the bottom of the sock up over the caterpillar's head, then pulled the sock off entirely to reveal a felt "big, beautiful butterfly," which was wrapped around her hand and was made to go "fly away." The children were delighted and, of course, wanted to make their own caterpillars and read the story.

Choral Reading*

Choral reading is an excellent way to share poetry and to link poetry to musical performances. Poems are selected by the teacher or children. As a poem is read, everyone thinks about its mood and its meaning to decide on ways to "orchestrate" its reading. The poem can be copied on an overhead transparency or a large piece of chart paper to identify the lines or refrains that are best suited to a single voice or small group interpretation and the lines that can be read by a larger group of voices. Directions such as fast/slow, loud/soft, or high/low can be incorporated, and sound effects or physical gestures can be added.

See Tierney, Readence, & Dishner (1985) for more information on choral reading.

Reading materials other than poems can also be considered. Rhymes, patterned books, epics, or other books having lusciously lyrical or rhythmically sensitive language can be tried through choral reading.

Readers' Theatre*

Readers' Theatre is an interpretive reading activity that allows us to relive the radio broadcasts of past or present. Unlike plays that require costumes, movement, stage sets, and so forth, the Readers' Theatre is mostly auditory although it is frequently complemented by facial expressions and a few gestures. It is well suited, therefore, to tape recording for later playback at listening posts. When different groups try the same passage (or the same group attempts repeated readings), children develop the notion of multiple interpretations. They come to see that reading is an active and open process of constructing meaning, not the accurate pronunciation of words. Because Readers' Theatre usually incorporates a practice before presentation, less proficient readers are able to be successful in oral reading.

Reader's Theatre provides an opportunity for reading orally. Attention is aurally focused.

Sloyer (1982)

A short story or a part of a book that has an exciting plot, compelling characters, and language that calls for visual images should be selected for Readers' Theatre. Some informational books such as Aliki's *A Medieval Feast* and Cole's *The Magic School Bus at the Waterworks* are also possible choices. Long descriptive passages or narration do not always work well and may need to be deleted or summarized; the "he saids" and "she saids" and other less essential passages can be omitted. A narrator and character roles are assigned, an introduction is prepared, and after careful rehearsal, the "play" is presented. Although commercial scripts are available, children can write their own scripts.

Aliki (1983); Cole (1986)

Story Theatre*

Like Readers' Theatre*, story theatre involves children in interpreting written material. Now, however, a visual element is added. For younger children, the teacher frequently reads a story and has children pantomime the action as it unfolds. An alternative is to let several children read character dialogue and narrative while another group interprets the readings through pantomime, each child acting a particular character role. The pantomimers do not use written scripts or texts but must listen carefully to the readers and interpret their character's action and feelings nonverbally. Criteria for choosing material for story theatre are similar to those for Readers' Theatre*, but now an element of character action is necessary. If a scene has characters sitting in chairs and talking, it might work well as Readers' Theatre* but not as story theatre.

Moffett & Wagner (1983)

Story Theatre provides an opportunity for movement interpretation.

Although most teachers choose stories for story theatre, other nonstory genres can also be used. For example, children can pantomime the informational books written by Gail Gibbons—*The Post Office Book: Mail and How It Moves* and *Department Store*—

Gibbons (1982); Gibbons (1984)

Some information books can also be used in Story Theatre.

that describe the movement of mail and the activities occurring at a department store on a typical day. Children also enjoy acting out a description of a chemical reaction, a plant's growth, or a frog's or caterpillar's metamorphosis.

MESSAGE BOARD*

See Boyd (1985) for a good classroom example of the use of a message board.

The message board is usually a bulletin board where the teacher and children exchange messages. The board fosters functional communication; it helps children to learn the range of purposes that literacy serves. Also, because both the teacher and children use the message board, it encourages a sense of community. The message board is usually placed near the door, so communications can't be missed. Paper and envelopes, writing implements, and thumbtacks are available nearby to facilitate its use. In the beginning of the year, the teacher introduces the message board by putting a welcoming note on it, along with a short set of directions for using it—for example, when it can be used, that it can be used for personal or general messages, that all exchanges must include the names of receivers and senders, that messages can be sealed in an envelope.

See Harste & Short (1988) for another discussion on message boards.

A range of teacher-children communications is possible on the message board: Children may leave notes for the teacher regarding decisions they have made, or a small group may indicate that it is now ready to share the findings of its project. The teacher may suggest a book that a particular child may find useful for study or provide permission for a group of students to survey the third graders on Tuesday on an issue related to some work they are doing in a thematic unit.

Most of the time, however, children use the message board to communicate with one another. They leave a new math story problem they have written and challenge others to solve it. They announce the creation of a particular response group, or they ask their classmates to help locate a book they had been using for a report they are writing. They can also write more personal messages addressed to particular children in the class.

MINI-LESSONS*

Calkins (1986)

The idea of mini-lessons was developed by Calkins to teach various aspects of the writing process. In integrated language classrooms, however, mini-lessons are much more broadly thought of; they can deal with *any* topic in the curriculum and in the class, not writing only.

Mini-lessons grow out of needs of children rather than being based on an artificial scope and sequence of skills.

A mini-lesson is a short meeting—usually five to ten minutes—with the whole class (or with a small group) during which the teacher addresses an issue that has arisen. While teachers observe children engaged in activities in various projects they have taken on, they identify ways they can support and extend the children's learning. They note problems or difficulties that children may be having, or they recognize children's learnings or strategies that they can build on or extend. Mini-lessons are specific occasions on which teachers share their knowledge or expertise.

Mini-lessons usually deal with three major issues: presenting procedural information, showing techniques, and teaching specific operations or conventions. Mini-lessons have been illustrated throughout this book, although they may not always have been labeled as such. Thus, the following examples summarize and clarify the range of possibilities.

Mini-lessons address various procedural concerns.

Presenting Procedural Information. As one could expect, mini-lessons on procedures occur most frequently in the beginning of the year or at the beginning of a thematic unit. They are the ways through which teachers communicate what they expect from children and what children can expect from them. The lessons can cover the way each day will be structured and the activities that are available for children. They may include some of the choices for children in a particular thematic unit, how to keep a

Learning Log*, or how to complete the forms in Authors' Folders*. Mini-lessons can cover the rules for using the Message Board*, explain how to set up a particular scientific experiment, or tell how to use Jackdaws*.

Demonstrating Techniques. Mini-lessons also involve teacher modeling and demonstrations. Children frequently don't revise because they don't know how. They don't know how to actually manipulate the page, how to delete information, or how to add information where there's no room between the lines or the margins, how to use carats and arrows, and so on. Thus, using a composition of their own or a text written in a Group Composed Writing* activity, teachers illustrate revision techniques. Mini-lessons can consist of various brainstorming sessions—helping children consider topics for their writing, problems they may want to pursue in individual or small group projects, and how they can go about tackling these questions in their inquiries. Mini-lessons can demonstrate how to construct Semantic Maps* or Comparison Charts*, or how to do Story Mapping*, Character Sociograms*, Book Talks*, or various Sketch to Stretch* activities. They can examine or compare certain authors' styles or how a particular written genre is structured or organized; they can evaluate ways several authors deal with the same topics or information.

Mini-lessons are opportunities for teacher demonstrations.

Teaching Specific Operations and Conventions. Mini-lessons can deal with teaching specific conventions and skills. They can cover ways to use the co-text to figure out or identify a word when reading (see General Problem-Solving Reading Strategies*). They can include how to structure a business letter and how to use quotation marks or other kinds of punctuation. Mini-lessons can show how to write up scientific observations, how to do certain mathematical operations or computations for a graph, or how to label and design a graph.

Mini-lessons deal with specific conventions, strategies, and so on.

In sum, mini-lessons offer help and instruction on many and various issues. It is important to know that they are rarely on procedures, techniques, or specific conventions only. Many mini-lessons include aspects of all these three major categories. Teachers plan certain mini-lessons ahead of time because they know the areas in which most children need guidance and support. However, many mini-lessons cannot be preplanned because they result from careful observations. They are conducted in a more spontaneous fashion because they address the needs of specific children in specific circumstances.

Mini-lessons can be preplanned, or they can occur spontaneously.

CONCLUSIONS

The activities and experiences described in this chapter are only suggestions. Teachers will make choices and draw on these strategies, depending on the children with whom they work and the circumstances in which they find themselves. The activities presented here are based on teaching practices that we have seen in a variety of settings; other teachers who want to try them are free to modify or reshape them to meet their own needs.

REFERENCES

Alberti, D., Davitt, R. J., Ferguson, T. A., & Repass, S. O. (1974). *Teachers guide for ice cubes: Melting rates of ice.* New York: McGraw-Hill.

Atwell, N. (1987). *In the middle: Writing, reading, and learning with adolescents.* Portsmouth, NH: Boynton/Cook.

Baratta-Lorton, M. (1976). *Mathematics their way.* Menlo Park, CA: Addison-Wesley.

Batchelder, M., & Comer, V. L. (1956). *Puppets and plays: A creative approach.* New York: Harper & Row.

Bauer, C. F. (1977). *Handbook for storytellers.* Chicago: American Library Association.

Bauer, C. F. (1983). *This way to books.* New York: Wilson.

Beaver, J. (1982). Say it, over and over. *Language Arts, 59,* 143–147.

Boyd, R. (1985). The message board: Language comes alive. In J. M. Newman (Ed.), *Whole language: Theory in use* (pp. 91–98). Portsmouth, NH: Heinemann.

Butler, A., & Turbill, J. (1984). *Towards a reading-writing classroom.* Rozelle, Australia: Primary English Teaching Association.

Byrnes, D. A. (1988). Children and prejudice. *Social Education, 52* (4), 267–271.

Calkins, L. M. (1986). *The art of teaching writing.* Portsmouth, NH: Heinemann.

Chambers, A. (1986). *The practical guide to marbelizing paper.* New York: Thames and Hudson.

Clay, M. (1979). *Reading: The patterning of complex behaviour.* Portsmouth, NH: Heinemann.

Cochrane, O., Cochrane, D., Scalena, S., & Buchanan, E. (1984). *Reading, writing and caring.* Winnipeg, Manitoba: Whole Language Consultants.

Cohen, D. (1968). The effect of literature on vocabulary and reading achievement. *Elementary English, 45,* 209–213.

Eidman-Aadahl, E. (1988). The solitary reader: Exploring how lonely reading has to be. *The New Advocate, 1,* 155–176.

Eldridge, J. L., & Butterfield, D. (1986). Alternatives to traditional reading instruction. *The Reading Teacher, 40,* 32–37.

Ellis, A. (1986). *Teaching and learning elementary social studies.* Boston: Allyn & Bacon.

Fulwiler, T. (1980). Journals across the disciplines. *English Journal, 69,* 14–22.

Fulwiler, T. (1982). Writing: An act of cognition. In C. W. Griffin (Ed.), *Teaching writing in all disciplines* (pp. 15–26). New Directions for Teaching and Learning, No. 12. San Francisco: Jossey-Bass.

Goodman, Y. M., & Burke, C. (1985). *Reading strategies: Focus on comprehension.* New York: Richard Owen.

Graves, D. H. (1983). *Writing: Teachers and children at work.* Portsmouth, NH: Heinemann.

Harste, J. C., & Short, K. G. (1988). *Creating classrooms for authors: The reading-writing connection.* Portsmouth, NH: Heinemann.

Hatano, G. (1988). Social and motivational bases for mathematical understanding. In G. B. Saxe & M. Gearhart (Eds.), *Children's mathematics* (pp. 55–70). New Directions for Child Development, No. 41. San Francisco: Jossey-Bass.

Heimlich, J., & Pittelman, S. D. (1986). *Semantic mapping: Classroom applications.* Newark, DE: International Reading Association.

Hepler, S. I., & Hickman, J. (1982). "The book was okay, I love you": Social aspects of response to literature. *Theory Into Practice, 21,* 278–283.

Hickman, J. (1981). A new perspective on response to literature: Research in an elementary school setting. *Research in the Teaching of English, 15,* 343–354.

Hillocks, G. (1986). *Research on written composition: New directions for teaching.* Urbana, IL: ERIC Clearinghouse on Reading and Communication Skills.

Holdaway, D. (1979). *The foundations of literacy.* Syndey, Australia: Ashton Scholastic.

Hornsby, D., & Sukarna, D. (1988). *Read-on: A conference approach to reading.* Portsmouth, NH: Heinemann.

Huck, C. S., Hepler, S., & Hickman, J. (1987). *Children's literature in the elementary school.* New York: Holt, Rinehart and Winston.

Hyde, A. A., & Bizar, M. (1989). *Thinking in context: Teaching cognitive processes across the elementary curriculum.* White Plains, NY: Longman.

Jackdaw. Grossman Publishers in association with Jackdaw Pub., Ltd., London, England.

Johnson, D. D., & Pearson, P. D. (1984). *Teaching reading vocabulary.* New York: Holt, Rinehart and Winston.

Johnson, L., & O'Neill, C. (1984). *Dorothy Heathcote: Collected writings on education and drama.* Portsmouth, NH: Heinemann.

Johnson, T. D., & Louis, D. R. (1987). *Literacy through literature.* Portsmouth, NH: Heinemann.

Kwak, W., & Newman, J. M. (1985). Activity cards. In J. M. Newman (Ed.), *Whole language: Theory in use* (pp. 137–144). Portsmouth, NH: Heinemann.

Levstik, L. S. (1986). The relationship between historical response and narrative in a sixth-grade classroom. *Theory and Research in Social Education, 14,* 1–15.

Lynch-Watson, J. (1980). *The shadow puppet book.* New York: Sterling.

Lytle, S. L., & Botel, M. (1988). *PCRP II: Reading, writing and talking across the curriculum.* Harrisburg, PA: Pennsylvania Department of Education. To be published in 1990 by Heinemann-Boynton Cook as *Frameworks for Literacy.*

Manning, G. L., & Manning, M. (1984). What models of reading make a difference? *Reading World, 23,* 375–380.

McCaslin, N. (1984). *Creative drama in the classroom.* White Plains, NY: Longman.

McKenzie, M. (1977). The beginnings of literacy. *Theory Into Practice, 16,* 315–324.

McKenzie, M. (1985). Shared writing: Apprenticeship in writing. *Language Matters, 1,* 1–5.

Moffett, J., & Wagner, B. J. (1983). *Student centered language arts reading, K–13.* Boston: Houghton Mifflin.

Morrow, L. M. (1988). Young children's response to one-to-one story readings in school settings. *Reading Research Quarterly, 23,* 89–107.

Mossip, J. (1985). It makes you feel needed: Students as teachers. In J. M. Newman (Ed.), *Whole language: Theory in use* (pp. 131–136). Portsmouth, NH: Heinemann.

O'Neill, C. (1985). Imagined worlds in theatre and drama. *Theory Into Practice, 24,* 158–165.

O'Neill, C., & Lambert, A. (1982). *Drama structures: A practical handbook for teachers.* Portsmouth, NH: Heinemann.

Pappas, C. C., & Brown, E. (1989). Using turns at story "reading" as scaffolding for learning. *Theory Into Practice, 28,* 105–113.

Reardon, S. J. (1988). The development of critical readers: A look into the classroom. *The New Advocate, 1,* 52–61.

Revel-Wood, M. (1988). Invitations to read, to write, to learn. In J. C. Harste & K. G. Short (Eds.), *Creating classrooms for authors: The reading-writing connection* (pp. 169–179). Portsmouth, NH: Heinemann.

Routman, R. (1988). *Transitions: From literature to literacy.* Portsmouth, NH: Heinemann.

Schlissel, L. (1982). *Woman's diaries of the westward journey.* New York: Schocken.

Siks, G. B. (1977). *Drama with children.* New York: Harper & Row.

Sloyer, S. (1982). *Readers' theatre: Story dramatization in the classroom.* Urbana, IL: National Council of Teachers of English.

Sonnenschein, F. M. (1988). Countering prejudiced beliefs and behaviors: The role of the social studies professional. *Social Education, 52* (4), 262–266.

Stone, L. (1986). International and multicultural education. In V. Atwood (Ed.), *Elementary social studies: Research as a guide to practice* (pp. 34–54). Washington, DC: National Council for the Social Studies.

Stratton, J. L. (1981). *Pioneer women: Voices from the Kansas frontier.* New York: Simon & Schuster.

Temple, C., Nathan, R., Burris, N., & Temple, F. (1988). *The beginnings of writing.* Boston: Allyn & Bacon.

Tierney, R. J., Readence, J. E., & Dishner, E. K. (1985). *Reading strategies and practices: A compendium.* Boston: Allyn & Bacon.

Unia, S. (1985). From sunny days and green onions: On journal writing. In J. M. Newman (Ed.), *Whole language: Theory in use* (pp. 65–72). Portsmouth, NH: Heinemann.

Wassermann, S., & Ivany, J. W. G. (1988). *Teaching elementary science: Who's afraid of spiders?* New York: Harper & Row.

Way, B. (1967). *Development through drama.* Atlantic Highlands, NJ: Humanities Press.

Weber, L. (1989). Teachers using historical fiction. In J. Hickman & B. Cullinan (Eds.), *Weaving Charlotte's web: Children's literature in the elementary classroom* (pp. 147–156). Needham Heights, MA: Christopher-Gordon.

Wells, G. (1986). *The meaning makers: Children learning language and using language to learn.* Portsmouth, NH: Heinemann.

Wilson, A. (1987). Cross-cultural experiential learning for teachers. *Theory Into Practice, 26,* 519–527.

CHILDREN'S LITERATURE

ALEXANDER AND THE TERRIBLE, HORRIBLE, NO GOOD VERY BAD DAY by J. Viorst. Illustrated by R. Cruz. Atheneum, 1972.

BEYOND THE DIVIDE by K. Lasky. Macmillan, 1983.

BIG CITY PORT by B. Maestro and E. DelVecchio. Illustrated by G. Maestro. Scholastic, 1983.

THE BORROWERS by M. Norton. Harcourt, 1953.

BRIDGE TO TERABITHIA by K. Paterson. Crowell, 1977.

BROWN BEAR, BROWN BEAR, WHAT DO YOU SEE? by B. Martin, Jr. Illustrated by E. Carle. Holt, 1983.

THE CABIN FACED WEST by J. Fritz. Coward, McCann, 1958.

CALEB AND KATE by W. Steig. Farrar, Straus & Giroux.

THE CAT'S PURR by A. Bryan. Atheneum, 1985.

THE CRANE MAIDEN by M. Matsutani. Illustrated by C. Iwasaki. Parents Magazine Press, 1968.

THE CRANE WIFE by S. Yagawa. Translated by K. Paterson. Illustrated by S. Akaba. Morrow, 1981.

DEEP IN THE FOREST by B. Turkle. Dutton, 1976.

DEPARTMENT STORE by G. Gibbons. Harper & Row, 1984.

THE DEVIL'S ARITHMETIC by J. Yolen. Viking Kestrel, 1988.

DIGGING UP DINOSAURS by Aliki. Crowell, 1988.

ENCHANTRESS FROM THE STARS by S. L. Engdahl. Atheneum, 1973.

EVOLUTION by J. Cole. Illustrated by Aliki. Crowell, 1987.

A GIRL CALLED BOY by B. Hurmence. Clarion, 1982.

GOLDILOCKS AND THE THREE BEARS by L. B. Cauley. Putnam, 1981.

GOLDILOCKS AND THE THREE BEARS by J. Stevens. Holiday House, 1986.

THE GREEN BOOK by J. P. Walsh. Farrar, Straus & Giroux, 1982.

THE HIGHWAYMAN by A. Noyes. Illustrated by C. Mikolaycak. Lothrop, 1983.

IN THEIR OWN WORDS by M. Meltzer. Crowell, 1977.

JAMES AND THE GIANT PEACH by R. Dahl. Knopf, 1961.

JOHNNY TREMAIN by E. Forbes. Houghton Mifflin, 1943.

JOURNEY OUTSIDE by M. Q. Steele. Viking, 1969.

LINCOLN: A PHOTOBIOGRAPHY by R. Freedman. Clarion, 1987.

THE MAGIC PORRIDGE POT by P. Galdone. Houghton Mifflin, 1976.

THE MAGIC SCHOOL BUS AT THE WATERWORKS by J. Cole. Illustrated by B. Degen. Scholastic, 1966.

THE MEDIEVAL FEAST by Aliki. Crowell, 1983.

MUMMIES MADE IN EGYPT by Aliki. Crowell, 1979.

MY BROTHER SAM IS DEAD by J. and L. Collier. Four Winds, 1974.

OX-CART MAN by D. Hall. Illustrated by B. Cooney. Viking, 1979.

THE PAPER MAKERS by L. E. Fisher. Godine, 1986.

THE POST OFFICE BOOK: MAIL AND HOW IT MOVES by G. Gibbons. Harper & Row, 1982.

THE SECRET GARDEN by F. H. Burnett. Lippincott, 1962.

THE SQUIRREL by M. Lane. Illustrated by K. Lilly. Dial, 1981.

SQUIRRELS by B. Wildsmith. Oxford University Press, 1974.

THE STORY OF THE GRATEFUL CRANE: A JAPANESE FOLKTALE by J. Bartoli. Whitman, 1977.

STREGA NONA by T. de Paola. Prentice-Hall, 1975.

SYLVESTER AND THE MAGIC PEBBLE by W. Steig. Windmill, 1979.

THE TEENY TINY WOMAN by P. Galdone. Clarion, 1984.

THUNDER AT GETTYSBURG by P. L. Gauch. Illustrated by S. Gammell. Coward, McCann & Geoghegan, 1975.

TIME OF WONDER by R. McClosky. Viking Penguin, 1957.
TIN LIZZIE by P. Spiers. Doubleday, 1978.
TO BE A SLAVE by J. Lester. Dial, 1968.
TUNNELS by G. Gibbons. Holiday House, 1984.
VOLCANOES by F. M. Branley. Illustrated by M. Simont. Crowell, 1985.
WILD AND WOOLLY MAMMOTHS by Aliki. Crowell, 1977.
WIZARD OF EARTHSEA by U. LeGuin. Parnassus, 1968.

9

Evaluation and Accountability

Imagine that after completing the detergent testing project described in Chapter 7, students took a fill-in-the-blank test. They listed formulas and matched results with products. They defined terms and ticked off a variety of true and false items. Although such an evaluation can tap some of what children learn, it also exaggerates the importance of specific bits of information, and it undercuts attention to the processes of science and the context within which information is important. As an assessment tool, this type of test ignores a wide range of significant learning activities and is incongruent with purposes and procedures in an integrated language classroom.

See Bussis & Chittenden (1987), Goodman, Goodman, & Hood (1989), Searle & Stevenson (1987), Valencia & Pearson (1987), Teale, Hiebert, & Vukelich (1988), and the report of the Education Commission of the States (1983) for other discussions of the necessity for rethinking assessment and evaluation in education.

Yet teachers in integrated language classrooms are just as accountable for the evaluation of pupil learning as are their peers in more traditional classrooms. They, too, must find ways to evaluate and assess that are congruent with their educational purposes. An integrated language classroom, then, requires evaluation and assessment that can reflect how children learn and think in context, how they connect what they have learned in various content domains, and how they progress over time. The following three interrelated features are important in such evaluation techniques:

Evaluate the level of development a child has reached in various aspects of learning. Evaluation of this kind has both formative and summative characteristics. It is formative in that it is used to help the teacher plan the kinds of topics, resources, activities, and organization children will need as they engage in thematic units. It is summative in that it can be used to interpret children's progress to the children and to their parents or guardians.

Evaluate the attempts a child has made to learn. One of the principles of an integrated language setting is allowing children to have opportunities to take intellectual risks and to move toward intellectual independence. The teacher attends not only to the end products of student investigations but to the path(s) the students took to get there.

Evaluate what a child has mastered. Teachers in integrated language settings need to know what children have mastered just as other teachers do. The difference is the way in which that information is collected and used. Although some teachers do use tests, they also use a variety of other end-product indexes. They evaluate the range of products—writing, art, reports, presentations—that grow out of ongoing work by relying on multiple measures rather than on a single test score.

Chapter 6 outlined various kid-watching procedures and techniques that can be used for evaluation, and we have also sprinkled other ideas about evaluation throughout this book. Inherent in an integrated language approach is a synergistic relationship between assessment and curriculum development; assessment and curriculum are fused. That is, children are assessed *in context* while they are engaged in projects and activities in various thematic units. This message has been illustrated throughout the book, so the rest of this chapter summarizes the major evaluation procedures we have discussed.

Assessment and curriculum are fused.

Wexler-Sherman, Gardner, & Feldman (1988); Wolf (1988)

ONGOING OBSERVATIONS AND PERIODIC DOCUMENTATIONS

In integrated language classrooms, teachers collaborate with children by supporting their choices of inquiries. As children pursue their investigations, teachers move around the room, interacting with individuals or with small groups of children to find out what the children are doing and how the teachers can support their efforts. Teachers are continually evaluating and teaching; these acts are reciprocal processes. In Chapter 6, we discussed ways by which these reciprocal processes of evaluation and teaching can be made more explicit. Through anecdotal or periodic target-child(ren) observations, teachers can decide what kinds of experiences or resources certain children need now, they know when a particular Mini-Lesson* is necessary, they are able to evaluate children's strategies in tackling a problem, and they can determine if a particular child needs to be encouraged to try something new.

Evaluation is continuous and covers all aspects of an integrated language classroom.

Teachers can also keep journals of classroom events, perhaps one for each thematic unit studied during the year. These accounts review and highlight significant experiences or patterns occurring in the classroom. The journals include the teachers' own observation sheets developed to examine small group inquiries (like the one quickly drawn up to document what was happening in the snails study described in Chapter 6). Journals can be complemented by incorporating class "before" and "after" Semantic Mappings* on some of the concepts learned in a thematic unit, snapshots of the growth of a Graffiti Wall* or of the artifacts constructed by children in the course of a unit, and a review of the Activity Cards* children have used, modified, or written on their own during a unit (see Chapter 8). Such a journal helps teachers to remember and reflect on how children participate in the culture or learning community of the classroom.

Teachers keep journals, too.

Hull (1988)

Keep "before" and "after" data.

CONFERENCES

Part of ongoing evaluation is having one-to-one conversations with children. Reading and writing conferences were discussed in Chapters 6 and 8, but brief conferences need not be limited to literacy activities. Because literacy is integrated across the curriculum in our perspective, these discussions always include specific content or a curricular domain. But conferences can be planned to focus on a particular mathematical or scientific problem or a certain issue in social studies, for example, and not concentrate on reading or writing per se.

One-on-one conversations with children are important evaluative tools.

Teachers can also have small group conferences as well. Periodic documentation of the dynamics of group interactions when children collaborate to investigate a common topic is essential in this perspective that emphasizes the social, contextual influences in learning. Tape recording or listening in on peer conferences (e.g., during Response Groups*—see Chapter 8) provides still another way to document and evaluate learning and language in the classroom. Children can also take turns being "reporters" whose job is to summarize the discussion and decisions of a peer conference to share with the teacher.

LEARNING PORTFOLIOS

Examining data over time is essential for a clear picture of development and progress.

See Cohen (1969), Cole & Scribner (1974), Dyson (1987), Heath (1983), and Heller, Holzman, & Messick (1982) for discussion of children's various ways of words and working styles as they are related to assessment and evaluation.

Gitomer (1988); Wexler-Sherman, Gardner, & Feldman (1988)

An important part of assessment and evaluation from an integrated language perspective is keeping individual portfolios on children. Children's abilities and strategies are developed in meaningful, familiar contexts, and their expertise and talents grow gradually and in different patterns. Thus, gathering an extensive collection of their work and other information provides a profile that documents children's learning. The portfolio approach has long been evident in the area of the visual arts and is now suggested for reading and writing. Because reading and writing are integrated across the curriculum from an integrated language perspective, portfolios must be conceived of even more broadly as *learning* portfolios.

Anything and everything can be included in students' learning portfolios: children's notes from their Learning Logs*, anecdotal or target-child observations, snapshots of artifacts children have constructed in the course of thematic units (topographical maps, dioramas, Comparison Charts,* etc.), Sketch to Stretch* productions, published texts in various genres, abandoned drafts, Semantic Mappings*, MMA summaries (or ATT or CAP assessments, etc.), evaluation sheets from Authors' Folders*, interviews done, child-made Jackdaw* materials, Graphs*, and on and on. Most teachers collaborate with children to decide what should be included in the portfolios. They choose what they think is indicative of children's best efforts; they also ask children to choose the work they feel best represents their work in a thematic unit, or what reflects the most difficult tasks they accomplished. Some schools keep portfolios of children's work over their years of attendance.

SELF-EVALUATION

A critical aspect of evaluation in an integrated language classroom is children's self-evaluation. This feature is usually incorporated into a child's learning portfolio, but it is such a critical factor in this perspective that we discuss it as a separate section. Self-evaluation can be seen as an extension of children's Learning Logs* (see Chapter 8) in which children jotted down their own questions, posed possible answers, and organized (and reorganized) their own ideas. Thus, Learning Logs* are ways to make children's thinking more explicit. Self-evaluation is similar; children pause to consider what they have learned, what has been important from each one's own perspective.

A good time for children to explicitly self-evaluate their own learning is at the end of a thematic unit, when they select the work to be included in their learning portfolios. For example, as they choose some particular writing, they explain why they thought it was their best work, why it represented significant work on a particular project, and so on. Children can also be encouraged to review their Learning Logs* periodically (perhaps at the end of a thematic unit), and write a summary of what stood out for them. Or they can include an evaluation as part of any big project they do. Even younger elementary children can evaluate their own work. The teacher can take notes as children tell what was the best thing they have done, or where they have done their hardest work. What children may think is significant in their learning may not be what teachers or parents or others deem valuable. Self-evaluation, therefore, is an important factor because it gives children opportunities to reflect on their own learning, thereby helping them to be independent, autonomous, and confident learners.

Even young children can self-evaluate.

Self-evaluation encourages student reflection.

TESTS AND EXAMS

Whether to give tests and exams is both an administrative and teacher decision. Many schools adopting an integrated language perspective do not use tests because they believe that the children's work produced in various thematic units is sufficient and provides more valid indicators of children's achievements and progress.

Others who have an integrated language perspective do not use teacher-made tests in the traditional sense. They conceive of tests in ways that make them more congruent with their instructional goals, rethinking the standard fill-in-the-blank and multiple-choice formats. For example, rather than having children give the answers to a list of math problems, teachers may ask them to analyze the problems they find the most difficult. These responses require that children identify the kind of problem and describe their approach to it. These analyses require the use of correct vocabulary, pattern recognition, and some knowledge of how to proceed. Another possibility is to have children identify five problems according to kind of problem and then give a brief analysis of the approach to each, with no actual problem-solving.

Hyde & Bizar (1989)

Particularly in science and social studies areas, such tests have the flavor of "laboratory" assignments. For example, they test for inquiry, one of the skills traditional tests fail to evaluate but that is critical in the integrated language perspective. It may seem difficult to construct a test that reflects inquiry skills, but it is possible. Observation and Inference*, two of the basic inquiry skills, can be tested by setting up a situation in which children are asked to observe carefully and then to make supported inferences. A test of these skills in science, for example, can include a demonstration in which children observe the teacher place two cubes in a clear liquid. One cube floats; the other sinks to the bottom. Students are then required to list three observations and then make two inferences that can be supported by their observations. Their responses are evaluated in terms of the accuracy of their observations (i.e., they are not inferences!), and the degree to which their inferences are supported by their observations.

Social studies and science use laboratory-like tests.

A test in social studies can use a political cartoon relevant to the students' recent studies. The children are asked to interpret the symbols used in the cartoon and to infer the cartoonist's "message." Their response is evaluated in terms of the way in which they draw on their recent study to interpret the cartoon and on the supportability of their inferences.

Another inquiry skill concerns children's ability to select and evaluate data. A test item following a unit on EXPLORATIONS can involve presenting children with a problem such as the following:

> You are considering inviting Mr. Erickson to speak to your class on the discovery of the New World. Which statements make Mr. Erickson most qualified to speak to your class? Explain your choices.
>
> A. He is related to Lief Erickson.
> B. He has written a book on the settlement of Greenland.
> C. He conducted some of the first research on Viking settlements in Newfoundland.
> D. He is director of the Viking museum in Oslo, Norway.

See also Hyde & Bizar (1989), Wassermann & Ivany (1988), Maxim (1987), and Ellis (1986) for further discussion of evaluation in science and social studies.

To answer this question, the students need to know something about the Viking explorations in North America, but they also need to be able to explain why some of Mr. Erickson's qualifications are better than others for the stated purpose. The question is embedded in both content and process, and it evaluates children's ability to make connections between the methods of study and the content studied.

Communicating data is also an important skill in inquiry, and it can be evaluated on a written test, especially if the test is open book or note. This kind of test is, to some extent, individualized. The teacher must know what questions and content children have been grappling with and then give them an opportunity to write about that. The children who found different interpretations of a historic figure, for instance, can be asked to use their notes to write an argument for accepting one interpretation over another. Another child may be asked to compare the way the textbook interprets an event in history with the way in which that event was interpreted in a piece of historical fiction.

Other possibilities are questions that ask children to construct a hypothesis to explain an observation in science or to select the most important thing they learned during a unit, and then to write a statement justifying their choice.

One primary teacher uses a film on the first Thanksgiving as a test of her third-graders' ability to compare and contrast sources after a study based on the MATCh unit,

Kresse (1979)

"The Indians Who Met the Pilgrims" (see Chapter 4). The film is quite short, offers a number of contrasts to the MATCh unit, and contains several inaccuracies that have been pointed out in other contexts. The test includes, among other things, having children identify three ways in which the film supports what they have learned and three ways it contradicts what they have learned.

Turner (1986)

Another primary teacher uses a "Can you spot the errors?" format for some of his testing in social studies. He constructs pictures that include errors that children's studies should enable them to identify. After a study based on Ann Turner's *Dakota Dugout,* he presents children with a picture of a prairie home and family. He asks students to draw a red circle around anything in the picture that would not have been there during the time of *Dakota Dugout.* Then students are asked to draw a blue circle around anything they think would not be there today. The children are thus required to use specific skills with a content they have been studying. The teacher does not assume that the children will know everything from the period, but he does know what the children have been studying and wants to evaluate the way in which they have been making sense of the time aspects of their study.

Thornton & Vukelich (1988)

A teacher could do a similar thing in science by drawing a series of pictures showing, say, plant growth under various conditions. The children circle the picture that ends a sequence (i.e., a plant bending in the direction of the sun after a series of pictures of a bean plant on a windowsill, or a long, white stem on a plant grown with little light). Some teachers give children a series of pictures representing a process they have observed, and the children paste the pictures in order on their test paper. A similar format can be used in math. Teachers can use data children have been collecting in a unit and construct several problems and possible solutions. Children would be asked to identify those aspects of the approach that are correct and incorrect by circling them with different colored pens.

Most tests in an integrated language classroom are not timed to test the speed of children's thinking. Instead, children are given time to think carefully about their answers and to go back and review their responses. Most tests also require students to develop ideas in writing, to justify or elaborate on responses. Such tests are closer to the way in which adults operate when they are working, and they are more congruent with the way in which the children have been working throughout the thematic units described in Chapters 3, 4, 7, and 8.

CONCLUSIONS

Evaluation should interrelate process and content.

Assessment and evaluation have to be consistent with principles of the integrated language perspective. Evaluation should interrelate process and content. It should also focus, not on children's weaknesses, but instead on those features of their behavior that demonstrate understanding and progress. Children are given many opportunities to monitor their own work, to revise and to evaluate it, to work with the teacher and peers to steadily improve it. Children review their work with a partner or the teacher; questions are raised about it *before* a grade is attached. With practice, the children learn to be more self-analytical about the quality of their work. Because it is the children who have to do the learning, it makes sense to teach them to be self-evaluative and then to evaluate their progress toward that goal. Thus, evaluation should provide insights into children's evolving personal restructuring of knowledge—what they know, how they have come to know it, what significance it has for them as members of the classroom community and the broader culture outside the classroom.

Practice produces higher-quality self-analysis by students.

Teachers become researchers when they document children's progress.

See Johnston (1987a, 1987b) and Moffett (1985) for more arguments for teachers as evaluators, and Goswami & Stillman (1987) regarding information on teachers as researchers.

This view of evaluation puts the teacher in a different role. Teachers are researchers in that they conduct their own inquiries about the language and learning constructed by children in their classrooms. They are also reflective and self-analytical as they document their own classroom practices and examine and reexamine their results and influences on children's learning. Thus, teachers are in a better position to document and interpret a wide range of student performance and can, therefore, provide a more accurate picture of children's learning and achievement than so-called objective tests or other instruments that attempt to assess children's understandings in "decontextualized" situations.

REFERENCES

Bussis, A. M., & Chittenden, E. A. (1987). Research currents: What the reading tests neglect. *Language Arts, 64,* 302–308.

Cohen, R. (1969). Conceptual styles, culture conflict, and non-verbal tests of intelligence. *American Anthropologist, 71,* 828–857.

Cole, M., & Scribner, S. (1974). *Culture and thought: A psychological introduction.* New York: Wiley.

Dyson, A. H. (1987). Individual differences in beginning composing. *Written communication, 4,* 411–442.

Education Commission of the States (1983). *A summary of major reports in education.* Denver, CO: Education Commission of the States.

Ellis, A. (1986). *Teaching and learning elementary social studies.* Boston: Allyn & Bacon.

Gitomer, D. H. (1988, April). *Assessing artistic learning using domain projects.* Paper presented at the annual meeting of the American Educational Research Association, New Orleans, LA.

Goodman, K., Goodman, Y., & Hood, W. J. (Eds.) (1989). *The whole language evaluation book.* Portsmouth, NH: Heinemann.

Goswami, D., & Stillman, P. R. (1987). *Reclaiming the classroom: Teacher research as an agency for change.* Portsmouth, NH: Boynton/Cook.

Heath, S. B. (1983). *Ways with words: Language, life and work in communities and classrooms.* Cambridge: Cambridge University Press.

Heller, K. A., Holzman, W. H., & Messick, S. (1982). *Placing children in special education: A strategy for equity.* Washington, DC: National Academy Press.

Hull, O. (1988). Evaluation: The conventions of writing. In K. Goodman, Y. Goodman, & W. J. Hood (Eds.), *The whole language evaluation book* (pp. 77–83). Portsmouth, NH: Heinemann.

Hyde, A., & Bizar, M. (1989). *Thinking in context: Teaching cognitive processes across the elementary school curriculum.* White Plains, NY: Longman.

Johnston, P. (1987a). Teachers as evaluation experts. *The Reading Teacher, 40,* 744–748.

Johnston, P. (1987b). Assessing the process, and the process of assessment, in the language arts. In J. R. Squire (Ed.), *The dynamics of language learning: Research in reading and English* (pp. 335–357). Urbana, IL: ERIC Clearinghouse on Reading and Communication Skills.

Kresse, F. H. (1979). "The Indians Who Met the Pilgrims," A MATCh unit. Materials and Activities for Teachers and Children. Boston: American Science and Engineering.

Maxim, G. W. (1987). *Social studies and the elementary school child.* Columbus, OH: Merrill.

Moffett, J. (1985). Hidden impediments to improving English teaching. *Phi Delta Kappan, 67,* 50–56.

Searle, D., & Stevenson, M. (1987). An alternative assessment program in language arts. *Language Arts, 64,* 278–284.

Teale, W. H., Hiebert, E. H., & Chittenden, E. A. (1987). Assessing young children's literary development. *The Reading Teacher, 40,* 772–777.

Thornton, S. J., & Vukelich, R. (1988). Effects of children's understanding of time concepts on historical understanding. *Theory and Research in Social Education, 15,* 69–82.

Valencia, S., & Pearson, P. D. (1987). Reading assessment: Time for change. *The Reading Teacher, 40,* 726–732.

Wassermann, S., & Ivany, J. W. G. (1988). *Teaching elementary science: Who's afraid of spiders?* New York: Harper & Row.

Wexler-Sherman, C., Gardner, H., & Feldman, D. H. (1988). A pluralistic view of early assessment: The project spectrum approach. *Theory Into Practice, 27,* 77–83.

Wolf, D. P. (1988). Opening up assessment. *Educational Leadership, 45* (4), 24–29.

CHILDREN'S LITERATURE

DAKOTA DUGOUT by A. Turner. Illustrated by R. Himler. Houghton Mifflin, 1986.

10

An Integrated Language Perspective Effecting Change

Why should the young child, so abundantly blessed with intellectual resources and so deeply committed to learning and exploration of the world, act so stupidly after a few years of school? . . . The problem . . . is to understand how something that begins so well can often end so badly. (p. 6)

Margaret Donaldson, 1978

BEGINNING WELL

Goodman, Goodman, & Hood (1989)

The first steps toward a more integrated perspective on teaching and learning often begin with a question very much like Margaret Donaldson's. Rethinking ways of teaching and learning, and then changing practice can be a risky enterprise. Although some schools adopt an integrated language approach and provide support for teachers during the transition to this new way of teaching, it is more common for integrated language teachers to find themselves alone or one of only a handful of teachers who share this perspective. Under these circumstances, a teacher may be unwilling or unable to leap into an entirely new program. Instead, a transition period is necessary. Gradually, teachers move toward their goal, seeking out colleagues at conferences and in other classrooms, testing their ideas, and building their expertise.

The transition process is helped by visits to integrated language classrooms, by talk to like-minded peers, and by reading the professional literature, but in the end, change happens in individual classrooms that are structured by the decisions of individual teachers and the reactions of particular groups of children. Variations occur according to the teacher's style, to school, district and state mandates, and to the nature of the community surrounding the school.

THE FIRST TEACHING POSITION

If possible, choose your school carefully.

A beginning teacher interested in working in an integrated language classroom may be in a position to screen prospective schools and districts, looking for an appropriate situation. Few schools have everything a new teacher may desire, but there are some things worth considering in deciding on a school or system. When you visit a school or interview for a position, consider the following questions:

1. Are children of all ages writing every day?
2. Does the school have a Sustained Silent Reading Program?
3. Is children's work prominently displayed, both in classrooms, and throughout the building?
4. Are invented spellings and other approximations accepted and displayed?

5. Are children grouped for many purposes, rather than by ability levels?
6. Are professional journals available in the library or teachers' room?
7. Are teachers encouraged to participate in professional organizations?
8. Do teachers take time to talk together about children in a positive way?

When characteristics such as these are present in a school, the implementation of an integrated language perspective is often much smoother. Do not assume, however, that without these characteristics already in place an integrated program cannot be implemented. If peers and administrators are supportive of such practices, a new teacher may still have found a good place to begin.

CHANGING ESTABLISHED PRACTICES

Not all teachers have the luxury of choosing their situations so carefully. Many start out in a traditional situation with which they are comfortable and gradually come to the realization that they are no longer satisfied with the status quo. When that is the case, the mechanisms for change may be more complex and take longer, but change can occur step by step.

Goodman (1987); Bailey (1988)

Those first steps can be both exhilarating and a bit frightening. As one second grade teacher explains, "Once you grow like this, there's really no turning back." As teachers increase their professional authority, they also raise their level of responsibility. They are responsible for staying informed to develop a sound base for classroom planning, practice, and decision-making. Their transition period begins, then, with the recognition that they desire a greater degree of responsibility. The next step is an assessment of current practice. This initial assessment is meant to establish which parts of an existing program already fit with intended changes, which could be modified for a better fit, and which could better be altered more radically or done away with entirely. The preceding chapters provide a basis for making these decisions. This chapter offers strategies for implementing changes on the basis of those decisions.

Hickman (1983)

Teachers who take their professional role seriously must stay informed.

Assess your situation.

The ideas that follow are suggestions from which teachers may choose, rather than a formula for converting traditional into integrated language classrooms. Some suggestions involve relatively simple changes; others require considerably more commitment. Each is a step toward creating an integrated language classroom. As one teacher who set out to transform her teaching suggests, "Do a little bit at a time. Learn to trust your children." Learn, too, to trust your own best knowledge about children and teaching, and take the first steps toward an integrated language classroom.

Hickman (1983)

REARRANGE THE ENVIRONMENT

Organizing for Cooperative Learning

One of the characteristics of an integrated perspective is cooperative learning. Reorienting children to this stance begins with changing the classroom environment. Room arrangement signals teacher intention and expectations regarding the flow of talk and activity in the classroom. Straight rows facing the front of the room make cooperative student efforts more difficult and encourage children to direct activity toward the teacher rather than toward their peers. The teacher easily slips into the position of dispenser of information and sole arbiter of talk. Think about the ways in which physical changes in the classroom environment foster child-child interactions.

Implementing change

Routman (1988); Goodman (1986)

Exchange desks for tables, or rearrange desks into table groupings. This organizes children for group work by shifting their focus toward sharing materials, spreading out projects, and cooperating with peers. Children need not be assigned a particular seat; rather, shifting groupings and activity patterns dictate seating.

Arrange for personal space. Teachers often make "cubbies" for children's personal supplies and books by covering ice-cream drums with contact paper and labeling each container with a child's name. This allows each child to have a place in the classroom that no one else may use, and it decreases problems with territoriality when seating patterns change. A child whose supplies are kept in a desk that also doubles as part of a group work table may become upset when someone else handles his or her materials. If supplies are kept in a personal cubbie away from the work area, such upsets are less likely to occur.

If keeping individual desks seems necessary, use tables or some desks as centers where children can work on projects. This also refocuses attention toward child-child interactions.

Establish a gathering or sharing area. As children become engaged in interesting and meaningful activities, they need to have a gathering place in the classroom separate from their work areas. A gathering place helps to reorient children when the teacher needs to focus the attention of the full class on a single event or activity. Children may gather to hear literature shared, to talk over matters of group concern, to observe a demonstration in science, or to share the results of a group project in social studies. Some teachers set off an area with a rug and cushions on the floor. Others use a bookcase to separate this area from other work spaces. One teacher simply marks off a semicircle with masking tape, and her kindergartners bring "sit upons" when they gather in the taped-off area.

Get rid of teacher-made and commercial room decorations. Let the classroom reflect children's work.

Display children's work aesthetically. When children see all the varieties of their work respected and beautifully displayed, they too tend to treat their work as being worthy of respect. Simply trimming and mounting poems, pictures, and other work and inviting children to write captions makes very pleasing displays. Displays of student work also broaden the audience with whom children share their work.

Accumulating Supplies

Another characteristic of an integrated language approach is the availability of multiple data sources. Because some of these resources may not be part of allocated classroom supplies, one transition step is beginning to build the rich resources on which integrated classrooms thrive.

See also Huck, Hepler, & Hickman (1987), Routman (1988), and Trelease (1985) for suggestions of good read-aloud literature.

Build a classroom library. Perhaps someone in the local community will donate issues of *National Geographic, Smithsonian,* or similar magazines. Try garage and library book sales and remaindered book stores, too. In addition, book clubs provide inexpensive paperback books, with free selections to teachers whose students purchase certain numbers of books. Invite parents to donate books in honor of a child's birthday. Contact Reading Is Fundamental or other community organizations and enlist their support for your school or classroom.

Build a personal collection of children's literature and resource books for possible thematic unit topics. Select a few good anthologies, and good read-alouds*. Visit a public library and ask the librarian for titles to share with students. Do not limit yourself to children's books. Look for well-illustrated adult books on topics of interest to children. Teachers can get information from these, and students can use the illustrations, captions, and other accessible parts of the books.

While traveling, collect artifacts. For instance, a trip to Fort Sumter, in Charleston, South Carolina, could provide reproductions of newspapers announcing the attack on Fort Sumter and South Carolina's secession from both a Northern and Southern perspective. For very little extra money, a historic map of Charleston and the harbor are available. With these, a Jackdaw* on the Civil War is under way.

Think, too, about the kind of artifacts that represent the daily life of the places you visit. On a trip to Mexico, one teacher saved cereal boxes, candy wrappers, a newspaper, a theatre program, a handful of coins, and a bus schedule—all in Spanish. She later used these artifacts as part of an activity on interpreting popular culture. Children also worked on problems involving currency exchanges in their math groups.

Ask for donations. Send home with the children a list of some suggested materials that can be used, including such things as egg cartons, scraps of wood, plastic meat trays, old jewelry, yarn, fabric scraps, leftover wallpaper, and so forth. Some teachers have found local merchants willing to donate used displays (cut off or cover advertising when possible). Let students organize this material as part of an activity on classification and categorization.

Students who organize classroom materials are more likely to feel responsible for those materials.

These kinds of activities also encourage students to invest in the new order of things and encourage more responsible care of materials. Students can begin to adopt new procedures by helping to establish them from the beginning. One fourth grade teacher begins each year by jointly planning with his students for a workable room and resources arrangement.

Alter the Teacher's Role

Changing teachers' classroom interactions

It is not enough to refocus children's attention on cooperative learning if the teacher is unable to change his or her interactions with the children in the classroom. Sometimes it is difficult to give up the center stage. There are, however, a few simple steps that can help teachers move off-stage just a bit.

Practice listening. During group sharing, allow the children to do most of the talking. Teachers who find this difficult sometimes allot themselves a specific number of comments per session. Audio taping some discussion sessions is also helpful in analyzing the teacher/student interactions.

Organize response groups. A teacher who moves from group to group can be the center of attention only during the brief interventions in each group. Brief visits in each group also encourage the teacher to listen to understand the flow of conversation.

Invite children to participate in establishing class rules together. Set up discussion groups to resolve management issues. If children have an investment in the organization of the class, the teacher is less likely to be arbiter of all disputes.

Turn over some of the homeroom functions to the students. Include money collection, attendance, and lunch counts among the jobs for which students have major responsibility. Check periodically, but encourage student responsibility for these activities.

CONFRONT THE BASICS

Goodman (1986)

One of the basic transitions from traditional to integrated language classrooms is rethinking the way in which reading and language learning occurs. Teachers must rethink the way in which basals, workbooks, and tests are used. If basal programs have been the focus of the reading program, there are several ways to move children toward more integrated approaches to reading.

Martinez & Teale (1989)

Reorganize the way in which time is allocated in the reading program. Spend time each day sharing literature with students. Allocate daily time, too, for children to read material of their own choice (Sustained Silent Reading*). The element of choice is crucial in developing life-long readers. It is also important that children have the opportunity to read many books at a comfortable level so that they begin to perceive themselves as successful readers. Moving away from basals means moving away from the feeling that it is always "better" to read "harder" books. Most people read for a variety of purposes—rarely because they want to prove to someone else that they are "good" readers. Providing both choice and guidance are characteristics of integrated language classrooms.

Choice and guidance are crucial features of an integrated setting.

Think of the basal as an anthology, not as a reading program, and use it accordingly. Carefully review the literature in the basal. Select texts that are good literature in their own right, rather than adapted or abridged versions of stories that are much better in their original form. Try forming critique groups to read and discuss these selections, and talk about these texts in the ways already suggested in other parts of this book. Use Reader's Theatre* instead of round-robin reading. Let the basal become one of many sources of literature, and provide opportunities for the same kinds of extensions already suggested for use with trade books. If some of the basal selections are not good literature, label them as such, and work with the children to rewrite a passage or make a story more interesting. Try Group Composed Writing* to improve such selections. This activity encourages careful reading by children, but it also acknowledges their right to good literature and to make judgments about the quality of the literature they are reading.

Critique groups foster good book talk.
Chambers (1985)

Eliminate ability groups. Set up Buddy Reading*, pairing weaker with stronger or older with younger readers (see Chapter 8). Look through the teacher's guide for additional reading selections, and collect other books that expand and complement the basal selection. The Reading Buddies* can then read and discuss worthwhile basal stories, but they can also share a variety of other literature together. Search out books or stories to contrast with or complement a basal selection. After children have read the basal story, organize groups to read and discuss other literature. For instance, a sixth grade class reading a basal selection on Jason and the Argonauts divided into groups that included analysis and comparison of other versions of the Argonaut legend, viewing a film of an excavation in Greece that appeared to confirm the historicity of another Greek legend that students then read, and a study of books of Greek mythology to learn more about some of the mythological characters Jason encountered.

Eeds & Wells (1989)

Organize Reading Buddies* and Response Groups*

In addition to Reading Buddies*, develop Response Groups*. Organize according to a topic children are studying and a basal or trade book story that relates to that topic. Select students or let students self-select so that a lively discussion will ensue.

Goodman (1986)

Stop assigning workbook pages. Have children work on literary extensions, including the creation of Semantic Maps* and Sketch to Stretch* extensions. Response Groups* can work on extensions that can be shared and that provide a backdrop for discussions of language use, literary interpretation, and so forth. Recall, for example, the children involved in activities with Big Books* or CLOZE* activities described in Chapter 8. The children were applying skills listed in the scope and sequence of any basal program, but they were applying them in context, rather than in isolation. They were using background knowledge, conventions of print, letter and sound relationships, word endings, letter clusters, sight words, and both meaning and graphic cues. They were also searching for meaning, confirming predictions, and self-correcting. In another instance, children working on a Comparison Chart* of Asian folktales engaged in comparing and contrasting, read for details, made inferences, sequenced events, identified cause and effect, and analyzed story structure.

Apply skills in context.

Generate thematic units from good basal passages. Most basal series include stories with particular themes—"Growing Up," "Friendship," or "Mythology," for instance. Review the basal series to see how units may develop from the passages in the readers and incorporate books and activities from other content areas in the same way you would in any thematic unit. Linking topics across the curriculum at this point may simply mean that you will be covering the units in content area texts out of the usual order.

Reduce the amount of time children spend in basal readers, and increase the time spent reading in literature of their choice, as well as in literature related to theme studies or shorter Mini-Lessons*. Confine work in the basals to one day, and use the rest of the week for integrated language work. If the school system requires that children complete the basal, send the basal home to be read and discussed with parents, or encourage its use as independent reading.

Goodman (1986)

During the time formerly allocated for reading groups, hold individual conferences, and sit in on Response Groups*.

Increase children's opportunities to write connected discourse. Instead of filling in the blanks in workbooks, have children write in Journals*, Learning Logs*, and the like. When children work on different activities, they have more to share, both orally and in writing. In the "No More Litter" example in Chapter 7, the children in the second grade class had already experienced school failures. Several were identified as having reading problems, some were receiving special education services, and a few had been retained several times in their short school careers. Most were reluctant readers and writers, yet they were excited about the prospect of working on a real problem in their community and were soon reading and writing extensively.

Graves (1983)

Set aside time when children share their work with one another—both work in progress and completed work (see Chapter 4 for specifics).

Display children's original work, rather than completed workbook pages, ditto sheets, or "100%" papers.

Send samples of this work home, too, so that parents have a sense of what their children are involved in learning.

Moulin (1988)

LOOK TO THE CONTENT AREAS

The transition to an integrated language classroom is made across the curriculum, not only in the areas of reading and language arts. In traditional curriculums, reading, language arts, and mathematics have had the lion's share of the elementary day. Social studies and science have had little or no instruction at all. Instead, they are generally relegated to the end of the day and regularly interrupted and dismissed for assemblies, announcements, and so forth. While this is nothing to celebrate, it does mean that you are probably freer to experiment and take risks in these two areas than in any other part of the curriculum. The content in these areas also lends itself especially well to the development of thematic units. In addition, most educators are more familiar with units in the content areas. The content areas, then, are a good place to begin in making the transition to thematic units.

Goodlad (1984)

Gamberg, Kwak, Hutchings, & Altheim (1988)

Content areas provide in-depth study and natural language use.

Begin with a mini-unit. Perhaps the science text has a unit on the water cycle. A mini-unit on water could begin with science concepts and then include information about areas of the world and how they are affected by rainfall patterns, water sources, and so forth. The unit could also expand to include other cycles in nature. In either case, the mini-unit covers material in at least two content areas and can be extended through a wide variety of literature.

Plan activities to fit the structure or time constraints required by your school or system. In most cases, this is simply a matter of presenting integrated activities in a more linear fashion and knowing that although the state may have minimum time requirements for language arts or social studies, you will be teaching some language arts during the period set aside for social studies and some social stud-

Learn how to present integrated activities to show how they meet state and local standards.

ies during language arts time. One school calls this approach to the development of an integrated language curriculum "toe-dipping" and has found it useful in introducing teachers to new ways of organizing instruction.

Organize the second half of the day—generally, the social studies and science portion of the curriculum—into long-term thematic units. Using some of the suggestions in this book, select topics that will have sustaining power for a four- to six-week period (or more), and that integrate social studies and science. Although portions of this theme may be integrated into other parts of the day, afternoons can be devoted to the kind of thematic study characteristic of an integrated perspective.

As teachers gain confidence in children's ability to work this way, and as they recognize that real learning is occurring, they broaden the type of inquiries children engage in. They begin to look for places where curricular areas overlap. A third grade teacher notices that the science curriculum calls for a study of living systems and the social studies curriculum includes a unit on communities. Why not combine these topics into a thematic unit? Time is set aside in the afternoon for theme studies, and both science and social studies textbooks are available, along with many trade books for student study.

Texts are one of many resources available to children.

Use textbooks as one of many sources in your room. Sometimes, teachers assume that an integrated language classroom does not use textbooks. Textbooks are often used, but they are used differently. The textbook is not the class authority and arbiter of scope and sequence; it is used as a resource in the same way that trade books are used. This is particularly true as teachers make the transition from textbook-based to integrated language classrooms. One of the "toe-dipping" teachers, for instance, began a thematic unit by using two textbook descriptions of the settlement of Jamestown and of the role of Pocahontas. The two versions conflicted. Which did students think might be correct? How could they check to find out? Soon, students were checking a variety of other sources, including Jean Fritz's biography of Pocahontas, high school and college textbooks, material from Jamestown Historic Park, and a local historian. Their final assignment was to rewrite their textbook description of Pocahontas and the settlement of Jamestown. The students were engaged in an interesting inquiry into a historical topic and a careful, critical reading of their textbook. Although they did not integrate many other aspects of the curriculum into their inquiry, they did use a variety of language, from discussion to oral reports and debates, and from taking notes to organizing those notes into a written form. The assignment did not require reorganizing the entire class or the curriculum, but it did allow the teacher to test the waters and to see what happened when children worked in an atmosphere of independent and small group inquiry. It also allowed the children to see the textbook as one of many sources available to them, rather than as the single most important authority on a subject. This may seem a slight shifting, but it is profoundly important in helping children to become more independent thinkers.

Fritz (1983)

Shifts toward independent thinking are crucial.

TEACH CHILDREN TO WORK IN GROUPS

Gamberg, Kwak, Hutchings, & Altheim (1988)

Children learn to work in groups just as they learned to work independently and to walk quietly through the halls. When children first begin small group work, tasks should be clear and specific, so that they know what is expected of them and can appropriately organize themselves. An assignment that is too broad ranging can result in disorder and frustration on the students' part and a sense of failure for the teacher. Remember that children need time to adjust to new routines, and they may respond initially with off-task behavior.

Involve children in establishing ground rules from the beginning. Debrief after activities, so that group problem-solving routines can be established and reinforced.

Hyde & Bizar (1989)

Do not assume that an initial problem in working cooperatively means that students are not able to handle this practice responsibly. Instead, reevaluate the activity in terms of the appropriateness and complexity of the activity and the children's interest in it and their motivation to participate. Then try again.

Start with short-term, clearly defined cooperative work. Teachers sometimes find that math is a good place to begin teaching children to work cooperatively. Begin by putting children in work groups, and give them problems to solve as a group. Encourage discussion, and make sure that the problem to resolve is one that can benefit from group processing. The tasks should be specific and focused enough to provide little opportunity for children to lose track of the task at hand. There should be immediate feedback, both on the problem-solving and the group dynamics.

Establish routines in one area that can be transferred to work in other areas. This is especially important in working on thematic units on which students may need more freedom of movement than, say, a math group might require.

SHARE RESULTS

Hickman (1983)

Teaching can be a very lonely activity, especially if one is swimming against the mainstream. It helps, then, to build understanding among peers. One way to accomplish this is to share students' work with the rest of the school. Hang displays in the hall, or invite other classes to some performance aspects of your children's work. Think about the ways in which you can establish recognition of the work your children are engaged in, both from your colleagues and from school administrators. The children in the "No More Litter" example in Chapter 7, for instance, shared their videotape with other classes and with the PTA. As a result, other people recognized the quality of the children's work and encouraged their continued efforts. This can establish a climate in the school in which the innovative teacher is viewed as a good and hard-working, if rather different, teacher. Such an attitude will make further changes less controversial and may even encourage a few peers to join in making changes.

Help to establish a climate supportive of innovation.

INVITE PARENTS TO PARTICIPATE

Moulin (1988)

Do not stop at the schoolhouse door. Parents have a vested interest in quality education for their children, and there is strong evidence that high levels of parent involvement are related to positive student attitudes and achievement. Too often, parents' information about what is going on in a classroom is based on student report and community gossip. This can create problems for a teacher trying to make changes that alter the kind of information going home to parents. For instance, some teachers have reported that parents complained when fewer dittoes came home because the parents felt that their children must not be "covering" as much material. It makes sense then, to create advocates rather than enemies by involving parents in your program at a variety of levels.

Involve parents as supporters, service givers, and facilitators. Develop a cadre of parents who collect materials from scrap lumber to computer software, donate time to help with putting on a play, or organize a culminating activity for a unit. Provide parents with positive access to the school and opportunities to observe classroom activity. They want their children to feel good about school, to be excited about learning, and to feel confident about themselves. An integrated language approach is often vigorously supported by parents once they understand its foundations and see its effects. Parents can be powerful advocates for teachers when they can speak on the basis of observation.

Goodman (1989); Potter (1989); Huck (1980)

Parents can be learners. Parents, especially those with younger children, may want specific help in fostering their children's education. Some schools and classrooms have successfully organized discussion sessions where parents and teachers can get together to talk about ways that the home and school environments can support each other. This situation also builds communication networks between parents and teachers that minimize misunderstandings. The teacher can show parents samples of student work and explain activities, so that parents understand what is happening in the classroom and can offer constructive feedback based on their knowledge of their own children. Local experts on language learning, children's literature, and child development can also be invited to parent meetings to provide additional background for the foundations teachers and parents are trying to build.

Parents can be learning resources in the classroom. Parents have talents that can be valuable resources in the classroom and that can encourage support for new programming. Some teachers use parent volunteers on a weekly basis to work in individual or small group situations with children. This is sometimes a matter of working with a small group on a special project that could use some expert assistance. Sometimes it is sharing literature; often it is working with children on organizing their thoughts into writing. You can see examples of this partnership as you read through the protocols in Chapter 4. Parents work as partners with the teacher to develop a sound educational program for their children.

WORK WITH ADMINISTRATORS

Teachers may be unaware of or confused by the plethora of guidelines and regulations for teaching and learning that exist at both local and state levels. In addition, school communities have their own share of myths about what is "required" just as many other communities have their own folk stories. Some of these myths include:

Myth 1. Teachers have to cover every unit of every textbook in the order in which they are written.
Myth 2. Teachers have to use the lesson plans in the textbooks.
Myth 3. Teachers have to use workbooks.
Myth 4. Children have to read every story and cover every lesson in every textbook.
Myth 5. Teachers teach reading for only one period a day.

Such regulations are neither good teaching practice, nor are they mandated in most districts. When confronted by such myths, do not accept them without checking things out.

Talk with the principal or the district subject coordinators to find out what is required, what is encouraged, and what is open to change in your state or district.

Honig (1988); Stedman (1987)

Become familiar with the state curriculum guides and state laws governing curriculum. Many teachers have been surprised to find that state and local guidelines are very much in harmony with practices recommended for integrated language classrooms.

If necessary, point out to the administration how the integrated language program matches state and local guidelines.

In some schools it is possible for a teacher to share plans and to explain the theoretical and research bases for them with administrators. Generally, teachers must be prepared to show how they will cover required skills and content in the context of the thematic unit approach. In other schools, administrators are more willing to believe successful practice than plans and theory. In these cases, inviting them in to see student activities or having them observe the products of student projects is more likely to garner their support.

INVITE THE COMMUNITY IN, AND TAKE CHILDREN INTO THE COMMUNITY

One of the most threatening aspects of an integrated language perspective is the feeling that the teacher must know so much and be able to draw on a vast array of resources beyond the confines of the textbook. When teachers make the transition to an integrated perspective, they quickly learn that they cannot be the source of all knowledge. They begin to shift their role from information giver to fellow constructor of meaning. To be most effective in this role, teachers need to think about the community resources waiting to be tapped.

Teachers cannot be the only source of knowledge in the classroom.

The surrounding community is a rich resource.

Invite community people into the classroom. Begin with the students' parents and guardians. A kindergarten teacher invites each of the parents or guardians of her students to spend some time with her students, sharing what that adult does for work or engages in as a hobby. One year, a full-time homemaker came to class with an apron stuffed full of symbols of all her jobs—a model car for her role as chauffeur, a tiny iron for her job as laundress, and so forth. Another parent who enjoyed woodworking taught children to make birdhouses. A grandfather taught the children to do dances popular in his youth.

Community officials are often willing to come and talk to school children, as are people involved in the business, service, arts, and recreational activities in the local area. When children in one school became interested in machinery, a local factory worker came to class and helped children build models of various kinds of machines. In another case, a local artist came and taught puppetry. Inviting all sorts of people into the life of the classroom lessens the teacher's and children's isolation, lifts some of the burden teachers often feel to be experts in everything, and models new ways of learning.

The community has a vested interest in schooling.

Take children into the community as much as possible. Try to lessen the barrier between school and the world by taking children to see people in nonschool environments. This sort of visibility introduces the teacher and the program of the class to the community and is one more way to build a support group. These expeditions need not require schoolbus trips or expensive transportation arrangements, either. There are plenty of things to study in the immediate environment of most schools. For trips within a more urban community, students can use public transportation. A fourth grade teacher arranged a bus trip to an art museum that was exhibiting African masks. As part of the class's study, students researched bus schedules, fares, distances, and transportation times, in addition to developing charts of symbols and techniques used in making masks of different regions of Africa. They developed a trip book that contained necessary information for planning the trip and for recording information about the uses of masks in various cultures.

Lessen the barriers between school and the "real" world.

Prepare your class for community contact. Well-prepared and well-behaved children are welcome in the community and are a pleasure to visit. Most people enjoy sharing their interests and respond well to children who have done some preparation before a visit. Work with children to establish ground rules for conduct and for gathering data. Successful field trips and visits from community members reinforce new patterns of student responsibility for their own learning.

Prepare children for responsible participation in the community.

FIND A FRIEND

Change is not always welcomed. If a teacher is going to be a change agent in a school, some people will resent such activity and will work to encourage a return to tradition. It is easier to resist those pressures if the teacher finds a companion who shares a

McLaren (1989); McNeil (1988a, 1988b, 1988c)

Even two can be a critical mass for change in a school.

similar perspective. Sometimes even a "critical mass" of two can provide enough strength to really make a difference, especially if both teachers are at the same grade level. In any case, it is a good thing to have someone to share and make plans with and to commiserate with when things don't go as well as one might like. Good teaching is hard work. Finding someone else who supports your efforts to be a first-rate teacher can help you to withstand pressures toward mediocrity.

GET INVOLVED!

To continue teaching, teachers must continue learning. Most states require some form of continuing education, but that is not the only way to grow as a teacher. Teachers also need to grow in experiences outside the classroom. A number of professional organizations provide scholarships and other incentives to enable classroom teachers to participate in a variety of special programs in specific content areas or for travel for educational purposes. In addition to the specific purposes of these programs, you have an opportunity to meet teachers from around the country and sometimes the world. They, too, form a support group for innovative teaching and add to your opportunities for enriching the learning of your students. Some of the organizations that support this type of growth include the National Council of Teachers of English, the National Council for the Social Studies, the International Reading Association, the National Science Teachers Association, and the National Council of Teachers of Mathematics. All these national organizations and their local and state affiliates welcome teacher participation and leadership. Individual enthusiasm coupled with such continued education recharge intellectual batteries so that teaching remains a stimulating and mind-expanding activity.

BECOME ASSOCIATED WITH A UNIVERSITY OR COLLEGE

As teachers move toward a more integrated model, they sometimes take advantage of the resources in nearby colleges and universities.

Enlist the help of a sympathetic faculty member. Invite that person to participate in your work. Collaborative efforts between college and university faculty and classroom teachers can be rewarding to all participants. The teacher can get some expert assistance without the threat of administrative evaluation, and the university representative has an opportunity to observe and participate in an important "laboratory" setting.

Let administrators know about college and university collaborations. An advocate from the university or college can sometimes encourage administrators to grant a classroom teacher a bit more leeway than might otherwise be the case. The university person can also document the class's progress, provide feedback, and serve as a resource person.

Make presentations at professional conferences. Collaborative efforts can result in presentations that put teachers in contact with like-minded colleagues and extend the needed support network.

EVALUATION AND ASSESSMENT

The procedures for evaluation discussed in Chapter 9 are appearing in a multitude of school settings. As a result, more holistic measures of evaluation may be relatively simple to implement and acceptable even in settings where letter or number grades must be assigned to the grade card. Teachers, then, can move toward incorporating assessments that are more compatible with an integrated language perspective.

Keep good records. The kid-watching techniques discussed in Chapters 6 and 9 require good recordkeeping. They help teachers plan, of course, but they also help explain to parents and administrators what children are learning and doing. In a sense, good recordkeeping helps validate good teacher intuition—that sense of how children are doing and where they are ready to go next that comes of careful observation, good practice, and professional judgment.

Keep plenty of records. Especially in schools where single grades or standardized tests are the major means by which children's learning is measured and reported, it is important to accumulate other data as evidence of the kind of thinking and learning that more fully represent the progress of an individual child. One simple way to do this is to keep a portfolio for each child that is periodically shared with parents. A child's story or poem, picture, or project can speak volumes about the kind of learning that is going on.

Goodman (1986)

Parents can also better understand the kind of documentation represented in a portfolio rather than the statistical interpretations required to make sense out of standardized measures. Even percentage scores on a teacher-made test do not tell a parent as much as does a book their child has created during a thematic unit.

Portfolios provide understandable feedback to parents.

Teach children how to take tests. If standardized tests are used with children in integrated language classrooms, it is helpful to prepare them for the format in which the test will be given. Placing a few practice sentences on the board periodically can help children get accustomed to the test format. Practicing what it is like to work within time constraints is also important for young children without much experience with timed tests. In most cases, however, children who are part of integrated language classrooms do as well or better on standardized tests than do children in more traditional classrooms.

Huck (1980); Tunnell & Jacobs (1989)

Involve children in self-evaluation. A relatively simple place to start in moving toward self-evaluation is to invite children to put together their own portfolio of work. Initially, it helps to provide some guidelines about what types of work can be sampled in a portfolio. For instance, a teacher may suggest that children include samples of the writing that they found the most interesting, or that they enjoyed doing the most, or that they found the most difficult. They may include an outline of the work they have been involved in over a particular period and provide samples of things representative of that work. Children may also include samples that represent something brand new that they have learned, or an example of something they had trouble with but think they are beginning to understand or to have mastered.

Gamberg, Kwak, Hutchings, & Altheim (1988)

Discuss evaluation with students. Some teachers provide check sheets for children to fill out that cover a child's activities for a particular period. The teacher fills out a similar sheet, and both meet to go over their evaluations. The child has an opportunity to provide feedback to the teacher, and the teacher can discuss areas of strength as well as areas of concern. In this way, even if the teacher must assign a number or letter grade, the child has a better understanding of where that grade came from and has an opportunity to provide evidence the teacher may not have considered.

Be patient. Good evaluative and assessment skills take time to acquire. They require continuous practice and careful reflection on that practice. Teachers have to be as patient with their own unfolding abilities as they try to be with children.

CONCLUSIONS

An integrated language perspective is accessible to many kinds of teachers in many kinds of situations. It is not a lockstep model but a belief about children and learning. No teacher enters the classroom with a perfect system in place; good teachers spend their entire careers building on decisions made as they confront the realities of life in classrooms.

This book has emphasized the importance of choices and ownership for teachers and children. Teachers generally make their choices because they care about children. Teaching requires careful thinking about the future we want for children. The debate over that future and over the ways to reach it have always been with us. We argue

Teachers share responsibility for building children's futures.

over whether it is enough to teach children to read and write or to achieve high scores on college entrance exams, or if there is some "cultural literacy" that will enable a diverse society to function as a democracy. We debate the impact of education on children's economic futures and on the political and economic future of our world. James Britton has said that "we want children, as a result of our teaching to *understand,* to be wise as well as well informed, able to solve fresh problems rather than have learnt the answers to old ones; indeed not only able to answer questions but also able to ask them" (p. 81). Choosing to teach from an integrated language perspective provides a context in which such goals are possible. Making the transition to that perspective can be an exciting and challenging experience.

Britton (1981)

REFERENCES

Bailey, J., Brazee, P. E., Chiavaroli, S., Herbeck, J., Lechner, T., Lewis, D., McKittrick, A., Redwine, L., Reid, K., Robinson, B., & Spear, H. (1988). Problem-solving our way to alternative evaluation procedures. *Language Arts, 65,* 364–373.

Britton, J. (1981). Talking to learn. In D. Barnes, J. Britton, & H. Rosen (Eds.), *Language, the learner and the school* (pp. 81–115). New York: Penguin.

Chambers, A. (1985). *Booktalk: Occasional writing on literature and children.* New York: Harper & Row.

Donaldson, M. (1978). *Children's minds.* Glasgow: Wm. Collins Sons.

Eeds, M., & Wells, D. (1989). Grand conversations: An exploration of meaning construction in literature study groups. *Research in the Teaching of English, 23* (1), 4–29.

Gamberg, R., Kwak, W., Hutchings, M., & Altheim, J. (1988). *Learning and loving it: Theme studies in the classroom.* Portsmouth, NH: Heinemann.

Goodlad, J. (1984). *A place called school.* New York: McGraw-Hill.

Goodman, D. (1987). TAWL topics. In *Teachers Networking: The Whole Language Newsletter, 1,* 5 & 9.

Goodman, G. (1989). Worlds within worlds: Reflections on an encounter with parents. *Language Arts, 66* (1), 14–20.

Goodman, K. (1986). *What's whole about whole language?* Portsmouth, NH: Heinemann.

Goodman, K., Goodman, Y. & Hood, W. J. (1989). *The whole language evaluation book.* Portsmouth, NH: Heinemann.

Graves, D. H. (1983). *Writing: Teachers and children at work.* Portsmouth, NH: Heinemann.

Hickman, J. (1983). Moving toward a literature based approach. *The W.E.B.: Spring Weather, 7* (3), 25–31.

Honig, B. (1988). The California reading initiative. *The New Advocate, 1* (4), 135–140.

Huck, C. (1980). Teacher feature. *The W.E.B.: Learning to Read Naturally, 4* (4), 14–17.

Huck, C., Hepler, S., & Hickman, J. (1987). *Children's literature in the elementary school.* New York: Holt, Rinehart & Winston.

Hyde, A., & Bizar, M. (1989). *Thinking in context: Teaching cognitive processes across the elementary school curriculum.* White Plains, NY: Longman.

Martinez, M. G., & Teale, W. H. (1989). Classroom storybook reading: The creation of texts and learning opportunities. *Theory Into Practice, 28* (2), 126–135.

McLaren, P. (1989). *Life in schools.* White Plains, NY: Longman.

McNeil, L. A. (1988a). Contradictions of control, part 1: Administrators and teachers. *Phi Delta Kappan, 69,* 333–339.

McNeil, L. A. (1988b). Contradictions of control, part 2: Teachers, students, and curriculum. *Phi Delta Kappan, 69,* 432–438.

McNeil, L. A. (1988c). Contradictions of control, part 3: Contradictions of reform. *Phi Delta Kappan, 69,* 478–485.

Moulin, N. (1988). Effect of parent involvement in classroom activities on parents' and children's attitude toward school. Paper presented at the Annual Meeting of the American Educational Research Association in New Orleans.

Potter, G. (1989). Parent participation in the language arts program. *Language Arts, 66* (1), 21–28.

Routman, R. (1988). *Transitions: From literature to literacy.* Portsmouth, NH: Heinemann.

Stedman, L. C. (1987). It's time we changed the effective schools formula. *Phi Delta Kappan, 63* (3), 216–224.

Trelease, J. (1985). *The read-aloud handbook.* New York: Penguin.

Tunnell, M. O., & Jacobs, J. S. (1989). Using "real books": Research findings on literature-based reading instruction. *The Reading Teacher, 42,* 470–477.

CHILDREN'S LITERATURE

THE DOUBLE LIFE OF POCAHONTAS by J. Fritz. Illustrated by E. Young. Putnam, 1983.

Index